Lecture Notes in Computer Science 1086

Edited by G. Goos, J. Hartmanis and J. van Leeuwen

Advisory Board: W. Brauer   D. Gries   J. Stoer

Springer
Berlin
Heidelberg
New York
Barcelona
Budapest
Hong Kong
London
Milan
Paris
Santa Clara
Singapore
Tokyo

Claude Frasson   Gilles Gauthier
Alan Lesgold   (Eds.)

Intelligent
Tutoring Systems

Third International Conference, ITS '96
Montréal, Canada, June 12-14, 1996
Proceedings

 Springer

Series Editors

Gerhard Goos, Karlsruhe University, Germany

Juris Hartmanis, Cornell University, NY, USA

Jan van Leeuwen, Utrecht University, The Netherlands

Volume Editors

Claude Frasson
Département d'informatique et de recherche opérationelle
Université de Montréal
C.P. 6128, succursale Centre-ville, Montréal, Québec H3C 3J7, Canada

Gilles Gauthier
Département d'informatique, Université du Québec à Montréal
C.P. 8888, succursale Centre-ville, Montréal, Québec H3C 3P8, Canada

Alan Lesgold
Learning Research and Development Center, University of Pittsburgh
Pittsburgh, PA 15260, USA

Cataloging-in-Publication data applied for

Die Deutsche Bibliothek - CIP-Einheitsaufnahme

Intelligent tutoring systems : third international conference ;
proceedings / ITS '96, Montréal, Canada, June 12 - 14, 1996. C.
Frasson ... (ed.). - Berlin ; Heidelberg ; New York ; Barcelona
; Budapest ; Hong Kong ; London ; Milan ; Paris ; Santa Clara
; Singapore ; Tokyo : Springer, 1996
  (Lecture notes in computer science ; Vol. 1086)
  ISBN 3-540-61327-7
NE: Frasson, Claude [Hrsg.]; ITS <3, 1996, Montréal>; GT

With 113 pages in French

CR Subject Classification (1991): K.3, I.2, D.2, H.5, J.1

ISBN 3-540-61327-7 Springer-Verlag Berlin Heidelberg New York

© Springer-Verlag Berlin Heidelberg 1996
Printed in Germany

Typesetting: Camera-ready by author
SPIN 10513097   06/3142 – 5 4 3 2 1 0   Printed on acid-free paper

Preface

ITS'96 is the third international conference on Intelligent Tutoring Systems. The preceding conferences were organized in Montréal in 1988 and 1992. These conferences were so warmly supported by the international community that it was decided to organize them every four years. In fact, ITS conferences are highly refereed international conferences. They are intended to serve as reference guidelines for the research community.

The program committee members came from 15 different countries and contributions were received from 23 different countries.

This proceedings volume contains 69 papers selected by the program committee from 128 papers submitted. They are preceded by six invited lectures from well-known speakers. The papers cover a wide range of subjects including advising systems, architectures for ITS, cognitive models, design issues, empirical studies, formal models, learning environments, real-world applications, software tools for tutoring, student modeling, teaching and learning strategies. The conference itself is preceded by three worshops on the role of qualitative reasoning techniques in ITS, simulation-based learning technology, and architectures and methods for designing cost-effective and reusable ITS. Four tutorials highlight important domains in ITS: creating educational software with Java, instructional design for collaborative distance learning, explanations in instructional systems (using task and causal models), student modeling (cognitive approaches).

We would like to thank all the members of the program committee who conscientiously reviewed all the papers which were sent so as to obtain a distributed and equilibrated point of view. We also thank the external reviewers who added their effort to complement the evaluations. A subset of the program committee met in February in Montréal to set up the final list of accepted papers.

The conference is supported by several scientific associations. We thank the Canadian Society for Computational Studies of Intelligence (CSCSI), the IEEE Computer Society, the Association for Computing Machinery (ACM), and the special interest groups SIGART and SIGCUE, the Association française des sciences et technologies de l'information et des systèmes (Afcet). They ensured a wide distribution of information regarding the announcement of the conference.

We would like to thank the Université de Montréal and the Université du Québec à Montréal for their support with the organization of the conference. We thank all those many people who gave their time and effort to make the conference a success, all the members of the organizing committee, a fantastic team who regularly spent numerous hours on all the details of the conference, all the students of the HERON laboratory in Montréal who helped with the practical organization of the conference. Finally, we appreciated the cooperation received from Springer-Verlag during the edition of this volume.

Montréal
June 1996

Claude Frasson
Gilles Gauthier
Alan Lesgold

Felisa Verdejo (U. Politecnica de Catalunya, Spain)
Martial Vivet (Université du Mans, France)
Gerhard Weber (University of Trier, Germany)
Barbara White (University of California, Berkeley, USA)
Beverly Woolf (University of Massachussets, Amherst, USA)
Kwok-Keung Yum (CSIRO, Australia)

Organizing Committee Chair
Gilles Gauthier (Université du Québec à Montréal, Canada)

Panels Chair
Beverly Woolf (University of Massachussets, Amherst, USA)

Exhibition Co-Chairs
Esma Aïmeur (Université de Montréal, Canada)
Guy Gouardères (Université de Pau et des Pays de l'Adour, France)
Anatole Kengne (Université de Montréal, Canada)

Tutorial Chair
Marc Kaltenbach (Bishop's University, Canada)

Workshop Co-Chairs
Gilles Imbeau (Université du Québec à Chicoutimi, Canada)
Suzanne Lajoie (McGill University, Canada)

Publicity Chair
Bernard Lefebvre (Université du Québec à Montréal, Canada)

Conference Treasurer & Registration Chair
Martine Gemme (Université de Montréal, Canada)

Local Arrangements
Carmen Alexe (Université de Montréal, Canada)
Martine Gemme (Université de Montréal, Canada)

External Reviewers
E. Aïmeur
C. Alexe
C. Frasson
G. Gauthier
J. Gecsei
G. Imbeau
M. Kaltenbach
B. Lefebvre
T. Mengelle

Submitted Papers Repartition

Africa	2
Algeria	1
Australia	6
Brazil	5
Canada	23
France	22
Germany	8
Hong Kong	2
Italy	1
Japan	9
Mexico	5
New Zealand	1
Republic of China	2
Singapore	2
Spain	2
Sweden	1
Switzerland	1
UK	8
United States	25
Ukraine	1
Yugoslavia	1

Table of Contents

Invited Papers

Architecture for ITS

Authoring and Software Tools for Tutoring

Cognitive Models

Collaborative Learning

Design Issues

Discovery Environments, Multimedia and WWW

Empirical Studies, Evaluation and Testing of ITS

Formal Models

Help and Advising Systems

Knowledge Representation in ITS

Learning Environments

Qualitative reasoning

Real World Applications

Simulation-Based Learning

Student Modeling

Teaching and Learning Strategies

Authors Index

Promoting the Transfer of Advanced Training Technologies

Charles P. Bloom

Human Computer Interaction Laboratory
NYNEX Science & Technology, Inc.
500 Westchester Avenue
White Plains, NY USA 10604
cbloom@nynexst.com

Abstract. As research into intelligent tutoring systems (ITS) passes the 25 year mark, it leaves behind a history full of technical accomplishments, yet unfulfilled expectations. Researchers have demonstrated that it is possible to build intelligent representations of domain, instructional, and student knowledge for a wide variety of domains. In addition, those representations can be used in concert with one another and with appropriate domain emulations to deliver individualized instruction. However, even given these significant technical accomplishments, the number of ITSs in use in actual educational situations in industry, academia, and government sectors is relatively few. If this is not due to insurmountable technical problems, than what is keeping the expectations of this promising technology unfulfilled? It is the premise of this paper that what is keeping the promise of ITS technology unfulfilled is the problem of technology transfer. The goal of this paper is to discuss barriers to successful technology transfer and approaches for overcoming those barriers, particularly as they apply to deploying intelligent tutoring systems in industry.

1   Introduction

Over the past 10 years I have worked in the research and development organizations of several major U. S. industries. My primary responsibility was to champion the development and transfer of advanced technology training applications into each corporation's operational environment. Twice in these 10 years our efforts have met with success. I say "our" because in both cases I was privileged to work with exceptional project teams. Our first technology transfer success started with the modest objective of trying to establish the credibility and feasibility of interactive learning systems technologies with our corporate clients (not to mention establishing our credibility to develop and deploy such systems). By the end of the project we had successfully developed and deployed a multimedia, PC-based training application that gained immediate widespread acceptance within the corporate user community. In addition, we had demonstrated a three month return on investment, and established a program to continue the development and maintenance of similar systems within the corporate training center (Bullemer & Bloom, in press). Our second technology transfer success was a little more ambitious. In this effort, our objective was to initiate a research and development program on intelligent tutoring systems with the goal of developing and deploying ITSs for specific client training needs. By the end of that project, we had developed and deployed the ITS platform, as well as developed authoring tools to support ITS application development and maintenance by domain experts and instructional designers. In addition, we succeeded in transferring the tools and capabilities into the operational environment (Bloom, Wolff, & Bell, in press).

The goal of this paper is to discuss barriers to successful ITS technology transfer that I have encountered over the past 10 years, and some approaches for overcoming those barriers. Before preceding it is important to define some of the boundary conditions of this discussion. For the purpose of this paper, technology transfer is defined as the process of transitioning technology innovations from research organizations (i.e., academic, government and industry research laboratories) to operational environments (i.e., training and maintenance organizations in industry). A complete discussion of the technology transfer process, including issues such as steps in the process or whether a linear or non-linear model of technology transfer is applied, is well beyond the scope of this paper. Rather, the focus of this paper will be on barriers or problems technologists will encounter during the technology transfer process. In addition, this paper adopts as its viewpoint the goal of transfer to industrial training settings (the domain with which I am most familiar). However, it may be that some (or all) of the discussion has more general application.

2   A Model of Technology Transfer

Most discussions of technology transfer focus on ensuring an appropriate fit to end-user needs through methodologies such as participatory design, usability evaluations, domain management, incremental, modular development, rapid prototyping, and using evaluation to inform tutor design. While I acknowledge that ensuring an appropriate fit to user needs is essential to succeeding at technology transfer, since numerous sources exist to guide technologists in these areas, this paper will not discuss these technical issues. Rather, my personal experience in technology transfer has led me to conclude that most failures in technology transfer are due to non-technical issues, such as resistance to change or general ignorance of technology.

Every technology transfer effort impacts multiple corporate organizations, from the organization responsible for its development, to the organizations that will eventually use and maintain the deployed technology. The first step in any technology transfer effort is to identify the different organizations involved in or impacted by the technology transfer effort. In the case of intelligent tutoring systems, impacted organizations include: researchers responsible for developing the technology, upper management responsible for funding (and sanctioning) both the development and delivery, members of the training organization (i.e., instructors who must incorporate the use of the ITS in their training plans, and training developers who must use the ITS to craft meaningful learning activities), end-users or workers to be trained using the ITS, and members of the deployment organization who will be expected to support, maintain and enhance the deployed platforms (both hardware and software). Each of these organizations comes to a technology transfer effort with their own agenda and their own criteria for success, which if not identified and addressed can result in the construction of barriers.

At the heart of most technology transfer barriers is resistance from the organization(s) most impacted, erected as a result of failure to attend to these differing agendas and criteria. Successful technology transfer requires dealing with these barriers, either proactively by addressing the differing criteria and agendas before they become barriers, or reactively once the barriers occur. Once a barrier is identified, as well as the organization(s) most impacted, technology transfer becomes an exercise in communication, collaboration, education and compromise. Although specific agendas, criteria, and barriers will change from case to case, enough commonalities have been observed across experiences to conclude that general lessons can be extracted. Therefore, it should be possible to give technologists a general awareness of where and why technology transfer problems arise, and what can be done to overcome them. In the sections that follow we will discuss technology transfer barriers in terms of the organization most impacted.

2.1 Upper Management

Management's agenda is based on profit and loss. Their criteria for success is a solution that will either significantly reduce operating costs or else increase profits, and to do so within a time period dictated by Wall Street. Training has traditionally been viewed in industry as a "cost-centered activity." In the short term, training consumes revenue, it does not generate revenue. As a result, training is typically seen as a last-ditch response to some crisis, such as a shortage of employees with critical skills. While corporate managers recognize that training is necessary to bring employees to a level that allows them to produce revenue, the traditional bias towards keeping training at the absolute minimum remains prevalent. The numbers are even more depressing: In 1992, it was estimated by the American Society for Training and Development that American companies spend in the neighborhood of $30 billion a year on training. While this number at first seems impressive, further examination shows that this expenditure represents spending on a tenth of the workforce by less than 1% of American companies. Additionally, most training dollars are spent on managerial positions and not on "front-line workers" (Economist, 1992).

As a result of this perspective, when confronted with the decision about investing in ITS, management seeks to determine whether there is a pressing business need, and what "price tag" they can tolerate for solving that business need. Unfortunately, ITS development costs are "front loaded" (i.e., most costs are up front with a high initial cost requirement and a fairly long payback period). Overcoming this barrier involves the accumulation and presentation of information to decision makers that demonstrates a clear business need, and both the technical and financial superiority of that solution over other possible solutions, including the status quo.

The first step in overcoming this barrier is to identify a domain where there is both a clear client need and a substantial business impact. This is not to advocate searching for a problem in need of an already-developed solution, but rather to emphasize the need to identify a match between a valid training need and the ability to provide an effective technical solution. Certainly, not all training situations require electronic delivery of training, but those that can benefit from such can show impressive improvements in training quality for an organization.

After identifying an "impact domain," the next step is to establish both business and technology cases. One mechanism of establishing a technology case is a *technology analysis* – an assessment of the feasibility of various options for solving the identified business need, as well as a domain assessment documenting the domain's requirements for any solution (see Bloom, Wolff, & Bell, in press). The mechanism for establishing a business case is the *cost-benefits analysis*. Cost-benefits analysis provides a financial basis for selecting among a set of actions or decisions. At the most simple level, cost-benefits analysis involves tabulating a set of costs and benefits associated with a set of competing options. When probability estimates regarding the likely outcomes of each option are considered (e.g., an outcome is estimated to have an X% probability of occurring), expected values for costs and benefits of each option can be computed. The option with the greatest value of the difference between expected benefits and expected costs is the option to choose (Wolff, in press). Should the results of these analyses provide evidence in support of ITS over all viable options, the final step is to communicate those results to decision makers in as convincing a manner as possible.

2.2   **Training Organization**

The second impacted group is the company's training organization – Instructors who must use the ITS and training developers who must craft meaningful learning activities into the ITS. Training organizations in industry are based on a zero dollar model – they are not expected to make money since their clients come from within their own corporation. Rather, they are expected to take in only the money they need to cover their costs. Training organizations exist only so long as some corporate client is willing to buy what they offer, either the delivery of courses from their existing library or the development of new training for specific needs. This creates an attitude of fear and suspicion within the training organization – fear that if no one wants what they have to offer their jobs will go away, and suspicion that every new technology is a threat to hasten their demise by making them obsolete. These attitudes are further fueled by the fact that most representatives of industry training organizations are not formally trained educators. This is not meant to imply that they do not care about the quality of the training they develop or deliver because they do believe very strongly in the value of education and in fact they are highly motivated to provide the best training they can. However, because of their lack of formal training in educational methods, most industry training organizations teach the way they learned -- under the traditional school-house model where courses are delivered in stand-up, instructor led fashion, with an emphasis on imparting facts, not job readiness, and where the student is viewed as a passive participant not an active learner (a particularly inappropriate method of performance oriented domains).   In addition, very few instruction developers in industry have any experience developing computer delivered training applications, let alone the knowledge representations required of an ITS. As such, and because of the technical complexity of ITS, most will view ITS as a threat, both to their established way of operating, as well as to their job security.   These attitudes produce an agenda of self-preservation and a criteria of only accepting technology they understand and can control. If these criteria are not met they will impose barriers of resistance -- resistance to change and resistance of the unknown.

The most effective way of dealing with these barriers is education -- Instructors and training developers need to be convinced of the benefits of intelligent tutoring systems, and of the need to broaden their approach to how training is done away from an exclusive school-house model towards a more experiential view of learning. In addition (and possibly more importantly), they need to be reassured (and convinced) that using ITSs and the changes they bring about are not a threat to their job status or security, but rather that ITSs are tools which when applied effectively, should enhance both.

2.3   End-User Organization

The third impacted organization is the actual workers for whom the training is developed. Most workers are motivated to do the best job they can, to both enhance their job skills and to eventually move up within the corporation. Their agenda is to get the best training they can that will help make this possible. Unfortunately, there is a high degree of cynicism and skepticism in the American workforce, especially towards management. Workers know that industry is a hierarchy, and their fate is primarily determined by their management. They also know that management can say one thing, but if their actions indicate something entirely different, they know the cost of failing to heed those implicit signals. For example, it is no good encouraging workers to take the time to "hone" their skills in an ITS if the time spent using that ITS (and away from their job) impacts their personal revenue. Workers have been promised many things in the past and will view the ITS as just another opportunity for the company to "trick" them. As a result, they will most likely resist its use.

The best approach to dealing with this barrier is to make the end-users feel part of the solution by involving them in meaningful ways during design and development. By obtaining their buy in and support, they also become advocates for the technology, and in industry, with its powerful unions, employee advocates are listened to and headed. However, even gaining their support is not sufficient by itself to overcoming their resistance. To truly overcome end-user resistance, workers need "signs" from management that there is a real commitment to this technology, and that they will not be punished or penalized for buying into the technology. Unfortunately, there is very little technologists can do to impact this deeper barrier other than acknowledging that it is a problem (which can help in relations with the end-user community), and trying to make the problem known to management.

2.4   Deployment Organization

Another impacted group is the deployment organization. Deployment organizations are among the most beleaguered in a corporation. About the only times they hear from a client is when something goes wrong requiring immediate attention, or when one of their clients needs something - yesterday. Because of this, agendas for deployment organizations are based around managing their workload. Their criteria is to accept only those applications they deem as "easily manageable" (i.e., fit their existing skill sets, do not overwhelm their workload, and can be easily understandable to facilitate to support, maintenance, and enhancement).

What complicates the transfer of an ITS, is that it does not fit any deployment organization criteria. ITSs are more complex than the types of systems deployment personnel normally encounter or are trained to handle. ITSs are generally a poor match to existing deployment organization skill sets. ITSs are special purpose systems that require that deployment personnel have backgrounds in topics like object oriented design, programming and languages, artificial intelligence, and human learning. In addition, even when the deployment organization has a background in these areas, the ITS will still be viewed as unmanageable because it requires too much effort to understand its inner workings (i.e., have a similar understanding of the way the system is supposed to work as the system's designers and implementers), essential to software support, maintenance and enhancements.

Given the complexity of an ITS, extraordinary measures are required to overcome these barriers and ensure that all parties responsible for deployment and maintenance have a sufficiently accurate understanding of the system. An accurate understanding of the system is important for at least two reasons. First, it helps deployment personnel see the ITS as manageable. Second, it can keep deployment personnel from introducing errors into the ITS by violating its basic design and purpose. These extraordinary measures include: integrating deployment personnel on the project with development personnel as early as possible, providing opportunities to educate deployment personnel on the system's basic design and purpose, and producing software documentation that captures both system requirements and design, as well as information about the way things are supposed to work.

The primary purpose for the integration of deployment and development personnel is to create an apprenticeship environment where deployment personnel will have the opportunity to learn about the system's basic design and purpose in the context of helping develop the system (Collins, Brown, & Newman, 1989; Lave & Wenger,

1991). Unfortunately, integrating deployment personnel into the project as early as possible is far from a simple matter. Deployment personnel and organizations are used to working with "familiar" systems. This has created an approach whereby they anticipate a very simple transfer that can be accomplished in short order and at the very last moment. This model does not leave them with much time or resources to dedicate to a long term technology transfer effort in which they must learn about a new type of system. Developers of advanced technology applications must educate managers and members of deployment organizations on the need to change their model of technology transfer from the traditional "hand-off" model to one where they become "partners" with developers.

Since it is not always possible for deployment personnel to spend the amount of time with development personnel required for apprenticeship learning to take place, it is necessary to take other measures to facilitate learning. One such method is to produce software documentation that enhances system requirements and design information with information about how the system is supposed to work in the form of use cases (Jacobson, Christerson, Jonsson & Overgaard, 1992) or scenarios (Carroll, 1995). Use cases or scenarios tell the reader what should happen in the application under certain circumstances. This information, primarily used as a source for design requirements, in addition to helping deployment personnel understand an application's purpose and utility, can provide them with a means of judging whether the application is operating as expected under particular situations.

2.5 Research Organization

The last group of impacted users to address is the research organization itself. It might seem strange to suggest that the developers of a technology might also erect barriers to successful technology transfer, nevertheless, there are barriers that developers themselves create or impose. The overriding agenda of members of research organizations is to work on technologies that are intellectually challenging, and to advance or contribute to communities of science. Another agenda should be to employ technology to help solve company problems, but that is not always the case.

Unfortunately, success at technology development and success at technology transfer can produce conflicting results. Success at technology development produces feelings of gratification, from internal feelings of accomplishment to external recognition from peers. On the other hand, success in technology transfer can produce feelings of diminished importance on the part of development personnel. A technology they have worked on, in many cases for years, now becomes "owned" by groups of employees who barely understand how to use it, let alone how to develop it.

In addition, in industry, innovation is often treated as commonplace by its recipients. Little (or no) recognition is given to the fact that something novel has been accomplished -- the ITS is enabling individualized instructional interactions via computer never before realized by employing powerful domain simulations and artificially intelligent reasoning mechanisms. To its new owners, the ITS is just another training option, no more accomplished than any other. Their method of dealing with innovation is to reduce it to manageable terms by lumping it in with stand-up lectures, distance learning classes, and computer-based training courses.

This sense of a loss (or the perception of an impending loss), can cause technology developers to erect barriers. These barriers manifest themselves mostly in difficult or strained interactions with members of the organizations who will be recipients of this technology. Developers begin to be less informative or helpful than they might ordinarily be. Common symptoms of this problem include long delays in responses to queries, shifting of priorities away from support activities, and missed milestones that pertain to technology transfer issues. The best approach to dealing with these barriers is a combination of awareness that they can occur, vigilance in monitoring when they occur (because they will occur), and openness in discussing both their occurrence and resolution. Developers need to be aware that people outside of their research field do not really care about the scientific impact of their technological innovations. In fact, most will see it as an increase to their already overwhelming workload. However, that in no way diminishes the value of their contribution.

3   Summary

Even though the development of a robust and appropriate application is prerequisite for successful technology transfer, good technology development by itself is insufficient to ensure successful technology transfer. Technology transfer in or to industry is a complex process involving the communication, cooperation and coordination of multiple and diverse corporate organizations. As with any complex process, each organization has its own agenda and criteria for success. If not dealt with up front (and many times even when they are), these differing agendas and criteria can result in the construction of barriers to successful technology transfer. Management needs assurances and data in support of cost-benefits decisions. The training organization needs education about the technology, and assurances that it is not there to replace them. The end-user organization needs assurances that this investment in technology is for real. The deployment organization needs education about the technology and the underlying skills necessary to maintain and enhance it. And finally the development organization needs to be aware that successful technology transfer means they personally lose control of their technology, and generally without fanfare. Attention to each of these issues is no guarantee for success, but it certainly increases the odds.

A good approach is to think of technology transfer as a "political" process where you are trying to get your technology "elected." Successful technology transfer requires satisfying all of your "special interest groups" in order to get their "vote." In addition, it also means that technologists' must take on the lion's share of the effort and do most of the compromising.

Specifically, technologists must first be aware that issues exist and be aware of the organizations raising the issues, including their own. Next, technologists must proactively educate and inform each organization on their area(s) of concern. However, even doing all of this proactive work, technologists must still be prepared to react to any barriers erected during the process. Finally, technologists need to learn how to accept defeat without accepting failure. Not all technology transfer efforts will be successful, even some where all agendas have been identified and attended to from the outset. Many times, technology transfer fails because the resistance put up is just too strong to overcome. In such cases, it is important to realize that certain amounts and types of change are beyond our abilities to influence, regardless of how much time and effort we put forth. Besides, in industry, the rule of thumb is you do not have long to wait before the management and/or personnel of the organizations you have to deal with changes, so you can always try again.

References

Bloom, C. P., Wolff, A. S., & Bell, B. (in press). Introducing Advanced Technology Training Applications into your Organization. C. P. Bloom & R. B. Loftin (Eds.), *Facilitating the Development and Use of Interactive Learning Environments.* Hillsdale, NJ: Erlbaum.

Bullemer, P. T. & Bloom, C. P. (in press). Transferring Learning Systems Technology to Corporate Training Organizations: An Examination of Acceptance Issues. In C. P. Bloom & R. B. Loftin (Eds.), *Facilitating the Development and Use of Interactive Learning Environments.* Hillsdale, NJ: Erlbaum.

Carroll, J. (Ed.) (1995). *Scenario-based design for human-computer interaction.* New York: John Wiley & Sons.

Collins, A., Brown, J. S., & Newman, S. E. (1989). Cognitive apprenticeship: Teaching the crafts of reading, writing, and mathematics. In L. B. Resnick (Ed.), *Knowing, learning, and instruction: Essays in honor of Robert Glaser* (pp. 453-494). Hillsdale NJ: Erlbaum.

Jacobson, I., Christerson, M., Jonsson, P., & Overgaard, G. (1992). *Object-oriented software engineering: A use case driven approach.* Wokingham, England: Addison Wesley.

Lave, J., and Wenger, E. (1991). *Situated learning: Legitimate peripheral participation.* Cambridge: Cambridge University Press.

"Training and the Workplace: Smart Work," *The Economist* (22 August 1992), 21-22.

Wolff, A. S. (in press). Cost-Benefits Analysis for Computer-Based Tutoring Systems. In C. P. Bloom & R. B. Loftin (Eds.), *Facilitating the Development and Use of Interactive Learning Environments.* Hillsdale, NJ: Erlbaum.

Learning Evolution and Software Agents Emergence

Guy Boy

European Institute of Cognitive Sciences and Engineering (EURISCO)
4, avenue Edouard Belin, 31400 Toulouse, France
Tel. (33) 62 17 38 38; FAX (33) 62 17 38 39
Email: boy@onecert.fr

Abstract. New information technology (IT) is a major challenge to human adaptability. A crucial issue for the integration of new IT in the education system is the enhancement of its role of preserving cultural heritage, improving knowledge transferal and social integration. Software agents are computer programs that can be used to improve learning. Learning is described by five attributes: pleasure, learning how to learn, efficiency, allowing for errors in order to learn, and memory retention. These attributes guide the design of software agents that extend and support understanding, motivation, memory and reasoning capabilities. We will provide examples of agents that add pragmatics to current educational materials. They improve cooperative learning and cooperative design of pedagogical documents. These issues are discussed in the context of a critical analysis of the French educational system and the emergence of new information technology and software agents.

Keywords. Software agents, active documents, pragmatics in learning systems, computer-supported cooperative learning, educational memory.

1 Introduction

When I was asked to write this position paper for ITS'96, I was both extremely honored and puzzled due to the fact that I am not a main-stream specialist on the topic. As a scientist, my fields of investigation are human factors and computer science with a particular emphasis (specialization) in the aerospace domain. As the Director of European Institute of Cognitive Sciences and Engineering (EURISCO), I coordinate applied research efforts on training in aeronautics. As a father of two children, I am very interested in the current evolution of the integration of new information technology (IT) in a local education system. In this paper, I will try to clearly distinguish between what is already known and what is plausible, but I will take the opportunity to touch on some important issues related to intelligent tutoring systems (ITSs) as I see them.

The first question that comes to my mind is: what is *intelligent* in intelligent tutoring systems? Is intelligence in the system itself? Is intelligence in the interaction between the system and its user? Is intelligence the only capacity of people that would be enhanced by a properly designed ITS? For me, a smart system is a system that is natural to use and enhances my capabilities without too many surprises. As Norman already pointed out: Technology should serve us (Norman, 1993).

When I try to figure out the evolution of basic tasks during the last two milleniums, I observe very little change content-wise. We still need to eat, sleep, work for food, take care of our children and grand parents, fight for our freedom, etc.

However, the nature of our artifact-based activities has drastically changed. These activities have become more cognitive as the number of artefacts has increased. Human beings need to extend their abilities for reasons such as survival, knowledge increase, or conquest. If I had to give only one attribute of human intelligence, I would say *adaptability*. People are able to adapt to almost anything: cold and hot weather, unexpected situations, etc. They can make decisions using very imprecise, incomplete and uncertain information. Today, new information technology is a major challenge to human adaptability.

A crucial issue for the integration of new IT in the education system is the enhancement of its role of preserving cultural heritage, improving knowledge transferal and social integration. It can be used for at least three reasons:

- to develop autonomy and individual learning;
- to remove barriers caused by social or geographical isolation;
- to open the education system to the external world and facilitate synergy with local resources.

Information technology is taken within a broad scope including its integration and use at school, home, work and public places for instance. The main issues that will be developed in this paper are the following:

- Will computer-mediated IT give birth to a new educational system?
- What would the role of human beings in this educational system be?
- What will be the repercussions of this evolution on the way human learn?

Humans are often the victims of new information technology because they do not assimilate or integrate it in the right way, and/or at the right time. The use of new IT leads to the creation of new cognitive functions enabling the management of knowledge and action. A major issue is the integration of computer technology with the current external memories as extensions of the human memory. Computer technology enables knowledge management and storage. The education system is certainly a good example of a generator of corporate knowledge that is reused for the benefit of students, teachers and parents.

This paper introduces a concept of *educational memory* (EM), i.e., corporate memory (CM) for the education system. CM work currently developed at EURISCO is multidisciplinary and multidomain. It is currently focused on the construction of CM concepts for the aeronautical industry (Attipoe & Boy, 1995; Boy, 1995; Durstewitz, 1994; Israel, 1996). In many ways, CM problems encountered in the industry domain are very similar to the CM problems encountered in the education domain, even if the productivity issues are not quite the same. CM is also related to the development of *Intranets*. Intranets will enable massive information transfer within an organization. But they do not solve the major problem of existence or availability of the right information at the right time in the right place, and in the right understandable format. In this perspective, we propose the use of *software agents* as *intelligent assistant systems* (Boy, 1991a) that are computer programs facilitating human-computer interaction, as well as human-human communication through new IT. Agents are taken in the sense of Minsky's terminology (Minsky, 1985).

The agent-orientation of human-machine interaction is not new. Autopilots have been commonly used since the 1930's. Such agents perform tasks that human pilots usually perform, such as following a flight track, maintaining an altitude, etc. Transferring such tasks to the machine modifies the original task of the human operator. Thus, the job of the human operator evolves from a manipulation task (usually involving sensory-motoric skills) to a supervisory task (involving cognitive processing and situation awareness skills) (Sheridan, 1992). Software agent technology enables users to center their interactions at the content level (semantics) partially removing syntactic difficulties. It also enables users to index (contextualize) content to specific situations that they understand better (pragmatics).

The evolution of learning technology shows that we are heading towards the construction of pedagogical tools that add pragmatics to current educational materials. Creating *software agents* involves new cooperation and coordination processes that were not explicitly obvious before. I will present my view on *computer-supported cooperative learning* (CSCL). A specific case of cooperative learning in physics will be given. I will then focus on the requirements for an educational environment based on the construction and exchange of documents. Examples of software agents for cooperative learning will be provided.

2 How can we improve the education system in France?

François de Closets describes learning in the French education system as follows (de Closets, 1996):

- learning is a job in itself: we spend at least twenty years of our life learning at school, and for some of us at university;
- learning is a social issue that takes a large percentage of our national budget;
- learning is a very precious right and an obligation: children need to go to school;
- learning has become a selection process that promotes the best students and eliminates the others;
- learning takes place during a limited period of time before entering the work place.

I would like to give a different perspective to this description of learning. In addition to the fact that learning is a necessity for survival and should be a life long experience, I propose five attributes of learning:

- pleasure;
- learning how to learn;
- efficiency;
- allowing for errors in order to learn from them;
- memory retention.

Learning should be a pleasure. It seems that rigid education systems do not encourage the pleasure of learning. We need to be motivated to learn. Today, children are motivated to buy things and to watch television for instance. They are less motivated to learn, read, discover scientific matters, discover music, etc. Adults too. How can we make people discover the pleasure of learning? Recently, the emergence of *Internet* raised new issues in this direction. People who are involved in

Internet know that it is empowering to explore new sites where they can find information that they would not imagine existed. There is a need for studying the future of organized knowledge supported by new IT (Floridi, 1995).

Learning should be learning how to learn. Did we learn how to learn? Do our children learn how to learn? No. In France, it is implicitly assumed as a given that learning is part of our intellectual capabilities, and learning how to learn is not necessary. Teachers should try to encourage learning how to learn by providing appropriate artifacts that help students to learn. Most of these artifacts are based on experience. They are very rarely discussed and transfered. They deal with pragmatics. We say that this teacher is good because he/she knows how to present the right artifact at the right time according to students' needs and reactions. Students need to learn how to state problems. « The essence of intelligence is to act appropriately when there is no simple pre-definition of the problem or the space of states in which to search for a solution » (Winograd & Flores, 1986).

Learning should be efficient. Most people stop learning when they find that it is not efficient. They usually think that they are wasting their time because they do not see much improvement in the quantity and quality of the results. Usually, students stop learning because they are not motivated and discouraged when confronted with unecessarily complexified matters. Learning should be made simple enough to afford rapid understanding. Learning should be more situational. Again, students should be pleased with themselves after completing successfully an exercise for instance. Of course, there are complex things to learn. They are often boring to learn because they are poorly presented. These should be made more attractive using metaphorical artifacts that break down the complexity.

Learning should allow making errors and learning from errors. Education systems are often designed for only good students mostly because they are designed by a national elite for training the future national elite. Many students rarely make errors because they learn what they are told to learn and repeat it in the right way (like robots). They obtain diplomas and eventually become part of the national elite. The other students make errors and feel bad about them. There is no room in the education system for errors. I claim that errors are good for people. Experiencing errors is enriching and should be better investigated. There are errors that need to be made and recovery strategies that are good to practice. Life is not linear. People will experience problems all troughout their life. They should be armed to solve them. For this reason, errors are good for contextualizing learning.

Learning should improve memory retention. What things that we learn should or should not be remembered? How is this possible and effective? Today, information is extremely volatile. The quantity of information that we have every day on television, for instance, is too much to be remembered in depth. People do not make effort to remember everything because not everything is relevant. In contrast, there is important information that needs to be remembered. For example, there are many people who studied a foreign language for several years at school, and who, ten years later, are unable to speak it. Memory needs to be reactivated in order to persist. Activation can be improved using appropriate methods. The *art of memory* taught by the Greeks relied on specific indexing mechanisms that I would like to recall here.

3 The art of memory and the Descartes' dream

The art of memory as an indexing mechanism

The *art of memory*, invented by the Greeks, is not used today. People have almost forgotten it after the invention and practice of printing. This art enables someone to memorize *loci* (locations) and images imprinted on his/her memory. It is usually considered as a mnemotechnique. A *locus* is easily remembered, e.g., a house, a balcony, an angle, etc. Images are forms, distinctive signs or symbols of things that we need to remember. The art of memory is like internal writing. Even if it is not necessary, people who know the letters of the alphabet are able to write and read. Similarly, people who know the mnemotechnique are able to put what they have heard into specific loci and repeat it by heart (Yates, 1966). If we want to remember many things, we need to have a number of loci. A major condition is that the loci must be organized into a series that needs to be remembered in order. This way, one can go forwards or backwards from any locus. Yates considers that the loci have attributes such as: put distinctive signs every five loci; create these loci in isolated places; create memory loci that are different from each other.

The art of memory is a particular *indexing mechanism* that enables people to invent loci and images (indices) that help remember things. Emotional events tend to facilitate the formation of such loci and images. Images can be shocking and unusual, beautiful or ugly, funny or rude. Good stories create emotions that are likely to create useful indices that will facilitate remembering.

« The reason that we remember the stories teachers tell is that human memory is set up to retrieve and tell stories, as well as to capture the stories that others tell. The story is a unit of memory. Furthermore, good stories contain good images, novel ideas, or particularly poignant passages that enable our memories to create indices that make retrieval of these stories easier. Storytelling depends on being reminded of a good story to tell. And, reminding depends on having labeled the stories we have heard or have created well enough so that when those labels appear naturally in the course of a day, we can use them to find relevant stories. » (Schank & Jona, 1991).

Descartes and the mathematized world

Despite the very rich background of the art of memory, our current world is dominated by rationality that was first introduced by René Descartes in 1619. The Discourse on the Method[1] developed by Descartes consists of:

- accepting only what is so clear in one's own mind as to exclude any doubt;
- splitting large difficulties into smaller ones;
- arguing from simple to the complex; and
- checking, when one is done.

---

[1] « Discours de la Méthode pour bien conduire sa raison et chercher la vérité dans les sciences. »

Highly selective exams leading to the best French Universities (Grandes Ecoles) are essentially based on the ability of students to solve complex problems using analytical conceptual tools derived from Descartes' dream, i.e., according to Descartes, his « method » should be applied when knowledge is sought in any scientific field (Davis & Hersh, 1986). This trend has induced an elitist selection process where the same content is proposed to very different students from primary schools to universities. There is none or very little adaptation of the education programs to students. Students must conform or fail. For instance, modern mathematics introduces young people to set theory. They have been invented by clever scientists and technocrats. Students are now selected according to their understanding of such mathematics, but they often do not know how to calculate a simple restaurant bill. In our diploma-oriented society, there is no mercy for people who do not have the « right » diploma. Furthermore, people who have the right diploma are not necessarily cultivated, they may be even unemployed, and worst, they may not be happy at all (de Closets, 1996).

Making two different perspectives complementary

Computers are the latest tools that have emerged from this mathematized world introduced by Descartes. Today, computers are everywhere: at work, in administration, in amusement places, at home, etc. Computer games have become so popular that children have skills that many adults could not pretend to have, e.g., rapid reactions, moving target traking, computer commands discovery by exploration, etc. These are positive arguments in favor of computers. On the negative side, computers define a mathematics-based world where reality is made of simulations. People may accommodate to the simulated world and not to the real world.

In the Cartesian approach, learning consists of problem decomposition. Knowledge is divided into chunks that can be learned individually. Quantitative assessments can be made. They are used to incrementally select students. In the art of memory approach, it is difficult to assess students progress using mathematical criteria. This approach deals with real world situations and problems. Investigations are performed in a open world. In contrast, the Cartesian approach deals with more academic problems dealing with closed world situations (otherwise mathematics could not be applied). New IT provides a chance to combine these two different approaches. Software agents are likely to facilitate cognitive linking between humans and machines. On the one hand, they enable people to enhance their memory capabilities with the crucial condition that people master these external memory extentions. Otherwise, there is a risk of relying too much on software agents and forgetting more than remembering. On the other hand, they provide analytical means to enhance reasoning.

4 Human-centered tools for learning and teaching

Software agents: evolution, emergence and rationalization

Norman (1993) refers to the motto of the 1933 Chicago World's Fair: « Science Finds, Industry Applies, Man Conforms. » This was a machine-centered view that was acceptable since artefacts were built to fit people's bodies. This was sometimes complex, however designers often found the right mathematics to solve related problems. Today, artefacts need to fit people's minds. There is no mathematics for representing and solving social and cognitive problems. Norman proposes a new human-centered motto: « People Propose, Science Studies, Technology Conforms. » This is a new trend to make technology humane. I would like to propose an alternative view addressing this socio-technical issue:

Humans and Societies Evolve,
Tools Emerge,
Science Rationalizes.

First, instead of talking about technology, let us talk about tools that are built to enhance human capabilities. Tools emerge from a process of trial and error. This concept of emergence is essential since isolated people have difficulties creating new tools without a social context. New tools usually emerge because they are needed and appropriate technology is available. Scientists rationalize both evolution and emergence. Scientific results are inputs for the evolution, but they are not the only ones. In particular, people's background and external events play an important role in the evolution of humans and societies.

Today, in most industrialized countries, human activities have become more cognitive. We have moved from doing to thinking. Interaction with modern tools is less energy-based, and more information-based. Human-machine interaction is mediated by computers. This interpretation is crucial for the design of new learning tools since people will need to learn how to interact with computer agents. In particular, students will need to learn how to communicate and cooperate with software agents in order to enhance learning.

Evolution of computer-based learning tools

The initial learning technology focused on individualized instruction, i.e., standalone tutoring. The current view has evolved to the point where training and education must support inquiry-based learning, collaboration and learning as it is integrated into doing and using. What is a learning environment? Let us try to summarize the evolution of learning technology from conventional computer-based training to cooperative learning.

Computer-based training (CBT) concerns training where students and instructors use computers to improve conventional training. Each instruction method is based on a model (Boy, 1993). This model involves knowledge that needs to be learned, the student and the way knowledge will be conveyed to the student. Thus, there are at least three major issues in CBT: (1) knowledge representation and elicitation; (2) student modeling; (3) computer-student interface. Domain knowledge representation can be more or less formal according to its degree of complexity. It is important to capture student knowledge in order to improve training. In addition, student background and personality need to be taken into account. The computer-student interface should include both domain and student knowledge.

Intelligent tutoring systems (ITS) have been studied for almost two decades. They involve CBT and include several human-like features in their software. An ITS has explicit models of tutoring and domain knowledge. It is more flexible in its system's response. The major problem in the ITS approach is due to the philosophy of the industrial age where the current model supports the fact that learning is knowledge transfer. *This model does not work today because we need to be change-tolerant, as the world changes every day.* In the information age, we need to go from facts to process, and from isolation to cooperation (Soloway, 1993).

Interactive learning systems should enable the student to manipulate cognitive artifacts (Norman, 1992a) from several perspectives or viewpoints. Viewpoints can be shallow (interface level) or deep (interaction level). For instance, an airplane artifact can be seen from several viewpoints: a picture or a text explaining how it should be used (user viewpoint); the way it is built (engineering viewpoint); or how much it costs (financial viewpoint).

Cooperative learning systems provide students with access to other people's ideas and concepts (SIGCUE, 1992). They make it possible to exchange, discuss, negotiate, defend and synthesize viewpoints. By using cooperative learning systems, we drastically depart from the usual one-directional way of learning. Students are placed in a dynamic environment where they can express their own viewpoints, and incrementally adapt initial viewpoints to more mastered concepts. In addition, cooperative learning systems are mediating tools that enhance cooperation between students, teachers, parents and other people involved in the education system. In this paper, we define a computer-supported cooperative learning (CSCL) environment as an *external memory* where knowledge is exchanged via *electronic documents*.

Learning is an active and constructive social process. An essential aspect of knowledge is that it is contextualized. This is the reason why knowledge is so difficult to acquire and represent. It is vivid. The paradox is that when we think that we have formalized it (e.g., written on paper), it is already deactivated! We have to recontextualize it to adapt it to a new situation and make it vivid again. Contextualization can be seen as indexing in the sense of connecting chunks of knowledge. The contextualization process is facilitated when people learn by doing. It follows that learning technology needs to be highly interactive.

Integrating software agents into active documents

In section 2 of this paper, we provided five attributes to learning. These attributes can be used to design and refine software agents as human-centered tools for learning and teaching in the same way as Nielsen's attributes to test usability of computer user interfaces (Nielsen, 1993).

One way to avoid the need for extra training is to produce software agents that can be naturally used by people. The CID project is an example of integration of software agents into *active documents* (Boy, 1991b). Direct manipulation improves the design and use of active documents. A user-centered answer to facilitate the integration of CSCL environments is to satisfy conditions such as consistency of knowledge, internal consistency of the system that insures human reliability, context-sensitivity to the task, expert advice when it is needed, etc. Current documents are constructed from a variety of knowledge sources. They may have various formats according to the target and the available technology. The form and content of a document are both task-dependent (context of use) and domain-dependent (content). One of the main difficulties in designing active documents is to anticipate a very large number of contexts of use. Context of use is usually related to other entities such as situation, behavior, viewpoint, relationships among agents, discourse, dialogue, etc. Contextualization is extremely difficult using the conventional paper technology. It is made easier using computer technology when appropriate software agents are available or easy to construct.

If active documents are understood by the user without external help, then they are self-explanatory. Complementary documents are commonly used to understand original documents. In active documents, explanations should be formalized and transferred into a software agent that will help the user to better understand. For instance, in physics lab exercises, diagrams are presented to the students with missing parts that the students need to add in order to complete a consistent electrical circuit. On paper, these diagrams are presented to the student with a text explanation to explain what he/she needs to do. Using the computer, the same diagrams are active, so that by clicking on each part of them, hypertextual information (text or graphics) appears and explains what to do.

5 External cognition on an example

In the following example, software agents are added to existing documents to enhance their usability. Software agents provide *pragmatics* to the existing documents where syntax and semantics are already defined and will not be modified. This feature corresponds to the French unified school program. Even if this approach fits well with the French education system, we think that the separation of semantics and pragmatics is a general and useful concept for the design of active documents, i.e., electronic documents that include software agents.

An example in physics

Let us take an example of a formal course on electrical tension. In this example, we show how a conventional physics exercise can be transformed into an active document by the addition of appropriate software agents. A conventional page describing the notion of potential difference or tension follows (Figure 1). Teachers may add appropriate agents such as *denotation* agents that show relevant parts of graphics explained in the text. These agents associate text descriptions to corresponding graphical objects, and conversely. For instance, by dragging the mouse on the sentence "We observe a river water current", the denotation agent shows the relevant part (Figure 2).

In the same way, a *definition* agent can be programmed to establish the correspondence between a text description and a mathematical formula. When the text "altitude difference between two points" is activated by putting the mouse on top of it, a mathematical formula appears in context. The context is defined by the corresponding picture and the denotation of the two points A and B (Figure 3).

NOTION OF POTENTIAL DIFFERENCE OR TENSION

We observe a river water current. The altitude difference between two points of the river causes the existence of a water current between these two points.

In the same way, we observe an electrical current in a closed circuit. The potential difference between two points of the circuit causes the existence of an electrical current between these two points.

This analogy is displayed in the following figure:

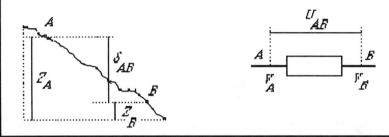

Figure 1. Basic pedagogical document.

NOTION OF POTENTIAL DIFFERENCE OR TENSION

We observe a river water current. The altitude difference between two points of the river causes the existence of a water current between these two points.

In the same way, we observe an electrical current in a closed circuit. The potential difference between two points of the circuit causes the existence of an electrical current between these two points.

This analogy is displayed in the following figure:

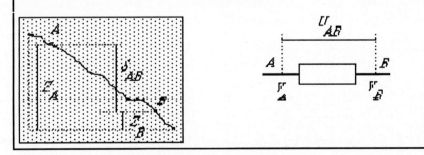

Figure 2. Use of a denotation agent.

An *analogy* agent gives the equivalence between various entities such as V_A and Z_A. By dragging the mouse on top of V_A, the altitude Z_A is highlighted and shows the analogy (Figure 4).

NOTION OF POTENTIAL DIFFERENCE OR TENSION

We observe a river water current. The altitude difference between two points of the river causes the existence of a water current between these two points.

In the same way, we observe an electrical current in a closed circuit. The potential difference between two points of the circuit causes the existence of an electrical current between these two points.

This analogy is displayed in the following figure:

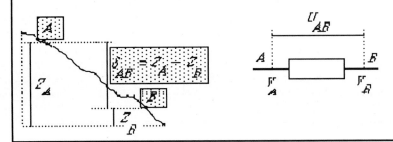

Figure 3. Use of a definition agent.

NOTION OF POTENTIAL DIFFERENCE OR TENSION

We observe a river water current. The altitude difference between two points of the river causes the existence of a water current between these two points.

In the same way, we observe an electrical current in a closed circuit. The potential difference between two points of the circuit causes the existence of an electrical current between these two points.

This analogy is displayed in the following figure:

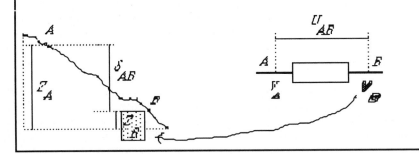

Figure 4. Use of an analogical agent.

These are very simple software agents that enhance the pragmatics of already designed physics courses. In this particular case, agents are basically hypermedia links between objects. Objects can be overlaid on top of graphical or textual parts of a conventional document to create active documents. There is a tool box of agent types that the teacher can choose to program his own agents by analogy. Agent types can be: denotation, definition, analogy, suggestive question, problem solving (decomposition of a problem into sub-problems), video management, evaluation, hypermedia link to another active document, etc. Once the teacher has chosen an agent type in the tool box, a procedure helps him/her to design the corresponding agent by clicking on appropriate objects or locations on the screen.

When in use, both students and teachers browse at their own speed active documents related to the lesson of the day. Individual backtracking is possible and encouraged. Eventually new agents can be created to enhance understanding of the concept to be learned. Students practice exercises by solving problems presented in active document exercises. In these documents, problem statements are put in context using agents in the same way as presented above. Suggestive questions guide the students. Hypermedia links to other relevant documents enable the student to remember concepts previously learned. An evaluation agent records students' paths in the various active documents, as well as the answers to the questions posed. By the end of a session active documents are collected and analyzed by the teacher either on-line with the students, or off-line.

An educational memory in use

Typical active documents such as those described above can be exchanged between teachers, students, parents, schools and homes. An educational memory is not a dead body of information but an actively growing accumulation of beliefs that have been put together (related or not) by people involved in the education process. These beliefs may evolve with time according to tests. An active document cannot become a stable and trustworthy knowledge entity[2] until it has been adequately communicated to and approved by other people. This is a reason to enhance the educational memory interactivity both within the education system itself, and with other parties such as industry and the civil organizations. The educational memory can be seen as a large set of interconnected active documents that are logically and historically organized. This logical and historical organization is performed using contextual descriptions of the documents as described previously. It also includes a classification of software agents. This classification is incrementally acquired using a concept clustering process applied to software agents constructed by teachers. The block representation handles the construction and re-construction of such documents' organization (Boy, 1991b).

Active documents should have appropriate indexing mechanisms. In the CID system, we have already developed an indexing mechanism that is suitable for incrementally updating descriptors of documents and attaching context to these descriptors. A descriptor is a partial description of the document that defines a particular semantic direction of search. A document is always partially described. This is why information retrieval is an *abduction* process (Peirce, 1931-1958). Abduction is the selection of a hypothesis from a predifined set. Context is added to the descriptors within a document to reduce the uncertainty characterizing the

---

[2]A trustable knowledge entity is garantied to work in a given context of validity. This is the case of physics formula such as Newton's law "f=ma" to measure forces at the surface of the Earth.

information retrieval process. Context is usually added either positively or negatively to descriptors after successful or unsuccessful document retrievals. When a document is retrieved, it not only provides content knowledge, but also contextual information such as who designed it, why it was designed the way it is (design rationale), who used it, who did not like it (user feedback), etc.

Let us take a scenario of active document search and reuse. First, a physics teacher decides to give a course on the notion of potential difference and tension. She decides to retrieve active documents generated by other people. She makes the assumption that using the educational memory, she will find interesting active documents that she can reuse and adapt to her course. She tries to describe what she needs by specifying a list of descriptors such as "potential difference" or "tension". After a first information retrieval attempt, she gets more than 100 active documents. She does not have time to examine the whole set. She then decides to add some context to the descriptors by specifying "tenth grade" and "physics course". She then gets 7 documents that she can browse. She sees that some of the documents mention that the evaluation feedback provided by other teachers on 4 of them is not acceptable. She decides not to consider these anymore. To decide which one of the 3 remaining documents she will keep, she reads the annotations provided by other teachers and uses the documents themselves. Once she has used the selected active document, she provides feedback information on her own use of it. She may say that some children could not understand some parts of it. Thus, she has made some modifications that are included and contextualized in the current active document. The document is returned to the educational memory.

In addition, a physics teacher may design a set of software agents that he/she can send to the educational memory for experimentation. Other teachers may use them and give their feedback. We think that this is a way to converge towards a normalization of pragmatics in the teaching of physics. The main problem is for teachers to carefully annotate the active documents that they create, modify or use. In the current project, we try to better understand the human factors involved in the use of such an educational memory, as well as the underlying mechanisms that are required to support it.

6 Conclusion and perspectives

In this paper, we assumed that technology is not a panacea for education. But, it can serve the proximal cause for mobilizing folks to actions (Soloway, 1995). Three main concepts have emerged: active documents, software agents and organization. Active documents are used as repositories of pedagogical knowledge. Both teachers and students should be able to easily create active documents, as well as modify old ones. To facilitate active document design and publishing, libraries of software agents need to be created and maintained[3]. Software agents are observers, information

---

[3]A major issue is the interoperability of software developed in a specific software environment. Software agents should be platform-independent. Furthermore, the combination of object-oriented techniques (a software agent is a software object) and component-based software has some essential benefits listed by Rappaport (1995): reuse, extendibility, customization, distributability, and standardization. An example

processors, and proposers. They can be active entities added to conventional documents transcribed into an electronic form. Some of them observe user's interactions. They are able to produce actions from the data they have acquired from the user. The action performed by a software agent ranges from the activation of other agents to the execution of (computational) operations. Software agents are easy to manipulate and relate to each others. They provide vivid behavior for a user interface. They can be visible (audible), or invisible (inaudible). When they are sensorial they have a presentation shape (usually called a metaphor) on the screen, or a sound, and a behavior. Otherwise, the user does not know that they exist. In the field of electronic documentation, agent adaptivity has been shown to be extremely useful in information retrieval (Boy, 1991b). In this case, software agents are knowledge-based mechanisms that enable the management of active documents. By manipulating active documents, it is anticipated that the education organization will evolve. It will produce a shareable memory that can be capitalized by the corpus of the teaching profession.

In the aeronautical domain, Airbus Training has implemented a procedure used by instructors that enables them to provide experience feedback, i.e., instructors ask for improvements or corrections of flaws in training tools based on the experience they have on these tools. Experience feedback is based on positive or negative experience that is interpreted by training specialists to generate or modify corporate knowledge. A corporate memory of the description of the various pedagogical tools is maintained using this procedure. The main point of such an organization is the optimization of the end product destined for the students.

The education system needs to better understand the notion of a product designed by a team of people for the needs of an evolving society. What do we want our children to learn? For doing what? Design rationale of educational products and experience feedback should be more explicit. In these conditions, teachers will be able to communicate about concrete descriptions of their pedagogical requirements by exchanging, using and refining software agents. The usability of an educational product could be tested using the learning attributes defined in section 2 of this paper.

It is widely recognized that humans will experience several changes in their professional life, because of technology changes as well as job changes. Training is no longer only a matter of an initial learning phase, but has become a life-time continuous process that can be based on intelligent assistance (Boy, 1991a) or performance support. Even if initial training (including theoretical courses) enables the acquisition of conceptual frameworks, intelligent assistance based on software agents can be seen as hands-on training with the possibility of zooming into deeper knowledge.

Back to the future

« Celestial navigation capitalized on the European virtues of mathematical theory and on instruments of high technological sophistication. In contrast, navigation in Oceania emphasized the deliberate refinement of people's intuitive sense of direction

---

of standardization of agent-based software is given in (General Magic, 1994).

and the learning of direct perceptual cues from the natural environment. From a seaman of Oceania, making a voyage is conceptualized as being within a pattern of islands, the positions of which are represented in his cognitive map » (Oatley, 1977).

Like the Polynesians who used dynamic cognitive maps to navigate across the Pacific more than 1,000 years ago, could we use software agents to extend our short-term and long-term memories to handle our « navigation » in our modern world? The *art of memory* may take a larger place within this framework in the future.

Acknowledgements

Many thanks to Jeffrey Bradshaw, Meriem Chater, Jean-Gabriel Ganascia, Mirella Huttunen, Rachel Israel, Alain Rappaport, Stéphane Sokorski and Helen Wilson for many useful and vivid exchanges on the topic.

References

Attipoe, A. & Boy, G.A. (1995). Modeling knowledge and access in corporate distributed information systems. Proceedings of the IJCAI'95 Workshop on Artificial Intelligence in Distributed Information Systems.

Boy, G.A. (1991a). *Intelligent Assistant System*. Textbook. Published by Academic Press, London.

Boy, G.A. (1991b). Indexing Hypertext Documents in Context. Proceedings *of the Hypertext'91 Conference*, San Antonio, Texas, December.

Boy, G.A. (1993). Operator and Student Models in Computer-Based Training. EURISCO Report no. T-93-005-GB-VI, Toulouse, France.

Boy, G.A. (1995). Supportability-based design rationale. *Proceedings of the IFAC Conference on Human-Machine Systems*, Boston, MA.

Davis, P.J. & Hersh, R. (1986). *Descartes' Dream. The World according to Mathematics*. Harcourt Brace Jovanovich, Inc.

de Closets, F. (1996). *Le bonheur d'apprendre*. Seuil, Paris, France.

Durstewitz, M.D. (1994). Reuse of Experience for Industrial Applications - A formal approach, *CSI'94, Cognitive Science in Industry*, Luxembourg, 28-30 September.

Floridi, L. (1995). The Internet and the future of organised knowledge. UNESCO Conference, Paris, France. March 14-17.

Israel, R. (1996). *L'oubli de l'oubli. Documents actifs et décision coopératives*. Mémoire de Diplôme d'Etudes Approfondies. Université Technologique de Compiègne. Rapport EURISCO.

Minsky, M. (1985). *The Society of Mind*. Touchstone Simon and Schuster.

Nielsen, J. (1993). *Usability engineering*. Academic Press. London.

Norman, D. A. (1992). Cognitive artifacts. In J. M. Carroll (Ed.), *Designing Interaction: Psychology at the Human-Computer Interface*. (pp. 17-38). Cambridge: Cambridge University Press.

Norman, D.A. (1993). *Things that make us smart*. Addison-Wesley Publishing Company, Reading, MA.

Oatley, K.G. (1977). Inference, navigation, and cognitive maps. In *Thinking - Readings in Cognitive Science*, P.N. Johnson-Laird & P.C. Wason, Cambridge University Press, Cambridge, UK, pp. 537-547.

Peirce, C.S. (1931-1958). *Collected Papers*, 8 vols. Edited by C. Hartshorne, P. Weiss, and A. Burks. Cambridge, Massachusetts: Harvard University Press.

Rappaport, A.T. (1995). Context, Cognition and Intelligent Digital Information Infrastructure. Personal Communication to be published.

Schank, R.C. & Jona, M.Y. (1991). Empowering the student: New perspectives on the design of teaching systems. *The Journal of the Learning Sciences*. Volume 1, Number 1, pp. 7-36.

Sheridan. T.B. (1992). *Telerobotics, Automation, and Human Supervisory Control.* MIT Press, Cambridge.

SIGCUE (1992). Computer supported collaborative learning. Bulletin of the Special Interest Group for Computer Uses in Education (SIGCUE). ACM Press, Spring, Vol. 21#3.

Soloway, E. (1993). *Interactive Learning Environments.* INTERCHI'93 Tutorial Notes, ACM, Amsterdam.

Soloway, E. (1995). Beware, Techies Bearing Gifts. Communications of the ACM, Vol. 38, No. 1, January.

Winograd, T. & Flores, F. (1986). *Understanding computers and cognition-A new foundation for design.* Addison-Wesley Pub. Comp., Inc. Reading, MA.

Yates, F.A. (1966). *The art of memory.* French translation by Daniel Arasse, 1975, Editions Gallimard, Paris, France.

Whither Technology and Schools: Collected Thoughts on the Last and Next Quarter Centuries

Allan Collins
BBN Educational Technologies
Cambridge, Massachussetts
U.S.A.

My talk will describe the evolution from Intelligent Computer Assisted Instruction to Intelligent Tutoring Systems to Interactive Learning Environments. I will theorize about why that evolution occurred and what are the critical characteristics of Interactive Learning Environments that will make them successful. I will then speculate about how Interactive Learning Environments will in the foreseeable future come to play a major role in education.

Instructional Design Tools Based on Knowledge Objects

David Merrill
ID2 Research Group
Department of Instructional Technology
Utah State University
Logan, Utah
U.S.A.

The ID2 Research Group is exploring the use of a knowledge-base consisting of specifically defined knowledge objects. In this architecture an instructional strategy represents various ways to show, or request the learner to provide, the elements of these knowledge objects. Because the elements (slots) of these knowledge objects are predefined, then an instructional strategy can be written once and reused to instruct a wide variety of subject matters, so long as the subject matter content can be partitioned into the slots of the knowledge objects.

In this presentation we will demonstrate the use of knowledge objects in the design of tutorial-based computer-based instructional systems and instructional simulations. We will demonstrate the Electronic TrainerOE and the ID2 Instructional Simulator. The underlying knowledge objects and instructional strategies used in these systems will be described.

A significant advantage of instructional design tools based on knowledge objects is a significant increase in the efficiency of the instructional development process.

Multi-Media Software Development and the Tools to Support It

Roger C. Schank
Institute for the Learning Sciences
Northwestern University
Evanston, Illinois
U.S.A.

One way to achieve the radical change needed by educational systems, both in business and schools, is to create new teaching devices. By attempting to build intelligent computers, we have learned a great deal about how people learn. By putting this knowledge about human learning to use in designing computer-based educational programs, we can create effective teaching devices for the future. The key aspect of computer-based learning environments is their ability to allow students to learn by doing. Computers can place students in new, different and interesting environments where they can direct their own learning, following their own interests and achieving goals they set for themselves. Most importantly, these environments can include large librairies of stories, on video, told by experts in particular fields. Of great importance to this process is the development of software tools which allow effective educational software to be built relatively quickly and efficiently. Examples of such tools developed at the Institute for the Learning Sciences and based on advanced research in cognitive psychology, computer science and education, will be shown.

Conceptual and Meta Learning During Coached Problem Solving

Kurt VanLehn

LRDC, University of Pittsburgh, Pittsburgh PA 15260, USA
http://www.cs.pitt.edu/~vanlehn vanlehn@cs.pitt.edu

Abstract. Coached problem solving is known to be effective for teaching cognitive skills. Simple forms of coached problem solving are used in many ITS. This paper first considers how university physics can be taught via coached problem solving. It then discusses how coached problem solving can be extended to support two other forms of learning: conceptual learning and meta learning.

1 Introduction

Coached problem solving occurs when a tutor and a student solve problems together. Sometimes the student takes the lead and the tutors merely indicates agreement with each step. At other times the tutor walks the student through particularly difficult parts of the solution. However, at all times they are focussed on solving the problem.

Coached problem solving is a kind of cognitive apprenticeship (Collins et al., 1989) wherein the activity is restricted to solving problems. When the coach is taking the lead in solving the problem, the coach is "modeling" the cognitive processes to be learned. A coach who seldom interrupts has "faded" her "scaffolding."

Simple forms of coached problem solving have been used by intelligent tutoring systems. For instance, model-tracing tutors (Anderson et al., 1995) use coached problem solving. As novice Lisp students enter each symbol, the tutor gives immediate negative feedback if the symbol is incorrect. If the student's second attempt to enter a correct symbol also fails, the tutor gives a hint. If the hint does not suffice to get the student to enter the correct symbol, the tutor tells the student what to enter.

By definition, coached problem solving does not include extended discussions of basic principles or concepts of the task domain. This is not to say that such discussion are valueless. Human tutors, even in procedural tasks domains such as Lisp coding, do interrupt coached problem solving with such discussions (Anderson et al., 1985; McArthur et al., 1990; Merrill et al., 1992). [1]

---

[1] During my talk, data from our current study of human physics tutors will be presented showing exactly how much time is spent on coached problem solving as opposed to other, more general discussions. A brief taxonomy of such "diversions" will be presented as well.

Coached problem solving is an effective form of instruction, especially for procedural knowledge. This is evident in the ubiquity of coached problem solving among human tutors (McArthur et al., 1990; Fox, 1993; Merrill et al., 1992; Lepper et al., 1993) and its success in machine tutors (Anderson et al., 1995; Lesgold et al., 1992; Mark and Greer, 1995; Shute, 1991; Shute and Psotka, 1996).

The success of coached problem solving is consistent with a widely accepted views on cognitive skill acquisition (VanLehn, 1996). Cognitive skill acquisition consists of three phases. (a) An initial phase wherein student acquire preliminary knowledge of the skill, primarily by reading descriptions of it. They do not actually try to apply the skill to solve problems during this relatively short stage. (b) The intermediate phase consists of learning how to solve problems by applying the knowledge first encountered in phase 1. This phase often lasts a long time. Students often need considerable help during at the beginning of this stage, and refer often to text, examples, teachers, peers or other sources of information about the skill. By the end of this phase, they can solve most problems without help. (c) Occasionally, a third phase occurs wherein students who can already perform the task continue to practice it until it becomes nearly automatic. During this phase, their speed and accuracy continues to increase, but the gains decrease according to a power law. Coached problem solving is relevant to the intermediate phase only, so we will confine subsequent discussion of learning theory to that stage.

During the intermediate phase, learning consists of two basic processes (Van-Lehn, 1996):

- *Practicing the application of existing knowledge.* This causes the knowledge to become easier to recall and apply on subsequent occasions.
- *Acquiring new knowledge.* This often occurs when students try to solve a problem, reach an impasse, realize that they are lacking some domain knowledge, and seek that particular piece of knowledge from a resource such as a textbook, solved example, teacher or peer.

If the instructional material presented during the initial phase were perfectly complete and students' understanding and memory for it were also perfect, then it would not be necessary to acquire new knowledge during the intermediate phase. But such perfection never occurs in practice, so students must often interrupt their problem solving to repair or extend their knowledge.

Coached problem solving encourages both forms of learning.

- The constant focus on solving problems maximizes the amount of practice that students get on applying their existing knowledge.
- The coach facilitates acquisition of new knowledge in two ways. (a) When the tutor provides immediate negative feedback own student errors, students find it easier to locate the incorrect or missing knowledge that caused the error. (b) When students have found an misconception in their thinking, the tutor is immediately available as a resource to aid the students' "debugging" of their knowledge.

Because coached problem solving encourages both forms of learning, one would expect it to accelerate learning, and that is indeed what one finds in the data.

In short, coached problem solving is a well understood, successful method of instruction. In the spirit of building on top of a success, rather than starting anew, this paper considers how coached problem solving can be extended to help students engage in two forms of learning that seem foreign to conventional coached problem solving, namely

- *conceptual learning*, which means acquiring the basic concepts of a task domain, using them precisely and recognizing their applicability in situations far removed from those studied in the classroom, and
- *meta learning*, which means acquiring new strategies for studying (learning) that are more effective than the ones that the student habitually uses.

This paper discusses our plans for encouraging these two kinds of learning in the context of a particular coached problem solving system, Andes, that is being built at LRDC and the US Naval Academy. The next section describes coached problem solving in Andes, and the sections following it describe extensions that will encourage meta learning and conceptual learning. Unfortunately, the implementation of Andes began just recently. The complete system is scheduled for testing in fall of 1997, although pieces of the system will be pilot tested as early as summer 1996. Thus, the following discussion is based on literature review and design. We hope it will be provocative.

2   Coached problem solving in Andes

This section first introduces the subject matter taught by Andes and the kinds of activities that students engage in when using Andes. It then begins to compare Andes to existing instructional systems for physics, indicating how its increased sophistication is needed in order to overcome their limitations.

2.1   An introduction to the task domain

The Andes system helps students learn classical Newtonian mechanics, a major part of university-level physics. This subject is arguably one of the most fundamental of all sciences. It is a prerequisite of virtually all advanced science and engineering courses in college.

A traditional physics problem asks the student to derive values for quantities. For instance, the problem in Figure 1, asks the student to find two quantities, an acceleration and a tension. At minimum, the solver must write down a system of equations and solve them. However, before writing the equations, a good solver will also produce force diagrams, such as those shown in Figure 1B, and will mentally plan the solution of the problem. For instance, the solver might say,

Okay, let's see what is going on here. The objects can either move clockwise, counterclockwise or not at all. I guess that the heavier object

Problem:

Consider two unequal masses connected by a
string that runs over a massless and
frictionless pulley, as shown in figure A.
Let m2 be greater than m1. Find the
tension in the string and the acceleration
of the masses.

Solution:

If the acceleration of m1 is a, the acceleration of m2 must be -a. The forces
acting on m1 and m2 are shown in figure B.

The equation of motion for m1 is
    T - m1*g = m1*a.

The equation of motion for m2 is
    T - m2*g = - m2*a.

Combining, we obtain

$$a = \frac{m2 - m1}{m2 + m1} g$$

and

$$T = \frac{2*m1*m2}{m1 + m2} g$$

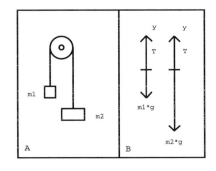

Fig. 1. A traditional physics example

will be the one going down, and that's m2. They want the acceleration
of the two blocks, which suggests applying Newton's law to them. They
move in opposite directions, so it won't work to put them together in a
single system. I'll have to use two systems, one for each block, and apply
Newton's law twice. So let's draw the forces for each system. [Draws the
2 force diagrams shown in pane B of Figure 1.]

This type of problem solving involves no algebraic manipulation. Therefore it
is called *qualitative analysis* in the physics education literature. It consists of 3
stages:

1. Determining how the objects will move over time. In the illustration just
   given, the student decided that one block would fall as the other block rose.
2. Planning a solution to the problem by choosing systems[2] and deciding which
   major principles, such as Newton's law or Conservation of Energy, to apply
   to each system. In the illustration, the student chose two systems, one for
   block 1 and one for block 2, and decided to apply Newton's law to each.

---

[2] A system consists of (1) a set of objects that are lumped together and treated as
a single body, (2) a period of time, and (3) a reference frame, which is used for
measuring velocity and other quantities. In the illustration, the student mentioned
the bodies of the two systems. Each body consisted of a single object, a block. The
student did not mention a time period or reference frame, as those details can be
added later if necessary.

3. Delineating the relevant mechanical quantities, such as forces, accelerations, energies, momenta, etc.

For complex problems, holding all this information in working memory may be difficult, so solvers may write some of it down. In the illustration above, for instance, the subject drew a force diagram.

Students often prefer to solve problems without first doing a qualitative analysis (Van Heuvelen, 1991a). They often do not even draw force diagrams (only 8% did on one of van Heuvelen's (1991a) tests). Students instead plunge right into writing and solving algebraic equations. The students' algebraic focus of attention often leads them to overlook important qualitative features of the problem (e.g., certain forces) and to make unwarranted but algebraically convenient assumptions.

Qualitative analysis can not only be used for planning the solution to problems, it can also be used alone to solve problems such as the ones shown in Figure 2. Such problems require no algebraic manipulation for their solution, so they are called *qualitative* problems.

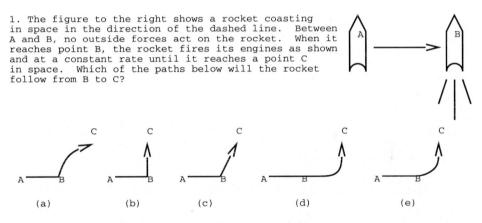

1. The figure to the right shows a rocket coasting in space in the direction of the dashed line. Between A and B, no outside forces act on the rocket. When it reaches point B, the rocket fires its engines as shown and at a constant rate until it reaches a point C in space. Which of the paths below will the rocket follow from B to C?

(a)   (b)   (c)   (d)   (e)

2. As the rocket moves from B to C, its speed is: (a) constant, (b) continuously increasing, (c) continuously decreasing, (d) increasing for a while, and constant thereafter, or (e) constant for a while, and decreasing thereafter.

Fig. 2. Some qualitative physics problems

Physics educators have adopted qualitative analysis as a primary instructional objective. There are several reasons for this:

— Physicists reason qualitatively not only on the simple problems used in physics courses (Chi et al., 1981; Larkin, 1983) but also when discussing physics with colleagues or presenting their results at conferences (Van Heuvelen, 1991a).

– After students leave their physics courses, those who do not become physicists will probably never solve another quantitative physics problem. Indeed, they probably couldn't even if they had to, because they will have forgotten many of the algebraic details of principles they had once mastered. However, they will have to do qualitative analyses, or at least partial analyses. They should be able to delineate forces, energies and momenta, and relate them to particle trajectories. Qualitative analysis is needed in many more scientific, technical and practical applications than quantitative analysis.

– Many students have misconceptions prior to physics courses, and these misconceptions survive intact when the instruction allows them to solve problems via algebraic reasoning (Halloun and Hestenes, 1985; Pfundt and Duit, 1991). When the instruction stresses qualitative analysis, fewer misconceptions escape remediation (Van Heuvelen, 1991b; Heller and Reif, 1984).

These are just some of the reasons that qualitative analysis has been adopted as an explicit instructional objective.

2.2 Student activities while using Andes

Andes must have a user interface that allows students to conveniently express their qualitative analyses. This interface serves two purposes. It reifies the abstract notion of a qualitative analysis, and that in itself can cause significant learning (Collins and Brown, 1990; Koedinger and Anderson, 1993; Singley, 1990; Merrill et al., 1992). Second, it allows students to show their qualitative analyses to the tutor so it can check them and offer advice. We are not yet sure what the user interface will look like, but one idea is to use textual forms. For instance, the following form might be generated by Andes for the qualitative analysis of the balloon-pulley problem of figure 1 (the italicized text is entered by the student):

– What happens?
  • Balloon A moves *straight up*
  • Mass A moves *straight up*
  • Balloon B moves *straight down*
  • Mass B moves *straight down*
  • Moving at the same speed are: *balloon A, mass A, balloon B, mass B*
– What is your solution plan?
  • Apply *Newton's law* to the system consisting of *mass A*.
  • Apply *Newton's law* to the system consisting of *mass B*.

Part of qualitative analysis is to delineate forces and other quantities. Forces are conventionally depicted on a diagram such as the ones in panes A and B of figure 1. Andes will have students display forces with such diagrams. Similar diagrams or textual forms will be invented for displaying other mechanical quantities, such as energies, momenta and motion vectors.

The students' activity when using Andes will consist of simply solving problems or studying problems that have already been solved (examples). When solving problems, students typically will enter a qualitative analysis using a form such as the one above and one or more vector diagrams, and then enter equations. They (or Andes) would then solve the equations algebraically. Some problems, such as the ones in figure 2, would require only a qualitative analysis. Other activities might provide a qualitative analysis but ask students to generate equations. Such activities serve partially as examples and partially as problems. Many such mixtures are possible.

2.3 Immediate feedback

The Andes system, as presented so far, does nothing that could not be done with pencil and paper. Physics educators have often used form-based scaffolding of qualitative problems solving, sometimes with remarkably good effects (Van Heuvelen, 1991b). Andes will go further in several ways, the first of which is providing a capability for immediate feedback.

Andes will know every possible correct solution path to the problems it presents. If a student's entry is not along any of the correct solution paths, the student can be given immediate negative feedback.

Sometimes the feedback will consists of simply highlighting the entry and saying that it is incorrect. However, Andes cannot use such "flag" tutoring with all errors, because many entries can be corrected by guessing (e.g., if the entry $sin(30)$ is flagged as wrong, some student immediately try $cos(30)$). When guessing seems likely to lead to a correct entry, the feedback will take the form of a question about the line of reasoning leading up to the correct entry (e.g., "Is the side adjacent or opposite?"). Although other physics tutoring systems have provided immediate feedback (Kane and Sherwood, 1980), they have not tried to prevent guess-based corrections to errors.

2.4 Fading

Fading is another feature of Andes that differentiates it from conventional physics instruction. Fading, which is the last phase in a cognitive apprenticeship (Collins et al., 1989), is the gradual removal of explicit supports for a cognitive process. Fading must be done in such a way that students continue to perform the target cognitive processes.

In the case of Andes, there are two forms of scaffolding: the user interface for qualitative analysis and the immediate feedback. Both should be faded. In particular, Andes will initially *require* that students enter a qualitative analysis before producing the equations, and it will gradually stops requiring such an explicit entry.

If a tutor does not successfully fade its scaffolding, then students may simply revert to their old bad habits as soon as they exit the tutor. This seems to have occurred with a physics tutoring system implemented by Bruce Sherwood and his colleagues as part of the Plato system (Kane and Sherwood, 1980). It was similar to Andes except that the solutions to problems were authored by humans instead of a model. In particular, it explicitly taught qualitative analysis and insisted that students do it before writing equations. When the final exam scores were compared, Plato students scored significantly higher than students taught conventionally, but the size of the effect was disappointing (approximate 35% of sigma) (Jones et al., 1983). Although the lackluster result is open to many explanations, the one that Sherwood endorsed during a recent talk (September, 1996) is that students simply did not use qualitative analysis on the final exam. Some students thought they didn't need to use it because they could correctly solve the problems without it and it would just slow them down. Other students thought that qualitative analysis did not apply to exam problems! Sherwood's interpretation corresponds with the experience of physics instructors who have explicitly and forcefully taught qualitative analysis in their classes and recitations, only to find students using purely algebraic problem solving on the homework and exams (Van Heuvelen, 1991a). In short, it is one thing to teach students how to do qualitative analysis, and it is quite another thing to get them to actually do it routinely. It is crucial that Andes fade its support for qualitative analysis in such a way that students continue to perform it either on paper or mentally.

Immediate feedback should also be faded, but for a different reason. Fading prevents students from becoming too dependent on feedback (Collins et al., 1989).

2.5   Procedural help

The features of Andes that have that has been described so far could be implemented with minor extensions to Olae, a student modeling and assessment system for physics (Martin and VanLehn, 1995b; Martin and VanLehn, 1995a; Martin and VanLehn, 1993). Olae could determine whether a students entry was correct and it could assess the student's probability of mastery for each physics rule. With the addition of a few heuristics, it could use rule-mastery to control fading of the scaffolding and immediate feedback. Although such a system would probably be better than its predecessors, it would occasionally be extremely frustrating to students because it would have no capability of providing helpful hints when they get stuck. As it turns out, providing such help requires a significant extensions.

In order to find out what kind of help students would need, we conducted a pilot study with a human tutor who played the role of Andes. The tutor sat in a different room from the student, but could see a copy of the student's screen. When the student wanted help, the student would type "help," and the tutor would pick up the phone and talk to the student. Notes were taken during the sessions with 9 students, and 73 help requests were observed.

Of the 73 help requests, 18 were simply requests for immediate feedback. The students often just asked, "Is that ok?" referring to their most recent entry. This kind of help could be provided by an Olae-based tutor.

The most common help request (27 occurrences) was the students' indication, in various ways, that they were lost and needed a hint about what to do next. Providing such a hint requires knowing which solution path the student has been pursuing so far and what would be the next reasonable step along it. This is a form a plan recognition. The Olae framework was extended to do this form of plan recognition and a new student modelling engine, Pola, was implemented (Conati and VanLehn, 1996; Conati and VanLehn, 1995). Pola will become the basis for the student modelling module of Andes. Once it has selected an appropriate next step for the student, Andes will construct a series of increasingly specific hints leading up to that step.

The next most common help request (14 occurrences) consisted of asking for help in achieving a specific goal. Some examples, paraphrased to make them easier to understand, are:

- How do I find the acceleration of block2?
- How can I find out which direction that force acts?
- How do I convert kilograms to Newtons?
- How to I eliminate mass from that equation?
- How do I solve that equation for acceleration?

Before giving help in achieving the goal, Andes should check that the goal is appropriate. Sometimes the proposed goal is not on a solution path. Sometimes the goal reveals a misunderstanding (e.g., one cannot convert kilograms to Newtons because kilograms measures mass and Newtons measure force). If the goal is appropriate, then a succession of increasingly more specific hints can be devised based on the goal tree for achieving the stated goal, as is done in many tutors (e.g., (Anderson et al., 1995)).

The remaining help requests (14) all revealed a conceptual misunderstanding of some kind. They will be discussed in the next section.

In most of the help requests ($27 + 14 = 41$ of 73), the students wanted to know what to do next. Andes will tell them, albeit obliquely via a series of hints. The hints will be based on Andes' data base of correct solution paths. Thus, this type of help is called "procedural."

The capabilities discussed so far make Andes similar to a model-tracing tutor (Anderson et al., 1995). Like the model-tracing tutors, Andes can give immediate feedback and procedural help. Unlike the model-tracing tutors, Andes intermingles example studying and problem solving, and it fades its scaffolding. Most importantly, Andes does not confine the students to only a small set of solution paths, as most of the model-tracing tutors do. Enforcing a rigid problem solving style on students is possible in physics, but it would be completely unacceptable to many physics instructors. Andes allows students to pursue any correct solution path, even though causes extraordinary combinatorial problems during student modeling (Conati and VanLehn, 1996; Conati and VanLehn, 1995).

Nonetheless, despite the high technology required to implement feedback, procedural help and the other Andes' features discussed so far, the students will see approximately the same level of support and the same kinds of activities as those afforded by a model tracing tutor. Thus, one would expect approximately the same pedagogical improvement over classroom instruction (Shute and Psotka, 1996). In order to obtain qualitatively greater benefits, we need to encourage new kinds of learning. The next sections describe them.

3   Conceptual help

In the discussion of types of learning, it was mentioned that coached problem solving, and model tracing tutors in particular, encouraged both acquiring of new knowledge and practicing the application of existing knowledge. How can we improve on that?

One answer arises from considering exactly how procedural help supports the acquisition of new knowledge. Suppose a student is lacking a particular rule (call it the target rule) and that hinting does not cause the student to invent it. Eventually, the procedural help system will simply tell the student what to do next. From this, the some students might induce a very specific version of the target rule. Other students might realize the need to generalize their experience, and ask the tutor to explain why the action it suggested is correct. The tutor prints the line of reasoning leading up to the action. Suppose our student is perceptive enough to determine which inference in the line of reasoning is due to the unknown (target) rule. The student asks the tutor to explain that inference. Now the tutor is at a loss for words. Its only representation of knowledge is the rule itself. It cannot explain or justify any of its rules simply because it has no representation of knowledge other than the rules themselves. In this respect, the tutor's knowledge is fundamentally shallow. The rules contain just enough information to allow them to solve problems correctly; they do not need to represent their intellectual heritage, so they do not.

Better students might be stimulated by the tutor to wonder about the veracity of its rules, seek information from a teacher or text, and end up learning just would one would like them to learn. But such good students probably do not need a tutor in the first place. Less capable or motivated students will simply accept the tutor's "rote" version of the rules. Perhaps the worst outcome may occur with students who seek a deeper explanation for rules but cannot find one; they may accept the tutor's rule in order to move forward on the problem solving, but doubt its veracity. Thus, if the tutor cannot explain individual rules, students may acquire "rote" rules whose veracity they doubt.

This assumes that individual rules actually have deep justifications that are worth knowing. This is not always the case. Some rules are just arbitrary. For instance, the Lisp tutor has many rules of the form "if you want to code a conditional statement, set the goal of entering COND." This rule reflects an arbitrary choice by John McCarthy, the inventor of Lisp, to start conditional statements with the word "COND." This rule cannot be proved via scientific experiments or mathematical logic. In order to learn Lisp, students must accept it "without proof" because it is not the sort of rule that needs proof.

Other rules are true by assumptions. For instance, an equation solving tutor has rules expressing the distributive law, the associative law and other fundamental postulates of arithmetic. Although a student could debate the truth of these rules, the debate would swiftly lead into the deepest parts of the foundations of mathematics where there are no easy answers to satisfy the curious student. For most students, it is better simply to treat the laws as extraordinarily useful assumptions and not to try to justify them further.

Most the model tracing tutors to date have been in mathematics or programming, where most of the rules are either arbitrary or true by assumptions. In physics, many rules are open to debate. For instance, many students find it difficult to believe that when an object rests on a surface, the surface exerts a force on it (called the normal force). Physics problem solvers typically represent this assertion as a single rule. The problem solver does not "know" why the normal force rule is true. If asked, it could not justify the rule to the student. Yet such a justification is exactly what some students need to hear in order to deeply understand the normal forces.

There is a converse problem as well. Students often have specific beliefs that are not true. Many of these have been observed. The Pfundt and Duit (1991) bibliography of the misconceptions literature is in its fourth edition and has thousands of entries. As Ploetzner and VanLehn (in press) demonstrated, many mechanics misconceptions can be easily represented as rules. For instance, one rule is, "If an object is moving in a certain direction, then there is a force on the object in that direction." As many investigators have found, simply telling the students that there is no such force will not convince them to abandon belief in it. Even producing experimental evidence against the belief is seldom convincing (Smith et al., 1993). Nonetheless, the tutor must do something to undermine belief in incorrect rules.

In short, we need to extend the model tracing paradigm in two ways. The tutor needs to be able to justify correct rules. It also must explicitly represent the most popular incorrect beliefs as rules and provide arguments against them.

Physics educators have tried many techniques to alter students' beliefs. There is a vast literature full of good ideas that we have only begun to tap. Our plan is to construct a library of "minilessons," where a minilesson is a short multimedia lesson on a particular concept.

Similar themes seem to occur in multiple minilessons. For instance, one theme is viewing the situation at the atomic level. Clement and his colleagues showed that students could be convinced to believe in the normal force rule showing the students that even the most rigid surface is springy at the atomic level (Murray et al., 1990). Placing an object on the surface causes it to indent ever so slightly. Once the students believe this (and they are generally more willing to accept statements about atomic phenomena than observable phenomena), then they can be easily convinced that normal forces exist.

Another common theme involves debugging confusions about the notion of differentiation with respect to time. Differentiation underlies several pairs of concepts that are often confused by students: Acceleration is the differential of velocity. Force is the differential of momentum. Work is the differential of energy. Students often confuse quantities related by a differential. For instance, many students believe that any object in motion has a force acting on it in the direction of motion, and that the faster the object moves, the stronger the force. Although there is no such force, any object in motion does have a momentum that is in the direction of motion and proportional to the object's speed. Thus, confusing force and momentum is one source for this misconception. (There are others.) Similarly, students often confuse acceleration and velocity (Reif, 1987). They think that the acceleration at the apex of a vertically thrown object is zero, when in fact it is the velocity that is zero. The minilessons that teach students to distinguish acceleration from velocity should appeal to the same differentiation sub-text as the minilesson that teaches students to distinguish force from momentum. We hope that this will encourage learning of the underlying abstraction. Similar comments apply to the underlying abstraction of constraint-based interactions (Chi, 1992; Chi et al., 1994b; Slotta et al., 1995), which seems to be involved in many difficult-to-learn concepts.

Minilessons will be initiated under a variety of circumstances. When the procedural help system's hints have finally gotten the student to make a correct entry, and the student model indicates that it is likely that the student did not know one of the rules involved in generating that action, then the conceptual help system will try to determine how ell the student learned the target rule. (Natural language interaction would be ideal for this interrogation, but well beyond the state of the art.) If the help system or the student feel that the rule is not adequately understood, either may initiate the minilesson.

Minilessons are also initiated during "terminology help," where terminology help is a simple hypertext technique based on Moore and Swartout (1990). Whenever the system prints anything substantive—including the statement of the physics problem, feedback messages, procedural help, etc.—most of the technical phrases in the text are underlined. Clicking on a underlined phrase causes a short explanation of its meaning in this context to be printed. This explanation will also have some underlined phrases. The need for terminology help became apparent in analyzing the 14 non-procedural help requests that we observed in the pilot study. Of these, 5 were requests for clarification of phrases in the problem statement. For instance, on one problem, which involved a parachute slowing the descent of a woman, mentioned "the retarding force on the parachutist." Students often did not realize that the parachute was pulling upward on the woman and thus was exerting a force on her, so they did not understand what the phrase "retarding force" was referring to. In 6 cases, students asked general questions about physics or algebra, such as "what is a system of equations?" Thus, in 11 of the 14 cases, some kind of terminology help would have been appropriate.

Some of the terminology help messages will have a minilesson button attached to them. Clicking on the button initiates a minilesson Thus, minilessons can be entered from both the procedural and terminology help systems.

3.1 Meta help

So far, we have assumed that the only goal of the tutor is to teach the students the task domain, which is physic in this case. However, if we expand the instructional goals, new kinds of learning will need to occur. This section proposes a new instructional goal for Andes, and discusses how it can be achieved.

Some student employ better strategies for studying than others. For instance, Chi et al. (1989) found that some student studied examples by explaining each line of the solution to themselves, whereas other students merely read the examples thorough in a cursory manner knowing that they could come back to them later if necessary. The students who self-explained the examples learned more not only during the example studying phase but also during a subsequent problem solving phase as well (VanLehn et al., 1992; VanLehn, 1995b). Thus, there is a correlation between a studying strategy, self-explanation, and the students' learning. This same correlation has been found in many other situations (Pirolli and Bielaczyc, 1989; Ferguson-Hessler and de Jong, 1990; Pressley et al., 1992; Chi et al., 1994a; Recker and Pirolli, 1995; Lovett, 1992). Protocol analysis and cognitive modeling have resulted in a thorough understanding of what the self-explanation strategy is and why it increases learning (VanLehn et al., 1992; VanLehn and Jones, 1995; Pirolli and Recker, 1994; Recker and Pirolli, 1995).

Recently, another naturally occurring studying strategy was discovered (Van-Lehn, 1995a). When solving problems, some students notice that the problem is similar to an already solved problem or example, but they do not immediately refer to it. Instead, they try to solve their problem without help, and refer to the example only when they reach an impasse and need help. This studying strategy is called Min analogy. Students using Min analogy learned more during problem solving than students who used a strategy called Max analogy, wherein they refer to the example as soon as they notice its relevance and continually refer to it as they work on the problem.

Other effective studying strategies have been observed, albeit less formally. For instance, Collins and Brown (1990) suggested that reflecting on ones' solution to a problem can speed learning. VanLehn (1991,1995b) suggested that adopting a wary, reflective stance while solving problems helps students notice opportunities for improvement in their methods.

There is evidence that studying strategies can be taught. Bielaczyc, Recker and Brown (1994) taught students how to self-explain in the classic cognitive apprenticeship manner. That is, they first demonstrated self-explanation (using a videotape of an actor), then helped the student practice self-explanation as they studied Lisp, then finally faded their help leaving the student to self-explain without prompting or help. The students who were taught to self-explain learned more than students who received an equivalent amount of time on the Lisp-learning task. Chi et al. (Chi et al., 1994a) showed that merely prompting a student to self-explain after each line caused them to learn the skill, and that in turn caused them to learn more of the target material (cardiophysiology). Shauble, Raghavan and Glaser (1993) taught students to reflect on their problem solving with a special tutoring system, and this caused increases in learning (Raghavan, personal communication, May 1995).

Andes will teach effective studying strategies not only because they should help the students learning physics, but also because they should help the students in their other courses as well.

For instance, in order to teach self-explanation, Andes will have students study examples using the "poor man's eyetracker," a software module developed for Olae. The example appears on the screen, but all its text, equations and diagrams are hidden by boxes that are the same shape as the hidden material. When the student clicks on a box, the box is removed and the material is exposed for the student to read. When the student clicks on another box, the first box is restored and the new box is removed. In this fashion, the student can read the example in any way desired but the machine can determine which lines the student has read, for how long the student spent contemplating the line, and whether the student went back to earlier lines while studying this line. On the basis of these data, the tutor decides whether the student has self-explained the example. If the student has not, then the tutor will not let them leave the example, but instead says, "You went through that example rather fast. There are some interesting things to learn from it. Perhaps you should seek them out." If the student goes back and studies the lines where, according to the tutor's analysis, rules unfamiliar to the student have been applied, then the tutor will decide that the student is self-explaining the example and learning from it. On the other hand, if the student again glosses the example, the tutor will make an even stronger suggestion, and perhaps even point out the line(s) that require attention. We are not yet sure of the details of the interaction (we need pilot subjects to find this out), but the intent is to use the eye-tracker to monitor the student's studying strategy and use blunt suggestions to modify it if necessary.

Because the sort of studying strategies that Andes will teach are sometimes called meta strategies (in order to distinguish them from problem solving strategies, such as means-ends analysis), we call this kind of tutoring *meta help*.

4   Conclusions

This paper has presented a plan for a tutoring system that goes several steps beyond the state of the art in model-tracing tutoring systems. The following are some of the less exciting but still important advances:

1. Andes will support a more flexible form of problem solving that allows students to pursue any correct solution path, rather than restricting them to ones that the tutor is prepared to recognize. This causes combinatorial difficulties in the student modelling module, which we have begun to conquer (Conati and VanLehn, 1996).
2. Andes will intermingle example studying and problem solving, which is intended to more closely approximate the kinds of mixed initiative problem solving that occurs during human-tutor coached problem solving.
3. Andes will fade its scaffolding by gradually removing both feedback and the requirement that students fill out a qualitative analysis form before doing algebraic manipulations.
4. Andes will provide terminological help by using hypertext for all substantive messages from the tutor; clicking on a confusing phrase will cause an explanation of it to be printed.
5. Andes will replace its customary minimal feedback with more focussed feedback whenever it is likely that receiving minimal feedback would allow students to guess the correct entry rather than figuring it out.

It is fairly clear how to implement most of these features. We expect them to provide minor enhancements either to students' learning or to the acceptance of the tutor by physics instructors.

However, our hope for major enhancements lies in two rather novel and risky forms of help: conceptual help and meta help. Conceptual help is based on the observation that in many task domains, problem solving rules only represent the minimal knowledge required to solve problems. In such domains, many rules have behind them a rich explanation and justification that students need to know. Such knowledge is often called "conceptual" knowledge. Andes' conceptual help system will consist of a library of minilessons and a variety of heuristics for invoking them. The most difficult part of the conceptual help system is coming up with minilessons that actually work. We hope to find several explanatory themes or techniques that can be used to design multiple minilessons.

Meta help is designed to get students to change their studying techniques. This is not simply another procedural skill that needs to be taught. Many students have a motivational set that emphasizes moving as quickly as possible thorough the material while getting as many problems correct as possible. In Carol Dweck's seminal work (Dweck, 1986), such students are called "performance oriented." Other students, whom Dweck calls "learning oriented," care less about getting the right answers than in learning the material. The overall goal of the meta help system is to not only teach students effective studying techniques but to change their orientation from performance to learning.

5 Acknowledgements

This research is supported by ONR's Cognitive Science Division under grant N00014-96-1-0260, and by DARPA's Computer Aided Education and Training Initiative under grant N66001-95-C-8367. The LRDC Andes team currently comprises Patricia Albacete, Cristina Conati, Marek Druzdzel, Abigail Gertner, Zhendong Niu and Anders Weinstein. The US Naval Academy Andes team comprises Dave Correll, Kay Schulze, Robert Shelby and Mary Wintersgill. This paper could not have been written without their crucial input during the long process of pulling the Andes design together.

References

Anderson, J., Farrell, R., and Saurers, R. (1985). Learning to program in Lisp. *Cognitive Science*, 8:87–129.

Anderson, J. R., Corbett, A. T., Koedinger, K. R., and Pelletier, R. (1995). Cognitive tutors: Lessons learned. *The Journal of the Learning Sciences*, 4(2):167–207.

Bielaczyc, K., Pirolli, P., and Brown, A. L. (1995). Training in self-explanation and self-regulation strategies: Investigating the effects of knowledge acquisition activities on problem-solving. *Cognition and Instruction*, 13(2):221–252.

Chi, M., Bassok, M., Lewis, M., Reimann, P., and Glaser, R. (1989). Self-explanations: How students study and use examples in learning to solve problems. *Cognitive Science*, 15:145–182.

Chi, M., de Leeuw, N., Chiu, M.-H., and LaVancher, C. (1994a). Eliciting self-explanations improves understanding. *Cognitive Science*, 18:439–477.

Chi, M., Feltovich, P., and Glaser, R. (1981). Categorization and representation of physics problems by experts and novices. *Cognitive Science*, 5:121–152.

Chi, M. T. H. (1992). Conceptual change within and across ontological categories. In Giere, R., editor, *Cognitive models of science: Minnesota studies in the philosophy of science*. University of Minnesota Press, Minneapolis, MN.

Chi, M. T. H., Slotta, J. D., and de Leeuw, N. (1994b). From things to processes: A theory of conceptual change for learning science concepts. *Learning and Instruction*, 4:27–43.

Collins, A. and Brown, J. S. (1990). The computer as a tool for learning through reflection. In Mandl, H. and Lesgold, A., editors, *Learning issues for intelligent tutoring systems*. Springer, New York.

Collins, A., Brown, J. S., and Newman, S. E. (1989). Cognitive apprenticeship: Teaching the craft of reading, writing and mathematics. In Resnick, L. B., editor, *Knowing, learning and instruction: Essays in honor of Robert Glaser*, pages 543–494. Lawrence Erlbaum Associates, Hillsdale, NJ.

Conati, C. and VanLehn, K. (1995). A student modeling technique for problem solving in domains with large solution spaces. In Greer, J., editor, *Proceedings of the 1995 Artificial Intelligence and Education Conference*. Association for the Advancement of Computers in Education, Charlotsville, NC. Abstract only.

Conati, C. and VanLehn, K. (1996). Pola: A student modeling framework for probabilistic on-line assessment of problem solving performance. In Chin, D. N., Crosby, M., Carberry, S., and Zukerman, I., editors, *Proceedings of UM-96, the Fifth International Conference on User Modeling*, pages 75–82. User Modeling, Inc., Kailua-Kona, Hawaii.

Dweck, C. S. (1986). Motivational processes affecting learning. *American Psychologist*, 41:1040–1048.

Ferguson-Hessler, M. and de Jong, T. (1990). Studying physics texts: Differences in study processes between good and poor solvers. *Cognition and Instruction*, 7:41–54.

Fox, B. A. (1993). *The Human Tutorial Dialogue Project: Issues in the Design of Instructional Systems*. Lawrence Erlbaum Associates, Hillsdale, NJ.

Halloun, I. A. and Hestenes, D. (1985). Common sense concepts about motion. *American Journal of Physics*, 53(11):1056–1065.

Heller, J. I. and Reif, F. (1984). Prescribing effective human problem-solving processes: Problem descriptions in physics. *Cognition and Instruction*, 1(2):177–216.

Jones, L. M., Kane, D., Sherwood, B. A., and Avner, R. A. (1983). A final-exam comparison involving computer-based instruction. *American Journal of Physics*, 51(6):533–8.

Kane, D. and Sherwood, B. (1980). A computer-based course in classical mechanics. *Computers and Education*, 4:15–36.

Koedinger, K. and Anderson, J. R. (1993). Reifying implicit planning in geometry: Guidelines for model-based intelligent tutoring system design. In Lajoie, S. P. and Derry, S. J., editors, *Computers as cognitive tools*. Lawrence Erlbaum Associates, Hillsdale, NJ.

Larkin, J. (1983). The role of problem representation in physics. In Gentner, D. and Stevens, A., editors, *Mental Models*. Lawrence Erlbaum Associates, Hillsdale, NJ.

Lepper, M. R., Woolverton, M., Mumme, D. L., and Gurtner, J. (1993). Motivational techniques of expert human tutors: Lessons for the design of computer-based tutors. In Lajoie, S. P. and Derry, S. J., editors, *Computers as Cognitive Tools*, pages 75–105. Lawrence Erlbaum Associates, Hillsdale, NJ.

Lesgold, A., Lajoie, S., Bunzo, M., and Eggan, G. (1992). Sherlock: A coached practice environment for an electronics troubleshooting job. In Larkin, J. and Chabay, R., editors, *Computer Assisted Instruction and Intelligent Tutoring Systems: Shared Goals and Complementary Approaches*, pages 201–238. Lawrence Erlbaum Associates, Hillsdale, NJ.

Lovett, M. C. (1992). Learning by problem solving versus by examples: The benefits of generating and receiving information. In *Proceedings of the Fourteenth Annual Conference of the Cognitive Science Society*. Lawrence Erlbaum Associates, Hillsdale, NJ.

Mark, M. A. and Greer, J. E. (1995). The vcr tutor: Effective instruction for device operation. *The Journal of the Learning Sciences*, 4(2):209–246.

Martin, J. and VanLehn, K. (1993). OLAE: Progress toward a multi-activity, Bayesian student modeler. In Brna, S. P., Ohlsson, S., and Pain, H., editors, *Artificial Intelligence in Education, 1993: Proceedings of AI-ED 93*, Charlottesville, VA. Association for the Advancement of Computing in Education.

Martin, J. and VanLehn, K. (1995a). A Bayesian approach to cognitive assessment. In Nichols, P., Chipman, S., and Brennan, S., editors, *Cognitively diagnostic assessment*. Lawrence Erlbaum Associates, Hillsdale, NJ.

Martin, J. and VanLehn, K. (1995b). Student assessment using Bayesian nets. *International Journal of Human-Computer Studies*, 42:575–591.

McArthur, D., Stasz, C., and Zmuidzinas, M. (1990). Tutoring techniques in algebra. *Cognition and Instruction*, 7(3):197–244.

Merrill, D., Reiser, B. J., Ranney, M., and Trafton, J. (1992). Effective tutoring techniques: A comparison of human tutors and intelligent tutoring systems. *The Journal of the Learning Sciences*, 2(3):277–306.

Moore, J. D. and Swartout, W. R. (1990). Pointing: A way toward explanation dialogue. In *Proceedings of the American Association of Artificial Intelligence Conference*. AAAI Press, Menlo Park, CA.

Murray, T., Schultz, K., Brown, D., and Clement, J. (1990). An analogy-based computer tutor for remediating physics misconceptions. *Interactive Learning Environments*, 1(2):79–101.

Pfundt, H. and Duit, R. (1991). *Bibliography: Students' alternative frameworks and science education*. Institute for Science Education, Kiel, FRG.

Pirolli, P. and Bielaczyc, K. (1989). Empirical analyses of self-explanation and transfer in learning to program. In *Proceedings of the Eleventh Annual Conference of the Cognitive Science Society*, pages 459–457, Hillsdale, NJ. Lawrence Erlbaum Associates.

Pirolli, P. and Recker, M. (1994). Learning strategies and transfer in the domain of programming. *Cognition and Instruction*, 12(3):235–275.

Ploetzner, R. and VanLehn, K. (1996). The acquisition of informal physics knowledge during formal physics training. *Cognition and Instruction*. In press.

Pressley, M., Wood, E., Woloshyn, V., Martin, V., King, A., and Menke, D. (1992). Encouraging mindful use of prior knowledge: Attempting to construct explanatory answers facilitates learning. *Educational Psychologist*, 27:91–109.

Recker, M. M. and Pirolli, P. (1995). Modeling individual differences in students' learning strategies. *The Journal of the Learning Sciences*, 4(1):1–38.

Reif, F. (1987). Interpretation of scientific or mathematical concepts: Cognitive issues and instructional implications. *Cognitive Science*, 11(4):395–416.

Schauble, L., Raghavan, K., and Glaser, R. (1993). The discovery and reflection notation: A graphical trace for supporting self-regulation in computer-based laboratories. In Lajoie, S. P. and Derry, S. J., editors, *Computers as Cognitive Tools*, pages 319–337. Lawrence Erlbaum Associates, Hillsdale, NJ.

Shute, V. J. (1991). Who is likely to learn programming skills? *Journal of Educational Comuting Research*, 6:1–24.

Shute, V. J. and Psotka, J. (1996). Intelligent tutoring systems: Past, present and future. In Jonassen, D., editor, *Handbook of Research on Educational Communications and Technology*. Scholastic Publications. In press.

Singley, M. (1990). The reification of goal structures in a calculus tutor: Effects on problem solving performance. *Interactive Learning Environments*, 1:102–123.

Slotta, J. D., Chi, M. T. H., and Joram, E. (1995). Assessing students' misclassifications of physics concepts: An ontological basis for conceptual change. *Cognition and Instruction*, 13(3):373–400.

Smith, J. P., diSessa, A. A., and Roschelle, J. (1993). Misconceptions reconceived: A constructivist analysis of knowledge in transition. *The Journal of the Learning Sciences*, 2(2):115–164.

Van Heuvelen, A. (1991a). Learning to think like a physicist: A review of research-based instructional strategies. *American Journal of Physics*, 59(10):891–897.

Van Heuvelen, A. (1991b). Overview, case study physics. *American Journal of Physics*, 59(10):898–907.

VanLehn, K. (1991). Rule acquisition events in the discovery of problem solving strategies. *Cognitive Science*, 15(1):1–47.

VanLehn, K. (1995a). Looking in the book: The effects of example-exercise analogy on learning. Submitted for publication.

VanLehn, K. (1995b). Rule learning events in the acquisition of a complex skill. Submitted for publication.

VanLehn, K. (1996). Cognitive skill acquisition. In Spence, J., Darly, J., and Foss, D. J., editors, *Annual Review of Psychology, Vol. 47*, pages 513–539. Annual Reviews, Palo Alto, CA.

VanLehn, K. and Jones, R. M. (1995). Is the self-explanation effect caused by learning rules, schemas or examples? Submitted for publication.

VanLehn, K., Jones, R. M., and Chi, M. T. H. (1992). A model of the self-explanation effect. *The Journal of the Learning Sciences*, 2(1):1–59.

Une architecture logicielle fondée sur le concept d'événement-logiciel: le cas de REPÈRES

Xavier DUBOURG

LIUM - Université du Maine
B.P. 535 - 72017 LE MANS Cedex - FRANCE
Tel : (33) 43 83 33 76 - Fax : (33) 43 83 35 65
E-mail : dubourg@lium.univ-lemans.fr

Résumé : La définition d'outils informatiques pour concevoir des ITS constitue un des apports des informaticiens dans un travail pluridisciplinaire de conception. Notre propos est de présenter une architecture logicielle pour gérer l'interaction dans un ITS. Cette architecture fondée sur les concepts d'événement-logiciel et de plan d'intervention repose sur deux principes définit au sein d'une équipe pluridisciplinaire (informaticiens, didacticiens) : la définition de deux niveaux d'interactions (niveau surface et niveau profond) ; l'apprenant et le dispositif informatique réalisent des actions à caractère intentionnelle, et se partage les initiatives.

1 Introduction

L'architecture des systèmes informatiques constitue un thème majeur dans la communauté scientifique des ITS. Au travers de l'architecture les conceptions des auteurs sur l'enseignement ou l'apprentissage transparaissent fortement. Nous pouvons ainsi distinguer différents types d'architecture correspondants à différentes familles de systèmes d'enseignement.

Dans ce cadre, nous nous intéressons à l'architecture des systèmes qui proposent des niveaux variables de suivi de l'activité des apprenants. Notre propos est de définir une architecture logicielle permettant une gestion paramétrable de l'interaction entre le système informatique et l'apprenant d'une part et la définition de modèle comportemental de l'apprenant de manière expérimentale d'autre part. La définition de cette architecture prend place dans un projet plus important - le projet REPÈRES - dont l'objectif principal porte sur la conception d'un environnement d'apprentissage destiné a favoriser chez des élèves l'acquisition des concepts mathématiques liés aux droites du plan en se basant sur les représentations graphiques et algébriques des objets mathématiques [Dubourg 95].

Dans cet article, nous présentons les principes que nous avons retenus pour la définition de cette architecture puis nous exposons l'architecture du système REPÈRES et le concept d'événement-logiciel.

2 Invariants Organisationnels

À partir de l'analyse de l'évolution des architectures des tuteurs intelligents, nous pouvons repérer des invariants dans leur organisation [Dubourg 95]. De manière très schématique, l'idée directrice des premiers travaux en EIAO [Clancey 83, Vivet 84, Anderson 85] est l'étude de l'utilisation pour l'enseignement d'un système expert couplé à un système tuteur. Le principe de conception est calqué sur celui des systèmes experts. La logique sous-jacente repose sur la transmission des connaissances du système expert vers l'apprenant. L'interaction est organisée de façon très rigide et l'apprenant dispose d'un faible degré de liberté.

L'architecture classique des tuteurs intelligents comporte quatre composantes : le module expert qui contient une représentation des connaissances du domaine et les mécanismes de raisonnement associés, le module pédagogique qui gère le déroulement des sessions en se référant à un paradigme d'apprentissage, le module dit "modèle de l'élève" qui contient la représentation que le système se construit des connaissances de l'élève et dont le rôle est de permettre l'individualisation de l'apprentissage, l'interface qui assure les échanges entre l'élève et le système informatique.

Suivant les réalisations et les objectifs de recherches, chacun de ces modules a été plus ou moins développé et certains problèmes ont été mis à jour. Nous distinguons trois grands axes dans l'évolution de ce type d'architecture :

• les difficultés à définir et à utiliser le modèle de l'élève [Self 88]. La conséquence principale est la réduction du modèle à une portion congrue malgré une volonté très présente d'adaptation individuelle des tuteurs aux apprenants.

• l'évolution de la technologie (capacité des machines) et des travaux sur l'interface homme-machine qui ont permis de développer des interfaces plus performantes (interfaces graphiques, manipulations directes). L'interface devient une partie de plus en plus importante, elle joue un rôle prépondérant dans l'acquisition des connaissances. En effet elle donne aux élèves un nouveau regard sur les connaissances du système et modifie ainsi leur comportement et leur manière de travailler.

• les conceptions pédagogiques des auteurs qui ont évoluées (en partie grâce au développement du travail pluridisciplinaires) vers une logique d'acquisition et de construction des connaissances par les apprenants en relation avec leur environnement.

Au niveau de l'architecture des tuteurs, nous pouvons remarquer la prégnance de deux éléments structurels importants : un environnement de travail qui constitue pour l'élève un système interactif simulé sur lequel il peut agir, et un module pédagogique.

Suivant les réalisations, chacun de ces éléments est organisé de manière plus ou moins complexe en fonction des conceptions des auteurs sur l'apprentissage et l'enseignement. L'environnement de travail peut ainsi être un système expert, un simulateur ou un micro-monde (au sens d'une représentation informatique d'une partie du monde réel - réalité virtuelle). Le module pédagogique peut également avoir des rôles très différents (tuteur, conseiller, "coach", perturbateur, co-apprenant, etc.). Ce module utilise, suivant les cas, des modules annexes (modèle de l'élève, historique de la session, système expert en explication, etc.).

Nous considérons que ces deux éléments (environnement de travail et module pédagogique) constituent chacun une source d'interaction avec l'élève. Le concept d'événement-logiciel - que nous présentons dans la quatrième partie - nous permet de *modéliser les échanges d'informations* entre ces deux éléments afin de rendre cohérentes et complémentaires les modalités d'interaction qu'ils induisent.

3 Principes de Conceptions et Architecture Générale

Suite au travail pluridisciplinaire sur la conception de "situations d'interaction" [Delozanne 94, Dubourg et al. 95], nous avons défini deux principes pour la gestion de l'interaction et l'élaboration de l'architecture logicielle de REPÈRES :

• l'interaction est composée de différents niveaux : interaction de surface (ou réflexe) et interaction profonde (ou intentionnelle),

• les élèves comme le système informatique réalisent des actions à caractère intentionnel. Les initiatives sont donc partagées entre les élèves et le système informatique.

Le premier principe vise à distinguer d'une part les représentations à l'interface des objets du domaine, des outils permettant de les manipuler (définition, modification, destruction, etc.) et les outils de contrôle mis à la disposition de l'apprenant et d'autre part l'utilisation par l'apprenant de cet environnement pour effectuer une tâche précise dans un contexte particulier. Ce principe nous a conduits à définir une architecture composée de deux modules (Cf. fig. 1). L'environnement de travail gère les interactions que nous qualifions d'interactions de surface (niveau réflexe). Le module pédagogique gère les interactions que nous qualifions d'interactions profondes (niveau intentionnel).

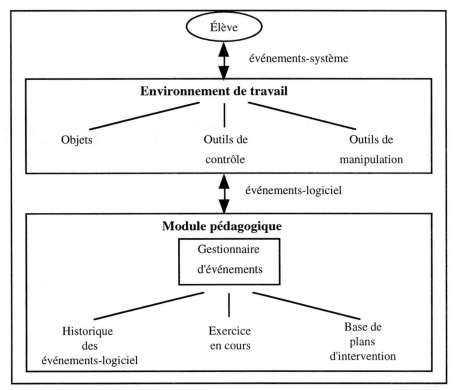

Fig. 1. Architecture de REPÈRES.

Le deuxième principe nous a amenés à concevoir une organisation fonctionnelle fondée sur la programmation événementielle pour donner le contrôle à l'utilisateur et à représenter de manière déclarative les connaissances permettant de gérer les interventions du module pédagogique (concept de plan d'intervention). Ce principe est également lié aux choix pédagogiques réalisées dans le projet concernant le rôle du système informatique : l'objectif est de donner aux apprenants les moyens de remplir des tâches et de leur donner les moyens de contrôler leur travail (en se basant sur différentes représentations d'un même concept mathématique). Le système ne doit jamais donner la solution d'un problème mais fournir les outils permettant de la trouver.

Pour assurer la communication entre les deux modules, nous avons défini le concept d'événements-logiciel. Dans la suite du texte, nous décrivons les aspects fonctionnels de cette architecture en insistant sur les concepts d'événement-logiciel et de plan d'intervention.

4 Événements-Logiciel

Un utilisateur communique avec un système informatique en créant des événements-système (par exemple, frappe d'une touche, clic avec la souris). Le noyau des applications interactives pilotées par événements est constitué par une boucle infinie qui attend de traiter un événement. Ce principe de gestion permet aux applications d'être à l'écoute de l'utilisateur. C'est l'utilisateur qui contrôle et décide du fonctionnement de l'application.

L'interprétation des événements-système permet de gérer efficacement le premier niveau d'interaction concernant la représentation des objets et des actions à l'interface du système. Mais les événements-système sont des observables de trop bas niveau pour rendre compte du contenu pédagogique des actions réalisées par l'apprenant dans l'environnement de travail. En effet, le module pédagogique doit avoir une représentation de l'activité des apprenants. C'est l'association d'un ou plusieurs événements-système dans un contexte précis qui prend une signification dans un objectif de résolution pédagogique.

Prenons un exemple (Cf. fig. 2) : un clic de la souris dans une fenêtre est interprété à un premier niveau pour qu'il ait un effet visible à l'interface (par exemple, désignation d'un point dans un repère orthonormé). Mais, par rapport à l'objectif de la tâche en cours (construire la représentation graphique d'une équation réduite), un clic de la souris ne signifie rien car il ne peut être interprété comme une action correspondant à une intention particulière de l'élève que dans un contexte bien défini.

Dans l'exemple de la figure 2, du point de vue informatique l'élève crée un point en cliquant une fois dans le repère mais par rapport à l'objectif et à l'environnement de travail, ce clic souris ne prend de signification que parce qu'il est précédé de la sélection d'un outil dans la palette. L'association de ces deux événements-système (sélection de l'outil et désignation d'un point dans le repère) prend une signification particulière dans l'environnement de travail (l'élève a défini un point).

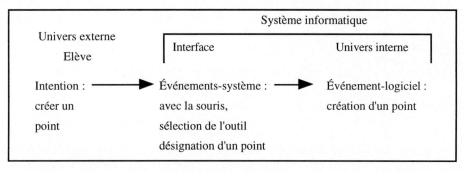

Fig. 2. Modélisation des actions des élèves par des événements-logiciel.

Nous définissons les événements-logiciel comme des séquences d'événements-système, dans un contexte précis, correspondants à une action significative par rapport à l'objectif pédagogique de la tâche en cours de réalisation. Les unités élémentaires dépendent du domaine d'application et correspondent aux actions élémentaires réalisables par les apprenants pour résoudre un problème du domaine.

Ce concept, qui réifie les actions exécutées par les élèves, est appelé événement-logiciel par analogie avec les événement-système. La fonction première de ces événements-logiciel est de *rendre compte au module pédagogique de l'activité des élèves dans l'environnement de travail.*

Dans REPÈRES, nous avons adopté la structure suivante pour représenter les événements-logiciel :
- l'origine de l'événement (élève ou REPÈRES),
- le type d'action (par exemple création d'objet, modification, outil utilisé),
- l'objet sur lequel porte l'action,
- la date de l'événement.

Initialement nous avons introduit le concept d'événement-logiciel pour réifier les actions de l'élève dans l'environnement de travail et informer le module pédagogique. Par la suite, il nous est apparu que ce concept pouvait être étendu. Dans la réalisation de REPÈRES nous avons utilisé la même structure d'événement-logiciel pour des fonctions différentes :
- d'une part les événements-logiciel permettent de représenter les actions du module pédagogique sur l'environnement de travail ainsi que l'analyse des actions des élèves,
- d'autre part, des événements de gestion (début d'un exercice par exemple) permettent de structurer le déroulement d'une session de travail,
- Enfin les événement-logiciel qui réifient les actions des élèves.

Les événements-logiciel du module pédagogique et les événements-logiciel de gestion sont différenciés par leur utilisation et leur fonctionnement mais possèdent la même structure.

4.1 Génération d'Événements par l'Environnement de Travail

Afin d'informer le module pédagogique de l'activité des élèves, l'environnement de travail génère des événements-logiciel correspondant aux actions réalisées par les élèves (événements-élève). À chaque type d'action est associée une classe d'événements-logiciel :
- création d'un objet (point, vecteur, marche d'escalier ou droite),
- modification d'un objet,
- destruction d'un objet,
- information sur un objet,
- utilisation d'un outil d'aide ou de contrôle,
- annulation d'une action précédente,
- tracé de la représentation graphique d'une équation.

Les modes de communication que nous avons définis en amont et le caractère intentionnel des actions des élèves permettent de simplifier la discrimination des événements-logiciel dans une série d'événements-système. Il n'y pas d'ambiguïté possible pour déterminer un événement-logiciel puisque l'élève choisit dans un menu ou dans une palette d'outils l'action qu'il veut réaliser. Nous posons comme hypothèse que les actions des élèves sont intentionnelles. Le système n'a pas à chercher quelles actions les élèves réalisent. Les analyses préalables permettent d'associer à chaque type d'actions un type d'événement-logiciel.

Il nous a semblé important de définir des événements-logiciel correspondant aux annulations pour marquer le fait que les élèves se sont engagés dans une action puis l'ont abandonnée avant d'arriver à son terme.

4.2 Génération d'Événements par le Module Pédagogique

Lors de l'exécution d'un plan d'intervention (Cf. § 5.3), le module pédagogique peut réaliser diverses actions sur l'environnement de travail : modification de l'interface (action sur les menus par exemple) ou action sur les objets de l'environnement (définition d'un objet, construction de la représentation graphique d'une équation). Les actions concernant les objets de l'environnement sont considérées comme "importantes" puisqu'elles peuvent être réalisées par les élèves. Un des principes de base de notre gestion de l'interaction est de donner aux élèves et au système informatique les mêmes possibilités d'actions. Nous avons donc choisi de représenter ces actions du module pédagogique sur l'environnement de travail par des événements-logiciel. L'objectif est de mémoriser l'ensemble des actions réalisées dans l'environnement de travail (par les élèves ou par le module pédagogique) afin d'utiliser cette base d'information pour gérer les interactions suivantes.

Ces événements-logiciel sont de la même nature que ceux réifiant les actions des élèves. Un des attributs permet de différencier l'origine de l'événement-logiciel (élève ou REPÈRES).

Le système crée également des événements-logiciel pour représenter l'analyse d'une action de l'élève dans un contexte précis. Ces événements sont des conséquences des actions précédentes (Cf. § 5.2).

5 Module Pédagogique

Le module pédagogique a pour fonction d'observer l'activité des élèves dans l'environnement de travail (en récupérant les événements-logiciel), d'analyser cette activité et de réagir lorsqu'il reconnaît un contexte particulier. Ce module intervient lorsque le contexte courant correspond à une description mémorisée dans un plan d'intervention. Dès la création d'un événement-logiciel le module pédagogique effectue plusieurs opérations dont : la mémorisation de l'événement dans un fichier, le calcul d'une intervention en fonction de l'événement et du contexte, et l'analyse de l'événement. Ces opérations générales sont redéfinies pour s'adapter à certaines classes particulières d'événements-logiciel.

Dans les paragraphes suivants nous détaillons deux de ces opérations : le calcul de la réaction et l'analyse d'un événement-logiciel ainsi que la structure des plans d'intervention.

5.1 Réaction à un Événement-Logiciel

Le gestionnaire d'événements-logiciel est un système opportuniste qui intervient lorsqu'il reconnaît dans l'environnement de travail un contexte décrit dans un plan d'intervention. Il cherche à réagir à chaque fois qu'un événement-logiciel est créé. En comparant cet événement et le contexte actuel avec les conditions des plans il décide de l'intervention à réaliser. Le choix du plan à exécuter est réalisé en trois étapes comme présenté dans la figure 3.

Première étape : à partir de la base de plans d'intervention, le système détermine la liste des plans actifs dont le déclencheur correspond à la classe de l'événement-logiciel qui vient d'être créé. Cette liste contient des plans d'intervention mais également les plans de gestion dont le déclencheur correspond à la classe de l'événement-logiciel.

Deuxième étape : le gestionnaire élimine de cette liste les plans dont les conditions ne sont pas vérifiées.

Troisième étape : des méta-règles permettent de choisir dans la liste des plans applicables le plan qui sera appliqué. Ces méta-règles correspondent aux stratégies d'intervention du système. Elles sont actuellement très rudimentaires.

Si, au cours de la sélection, la liste des plans devient vide, le système ne réalise aucune intervention.

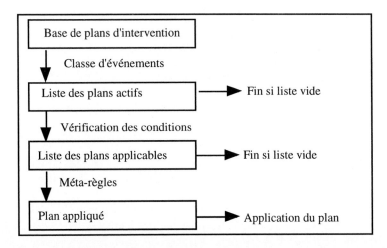

Fig. 3. Sélection du plan d'intervention.

5.2 Analyse d'un Événement-Logiciel

Lorsqu'un événement-logiciel est créé, le module pédagogique l'analyse pour évaluer sa pertinence en fonction du contexte mais isolément des événements-logiciel précédents. Cette analyse dépend du contexte de la situation et du type de l'événement-logiciel. Elle est réalisée par des méthodes associées à chaque classe d'événement-logiciel. Nous avons choisi de représenter le résultat de ces analyses par des événements-logiciel que nous avons nommés événements-REPÈRES.

Par exemple, si l'élève définit un point A (x_a, y_a) dans une situation où il doit construire la représentation graphique d'une droite, alors le système analyse l'événement-logiciel correspondant pour voir si le point appartient à la droite. Dans le cas contraire, le système tente de définir si un des points suivants appartient à la droite : $(-x_a, -y_a)$, (y_a, x_a), $(-y_a, -x_a)$, $(x_a, -y_a)$, $(-x_a, y_a)$.

L'objectif est d'analyser la nature de la difficulté des élèves afin de pouvoir proposer des réactions adaptées. Le résultat de cette analyse est représenté par un événement-logiciel. C'est sur cet événement que le gestionnaire réagit pour proposer une intervention.

5.3 Plans d'Intervention

Les événements-logiciel permettent de représenter les actions de l'élève dans l'environnement de travail. Ils constituent une base de connaissances (sous la forme d'un historique) qui permet au système de calculer ses interventions et de déterminer sa stratégie. Ces interventions sont adaptées au contexte de la situation et sont cohérentes par rapport aux actions précédentes des élèves et aux interventions précédentes du système. Les interventions du système ne se limitent pas à une action mais consistuent parfois une succession d'actions dans un contexte particulier. Nous avons adopté une structure de plans d'intervention qui permet de représenter une intervention du système en précisant le contexte dans lequel elle est intéressante. Cette structure est fondée sur les plans KEPLER [Labat et Futtersack 90] issus des systèmes CAMELIA et AMALIA [Vivet 88].

L'objectif de ces plans d'intervention est de modéliser les connaissances nécessaires au module pédagogique pour répondre aux deux questions suivantes :

• Dans le contexte courant, faut-il intervenir ?
• Si oui, quelle intervention (suite d'actions) faut-il réaliser ?

Les plans KEPLER-REPÈRES sont donc constitués de deux parties. La première partie permet de décrire le contexte d'application du plan. La deuxième partie décrit l'enchaînement des actions à réaliser pour appliquer le plan. La figure 4 montre un exemple de plan KEPLER-REPÈRES.

```
[Plans cree ()
event-cree-point                          ; déclencheur
()                                        ; varaibles

((exercice (objectif initiation))         ; conditions
  (activité (type al->gr))
  (nb-event (event-cree-point) > = 2))

((afficher t28 fm)                        ; actions
(si ((event-aide ((objet it-verif7))))
        (activer it-cours8))
        (activer it-verif7))))]
```

Fig. 4. : Exemple de plan d'intervention.

Le contexte est décrit par le déclencheur et les conditions du plan. Le déclencheur correspond à une classe d'événements logiciel. Les plans sont regroupés en fonction de la valeur de leur déclencheur. Lorsqu'un événement est créé, tout un ensemble de plans est envisagé.

Les variables sont l'ensemble des mémoires auxiliaires dont l'interpréteur de plans a besoin pour exécuter le plan.

Le troisième champ, "Condition", permet de spécifier les conditions précises d'application du plan. Ces conditions sont facultatives et portent sur le contexte de la situation (l'exercice en cours, le dernier événement-logiciel) et sur l'historique des événements-logiciel depuis le début de la session. Les conditions qui portent sur le contexte sont de la forme attribut-du-contexte valeur. Ce champ possède la structure suivante :   (Exercice (<champs> <valeur>) (<champs> <valeur>) …)
        (Événement (<champs> <valeur>) (<champs> <valeur>) …)

Les actions sont exécutées en séquence. Elles agissent à plusieurs niveaux :
  • modification des menus par ajout ou retrait des items,
  • modification des fenêtres graphique et algébrique par ajout ou retrait d'objets,
  • apparition de messages d'aides,
  • prise de contrôle pour placer les élèves dans les modules d'aides.

Le langage d'interprétation des plans KEPLER adapté à REPÈRES permet de représenter explicitement le comportement pédagogique du système à l'aide des structures de contrôle classiques (Si Alors, Tant que, etc.).

6 Conclusion

La gestion dynamique de l'interaction que nous proposons repose sur la séparation entre l'environnement de travail et un système d'observation de l'activité des élèves (module pédagogique). Le système produit une interaction de qualité si plusieurs conditions sont vérifiées :

• l'environnement de travail propose aux apprenants une représentation fidèle et cohérente du monde. Cette représentation permet aux apprenants de donner du sens aux actions qu'ils réalisent ;

• l'observation réalisée par le module pédagogique à partir des événement-logiciel fournit "suffisamment" d'informations. Il est essentiel ici (comme dans tous systèmes d'observation) de définir avec précisions quelles sont les observables. Le travail pluridisciplinaire avec les didacticiens et les enseignants a pour objectif de définir les observables et leur granularité ;

• les interventions produites par le module pédagogique sont cohérentes et calculées en fonction du contexte et du niveau d'interaction souhaité.

La réalisation du système REPÈRES nous a permis de mettre en œuvre les principes que nous avons présentés ci-dessus. Actuellement nous avons développé deux activités (construction de la représentation graphique d'une droite à partir de son équation algébrique et recherche de l'équation algébrique d'une droite à partir de sa représentation graphique). Ces deux activités utilisent des bases de plans d'interventions d'environ cent plans.

Une perspective importante de nos travaux, consiste dans un premier temps à utiliser la version actuelle de REPÈRES pour recueillir un corpus de modèles comportementaux. Il nous semble important de nous appuyer autant sur les résultats produits par les élèves que les mécanismes qu'ils mettent en œuvre pour les produire. Il apparaît que l'utilisation du concept d'événement-logiciel constitue une réponse au modèle comportementale de l'élève. Dans un deuxième temps nous souhaitons exploiter ces corpus avec les didacticiens afin de compléter et d'affiner les bases de plans d'interventions et de définir des modèles épistémiques d'élèves en compilant les modèles comportementaux. En effet, d'une session à l'autre le modèle épistémique permet de conserver les informations essentielles sur l'élève pour lui proposer des exercices ou des activités lui permettant de mieux progresser.

7 Bibliographie

[ANDERSON 85] J.R. Anderson, The geometry tutor, In Proceedings of the International Joint Conference of Artificial Intellingence, p. 1-7, Los Angeles, 1985.

[CLANCEY 83] W. Clancey, The epistemology of a ruled-based expert system: a framework for explanation, Artificial Intelligence, vol 20, p. 215-251.

[DELOZANNE 94] E. Delozanne, Un projet pluridisciplinaire : ELISE un logiciel pour donner des leçons de méthodes, Recherches en Didactique des Mathématiques, Vol 14/1.2, p. 211-249, Grenoble, La Pensée Sauvage, 1994.

[DUBOURG et al 95] X. Dubourg, E. Delozanne, B. Grugeon, Situations d'interaction en EIAO : le système REPERES, in D. Guin, J-F. Nicaud, D. Py, Environnements Interactifs d'Apprentissage avec Ordinateur, tome 2, Quatrièmes Journées EIAO de Cachan, Eyrolles, p. 233-244, 1995.

[DUBOURG 95] X. Dubourg, Modélisation de l'interaction en EIAO, une approche événementielle pour la réalisation du système REPÈRES, Thèse de l'Université de Caen, 242 p., Caen, Octobre 1995.

[LABAT et FUTTERSACK 90] J-M. Labat, M. Futtersack, QUIZ : un système pour enseigner le bridge, Actes des journées EIAO de Cachan, ENS, 1990.

[SELF 88] J. Self, Bypassing the intractable problem of student modelling, ITS 88, Montréal, Juin 1988, p. 18-24.

[VIVET 84] M. Vivet, Expertise mathématique et informatique : CAMELIA, un logiciel pour raisonner et calculer, Thèse d'État, Université Paris 6, 1984.

[VIVET 88] M. Vivet, Knowledge based tutors : towards the design of a shell, International Journal of Educational Research, 1988, vol 12, n° 8, p. 839-850.

An Actor-Based Architecture
for Intelligent Tutoring Systems

Claude Frasson[1], Thierry Mengelle[1], Esma Aïmeur[1], Guy Gouardères[2]

[1] Université de Montréal, Département d'informatique et de recherche opérationnelle
2920 Chemin de la Tour, Montréal, H3C 3J7, Québec, Canada
E-mail: {frasson, mengelle, aimeur}@iro.umontreal.ca
[2] Université de Pau, IUT Informatique, Bayonne, France
E-mail: gouarde@larrun.univ-pau.fr

Abstract. The evolution of intelligent tutoring systems (ITS) toward the use of multiple learning strategies calls on a multi-agent architecture. We designed an ITS where several agents assume different pedagogical roles; consequently, we called them actors. We first describe the conceptual architecture of an actor which allows it to be reactive, instructable, adaptive and cognitive. We then provide a detailed view of this architecture and show how it functions with an example involving the different actors of a new learning strategy, the learning by disturbing strategy.

1. Introduction

Learning in intelligent tutoring systems (ITS) has evolved during the last two decades. The goal of an ITS was to reproduce the behavior of an intelligent (competent) human tutor who can adapt his teaching to the learning rhythm of the learner. Initially, the control of the training was assumed by the tutor (prescriptive approach), not the learner. More recent ITS developments consider a co-operative approach between the learner and the system which can simulate various partners, such as a *co-learner* [6], a *learning companion* [4]... In fact this evolution progressively highlighted two fundamental characteristics: (1) learning in ITS is a constructive process involving several partners, (2) to improve it various learning strategies can be used such as one-on-one tutoring, learning with a co-learner [6], learning by teaching [12, 13], learning by disturbing [1]. To fulfill these goals we have designed a multi-agent architecture in which each learning strategy is supported by several agents. In this paper, we will illustrate how the learning by disturbing strategy works with three agents: the *tutor* who supervises the learning session, the *troublemaker*, a "particular" companion who can decide to give correct solutions or wrong information in order to check, and improve, learner's self-confidence, and the *artificial learner* which allows to synchronize human learner's activity with the two other agents. The capability for an agent to play different roles and the necessity to learn from the behaviour of the other agents will incline us to consider agents as *actors*.

We first present the main properties of an actor as a specific intelligent agent, then we describe the architecture of an actor, both at conceptual and technical levels. We illustrate this architecture in giving implementation details of the troublemaker, the main actor of the learning by disturbing strategy.

2. The Actor Paradigm

Like other agents, actors are *autonomous* entities; they can operate without human control [3] and interact with other agents (they have *social ability*) using an agent-communication language. Like *reactive agents*, actors can provide immediate responses to stimuli without reasoning. They can also handle situations that require planning, prediction and diagnosis capabilities [11].

In order to allow the pedagogue to design new strategies, or to adapt existing ones, actors need to be *instructable* [2, 9] and so able to dynamically receive new instructions or algorithms. The properties of *adaptive agents* [7] are also requested for actors; they need to adapt their perception of situations and modify their decisions by choosing new reasoning methods.

Beyond these different properties and to dynamically improve the behavior or the ITS, actors need to be *cognitive*. The cognitive aspect of an actor relies upon its capability to learn and discover new facts or improve its knowledge for a better use. An actor should learn by experience.

To sum up, an *actor* is an intelligent agent which is *reactive*, *instructable*, *adaptive* and *cognitive*.

3. Global Architecture of an Actor

The architecture (Figure 1) we need contains four modules (Perception, Action, Control and Cognition) distributed in three layers (Reactive, Control and Cognitive). It is similar (but extended) to the *Touring Machines* [5], consisting in *perception* and *action* subsystems that interface with the environment of the agent and three control layers (reactive, planning and modelling layers). Our architecture contains also a *reactive layer*, with direct association between perception and action modules, and a *control layer* which corresponds to the planning layer. However, the third layer (*cognitive layer)* is not restricted to solving goal conflicts (as in Touring machines) but supports the ability to learn from experience which is an important element of an intelligent entity [8].

An original point of this architecture is that each actor has the possibility to observe the *previous behavior* of the other actors, their trace of actions (and not only the results of actions). To allow such capability each actor has an external view on the other actors and an internal view allowing other actors to consult its own behavior. In addition, an actor can decide to hide part of its behavior to the other actors.

- The *perception* module detects a change of the environment of the actor and identify the situations in which the actor may intervene. The environment of an actor is composed by all the other actors and a common memory. Changes of the environment result from the activity of the other actors (for instance, the fact that the troublemaker has just given a wrong information or that an answer of the learner becomes available in common memory).
- The *action* module regroups all the actions (functions) which allow the actor to operate on the environment, for instance : display an answer, submit a problem, congratulate, mislead,...

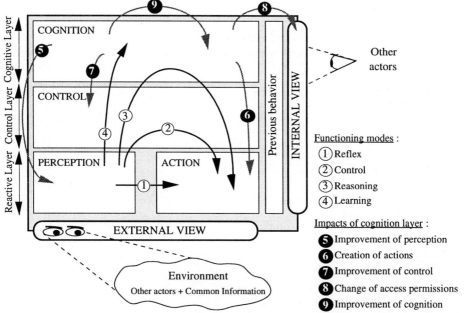

Fig. 1. Conceptual architecture of an actor.

- The *control* module handles situations which imply a planning aspect in order to determine the actions to be activated. For instance the tutor can decide to stop or continue the tutoring session, the troublemaker may give the right or wrong solution,...
- The *cognition* module allows the actor to improve its performance according to several aspects such as: improve actor's perception (❺), expand the control (❼), complete the set of actions (❻), modify the view of the other actors on its internal activity (❽), and finally improve its own reasoning strategies (improvement of cognition (❾)). This module includes several reasoning strategies and learning mechanisms intended to modify or create new reasoning strategies.

These modules can be used according to different *functioning modes* which can involve one or several modules.
- The r*eflex mode* (①) involves perception and action modules; in that case there is a direct association between an identified situation and a specific action (spontaneous action) without reasoning capabilities. This mode avoids to call a higher level layer to generate control actions.
- The *control mode* (②) involves perception, action and control modules. Starting from a given situation the control module takes a decision among possible alternatives, it constructs plans and selects actions to execute.
- The *reasoning mode* (③) involves the four modules; it intervenes when, after learning, the cognition module decides to override some knowledge in the control layer (❼) in order to influence the current decision.
- The *learning mode* (④) involves only perception and cognition modules. In that case, the single objective of the actor is to improve its expertise; it has no social behavior (interaction with other actors) but only internal modification as objectives.

4. Functional Design

Now we can give more details on each module and precise the interactions between the different layers (Figure 2). An example of the whole behavior of actors is given in section 5.3.

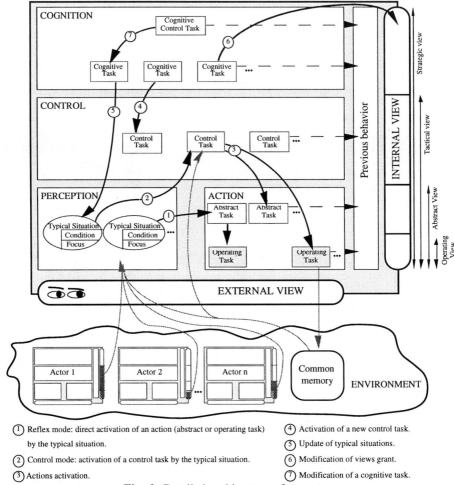

Fig. 2. Detailed architecture of an actor.

- The *perception module* contains a set of *typical situations* [10]. A typical situation corresponds to a condition of activation according to characteristics of the environment. Each external actor is observable through the external view and actions can update the common memory. Most of these typical situations are defined by the pedagogical expert for each actor (for instance all the conditions of activation for the troublemaker). However a typical situation can be also induced by the cognitive layer (Figure 2, ⑤).

Each typical situation is described by an object with three parts: a focus, a condition, and a conclusion. The focus allows to restrict the view of the environment in order to only consider information that are relevant for the evaluation of the condition. The condition is a logical proposition. The conclusion refers to the task to be activated when the condition is true. This task can be situated either at the action level (①) or the control level (②), as indicated on Figure 2. An example of a typical situation is given in section 5.2.

All the activities that the actor can perform (actions, control or cognitive decisions) are supported by tasks situated in action, control and cognition modules. Four categories of tasks are distributed among these modules: operating, abstract, control and cognitive tasks.

• The *action module* consists of a set of tasks that the actor can perform to act on the environment. There are two types of action tasks: *operating tasks* that are perceptible by the other actors and *abstract tasks* which are not perceptible. *Operating tasks* (gray boxes on Figure 2) are elementary tasks (for instance Give-Problem, Display-Answer). *Abstract tasks* (white boxes on Figure 2) include both elementary tasks (e.g. Find-Right-Answer (this task allows the tutor to get the solution of a problem)) and tasks that lead to the activation of an operating task (for instance, in the case of the troublemaker, Mislead calls the Display-Answer operating task with a wrong answer as a parameter).

• The *control module* contains several *control tasks* which are activated by typical situations and allow to trigger action tasks. The goal of a control task is to participate in a decision process which aims to select and activate a sequence of action tasks. A control task can also call another control task before activating an action task. For instance, regarding the troublemaker (see section 5.2), the Scene2: React-To-Answer control task calls another control task (Choose-An-Attitude) which sends back a decision. According to this decision, Scene2: React-To-Answer finally calls a specific action task (e.g. Tell-lies, Remain-silent).

• The cognition module consists of several *cognitive tasks* and a single *cognitive control task*. In order to ensure the various functions of the cognitive layer, each cognitive task is in charge (specialized) of improving a specific aspect of the actor (improving a specific module or modifying the views grants). Cognitive tasks are not activated from other components (typical situations and tasks) but are permanently running; they possess two distinct parts: a learning algorithm and an action part. The learning algorithm can in fact use one among three learning mechanisms: analogy, deduction and induction. Cognitive tasks allow to analyze the results of previous actor's performance, and decide how to improve it (learning by experience). The role of the cognitive control task is to modify the expertise of the cognitive tasks (actions and learning mechanisms).
Let us take two examples of cognitive tasks. A cognitive task specialized in improving the control module can observe the previous decisions of a control task that has to choose among several alternatives (see section 5.2: Choose-An-Attitude). The learning algorithm of the task (for example an induction mechanism) can infer that these decisions are not justified and decide to create a *new control task*. When the conditions of activation (typical situation) of the control

task will be satisfied, the cognitive task will dynamically replace the old control task by the new one. Similarly a cognitive task intended for improvement of perception will be able to modify typical situations (focus, condition or conclusion) or to infer some new ones.

To keep a trace of the activity of the actor (also called behavior) each activation of a task is stored in the *previous behavior area* indicated on the right side of Figure 2. As tasks are classified according to four categories, the actor behavior can be observed according to several levels of abstraction or *views*. Thus, it is possible to observe the actor's behavior within 4 views: operating view (operating tasks only), abstract view (operating and abstract tasks), tactical view (operating, abstract and control tasks), strategic view (all the tasks). Schematically, the operating view of an actor shows *what* the actor has done while the other views explain *why*. So actors can have a more reliable behavior knowing the reasons of activities of the other actors. By default, an actor has only an operating view on the others. Moreover, an actor can still decide to restrict the internal view on its behavior.

5. Example: the Learning by Disturbing Strategy

5.1. Informal description of the learning by disturbing strategy

As indicated in section 1, this strategy involves three actors in order to strengthen the learner self-confidence. The *tutor* submits a problem both to the *learner* and the *troublemaker*. The troublemaker, can give right or wrong solutions. It can react only once to each request of the tutor (intervention before the learner, after the learner, or remain silent). If the learner is unable to give a correct solution the tutor finally gives him the right solution.

5.2. Design and Implementation

The implementation of this strategy requires to define a set of tasks and a list of typical situations for each of the three actors mentioned above. Figure 3 shows all the typical situations and tasks for the troublemaker. The perception module involves two typical situations TM-TS1 and TM-TS2, which respectively allow the actor to intervene before and after learner's answer. We describe below the implementation of the typical situation TM-TS2:

Focus	*Condition*	*Conclusion*
Access to behaviors: Yes From: TUTOR last Operating Task *Only:* Common memory: Yes	Learner-answer is-in Common Memory Operating-View (Behavior (TM)) = ∅	Scene2: React-To-Answer

The *focus part* restricts the view of the environment to the information that are relevant for the evaluation of the condition: the behavior of all actors since the tutor has given the problem, and the common memory. According to the previous description of the strategy, the *condition part* checks the presence of the learner's answer in the common memory, and the fact that the troublemaker has not already reacted on the current problem (last proposition). When the condition is true, the *conclusion part* calls the `Scene2: React-To-Answer` control task.

The algorithm of the `Scene2: React-To-Answer` control task (described bellow), calls another control task `Choose-An-Attitude`, which decides of the activation of the suitable action task:

```
attitude := Choose-An-Attitude
if (attitude = be negative) then Mislead
else if (attitude = be positive) then
    Get the learner's answer in the Common Data Area.
    Analyse the answer.
     if (right answer) then Approve else Give-Solution
else if (attitude = be neutral) then Remain-Silent
```

5.3. Example of Functioning

To illustrate the functioning of the learning by disturbing strategy, and especially of the troublemaker, Figure 3 considers the following situation :

We are at time t4; none of the actors is active. At time t1, the tutor submitted a first problem to the learner; at time t2, the troublemaker has decided not to react before learner's answer; and, at time t3, the learner has given the right answer which is now available in common memory.

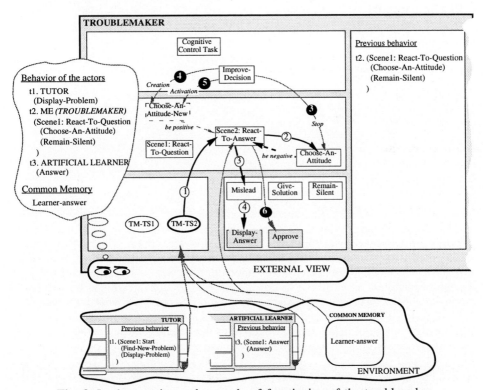

Fig. 3. Implementation and example of functioning of the troublemaker.

Figure 3 presents two possible scenarios: the first one (arrows labelled with white circles) gives an example of the control mode, while the second one (arrows labelled with black circles) concerns the reasoning mode.

First scenario. In its attempt to rebuild, step by step, the behavior of all the actors the troublemaker accesses to the previous behavior areas according to its view grant. This explains why the result of this operation (behavior of the actors indicated on the left side of the troublemaker) contains only the *operating tasks* of the tutor and the artificial learner. This view on the environment makes the TM-TS2 typical situation triggerable; so the Scene2: React-To-Answer control task (that is linked with TM-TS2) is activated (①). As previously mentioned this task calls another control task: Choose-An-Attitude (②) which returns a negative position to Scene2: React-To-Answer. This last one activates the Mislead abstract task (③); this task calls the Display-Answer operating task with a wrong solution as a parameter (④). Consequently, a wrong solution is displayed on the learner's screen.

Second scenario. This second scenario begins like the first one, however when the Choose-An-Attitude control task is activated, a cognitive task (Improve-Decision) intervenes to change the expertise for selecting an attitude. It stops the current control task (❸), creates a new control task (❹) allowing to take the same kind of decision but with a new expertise, and activates this last one (❺). Unlike the first scenario, the decision is now to be positive; so, because learner's answer is right, Scene2: React-To-Answer calls the Approve operating task (❻).

Finally the result of all these operations on the troublemaker behavior will be updated with the following information:

- First scenario
```
t4. (Scene2: React-To-Answer
        (Choose-An-Attitude)
        (Mislead
            (Display-Answer))))
```

- Second scenario
```
t4. (Scene2: React-To-Answer
        (Choose-An-Attitude [Cancelled])
        (Improve-Decision)
        (Choose-An-Attitude-New)
        (Approve))
```

6. Conclusion

We have presented an ITS architecture based on actors, a type of intelligent agents with suitable properties for ITS. The actors characteristics have been particularly detailed for the pedagogical component of the ITS architecture in which various actors can interact dynamically. This architecture has multiple advantages. First, it provides a high degree of flexibility in terms of interaction between the learner and actors in various strategies. This allows a co-operative approach in which the learner is involved with a constructive knowledge elaboration. Second, the actor improves itself by interacting with the other actors. The learner is not the only participant who learns but the community of actors that is attentive to the behavior of the learner and learns by experience. Third, the cognitive layer has learning mechanisms to cope with new situations that cannot be processed at lower levels. Learning by experience allows the actors to evolve from the reasoning mode to the control mode and even to the reflex mode, using a permanent learning process.

We have designed this architecture in the context of the SAFARI project, a multidisciplinary project aiming at developing various ITS. We have already implemented a basic prototype using the Smalltalk object-oriented language. In the present state, this prototype supports all the functionalities described above, except those of the cognitive layer. It includes a simplified version both of the one-to-one tutoring, and the learning by disturbing strategies. We are now focusing our work on the implementation of the cognitive layer and on the refinement of the pedagogical expertise of new tutoring strategies.

Acknowledgments

This work has been supported by the Ministry of Industry, Trade, Science, and Technology (MICST) under the Synergy program of the Government of Québec.

References

1. Aïmeur, E., Frasson, C., Stiharu-Alexe, C.: Towards New Learning Strategies In Intelligent Tutoring Systems, *Brazilian Conference of Artificial Intelligence SBIA'95* (1995) 121-130
2. Altermann, R., Zito-Wolf, R.: Agents, Habitats and Routine Behavior, *Thirteen International Conference On Artificial Intelligence* (1993)
3. Castelfranchi, C.: Garanties for autonomy in cognitive agent architecture. In Wooldridge, M. & Jennings, N.R. (Eds), *Intelligent Agents: Theories, Architectures and Languages*, LNAI, vol 890, Springer Verlag: Heidelberg, Germany (1995) 56-70.
4. Chan, T.W., Baskin, A.B.: Learning Companion Systems. In C. Frasson & G. Gauthier (Eds.) *Intelligent Tutoring Systems: At the Crossroads of Artificial Intelligence and Education,* Chapter 1, New Jersey: Ablex Publishing Corporation (1990)
5. Ferguson, I. A.: Touring Machines: An Architecture for Dynamic, Rational, Mobile Agents. *PhD Thesis*, Clare Hall, University of Cambridge (1992)
6. Gilmore, D., Self, J.: The application of machine learning to intelligent tutoring systems. In J. Self, (Ed.) *Artificial Intelligence and Human Learning, Intelligent computer-assisted instruction,* New York: Chapman and Hall (1988) 179-196
7. Hayes-Roth, B.: An architecture for adaptive intelligent systems. *Artificial Intelligence: special issue on agents and interactivity* (1995) 327-365
8. Honavar, V.: Toward learning systems that integrate different strategies and representations. In *Symbol Processors and Connectionist Networks for Artificial Intelligence and Cognitive Modelling: Steps toward Principled Integration*, Honavar, V. & Uhr, L. (Eds), New York, Academic Press (1994)
9. Huffman, S.B.: Instructable Autonomous Agents. *PhD Thesis*, University of Michigan, Dept of Electrical Engineering and Computer Science (1994)
10. Mengelle, T.: Etude d'une architecture d'environnements d'apprentissages basés sur le concept de préceptorat avisé. *PhD Thesis*, University of Toulouse III (1995)
11. Morignot P., Hayes-Roth, B.: Why does an agent act ?. In M.T. Cox & M. Freed (Eds.), *Proceedings of the AAAI Spring Symposium on Representing Mental States Mechanisms.* Menlo Park, AAAI (1995) in press.
12. Palthepu, S., Greer, J., McCalla, G.: Learning by Teaching. *The Proceedings of the International Conference on the Learning Sciences,* AACE (1991)
13. Van Lehn K., Ohlsson, S., Nason, R.: Application of simulated students: an exploration. *Journal of artificial intelligence in education*, vol 5, n 2 (1994) 135-175

A Highly Flexible Student Driven Architecture for Computer Based Instruction

Denis Gagné[1] and André Trudel[2]

[1] IntelAgent R. & D. Inc.
1930, rue Gagnon
Lachine, Québec, Canada, H8T 3M6
dgagne@alex.qc.ca

[2] Jodrey School of Computer Science
Acadia University
Wolfville, Nova Scotia, Canada, B0P 1X0
Andre.Trudel@AcadiaU.ca

Abstract. We propose a domain independent framework for computer based instruction systems capable of generating custom courses. A salient property of our framework is that the corpus content, pedagogical course structure, and course delivery are independent. The system does not use a student model. We believe that the student is the best model of himself and provide him with the power to dynamically change the course's delivery.

1 Introduction

Mass, anytime, anywhere delivery of tailored self-paced Computer Based Instruction (CBI) has potential cost benefits for commercial, industrial and military applications. For years, the predominant paradigm for CBI was primarily that of an electronic book. These systems were, a priori, passive, only allowing students to push buttons to turn pages (Schank 1993). CBI should be more than an electronic book in the hands of a student. The student should become an active participant, and be given the power to modify the intruction's delivery. Modern CBI systems aspire to user-centered, interactive tailored instruction that fully utilises still graphics, pictures, sound, computer animation and full motion video.

The advantage of one on one instruction is that instruction is tailored to the needs of an individual. The current trend in CBI research is to assign the responsibility of tailoring instruction to some Intelligent Tutoring System (ITS) (e.g., (Kono et al.1994, Huang et al. 1991)). The basis of the ITS paradigm is that instruction should be tailored based on some model of the student. The model is built and updated by the system and contains the systems perception of the student's expertise or knowledge of the course content. We believe that the student is the best model of himself and propose a "learner empowerment approach" to tailoring instruction. Within this paradigm, emphasis is placed on the adaptiveness of the CBI system to the student's explicit directions. The student is given the power to dynamically change different apsects of the course's delivery.

Updating CBI applications is an expensive and time consuming process that often leads to the complete redesign and rewrite of the application. The problem is that the pedagogical organization of the content of a subject matter is often inseparable and indistinguishable from the media used to convey the concepts. Changing the course content often impacts its delivery and vice versa. It should be possible to update the course's content and delivery independently of each other. This separation between the "what" and the "how" appears in other areas of Artificial Intelligence. For example, the old debate between procedural and declarative representations (Winograd 1985), and Kowalski's (1979) view that algorithms consist of logic plus control.

We propose a framework that clearly seperates the pedagogical organization of the content and the media used to convey the different concepts. This framework allows for the diffusion of highly adaptive CBI applications. The end result is an environment providing for easy evolution of the CBI application content and fully individualized diffusion of content to the student within an interactive and adaptive environment.

2 Proposed Framework

The most important feature of the proposed framework is its capability of doing personalised pedagogical planning. Once the student's level of expertise has been obtained for the different topics in the course, the planner will generate a custom course to meet some preset objectives.

Three activities must take place prior to the personalised planning process: creating a corpus of knowledge, instantiating a course, and creating a competency profile.

Creating a corpus of knowledge: A corpus of knowledge consists of a collection of concepts defining or relating to a subject matter. Precedence relations may be specified between the concepts. Associated with each concept are different expertise abstractions or proficiency levels. The abstractions or levels are cumulative and sequential. That is, to attain the highest level, one begins at the lowest and studies each level in order. The actual number of levels and names given to each is not set a priori. These are decisions to be made by the course engineer. For example, the levels can be associated with Bloom's hierarchy (1956). To summarize, a concept is made up of levels. Information is associated with each level, we call this information *mediatic learning resources.* One or more mediatic learning resources are assigned to each level. The media used for the mediatic learning resources is varied (e.g., text, still graphics, pictures, sound, computer animation, full motion video, quiz etc.).

Instantiating a course: Concepts from the knowledge corpus can be grouped together to form units. For example, the board game unit may consist of the chess and checkers concepts. We then in turn group together units to form a course. We can also specify precedence relationships between the units. The knowledge corpus and courses are stored in a *pedagogical knowledge base.*

Creating a competency profile: Once a student and a course have been paired up, we create a competency profile. The profile has two parts. The first are learning objectives or standards set by the course designer. Objectives are set for each concept or alternatively, objectives can be set at the unit level which are then inherited by the concepts. A concept objective is a performance expectation that the designer wishes the student to attain for that particular concept. It is important to note that the objective is independent from the proficiency levels associated with a concept. The person specifying the objective may have no idea what the particular proficiency levels are. The system takes care of translating an objective into a proficiency level. The second component of a competency profile is an assessment or estimate of the student's knowledge level for each concept. The assessments can either be objective or subjective. An objective assessment can be obtained via placement tests. A subjective assessment can be supplied either by the course designer or by a student's self-evaluation. The accuracy of the student assessments is not crucial as they can be easily modified during course delivery.

The competency profile identifies knowledge gaps for each concept. Usually, the student will be assessed at a level lower than the objective set by the designer. The pedagogical planner will identify each of these gaps and propose to the student a series of proficiency levels to be studied for each concept. Successful completion of the levels will bridge the gap.

If at any point during course delivery the student feels the material is being presented at an inappropriate level, the student can stop the delivery and ask to change his/her student assessment. This causes re-planning, and the course is modified accordingly. Note that a sophisticated student model is not maintained. The student is his/her own best model and has control over the course delivery.

In the next section, we describe the pedagogical knowledge base which contains the knowledge corpus and the courses. We then present the pedagogical planner and conclude with a description of a working prototype.

3 Pedagogical Knowledge Base

The pedagogical knowledge base contains mediatic learning resources, concepts, the corpus, units, and courses. Each of these is described mathematically below. This is followed by a semantics for the notation. We conclude the section with a discussion of the pedagogical knowledge base's features.

3.1 Syntax

A pedagogical knowledge base PKB is a tuple

$$PKB = (MR, SC, x, y, C, \Psi, U, \Gamma)$$

where:

$MR = \{mr_1, \ldots, mr_n\}$ where each mr_i is a mediatic learning resource.

$SC = (V, E)$ a directed acyclic graph (not necessarily connected) where $V = MR$.

x, y are integers where $0 \le x < y$.

$C = \{c_1, \ldots, c_n\}$ where each concept c_i is a tree consisting of a root and one or more leaves (see figure 1). The root node contains the labels $p_0, \ldots, p_m$ where $m \ge 1$, $p_0 = x$, $p_m = y$, and $p_0 < \ldots < p_m$. The value of m can vary between concepts. Between each label in the root is a pointer to a leaf (c.f., a B-tree). Each leaf l_i is different and is a subgraph of SC and is called a sub-concept.

$\Psi = (V', E')$ a directed acyclic graph (not necessarily connected) where $V' = C$.

$U = \{u \mid u \text{ is a sub-graph of } \Psi\}$. Each element is called a unit.

$\Gamma = \{\gamma \mid \gamma = (V'', E'') \text{ is a directed acyclic graph (not necessarily connected)}$ where $V'' \subseteq U\}$. Each element is called a course.

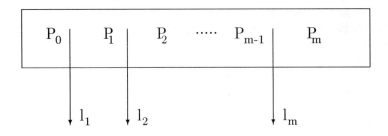

Fig. 1. Concept c_i

3.2 Semantics

The intended interpretation of:

$$PKB = (MR, SC, x, y, C, \Psi, U, \Gamma)$$

is as follows:

MR: A mediatic learning resource is information in any media about a narrow topic. For example, the set MR can contain the following:

mr_1: text file which describes breadth first search (BFS).

mr_2: video on BFS.

mr_3: quizz on BFS.

mr_4: mathematical complexity analysis of BFS.

Usually, each mr_i will be stored in a separate file. If the subject domain is fairly complex, the set MR will be large.

SC: Each node in the graph SC is an mr_i from the set MR. The edges represent precedence constraints.

C: Each concept $c_i \in C$ deals with a particular topic. The labels in the root (see figure 1), taken as pairs, represent levels of expertise. The lowest level is associated with the pair (p_0, p_1), the next highest with (p_1, p_2), and the highest with (p_{m-1}, p_m). Associated with each level of expertise is a leaf node. For example, (p_0, p_1) has a pointer to leaf l_1 (sub-concept). Successful completion of the material contained in sub-concept l_i guarantees that the student has a level of expertise equal to (p_{i-1}, p_i). A specific example of a BFS concept is shown in figure 2. Here we have two levels of expertise. To attain a level of (x, p), the student must complete the leaf node attached to it. Note that the leaf is itself a tree. The student must complete mr_1, mr_2, mr_3 in that order. To gain more expertise (i.e., be at level (p, y)), the student must then complete the second leaf which consists of only mr_4. Note that the two leaves are related to the same topic. Also, expertise level (x, p) is a pre-requisite to expertise level (p, y). The student cannot skip between expertise levels, they must be studied sequentially.

Ψ: is a directed acyclic graph whose nodes are concepts. The edges represent precedence relations between the concepts.

U: is a set of units. Each unit is a subgraph of Ψ. Units are used to group together concepts that share a common theme.

Γ: is a portfollio of courses. Each course is a directed acyclic graph whose nodes are units. The edges between the units represent precedence relations.

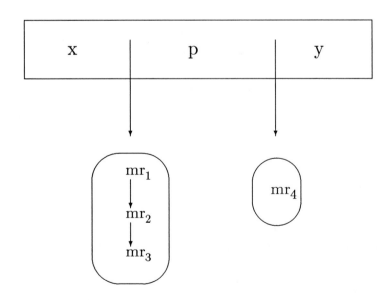

Fig. 2. BFS concept

3.3 Independence

The pedagogical knowledge base makes a clear and distinct separation between the "what" and the "how". A salient property of our framework is that the corpus content, pedagogical course structure, and course delivery are independent. Any one of the content, structure, or delivery can be updated without adversely affecting the others.

One can make changes to the content of the corpus without having to worry about how the content will be used. For example, changes could be made to mediatic learning resources without requiring any updates to the structure of the courses that contain them. Another form of independence involves the refinement of concepts. The knowledge base can evolve by adding proficiency levels to concepts. For example, we could add a proficiency level to the BFS concept in figure 2. These three proficiency levels could represent the availability of mediatic learning resources at the beginner, intermediate and expert level. This change would have no affect on the structure of the courses that contain this concept. But, course delivery would automatically take this change into consideration when preparing a personalised learning plan. Note that the course planner would be aware and possibly even use the extra proficiency level when planning with competency profiles that were prepared before the proficiency level was added.

One can also make changes to the pedagogical structure at the corpus, unit and course level without affecting the pedagogical content. Structural changes are realized by adding and/or deleting precedence edges in the various graphs. For example, we can change the presentation order of concepts in a course by modifying the links between the units in the course. This change does not percolate down to the concept or the mediatic learning resource level.

Two basic concerns are important in our structure of the subject matter. The first concern is the interdependence of individual concepts which form the basis of the epistomological organisation of the subject matter. The second concern is the proficiency or expertise abstraction levels which can be defined for individual concepts and the different mediatic learning resources that can be assigned to each proficiency or expertise level of an individual concept.

4 Pedagogical Planner

The algorithm for the delivery of custom courses requires a special graph traversal which we call *ancestor first traversal*. Recall that the edges in all our graphs represent precedence constraints. The ancestor first traversal guarantees that these constraints are satisfied.

Below we present the graph traversal, followed by the planning algorithm.

4.1 Ancestor First Traversal

The ancestor first traversal of a directed acyclic graph (not necessarily connected) visits all the ancestors of a vertex v before visiting v. Whenever more than one vertex can be traversed next, the user is asked to choose one.

4.2 Planning Algorithm

Given a pedagogical knowledge base $PKB = (MR, SC, x, y, C, \Psi, U, \Gamma)$ and a particular course $\gamma \in \Gamma$, we must first construct a competency profile:

> For each concept $c \in \gamma$, associate integers i_c and s_c with c where $x \leq i_c, s_c \leq y$. i_c is the objective obtained from the instructor. s_c is an estimate or assessment of the student's knowledge level of c.

The planner then performs a gap analysis on each concept:

We do an ancestor first traversal of the course in order to get at each unit. A unit is itself a graph of concepts. We in turn do an ancestor first traversal of the unit in order to access each concept in the course. For each concept, we must perform a gap analysis which is contained in the while loop. A gap analysis of a concept c simply presents to the student all the sub-concepts that are between s_c and i_c. For example, if in figure 1 s_c lies between p_1 and p_2, and i_c lies between p_{m-1} and p_m, then for the student to get from a competency level of s_c to i_c he/she must cover sub-concepts $l_2, \ldots, l_m$. Note that if initially the student's rating (s_c) is greater than the instructor's (i_c) then the concept is skipped altogether because the student already knows more than what is required.

The delivery of the course is dynamic. At any time during the execution of the while loop within step 2, the student can stop execution. The student would do this when he/she feels the material being presented is either too difficult or easy. In either case, the student usually feels frustrated. Once halted, the system will ask the student to re-enter his/her personal assessment. The student enters a smaller value if the course is too difficult. This results in easier sub-concepts being presented to the student. If the course is too easy, a larger value is entered. This will cause the system to skip some sub-concepts and move on to more challenging material.

4.3 Custom Delivery

An interesting feature of this framework is that from a fixed course γ in the knowledge base, we can generate many custom courses by varying competency profiles. Customization of a course can come from varying learning objectives and/or standards, varying students' assessments or a combination thereof. This feature allows custom runtime course delivery from multiple perspectives without changing the course structure.

Proficiency expectations may be defined for an individual, providing the basis for personalized instruction based on expectations specific to an individual, or be defined for a group as is the case for classroom teaching. When taken with an individual student assessment, personalised or group expectations still lead to personalised pedagogical planning and thus delivery.

As an example of setting group expectations, a pedagogical structure for a course on AI could be instantiated as AI101 and AI201 by simply defining two different proficiency expectation patterns for the same course structure. The

AI201 may address the same subject matter at a generally higher proficiency expectation level. Concepts can be skipped within a course instantiation by setting a null expectation on specific concepts. Note that setting null expectations on different concepts will affect course delivery, but will not change the pedagogical structure of the course itself. A student would then be presented a personalised learning plan based on his personalised assessment with respect to the course's concepts. Alternatively, a "classroom" course could be provided by generating a common assessment to a group of students.

We re-iterate the fact that course delivery is totally independent from the pedagogical knowledge base. There is no delivery code embedded in the content. Also note that the proposed framework can support directed, guided and exploratory learning.

5 Prototype and Potential Applications

To test the feasibility of our proposed framework, we built a simple pedagogical knowledge base with an "internet" theme. Each mediatic learning resource is a short text file which describes an aspect of the internet (e.g., history, ftp, email, etc.). The proficiency levels of a concepts are represented by a slide bar. The slide bar is sub-divided into regions. With each sub-region, we associate a sub-concept.

Using ToolBook, we then implemented a custom course generation and delivery system which uses the internet knowledge base. To obtain the objectives for a course, we present the instructor with a two column window. In the first column is a list of the concepts. Beside each concept is a slide bar used for entering an assessment. The student is also presented with a similar window. The student can also see the instructor's assessment (represented by arrows), but cannot change it. Note that the concepts and assessments all use the same slide bar representation. Once the assessments have been entered, the system will generate and present a custom course.

Based on our initial successes with the prototype, we plan to build a full blown version of the system.

Besides the traditional business applications (e.g., training and re-training employees), our proposed framework can naturally be used for distance education (Web Based Training). To deliver the course over the internet, WWW browser software could be used. By adding gap analysis features to a WWW browser, it could be used for custom course planning and delivery. Students would then surf the course!

Another application, is to view the pedagogical knowledge base as a database on some subject matter. The planner would be used to query the database. Before posing a query, the user would set his/her personal levels of actual and desired expertise (i.e., a competency assessment). The result of the query would be tailored to the user's level of expertise. Different users would get varying views of the same database. For example, a client, secretary and lawyer that query a legal database about liens expect and require information at different levels of expertise. Another example is the custom presentation of WWW home pages. A large computer company may wish to present different versions of its home page to a non computer science person, and a software engineer.

6 Conclusion

We described a framework for a computer based instruction system capable of delivering highly flexible custom courses. This is accomplished without the use of a student model. Instead, the student is given the power to customize the course during delivery.

Our framework is suitable for both small and large scale systems. Also, the framework is domain independent (unlike (Chandler 1994)).

A salient property of our framework is that the corpus content, pedagogical course structure, and course delivery are independent. Any one of these three components can be modified without adversely affecting the others. This permits the maintenance of the system by non-system experts.

Acknowledgements

The authors would like to acknowledge the excellent work of Francois Otis in implementing the validating prototype. The second author is supported by IntelAgent R. & D. Inc. and NSERC research grant 46773.

References

Bloom, B.: Bloom taxonomy of Educational Objectives: Book 1. Cognitive Domain. Longmans Green, New York, (1956).

Chandler, T.: The Science Education Advisor: Applying a User Centered Design Approach to the Development of an Interactive Case-Based Advising System. *Journal of Artificial Intelligence in Education,* **5:3**, (1994), 283–318.

Huang, X., McCalla, G., Greer, J. and Neufeld, E.: Revising deductive knowledge and stereo-typical knowledge in a student model. *User Modeling and User-Adapted Interaction,* **1**, (1991), 87–115.

Kono, Y., Ikeda, M. and Mizoguchi, R.: THEMIS: A Nonmonotonic Inductive Student Modeling System. *Journal of Artificial Intelligence in Education,* **5:3**, (1994), 371–413.

Kowalski, R.: Algorithm = logic + control. *Communications of the ACM,* **22** (1979), 424-431.

Schank, R.C.: AI, Multimedia, and Education. IJCAI-93, (1993), 1667–1672.

Winograd, T.: Frame Representations and the Declarative/Procedural Controversy. *Readings in Knowledge Representation,* R. Brachman and H. Levesque (Eds), (1985), 357-370.

A Generic Architecture for ITS Based on a Multi-agent Approach

Stéphane Leman[1], Pierre Marcenac[1] and Sylvain Giroux[2]

[1] IREMIA, Université de La Réunion, La Réunion, France
[2] LICEF, Télé Université, Montréal, Québec, Canada

Abstract. This paper present a generic architecture for Intelligent Tutoring Systems. First, learning is described with three hierarchic level: curriculum, lesson and problem. We describe an agent model to represent knowledge at problem level. This agent model contain a definition of intern archictecture and a description of the different algorithms for collaboration between agents. After we see that this model is an autosimilar one. We can use the same model for different level. Multi-agent systems can be see as primitif agents in the upper level and a multi-agent can be described with the same model as its components.

Résumé. Cet article présente une architecture multi-agents générique pour des systèmes tuteurs intelligents. L'enseignement est tout d'abord décrit en fonction de trois niveaux hiérarchiques : cursus, sessions, problèmes. Nous décrivons ensuite en détail un modèle d'agent pour la représentation de l'apprenant au niveau hiérarchique le plus faible, correspondant à la résolution d'un problème par un apprenant. Ce modèle d'agent consiste en la définition interne des agents, mais aussi des différents algorithmes permettant de gérer leur collaboration. Nous montrons ensuite comment, en utilisant plusieurs points de vue, ce modèle peut être généralisé pour représenter l'apprenant pendant tout le cursus.

1 Introduction

L'objectif primordial de notre recherche est de construire une architecture générique de Systèmes Tuteurs Intelligents (STI). Il s'agit de décrire un modèle de STI, le plus indépendant que possible de l'expertise à enseigner et qui s'adapte donc facilement à un grand nombre d'entre elles. Le problème est alors de décrire des fonctionnalités et des comportements génériques à tous les STI.

Nous avons choisi une approche multi-agents pour décrire cette architecture générique. En effet, l'approche multi-agents permet d'aborder une expertise de façon distribuée et de représenter celle-ci par des agents autonomes réduisant ainsi sa complexité. De plus, un STI décrit avec une approche multi-agents offre des avantages indéniables en terme d'évolutivité, d'opportunisme [1], d'adaptabilité de l'enseignement et de la modélisation de l'apprenant [9].

Notre modèle comporte deux facettes : les agents et la société. Aussi, notre modèle identifie un ensemble de propriétés et de comportements autonomes des agents ainsi que les comportement émergeants des communications entre les agents au sein de la société. Par ailleurs, l'approche privilégiée ici n'est pas uniquement une approche de type modulaire [8], mais est totalement distribuée. Chacun des agents contient en son sein une part de l'expertise, une part de la représentation de l'apprenant et une part des stratégies tutorielles. Enfin, notre modèle est auto-similaire : il permet de représenter une expertise selon plusieurs niveaux de complexité décroissante.

La décomposition choisie pour décrire le cursus enseigné est basée sur des idées décrites dans [3], où l'expertise est décomposée en objectifs correspondant chacun à une session. Chacune de ces sessions est constituée par un ensemble de problèmes. Enfin, la résolution de chaque problème nécessite un ensemble de connaissances. Cette décomposition permet de décrire l'expertise par trois niveaux hiérarchiques, auxquels sont rattachés des systèmes multi-agents. La section 2 présente une telle décomposition. Dans la section 3, nous définissons le modèle d'agent au niveau problème. Enfin, la section 4 montre comment le modèle d'agent défini pour le niveau problème peut être généralisé aux différents niveaux hiérarchiques composant le cursus.

2 Organisation du cursus

Nous nous plaçons dans le cadre d'un STI pour le transfert d'une expertise complexe. Il est alors nécessaire de représenter cette expertise complexe dans le système. L'ensemble de l'enseignement est représenté généralement par une expertise brute pouvant prendre diverses formes (bases de règles, texte). Une étape importante de la production d'un STI consiste en la transformation de cette expertise selon un formalisme reconnu par le système [4].

La méthode classique que nous adoptons est une décomposition de l'expertise en plusieurs niveaux décroissants de complexité. Ainsi, le cursus d'enseignement, représentant l'ensemble de l'enseignement proposé à l'apprenant, est décomposé en un ensemble de sessions d'enseignement correspondant chacune à un objectif pédagogique. Cette décomposition du cursus par un ensemble de sessions peut s'exprimer par un graphe hiérarchique décrivant l'ordre dans lequel les sessions doivent être exécutées. L'ordre adopté est un ordre partiel exprimant un ensemble de précédences pédagogiques.

De la même façon que le cursus est décomposé en sessions et une session peut être elle-même décrite par ensemble de problèmes. Les problèmes inclus dans une session sont également organisés dans un graphe hiérarchique décrivant la stratégie adoptée concernant l'ordonnancement partiel des différents problèmes. Un tel graphe est appelé graphe de stratégie.

Enfin, chaque problème est décrit par l'enchaînement des différentes connaissances nécessaires à sa résolution. De même, il existe un ordonnancement des connaissances, exprimé au sein d'un graphe de raisonnement et, pour un même problème, plusieurs graphes de raisonnement peuvent coexister.

Pour prendre en compte cette décomposition de l'expertise en trois niveaux hiérarchiques, l'approche multi-agents apparaît idéale. En effet, une telle approche permet à la fois de décrire aisément plusieurs niveaux d'abstraction d'une expertise par des agents de granularité décroissante, réduisant ainsi la complexité de la représentation, mais également de faire cohabiter dans un même système plusieurs sous-systèmes autonomes représentant plusieurs points de vue du même objet.

Ainsi, dans notre système, le cursus est décrit comme un système multi-agents dont les composants correspondent à des sessions d'apprentissage. En effectuant un agrandissement sur ces sessions, chacune d'elles est vue comme un système multi-agents dont les composants modélisent les problèmes qui permettent l'assimilation de l'objectif pédagogique. Enfin, chaque problème est lui aussi décrit comme un système multi-agents, dont les agents représentent les connaissances primitives sur l'expertise nécessaire à la résolution du problème.

L'architecture générale de notre système comprend donc trois niveaux de descriptions. Nous allons maintenant présenter le modèle d'agent correspondant au niveau de complexité hiérarchique le plus bas. La section 4 reviendra sur cette architecture en montrant que le modèle du niveau problème s'applique aux niveaux session et cursus.

3 Le modèle d'agent au niveau problème

3.1 Composition interne

La composition interne des agents de notre système est principalement définie par trois caractéristiques essentielles : les connaissances, les accointances et les croyances.

Connaissances Dans notre système, chaque agent représente une connaissance. Nous distinguons les connaissances statiques qui décrivent les connaissances conceptuelles et les connaissances dynamiques qui décrivent le savoir-faire dans le domaine. Les connaissances statiques et les connaissances dynamiques sont représentées par des agents de deux types : d'une part, les connaissances statiques seront représentées par des S-agents et d'autre part, les connaissances dynamiques seront représentées par des D-agents.

La connaissance modélisée par un agent S ou D correspond à une partie indivisible de l'expertise à enseigner. La granularité de cette expertise est fixée conjointement par un expert du domaine et un pédagogue, en fonction du niveau supposé de l'apprenant et du niveau d'expertise à atteindre.

Accointances Dans un système multi-agents, chaque agent ne possède que des informations locales. Ainsi, en ce qui concerne les communications, un agent ne peut s'adresser qu'aux agents dont il connaît l'existence : ses accointances. Conformément à la philosophie multi-agents, et pour laisser à chaque agent une grande autonomie de fonctionnement, les communications entre agents se font uniquement par envoi de messages asynchrones. Dans notre modèle, les agents n'ont qu'une représentation partielle de leur environnement et la vue qu'ils possèdent sur le système reste donc très locale. Les accointances sont les agents avec lequel l'agent est lié au travers du graphe de raisonnement (Cf 3.2).

Croyances Les agents S et D sont utilisés pour modéliser l'apprenant. La maîtrise d'une connaissance par l'apprenant ne peut être représentée de façon "booléenne". Ainsi chaque connaissance de l'apprenant est modélisée par un agent de type S ou D avec une certaine valeur de croyance propre (Cp) représentant le degré de maîtrise de l'apprenant pour cette connaissance[1].

Les agents S et D permettent de représenter la maîtrise des connaissances par l'apprenant sur le domaine enseigné. Cette représentation des connaissances sur le domaine constitue l'ébauche de la modélisation d'un apprenant, mais les connaissances statiques et dynamiques prises individuellement ne suffisent pas pour résoudre un problème. Aussi il est fondamental de pouvoir modéliser l'enchaînement des connaissancesdans un raisonnement.

3.2 Organisation de la société

Si les agents représentent les connaissances, une société d'agents communiquants représente un raisonnement. En effet, un raisonnement est constitué par l'enchaînement dynamique de connaissances statiques et dynamiques. En conséquence, les raisonnements sont représentés dans notre système par des graphes de raisonnements dont les noeuds sont constitués par des agents S et D et dont les arcs correspondent aux accointances entre ces agents. Chaque étape de la progression est signifiée par l'un des noeuds du graphe et à chacun de ces noeuds correspond un agent du système.

En général, pour la résolution d'un même problème, il existe plusieurs solutions. A chacune de ces solutions va correspondre un graphe de raisonnement. Le système est alors composé de plusieurs sous-systèmes multi-agents parallèles correspondant aux diverses possibilités de raisonnements. Lors de la résolution du problème, l'apprenant ne suit pas forcément un seul raisonnement, il commence ainsi plusieurs solutions possibles. Chacune des actions de l'apprenant est traitée en parallèle dans les différents sous-systèmes multi-agents. De cette façon, la solution choisie par l'apprenant n'est pas prédéfinie dans le système. Les différentes solutions sont examinées en parallèle et celle qui est effectivement choisie par l'apprenant émerge.

3.3 Construction dynamique du modèle de l'apprenant

La construction du modèle de l'apprenant reste un problème difficile et complexe [6]. La caractéristique principale de notre modèle de l'apprenant est sa distribution dans les différents agents. Il n'existe pas de représentation centralisée de l'apprenant, mais des informations propres aux agents et réparties dans l'ensemble du système. La construction du modèle repose sur un algorithme de recouvrement [2] mais cette fois distribué car étendu aux systèmes multi-agents. Les connaissances de l'apprenant sont vues comme un sous-ensemble

---

[1] Deux autres valeurs de croyances existent dans le modèle d'agent, elles ne seront pas abordées ici. Il s'agit de Cg : Croyance globale qui représente l'importance relative de la solution à laquelle appartient l'agent par rapport aux autres solutions possibles et Cr : Croyance relative qui mesure l'importance relative de l'agent dans la solution.

des connaissances expertes. La modélisation des connaissances de l'apprenant se fait donc en agissant sur les agents par deux types de modification : au niveau interne, l'agent directement concerné par l'action de l'apprenant va voir sa connaissance mise à jour et au niveau externe par propagation de cette information aux autres agents du système modélisant la même connaissance.

Évolution directe du modèle Initialement, les connaissances de l'apprenant sur le domaine enseigné sont complètement inconnues dans le modèle. Le modèle de l'apprenant est "vide". De ce fait, le système est alors constitué d'un ensemble d'agents correspondant aux différentes solutions expertes, mais dans lequel tous les coefficients de croyances propres ont des valeurs inconnues. Ensuite, en fonction des actions de l'apprenant, cette croyance évolue de façon dynamique. Pour un agent-S, chaque fois que l'agent est sollicité dans des contextes différents, sa valeur de croyance propre est renforcée. Pour un agent-D, la nouvelle valeur de croyance propre est la résultante de l'ancienne valeur et de l'évaluation par le système de la maîtrise de la connaissance.

Évolution par propagation Pour les deux types d'agents, après la mise à jour de sa valeur de croyance propre, l'agent diffuse cette valeur aux agents qui modélisent la même connaissance. Ceux ci prennent en compte cette nouvelle information et modifient leurs propres valeurs de croyance. Il n'y a pas de mécanismes de négociations comme dans [7], toutes les informations transmises sont considérées comme valides. Cette diffusion aboutit à une harmonisation des différentes valeurs de croyances et permet ainsi le maintien de la cohérence du système.

Expertisation Nous avons jusqu'à présent montré comment modéliser l'apprenant dans les cas simples, c'est-à-dire lorsque l'action de l'apprenant correspondait à une action attendue par un des agents. L'apprenant suivait étape par étape, une des solutions expertes. Toutefois, il est possible que l'apprenant effectue un saut dans le raisonnement correspondant à la maîtrise d'un nouveau type de connaissance : un raisonnement. Pour le modéliser, nous introduisons les agents-R.

Toutefois, il n'est pas approprié de créer un agent de type R à chaque fois que l'apprenant effectue un saut dans le graphe de raisonnement. Il faut en effet vérifier que les connaissances sautées par l'apprenant dans ce raisonnement sont bien maîtrisées. Pour résoudre le problème de la validation du raisonnement de l'apprenant, l'algorithme, dit d'expertisation, comprend deux parties. Tout d'abord, il faut reconnaître le raisonnement de l'apprenant dans l'un des graphes de raisonnement. Ensuite, il faut, dans le cas où le raisonnement est valide, le modéliser par la création d'un agent R défini lui aussi par ses connaissances, accointances et croyances. Cette opération modélisant l'expertisation de l'apprenant est décrite en détail dans [10].

Le modèle d'agents défini dans cette section permet de décrire à la fois les connaissances et les raisonnements d'un apprenant au niveau de la résolution du problème. Nous allons maintenant montrer que ce modèle est auto-similaire, et qu'il permet aussi de représenter les connaissances et les raisonnements au niveau d'une session.

4 Auto-similarité du modèle

L'auto-similarité est une propriété fondamentale et bien connue dans l'étude des courbes et des ensembles fractals [11]. Cette propriété s'applique à un objet mathématique dont toute partie est semblable à la totalité (par exemple, l'ensemble de Cantor). Par extension, un objet est dit auto-similaire si chacune de ses parties peut se représenter avec les mêmes caractéristiques que son tout (par exemple, un chou-fleur).

De même, par extension, l'auto-similarité peut être définie pour des systèmes multi-agents comprenant plusieurs niveaux de description hiérarchiques. Le premier niveau décrit le but global du système ainsi que l'organisation, décrite par un graphe, des différents agents de niveau 2 qui le composent. De la même façon, un agent du second niveau possède un but et décrit l'organisation des agents de niveau trois dont il est composé. Le modèle d'agents est alors dit auto-similaire, si un agent de niveau n peut être perçu comme un système multi-agents de niveau n-1 ayant les mêmes propriétés et si, réciproquement, un système de niveau n peut être perçu comme un simple agent du niveau n+1. De cette façon, l'auto-similarité permet d'unifier systèmes et agents. Les propriétés du modèle d'agent définies à un niveau hiérarchique restent alors valables pour tout le système. Contrairement à la définition mathématique, la notion d'auto-similarité ne se répète pas à l'infini, mais s'applique dans notre architecture pour un nombre fini de niveaux de description. Ainsi, le niveau cursus est uniquement vu comme une société d'agents et réciproquement, pour les agents représentant les connaissances, seul le modèle agent peut être appliqué.

Les avantages d'une telle architecture auto-similaire se retrouvent à plusieurs niveaux. Tout d'abord, en terme de conception, un avantage immédiat provient de la réutilisabilité des différents algorithmes. Les algorithmes fonctionnant à plusieurs niveaux hiérarchiques ne sont pas liés aux connaissances modélisées par les agents et sont, de ce fait, en grande partie génériques. Le fonctionnement similaire du système aboutit ainsi à une simplification notoire des problèmes de conception, et en réduit ainsi la complexité. Par ailleurs, chaque agent étant décomposé et défini comme un système multi-agents au niveau inférieur, la décomposition hiérarchique que nous proposons est assez naturelle.

Nous montrons dans les paragraphes suivants que les agents du niveau session, les Pb-agents, sont auto-similaires aux agents S et D. Le niveau session et les Pb-agents sont détaillés ci dessous en trois points : composition interne des agents, organisation de la société et modélisation de l'apprenant.

4.1 Composition interne des agents

Au niveau session, nous définissons les agents primitifs correspondant à un problème : les Pb-agents. Les Pb-agents sont similaires aux agents primitifs connaissances (S-agents et D-agents) du niveau problème. un Pb-agent peut être vu comme un système multi-agents et il possède les mêmes caractéristiques internes que les agents qui le composent. Il peut en effet être défini par ses accointances, ses connaissances et ses croyances.

Connaissances La connaissance modélisée par un agent problème correspond à l'ensemble des connaissances nécessaires à sa résolution. Il s'agit donc en fait de l'agrégat des connaissances représentées par les agents S et D qui le composent ainsi que de leur organisation au sein des différents graphes de raisonnement.

Accointances Un agent problème possède le même type d'accointances que les agents S et D. Il s'agit des agents avec lesquels il est lié dans le graphe de stratégie auquel il appartient : l'ensemble des pères, l'ensemble des fils et le sommet du graphe de stratégie. Comme pour les agents du niveau problème, les accointances sont les seuls agents avec lesquels un Pb-agent peut communiquer.

Croyances La croyance propre représente le degré de maîtrise par l'apprenant du problème. La valeur Cp dépend de la valeur de Cp des différents agents S et D qui composent l'agent. En effet, mieux les connaissances nécessaires à la résolution de l'exercice seront maîtrisées par l'apprenant, et meilleures seront ses chances de réussir à résoudre le problème.

4.2 Organisation de la société

Une session est définie par un objectif pédagogique que doit atteindre l'apprenant. Pour atteindre cet objectif, plusieurs stratégies d'enseignement peuvent être employées. Les différentes stratégies sont initialement décrites par des experts qui décomposent ainsi l'objectif pédagogique complexe en une succession de problèmes plus simples qui peuvent être résolus par l'apprenant. L'organisation de la session se fait donc par l'intermédiaire d'un graphe similaire au graphe de raisonnement que nous appelons graphe de stratégies. A chacun des noeuds du graphe de stratégies correspond un agent du système correspondant à un problème : les Pb-agents. Les graphes de stratégies sont hiérarchiques comme les graphes de raisonnement, et indiquent donc l'ordre partiel dans lequel les problèmes doivent être exécutés.

Pour atteindre l'objectif pédagogique de la session, plusieurs stratégies peuvent être employées. A chacune de ces stratégies va correspondre un graphe de stratégie. Au niveau session, le système multi-agents est ainsi composé de plusieurs sous-systèmes correspondant aux diverses stratégies recensées. Il est ainsi possible qu'à l'intérieur d'une même session cohabitent deux Pb-agents représentant le même exercice, mais utilisé dans des contextes différents. Si on laisse à l'apprenant une liberté dans le choix de ses exercices, ce qui nous semble une hypothèse intéressante, il est possible que celui-ci commence plusieurs stratégies différentes. Dans ce cas, le système examine les différentes stratégies en parallèle jusqu'à ce que celle qui a été effectivement choisie émerge, les autres stratégies étant abandonnées en cours de route.

L'avantage d'avoir un modèle d'agent auto-similaire apparaît clairement à ce niveau : alors que la complexité des agents s'est accru (chaque agent correspondant maintenant à un système du niveau inférieur), les propriétés de ces agents sont conservés et les algorithmes utilisés sont réutilisables.

4.3 Construction dynamique du modèle de l'apprenant

Ici encore, la construction de la modélisation de l'apprenant se fait en utilisant le même algorithme de recouvrement distribué qui modifie dynamiquement les Pb-agents. Cette modification des valeurs de croyances peut s'effectuer de deux façons, soit par modification directe lorsque l'apprenant résout le problème représenté par l'agent, soit par propagation, lorsqu'un Pb-agent représentant le même exercice dans une autre stratégie a modifié sa valeur et diffusé cette nouvelle valeur dans le graphe de stratégie.

Enfin, l'algorithme d'expertisation défini au niveau problème peut également être réutilisé au niveau d'une session, lorsque l'apprenant effectue un saut dans le graphe de stratégie. Ce saut correspond à un ensemble de problèmes que l'apprenant choisit de ne pas résoudre pour atteindre l'objectif pédagogique de la session. Néanmoins, si ces mêmes problèmes ont été correctement exécutés dans le cadre d'autres stratégies, il est légitime de penser que l'apprenant est suffisamment entraîné pour passer à autre chose. Dans ce cas, il convient de modéliser cet état, tout comme nous l'avions fait au niveau problème avec les R-agents, par la création d'un St-Agent. L'algorithme d'expertisation peut donc être à nouveau utilisé à ce niveau. Les calculs liés aux croyances du nouvel agent sont les mêmes qu'au niveau problème. Le St-Agent se comporte ainsi de la même manière que le R-agent, et la propriété d'auto-similarité de notre modèle est ainsi conservée.

5 Conclusion

Cet article propose une architecture de type multi-agents pour les systèmes tuteurs intelligents. L'enseignement est décrit en fonction de trois niveaux hiérarchiques. Le cursus est décomposé en sessions de travail, qui sont elles-mêmes scindées en plusieurs problèmes. Nous proposons alors une modélisation des connaissances et des raisonnements d'un apprenant. Au niveau problème, le modèle utilise des agents de base modélisant les connaissances statiques et dynamiques de l'apprenant. Ces agents sont enchaînés dans des graphes de raisonnement et sont modifiés dynamiquement au cours de la résolution par l'apprenant des problèmes qui lui sont proposés. Enfin, la reconnaissance de raisonnements plus complexes de l'apprenant est également décrite ainsi que la modélisation de ces raisonnements par des agents. Le modèle multi-agents est générique (les agents ont un comportement indépendant de l'expertise) et auto-similaire (le modèle d'agent défini au niveau problème est étendu à l'ensemble du cursus).

L'implémentation du modèle multi-agents avec l'aide de la plate forme de programmation que constitue Epitalk [5] est en cours. une expérimentation de la construction dynamique du modèle de l'apprenant est actuellement mise en oeuvre dans le cadre d'une expertise de diagnostic d'un jeu de tarot.

Les perspectives de recherche sont maintenant axées sur l'intégration, au sein du modèle d'agent, d'un ensemble de stratégies tutorielles. Ces stratégies implémentées au plus bas niveau ne modifient pas le caractère auto-similaire du modèle d'agent. En effet, s'il est nécessaire d'intervenir pour guider l'apprenant au cours de la résolution d'un problème, il faut être également capable de fournir une intervention tutorielle pour l'aider à choisir un exercice au niveau de la session.

References

1. M. Baker, K. Bielaczyc : Missed opportunities for learning in collaborative problem-solving interactions. 7th World Conference on Artificial Intelligence in Education Washington USA (1995) 210–217
2. B. Carr, I. Goldstein : Overlays, a theory of modelling for CAI. AI memo 406 MIT Press (1977)
3. C. Frasson, G. Gauthier, G. Imbeau : Architecture d'un système tutoriel basé sur un curriculum. Génie Educatif 4-5 (1992) 23–37
4. E. Gavignet, M. Grandbastien : Représentation des connaissances dans un générateur de systèmes d'EIAO. International Conference on Intelligent Tutoring Systems Montréal Canada (1992) 209–216
5. S. Giroux, F. Pachet, G. Paquette : Des systèmes multi-agents épiphytes. Revue d'Intelligence Artificielle (1995)
6. P. Holt, S. Dubs, M. Jones, J. Greer : The State of Student Modelling Student Modelling: The Key to Individualized Knowledge Based Instruction. Springer Verlag (1994) 3–35
7. P. Jambaud, D. Hérin-Aimé : Contribution to negotiation studying : a knowledge items approach. 7th World Conference on Artificial Intelligence in Education Washington USA (1995) 250–257
8. S. Levesque, C. Frasson, J. Gescei : Perspectives multi-agents des systèmes tuteurs intelligents. Journées Françaises IAD & SMA Voiron France (1994) 55–66
9. S. Leman, S. Giroux, P. Marcenac : A Multi-Agent Approach to Model Student Reasoning Process. 7th World Conference on Artificial Intelligence in Education Washington USA (1995) 258–265
10. S. Leman, S. Giroux, P. Marcenac : When the student surpasses the master. International Conference on Computer Aided Engineering Education Bratislava Slovaquie (1995) 21–26
11. H.O. Peitgen, H. Jurgens, D. Saupe : Chaos and Fractals. New Frontiers of Science. Springer Verlag (1992)

LearnMedia : A Co-operative Intelligent Tutoring System
for Learning Multimedia[*]

Huaiqing Wang

Department of Information Systems, City University of Hong Kong
Tat Chee Ave., Kowloon, Hong Kong

Abstract. Intelligent Tutoring Systems (ITSs) have become increasingly important for enabling students to understand and solve specific problems. It is realised that today's state-of-the-art ITSs still lack the collaboration and co-operation aspects in a real life classroom. This paper describes the LearnMedia, a co-operative ITS for learning multimedia. The architecture of LearnMedia consists of three layers, the educational agent layer, the knowledge server layer and the repository layer. By deploying repository technology, the architecture provides the means for multiple educational agents to conduct co-operative and collaborative interactions between students and teachers and among students. The LearnMedia prototype demonstrates the need for multi-agent co-operation and collaboration in future ITSs.

1. Introduction

Computer assisted learning (CAL) and computer based training (CBT) have evolved through many stages since their beginning in the 1950's [Frasson90]. The promise of CAL and CBT is that they can make benefits of individualized instruction available to all students at affordable costs. The evolution from CAL and CBT to intelligent tutoring systems (ITS) was the first step by which educational and artificial intelligence (AI) communities began to look at each other's work [Frasson90]. The important contributions from AI came from the studies on knowledge: knowledge acquisition, knowledge communication, knowledge models, knowledge misunderstanding, etc. Since then, a variety of intelligent tutoring systems have appeared since the 1970s [Bos94; Frasson90].

Even today's state of the art ITSs ([Bos94; Corbett92; Kushniruk94; Wang92; Wang93; Wang94]) still apply the simplistic model of one student being tutored by a single educator. Recent researches in the area of Computer Supported Collaborative Learning (CSCL) have demonstrated the important role that collaborative interactions play in any learning process. In order for the next

[*] This research is supported by the quality enhancement fund (No. 871-060) from the City University of Hong Kong.

generation of ITSs to provide a realistic learning environment, such futuristic ITSs must be able to incorporate the ability for such collaborative learning interactions, which might be among students, among teachers, or between teachers and students. Consequently, it is hoped that within such an integrated co-operative learning environment, a student can be educated in a much more effective and efficient manner.

This paper focuses on addressing the architecture within next generation ITSs by integrating co-operative facilities into them. The next section gives a brief overview, while section 3 describes the knowledge representation issue. Section 4 presents the architecture of the LearnMedia system. Section 5 describes the implementation of the LearnMedia, a prototype system, in detail through an example. Conclusions are presented in the last section.

2. Background

2.1 Vision of "Virtual Classroom"

The vision of a distributed intelligent "Virtual Classroom" is compelling [Hiltz93]. Such futuristic computer aided education systems would involve large numbers of heterogeneous, intelligent educational agents distributed over large computer and telecommunication networks [Girard92]. Such educational agents are computer programs that serve students, teachers, and other multimedia educational information providers. It would be expected that within such a "Virtual Classroom", not only a large number of educational sessions may be present at any given time, but also that a wide variety of educational services on vastly different subjects be provided. Each of the educational *agents* within the "Virtual Classroom" should provide the means and the capabilities to achieve a particular goal cooperatively. For instance, if a student agent that serves a college-level physics student discovers that the student has a particularly hard time in solving differential equations, then the agent may be wise to collaborate with another agent, that serves a mathematics teacher, to achieve the goal of making the student familiar with such a type of problem solving. In general, information concerning any particular educational activity may be shared by one or more educational agents. Each educational agent in the "Virtual Classroom" must be able to interoperate with other educational agents to achieve the grand vision.

2.2 Cooperation and intelligent agents

The findings from Qin's paper [Qin95] indicated that cooperative efforts resulted in better problem solving than did competitive efforts. An example in this paper [Qin95] shows that the number of findings in which cooperation outperformed competition was 55 while only 8 findings found competition to outperformed cooperation. On average, cooperators outperformed competitors by over one half of a standard deviation. The possible reasons why cooperation may increase problem-solving successes include the exchange of information and insights among cooperators, the generation of a variety of strategies to solve the problem, and the development of a shared cognitive representation of the problem.

A typical co-operative ITS should support a large number of students, human teachers, and support staffs at the same time. It should also support co-operation among them, e.g. the question/answer between students and teachers, the discussion among students, the co-operation between users (i.e. students and teachers) and the systems, etc. Such systems will involve large, complex computer and communication networks and will potentially involve many processes and/or many machines, that cooperate with each other. The concept agent has become important in both artificial intelligence and computer science [Wooldridge95]. The term agent is used to denote a software-based computer system that enjoys the following properties: (1) autonomy (agents operate without the direct intervention of humans) (2) social ability (agents communicate with other agents) (3) reactivity (agents perceive their environment and respond in a timely fashion to changes that occure in it) (4) pro-activity (agents do not simply act in response to their environment, they are able to exhibit goal-directed behaviour by taking the initiative).

The main co-operation features of such agents in a cooperative ITS are listed as the following:

- Each educational agent plays a particular role within the entire ITS framework. Such agents may rely on one or more other agent' services. For instance, a student may ask a teacher some questions and the teacher wants to give answers. Consequently, it is necessary for each of the agents to interoperate with others for the purpose of sharing information.

- Educational agents are able to communicate with each other via messages. However, in order for each agent to interpret each message in exactly the same manner (a common confusion of different interpretations is the meaning of the phase "above average", compared to what), it is essential for all agents to share a common vocabulary.

3. Knowledge Representation

The basic problem of KR is the development of a sufficiently presentation notation with which to represent knowledge. In the following sections we shall refer to such notations as a knowledge representation scheme.

The knowledge representation scheme to be used to model CITSs is based on the Knowledge Representation language Telos, developed at the University of Toronto [Mylopoulos90]. The Telos knowledge representation language adopts a representational framework which includes structuring mechanisms analogous to those offered by semantic networks and semantic data models namely classification (inverse instantiation), aggregation (inverse decomposition) and generalization (inverse specialization). Another important novelty of Telos is its treatment of time.

This feature facilitates the natural modelling of dynamically changing domains, including the case where definitions of concepts change over time. The functional operations in Telos is a very powerful feature in which operations ASK, TELL, UNTELL and RETELL allow the user to query and update CITSs, and serve as primitives in terms of which CITSs can be defined.

In addition, Telos offers an assertional sublanguage which can be used to express both deductive rules and integrity constraints with respect to a given knowledge base. Two novel aspects of Telos are its treatment of attributes (i.e. attributes can be defined analogously to entities and can have their own attributes), and the provision of special representational and inferential facilities for temporal knowledge.

This paper uses the Telos knowledge representation scheme to represent and model the variety of types of knowledge required by a CITS within a consistent framework. Using Telos, each category of knowledge is treated as a class (with its instances being its specializations). All classes of information contained in a sample CITS can be organized within the hierarchy which is described in the next section.

A few example classes and instances are shown in Figure 1:

```
SimpleClass Questions
  IsA Topics
  WITH
    ATTRIBUTE
       sender: StudentAgents
       destination:
          EducationalAgent
       topic: Topics
      question: String
      send_time: Date
END

SimpleClass StudentAgents
  IsA EducationalAgents
  WITH
    ATTRIBUTE
      study_history: Topics
      current_courses: set of Topics
      question_history: set of Questions
    CONSTRAINTS
      (forall x/StudentAgents
      (x.current_topics.size < 6))
END

Token Q1
  IN Questions
  WITH
```

sender:
  AgentForJohn
destination:
  AgentForMary
topic:
  VB_Form
question:
  "How to load a picture into a VB Form?"
  ....
END

Figure 1: Two classes and an instance

The class Questions in Figure 1 is a subclass of the class Topics and has five local attributes (members). All the necessary information about a question that a student wants to ask is stored in a Questions object. For example, the attribute "sender" presents that an instance of StudentAgents is the "sender" of this message. When a teacher agent receives a Questions object, it knows everything about the question, because the student agent (sender) and the teacher agent (receiver) have the same definition of the class Questions. If it is necessary, questions could be stored in the repository for further use. Similarly, when a teacher agent gives an answer, an instance of TeacherAnswers will be created and will be sent to the student agent. The constraint in the class StudentAgent constrainses that each student can take six topics at the same at most.

4. Architecture

The architecture of the LearnMedia is shown in Figure 2.

There are three layers in the architecture: the agent layer, the server layer and the repository layer. The agent layer contains all the application agents, i.e. students interface agents, teachers interface agents, and technicians interface agents, etc. The function of the knowledge server is to glue all the other components together. The server is responsible for communication between application agents and the communication between agents and the repository. The repository layer can provide a centralised representation, consequently, information relevant to the management, evolution, operation and maintenance of the LearnMedia can be shared in a transparent fashion.

When a student learns, he/she attaches him/herself into the LearnMedia Virtual Classroom system. The LearnMedia will create an active educational agent that interacts with the student. For example, when the student John starts to learn, an instance AgentForJohn of the class StudentAgents will be created. Through the agent, the student is able to navigate sections and/or topics. When he/she needs to

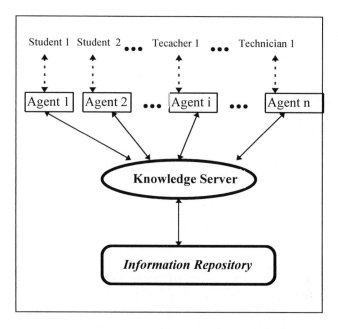

Figure 2: The architecture of the LearnMedia

ask any questions, he/she should ask the agent to pop-up a Questions form to fill. After the form is filled, an instance of Questions will be created locally and will be sent to the Knowledge Server. The Knowledge Server will receive the Questions object, and send it to the right destination. When a student want to discuss a topic with his classmates, he/she will fill a discussion form provided by the agent and a corresponding object will be created and sent to the server. The knowledge server will distribute the discussion object to relevant students.   Students can also do exercises and assignments on line.   The knowledge server will store some necessary information in the repository, based on pre-defined rules. Such information, e.g. the navigation history of a student, the problems that a student had during exercises, the questions that a student asked,   will be stored in the repository. Such historical information is very useful for teachers as well as for students themselves.

Through teacher interface agents, teachers are able to make/update lecture notes, ask students to do assignments, mark student assignments, review student learning records, etc. When a teacher makes/updates lecture notes, he/she logs into the LearnMedia and a teacher interface agent will be created. Based on the teachers requests, the agent will   load the relevant sections, update them and store these sections (objects) back to the repository. During operation, when a teacher receives a question from a student, he/she can fill in an answer form and then send the answer form (an instance of the TeacherAnswers class) back to the sender or send the object to all the students who are in the same class as the sender. Teachers can easily query the repository (via the server) about student progress and difficulties.

5. Implementation

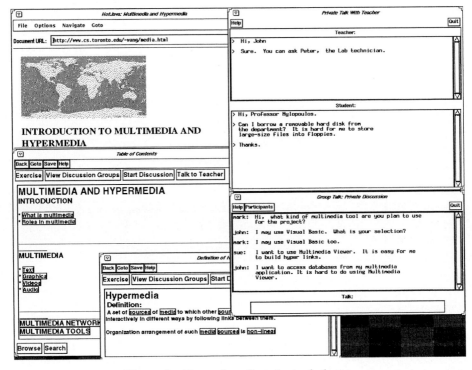

Figure 3 : Examples of student windows

LearnMedia provides help to those learning multimedia and hypermedia. LearnMedia includes novel features that provide means for multiple user interactions via a repository. Within the LearnMedia, the repository provides a central vocabulary that is shared by all the educational agents. Consequently, information relevant to the management, evolution, and maintenance can also be shared across the entire system in a transparent fashion. In addition, each educational agent can also take advantage of the meta-level retrieval services provided by the repository to enhance system wide co-operation, collaboration and deep understanding.

In order to demonstrate the novel architecture described in Figure 2, a prototype tutoring system, Figure 3 shows an example tutoring session under the LearnMedia. The student, upon invoking the LearnMedia, will face a window containing tutoring information presented as hypermedia documents. In figure 3, the window is located at the left. The student is free to browse and navigate through the hypermedia space following hypermedia links.

The multiple agent collaboration facilities in the LearnMedia are provides in two manners. In the first case, a particular student view currently active discussion groups and join one of them. In a discussion group, numerous students join together to conduct live discussions on a topic of shared interest. Teachers may join such discussion groups to give appropriate advice. A student can start a new discussion group on a new topic, if such discussion group does not exist. On the other hand, they may initiate private one-to-one interaction with the particular teacher who is responsible to this particular topic. Examples of discussion group and private interaction with a teacher are at the button of figure 3.

6. Conclusions

This paper's contributions to the ITS research community is to demonstrate the new architecture offered by the integration of repository technology, multiple agent technology with future co-operative ITSs. The architecture of LearnMedia consists of three layers, the educational agent layer, the knowledge server layer and the repository layer. By deploying repository technology, the architecture provides the means for multiple educational agents to conduct co-operative and collaborative interactions between students and teachers and among students. The LearnMedia prototype demonstrates the need for multi-agent co-operation and collaboration in future ITSs.

References

[Bos94] Bos E. And Plassche, J., "A Knowledge-Based, English Verb-Form Tutor", Journal of Artificial Intelligence in Education, 5(1), 1994, pp 107-129

[Corbett92] Corbett, A., and Anderson, J, "Student Modelling and Mastery Learning in a Computer-Based Programming Tutor", in "Intelligent Tutoring Systems", edited by C. Frasson, G. Gauthier and G. McCalla, Springer-Verlag, 1992, pp 413-420.

[Frasson90] Frasson C. And Gauthier G., "Intelligent Tutoring Systems", Ablex Publishing Corporation, 1990.

[Girard92] Girard J., Gauthier G., and Levesque S., "Une architecture multiagent", in "Intelligent Tutoring Systems", edited by C. Frasson, G. Gauthier and G. McCalla, Springer-Verlag, 1992, pp 172-182.

[Hiltz93] Hiltz, S. R., "The Virtual Classroom: A New Option for Learning", Norwood, N. J., Ablex Pub. Corp., 1993.

[Kushniruk94] Kushniruk, A. and Wang, H., "A Hypermedia-Based Educational System With Knowledge-Based Guidance", Proceedings of the World Conference on Educational Multimedia and Hypermedia, June 25-29, 1994; Vancouver, Canada, pp 335 - 340

[Mylopoulos90] Mylopoulos, J, etc, "Telos: A Language for Representing Knowledge About Information Systems", ACM Trans. on Information Systems, Vol. 8, No. 1, Oct. 1990, pp 325 - 362.

[Qin95] Qin Z., Johnson D., and Johnson R., "Cooperative Versus Competitive Efforts and Problem Solving", Review of Educational Research, Vol. 65, No. 2, 1995, pp 129 - 143.

[Wang92] Wang, H., and Kushniruk, A., "The UNIX Tutor", in "Intelligent Tutoring Systems", edited by C. Frasson, G. Gauthier and G. McCalla, Springer-Verlag, 1992, pp 317-324.

[Wang93] Wang, H., and Kushniruk, A., "An Intelligent Tutoring System for UNIX", Proceedings of PEG93 (AI Tools and Classroom: Theory into Practice), Edinburgh, UK; July 1993; pp 261 - 269.

[Wang94] Wang, H., and Kushniruk, A., "The SQL Tutor: An intelligent tutoring system for relational databases", Proceedings of The Second World Congress on Expert Systems, Lisbon, Portugal, January 1994; CD-ROM IXA1.

[Wooldridge95] Wooldridge, M. And Jennings, N., "Intelligent agents: theory and practice", The Knowledge Ebgineering Review, Vol. 10, No. 2, 1995, pp 115-152.

Having It All, Maybe:
Design Tradeoffs in ITS Authoring Tools[1]

Tom Murray

Center for Knowledge Communication
University of Massachusetts
tmurray@cs.umass.edu , www.cs.umass.edu/~ckc/

Abstract. While intelligent tutoring systems are becoming more common and proving to be increasingly effective, each one must still be built from scratch at a significant cost. ITS Authoring tools, developed to address this issue, have a variety of purposes and intended users, and their design must account for tradeoffs among four overall goals: scope, depth, learnability, and productivity. We discussed how our system approaches these overall goals in terms of the four functional components of ITSs: the learning environment, the domain model, the teaching model, and the student model. Our research tires to find a balance among the goals which will yield a high level of all four, or at least investigate the possibility of excelling in all four areas.

Introduction

In the last half decade Intelligent Tutoring Systems (ITSs, or knowledge based computer tutors) have moved out of the lab and into classrooms and workplaces, where some have proven to be highly effective as learning aides (Shute and Region 1990). For example, students working with an Air Force electronics trouble shooting tutor for only 20 hours gained proficiency equivalent to that of trainees with 40 months (almost 4 years) of on-the-job experience (Lesgold et al., 1990). In another example, students using the LISP tutor (Anderson & Reiser 1985) completed programming exercises in 30% less time than those receiving traditional classroom instruction and scored 43% higher on the final exam. While intelligent tutoring systems are becoming more common and proving to be increasingly effective, each one must still be built from scratch at a significant cost. Little is available in terms of authoring tools or shells for these systems.[2] Some (Youngblut, 1995) say there are not enough ITS's to make informed design decisions about ITS shells and authoring tools. There is certainly a grain of truth to this, but it is also true that so few ITSs exist for evaluation and generalization because they are so difficult and expensive to build. Some of us must build chickens, and some of us must build eggs, all artifacts limited by the nascency of the field, if the field is to mature.

A number of ITS authoring systems have been prototyped (see discussion below), and their diversity attests to the lack of any consensus in the field on what mechanisms or interfaces are most appropriate. This is true for ITSs, so it is no surprise that it is even more pronounced for ITS authoring systems. This is due in part to the large and under constrained design space. There is rough consensus on the nature of the tradeoffs involved, but not on how to balance those tradeoffs to produce useful and usable systems. Designing for power/flexibility vs. usability are usually at odds with each other. Power/flexibility relates to both scope (breadth) and depth of knowledge. Knowledge *depth* is the depth to which a system can reason about and teach the knowledge, and the depth to which it can infer a student's knowledge and respond accordingly. *Scope* is how general the framework is for building tutors for diverse subject areas and instructional approaches.

Usability also has two aspects: learnability and productivity. Learnability is how easy a system is to learn how to use. Productivity is how quickly trained users can enter information and produce tutoring systems. Learnability and productivity are often at odds, since a system that is designed to be picked up quickly by novices may not provide the powerful features that

---

[1] This research is based on work supported by the National Science Foundation and the Advanced Research Projects Agency under Cooperative Agreement No. CDA-940860.

[2] An ITS "shell" is a domain independent framework for building ITS's and representing the necessary knowledge; an ITS "authoring system" (or authoring tool) is an ITS shell along with a user interface that allows non-programmers to formalize their knowledge and build ITS's.

experienced users need to efficiently produce large systems. Scope and Depth are also often at odds, because one must often limit the generality of a system to be able to represent deep causal knowledge. Hypercard, for example, is an authoring tool with huge knowledge scope and minuscule knowledge depth. Note also that Power/flexibility in ITS authoring tools is mostly concerned with the "shell" aspect of the system, while usability is more concerned with the interface and "tool" aspect. Clearly, shell and tool are highly interdependent, since a bad tool can make an important aspect of the representational framework practically inaccessible, and a representational framework the is too ambitious or arcane will lead to tools that are visually and conceptually incomprehensible.

Traditionally, ITSs are described as having four major components or functions (Wenger, 1987). The first three are attempts to model the cognitive skills of good human tutors: expertise in the domain begin taught, the expertise of teaching, and the ability to infer something about what the student knows or feels. The fourth component is the student's interface or learning environment, and is the part of an ITS that can go beyond normal human-to-human teaching by immersing students in powerful interactive environments and simulations of phenomena that are not practical to experience in real life.

The state of the art is such that no system yet excels in all four of these areas, and those that excel the most in one or more areas teach a comparatively limited skill or content area. In order to more concretely discuss the tradeoffs of power/flexibility and usability, we will focus on how these tradeoffs play out in the four ITS component areas. The table in Figure 1 illustrates the factors involved.[3] We will organize the discussion around the Eon authoring tool (actually a suite of authoring tools) which we are developing, describing why we made our design decisions, and comparing Eon with other systems.

		Domain Model	Teaching Model	Student Model	Learning Environment
Power/ Flexibility	Scope				
	Depth				
Usability	Learnability				
	Productivity				

Figure 1. ITS Authoring Tool Design Tradeoffs

Defining the User

Many of the design decisions for ITS shells (all still in prototype form) depend critically one the nature of the intended user (i.e. author). Authors can have differing skill levels in three areas: programming, instructional design, and knowledge engineering.[4] Some systems (Merrill 1989) walk the user through a pre-defined knowledge acquisition dialog, asking the user a series of questions. This removes knowledge engineering from the design process, making the system much more usable, but such systems tend to be inflexible and tedious to use compared with open ended systems which provide a framework and allow the author to mix top down and bottom up design in an opportunistic fashion. Other systems (Jones & Wipond 1991) allow free-form design but can also critique the design for completeness, constancy, and even instructional validity (if you agree with the instructional model they include).

To build a tutor of any reasonable level of sophistication will usually require the efforts of a design team rather than an individual, and will require a tool with complexity at least on the order of magnitude of Photoshop, or AutoCAD. Therefor, for the foreseeable future, we do not expect the "average" classroom teacher or industrial trainer to be able to author an ITS any more than we expect every teacher to author a textbook in their subject area. The "master" teachers or

---

[3]The design space is not 2 dimensional, but many dimensional, since every box in the table represents a dimension along which the design can vary.

[4]We will assume that subject matter expertise is a given, and that graphic design skills and good intuitions about human-computer interfaces will also be needed on the design team.

trainers who become ITS authors will have to be able to invest significant time in building the systems, and invest additional startup time on the learning curve for these sophisticated tools.[5] But whereas now building an ITS is restricted to a few initiates, the right tools could allow every company and every school to have at least one person or team capable of ITS authoring. These teams could work with teachers and subject matter experts to rapidly produce ITSs.

Another class of potential users are educational theorists. ITS authoring tools should allow theorists to rapidly prototype ITSs and easily modify their teaching strategies and content to experiment with alternative curricula and instructional methods (Winne 1991). This is crucial because there is still little known about the form or applicability conditions of instructional strategies for ITSs, and whether such strategies are best acquired from practicing teachers or instructional design theories (Ohlsson 1987, Major 1993).

In order to define the intended user for the Eon tools, we must first describe our notion of a meta-authoring tool.

Eon as a Meta-Authoring Tool

It is at this point that we reveal our vision to "have it all, maybe." The depth vs. breadth tradeoff seems to imply that, 1) ITS authoring tools that can build powerful tutors that closely matching the pedagogical needs of the domain must have a narrow scope, and that 2) an all-purpose ITS shell, by necessity, must have a shallow knowledge representation and that the learning environment it creates will have little conceptual fidelity (Dooley et. al 1995). Yet, a programming language, SmallTalk for example, is an authoring tool for creating *any* ITS, albeit a tool with minimal learnability and productivity. So scope and depth are achievable simultaneously in an authoring environment, but at the cost of usability. A programming language does not provide the correct level of abstraction for efficient or easy authoring.

Our approach to these tradeoffs is to create a three-tiered suite of authoring tools, at three levels of abstraction. At the first tier is a general purpose ITS authoring system that requires moderate knowledge engineering and instructional design expertise to use. At the second tier are special purpose ITS authoring systems that require minimal knowledge engineering and instructional design expertise. The third tier involves the average teacher using an ITS in her class.

Eon incorporates a knowledge object which call an "Ontology" which allows both generality (scope) and domain specificity (depth). The first step in building an Eon ITS is to define the Ontology, which specifies the conceptual vocabulary and underlying structure for the domain. Eon uses a semantic net representation of the tutor's knowledge called the "Topic Network". The Ontology defines the types of topics and topic links allowed in the network.[6] For example, our Statics Tutor has topic types Fact, Concept, Procedure, and Misconception, and topic links Prerequisite, Generalization, and Sub_Concept; while our Manufacturing Equipment tutor has topic types Safety, Maintenance, Operation, Theory, and Common Failures, and topic links Sub_Part and Similar_Part (both of these tutors are early prototypes, and their ontologies are still in flux). Eon Ontologies specify a number of other things, such as topic properties (e.g. difficulty, importance), and default student model rules (see Murray 1996b for more detail). Our goal is to be able to provide special purpose ITS shells with pre-defined Ontologies tailored to domain or task types. For example, ITS authoring shells could be produced for science concepts, human service/customer contact skills, and equipment maintenance. Designing these ontologies is a first tier activity. Using pre-defined ontologies to build tutors is a second tier activity. The ontologies could be tweaked by the second tier user, but otherwise the instructional designer could immediately start constructing a tutor in an environment that supports and helps structure the knowledge acquisition process.

---

[5]The REDEEM system (Major 1995) has some promise as a shell which could allow the average teacher to build a low-fidelity ITS with minimal training.

[6]The ARPA Knowledge Sharing Effort (KSE) described in Gruber (1993) is exploring the use of standardized ontologies for sharing knowledge in knowledge-based systems. Our work is related, but currently we are focusing on ontologies that support knowledge authoring rather than sharing, and we focus on pedagogical knowledge, where the KSE deals with performance knowledge.

Though we recognize that a special purpose shell programmed from scratch is likely to be more powerful than a shell built with a general meta-shell, the meta-shell approach allows for the proliferation of special-purpose shells with a common underlying structure, so inter-domain commonalties can be exploited in both content creation and in training authors to use the shells.

At the third tier we will provide a simplified subset of the authoring tools, so that once an ITS is built *any* teacher can customize the it for a particular class or student. For example by modifying hint's text, replacing a picture with a more recent version, making a teaching strategy more verbose, or by changing a prerequisite relationship between topics. This is important because teachers will be reluctant to use instructional systems that they can't understand or adapt.

In summary, by incorporating Ontology objects and tools specialized for users at all three tiers, we hope to "have it all, maybe." We can address a range of usability levels, and hope for a fair degree of both scope and depth. Our project is still in an early stage (all of the tools have been prototyped and we have begun creating Ontologies and Tutors), and we expect the feedback we are getting from our participatory design process to provide more information about how far an author can get with a given level of training, and how reusable the Ontologies will be.

Next we will discuss some tradeoffs and design decisions for the Eon system, and compare Eon with other ITS authoring tools, by focusing on each of the four ITS components: learning environment, domain model, teaching model, and student model. Refer to the four tools in Figure 2 for the following descriptions.

Authoring the Learning Environment

The aspect of most ITS authoring shells that is most sorely lacking in relation to off the shelf tools for building traditional CAI (computer-based instruction) is student interface design. Eon, however, allows authors to completely customize the student interface and learning environment to create a wide variety of highly interactive learning environments. Eon's Interaction Editor tool contains a hierarchical pallet of user interface components called widgets. There are simple widgets such as buttons, text, pictures, movies, and hot-spots, and more complex widgets such as multiple-choice dialogs, tables, and graphs. In addition, by adhering to a simple inter-module protocol, arbitrarily complex widgets can be programmed outside of Eon, and "dropped in" as needed for special purpose authoring tools or specific domains.[7] These custom widgets can be device simulations or whole learning environments, for example, our Statics Tutor has a "crane boom" widget which lets students manipulate positions of objects and cables and observe the resulting static forces. The widget protocol involves specifying the "parameters" used to set a widget's properties, and the student "events" that the widget recognizes. The events can be simple as "button-pushed," or require some processing as in a multiple choice "correct answer" event, and in the case of custom built widgets, can be arbitrarily sophisticated, as in a "student has moved the load past the tension limit of the cable" event in the crane boom widget.

Our design base-line for the Interaction Editor is highly usable widely available tools such as Authorware and Icon Author. The major difference between these systems and Eon for interface building (other than the fact that Eon is still a prototype) is that they use a "story board" paradigm for representing instructional content, and Eon uses a knowledge based paradigm (Murray 1996a). Student screens built with off the shelf authoring tools have fixed content (which can be modified somewhat via programming), while in Eon, each screen is a reusable template, and the author creates "content" objects to fill in these templates. The values of widget parameters can be bound to scripts or functions, allowing the student screens to be generated dynamically as well as containing canned material. Still, Eon is not as facile at authoring complex device simulations as tools built specifically for this purpose, such as RIDES (Munroe et al. 1994). RIDES allows widgets such as simulated meters, levers, faucets, and motors to

---

[7]Eon is built using Apple's Tool Builder. The special purpose widgets can be fairly easily build in Tool Builder, or they can be programmed in some other language and linked in.

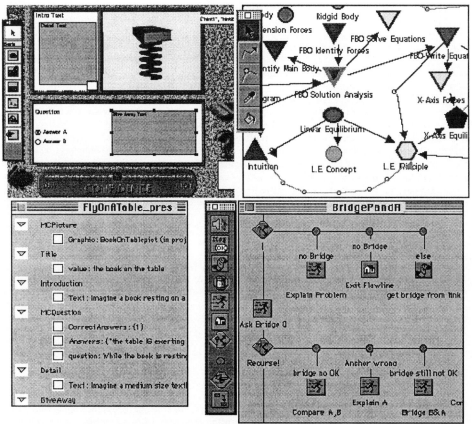

Figure 2: Interaction Editor (UL), Topic Network Editor (UR), Contents Editor (LL), and Strategy Editor (LR)

be connected by wires or pipes, and represents the interactions between these components in such a way that students can inspect how the device operates. RIDES, like other special purpose authoring tools built to date, has only limited abilities to represent curriculum, content abstractions, or multiple teaching strategies.

Authoring the Domain Model

A major difference between ITSs and conventional CAI systems is that ITSs contain an inspectable model of domain expertise. This expertise can be either runnable (is in an expert system) or non-runnable. The domain model also contains two types of information: content (or performance) information, which represents knowledge about the subject matter area, and pedagogical information (some times called propeaudic information) which is information about learning or teaching the content. Pedagogical information is declarative, for example: prerequisite relationships, information about recognizing and remediating common misconceptions, and topic importance and difficulty. Most ITS systems contain either an expert system model with little pedagogical information, or a more curricular model which represents domain content relationships and pedagogical information, but is not runnable. (Though an ITS could conceivably excel in both areas.)

To date, expert systems building is still a black art requiring significant knowledge engineering skills. Powerful AI techniques such as plan recognition, case-based reasoning, natural language understanding, neural networks, fuzzy logic, and rule-based problem solving must be used sparingly and cautiously if the goal is to produce tutors efficiently, since the inclusion of these technologies into tutoring systems dramatically increases the complexity of the necessary authoring tools, and the amount of training needed to use them. AI models of expertise are said to be powerful because of their generality and modularity, but in practice, the amount of complexity and experience needed to build and maintain a working expert system is at odds with the level of simplicity needed for a truly usable ITS shell.

Our goal is to build highly usable systems, and since no generic expert system framework has yet been devised which lowers the complexity level sufficiently, Eon does not support the authoring of rule based expertise (though Eon-built tutors can be interfaced with expert systems). This means that examples, "why" and "how" inquiries, hints, explanations, and problem solving demonstrations, which can be generated from first principles in more AI-intensive ITSs (e.g. Lesgold et al. 1990), must be generated with canned information and parameterized properties in Eon tutors (one area of many in which we can't "have it all"). The lack of a runnable model also limits the student model's depth (as explained later). Authoring tools are being developed for Model Tracing tutors, which incorporate expert systems for relatively simple skills, and maintain fine grained models of student knowledge (Anderson & Pelletier 1991).

Topics and topic relationships are created with Eon's Topic Network Editor. A node's shape represents topic type, for example as concept, fact, or procedure. The color, border color, fill pattern, and border thickness can be used to visually portray up to four other topic properties. Topic links of various types have different colors. As mentioned above, Eon Ontology objects specify the knowledge types, topic properties, and link types for a specific domain or class of domains. Murray 1996b describes how "Topic Levels" are used to allow more representation flexibility than is possible in a traditional semantic network paradigm. Topic Levels can specify different types of performance (e.g. knowing vs. *using* a fact), different levels of mastery (novice vs. expert), and different instructional functions (motivate, teach, test, summarize) within a single topic.

Authoring the Teaching Model

A variety of representational formalisms have been used for control and strategic knowledge in ITS shells. Some employ relatively sophisticated AI techniques such as goal-based planning (Russell et al. 1988), black board architectures (W. Murray 1990), agents (Chiekes 1995), task decomposition (Van Marcke 1995), and production rules (Anderson & Pelletier 1991, Major 1995). Similarly to the domain knowledge discussion above, no framework or visual editor has yet been devised for any of these formalism which lowers the complexity level sufficiently for our intended users. These formalisms are highly modular, but control information elicited from human experts often has clearly defined structure (Gruber 1987), and high modularity can hide the structure of strategic knowledge, obfuscate the context of strategy decisions, and make strategy design unwieldy (Lesser 1984).

We use a graphically portrayed procedural representation of strategic knowledge, which explicitly shows structural and contextual control information. Our Strategy Editor has a look and feel similar to commercially available authoring tools such as Authorware and Icon Author. The "flow line" paradigm for visual authoring of control or strategic knowledge has proven to be highly understandable and usable. It is not as powerful as the more AI-intensive methods mentioned above, because it does not allow for a tutor to reason about what it plans to do or could do further along in the session and optimize the current action accordingly, or to search a large space of potential instructional actions. But in our experience we have not yet found that such power is necessary.

There are two major difference between Eon flow lines and those used in commercially available authoring tools. First, Eon flow lines, unlike the others, are real procedures, with parameters and local variables, and they can return a value. Second, the Eon system allows for the representation of alternate teaching strategies and meta-strategies. The diamond shaped icons in the flow line in the Figure show decision or branching points (they are also used to create repeat loops). Branching conditions, stored with the small circles above each branch, can be responsive to user actions (i.e. widget events), student model values (described below), content properties (such as a topic's difficulty), and other arbitrary conditions (using a flow line's local variables).

Effective teaching systems will need multiple instructional strategies, and meta strategies for choosing among them, to be able to respond to a variety of learning conditions and types of knowledge (Ohlsson 1987). Spensley et al. (1990) describe a shell which allows meta-strategies to choose among pre-defined general strategies, including cognitive apprenticeship, successive refinement, discovery learning, abstraction, practice, and Socratic diagnosis. The strategies themselves are fixed however, and fine grained decisions can not be modified. Major (1995) describes a highly usable authoring tool (REDEEM) that allows teachers to set a number of teaching strategy parameters to customize and select applicability conditions for teaching actions. In this system some flexibility is traded for usability, since the underlying instructional strategies are pre-defined (though parameterized).

Eon also uses a parameterized approach, but is more flexible since the strategies can be built from scratch. Users define a number of "strategy parameters", for example, "degree of hinting," "degree of interruption," "preference for general vs. specific information," and "amount of information". Then they create meta strategies, which specify combinations of these, e.g. "moderate hinting; give general information before specific; and skim (don't give much information)." These global variable are used in the decisions of teaching strategy flow lines to, for example, take one branch for moderate hinting and another for maximum hinting. Unlike REDEEM, which is in late a prototype stage and has proven to be usable by teachers, the Eon meta-strategy mechanism is still being developed.

The strategy parameters, being a component of the vocabulary for describing instructional decisions, are part of the Ontology. Since some teaching knowledge is general in nature (Van Marcke 1992, Jona 1995), default teaching strategies and meta-strategies are incorporated into special-purpose (Eon-derived) authoring systems.

Authoring the Student Model

In general, ITS Student Models come in two flavors: runnable models and overlay models (VanLehn 1988). Runnable models, such as those used in Model Tracing tutors (Anderson & Reiser 1985) represent student knowledge as a subset of the expert system rules, along with buggy rules, and can compare these rules to the student's behavior in precise ways. Overlay models assign competency (and sometimes certainty) values to curriculum topics according to inferences made during the tutorial. Runnable models are used with expert-system based ITSs, and overlay models are used with non-runnable or curriculum-based ITSs. The same problems in complexity apply to authoring runnable student models as apply to authoring expert systems, as described above. Therefor Eon does not support Model Tracing or similar methods.

Among ITS shells that support overlay models (the vast majority of them), interfaces for authoring student models are almost completely lacking. Eon allows authors to specify in detail how the student model will infer student knowledge from student behavior. Of course, this level of authoring is at the "first tier" mentioned above, and most authors will be using a default set of student modeling rules (and perhaps making minor adjustments). The overlay model for most ITSs assigns a single value to curriculum topics at the same level. Eon's overlay model is more sophisticated. Values can be assigned to entities at several "decision layers:" Lesson, Topic, Topic Level, Presentation, and Transactions. Events and objects at each layer are composed of events and objects at the next lower layer, for example, running a lesson will invoke the teaching of a number of topics, teaching a topic will run a number of its topic levels, and each topic level consist of a number of presentations (representing student interactions or blocks of information). Within a presentation, a multiple choice question for example, a number of low level student and tutor transactions will occur, such a selecting an answer or asking for help (the student), or giving a hint (the tutor). The author assigns a set of allowed values to each layer, then creates rules which show how the values of one layer are calculated based on the values of the next lower layer. The Ontology stores the allowed values, and some default student model rules. Teaching strategies query the information in the Student Model to make decisions based on, for example, whether a topic is "mastered" or whether a presentation have been "given" already.

Conclusion

ITS Authoring tools can have a variety of purposes and intended users, and their design must account for tradeoffs among four overall goals: scope, depth, learnability, and productivity. We have discussed how our system approaches these overall goals in terms of the four functional components of ITSs: the learning environment, the domain model, the teaching model, and the student model. Though designing to maximize any of the four overall goals could compromise the other three, our research tires to find a balance among the goals which will yield a high level of all four, or at least investigate the *possibility* of excelling in all four areas. Our approach to "having it all, maybe" has four principles: 1) use appropriate representational formalisms, 2) provide highly visual authoring tools, 3) create Ontology objects for each class of domains, and 4) provide authoring tools for "three tiers" of users, as summarized below:

1) A long standing aphorism in Artificial Intelligence is that once an appropriate knowledge representation is found for a problem, the task of solving the problem, or of programming an intelligent system to solve the problem, is half complete. We in the field of ITS are still searching for powerful representational formalisms. So although designing general ITS shells requires many compromises, additional levels of excellence on all fronts will be realized as better formalisms are developed over time. We have much to learn about appropriate levels of abstraction, conceptual structures, and conceptual vocabularies for general and special purpose systems. We are in the process of designing a conceptual vocabulary of primitive tutorial actions pedagogical parameters, and a knowledge classification scheme that authors can use to organize and codify domain knowledge and teaching knowledge.

2) We believe that all conceptual and structural elements of a representational formalism must be portrayed graphically with high visual fidelity if ITS Authoring systems are to be used by non-programmers without a high degree of knowledge engineering expertise. Such an interface relieves working memory load by reifying the underlying structures, and assists long term memory by providing remindings of this structure.

3) We have introduced authorable objects called Ontologies which define the underlying conceptual vocabulary for a class of domains, and thus allow Eon to be used as a meta-authoring tool for creating special purpose authoring tools.

4) Meta-authoring allows us to satisfy the needs of three groups of users: those who use meta-authoring to create special purpose authoring tools, those who use special purpose authoring tools to create ITSs, and teachers who use ITSs in their classes. Authoring tools, or variations of tools, will be provided for all three types of users.

Eon is currently being used to build five tutors. The Statics Tutor teaches introductory Statics concepts, and includes a "crane boom" simulation. The Bridging Analogies Tutor incorporates a Socratic teaching strategy developed and tested by cognitive scientists to remediate common persistent misconceptions in science. The Chemistry Workbench tutor provides a more open ended learning environment for learning about solvency and chemical reactions by interactively mixing chemicals and measuring the results. The Keigo Tutor teaches a part of Japanese language called "honorifics," dealing with the complicated rules used to determine verb conjugation which appropriately honors the listener and topic of a conversation. For this tutor Eon is interfaced with a rule based expert system. The Refrigerator Tutor explains the thermodynamic principles underlying refrigeration. All of these systems are in prototype stages.

References

Anderson, J. R. & Pelletier, R. (1991). A development system for model-tracing tutors. In *Proceedings of the International Conference on the Learning Sciences* , (pp. 1-8), Evanston, IL.

Anderson, J. R. & Reiser, B. (1985). The Lisp Tutor. BYTE, April 1985, pg. 159-175.

Bonar, J., R. Cunningham, and J. Schultz, (1986). An Object-Oriented Architecture for Intelligent Tutoring. *Proceedings of the ACM Conference on Object-Oriented Programming Systems, Language and Applications*. ACM, New York.

Cheikes, B. (1995). Should ITS Designers be Looking for a Few Good Agents? In AIED-95 workshop papers for Authoring Shells for Intelligent Tutoring Systems.

Dooley, S., Meiskey, L., Blumenthal, R., & Sparks, R. (1995). Developing reusable intelligent tutoring system shells. In AIED-95 workshop papers for Authoring Shells for Intelligent Tutoring Systems.

Gruber, T. (1987). "A Method for Acquiring Strategic Knowledge from Experts." University of Massachusetts Dissertation.

Gruber, T. (1993). Toward Principles for the Design of Ontologies Used for Knowledge Sharing. In *Formal Ontology in Conceptual Analysis and Knowledge Representation*, Guarino & Poli (Eds.). Kluwer Academic Publishers.

Jona, M. (1995). Representing and re-using general teaching strategies: A knowledge-rich approach to building authoring tools for tutoring systems. In AIED-95 workshop papers for Authoring Shells for Intelligent Tutoring Systems.

Jones, M. & Wipond, K. (1991). Intelligent Environments for Curriculum and Course Development. In Goodyear (Ed.), *Teaching Knowledge and Intelligent Tutoring*. Norwood, NJ: Ablex.

Lesgold, A., Lajoie, S., Bunzo, M., and Eggan, G., (1990). A Coached Practice Environment for an Electronics Troubleshooting Job, in J. Larkin, R. Chabay and C. Sheftic (Eds.) *Computer Assisted Instruction and Intelligent Tutoring System: Establishing Communication and Collaboration.*. Erlbaum, Hillsdale, NJ.

Lesser, V. (1984). Control in Complex Knowledge-based Systems. Tutorial at the IEEE Computer Society AI Conference.

Major, N. P., (1993). Teachers and Teaching Strategies. *Proc. of the Seventh International PEG Conference*, Heriot-Watt Univ., Edinburgh.

Major, N. (1995). REDEEM: Creating Reusable Intelligent Courseware. *In Proc. of AI-ED 95*, Washington, D.C., August, 1995.

Merrill, M. D. (1989). An Instructional Design Expert System. *Computer-Based Instruction*, 16: 3, pp. 95-101.

Murray, T. (1996a). From Story Boards to Knowledge Bases: The First Paradigm Shift in Making CAI "Intelligent." To appear in *Proc. of ED-MEDIA 96.*, Boston, MA, July 1996.

Murray T. (1996b). Special Purpose Ontologies and the Representation of Pedagogical Knowledge. To appear in *Proc. of the International Conf. on the Learning Sciences*. Evanston IL, July 1996.

Murray, W.R. (1990). A Blackboard-based Dynamic Instructional Planner. In *Proc. of AAAI-90*.

Ohlsson, S. (1987). Some Principles of Intelligent Tutoring. In Lawler & Yazdani (Eds.), *Artificial Intelligence and Education*, Volume 1. Ablex: Norwood, NJ.

Russell, D., Moran, T. & Jordan, D. (1988). The Instructional Design Environment. In Psotka, Massey, & Mutter (Eds.), *Intelligent Tutoring Systems, Lessons Learned*, Hillsdale, NJ: Lawrence Erlbaum.

Shute, V.J. and Regian, J.W. (1990). Rose Garden Promises of Intelligent Tutoring Systems: Blossom or Thorn? Presented at Space Operations, Automation and Robotics Conference, June 1990, Albuquerque, NM.

Spensley, F., Elsom-Cook, M., Byerley, P., Brooks, P., Federici, M. and Scaroni, C. (1990). "Using multiple teaching strategies in an ITS", in Frasson, C. and Gauthier, G. (eds.), *Intelligent Tutoring Systems: At the crossroads of Artificial Intelligence and Education*. Norwood, NJ: Ablex.

Towne, D.M., Munro, A., (1988). The Intelligent Maintenance Training System. In Psotka, Massey, & Mutter (Eds.), *Intelligent Tutoring Systems, Lessons Learned*, Hillsdale, NJ: Lawrence Erlbaum.

Van Marcke, K. (1992). Instructional Expertise. In Frasson, C., Gauthier, G., & McCalla, G.I. (Eds.) *Procs. of Intelligent Tutoring Systems '92*. Springer Verlag, Berlin.

VanLehn, K. (1988). "Toward a Theory of Impasse-Driven Learning." In Mandl, H. & Lesgold, A. (Eds.), *Learning Issues for Intelligent Tutoring Systems*. New York: Springer-Verlag.

Wenger, E. (1987). *Artificial Intelligence and Tutoring Systems*. Los Altos, CA: Morgan Kaufmann.

Winne P.H., 1991. Project DOCENT: Design for a Teacher's Consultant. In Goodyear (Ed.), *Teaching Knowledge and Intelligent Tutoring*. Norwood, NJ: Ablex.

Youngblut, C., 1995. Government-Sponsored Research and Development Efforts in the Area of Intelligent Tutoring Systems: Summary Report. Inst. for Defense Analyses Paper No. P-3058, Alexandra VA.

Teacher-Usable Exercise Design Tools

Michael Schoelles[1] and Henry Hamburger[1]

[1] George Mason University, Fairfax,VA, 22030, USA

Abstract: We present software tools with which a language teacher can specify exercises for the Fluent-2 two-medium conversational language learning environment. The tools permit creation of tutorial schemas, language usage structures and graphical properties of objects. These data structures play major roles in guiding the execution of an exercise on a particular grammatical topic. The tools support our goal of immersing the learner in realistic situations with varied language constructions and conversational styles. They give a teacher some control over the situation, style and variety and let her construct exercises for particular grammatical topics.

1 Introduction

Fluent-2 is an intelligent tutoring system and learning environment for second language, featuring multi-medium dialogue in written and spoken language and animated graphics [4, 5]. Here we describe our tools that let a language teacher tailor the system's behavior to particular pedagogical requirements. One tool lets the teacher specify language usage in familiar terminology (what Odlin [7] calls the level of pedagogical grammar). Another tool permits specification of the sequence and pattern of microworld actions and conversational styles as well as their coordination with the language aspects. A third simplifies the development of the graphic representations.

These tools permit what is called knowledge acquisition, in the parlance of expert systems. The word "teacher" is used here and throughout the paper to mean the individual who specifies exercises to the system. This individual may in fact be a language teacher, an expert in language pedagogy or a second language researcher. The role is analogous to that of a domain expert for an expert system. The remainder of this section introduces the Fluent-2 two-medium conversational language learning environment, as a system and from the learner viewpoint. The next three sections treat the three tools. Section 5 is a pointer to the future.

1.1 System Overview

This section provides a general overview of the Fluent-2 system and its relationship to the tools. This relationship can be seen in the architecture depicted in Figure 1. The tools in the outer ring provide knowledge transfer pathways from the teacher to the knowledge base of the system in the second ring. The four processors in the next ring perform the tutoring and learning environment functions of the system. These processes – which are data-driven by the knowledge base and event-driven by the student – are governed by the executive, which also interacts with the student.

In figure 1 the bold ring between the tools and the knowledge base represents the boundary of the system during a learning session, with the tools deactivated. The bold spokes separate the different modules. They represent the conceptual boundaries of the system objects that encapsulate the various components of knowledge with their corresponding processes.

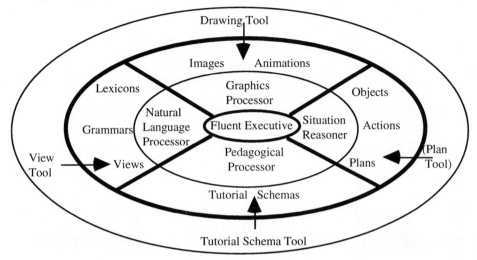

Fig. 1: Fluent-2 Architecture

The outer ring of the detailed architecture diagram identifies existing tools for building (i) tutorial schemas, (ii) language usage structures and (iii) the graphics of objects. A fourth tool, for building microworld plans, is shown in parentheses. The teacher manipulates a graphical user interface in order to input data to the tools, which process this input to produce instantiated objects for the next ring.

The knowledge base appears in the second ring. Tutorial Schemas coordinate the plans, conversational style and conversational variety when the system is in ITS mode. Views provide language specifications and constraints to achieve the conversational variety within of a tutorial schema. Plans and actions are rules that specify how the tutor organizes activity in the microworld, how the student initiates actions and how the microworld state is altered. The Microworld object hierarchy specifies the objects in a microworld.

The third ring shows the processes that operate on the knowledge base to provide language tutoring or a learning environment. The pedagogical processor decides what the tutor will do and say next by selecting a tutorial schema from the knowledge base and executing it. The natural language processor is a generative system that constructs a semantic structure based on the current view. The semantic structure is processed by the language generation system to generate a sentence in the specified language. The situation reasoner instantiates and executes the plan and action rules based on the current situation. Microworld Processing maintains object information and performs the graphical actions in the microworld.

The system executive controls the interaction between the student and the system and coordinates the main processes (in the adjacent ring) based on this interaction. The student's interaction with the system takes two forms, learning and control. In a learning interaction, the student causes linguistic and graphical events in the microworld. In a control interaction the student can take control of choices about the plans and actions, the conversational style and the degree of linguistic variety. For more on Fluent-2, see [5]

1.2 Student View

Learning with Fluent-2 comes from conversations that are generative with respect to both natural language and graphics. The conversations take place in microworlds, where descriptions, questions and commands are tied to microworld events and their resulting conditions. These events and conditions are visible on the computer screen, as animations and graphical properties of the objects in a microworld. Several microworlds have now been implemented. One has an animated person that can walk, turn around and do things with its hands, as shown in Figure 2.

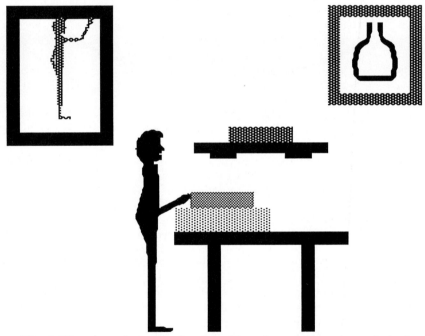

Fig. 2 The person has walked to the table and reached out to touch the box.

Dialogue 1 is an actual interaction between the tutor and the student for the situation shown. Generation of the tutor's side of this dialogue was the end result of the system executing a tutorial schema. That schema was created using the tutorial schema tool and the language specification tool. The student types in responses which are then examined for correctness in straightforward ways that do not yet use the language representation. Dialogue 1 is an exercise in definiteness, which is notoriously difficult for learners of English; see, for example, Swan and Smith [10].

Tutor: I am walking to the table...   There is a box on the shelf... There is another box on the table... What is on the shelf ?
Student: A box

Tutor:	Correct... Touch a box ... You are touching the box on the table... Which box did you touch?
Student:	The big one
Tutor:	Correct.
Cloze:	There are two boxes. _____ box on the table is big. There is also ___ box on the shelf.
Student:	There are two boxes. The box on the table is big. There is also a box on the shelf.
Tutor:	Good.

Dialogue 1 Definiteness

The system is multi-medium in both directions, with the graphical and linguistic communication both available for use by both the student and the tutoring system. It is the immediacy and responsiveness of this interaction, its flexibility and its opportunity for active learning in a realistic context that motivate the entire approach. On the pedagogical importance of such properties, see [2]. The flexibility arises from our use of techniques and concepts of artificial intelligence. Clancey and Soloway [1] list nine "new perspectives" for artificial intelligence and learning environments, all of which remain significant and four of which – graphics, discourse, tools and exploration – play central roles here.

A learner of any language needs to master a very large number of grammatical forms along with their meaning and usage patterns. In all or most languages, one needs to be able to formulate questions, commands and descriptions, use pronouns and tenses, express quantification and uniqueness, and so on. Rather than build a large and inflexible array of exercises, we have adopted an approach based on pedagogical tools. This strategy has the advantages of flexibility, extensibility and teacher involvement.

Specifically, in section 2 we show how to build exercises for definiteness and prior action in English. Ultimately, we want to be able to present these and other grammatical topics in many different situations and in the many languages for which they are relevant. This quest for flexibility that we have adopted is rare among CALL systems. Carrying it out requires mutual independence of the tutorial schemas, the microworlds and the language processing. Indeed two of the dialogues presented below are the result of a single tutorial schema - for practice with definiteness - that is put to use in two different microworlds. Flexibility of language implies a multilingual language processing design, which we have [3], and suggests discussing grammatical topics from a cross-linguistic perspective, which we do [8].

2 Tutorial Schema Tool

To give a concrete sense of how tutorial schemas control the pedagogical behavior of the system we present two more dialogues and the exercise or tutorial schema underlying one of them. We then describe the use of the tutorial schema tool to build that exercise. The exercises use a variety of interaction types including: introductory descriptions accompanied by demonstrative actions; questions followed by answers and then responses to answers; commands followed by actions responsive to the commands; and finally a cloze (fill in the blanks) test. We believe that the flexibility of this approach transcends that of other authoring capabilities, like the templates of Kreyer and Criswell in [6].

2.1 Dialogues and Teacher Interface

Tutorial schemas transcend microworlds, in the sense that a suitably designed tutorial schema can be applied in multiple microworlds. For example, whereas Dialogue 1 (above) takes place in the microworld of Figure 2, Dialogue 2 takes place in an entirely different microworld. Inspection of the two dialogues reveals a certain structural similarity between them. The similarity arises because the knowledge representation underlying both is the same tutorial schema, but with different plans, and therefore different objects.

Tutor:	I am picking the cup up from the sink...There is a cup on the table...There is another cup on the sink...What is on the table ?
Student:	A cup
Tutor:	Correct...Pick up a cup . ..You are picking the cup up from the table...Which cup did you pick up ?
Student:	The empty one
Tutor:	Correct.
Cloze:	There are two cups. _____ cup on the table is empty. There is also ___ cup on the sink.
Student:	There are two cups. The cup on the table is empty. There is also a cup on the sink.
Tutor:	Good.

Dialogue 2 Definiteness in another microworld

Dialogue 3 makes it clear that using a visual means of communication does not limit the teacher creating the tutorial schema to the present tense. Indeed one can even go so far as to distinguish different kinds of prior action, here a difference between what is expressed by the simple past and the present perfect in English. We believe that the immediacy of the visual medium will keep down cognitive load and permit the factors underlying the linguistic distinction to be recognized. On visual advantages of this sort, see [9].

Tutor:	Turn on the faucet...You have turned the faucet on...Pick up the cup from the sink...You have picked up the cup from the sink...What did you do first ?
Student:	I turned the faucet on
Tutor:	OK...What did you do next ?
Student:	I picked up the cup from the sink
Tutor:	OK....Fill the cup with the water...You have filled the cup with the water...What have you done ?
Student:	I have filled the cup.
Tutor:	OK.

Dialogue 3 Prior Action: simple past vs. present perfect

Now we turn to how a teacher actually creates the knowledge representation that drives dialogues, thereby transforming an idea for an exercise into a schema that then guides actual system execution. Figure 3 shows the screen after using the Tutorial Schema Tool to create the Definiteness Tutorial Schema that produced Dialogue 2. For Dialogue 1, the screen looks identical except for the left-hand column, where the plans/actions are walking and touching rather than picking up and putting down.

○ **Select plan**　○ **Show args**　○ **Define Cloze**　┌─────────────┐
○ **Expand plan**　　　　　　　　　　　　　　　　　　　│ **Create TS** │
　　　　　　　　　　　　　　　　　　　　　　　　　　　　　└─────────────┘

Plan	Style	View	Success	Failure
PICKUP	TOURGUIDE	PRESENT-ACT		
PUTDOWN	TOURGUIDE	LOC-STATE	LOC-STATE-OTHER	
NONE	QUIZMASTER	WH-ON-TOP		
PICKUP	COMMANDER	CMD-ACTION	PRESENT-ACT	CMD-FA IL
NONE	QUIZMASTER	WH-PRES-SPEC		

Figure 3 Tutorial Schema Interface

The key design decisions are in the cycle of steps numbered 2-5. Recall that the objective of the exercise is to stress the distinction between definite and indefinite articles in English, and to get the student actively involved in using them correctly. Therefore, the teacher should create situations that require one or the other in both the system's and then the student's use of language.

Here, in the second line of figure 3, the teacher chose the PUT-DOWN plan/action, and repeated the choice of the TOURGUIDE conversational style, this time using two views, namely LOCATION-STATE and LOCATION-STATE-OTHER. The first view causes the system to generate language about the location of the object that was just picked up and put down. This particular view specifies that the reference should be indefinite, which together with the notion of location, makes the system generate a *There is* sentence in line 2 of Dialogue 2. The second view causes the system to generate language about the location of some other object of the same type. For more about the specification of views, see section 3.

In the third line of the schema, the teacher has switched from TOURGUIDE to QUIZMASTER in order to follow up with a question about the current state of the microworld and give the student a chance to answer. In this case no plan/action is specified, since QUIZMASTER is a language-only conversational style. Selecting WH-question as the view leads to a question about the cup, the answer to which requires use of the definite article.

The fourth line specifies COMMANDER as the conversational style, so the system will tell the student what to do and the student will then be allowed to try to do it by acting in the microworld. To generate an indefinite here, the teacher chose COMMAND-INDEF as the view. To follow up the command with additional dialogue after the student completes the action follow-up views for both failure and success were selected. The WH-PRES-SPEC view in the last line of the schema will generate a *which* question, which will make it appropriate for the student to respond with the definite and the system will evaluate the student's response accordingly.

Additional options allow more detailed control over exercises than so far described. As seen above the Create Schema screen provides the capability to specify a conversational style and one or more views at a plan level. Typically a plan consists of a series of subplans or actions. To achieve a finer degree of control over the system's language and the detailed steps of the plan the Expand Plan button expands the current plan into its subplans and individual actions. For each of these, a conversational style and view(s) may be specified.

The Show Args button provides information about the plan/action arguments. It displays the plan/action header used by the system. This header contains the language-independent meaning of the plan or action and a list of its arguments in the form of (variable symbol, class constraint) pairs.

The Define Cloze button allows the teacher to enter a cloze test, like those at the end of Dialogues 1 and 2. When this button is pressed, an edit box is displayed in which the test can be entered. Quotes surround the text in the cloze that will be replaced by blanks for the student to fill in. The teacher selects tutorial schema management functions (define, list, save and restore) from a menu bar.

3 The Language Tool

The language tool lets the teacher strongly influence the language that the natural language processor generates from a particular tutorial schema. Using the tool, the teacher specifies a language representation called a view. A view may be simple or complex. Simple views result in single clauses, while complex views combine two simple views via some relation to yield a complex sentence. A simple view may reflect an action or a state. Action views yield language that indicates what action is taking place, while for a state view, some state of the microworld will be the focus. At a more detailed level, simple views have three parts: a context level description, an event level description and an object level description. It is at this level that we begin our description of the language tool.

The definition screens for the language tool are all GUIs with radio buttons and edit boxes for making choices. At the context level the choices available are: the tense (present or past), polarity (positive or negative), aspect (none, on-going or prior action) and modality (factual, possible, necessary or obligative) parameters of a clause. The following examples illustrate the use of this level. Each example consists of a sentence and the button(s) used to obtain it. Any buttons not mentioned in an example uses a default.

Sentences	Button Pushed
Pick up the cup.	Imperative
The cup was on the table.	Past
You did not pick up the cup	Past, Negative
Can you pick up the cup?	Possible, Question (Yes/No)
Should I pick up the cup?	Obligative, Question (Yes/No)
What cup have I not picked up?	Past, Question (Wh), Prior Action

The choices for the event level are: what action (student did or tutor did), what arguments (minimum or maximum), pre/post action (state before or after action), which argument (teacher enters) or which attribute (teacher enters). Again examples are the best way to illustrate the use of these parameters.

Clause	Parameters	Settings
Pick up the cup.	What arguments	Minimum
Pick up the cup from the table.	What arguments	Maximum
The cup was on the table.	Pre/Post Action	State after action

The cup is in your hand.	Pre/Post Action	State before action
	Which Argument	Patient
	Which Attribute	Location

At the object level one specifies information on how to refer to a particular microworld object. The object is identified in the Which Argument slot of the event level view. The Precision option specifies whether to talk about the object itself (Distinct), about its class (Direct), the parent of that class (Parent) or the topmost class (Top). The Definiteness options specify whether to make a definite or an indefinite reference to the object. The following examples, illustrate the use of this level.

Clause	Buttons Pushed
Pick up a cup.	Indefinite
Pick up the cup on the table.	(none)
There is another cup on the sink.	Direct
	Indefinite
Which cup did you pick up?	(none)
What did you pick up.	None
Fill a container.	Parent
	Indefinite

To create action and state views from these basic building blocks the teacher enters the name of the context, event and object level views and then assigns a name to the action or state view. To create a complex level view a similar screen is displayed with entries for the names of two simple views and a relation that connects them.

4 The Drawing Tool

The motivations for a microworld tool are extensibility, development efficiency and the acquisition of knowledge from a subject matter expert. In other words, we want a large number of microworlds and we want a teacher to construct them. A new microworld may support exposure to new aspects of the target language and may also provide new situations in which to practice existing knowledge. (On the role of situation in second language acquisition, see [2]).

To build a teacher usable tool for a system component that is tightly coupled to the other components of the system is an ambitious goal. In Fluent-2 the microworld and the lexicon have a tight coupling since language must be generated for the actions and objects that make up the microworld. In light of this, our approach is to build the microworld tool incrementally.

The first step, building the drawing tool for creating graphical images, has been completed. This tool, with its 40 operators, was used to create the animation of a person in Figure 2. The tool made it easy for us to reshape portions of this complex polygonal figure 2 while keeping intact the various relationships among the parts, as one must to allow animations by interpolation. In particular the drawing tool made it manageable to create the forward and side views and to make these two views compatible for the action of turning around. This was done with the operator that permits selecting a single point (or several) at a time and moving it (or them) a tightly controlled distance in a precise direction. Resulting changes appear instantaneously. Another operator lets the user rotate a selected contiguous segment of the figure's outline about any selected center or rotation. The amount of rotation can then be adjusted by successive clicks. To get the extreme position of a swinging arm for walking, we began by putting the rotation icon at the shoulder. Other operators let us now make additional people of various sizes, shapes and colors at will, and all of them can be imported into microworlds where they will be able to walk, turn around, touch things, and so on.

5.0 Future Directions

This paper reports progress in readying FLUENT-2 for the classroom. The screen designs represent a first cut at an operationally effective interface between a teacher and the FLUENT-2 system. We plan to continue to work closely with teachers in order to improve the usability of the tools and the system from their point of view.

One of the design principles that has guided the development of FLUENT-2 is that whenever possible the system should reason about the situation in order to choose the appropriate thing to say, in order to relieve the teacher of decisions about details, letting him/her focus on the more general specifications and pedagogically meaningful aspects of an exercise. We are developing more situation reasoning and discourse reasoning capabilities in order to achieve this goal. "Introduce all objects that can support other objects" is an example of the type and level of specification that should be available to the teacher. However, it should be kept in mind that the more general the exercise specification the less knowledge the teacher has about exactly what the system will say.

References

1. Clancey, W. J. and Soloway, E. (1990) Artificial intelligence and learning environments: Preface. Artificial Intelligence, 42, 1, 1-6.
2. Ellis. R. (1986) Understanding Second Language Acquisition. Oxford: Oxford University Press.
3. Felshin, S. (1993) A Guide to the Athena Language Learning Project Natural Language Processing System, MIT.
4. Hamburger, H. (1994) Foreign language immersion: Science, practice and a system. J. Artificial Intelligence in Education.
5. Hamburger, H. (1995) Structuring two-medium dialog for language learning. In Holland, M., Kaplan, J. and Sams, M. (Eds.) Intelligent Language Tutors: Balancing Theory and Technology. Hillsdale, NJ: L. Erlbaum Associates.
6. Kreyer, s. and Criswell, E. (1995) Instructor as author in an adaptive, multimedia, foreign language tutor. In Holland, M., Kaplan, J. and Sams, M. (Eds.) Intelligent Language Tutors: Balancing Theory and Technology. Hillsdale, NJ: L. Erlbaum Associates.
7. Odlin, T. (1994) Perspectives on Pedagogical Grammar. Cambridge: Cambridge University Press.
8   Schoelles, M. and Hamburger, H. (in press) Cognitive tools for language pedagogy. Computer-Assisted Language Learning
9. Stenberg, G., Radeborg, K. and Hedman, L. R. (1995) The picture superiority effect in a cross-modality recognition task. Memory and Cognition, 23, 4, 425-441.
10. Swan, M. and Smith, B. (1987) Learner English. Cambridge: Cambridge University Press.

Modèles cognitifs pour l'apprentissage en thermodynamique

Jean-Marc Charlot, Bernard Marcos, Jean Lapointe

Faculté des sciences appliquées, Université de Sherbrooke,
Sherbrooke (Québec), Canada, J1K 2R1. charlot@graco.gme.usherb.ca

Résumé. Notre étude porte sur la collecte, la formalisation et la comparaison des modèles mentaux d'étudiants en thermodynamique. Elle s'appuie sur des résultats provenant de la psychologie cognitive et des outils développés en intelligence artificielle. Elle rapporte les observations sur des entretiens que nous avons menés auprès de Novices et d'Experts afin de saisir leurs modèles mentaux, et propose un formalisme de représentation de ces modèles qui interviennent dans le processus de résolution de problèmes en thermodynamique. On utilisera ce formalisme pour suivre l'évolution de l'apprenant dans un système tutoriel d'aide à l'apprentissage.

1   Introduction

Les étudiants entreprenant des études en sciences appliquées éprouvent de réelles difficultés à développer des représentations mentales appropriées, nécessaires à une bonne compréhension des phénomènes. Cet article décrit l'approche suivie pour le recueil et la formalisation des modèles mentaux de novices et d'experts en thermodynamique. Notre approche s'appuie sur des techniques d'intelligence artificielle comme l'intégration et la manipulation de connaissances qualitatives. Elle doit ensuite permettre de comparer ces modèles mentaux; cette comparaison sert de point de départ à un diagnostic sur l'évolution de l'apprenant.

La section 2 de cet article rappelle quelques caractéristiques importantes des modèles mentaux et leurs liens avec les systèmes tutoriels. La section 3 présente le recueil des modèles mentaux à partir des entretiens que nous avons menés auprès des Novices, Étudiants et Experts. Enfin, nous exposons le formalisme pour représenter le modèle mental ainsi que son évolution durant l'apprentissage.

2   Modèles mentaux

Depuis quinze ans, la psychologie cognitive n'a pas cessé d'influencer les conceptions et les pratiques de l'enseignement qu'elle considère comme la science de la construction du savoir [1]. Elle est la seule à étudier de manière complète l'apprentissage, l'acquisition, l'intégration et la réutilisation des connaissances.

L'un des apports importants est la notion de modèle mental [2], qui correspond à la manière dont nous percevons le monde réel [3]. Les novices et les experts utilisent des modèles mentaux différents pour représenter les phénomènes physiques présents en thermodynamique. Ils se distinguent par la nature de leurs connaissances [1, 4, 5] et aussi par la manière dont ils se représentent les phénomènes [6]. Le novice peut aussi avoir de mauvaises représentations qu'il tient de l'expérience de tous les jours; par exemple, il confond masse et poids [7]. Il est possible d'agir sur ses connaissances afin d'arriver à un raffinement ou à une correction de sa représentation des phénomènes [8].

Généralement, les systèmes tutoriels comprennent un module expert, un module étudiant, un module tuteur et une interface entre le système et l'apprenant [4]. Le module étudiant peut être un sous-ensemble du modèle de l'expert, auquel on ajoute une liste d'erreurs pour rendre compte des notions mauvaises et manquantes du novice. Une autre approche consiste à classer les erreurs en deux catégories : celles qui dépendent du domaine traité et celles qui relèvent plutôt du processus général de résolution de problèmes, d'interprétation et de transcription de l'énoncé [9].

Le formalisme proposé permet de recueillir, de mettre à jour et d'utiliser les modèles mentaux de l'étudiant afin de faire progresser ses connaissances et ses stratégies de résolution de problèmes vers celles de l'expert. Pour White et Frederiksen, cette évolution est vue comme une succession de modèles mentaux prédéfinis et plaqués les uns à la place des autres [10]. Cependant, cette conception ne reflète absolument pas l'évolution continue et dynamique du modèle mental de l'apprenant. De plus, nous n'avons pas retrouvé ce concept d'évolution dans d'autres travaux.

3   Le recueil des modèles mentaux

Nous décomposons la phase d'apprentissage en trois stades : le Novice, l'Étudiant et l'Expert. L'apprenant est tout d'abord Novice, et idéalement, lorsque les objectifs d'apprentissage sont atteints, il est Expert. Durant toute la période d'apprentissage, qui s'étend du stade de Novice à celui d'Expert, il est Étudiant. Une étude expérimentale a mis en évidence l'existence de différences de perception des principes de base en thermodynamique et de notions liées au sens commun entre étudiants suivant le même cursus. Recrutés sur une base volontaire, douze candidats ont participé à deux séances d'entretiens individuels enregistrés sur cassettes vidéo pour être analysés ultérieurement. La première séance a eu lieu avant le début du cours de thermodynamique. Elle visait à mettre en relief les différences de perception et la persistance du sens commun des notions utilisées dans un contexte scientifique. La seconde séance a eu lieu à la fin du cours et avait pour objet d'évaluer l'effet de l'enseignement sur les connaissances et les croyances a priori des étudiants. Chacun devait exprimer les raisonnements lui permettant d'aboutir à la conclusion qui lui semblait correcte à la situation présentée.

Pour élaborer les questions de l'entretien avec les Novices, nous avons consulté trois professeurs ayant enseigné le cours de thermodynamique du tronc commun. Cette démarche visait deux buts : connaître les raisonnements auxquels ont recours les Novices lorsqu'ils sont confrontés à des problèmes de thermodynamique et imaginer des problèmes pouvant mettre en évidence ces raisonnements. Selon ces professeurs, il semble que les représentations scientifiques des étudiants sont très pauvres. Des lacunes dans les concepts de base comme l'accélération de la pesanteur, la pression atmosphérique, la notion de vide, ne leur permettent pas de bien asseoir les concepts nouveaux vus dans le cours. Par exemple, on mélange conservation de la masse et conservation du volume, chauffer signifie augmenter la température, etc. Le cours apporte de nouvelles notions telles l'enthalpie, l'entropie et l'énergie interne. Pour assimiler correctement ces concepts, il faut bien maîtriser les concepts de base préalables comme la pression, la température et la densité.

3.1   Entretiens avec les Novices

Deux questions de l'entretien sont présentées ci-dessous, et une analyse complète et détaillée est effectuée dans Charlot [11].

Situation 1 : *On chauffe un glaçon sorti d'un congélateur à -18°C. Tracez la température de ce corps au cours du temps.*
   Cette question permet d'évaluer la représentation mentale qu'un novice a de la notion de chaleur. Pour certains, les réponses présentées à la figure 1 montrent que le mot chauffer est synonyme d'augmentation de température, quel que soit l'état dans lequel se trouve le corps. De même, la notion de changement de phase est floue pour beaucoup d'entre eux.

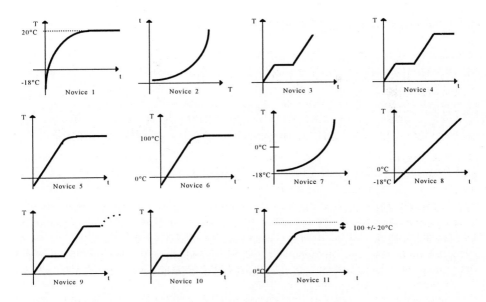

Figure 1 Les réponses des novices

Situation 2 : *On prend un cylindre fermé à une extrémité que l'on bouche, à l'autre extrémité, par un piston qui peut se déplacer librement tout en assurant l'étanchéité du système. Ce piston-cylindre contient de l'eau et de la vapeur d'eau. On le chauffe. Expliquez ce qui se passe.*

Cette question présente un système piston-cylindre couramment utilisé dans les problèmes de thermodynamique. Elle permet de connaître la représentation mentale qu'ont les Novices des variables P, T et V et de leurs relations, lors d'une évolution avec transfert de chaleur. Voici la répartition des réponses :

P↗ T↗, V↗	P↗, T↗, V↗, donc P↘, V↘ mais P devrait↗	T↗, V↗, P = constante	P↗
5 novices	3 novices	1 novice	2 novices

Elles montrent que les novices ont de la difficulté à concevoir un système où il y a un mélange d'eau et de vapeur d'eau, car pour eux, il y a également de l'air sous le piston. Tous indiquent que le piston monte, même si cette conclusion arrive après quelques hésitations, voire après une affirmation contraire. Par contre, presque tous voient dans ces évolutions une augmentation des variables P, T, V; car selon eux, si P n'augmente pas, V ne peut pas augmenter, donc le piston reste à sa place. Ils ont l'intuition que le piston doit monter, donc P doit augmenter pour que V augmente!

3.2   Entretiens avec les Étudiants

Huit étudiants parmi les onze Novices ont participé à ces entretiens qui reprennent les concepts abordés lors de la première série d'entrevues sous une forme plus académique, à la manière des questions constituant les examens du cours. Ces entretiens ont montré que des perceptions liées au sens commun n'ont pas disparu. En effet, dans le cadre du cours, l'étudiant se rattache aux équations et aux principes énoncés, mais dés qu'un raisonnement qualitatif lui est demandé, il réutilise les modèles mentaux erronés que nous avions relevés lorsqu'il était Novice. Les modifications apportées à son modèle mental par le cours semblent donc fragiles.

3.3   Entretiens avec les Experts

Ces entretiens nous permettent de construire le modèle mental de l'Expert qui correspond aux objectifs du cours et au niveau d'expertise que les professeurs désirent pour leurs étudiants. En particulier, ils décrivent comment on présente chaque notion dans les différentes activités académiques ainsi que la stratégie générale de l'expert pour résoudre des problèmes de thermodynamique.

4   La représentation des connaissances

Dans l'approche traditionnelle de construction des systèmes tutoriels, une étude détaillée et des rencontres avec les experts permettent de cerner les connaissances, de les organiser, de les hiérarchiser et de les intégrer au tutoriel. Une fois élaborée, la base de connaissances est fixe et sa structure immuable. Ce sont les connaissances correspondant au stade Expert.

En ce qui concerne l'Étudiant, la tâche est tout autre, car la structure de ses connaissances n'est pas définie a priori. Le tutoriel doit donc découvrir le modèle mental de l'étudiant, représenter la structure de ses connaissances (concepts et méthodes) et agir sur ces objets durant l'apprentissage. De ce fait, la structure de la base de connaissances relative au modèle mental ne peut être définie que pendant l'exécution du logiciel. Il faut donc procéder à la définition dynamique des objets auxquels l'étudiant a recours. Pour cela, nous utilisons la logique des prédicats, ce qui permet une grande flexibilité. Ces objets sont structurés et hiérarchisés en réseaux sémantiques et ils rendent compte de l'organisation du modèle mental de l'Étudiant et de l'Expert. Le domaine englobe les connaissances impliquées dans la résolution de problèmes de thermodynamique.

À partir des constatations émanant de notre collecte des modèles mentaux relatifs aux trois stades de l'apprentissage, nous avons retenu une structure tripartite pour modéliser les représentations mentales d'un sujet. Chacune des parties touche à un type particulier de connaissances : générales au domaine, spécifiques au problème et concernant la démarche de résolution du problème.

4.1   Les connaissances générales relatives au domaine

Il s'agit des connaissances statiques et dynamiques telles que définies par Tardif [1] et Ermine [12], c'est-à-dire les concepts utilisés, leurs interrelations, leurs attributs ainsi que les méthodes et les procédures qui s'y rattachent. En effet, tout problème du domaine peut être ramené à un système qui subit une succession de zéro, d'une ou de plusieurs transformations. La modélisation du domaine peut donc être vue comme deux réseaux sémantiques : l'un représentant un système, l'autre, une transformation, les deux étant reliés par le concept « un état ». La Figure 2 présente cette catégorie de connaissances pour l'Expert. Pour un étudiant, ce module de connaissances aura la même structure, c'est-à-dire les mêmes types de lien, mais le réseau sera moins complet et n'aura pas forcément la même organisation. Ces connaissances correspondent aux connaissances statiques des systèmes experts telles que définies dans la méthode MOISE [12, 13]. Dans notre cas, le qualificatif statique perd son sens, car c'est justement l'apprentissage qui permettra de raffiner le modèle du domaine qu'a l'étudiant. Ce réseau aura la même structure, mais il n'est pas défini a priori. Il faudra donc essayer de le bâtir en accord avec les connaissances initiales du Novice et avec celles qu'il acquiert. Nous formulons l'hypothèse que cette représentation du domaine permet d'aborder la majeure partie des problèmes posés dans le cadre du cours de thermodynamique.

Les liens hiérarchiques sont au nombre de trois :
- *aUn* : est composé de , « un système *aUne* substance » signifie que le concept « une substance » est une partie constituante du concept « un système ».

- *estUn* : est une sous-classe de, « un état initial *estUn* état » signifie que « un état initial » est un concept de même nature que « un état ». En d'autres termes, il s'agit de la définition d'une sous-classe d'un concept. « un état initial » est une sous-classe de « un état ».

- *valDans* : prend ses valeurs dans, « une substance *valDans* {air, eau} » définit le domaine dans lequel un attribut prend ses valeurs. Ce lien permet le typage des attributs. Il s'applique à un attribut d'un concept qui peut prendre une valeur. Un lien *valDans* ne peut donc provenir que d'un noeud terminal.

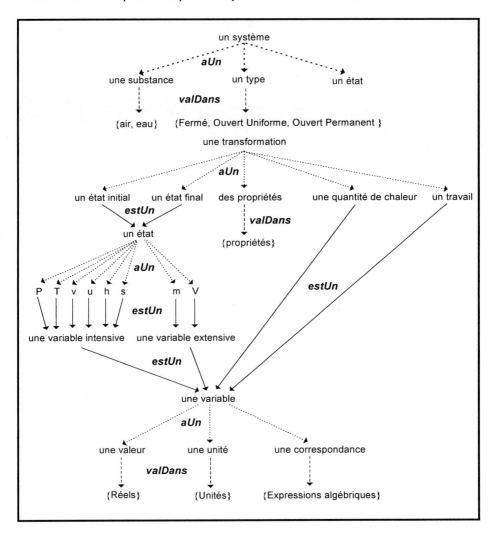

Figure 2 Réseau sémantique traduisant le domaine

Les domaines sont définis en extension ou en compréhension. L'héritage des liens s'exprime ainsi en notation *Backus-Naur* :

- X *est une sous-classe de* Y ::= X {*estUn* Y$_i$} *estUn* Y
- X *est composé de* Y ::= X {{*estUn* X$_i$}{*aUn* Y$_i$}} *aUn* Y

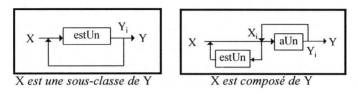

X *est une sous-classe de* Y   X *est composé de* Y

Figure 3 Héritage des liens

Chaque concept constitue un noeud du réseau. On distingue deux types de noeuds : les noeuds terminaux et les noeuds non terminaux. Un noeud est dit terminal si aucun lien sémantique des types *aUn* et *estUn* ne part de ce noeud. Seul un lien *valDans* peut partir d'un noeud terminal. Un noeud duquel part au moins un lien *aUn* ou *estUn* est un noeud non terminal.

En plus du réseau de définition hiérarchique des concepts, cette modélisation du domaine comprend également les relations, des méthodes ou tâches s'appliquant sur ces concepts dont les procédures de changement d'unité pour une variable, les procédures de recherche dans une table de thermodynamique, les procédures de résolution d'une équation à une inconnue, etc.

4.2   Les connaissances spécifiques au problème

Il s'agit de l'adéquation du modèle au problème posé. Toutes les connaissances du domaine ne sont pas forcément nécessaires pour résoudre le problème. Certaines doivent être précisées, des valeurs doivent être données aux attributs, d'autres n'interviennent pas. De nouveaux liens sont donc requis :

- *ins :* est une instance de, par exemple, X *est une instance de* Y. C'est sur l'objet X, qui est une instance du cas particulier du concept Y, que l'on va travailler pour le problème. Les concepts généraux définis dans le modèle du domaine doivent être précisés pour le problème traité. Un système et une transformation seront toujours définis par un lien *ins*. Par exemple, le piston-cylindre *est une instance de* un système.
- *syn :* permet de relier un concept du domaine à une instance de ce concept pour le problème. Le lien *ins* est utilisé pour définir une instance d'un concept du domaine auquel aucun lien sémantique n'aboutira. Les liens *syn* sont créés automatiquement, par rapprochement de l'instance définie avec le réseau du domaine.
- *pour :* est un connecteur qui fait hériter les caractéristiques d'un concept à un autre. Pour reprendre l'exemple de la situation 2, il faut préciser l'état du piston-cylindre, car un système *aUn* état, et l'état du piston-cylindre *estUn* état en particulier qui lui est propre. Il faut donc créer une instance d'un état pour le

piston-cylindre. Ainsi, l'état du piston-cylindre *est synonyme de* un état *pour* le piston-cylindre. De ce fait, le concept « l'état du piston-cylindre » héritera de toutes les caractéristiques du concept « un état », et cet état est propre à l'objet « le piston-cylindre ».

- *val :* précise la valeur donnée à un attribut instancié. Par exemple, une unité *vaut* kPa *pour* P1.

Ainsi donc, un réseau spécialisé pour le problème se bâtit en accord avec le modèle du domaine. Une interface a été développée afin de faciliter l'acquisition, la modification et l'utilisation de ces modules de connaissances. Des outils ont été mis au point afin de suivre l'évolution de la base de connaissances. Un analyseur et un interpréteur permettent de transcrire ces connaissances énoncées dans un pseudo-langage en logique des prédicats.

Enfin, les connaissances concernant la démarche de résolution du problème doivent être analysées. Il s'agit du plan ou de la stratégie qu'il faut suivre pour aboutir à la solution. En d'autres termes, quels objets doivent être considérés, quelles méthodes leur appliquer et dans quel ordre? Cette partie est en cours d'élaboration. Il faut définir les moyens de codages des tâches, leur mode de représentation et le processus d'acquisition pour le logiciel (tables thermodynamiques, résolution d'équations, etc.). Voici une portion du réseau sémantique présenté à la Figure 2 :

```
une valeur estUn concept
    prend ses valeurs dans {Reels}
une unite estUn concept
    prend ses valeurs dans {Unites}
une correspondance estUn concept
    prend ses valeurs dans {Expressions algebriques}
une variable estUn concept
    aUne valeur
    aUne unite
    aUne correspondance
une variable intensive estUne variable
un volume massique estUne variable intensive
une temperature estUne variable intensive
...
un etat estun concept
    aUne pression
    aUn volume massique
    aUne temperature
...
un etat initial estUn etat
un etat final estUn etat
une propriete estUn concept
    prend ses valeurs dans {proprietes}
une transformation estUn concept
    aUn etat initial
    aUn etat final
```

Voici une partie d'un réseau résultant de l'instanciation des concepts en objets nécessaires à la résolution d'un problème :

```
transfo1 est une instance de une transformation
transfo2 est une instance de une transformation
etat1 est synonyme de un etat initial pour transfo1
etat2 est synonyme de un etat final pour transfo1
```

```
T1 est synonyme de une temperature pour etat1
m1 est synonyme de une masse pour etat1
une valeur vaut 20 pour T1
une unite vaut Celcius pour T1
une valeur vaut 1 pour m1
une unite vaut kg pour m1
```

5   Conclusions et orientations futures

Pour la suite de cette étude, nous continuerons d'améliorer le formalisme de représentation des différents modules de connaissances. Nous cherchons également à définir la notion de distance entre deux représentations mentales. Outre la mise en place de la structure pour rendre compte du modèle mental, la comparaison des modèles mentaux relatifs aux Étudiants et aux Experts constitue l'une des difficultés majeures de ce projet. Nous devons aussi évaluer l'adéquation du modèle mental de l'Étudiant avec celui de l'Expert, c'est-à-dire avec le but visé par l'objectif du cours.

Bibliographie

1   Tardif, J. (1992) Pour un enseignement stratégique: L'apport de la psychologie cognitive, Montréal, Éditions Logiques, 474 p.
2   Craik, K.J.W. (1943) *The nature of explanation*, Cambrige, U.K., Cambridge University Press, 123 p.
3   Norman, D.A. (1983) *Some observations on mental models*, dans D. Gentner et A.L. Stevens (1983), *Mental Models*, Lawrence Erlaum Associates, Hillsdale NJ, p. 7-14
4   Anderson, J.R. (1988), *The expert module,* dans M.C. Polson & J. J. Richardson (Ed.), *Foundations of Intelligent tutoring systems*, Lawrence Erlbaum Associates, Hillsdale NJ, p. 21-53.
5   Larkin, J., McDermot, J., Simon, D.P., Simon, H.A. (1980*) Expert and Novice performance in solving physics problems*, Science, Vol. 208, p. 1335-1342.
6   Vanlehn, K. (1988) *Student modelling*, dans M.C. Polson, J.J. Richardson (Ed.), *Foundations of Intelligent tutoring systems*, Lawrence Erlbaum Associates, Hillsdale NJ, p. 55-78.
7   Champagne, A.B., Klopfer, L.E., Gunstone, R.F. (1992) *Cognitive research and the design of science instruction*, Educational-Psychologist, Vol. 17, No. 1, p. 31-53.
8   Mestre, J., Touger, J. (1989) *Cognitive research, What's in for physics teachers*, The physics teacher, september, p. 447-456.
9   Therien, L., Lapointe, J., Marcos, B., Pirmoradi, S. (1990) *Des erreurs instructives*, Bulletin de l'Association Mathématiques du Québec, Vol. 4, No. 3, p. 5 - 11.
10 White, B.Y., Frederiksen, J.R. (1990*) Causal model progressions as a foundation for intelligent learning environments*, Artificial Intelligence, Vol. 42, No. 1, p. 99-157.
11 Charlot, J.-M., Marcos, B., Lapointe, J. (à paraître) *Novices Mental Models in Thermodynamics*, soumis au Canadian Journal of Educational Communication.
12 Ermine, J.-L. (1993) *Génie logiciel & génie cognitif pour les systèmes à base de connaissances*, Vol. 1, Technique et Documentation Lavoisier, Paris 1993.
13 Alkhatib, B. (1993), *Étude et réalisation d'un système d'exploitation des connaissances. Application au domaine de l'Automatique*, Thèse de l'Université Bordeaux I, France.

Plan Scaffolding:
Impact on the Process and Product of Learning

Albert T. Corbett and Stefanie Knapp

Human Computer Interaction Institute, Carnegie Mellon University,
Pittsburgh, PA 15213, USA

Abstract. This paper examines a plan scaffolding interface in the ACT Programming Tutor. This interface is derived from a cognitive analysis of the task structure and has been shown to accelerate the acquisition of skill. This study examines the impact of the planning interface on the learning process and on the structure of the knowledge that results. Several measures of students' declarative knowledge of programming are developed to predict tutor learning rates. The tutor's predictions of students' quiz performance are also examined. Results indicate that the planning interface speeds learning because students can more readily apply relevant knowledge acquired in simpler contexts. However, the resulting programming knowledge is similar for the scaffolding and standard coding conditions.

1 Introduction

This paper explores the impact of a plan scaffolding interface on skill acquisition in the ACT Programming Tutor (APT). A major issue in education is the extent to which a complex skill can be decomposed into a hierarchy of component skills and the extent to which prerequisite skills in the hierarchy can be mastered in isolation (Resnick & Resnick, 1992; Shepard, 1991). We recently addressed this issue in the context of APT (Corbett & Anderson, 1995a). We examined a challenging programming task that arises early in the Lisp programming curriculum and argued that it could be decomposed into coding rules that can be practiced in isolation and planning rules that are intrinsic to the complex task. We presented evidence that learning rate for the complex task is optimized when the coding rules are mastered ahead of time, and when a plan scaffolding interface is provided that maps each planning rule onto an overt action.

In this paper we examine more closely the impact of plan scaffolding on the learning process and on students' resulting knowledge states. We develop measures of students' knowledge of declarative information and examine whether these measures differentially predict learning rate when students work with the plan scaffolding interface vs. the standard coding interface. We also examine the tutor's predictions of quiz performance. Much of the recent research with APT has been directed at enhancing the tutor's accuracy in predicting individual differences in test performance (Corbett & Anderson, 1995b). In this study we examine whether the use of the plan scaffolding interface results affects the accuracy of test predictions. If so, it could indicate that students are acquiring structurally different programming knowledge.

In the following sections we briefly review the modeling assumptions that underlie APT, review the plan decomposition and scaffolding analysis, describe the measures of students' declarative knowledge, and finally, report the study.

1.1 The Cognitive Model and Learning Model

ACT-R (Anderson, 1993) assumes that a cognitive skill such as programming can be modeled as a set of independent production rules that associate problem states and problem solving goals with actions and/or subgoals. APT is constructed around a set of several hundred language-specific rules for writing programs called the *ideal student model*. The tutor attempts to match the student's action at each problem solving step to an applicable rule in the ideal model in a process we call *model tracing*. If a match is found, the assumption is made that the student has applied an analogous cognitive rule and the tutor's representation of the problem state is updated accordingly. If not, the tutor notifies the student of the error and allows the student to try again.

As the student works, the tutor estimates the probability that the student has learned each rule in the ideal model in a process we call *knowledge tracing*. At each opportunity to apply a rule, the probability that the student knows the rule is updated, contingent on whether the student's action was correct or not. The learning and performance assumptions and Bayesian computational procedure are described elsewhere (Corbett & Anderson 1995b). In knowledge tracing two learning parameters are estimated empirically for each rule in the model, as shown in Table 1.

Table 1. The learning parameters employed in knowledge tracing.

P(L0)	The probability a rule is in the learned state prior to the first opportunity to apply the rule (i.e., from reading the text)
P(T)	The probability a rule will make the transition from the unlearned to the learned state following an opportunity to apply the rule

The tutor uses the knowledge tracing mechanism in an attempt to implement mastery learning. The tutor curriculum is structured around production sets. In each curriculum section students read text that introduces a small set of production rules. Then the tutor provides practice problems that exercise those rules. The student completes a fixed set of required exercises in each section that cover the rules, then continues working on remedial exercises in the section until the probability that the student has learned each rule in the section has reached a criterion value, 0.95.

1.2 Test Predictions and Individual Differences

The learning and performance assumptions that underlie knowledge tracing can be used to predict student programming performance both in the tutor and in a posttest environment. A series of studies demonstrated the need to incorporate individual differences among students in learning and performance to accurately predict test performance (Corbett & Anderson, 1995b). Individual differences are incorporated in the form of four weights, one for each of the four parameter types, wL0, wT, wG and wS. In this model each of the four probability parameters for each rule is converted to odds form (p/(1-p)), multiplied by the corresponding subject-specific weights and the resulting odds converted back to a probability. A best fitting set of weights for each subject can be generated with a curve-fitting program for research purposes. In the tutor, these weights are estimated dynamically by means of regression equations based on raw error rates. In either case, the test predictions of the weighted model are very sensitive to individual differences.

1.3 Knowledge Decomposition and Planning Productions

Table 2 presents four hypothetical problem descriptions and solutions from the APT Lisp Tutor. The first two exercises are drawn from the first curriculum section that introduces three extractor functions, *car*, *cdr* and *reverse*. Each of these operators takes a list and returns components of, or a transformation of, the list. In the first exercise the student applies the operator *car* to the list *(a b c)* to return the first element, *a*. In the second exercise, the student applies the operator *reverse* to *(d e f)* to return the *(f e d)*. The third exercise is drawn from the second curriculum section that introduces three constructor functions, *append*, *cons* and *list*. These functions take two or more arguments and create new lists. In this exercise the student uses the operator *cons* to insert the atom *a* at the beginning of *(f e d)*.

Table 2. Three simple exercises and a more complex subsequent exercise.

Exercise Description	Solution
(1) Write a function call that takes (a b c) and returns a.	*(car '(a b c))*
(2) Write a function call that takes (d e f) and returns (f e d).	*(reverse '(d e f))*
(3) Write a call that takes a & (f e d) and returns (a f e d).	*(cons 'a '(f e d))*

(4) Write a function call that takes (a b c) and (d e f) and returns (a f e d).
Subgoals:
    Planning Goal 1: Recognize that a must be extracted from (a b c)
    Planning Goal 2: Recognize that the list (d e f) must be reversed
    Planning Goal 3: Recognize that a and (f e d) must be combined in a list
    Coding Goal 1: Code a call to *cons*
    Coding Goals 2&3: Code a call to *car* with the 1st given as an argument
    Coding Goals 4&5: Code a call to *reverse* with the 2nd given as an argument
Solution: *(cons (car '(a b c)) (reverse '(d e f)))*

This study focuses on the more complex fourth exercise at the bottom of Table 2, drawn from the fifth curriculum section. Unlike the earlier exercises, the student must apply extractor functions to the given lists *and* combine the results into a new list.

The subgoal structure of this exercise is depicted in the table. It begins with three planning goals in which the student analyzes the relationship between the given and goal lists. The goal structure concludes with five coding goals. These coding goals can be satisfied by the same five production rules required in the three simple exercises at the top of the table. However, this complex task does not simply reduce to these five coding rules. Corbett and Anderson (1995a) demonstrated that if the five rules are mastered in early curriculum sections it speeds learning in these complex exercises, but does not yield immediate mastery of the more complex exercises.

1.4 Reifying Planning Subgoals

We developed a variation of the tutor interface for the fifth curriculum section to reify the first two subgoals in Table 2. The standard interface is depicted in Figure 1a and the new interface is depicted in Figure 1b. In the standard interface the student codes the solution, *(cons (car '(a b c)) (reverse '(d e f))),* directly. Code is entered top-down, so the student begins by coding *cons*, then codes the embedded calls to the extractor functions *car* and *reverse*, along with their literal list arguments. Students receive immediate feedback on each of the five coding actions and only correct coding actions are accepted by the tutor, so the student always remains on a successful solution path.

In the plan reification interface the student fills in two subgoal nodes to indicate what expressions must be extracted from the given lists before entering any code. In this example students must type the expression *a* for <subgoal1> and *(f e d)* for <subgoal2> before entering the code *(cons (car '(a b c)) (reverse '(d e f)).* Again, students receive immediate feedback on each of the two planning and five coding actions and remain on a correct solution path. This planning interface is reminiscent of the programming environment GIL (Reiser, Beekelaar, Tyle & Merrill, 1991), which has been shown to be an effective learning environment. After coding each Lisp function in GIL's graphical interface, students post the input arguments and output values. However, the goals of the two interfaces differ. The emphasis in GIL is to foster comprehension of each coding step, while in the present interface the goal is to map implicit rules in planning chains onto observable actions. By doing this we can (1) reduce the problem solving complexity for the student and (2) simplify the attribution task in modeling the student's knowledge.

Write a function call that takes the lists (a b c) and (d e f) and returns the list (a f e d).	Write a function call that takes the lists (a b c) and (d e f) and returns the list (a f e d).
<code>	Subgoals: <subgoal1> <subgoal2> Code: <code>

Fig. 1a. The standard interface.   **Fig. 1b.** The planning interface

Corbett and Anderson (1995a) demonstrated that the plan reification interface increases learning rates and that the knowledge acquired transfers to the standard coding interface in testing. In this paper we examine more closely the impact of scaffolding on learning, by assessing students' use of declarative knowledge and examining the tutor's predictions of individual differences in test performance.

1.5 Declarative Knowledge

Students read text in each curriculum section before completing programming problems. In this study the tutor administered tests to assess students' encoding of the declarative information in the text. Each test consisted of 20 to 30 questions with no feedback on answers. Four of these tests assess knowledge that is relevant to the section 5 problems. In this study we examine whether these four tests predict learning rates in the planning and standard interfaces. These tests are described here.

Factual Constructor Knowledge. The first task presents True/False questions on basic factual knowledge of constructor functionality, e.g.,

    (cons 'a '(b c)) returns (a b c)   [answer: true]

Factual List Structure Knowledge. The second task presents short answer questions in which students indicate the number of, and identity of, elements in a list, e.g.,

    (a (b c) d (e (f)))   [answer: 4 elements: a, (b c), d, (e (f))]

Extractor Algorithm Evaluation. The third task assesses students' understanding of the evaluation of nested extractor function call. This knowledge is a prerequisite to planning the section 5 problems and taps the students' success in applying explicit rules in the text. In this task short answer questions are presented in which students type the result of extractor algorithm function calls, e.g.,

    (car (cdr '((a b) (c d) (e f)))) returns ?   [answer: (c d)]

This task was presented twice, just before and just after section 4 in which students write extractor algorithm function calls.

Constructor Programming Problem Similarity. The fourth task is a problem similarity rating task. In each question of this task, two hypothetical programming exercises are presented and students are asked to rate how similar these the programming problems are on a scale from 1 to 7. For example, students judge all 6 pairwise comparisons of these four hypothetical programming exercises:

	Given expressions	Goal list to construct
(1)	a b c	(a b c)
(2)	(a) (b) (c)	((a) (b) (c))
(3)	a b c	((a) (b) (c))
(4)	(a) (b) (c)	(a b c)

[judgment ratings - no correct answers]

This task does not directly assess declarative knowledge. Instead, it is designed to assess how students reason with this knowledge in problem solving. In this example, the first two problems are solved by applying the same operator, *list.* In none of the other five pairings do the two problems require the same operator. If students apply the factual knowledge of list structure and constructor functionality tapped in the first two tasks to reason about these programming problems, the first pair should receive the highest similarity ratings. The problems in four of the remaining five pairings share either common given expressions or common goal expressions. To the extent that students are influenced by surface similarity, we would expect these four pairings to receive higher ratings. This task was presented twice during the study, just before and just after section 3 in which students write constructor function calls.

2 The Design of the Study

Students in this experiment worked through the early sections of the APT Lisp curriculum and completed three posttests. This study focuses on the fifth curriculum section with problems similar to problem 4 in Table 2.

2.1 Subjects

Thirty-eight students were recruited to participate in the study for pay. These students had an average Math SAT score of 665 and had completed an average of 2.0 prior programming courses, although none had prior experience with Lisp. Both of these variables were controlled in assigning students to two groups.

2.2 Design

Students worked through seven curriculum sections in this study. This curriculum introduces two data structures, *atoms* and *lists,* and introduces *function calls.* The first section introduces three extractor functions, *car, cdr* and *reverse.* The second and third sections introduce three constructor functions, *append, cons* and *list.* The fourth section introduces extractor algorithms - nested function calls that apply successive extractor functions to extract components of lists. This study focuses on the fifth section in which students embed extractors and extractor algorithms as arguments to constructor functions as exemplified in exercise 4 above. These five curriculum sections contain 30 required tutor exercises. Students completed one or two declarative knowledge tests after reading the text but before completing programming exercises in each of the first five sections. Students completed cumulative programming tests following the first, fourth and fifth sections. These tests contained six, twelve and eighteen programming exercises respectively.

All students worked to mastery in the five curriculum sections under the control of knowledge tracing and used the standard coding interface through the first four curriculum sections. Nineteen students employed the planning interface in section 5, while nineteen students continued with the standard coding interface.

2.3 Procedure

In each section, students read text describing Lisp, completed one or two sets of questions on the text, then completed a set of required programming exercises that covers the rules being introduced. Students then completed remedial exercises as needed to bring all production rules in the section to a mastery criterion (knowledge probability > 0.95). The cumulative posttest exercises were similar to the tutor exercises and the test interface was identical to the tutor interface, except that students could freely edit their code and received no tutorial assistance. No plan scaffolding was provided in the posttests; all students used the standard interface.

3 Results

Two students in the planning condition inadvertently completed one posttest before the prerequisite tutor sections and were excluded from analysis. Students averaged 41 remedial exercises overall (range = 0 to 164) in addition to the 30 required exercises.

3.1 Plan Scaffolding Impact

The dependent measures of plan scaffolding effectiveness in learning is the number of remedial exercises needed to achieve mastery in section 5 of the tutor and time to complete that section. Students in the planning condition required an average of 2.65 remedial exercises to reach mastery in section 5, while students in the standard coding condition required 10.32 remedial exercises. This advantage for the planning condition is marginally reliable, $t(34) = 1.91$, $p < 0.06$. Students in the planning condition required 22.6 minutes to complete these exercises, while students in the standard condition required 32.2 minutes. This 43% increase from the planning to standard coding condition is not reliable, because of the large variance, $t(34) = 1.03$.

3.2 Parameter Weights

We computed a best fitting set of individual difference parameter weights for each subject's tutor performance in order to predict test performance. The average weights for the learning parameters within each group are an alternative measure of plan scaffolding effectiveness. The logarithm of these multiplicative weights is presented in Table 3. As can be seen, the weights for both learning parameters are substantially larger in the planning condition. Students in the planning condition were much more likely to have an encoded the correct procedural rule prior to the first practice opportunity and to learn a correct procedural rule at each opportunity in practice.

Table 3. Average individual difference weights for the two learning parameters.

Group	$\ln(wL_0)$	$\ln(wT)$
Plan Scaffolding	3.22	2.34
Standard Coding	1.51	-0.17

3.3 Textual Knowledge Measures

Accuracy measures (percent correct) were computed for the first three types of declarative tasks. The ratings that students generated in the constructor problem similarity task (Task 4) were converted into a measure of the extent to which the student relied on the functional information relevant to problem solving, rather than surface similarity as follows: (mean similarity rating for the problem pairs with the same functional solution) minus (mean similarity rating for the other five problem types). We submitted the six measures of textual knowledge along with two subject variables (Math SAT and number of prior programming courses) to a factor analysis to simplify the structure of predictor variables. Table 4 displays the factor structure that emerged.

Table 4. Factor loadings of Six Knowledge and Reasoning Measures.
(Values 0.5 or greater are reported)

Variable	Factor 1 (Reasoning)	Factor 2 (Factual Knowledge)	Factor 3 (Prior Knowledge)
Factual Knowledge of Constructors		0.85	
Factual Knowledge of List Structure		0.77	
Extractor Algorithm Evaluation 1	0.49	0.54	
Extractor Algorithm Evaluation 2	0.54	0.56	
Constructor Problem Similarity 1	0.75		
Constructor Problem Similarity 2	0.88		
Math SAT		0.76	
Number of Programming Courses			0.92

This factor structure reflects a distinction between having and using factual knowledge. Factual knowledge of list structure and constructors load heavily on Factor 2. The problem similarity measures, which reflect the extent to which the students use list structure and functionality in rating problem similarity, load heavily on Factor 1. Interestingly, the extractor evaluation measures load moderately on both factors. Students Math SAT scores load on the factual knowledge factor, while prior programming knowledge loads on an entirely separate factor.

We correlated the three sets of factor scores with the log individual difference learning weights, as displayed in Table 5. As can be seen, the factual knowledge and reasoning factors correlate in an orderly fashion with the individual difference weights for the plan scaffolding condition. Factor 2, which reflects factual knowledge correlates positively with $\ln(wL_0)$, which corresponds to the probability of learning an appropriate rule prior to the first practice opportunity, $r = 0.65$, $t(15) = 3.31$, $p < .01$. Factor 1, which reflects effective reasoning about constructors correlates reliably with $\ln(wT)$, which corresponds to the probability of learning a rule during procedural practice, r = 0.52, t(15) = 2.35, p < .05. None of the factors correlates reliably with either individual difference weight in the standard coding condition.

Table 5. Correlation of Factor Scores and Individual Difference Learning Weights across Subjects in the Plan Scaffolding and Standard Coding Groups

	Plan Scaffolding		Standard Coding	
	$\ln(wL_0)$	$\ln(wT)$	$\ln(wL_0)$	$\ln(wT)$
Factor 1 Reasoning	0.20	0.52	0.07	0.13
Factor 2 Factual Knowledge	0.65	0.34	0.21	0.05
Factor 3 Prior Programming	-0.01	-0.06	-0.05	0.19

3.4 Test Measures

The third test contained six exercises drawn from section 5. All students completed these test exercises in the standard coding interface without tutorial support. Table 6 displays the mean actual test performance, mean predicted test performance and the correlation of actual and expected accuracy across subjects in the two groups. As can be seen, students in the plan scaffolding condition completed 64% of the exercises correctly, while students in the standard condition completed 62% correctly. Thus, the knowledge that students acquired with the plan scaffolding interface fully transferred to the standard coding interface used in the test. Moreover, there is little difference in the predictive accuracy of the tutor's student model in the two conditions. The student model over predicts test performance in each condition by 15-20% and in each condition the model is quite sensitive to individual differences. The correlation of actual and expected performance is 0.63 in the planning condition and 0.74 in the standard condition. The difference between these two correlations is not significant.

Table 6. Actual and expected proportion of exercises completed correctly across subjects in the two groups.

	Mean Proportion Correct		Correlation
Condition	Actual	Predicted	r_{AP}
Plan Scaffolding	0.64	0.76	0.63
Standard Coding	0.62	0.71	0.74

4 Conclusion

This study replicates the results of Corbett & Anderson (1995a): model-guided plan scaffolding accelerates learning rate and yields essentially complete transfer to the standard coding interface in testing. The results also begin to shed light on why plan scaffolding is effective in learning. By reifying the subgoal planning process, the interface allows students to directly apply their basic knowledge of functions acquired in isolation earlier in the curriculum. As a result, the declarative assessments of students factual knowledge and similarity judgments predict students learning weights, wL0 and wT, in an orderly fashion. No such orderly relationship emerged in the standard coding condition in which multiple reasoning steps mapped onto a single coding actions. While students apparently follow very different problem-solving paths in the two conditions, the posttest evidence nevertheless suggests they arrive at very similar knowledge states. Average test accuracy in the two conditions was essentially identical and the underlying cognitive model predicted posttest performance equally well in the two conditions. These results further support the position that a careful cognitive analysis can be useful in both curriculum and interface design.

References

Anderson, J.R. (1993). *Rules of the mind.* Hillsdale, NJ: Lawrence Erlbaum Associates.

Corbett, A.T. and Anderson, J.R. (1992) Student modeling and mastery learning in a computer-based programming tutor In C. Frasson, G. Gauthier, G. McCalla, (Eds.) *Intelligent tutoring systems: Second international conference on intelligent tutoring systems* (pp. 413-420). New York: Springer-Verlag.

Corbett, A.T. and Anderson, J.R. (1995a). Knowledge decomposition and subgoal reification in the ACT programming tutor. In J. Greer (Ed.) *Artificial Intelligence and Education, 1995: The Proceedings of AI-ED 95.,* 469-476. Charlottesville, VA: AACE.

Corbett, A.T. and Anderson, J.R. (1995b). Knowledge tracing: Modeling the acquisition of procedural knowledge. *User modeling and user-adapted interaction,4,* 253-278.

Reiser, B.J., Beekelaar, R. Tyle, A., & Merrill, D. (1991). GIL: Scaffolding learning to program with reasoning-congruent representations. In L. Birnbaum, (Ed.) *The International Conference of the Learning Sciences: Proceedings of the 1991 Conference.* Charlottesville, VA: AACE.

Resnick, L.B. & Resnick, D.P. (1992). Assessing the thinking curriculum: New tools for educational reform. In B. Gifford & M. O'Connor (Eds.) *Changing assessments: Alternative views of aptitude, achievement and instruction.* Boston: Kluwer Academic Publishers.

Shepard, L. A. (1991). Psychometrician's beliefs about learning. *Educational Researcher*, 20, 2-16.

Acknowledgments

This research was supported by the Office of Naval Research grant N00014-95-1-0847. We thank Dana Heath and Michele Mellott for assistance in data collection.

A Model of Tutoring:
Based on the Behavior of Effective Human Tutors

Ramzan Khuwaja[1], Vimla Patel[2]

[1]Cognologic Software Inc.,
3620 Lorne Crescent, #216, Montreal, Qc, H2X 2B1
Phone: (514) 842-1527
Email: khuwaja@steve.iit.edu

[2]Center for Medical Education, McGill University,
1110 Pine Avenue West, Montreal, Qc, H3A 1A3
Phone: (514) 398-4987; Fax: (514) 398-7246
Email: patel@hebb.psych.mcgill.ca

Abstract. Research has shown that tutoring by humans provide the most effective method of instruction. One school of thought in the Intelligent Tutoring Systems (ITS) community believes that studying human tutors is the best way to discover how to build effective machine tutors. This paper describes a conceptual model of tutoring that is based on a study of skilled human tutors in the domain of cardiovascular physiology. This model is developed as a part of research to develop an ITS, CIRCSIM-Tutor, for first year medical students at Rush Medical College, Chicago. The major theme of this model of tutoring is that, in a problem-solving environment, it facilitates the student to integrate his/her knowledge into a coherent qualitative causal model of the domain and solve problems in the domain. The key feature of this model is that it uses multiple models of the domain in the process of facilitating knowledge integration.

1 Introduction

Tutoring by humans is the most effective method of instruction [1], although not all human tutors are equally effective [2]. Some human tutors are even less effective than the instruction provided via group instruction method [3]. One explanation for the effectiveness of human tutoring is that it is the "skilled tutoring which provides the magic" [3]. Skilled tutoring requires expertise in both the *domain* and in the *process of tutoring* [6].

One of the major goals of the field of Intelligent Tutoring Systems (ITS) is to develop machine tutors that are at least as effective as human tutors. One school of thought in the ITS community believes that studying human tutors is the best way to discover how to build effective machine tutors [3]. A number of human tutoring studies have been conducted in this regard. Most of these studies have implicitly assumed that the human tutor being studied need not be an *expert* in the domain or in the process of tutoring. No ITS built to date has outperformed skilled human tutors [3]. We are convinced from our research that in order to build an ITS that is as effective as a skilled human tutor, we need to base its development on the observations of *skilled* human tutors.

This paper describes a conceptual model of tutoring which is based on a study of skilled human tutors in the domain of cardiovascular (CV) physiology. This study has provided a comprehensive set of data reflecting their behavior in a tutoring situation. This data is used to develop the model of tutoring described in this paper. This model is developed as a part of research to develop an ITS, CIRCSIM-Tutor (CST), for the first year medical students at Rush Medical College, Chicago. A version of CST that uses this conceptual model of tutoring is currently under development.

The major theme of this model of tutoring is that, in a problem-solving environment, it facilitates the student to integrate his/her knowledge into a coherent qualitative causal model of the domain and solve problems in the domain. The key feature of this model is that it uses multiple models of the domain in the process of facilitating knowledge integration.

2 Background

ITSs are complex systems. It is always helpful to use tools that break complex behavior into parts in order to manage complexity. The multiple expert metaphor is one such tool that at a very high level of abstraction, breaks complex tutoring behavior into four, commonly accepted, parts - *domain expert*, *student expert* (or student modeler), *pedagogy expert*, and *communication expert* [8; 2]. The domain expert characterizes the knowledge and strategies needed for expert performance in a domain. The student expert is also called a student modeler because it represents the tutor's estimate of the student's understanding of the material to be taught. The pedagogy expert, using a theory of tutoring, provides assistance to the student, monitors and criticizes the student, and selects problems and remedial material for the student. The communication expert processes the flow of communication in and out of the system. According to this metaphor, in an ITS these experts communicate with each other and coordinate their activities to create effective tutoring behavior. This metaphor is so popular that it has served as a design model for many ITS projects during all phases of their development [4].

We have also used the multiple expert metaphor to classify the functional complexity of CST. But for the purposes of the model of tutoring described here we have limited to consider only the functionality of the *domain* and the *pedagogy* expert of this metaphor. From now on when we refer to our model of tutoring we will mean a model with only the above mentioned functionality.

In this paper we will also describe an analysis of the behavior of our tutors while performing different task in a tutoring situation. An evaluation study conducted at the Rush Medical College has clearly demonstrated the effectiveness of the tutoring method of our tutors. For a detailed description of this evaluation study, the reader is referred to [4]

One of the fundamental assumptions behind our model of tutoring is that an effective tutor requires *expertise* in both the domain and in the process of tutoring. Traditionally these behaviors have been analyzed in isolation of each other. Here we have made an attempt to analyze these two roles both in isolation and in light of each other's underlying theoretical orientation. We hope that this approach will bridge the gap between various experts of the multiple expert metaphor [2].

CST uses a Socratic style [8] to communicate with the student. In this style the tutor frequently asks questions and responds to the student's queries. The knowledge domain of CST is cardiovascular physiology, specifically the baroreceptor reflex, which maintains a more or less constant blood pressure using a negative feedback mechanism. While tutoring in this domain the system forces the student to concentrate only on the qualitative and causal nature of the working of the baroreceptor reflex.

3 Methods Used to Capture Data about Domain and Pedagogical Expertise

This section, very briefly, describes the methods of getting expert information to develop our model of tutoring. We have worked with two tutors (Allen Rovick and Joel Michael) who are professors in the Department of Physiology at Rush Medical College; they have worked together to develop automated tutors for more than ten years.

Most information that is used to develop different domain models (for the domain expert) has been obtained by interviewing our tutors. We have also used the keyboard-to-keyboard tutoring method [7]. This method uses two linked computers with the student and the tutor communicating by typing at the keyboard and reading the comments of the other on the computer screen. This method captures the actual interaction used by the tutor while tutoring the student in the domain. Here the expert mimics as much as possible the function of the prospective system.

In concurrent verbalization, the expert thinks aloud, while solving a problem. This method is particularly suited to elicit information about the control aspects (the task structure and the strategy) of the reasoning process. We have conducted a set of think-aloud sessions using this method to capture the problem-solving behavior of our tutors. Please refer [4] for a detailed description of all methods used to capture data for our research.

4 A Cognitive Model of Tutoring

This section describes the model of tutoring that we have developed for CST. Here we will sketch a broad picture of this model by classifying its major components.

Fig. 1 schematically shows the two major experts whose behavior is considered for this model of tutoring. Here our hypothesis is that it is the domain expert that provides domain intelligence to the pedagogy expert, which in turn provides the tutoring expertise and communicates with the student. Because of the nature of the activity of our tutors in the keyboard-to-keyboard sessions, from the transcripts of these sessions one can only observe the composite behaviors of these two experts. It would be extremely advantageous if we could capture the behavior of one of these experts in isolation and then take it as a reference to analyze the behavior of the second expert from the keyboard-to-keyboard session. Fortunately in our research framework our tutors play multiple roles. The two roles that we are concerned with require them to act as expert in the domain and in the process of tutoring as well. So here it is possible to capture the behavior of the domain expert by letting our tutors verbalize while solving the kind of problems they give to the student in a keyboard-to-keyboard session. This is exactly what we have done to capture the problem-solving method of our tutors.

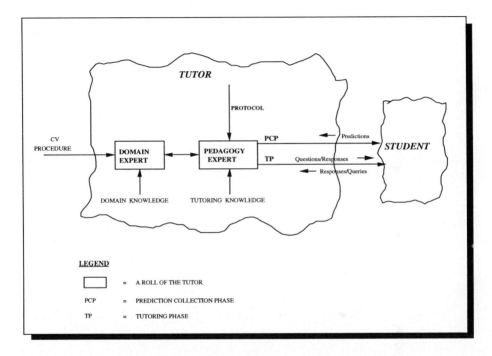

Fig. 1. Schematic View of a Cognitive Model of Tutoring

The domain expert, in our case, uses multi-level and multi-perspective qualitative causal model of CV physiology to perform domain reasoning. Readers are advised to refer [4; 5] for detail information about the nature and functioning of the domain expert used in our system.

In our context human tutors perform a considerable amount of activity before a tutoring session starts. This activity mainly concentrates on creating the tutoring environment (and hence the tutoring protocol) in which the tutor and the student communicate. We classify this as *pre-session* activity of the tutor. The *in-session* activity is the activity performed by the tutor while a tutoring session is underway. The model of tutoring we are describing considers both pre-session and in-session activities of the tutor. These activities are part of the behavior carried out by the pedagogy expert. During tutoring, the pedagogy expert performs three major decisions: What to teach, When to teach, and How to teach. These activities are performed in order to achieve the goals of the system. Sec. 5 and 6 describe the pre-session and in-session behavior of our tutors (and hence our model of tutoring) respectively.

5 Pre-Session Behavior of the Pedagogy Expert

Tutoring a problem-solving task effectively in virtually any structured domain requires the tutor to create a problem-solving *environment* so that he/she can communicate effectively in the domain. The creation of a problem-solving environment requires the development of a set of rules that govern the interaction of the tutor and the student in the environment. This set of rules does not constrain the behavior of the tutor or the student in each step in the problem-solving process but rather emphasizes higher level constraints of the problem-solving task in the domain and a generic way of proceeding in it. We call this set of rules the *tutoring protocol* [6]. In other words, the pre-session behavior of the tutor consists of developing a tutoring protocol to allow him/her to exercise control over the tutoring environment. The tutoring protocol is a very high level plan of the tutor, which is developed *before* the actual interactive communication with the student starts. But it is flexible and carefully thought out to ensure that optimal knowledge communication takes place during the tutoring session.

Our tutors have conducted 47 keyboard-to-keyboard sessions during the last five years. Over this span of time three different tutoring protocols have been used. These protocols are alike in many ways, but their differences have noticeable different effects on the tutoring process [6].

Every tutoring session alternates between two phases: a prediction collection phase (PCP) and a tutoring phase (TP) (see Fig. 1). In the prediction collection phase the tutor collects the student's predictions for the current problem and in the tutoring phase the tutor tries to remediate the student's misconceptions about the domain subject matter.

In the first protocol our tutors responded immediately to every student prediction. Their instincts told them to give each student as much immediate feedback as possible. In the second protocol the tutor reduced the amount of feedback during problem-solving. The behavior of the tutor here is more like a coach. He watches the student's sequence of predictions and interrupts only if a violation takes place. In the third protocol no help is provided in the PCP. This protocol provides the student full freedom to use his/her mental model to practice problem-solving under the watchful eyes of the tutor, who waits until the second phase to try to remedy the student's misconceptions. Our model of tutoring uses the third protocol. Please refer [6] for a detailed discussion on these three protocols and their influence on the tutoring process.

6 A Conceptual Model of the Pedagogy Expert: In-Session Behavior

The in-session behavior of the pedagogy expert deals with the activities in the tutoring phase (see Sec. 4). In the tutoring phase the pedagogy expert makes three major decisions: *What* to teach, *When* to teach, and *How* to teach.

During tutoring, the CST alternates between two major phases: the diagnostic phase and the pedagogic phase. In the diagnostic phase the student modeler builds a model of the student. Based on this model, the pedagogy expert in the pedagogic phase engages either in confirmatory/exploratory activity or remediation activity. Interestingly these two phases also alternate in the pedagogic phase. In the confirmatory/exploratory phase either the tutor *confirms* a hypothesis about the knowledge state of the student or it *explores* the underlying cause of a student's error in prediction. If the tutor is successful in achieving either of these goals then the remediation phase is invoked. Here the tutor tries to remediate the current misconception of the student. On the other hand if the tutor fails in its diagnostic endeavor, a default remediation strategy is selected to tutor the student for his/her current problem(s).

6.1 A Tutor's View of the Student

We assume that the student who comes for tutoring (i.e., for a keyboard-to-keyboard session) may possess a number of misconceptions that are the main source of his/her incorrect predictions for a CV problem. In order to discover the actual misconceptions confusing this student, the tutor adopts a layered approach to diagnosis. Because of the constraints of the third protocol the only form of information available to the tutor, at first, is a set of errors (more specifically, wrong predictions of the student). These errors, based upon their individual characteristics, determine a number of error patterns. These are not the actual misconceptions of the student but rather bring the tutor one step closer to finding the actual cause of the student's error. In the next step of diagnosis the tutor uses these error patterns to hypothesize a number of causes (we call them student difficulties) that could be the actual source of sub-optimal behavior of the student.

It is the error pattern level that substantially reduces the space of potential misconceptions of the student for the tutor's diagnostic process. A large space of potential causes exist for each error in the student's predictions. The error pattern level forces the tutor to view the student only through a limited set of possibilities that are related to the steps in the problem solving process. Thus, only the student difficulties that are related to these steps are considered as the potential causes for the student's sub-optimal behavior.

6.2 Pedagogy Expert in Action

This section describes the in-session decision making process of the pedagogy expert in the form of a flow chart. This flow chart is shown in Fig. 2. Here we assume that the student has completed predicting for a phase of CV system. This dynamic behavior of the pedagogy expert is explained as follows. In order to facilitate the explanation of this behavior, various steps in Fig. 2 are tagged with numbers in small circles.

136

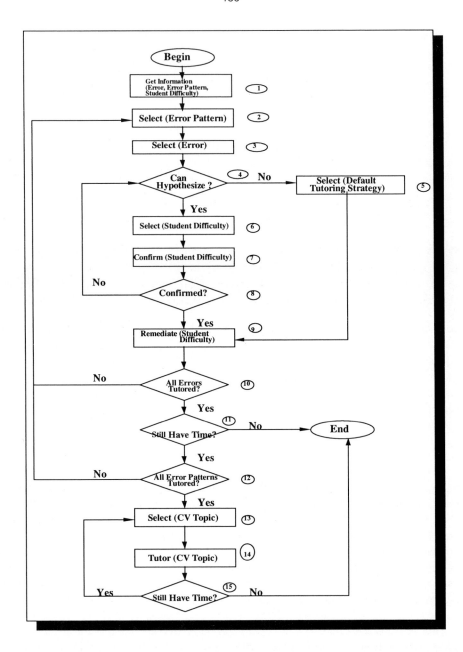

Fig. 2. Flow Chart Representing the Dynamic Behavior of the Pedagogy Expert

The decision making process in Fig. 2 starts at "1" where the pedagogy expert collects information about the student's errors, error patterns, and student difficulties from the student modeler. Next at "2" it selects an error pattern for consideration. Let's call this the current error pattern. At "3" if the current error pattern has multiple errors associated with it then the pedagogy expert selects one of them for consideration. Let's call this the current error. Next considering the current error pattern, the pedagogy expert decides, at "4," whether it can form a hypothesis about the cause of the current student error. If it forms a hypothesis then a student difficulty is selected at "6." If it does not form a hypothesis then a default tutoring strategy is selected (at "5") to remediate (at "9") the student's current error.

In the case when the pedagogy expert can hypothesize about the student's underlying problem, at "7," it tries to confirm this hypothesis. If this hypothesis is confirmed, at "8," then a remediation phase (at "9") is invoked. If the tutor's effort is not successful at "8" then it again decides, at "4," whether it can make another hypothesis about the student.

As soon as the remediation phase is completed at "9," the pedagogy expert checks (at "10") whether all errors are tutored or not. If all are not yet covered then the tutor, at "2," repeats the above mentioned process. On the contrary if the tutor has completed tutoring for all the student's errors then, at "11," considering the time elapsed during this tutoring, it decides whether to continue tutoring about the current phase of CV system or not. If time does not permit the system to do that then this decision making process halts until a new set of predictions for the next phase of CV system is available. On the other hand if there is time available for the current phase of the CV system then at "12" the tutor checks for the current list of error patterns. If some error patterns are still left then, at "2," it repeats the above mentioned cycle, else, at "13," the system selects a generic topic that it considers important for the student to learn. At "14" this topic is planned for tutoring with the student. At "15," the pedagogy expert again looks at the clock. If time permits then it selects another topic, else this process is halted for the current phase of the CV system.

7 Conclusion and Summary

The model of tutoring described in this paper is based on a study of skilled human tutors. This study has shown that our tutors perform a variety of tasks that are elegantly coordinated to create an effective tutoring behavior. We believe that basing the development of an ITS on the behavior of skilled human tutors provide one method of creating effective machine tutors.

The model described here considers only the domain and the pedagogy decision making process of our tutors. The domain expertise is based on a use of a multi-level and multi-perspective qualitative causal model of CV system. This domain model is then used by the pedagogical process.

The pedagogical expertise consider both the pre-session and the in-session behaviors. The pre-session behavior is the most overlooked functionality in current ITSs. We believe that incorporating this behavior in an ITS will facilitate its deployment in a real world educational environment [6]. The in-session behavior of our model uses a multi-level view of the student's misconceptions. The pedagogical process is driven to facilitate the student to integrate his/her domain knowledge. This process uses multiple qualitative models of the domain to generate feedback for the student.

Only basing the development of our model on the behavior of effective human tutors is not enough, we clearly need to test our system to evaluate its effectiveness in a real world educational environment.

References

1. Bloom, B. S. (1984). The 2-sigma problem: The search for methods of group instruction as effective as one-to-one tutoring. *Educational Researcher*, 13, 4 - 16.
2. Breuker, J. (1990). Conceptual model of intelligent help system. In Breuker, J. (ed.), *EUROHELP: developing intelligent help systems* (pp. 41-67). Copenhagen: EC.
3. Galdes, D. K. (1990). *An empirical study of human tutors: The implications for intelligent tutoring systems.* Unpublished Doctoral Dissertation, Department of Industrial and Systems Engineering, Ohio State University, Ohio.
4. Khuwaja, R. A. (1994). *A Model of Tutoring: Facilitating Knowledge Integration Using Multiple Models of the Domain.* Ph.D. Thesis, Computer Science Department, Illinois Institute of Technology, Chicago, Illinois.
5. Khuwaja, R. A., Evens, M. W., Rovick, A. A. & Michael, J. A. (1992). Knowledge representation for an intelligent tutoring system based on a multilevel causal model. *Proceedings of the ITS'92* (pp. 217-224). New York: Springer-Verlag.
6. Khuwaja, R. A., Rovick, A. A., Michael, J. A. & Evens, M. W. (1995). A tale of three protocols: The implications for intelligent tutoring systems. In the *Proceedings of the GW International Conference on Intelligent Systems.* Las Vegas, NV.
7. Li, J., Seu, J., Evens, M., Michael, J. & Rovick, A. (1992). Computer dialogue system (CDS): A system for capturing computer-mediated dialogue. *Behavior Research Methods, Instruments, & Computers*, 24, 535 - 540.
8. Wenger, E. (1987). *Artificial intelligence and tutoring systems.* Los Altos, CA: Morgan Kaufman.

Acknowledgments

The model of tutoring described here is based on the first author's Ph.D. research work at the Illinois Institute of Technology, Chicago. The first author is very thankful to Martha Evens, Allen Rovick, and Joel Michael for their guidance, support and encouragement during the course of this research.

This work was supported by the Cognitive Science Program, Office of Naval Research under Grant No. N00014-89-J-1952, Grant Authority Identification Number NR4422554, to Illinois Institute of Technology. The content does not reflect the position or policy of the government and no official endorsement should be inferred.

Motivation System and Human Model for Intelligent Tutoring

Yukihiro Matsubara and Mitsuo Nagamachi

Faculty of Engineering, Hiroshima University
1-4-1, Kagamiyama, Higashi-Hiroshima 739, Japan

Abstract. In this paper, we focus on the student's "motivation level" in his learning situation, and we propose the ergonomic design of ITS framework as the motivation system. The aim of this system is motivating the student for his/her learning process to give the appropriate encouragement, praise or reproach messages. It is important to represent the student's internal psychological state. Therefore, we propose the human model which consists of several element for pshycological characteristics and prepares the fuzzy if-then rules to infer the message policy as the adequate strategy knowledge. In general, it is difficult to identify the fuzzy if-then rules and membership functions, so we introduce the automatic fuzzy rule acquisition system, called FREGA, which is our new knowledge acquisition system combining ID3 method and Genetic Algorithm. Finally, we give the estimation of this system.

1 Introduction

In the previous studies of intelligent tutoring systems, many researchers focused on the constructing method for a student model which represents the knowledge acquisition aspects of student, and most systems carry out teaching based on this student model (Wenger 1987, Sleeman 1982). On the other hand, considering the actual teaching environment, human teachers try to teach the student referring not only student's domain knowledge acquisition level but also his/her internal psychological state, which is the "motivation level". In this view, Soldato (1992) introduced the motivation concept into the intelligent tutoring system but not utilizing the student's psychological characteristics. On the other hand, we proposed the motivation model for intelligent tutoring system (Matsubara, et al., 1991,1994). This model was a kind of student model and expressed the student's mental state and psychological characteristics. Using this model, we could construct a more efficient tutoring system to motivate the student. This technique would lead to achieving the development of a more human-like system.

In this paper, we focus on the student's "motivation level" in his/her learning situation, and we propose the ergonomic design of ITS framework as the motivation system. The aim of this system is motivating the student's learning process to give the appropriate encouragement, praise or reproach messages. It is important to represent the student's internal psychological state. Therefore, we propose the human model which consists of several elements for psychological characteristics which can be measured easily using a questionnaire method and preparing the fuzzy if-then rules to infer the message policy as the adequate strategy knowledge. In general, it is difficult to identify the fuzzy if-then rules and membership functions, so we introduce the automatic fuzzy rule acquisition system, called FREGA, (*Fuzzy Decision Tree Generator based on Genetic Algorithm*: Kunisa, et al., 1993), which is our new knowledge acquisition system combining ID3 method (Quinlan, 1984) and Genetic Algorithm (GA).

In the following, we explain the motivation theory and propose the human model. Next, we show the motivation system as the ergonomic design of ITS framework and propose the human model and FREGA algorithm. Finally, we give the estimation of this system.

2 Tutoring System And Motivation

2.1 Motivation Theory

In general, there are two kinds of motivation methods, intrinsic motivation approach and extrinsic one. Intrinsic motivation method is focused on the student's interest and curiosity, and as a result, the student becomes to study himself. On the other hand, extrinsic motivation method is focused on the external target or outcome (e.g. praise and reproach), and it is useful to motivate the student immediately. In the view of ITS, it is difficult to utilize the intrinsic motivation method because that method must depend on the each domain knowledge aspect. On the other hand, extrinsic one does not depend on it, and can get efficient effect for the student. Therefore, it is said that extrinsic motivation method is a good approach to motivate the student to give the appropriate praise message or reproach message in the specific learning situation. It is a useful tool because it is easy to bundle the function with the general ITS framework.

2.2 Human Model

The tutoring system must consider and grasp the student's internal psychological state to give efficient motivation messages for the student. In previous research, we treated the three psychological elements (type of achievement motive, the level of satisfaction, and the information of success-fault history) and tried to construct the human model to motivate the student (Matsubara, et al., 1991). However, it is not enough to identify the student's psychological state. In this research, we extend this human model and consider more psychological element shown in Figure 1.

The element category I represents the student's psychological characteristics, and category II shows the psychological state in the learning process. These elements and each parameter are identified by Questionnaire method which can get the subjective data for the student. We select fuzzy if-then rule as the knowledge representation method (Figure 2) for the inference knowledge (called motivation knowledge).

Rule 1 means that if the system gives the praise message in the next phase for the specific type of student (i.e. achievement motivation level is very high, and so forth), then the student's motivation level will grow to very high. This rule type has some characteristics that the element of human model and the message style which will be selected in the next phase are found in the condition part of the rule, and the motivation level for the student is represented on action part. Therefore, the human model has 4 kinds of rules (i.e. praise, reproach, encourage, and nothing) in each combination of psychological state.

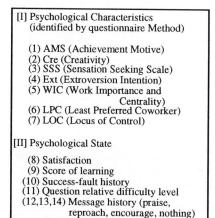

```
[I] Psychological Characteristics
    (identified by questionnaire Method)

    (1) AMS (Achievement Motive)
    (2) Cre (Creativity)
    (3) SSS (Sensation Seeking Scale)
    (4) Ext (Extroversion Intention)
    (5) WIC (Work Importance and
                Centrality)
    (6) LPC (Least Preferred Coworker)
    (7) LOC (Locus of Control)

[II] Psychological State

    (8) Satisfaction
    (9) Score of learning
    (10) Success-fault history
    (11) Question relative difficulty level
    (12,13,14) Message history (praise,
                reproach, encourage, nothing)
```

Fig.1. Element of the Human Model

Rule1: IF Achievement Motive:: Very High
    & ....
    & Next Message:: Praise

THEN Motivation:: Very High

Rule2: IF Achievement Motive:: $18 \leqq x_1 < 50$
    & ....
    & Next Message:: Praise

THEN Motivation:: $50 \leqq y < 65$

Fig.2. An example of motivation knowledge (Fuzzy if-then rule)

3 Motivation System: Ergonomic Design of ITS

3.1 Overview of The System

The architecture of the motivation system is shown in Figure 3. The system consists of 10 sub modules, which are domain knowledge, motivation knowledge, tutoring knowledge, domain expert module, human model, student model, motivation knowledge acquisition module (FREGA), tutoring module, text generator, and interface. At first, the tutoring module decides the tutoring strategy referring to the tutoring knowledge and user model which includes both the student model and human model. Next, the domain expert module selects and gives the appropriate problem for the student based on the selected tutoring strategy, student model, and domain knowledge, and gets the student's answer. Finally, the system infers and judges the learning result of the student and the text generator module makes the appropriate message to motivate the student, referring to the motivation knowledge and human model. On the other hand, it is difficult to construct the motivation knowledge, the system bundles the knowledge acquisition system (FREGA), and utilizes an off-line phase of the tutoring system. In this paper, we apply it to the domain of an English Grammar problem, and construct the tutoring system based on the concept of motivation system. The system is implemented on the Macintosh using the C language, and FREGA is implemented on the Sun Sparc Station.

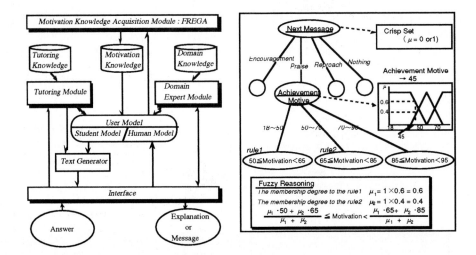

F i g . 3 . The architecture of motivation system   **Fig.4.** An example of fuzzy decision tree

3.2   Motivation Rule and Human Model

The system constructs the motivation knowledge using the FREGA automatically. It is impossible to make the rule manually because there are a lot of combinations in the condition part of motivation knowledge. The FREGA system makes up the refined rule from the case-based data using the mechanism of ID3 and GA, and constructs the fuzzy decision tree. In the following procedure, the system collect the case-based data.

Step1. Give the questionnaire concerned with the human model element (category I, (1)~(7)) to the student, and get the estimation results on the SD scale.

Step2. Subject (student) to the learning using the motivation system which we prepared.

Step3. In the specific phase of learning process, the system gives 4 kinds of messages. The subject estimates for each kind of message, whether each message is efficient or not in motivating him/her at that phase and identified motivation level as the action part of the motivation knowledge.

In this way, the system can get case-based data. Using these data, the FREGA can construct a refined fuzzy decision tree as shown in Figure 4. This tree represents some rules in it like rule 2 shown in Figure 2 and formalized as follows.

$$R_k : \text{If } x_1 = A_1 \text{ and } \dots x_i = A_i \text{ and } \dots \text{ and } x_n = A_n$$
$$\text{Then } min\_w_k \leq y \leq max\_w_k \tag{1}$$

where; k=1,...,NR (NR: number of rules), i=1,...,n (n: number of attribute for rule k)

For example, if a student whose the achievement motivation level is "45" uses this system, the system infers the motivation level in the case of "praise message" using the fuzzy inference method. Using the following equation, the system infers and calculate the certainty factors and y^*.

$$\mu_k = \prod_i A_i (x_i) \ , \ min\_y \ = \frac{\sum_k \mu_k \cdot min\_w_k}{\sum_k \mu_k} \ , \ max\_y \ = \frac{\sum_k \mu_k \cdot max\_w_k}{\sum_k \mu_k}$$

$$min\_y \ \le y^* \le \ max\_y \qquad\qquad (2)$$

As the same method, the system infers the other cases (reproach, encouragement, nothing) of motivation level. Finally, the system selects the appropriate inference result which has the highest value and the smallest range of motivation level.

3.3 FREGA: Motivation Knowledge Acquisition based on ID3 Algorithm

To get the motivation knowledge, we propose the ID3 based knowledge acquisition system. ID3 is a machine learning method which automatically generates a decision tree from a set of training examples represented by a number of attributes and a decision class (Quinlan, 1984). The generated tree is transformed equivalently into production rules. The feature of ID3 is to select an attribute so that the greatest information gain can be obtained and to find the minimum number of nodes of a decision tree as a result. ID3 can only treat nominal attributes, and so all numerical attributes must be divides into several classes to apply them to the ID3 algorithm. Accordingly we try to take advantage of FIND algorithm (Araki, D. et al., 1992) which has a labeling procedure for numerical attributes. The feature of this algorithm is to collect numerical data into data clusters according to its decision class to make borders for the adjacent data clusters by calculating maximum information gain and to decide the number of data clusters by a dividing operation and unifying operation for them. However, ID3 and FIND algorithm can not treat numerical decision. We then introduce a new algorithm which integrates ID3 and FIND algorithms, which can treat both numerical decision and numerical attributes, called FREGA. This algorithm can search the borders of numerical decision using the genetic algorithm based searching procedure. The outline of FREGA algorithm are shown in Figure 5.

Step1. Declare the population size (PS), the number of borders (NB), string length per border (SL), and the number of maximum generations (MG) as in Figure 6.

Step2. Replace bit strings by a real type variable r_{jj} (jj=1,...,NB). Moreover exchange the real type variable for the real numerical decision as follows.

144

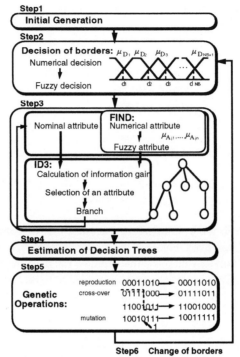

Fig.5. The processing diagram of FREGA

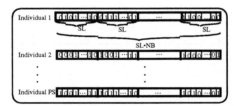

Fig.6. An occurrence of the initial population

$$d_{jj} = r_{jj} \cdot \frac{max\_dec - min\_dec}{2^{SL}} + min\_dec \tag{3}$$

where; *max_dec* is the maximal number of numerical decision data and *min_dec* is the minimal number of numerical decision data.

Step3. Execute the ID3 algorithm. If there are numerical decision attributes, utilize FIND algorithm to calculate the information gain on each numerical attribute.

Step4. Calculate the fitness value of each individual on the basis of an objective functions as follows.

$$fitness = \sum_{j=1}^{N} \left(y^{(j)} - \frac{min\_y^{(j)} + max\_y^{(j)}}{2} \right)^2 + Penalty \tag{4}$$

where; j=1,...,N (N: number of training data)

Step5. Execute reproduction and cross-over on the basis of each fitness value. Moreover execute mutation at random.

Step6 If the present generation is equal to MG, then stop, else go to Step2.

4 System Evaluation

4.1 Generated Motivation Rule

We collect about 2,300 case-based data from 10 subjects and attempt to construct the motivation knowledge applying to the FREGA. A part of the identified rules are shown in Figure 7, and major used elements in motivation knowledge are show in Table 1. Mainly, in the category I elements, LOC (7), achievement motivation level (1), and creativity (2) are used in the rules. On the other hand, score of learning (9), question difficulty level (11), and message history (12, 13, 14) are used as the category II elements. These results indicate that FREGA can distinguish the useful and important elements of the rule condition part and can reduce the searching space of the inference phase adequately.

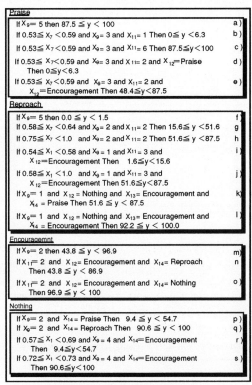

Fig.7. Extracted Rules

Table 1. Used Elements in Motivation Rules

Message / Method	Praise	Reproach	Encour.	Nothing
NB=5 PS=50	7, 9,11,12,13,14	1, 2, 4, 7, 9,11,12,13,14	8,9,11,12,13,14	1, 2, 3, 7, 9,11,12,13,14
NB=7 PS=50	7, 9,11,12,13,14	2, 3, 7, 8,9,10,11,12,13,14	4, 7, 8,9,11,12,13,14	1, 2, 4, 7, 9,11,12,13,14
NB=7 PS=100	2, 7, 9,11,12,13,14	2, 3, 7, 8,9,10,11,12,13,14	3, 7, 9,11,12,13,14	1, 2, 4, 7, 9,10,11,12,13,14

4.2 Execution Example

Table 2 shows the execution example in the case of 30 trials (150 problems) and Figure 8 shows the example of the screen. We assume two patterns of student type, one is high level LOC (=0.75) and the other is low level (=0.25), and Max score is "5". For example, in the case of the 8th trial, if the question level is low (=1) and performance score is very high (=4), the system give the "encourage type of message" to the "Low LOC" type student and "nothing (only the success-fault information) type of message" to the "High LOC" type of student. The highlight part of the Table 2 indicates that different message types are selected between the low and high LOC type of student in spite of the same situation. Therefore, we can say that the motivation system can generate the appropriate message considering the human model and motivation knowledge.

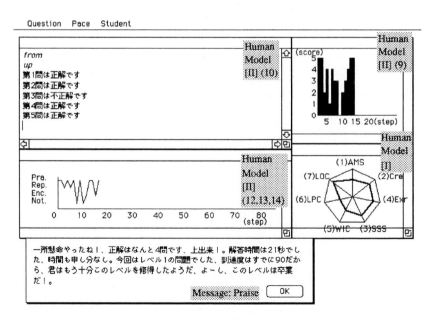

Fig.8. An example of screen

Table **2** . An example of Simulation

Trial	1	2	3	4	5	6	7	8	9	10	11	12	13	14
Score	5	4	4	5	0	1	0	4	5	4	5	5	2	0
Level	1	1	1	1	1	1	1	1	1	1	1	2	2	2
Low LOC	Pra.	Rep		Pra.	Not.				Not.		Not.			Enc.
High LOC	Pra.	Rep		Pra.	Not.				Not.		Not.			Enc.

15	16	17	18	19	20	21	22	23	24	25	26	27	28	29	30
1	5	4	5	4	5	0	0	0	3	3	5	3	5	2	0
2	2	2	2	2	2	5	5	5	5	5	5	5	5	5	5
Rep.	Pra.	Rep.	Pra.	Rep.	Pra.	Not.	Not.	Not.			Pra.		Pra.	Rep.	
Rep.	Pra.	Rep.	Pra.	Rep.	Pra.	Not.	Not.	Not.			Pra.		Pra.	Rep.	

5 Conclusion

In this paper, we focus on the importance of motivation function for the intelligent tutoring system and propose the human model which represents the student's internal psychological state. We construct the motivation system as a new concept of ITS framework. We apply this to the domain of an English Grammar problem and construct the prototype system. We bundle the motivation knowledge acquisition system (FREGA) with the motivation system. In the system evaluation, we confirm that the system can generate the appropriate message considering the human model and motivation knowledge which are identified by FREGA.

This work is supported in part by Grand-in-Aid for Scientific Research 07780162 from the Ministry of Education, Science and Culture.

References

1. Araki, D., and et al., Inductive decision tree learning from numerical data, Journal of Japanese Society for Artificial Intelligence, Vol.7, No.6, pp.992-1000 (1992).
2. Kunisa, A., Tsuchiya, T., Matsubara, Y. and et al., An expert system for sales forecast on the basis of a decision tree, Proceedings of the Second China-Japan International Symposium on Industrial Management, pp. 355-360 (1993).
3. Matsubara, Y. and Nagamachi, M., A motivation model for intelligent tutoring system, Proceedings of 11th Congress of the International Ergonomics Association, pp.634-636 (1991).
4. Matsubara, Y. and Nagamachi, M., Ergonomic design of intelligent tutoring system: the decision method for tutoring strategy based on the motivation model, Proceedings of the 3rd Pan-Pacific Conference on Occupational Ergonomics, pp.585-589 (1994).
5. Payne, S.J., Methods and mental models in theories of cognitive skill, In Self, J. (eds.), Artificial Intelligence and Human Learning, Chapmann and Hall Computing, pp.69-87 (1988).
6. Quinlan, J.R., Learning efficient classification procedures and their application to chess end games, In Michalski, R.S., Carbonell, J.G., and Mitchell, T.M. (eds.), Machine Learning - An Artificial Intelligence Approach, Springer-Verlag, pp. 463-482 (1984).
7. Sleeman, D., Brown, J.S., Intelligent tutoring systems, Academic Press (1982).
8. Soldato, T.D., Detecting and reacting to the learner's motivation state, In Frasson, C. and et al. (eds.), Intelligent Tutoring Systems, Lecture Notes in Computer Science 608, Springer- Verlag, pp.567-574 (1992).
9. Thomas, L., and et al., Cognitive modeling and the development of an ITS, Proceedings of 11th Congress of the International Ergonomics Association, pp.616-618 (1991).
10. Wenger, E., Artificial intelligence and tutoring systems, Morgan Kaufmann (1987).

La modélisation fine du processus résolution de problème dans Miace

André Mayers[1] et Bernard Lefebvre[2]

[1]Département d'informatique et de recherche opérationnelle, Université de Montréal

[2]Département d'Informatique, Université du Québec à Montréal

RÉSUMÉ[1]: Miace est une architecture cognitive dont un aspect original est l'intégration de l'environnement dans lequel le tuteur et Miace communiquent. Cette intégration permet de tenir compte des limites de la mémoire de travail et de créer, ainsi, une simulation plus réaliste. Dans le but d'avoir une meilleure estimation des difficultés cognitives que pose la résolution d'un exercice par un élève, cet article présente une recherche de moyens adéquats pour modéliser finement le processus de résolution de problème. Il expose, dans cet objectif, la mise en oeuvre des connaissances procédurales à l'intérieur de Miace. Il met en relief l'interaction entre les connaissances déclaratives, les connaissances épisodiques et les connaissances procédurales lors de l'exécution de ces dernières. Cet article montre en particulier que l'intégration de l'environnement permet de modéliser les déplacements de l'attention nécessaires pour résoudre un problème.

Introduction

La qualité du modèle de l'étudiant que le tuteur se construit est un des facteurs clés de l'efficacité de son enseignement. C'est à partir de ce modèle que le tuteur élabore ses activités pédagogiques (choix des exercices, contenu des interactions...) afin de maximiser l'apprentissage de l'étudiant.

La construction d'un modèle théorique et computationnel de l'étudiant est donc un domaine crucial de recherche pour les systèmes tutoriels intelligents. Miace, un modèle de ce type conçu spécialement pour étudier l'efficacité des stratégies pédagogiques, se distingue de la majorité des théories d'apprentissage par l'attention qu'il porte à l'environnement dans lequel le tuteur et l'élève communiquent.

MIACE, en tant que système informatique modélisant un étudiant, communique avec le tuteur à l'aide de fenêtres dans lesquelles ils peuvent lire et écrire. Deux publications antérieures [14., 16.] décrivent l'architecture et l'importance de l'environnement d'apprentissage. Une autre [15.] montre comment Miace acquiert de nouvelles connaissances déclaratives à partir de stimuli dans une fenêtre. Le présent article expose la mise en oeuvre des connaissances procédurales. Il met en relief l'interaction entre les connaissances déclaratives, les connaissances épisodiques et les connaissances procédurales lors de l'exécution de ces dernières. Le présent article montre aussi comment l'utilisation de la fenêtre permet une modélisation plus précise du processus de résolution de problème.

Les systèmes qui forment l'architecture cognitive ont été proposés par des auteurs avec des objectifs de recherche souvent différents. Ces auteurs ont, en outre, des méthodes de classification différentes pour déterminer les composantes de leur architecture cognitive. Certains définissent les systèmes sur la base des corrélations entre le comportement cognitif et les processus du cerveau[23.]. D'autres regroupent dans un système un ensemble de processus qui interagissent intimement dans le comportement[23.]. Le résultat est qu'il n'y a pas de consensus sur le nombre de ces systèmes ni sur leurs définitions .

Miace est conçu dans un but pragmatique, c'est-à-dire pour tester des stratégies pédagogiques

---

1. Cette recherche a bénéficié d'une aide du programme Synergie du Ministère de l'Industrie, Commerce, Science et Technologie (MICST) du Gouvernement du Québec.

visant l'apprentissage de domaine comme les mathématiques ou l'électronique. Miace apprend comme l'étudiant à l'aide de définitions, d'exemples et d'exercices qu'il peut réaliser seul ou avec l'aide du tuteur. L'objectif est d'expliquer pourquoi un ensemble de définitions, d'exemples et d'exercices a permis ou n'a pas permis à un étudiant de maîtriser un concept ou une habileté en terme des composantes cognitives les plus acceptées.

1 L'architecture cognitive de Miace

L'architecture de Miace peut être perçue selon 3 points de vue: 1) temporel: mémoire à long terme vs mémoire de travail; 2) rôle dans l'activité cognitive: mémoire déclarative vs mémoire procédurale vs mémoire épisodique; 3) forme: générique vs exécutable.

Le point de vue temporel divise l'architecture en une mémoire à long terme et une mémoire de travail. La mémoire à long terme contient les connaissances acquises du domaine et se divise en deux parties: la mémoire générique qui contient l'information générale et la mémoire épisodique qui utilise les éléments de la mémoire générique pour enregistrer les événements vécus. La mémoire de travail contient les éléments de connaissance qui font l'objet de l'attention de Miace. Ses principales fonctions à l'intérieur de l'architecture sont l'interprétation des stimuli de l'environnement, l'intégration des nouvelles connaissances dans la structure des connaissances déjà acquises et l'enrichissement des liens entre les éléments de la mémoire à long terme.

Selon leur rôle dans l'activité cognitive, Anderson [1., 3.] distingue les connaissances procédurales (appelés procédures par la suite) qui concernent le comment faire des connaissances déclaratives qui font référence à l'information que nous possédons sur les objets (abstraits et concrets) et la façon de les manipuler. La distinction entre les connaissances déclaratives et procédurales dans Miace s'appuie aussi sur ces critères. Cependant, à la différence d'Anderson, Miace distingue les connaissances sémantiques et les connaissances épisodiques. Les premières représentent les informations nécessaires au langage et à la représentation cognitive du monde. Les connaissances épisodiques, selon la définition de Tulving [24.], sont reliées au souvenir d'événements et d'expériences personnelles. Pour d'autres [11., 20., 25.], la connaissance épisodique est utilisée sans référence à la conscience et permet d'encoder sous forme brute l'activité cognitive. Elle a pour rôle d'amener dans la mémoire de travail les représentations d'expériences passées de façon à permettre à l'individu de choisir l'action la plus profitable dans le présent contexte. Selon une analyse [9., 10.], les architectures qui utilisent les mêmes représentations pour les connaissances sémantiques et épisodiques n'arrivent pas à distinguer les différentes occurrences d'un concept. Grâce à cette distinction, Miace différencie le particulier du général. L'occurrence du nombre 234 dans l'addition de 234 + 956 est une cognition expérimentée à un moment particulier. Elle forme une des composantes d'un autre objet bien défini (l'addition) que Miace peut distinguer du concept général associé à ce nombre.

Le troisième point de vue réfère à la distinction entre les connaissances génériques, qui sont des structures abstraites, et leurs instances qui interviennent dans les activités cognitives et dont les traces sont conservées dans la mémoire épisodique. Les formes génériques de la mémoire déclarative sont des outils qui permettent à l'individu de construire des représentations d'objets réels ou imaginaires. L'ensemble de ces formes constitue la mémoire sémantique, et les instances de ces dernières sont donc les représentations construites par la mémoire de travail. Les procédures génériques sont l'équivalent des procédures des langages informatiques, et les instances de ces procédures sont les processus exécutés par le microprocesseur qui joue le rôle de la mémoire de travail.

2 Les 3 types de représentation des connaissances

2.1 La mémoire déclarative

Comme les connaissances déclaratives et leurs processus d'acquisition ont déjà été présentés ailleurs [14., 16.], nous insistons dans cette communication sur la classe des buts, une sous-classe particulière des connaissances déclaratives, à cause de ses rapports étroits avec les procédures. La connaissance déclarative qui décrit l'état à atteindre et que l'on appelle but fait le lien entre les connaissances déclaratives et les procédures. Sa mise en oeuvre diffère des autres connaissances déclaratives qui décrivent les objets et les relations du domaine d'apprentissage.

Les connaissances déclaratives permettent à Miace de se représenter les objets et les relations du domaine. Si le domaine est l'arithmétique, les structures qui symbolisent les nombres, les opérateurs d'addition et de soustraction sont des exemples de connaissances déclaratives. Elles permettent aussi à Miace de se représenter les objectifs qu'il poursuit ou qu'il pourrait poursuivre comme «additionner deux entiers». La possibilité de les communiquer verbalement est souvent utilisée comme critère pour distinguer les connaissances déclaratives des procédures.

Les buts d'un élève déterminent la direction de ses actions. À l'intérieur de l'architecture cognitive Miace nous prenons pour acquis que l'élèves est motivé à apprendre, c'est-à-dire à intégrer les définitions, à comprendre les exemples et à résoudre les problèmes que lui présente le tuteur. Dans la résolution d'une équation comme $3x + 7 = 5$ le but est d'atteindre une équation dont la forme générique est $x = ?$. Dans la reconnaissance des visages, le but est de donner le nom de la personne.

La réaction de Miace à son environnement dépend du but actif. S'il y a deux nombres dans une fenêtre, Miace les additionne si le but est d'effectuer cette opération, il les multiplie si le but est d'effectuer une multiplication, et il les néglige si ces nombres n'ont aucune relation avec le présent but. Les autres connaissances deviennent donc actives en fonction de leur pertinence pour le but actif.

L'utilisation d'une procédure fait toujours suite à la création d'une forme exécutable d'un but générique. Cette forme générique n'est pas une classe, mais une instance d'une des sous-classes de la classe *but*. À partir de celle-ci, Miace crée la forme exécutable à l'aide d'un appel de fonction LISP.

La figure 1 décrit à l'aide d'un exemple les attributs de la forme générique d'un *but*. Cet exem-

---

Fig. 1 Le but additionner

fonction-but: #'fonction-but
; Une fonction générique CLOS qui prend comme paramètres, un but, par exemple l'instance

nom : «additionner»
; Le protocole génère automatiquement (ou avec le concours du tuteur) un nom qui identifie
; cette instance et la fonction (ou la macro) utilisée pour la forme exécutable.

mémoire-associative :
  (((nat23 nat15)((nat38) 247))…
  ((nat3 nat5) ((nat8) 244 167 189…)
          ((nat7) 65 22))…)
mémoire-procédurale :
  ((proc17   247   …) (proc5   244
  167…))

; Elle permet d'accéder directement à la réponse à partir
; d'épisodes antérieurs. Ex. la 2°ligne indique que l'addi-
; tion de 3 et 5 a donné 8 pour les épisodes 244,167, 189 …
; La 3°ligne indique que l'addition de ces même nombres a
; donné le résultat erroné 7 lors des épisodes 65 et 22.
; Elle permet d'identifier les procédures qui permettent
; d'additionner et les épisodes où ces procédures ont été
; utilisées. Proc5 permet d'additionner par incrément suc-
; cessif. Proc17 est la procédure conventionnelle.

ple est utilisé plus tard pour illuster d'autres construits. L'expression *(additionner nat23 nat15 :fenêtre t)* est une forme exécutable du but décrit dans la figure. Dans cette expression, *nat23* et *nat15* sont des schémas déclaratifs représentant les nombres naturels 23 et 15 que Miace a lus et reconnus dans une fenêtre, et ils forment les paramètres de la fonction *additionner*. La forme exécutable spécifie aussi le contexte à l'aide de mots clés comme *:fenêtre* dont la valeur *t* dans l'exemple signifie que Miace peut effectuer l'addition dans une fenêtre. La fonction *additionner* est générée automatiquement lors de la création de l'instance *additionner,* et son code ne contient qu'une ligne: un appel à la fonction contenu dans l'attribut *fonction-but*. Les méthodes de cette fonction générique sont responsables du choix de la procédure à exécuter pour atteindre le but et de coder le déroulement de cette procédure dans un épisode.

2.2 La mémoire épisodique

La mémoire épisodique a été introduite dans l'architecture pour expliquer la création des procédures et des connaissances sémantiques. Miace, en effet, comme plusieurs autres théories modernes, dont les modèles connexionnistes [4., 5.], les théories de l'induction [8., 12.] , le chunking compétitif [21.], émet l'hypothèse que les connaissances déclaratives et procédurales sont abstraites de la mémoire épisodique [14].

Fig. 2 Les attributs d'un épisode
temps : 346
but: additionner
procédure : assoc-1
paramètres: (nat3 nat4 :table nil)
état : succès
super-episode : 300
événements : ()
coût : 1
résultats : nat7

La mémoire épisodique est, dans Miace, le dépôt des événements vécus par le sujet. L'épisode courant relate l'activité actuelle de la mémoire de travail. Il commence par l'évaluation de l'accessibilité du but et de ses paramètres en fonction de leur potentiel d'activation. Cette évaluation est relativement simple parce que ce sont des schémas déclaratifs qui contiennent, dans une facette, les épisodes où ils ont été utilisés et leur position dans l'environnement. L'accessibilité du but est fonction du potentiel d'activation de la procédure qui l'appelle. Plus la procédure a été exécutée, plus son potentiel d'activation est élevé, et plus la distance temporelle entre l'exécution de ses sous-buts peut être grande.

La structure hiérarchique des épisodes reflète la décomposition naturelle des tâches en sous-tâches puisque chaque but crée un épisode et chaque sous-but, un sous-épisode. Comme le montre la figure 2, un épisode précise le moment où il se déroule, le but, la procédure utilisée (la méthode est expliquée dans la prochaine section), les paramètres du but, l'état, le super-épisode, les sous-épisodes, le coût d'utilisation de la procédure et les résultats.

2.3 La mémoire procédurale

Les procédures sont les manipulations cognitives ou comportementales que l'on effectue pour atteindre un but. Dans le paradigme de la résolution de problème, les problèmes sont présentés comme un réseau. L'un des noeuds, appelé l'état initial, constitue la donnée du problème. Le noeud à atteindre, appelé l'état final, est le but. Les opérateurs qui sont l'équivalent des procédures permettent de passer d'un état à l'autre. Il y a cependant une différence entre les procédures et les opérateurs: les premières sont des entités psychiques et les seconds sont des entités qui appartiennent à un domaine de connaissance.

Les procédures n'ont pas une forme déclarative et, par conséquent, Miace ne peut examiner leur contenu. Anderson (1993) utilise l'exemple suivant pour bien faire saisir la différence entre procédure et schéma déclaratif. Un individu, qui peut décrire la topographie d'un clavier, possède une représentation déclarative du clavier, mais est un dactylographe inefficace s'il ne possède pas les procédures pour dactylographier.

Les procédures dites primitives s'exécutent sans utiliser les ressources de l'attention sauf pour encoder la donnée initiale, puis le résultat, comme c'est le cas lors de la reconnaissance de visages connus. Celles qui sont dites complexes s'exécutent en précisant des sous-buts comme dans la résolution d'une équation. Ces sous-buts sont des connaissances déclaratives qui utilisent les ressources de l'attention. De façon récursive ces sous-buts peuvent être atteints par l'exécution d'autres procédures qui peuvent elles-même être constituées de sous-buts. La récursion s'arrête lorsque les sous-buts peuvent être exécutés par des procédures dites primitives. Il faut remarquer que les procédures complexes ne sont pas des connaissances déclaratives et ne peuvent pas être examinées. Un élève qui résout une équation à l'aide d'une procédure ne peut décrire à priori sa démarche, il prend conscience des sous-buts au fur et à mesure qu'il résout le problème.

Les procédures sont extraites d'épisodes antérieurs où Miace essaie de comprendre un exemple du même but[1]. Le contexte d'exécution de la procédure est une généralisation des conditions existantes au moment de l'exemple. Il s'ensuit que les procédures initiales que Miace construit pour atteindre un but sont souvent imparfaites, à la suite d'une généralisation incorrecte des conditions initiales. Ces généralisations erronées correspondent aux erreurs que font des étudiants réels pour la même raison.

Les procédures primitives

Le comportement réel de Miace est le résultat de l'exécution de procédure primitive. En effet, toutes les activités cognitives ou comportementales, même les plus complexes, se décomposent en une suite de procédures primitives. Le choix de ces dernières est donc important pour une simulation fine et réaliste du comportement de l'élève. La granularité doit être suffisante pour expliquer pourquoi l'addition d'entiers se réalise plus facilement si les opérandes sont disposés verticalement plustôt qu'horizontalement.

Dans Miace, les procédures primitives peuvent être divisées en deux ensembles. Le premier est relatif aux habiletés de base que possède un élève typique de la population (âge, sexe, milieu culturel,...). Cet ensemble peut varier en fonction de la population ciblée. Le second permet de simuler l'interaction entre la mémoire de travail de Miace et l'environnement. Dans ce but, Miace adopte et adapte la «théorie épisodique de la dynamique de l'attention spatiale» proposée par Sperling et Weichselgartner [19.]. Selon cette théorie, l'attention ne se déplace pas d'un objet à un autre de façon continue mais de façon discrète.

Dans la mise en oeuvre, deux fenêtres constituent, avec les régions (ligne, colonne et rectangle) que Miace définit dans ces fenêtres, l'environnement dans lequel Miace peut lire et écrire. Dans l'une de ces fenêtres, appelée *tableau noir*, Miace lit les questions, les exemples, et les définitions que le tuteur a écrits; dans l'autre, appelée *cahier d'exercice*, Miace lit et écrit, comme tout autre élève pour solutionner des exercices.

Lorsque Miace lit (ou écrit), en accord avec la théorie énoncée ci-dessus, il doit au préalable porter son attention visuelle sur la région où est (ou sera) l'objet. Ceci s'accomplit au moyen de buts et de procédures primitives prédéfinies dans l'architecture. Ces procédures sont construites avec les outils du langage d'implantation. La fenêtre active est identifiée par une variable globale *centre-fenêtre* qui pointe sur un pipeline bidirectionnel. Déplacer la fenêtre d'attention de Miace consiste à changer le pipeline sur lequel pointe cette variable. Il existe quatre autres variables globales *centre-rectangle*, *centre-colonne*, *centre-li-*

---

1. Présentement les procédures sont créées par le programmeur à partir de protocoles.

gne* et **centre-objet**, qui permettent de focaliser l'attention de Miace à une colonne de chiffre à additionner ou encore sur les chiffres successifs à l'intérieur de cette colonne. Par contre, il n'existe pas de procédures primitives qui permettent de porter l'attention successivement sur les chiffres des dizaines de deux nombres écrits sur une seule ligne; et c'est ce qui explique pourquoi, il est plus facile d'additionner lorsque les entiers sont écrits en colonne. D'autres buts et procédures, qui correspondent à des tâches survenant fréquemment et naturellement, ont été construits à l'aide des outils du langage pour permettre à Miace de lire et écrire des objets consécutifs horizontalement ou verticalement.

Les schémas déclaratifs possèdent une facette *lieu* qui identifie la fenêtre, la ligne et la colonne où apparaît un objet dans l'environnement. Le centre d'attention peut être élargi à l'objet, dont l'objet courant est une composante, en utilisant la facette *partie-de* du schéma déclaratif de l'objet courant. Le centre d'attention peut aussi être réduit à une des composantes de l'objet courant en se servant de la facette *r-concept* qui contient les composantes de l'objet courant.

Le schéma déclaratif de l'objet, qui est au centre de l'attention, fait partie de l'épisode courant et s'ajoute ainsi au contenu de la mémoire de travail. Comme pour les autres schémas déclaratifs, Miace a accès aux différentes propriétés de l'objet en fonction de leur utilisation antérieure. Cependant, les composantes de l'objet, parce qu'elles sont visibles, peuvent être utilisées sans contrainte par un rétrécissement de l'attention visuelle.

Les procédures complexes

L'exécution des procédures complexes met en relief la structure hiérarchique des buts. Cette structure hiérarchique correspond comme le fait remarquer Anderson [3.] à la décomposition naturelle des tâches à exécuter dans la vie de tous les jours. La structure des procédures complexes, en spécifiant les sous-buts à atteindre, est, selon Anderson, le résultat d'une adaptation rationnelle de l'organisme à l'environnement.

Les procédures complexes et les procédures primitives sont mises en oeuvre sous forme d'instance

> **Fig. 3 Les attributs d'une procédure**
> ```
> lambda-list:
>   '((op1 (and nombres-entiers-positifs-cl
>           (satisfies in-window-p)))
>     (op2 (and nombres-entiers-positifs-cl
>           (satisfies in-window-p))))
> fonction-procedure :
>   #'(lambda (op1 op2)
>     (focus-sur-fenêtre-exercice)
>     (set-focus-rectangle
>       (make-box-for-addition op1 op2))
>     (laisse-ligne-vide) ; pour la retenue
>     ...
> ```

d'une classe CLOS. La figure 3, présente la procédure utilisée par Miace pour additionner deux entiers donnés par le tuteur dans une fenêtre. L'attribut *lambda-list* spécifie les paramètres et les conditions d'utilisation de la procédure en terme de type LISP et l'attribut *fonction-procedure* spécifie le code LISP à exécuter. Pour respecter la définition des procédures primitives, le code de ces dernières ne doit contenir aucune forme exécutable d'instance de la classe *but,* puisque l'utilisation de ces formes exécutable nécessite la création d'un épisode. Inversement, comme dans l'exemple présenté, le code d'une procédure complexe doit être entièrement composé de sous-buts, puisqu'il doit être possible à partir de sa trace dans la mémoire épisodique de reconstituer fidèlement le scénario de son exécution.

L'évaluation d'une procédure

Miace utilise une fonction qui, étant donné le but (additionner), les paramètres (nombres) et le contexte (examen, devoir, utilisation des manuels, calculatrice, papier, crayon) retourne une procédure équivalente à la procédure qu'aurait choisie un étudiant réel pour effectuer la tâche.

Ce choix repose sur le «principe général de rationalité» proposé par Anderson [2.] qui s'énonce comme suit: «le système cognitif opère en tout temps pour optimiser l'adaptation du comportement de l'organisme» (p. 28). Dans ces conditions, Anderson précise que le terme rationalité ne signifie pas que l'organisme s'engage dans un raisonnement logiquement valide pour choisir la procédure à exécuter, mais plutôt que le comportement humain est maximisé pour accomplir ses buts à meilleur coût. La valeur d'une procédure dans ce contexte se calcule, selon Anderson, comme l'espérance de profit E(P). Si nous notons par s, le degré de sécurité de la procédure qui s'évalue comme étant la probabilité que la procédure atteigne le but, et par $1-s$ la probabilité qu'elle n'atteigne pas le but, puis par G le gain si la procédure atteint son but, enfin par C le coût pour exécuter la procédure, alors le profit, si la procédure atteint son but, est $G-C$. Dans le cas contraire, il est de $0-C$. L'espérance de gain est $E(P) = (G-C)S + (0-C)(1-S) = GS-C$.

Le coût (C) — La notion de coût réfère au temps et à l'énergie nécessaires pour exécuter la procédure. Les coûts des procédures primitives sont définis de façon ad hoc. Ainsi les procédure primitives permettant de déplacer l'attention de Miace ou d'effectuer des opérations élémentaires comme «extraire la retenue d'entiers supérieurs à 9» est de 1; celui d'une procédure de lecture est de 2; celui d'une procédure d'écriture est de 4.

Le coût d'une procédure complexe est la somme des coûts des procédures choisies pour exécuter ses sous-buts. Il est, cependant, impossible de connaître le coût d'exécution d'une procédure complexe avant de l'avoir exécutée puisque qu'en général, il y a de fortes chances qu'un de ses sous-buts puisse être réalisé par plus d'une procédure, et que le choix de cette procédure ne peut être fait qu'au moment de l'appel de ce sous-but. En conséquence, Miace utilise la moyenne des coûts antérieurs comme estimation du coût a priori.

Pour réaliser l'addition de 23 et 15 Miace a le choix entre 3 procédures pour atteindre ce but (figure 1): *proc*17, *proc*5 et une procédure associative. Le coût de la procédure associative est de 1 puisque les procédures associatives sont traitées comme des procédures primitives. Ceci correspond au cas où l'on se souvient d'un résultat calculé auparavant. La procédure *proc*17 consiste à additionner les nombres colonne par colonne dans une fenêtre. Il n'est pas possible de savoir a priori le coût exact d'utilisation de cette procédure. En effet, lors de l'exécution, Miace a pour but à un moment donné d'additionner les unités 3 et 5. Pour atteindre ce but, il y a 4 procédures *proc*17, *proc*5 et deux procédures associatives, et le choix dépend de l'état du système au moment du traitement. Le coût a posteriori de l'évaluation de *proc*17 s'évalue par la somme des coûts des procédures choisies dans les sous-épisodes qui ont mené à son exécution.

Le Gain (G) — L'intérêt de l'élève à réaliser l'exercice est défini par un paramètre dont la valeur est choisie de façon ad hoc par le tuteur au moment de poser la question. Il peut par exemple donner une valeur de 30 pour un exercice en classe (qui ne compte pas pour l'évaluation), donner une valeur de 50 à un devoir qui sert à son évaluation et donner une valeur de 80 à une question d'examen.

La sécurité (S) — Dans le scénario de la figure 1 Miace a, lors d'épisodes antérieurs, utilisé différentes procédures pour additionner. Certains de ces épisodes se sont terminés avec succès et d'autres ont mené à des impasses ou des résultats erronés.

Comme Miace ne peut découvrir par lui-même les erreurs qu'il a commises, la facette *état* d'un épisode où le but est atteint normalement à l'aide d'une procédure a, par défaut, la valeur succès. Cependant, si le tuteur s'aperçoit d'une erreur, il peut modifier cette valeur. C'est à partir de ces données que Miace évalue ses chances d'atteindre un but avec une procédure. Ce jugement est réévalué après l'exécution de la procédure.

Sous l'hypothèse que dans un espace de temps donné le nombre de succès S: et le nombre d'échecs **E**: sont deux variables aléatoires indépendantes de distribution gamma (Γ(s, 1), Γ(e, 1)) alors la sécurité **S / (S+E)**: , qui est la probabilité subjective d'atteindre le but, suit une distribution bêta β(s, s + e) [7., 6., 17., 18.]. Afin de pouvoir associer une valeur précise à la probabilité subjective plutôt qu'une distribution, Miace, comme le suggère Thiétart [22.], considère l'espérance mathématique $s/(s + e)$.

Après avoir effectué la procédure, Miace révise la chance d'atteindre le but avec cette procédure selon un processus Bayesien. Après *m* succès et *n* échecs, les paramètres de la distribution sont (s + m, e + s + m + n) et son espérance mathématique est $\frac{s + m}{s + e + m + n}$.

Le choix a priori des paramètres *s* et *e* lors de la première utilisation permet de modéliser le degré d'optimisme de l'élève et la vitesse à laquelle un individu change d'opinion. Plus *s* est grand par rapport à *e*, plus le rapport $s/(s + e)$ s'approche de 1, plus la probabilité subjective que la procédure atteigne son but est grande. Plus *s* et *e* sont initialement grands, moins le résultat de l'exécution de la procédure affecte le rapport $s/(s + e)$.

Dans le scénario de la figure 1, la sécurité de *proc*17, est de $\frac{1 + 15}{1 + 5 + 15 + 3}$ ou 0,67. Dans le cas de cet exemple, la facette *mémoire-procédurale* a été définie en remarquant que *proc*17 a été utilisé dans 18 épisodes, dont 15 avec succès, par un élève pessimiste modélisé par les paramètres *e* = 5 et *s* =1. Avec ces paramètres, la procédure avait initialement moins de 17 % ($1/(1 + 5)$) de chances d'atteindre son but pour l'élève modélisé.

Le choix de la procédure

Pour choisir une procédure, Miace crée, premièrement, une liste des procédures applicables qu'il ordonne selon les valeurs décroissantes du potentiel d'activation, tout en éliminant les procédures dont le potentiel d'activation est en dessous d'un certain seuil. Cette liste est construite selon un protocole d'appariement des paramètres actuels du but avec les paramètres formels définis pour chaque procédure. L'idée de base de ce protocole provient d'une vision des buts, comme étant des fonctions génériques, et des procédures, comme étant des méthodes du langage CLOS. Cependant, l'algorithme pour trouver les procédures (ou méthodes) applicables a été adapté aux contraintes psychologiques.

Dans le langage CLOS, la définition suivante *(defmethod additionner ((op1 integer) (op2 (eql 0)) &key (table nil)). . .)* spécifie qu'*op*1 doit être un entier et qu'*op*2 doit être égal à 0. Il n'est cependant pas possible de spécifier davantage les conditions que doivent respecter les paramètres. Miace permet l'utilisation de prédicats et de connecteurs logiques pour préciser ces contraintes. L'expression suivante *(defprocedure ((op1 (and integer (satisfies in-window-p))) (op2 (eql 0)) &key (table nil)) . . .)* spécifie qu'*op*1 doit être un entier et être dans une fenêtre de l'écran. En outre l'utilisation de certains mots clés dans le but servent à indiquer comment l'atteindre. Il est possible de préciser qu'une addition doit se faire sans l'utilisation d'une fenêtre ou qu'un objet doit être écrit à un endroit spécifique ou relatif à un autre objet. Lorsque ces mots clés ne sont pas spécifiés, Miace utilise la première procédure qui satisfait les autres paramètres. Il existe aussi d'autres adaptations. Le nombre de paramètres formels n'est pas nécessairement le même pour toutes les procédures utilisables pour un même but; et les mots clés acceptables pour une procédure ne sont pas nécessairement acceptables pour une autre.

Après avoir créé la liste des procédures applicables, Miace en évalue l'espérance de profit jusqu'au moment où il trouve une procédure dont le profit dépasse un seuil prédéterminé.

Si aucune procédure n'est choisie, Miace demande l'aide du tuteur qui doit a) suggérer une procédure existante; ou b) modifier interactivement une procédure existante; ou c) en construire une nouvelle en fournissant explicitement à Miace les sous-buts à atteindre; ou d) donner la réponse. Dans le premier cas, un nouvel épisode s'ajoute à la liste des épisodes où cette procédure a été utilisée. Ceci augmente son potentiel d'activation et, en conséquence, sa probabilité d'être choisie dans une situation similaire sans l'intervention du tuteur. Dans les deux cas suivants une nouvelle procédure est créée. Elle est ajoutée à la liste des procédures utilisables pour additionner. Il est important de noter que la procédure initiale coexiste avec la nouvelle procédure et qu'elle peut encore être utilisée, si son potentiel d'activation se retrouve après un certain temps, supérieur à celui de la nouvelle procédure. Miace explique d'ailleurs à partir de ce mécanisme, comment une conception ou un comportement erroné mais corrigé peut réapparaître après un certain temps. Dans le dernier cas, Miace n'apprend aucune procédure, mais il ajoute un nouvel épisode à la liste des épisodes pour la réponse *nat*38 à l'entrée (*nat*23 *nat*15), ce qui augmente la probabilité qu'il puisse accéder directement à la réponse si la même question lui est à nouveau posée.

Conclusion

Miace est un modèle étudiant construit à partir d'autres théories. Miace est particulièrement redevable à la famille de théories ACT [1., 3.] pour la définition des connaissances déclaratives et procédurales.

La vision des buts en terme de fonction générique, et des procédures en terme de méthodes du langage CLOS offre une alternative intéressante à celles qui, comme ACT, voient les procédures en terme de système de production.

La distinction entre procédures primitives et complexes faites à l'intérieur de Miace met en évidence les différences entre les utilisations des ressources de la mémoire de travail. Pour les procédures primitives l'utilisation de ces ressources est nulle. Pour les procédures complexes, l'enchaînement des sous-buts se fait également sans les utiliser. L'individu passe ainsi d'un sous-but à l'autre sans chercher. Ce sont ces sous-buts qui, comme toute autre connaissance déclarative, utilisent ces ressources. Leur utilisation n'est donc pas attribuable à la procédure en soi, mais aux sous-buts qu'elle précise. La modélisation des procédures complexes a amené à préciser qu'elles devaient dans leur exécution être une suite ininterrompue de sous-buts.

La recherche de moyens plus précis pour modéliser les processus de résolution de problème est un apport important pour les systèmes tutoriels intelligents. L'évaluation fine des difficultés que peut poser la résolution d'un problème pour l'élève, permet à un tuteur intelligent de mieux calibrer la progression des exercices qu'il donne. Cet article montre en particulier que l'intégration de l'environnement d'apprentissage à l'architecture cognitive permet de modéliser les déplacements de l'attention nécessaires pour résoudre un problème.

La modélisation fine des processus de résolution de problème permet de percevoir des éléments qui échappent autrement à l'attention du pédagogue. Par exemple, lorsque l'élève additionne colonne par colonne, il écrit les chiffres sans que son attention porte sur l'ensemble qui est la réponse. Il doit donc, à la fin, lire la réponse pour la connaître, même s'il en a écrit chacun des éléments.

Les essais en cours montrent aussi la nécessité de transformer progressivement les procédures complexes en procédures primitives. Au fur et à mesure que Miace apprend des tâches plus complexes, les procédures nécessitent des ressources qui dépassent les capacités normales de la mémoire de travail. En outre, le coût d'utilisation de ces procédures dépasse les gains espérés de leur utilisation et provoque l'arrêt de la résolution de problème.

Bibliographie

1. Anderson J. R.: *The architecture of Cognition*. Cambridge, MA: Harvard University Press (1983)

2. Anderson J. R.: *The adaptative character of thought*. Hillsdale, NJ : LEA (1990)
3. Anderson J. R.: *Rules of the Mind*. Hillsdale, NJ : LEA (1993)
4. Cleeremans, A., & McClelland, J. L.: Learning the structure of event sequences. *Journal of Experirnenral Psychology: General* 120 (1991) 235-253
5. Dienes, Z.: Connectionist and memory array models of artificial grammar learning. *Cognitive Science* 16 (1992) 41-79
6. Edward W.: Behavioral decision theory. *Annual Review of Psychology* 12 (1961) 473-498
7. Hogg R. V. & Craig A. T.: *Introduction to mathematical statistics*. NY : The Macmillan Compagny (1965)
8. Holland, J. H., Holyoak, K. J., Nisbett, R. E., & Thagard, R R. *Induction: Processes of inference, learning, and discovery*. Cambridge, MA: MIT Press (1986)
9. Humphreys M. S., Pike R., Bain J. D. & Tehan G.: Global Matching: a Comparaison of the Sam, Minerva II, Matrix, and Todam Models. *J. of Mathematical Psychology* 33 (1989) 36-67
10. Humphreys, M. S., Bain, J. D. & Pike, R.: Different ways to cue a coherent memory system: A theory for episodic, semantic and procedural tasks. *Psychological Review* 96 (1989) 208-233
11. Lachman, R., & Naus M. J.: The episodic/semantic continuum in an evolved machine. *Behavioral and and Brain Sciences* 7 (1984) 244- 246
12. Mathews, R. C.: The forgetting algorithm: How fragmentary knowledge of exemplars can abstract knowledge. *Journal of Experimental Psychology: General* 119 (1991) 117-119
13. Mathews R. C. & Roussel L. G.: Automatic Abstraction of Stimulus Structure From Episodes: Comment on Whittlesea and Dorken (1993). *Journal of Experimental Psychology: General* 122 (1993) 397-400
14. Mayers A. & Lefebvre B.: Une modélisation de l'architecture cognitive d'un étudiant pour un système tutoriel intelligent. *Dans* Frasson C., McCalla G. I. & Gauthier G. (*Eds.*) *Intelligent Tutoring Systems : Second International Conference, ITS'92*. Montréal, Canada, Juin 1992. Springler-Verlag 277-285
15. Mayers A. & Lefebvre B.: The dynamic Construction of Cognition in a Computerized Architecture of Learning. *Proceedings of Fourth International Conference on User Modeling*. Bedford, MA: The MITRE Corporation. (1994) 169-174
16. Mayers A. & Lefebvre B.: La construction dynamique des cognitions dans une architecture informatisée de l'apprentissage. *Les Actes du colloque «L'en-quête» de la créativité, 6 °colloque de l'ARC: La recherche au collégiale*. Joliette, 5-6-7 mai 1994: Cégep de Lanaudière 143-156
17. Peterson C. R. , Schneider R. I. & Miller A.J.: Sample size and the revision of subjective probabilities. *Journal of Experimental Psychology* 69 (1965) 522-527
18. Phillips L. D. & Edwards W.: Conservatism in a simple probability inference task. *Journal of Experimental Psychology* 72 (1966) 346-357
19. Sperling G. & Weichselgartner E.: Episodic Theory of the Dynamics of Spatial Attention. *Psychological Review* 3 (1995) 503-532
20. Seamon, J. G.: The ontogeny of episodic and semantic memory. *Behavioral and Brain Sciences* 7 (1984) 254
21. Servan-Schreiber, E., & Anderson, J. R.: Learning artificial grammars with competitive chunking. *Journal of Experimental Psychology: Learning, Memory, and Cognition* 16 (90) 592-608
22. Thietart R. A.: *La dynamique de l'homme au travail*. Paris : Les éditions d'organisation (1977)
23. Tulving E. Varieties of consciousness and levels of awareness in memory. *In* A. D. Baddeley & L. Weiskrantz (*Eds.*) *Attention: Selection, Awareness, and Control (A tribute to Donald Broadbent)* . Oxford : Clarendon Press. (1993) 53-71
24. Tulving E.: Episodic and semantic memory. *In* Tulving E., Donaldson W.: (*Eds.*) *Organisation and Memory* NY : Academic Press (1972) 381-403
25. Wolters, G.: Memory: Two systems or one system with many subsysterns? *Behavioral and Brain Sciences* 7 (1984) 256- 257

Learner Models for Supporting Awareness and Collaboration in a CSCL Environment

AYALA Gerardo and YANO Yoneo

The University of Tokushima, 2 - 1 Minami Josanjima Cho, Tokushima, Japan 770.
{ayalasan,yano}@is.tokushima-u.ac.jp

Abstract. In this paper we present our approach in learner modelling for CSCL environments. Learner models provide the information needed in order to support awareness and promote opportunities of effective collaboration and learning in a networked community of practice. The learner model is proposed as a set of beliefs hold by a software agent about the capabilities, commitments and learning goals of the learner. By exchanging their beliefs about the capabilities of their learners the software agents promote the creation of zones of proximal development in the learning group, by proposing tasks based on the group-based knowledge frontier of their learners, which represents the assistance and learning possibilities of the learner in a community of practice.

1 Introduction

GRACILE, a Japanese GRAmmar Collaborative Intelligent Learning Environment, has been developed as part of our research on the structures and procedures needed for the effective collaboration between learners of a networked small community of practice. In GRACILE foreign students in our university collaborate writing a dialogue in Japanese, assisting each other in the application of language patterns and expressions of the Japanese language. The learner interacts with two software agents: a *mediator agent* and a *domain agent* [1]. The domain knowledge in the environment consists of a set of Japanese language patterns, expressions and vocabulary distributed among domain agents in the network. The mediator agent supports the communication and collaboration between learners by promoting learning tasks considering the knowledge development of the learner as a member of a learning group.

In this paper we present our approach in learner modelling for CSCL (computer-supported collaborative learning) environments. We propose that learner models in CSCL environments must provide the information needed in order to support awareness and promote opportunities of effective collaboration and learning in a group. We first introduce the need and structure of the learner model in our CSCL environment, then we discuss the use of the learner model, and finally we present the main aspects of the learner modelling process.

2 Learner Models in Collaborative Learning Environments

A learner model has been considered a set of beliefs hold by the system about the learner [2]. In CSCL environments the issue of learner modelling has not been discussed in detail. In CLARE, a CSCL environment that facilitates knowledge construction [3], learners work on the construction of a group knowledge base from research papers. While learner derive a representation of an artifact and an evaluation of its content, they are not allowed to see what others are doing or have done. Later they compare, discuss and integrate their individual representations. CLARE includes a representation of the group's knowledge base, but there is not an individual learner model in the framework. A proposal for collaborative intelligent learning systems [4] also implies the representation of a group model, but not an individual one.

In the Learning Web, the multi-agent framework presented by Norrie and Gaines [5] software agents are designed to make intelligent decisions based on the content of their knowledge bases and the messages they receive. In the Learning Web an interface agent learns from the user's actions, working as an intelligent assistant, while a tutor agent provides scaffolding to the learner, progressively removing it as the learner internalizes the knowledge. Those agents require a model of the learner in order to perform their tasks.

We propose that the role of the learner model in CSCL environments should not be to support tutoring or diagnosis, but to enhance awareness and the effective collaboration between learners. Based on the idea that effective and successful collaboration between learners depends on the understanding of their mental states [6] we propose to model the learner as an agent, in terms of her/his mental state, which refers to her/his commitments, learning goals (intentions) and capabilities.

3 Structure of the Learner Model

Since in a CSCL environment the learner is an active agent collaborating with other agents, we propose that the learner model should be based on the basic concepts of agent modelling in distributed AI [7]. In GRACILE the learner model is a set of beliefs the mediator agent holds about its learner. These beliefs are organized as follows:

a) The learner's capabilities (representing her/his actual and potential capabilities).
b) The learner's commitments (the promises to perform tasks for the common problem and to assist other learners).
c) The learning goals or intentions (the tasks s/he would like to perform).
d) The learner's group-based knowledge frontier which represents the opportunities of progress and assistance the learner has by applying the domain knowledge elements together with the other learners in the group.

3.1   Domain Knowledge Representation

In GRACILE the domain agents are able to construct and analyze sentences constructed by the learner, applying a set of Prolog rules that represent Japanese language patterns and expressions. These grammar patterns are pedagogically organized, being related by *part-of* relations and grouped into classes which represent the *communicative situations* where they are appropriately applied. Each one of these situations refers to a communicative act, like *greeting, affirmative request, ask for opinion, refusal,* etc. A dialogue constructed collaboratively by the learning group is a sequence of these communicative acts, each one corresponding to the application of a domain knowledge element. The part-of relations are used by the mediator agent in order to promote the learner's progress from simple to more complex language patterns and create its beliefs about the learning and assistance opportunities of the learner in the group.

3.2   The Learner's Capabilities

Mediator agents in GRACILE support the collaboration and learning possibilities of the learners, by promoting the creation of *zones of proximal development*. Vygotsky defined the concept of zone of proximal development as the distance between the *actual development level* and the *potential development level* of the learner [8]. In terms of Vygotsky's theory of social learning, knowledge internalization occurs when an interpersonal process, at the social level, is transformed into an intrapersonal process, at the individual level.

In GRACILE the actual development level is represented by the knowledge elements that the mediator agent believes have been internalized by the learner. This is the set of knowledge elements that the mediator agent believes have been applied by the learner *without the assistance* from other learners or the domain agents in the network. The potential development level corresponds to that knowledge elements the mediator agent believes the learner has applied correctly *with the assistance* of other learners or the domain agents.

3.3   The Learner's Group-Based Knowledge Frontier

In order to represent the learner's assistance and learning opportunities in a CSCL environment we have defined the learner's *group-based knowledge frontier* (here after referred as GBKF) as the union of the following two sets:

a) The set of complex knowledge elements related (by part-of relations) to simpler elements believed to be already internalized by the learner.
b) The set of knowledge elements believed to be internalized by other members of the current learning group, but still not believed to be internalized by the learner.

The learner's *candidate knowledge for relevant collaboration* (hereafter referred as CKRC) consists of the intersection of these two sets. The CKRC is

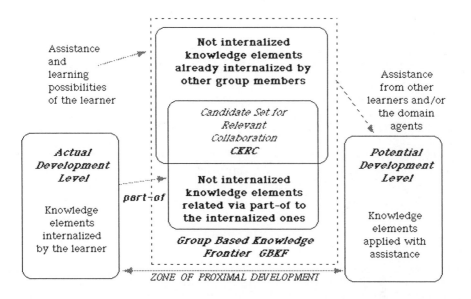

Fig. 1. The learner's group-based knowledge frontier.

then a subset of the GBKF which represents those knowledge elements still not internalized that have been internalized by other learners and which are structurally related to the learner's internalized elements (see figure 1).

Each mediator agent will propose to its learner those tasks where knowledge elements in the CKRC (or in the GBKF if the case when the CKRC is empty) are applied. This results in the enhancement of possibilities of effective collaboration in the group and the creation of zones of proximal development within which the learner can work and be assisted by more experienced learners. In order to construct the GBKF and the CKRC sets the mediator agents cooperate by exchanging their beliefs about their learners' capabilities.

3.4 The Learner's Commitments and Goals

Since the learner is an active social agent in GRACILE, her/his behavior not only implies the construction of sentences for the group's dialogue, but also her/his commitments to other learners and her/himself. The learner's commitments represented in the learner model are:

a) The commitments to perform a task for the common problem, which refers to the construction a sentence for a specific situation in the common, applying a specific knowledge element.
b) The commitments to assist other learners in the application of knowledge.

In addition, the mediator agent holds beliefs about the explicit presentation of the learning goals of the learner, which refer to her/his intentions to construct a sentence for a specific situation in the dialogue. At any time the learner can explicitly presents her/his learning goals to the mediator agent, by selecting them form a list of situations and knowledge elements. The learning goals and commitments of the learner are represented in terms of the situations in the dialogue where knowledge elements need to be applied.

3.5 The Learner's Beliefs on her/his Capabilities

The beliefs of the learner about her/his capabilities are not represented explicitly in the learner model, but only considered as a reason to determine inconsistent behaviour of the learner, which results in the revision of the mediator agent's beliefs about the learner's capabilities. For example, if the learner asks for assistance from the domain agents or other learners in the network, about the application of a knowledge element considered in her/his actual development level, then the mediator agent considers to stop believing that the learner believes that s/he has internalized such knowledge element.

4 The Use of the Learner Model

Based on the information from their learner models the mediator agents in GRACILE are able of the following activities:

a) Support awareness, by allowing the communication of the learning goals (intentions), commitments, capabilities and constructions of the learners in the networked community of practice.
b) Give information to other mediator agents about the capabilities of its learner, so they can construct the GBKF and CKRC of their learners.
c) Make an intelligent task proposal to the learner, considering the knowledge elements in the GBKF and CKRC sets, promoting zones of proximal development.
d) Decide to present or not to its learner a request of assistance from other learner in the network, based on the learner's current commitments (task load) and capabilities.
e) Look for consistency in its beliefs about the capabilities of the learner, by considering the learner's beliefs about her/his own capabilities and the evaluation of the learner's constructions, provided by the domain agent. The representation of the GBKF, the CKRC and the potential development level are also used in the creation and justification of basic and derived beliefs, as well as in the decision to discard beliefs about the learner's capabilities.

4.1 Learner Models for Supporting Awareness

In order to collaborate effectively learners require to be aware of the intentions, commitments and capabilities of the other learners in the environment. Gutwin et al. have proposed a framework for awareness in CSCL environments [9] where workspace awareness has been defined as the up-to-the-minute knowledge that the learner needs about other learners, in order to collaborate effectively.

The role of the student model in ILE as an external focus of discussion, built by some interaction with the student rather than by an internal analysis [2], has been implemented by Bull in a collaborative approach for student modelling, based on the cooperation between student and the system, which enhance reflection and language awareness in a second language learning environment [10]. Awareness is a result of the openness of the model to the learner.

In GRACILE all learner models are *freely accessible* to the learners at any time, via the mediator agents (see figure 2). In this way the learner is invited to reflect on her/his own capabilities and locate her/his own level with regards to the rest of the group. Learners become aware of who would be able to assist them in the application of a knowledge element in a given situation. When learners have to make a commitment of a learning task as part of the group's common problem they tend to select tasks where they can practice those knowledge elements considered used and acquired by other learners in the group, so they can get assistance from them, if necessary. Supporting awareness increases the realistic collaboration and therefore motivation and learning possibilities in the group.

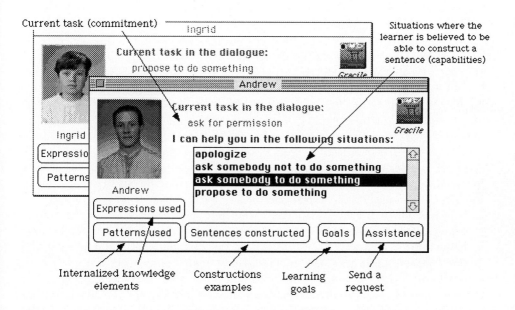

Fig. 2. Accessible learner models.

4.2 An Example of Interaction with the Mediator Agent in GRACILE

The capabilities of the mediator agent are performed based on their beliefs about the learner and the messages they get from other mediator agents [11]. In this example a group of foreign students (Ingrid, Brigitte and Andrew) is writing a dialogue in Japanese, working with Macintosh computers connected via Ethernet. The mediator agents of Ingrid, Brigitte and Andrew exchange their beliefs about their learner's capabilities. Thanks to such cooperation the mediator agent of Ingrid is able to create her GBKF and CKRC sets and make an intelligent task proposal to her. But before Ingrid makes a commitment to construct a sentence for the dialogue under construction by the group, she asks her mediator agent to present information about Andrew (see figure 2). She becomes aware that Andrew is believed to be able to construct sentences in Japanese for the situations *apologize, ask somebody to do something, ask somebody not to do something and propose to do something.* Ingrid considers that Andrew may be able to help her in the application of the language patterns needed for such situations, and that he is currently working on the construction of a sentence for the situation *ask for permission.* By selecting the situation *ask somebody to do something* and clicking on the "Expressions Used" and "Patterns Used" buttons, she can see the knowledge elements applied by Andrew in that situation, or take a look to the sentences previously constructed by him by clicking on the "Sentences constructed" button. Another aspect that Ingrid can consider for her task commitment is Andrew's learning goals or intentions.

The mediator agent presents to Ingrid its task proposal as a list of situations where knowledge elements in the CKRC (or the GBKF if the CKRC is empty) of Ingrid can be applied. These situations imply the application of knowledge believed to be already internalized by Andrew and Brigitte and structurally related to Ingrid's actual knowledge. The situation *apologize* appears in the list and she makes a commitment to construct a sentence for that situation in the dialogue. Ingrid makes such decision maybe because she is aware that Andrew may help her. She can send a request of assistance to him by clicking on the "Assistance" button or send a request of assistance to the domain agents via her mediator agent, which works as a facilitator. Brigitte, also cooperating in the dialogue construction, sends a request of assistance to Ingrid concerning a situation where Ingrid is believed to be able to construct a sentence, however Ingrid refuses to provide assistance since she considers herself not capable to help. Ingrid constructs the sentence for the dialogue and the domain agent analyses it, sending a message to her mediator agent indicating if the sentence constructed is correct and appropriate as an apologize in Japanese. These last three actions of Ingrid imply a revision of the mediator agent's beliefs about her capabilities. Finally her mediator agent informs the changes in its beliefs to the mediator agents of Andrew and Brigitte and makes the corresponding changes in the GBKF and CKRC of Ingrid, taking into account the changes in its beliefs and after receiving new information concerning the capabilities of Andrew and Brigitte from their mediator agents.

5   The Learner Modelling Process

For an ITS (Intelligent Tutoring System) learner modeling has been considered as a cognitive diagnosis process, where the computer system infers the learner's knowledge by analyzing her/his behavior [12]. The learning modelling process in GRACILE implies the following actions by the mediator agent:

1) Include the learning goals (intentions) explicitly presented by the learner.
2) Determine the learner's task commitments based on her/his selection of a task from the mediator agent's proposal, constructed based on the CKRC or GBKF sets.
3) Include the learner's beliefs on her/his capabilities and the respective commitment, after the learner makes a commitment of assist other learner.
4) Revise its beliefs about the capabilities of its learner, creating basic and derived beliefs with their respective justifications, as well as discarding those considered inconsistent with the learner's behaviour. The mediator agent takes into account the information from the domain agent about the learner's constructions, the actual learner model and the GBKF and the CKRC.

5.1   Revision of the Learner Model

Learner modeling is a process of beliefs revision since the learner model is a set of beliefs the mediator agent holds about the learner. In GRACILE, the justification of beliefs on the learner's capabilities includes not only the structural aspects of knowledge progress (part-of relations) but also the social aspects represented by the potential development level, the GBKF and the CKRC of the learner.

5.2   Creating Beliefs

During the belief revision process the mediator agent applies a set of rules in order to decide to create or discard its beliefs. These rules create basic and derived beliefs about the learner's capabilities with their respective justification. The conditions of these rules refer to the result of the analysis from the domain agents of the learner's construction, the current state of the beliefs about the capabilities of the learner, represented in the learner model, and the structural relations between knowledge elements, represent by their part-of relations. In addition, the potential development level, the GBKF and the CKRC are used by the mediator agent in order to justify the beliefs created and decide when to create a derived belief from a basic one.

Here we present one of these rules which creates a belief about the internalization of a knowledge element, when the learner correctly applies a knowledge element without help from the domain agents or other learners in the network:

IF
a) *the domain agent indicates that the learner was able to apply knowledge element K without assistance from the domain agent or other learners and*
b) *the learner was not believed capable to do it and*
c) *K is in the learner's candidate knowledge for relevant collaboration (CKRC)*
THEN
1) *creates the basic belief that the learner is able to apply knowledge element K and*
2) *justifies it with the fact was applied without help and that K was in the learner's CKRC.*

One example of a rule that create a derived belief is:

IF
a) *there is a basic belief that the learner is capable of apply knowledge K and*
c) *there is a knowledge element X which is part-of K and*
d) *X is in the learner's potential development level*
THEN
1) *creates the derived belief that the learner is able to apply knowledge element X and*
2) *justifies it with the fact that X is part-of K and has been applied before with the assistance of other agent in the environment.*

5.3 Discarding Beliefs

The beliefs about the learner's capabilities are considered to be discarded when the mediator agent notices inconsistencies in the learner's behaviour. This happens when the learner asks for assistance to another learner or to a domain agent about the use of a knowledge element believed to be in her/his actual development level, or when s/he makes an incorrect construction, applying a knowledge element incorrectly which is believed to be in her/his the actual development level.

Discarding a derived belief implies discarding at least one of the basic beliefs which gave origin to it [2]. The mediator agent reasons with rules that consider the justification of the beliefs to be discarded, such as:

IF
a) *the domain agent indicates that the learner was not able to apply knowledge element K and*
b) *there is a derived belief that the learner is capable to apply K and*
c) *the justification of the derived belief does not indicate that knowledge element K was in the CKRC when the belief was created and*
d) *there is a set of basic beliefs that support this derived belief*
THEN
1) *discards that derived belief and*
2) *discards the less justified belief of the set of basic beliefs.*

In order to determine the less justified belief the mediator agent applies some heuristics about the strength of a justification. The strongest justification concerns those knowledge elements that were in the learner's potential development level when the belief was created, then those that were in the learner's CKRC, next those in the learner's GBKF, (but not in the CKRC) and finally (the less justified) those not related.

6 Conclusions

We have presented our approach in learner modelling for CSCL environments, proposing that the role of the learner model in these environments should be support awareness and enhance the effective collaboration between learners. In GRACILE the learner model is considered a set of beliefs held by the mediator agent about the learning goals, commitments and capabilities of the learner. In the environment learner models accessible to the learners at any time. The group-based knowledge frontier (GBKF) and the candidate knowledge for relevant collaboration (CKRC) of the learner are generated by the mediator agents in order to decide which tasks are proposed to the learners, promoting effective collaboration and learning possibilities in the group.

References

1. Ayala, G., Yano, Y.: Interacting with a mediator agent in collaborative learning environments. Symbiosis of Human and Artifact: Future Computing and Design for Human-Computer Interaction, A20. Y. Anzai, K. Ogawa and H. Mori (eds.), Advances in Human Factors/Ergonomics. Elsevier Science Publishers (1995) 895-900.
2. Self, J.: Formal approaches to student modelling. Student Modelling: The key to individualized knowledge-based instruction. Greer, Jim E. and McCalla, Gordon (eds.) NATO ASI Series. Springer Verlag. (1994) 295-352.
3. Wan, D., Johnson, P.: Experiences with CLARE: a computer-supported collaborative learning environment. Int. J. Human-Computer Studies 41, (1994) 851-879.
4. McManus, M., Aiken R. M.: The group leader paradigm in an intelligent collaborative learning environment. Proceedings of AI-ED 93, AACE. Paul Brna, Stellan Ohlsson and Helen Pain, (eds.) (1993) 249- 256.
5. Norrie, D. H., Gaines, B. R.: The learning web: a system view and agent-oriented model. International Journal of Educational Telecommunications, 1(1), (1995) 23-41.
6. O'Malley, C.: Designing computer support for collaborative learning. Computer Supported Collaborative Learning. Claire O'Malley (ed.). Springer-Verlag, (1995) 283-297.
7. Shoham, Y.: Agent-oriented programming. Artificial Intelligence 60, (1993) 51-92.
8. Vygotsky, L. S.: Mind in society: the development of higher psychological processes. Harvard University Press. London (1978).
9. Gutwin, C. Stark, G., Greenberg, S.: Support for Workspace Awareness in Educational Groupware. Proceedings of CSCL '95. Indiana University. http://www-cscl95.indiana.edu/cscl95/gutwin.html (1995)
10. Bull, S., Pain, H., Brna, P.: Student modelling in an intelligent computer assisted language learning system: the issues of language transfer and learning. Proceedings of the International Conference on Computers in Education ICCE'93. Chan Tak-Wai (ed.) (1993) 121-126
11. Ayala, G., Yano, Y.: Intelligent agents to support the effective collaboration in a CSCL environment. Proceedings of the ED-MEDIA/ED-TELECOM 96 Conference, Boston, Mass. AACE (ed.) (1996) (to appear).
12. Dillenbourg, P., Self, J.: A framework for learner modelling. Interactive learning environments, Vol. 2, Issue (2), (1992) 111-137.

Modeling the Cooperative Interactions in a Teaching/Learning Situation

Evandro de Barros Costa[1] and Angelo Perkusich[2]

[1] Departmento de Informática e Matemática Aplicada
Universidade Federal de Alagoas
[2] Departamento de Engenharia Elétrica
Universidade Federal da Paraíba
Caixa Postal 10105 - 58109-970 - Campina Grande - PB - Brazil
Fone: +55 83 333 1000 R-412, Fax: +55 83 333 1650
e-mail address {perkusic,evandro}@dsc.ufpb.br

Abstract. This paper describes the interaction model within a computer-based intelligent learning environment based on a multi-agent architecture called MATHEMA. In MATHEMA, we have a micro-society of artificial tutoring agents that interacts with the human learner, aiming to involve him in a cooperative learning situation. We are interested in the modeling of two types of interaction: among the agents of the micro-society, and between a human learner and a tutoring agent. In this paper the interaction in the micro-society is focused.

1 Introduction

One of the central issues in the research on AI in Education is related to the possibility of the adaptation of an artificial tutor to individual students, in a learning situation. This possibility has been considered from 70s through the ITS category. Recently, the category of the Intelligent Learning Environment (ILE) has been designed to tackle this problem as well. An ILE can be seen as a combination involving aspects of traditional ITS and aspects of Microworld [1]. The difference between traditional ITS and ILE is basically related to the tutorial interaction style. While traditional ITS is based on rigid interaction style, where the initiative and control of the interaction are prerogatives of the system [7]. The ILE is based on a flexible interaction style related to notion of cooperative learning, where the initiative can be shared in function of a negotiation dialogue.

As a solution to the above mentioned problem, we first define, in our work, an ILE (one-to-one), where the teaching/learning process is achieved through the interaction, and then we extend it to an ILE based on multi-agent architecture [1]. This ILE is called MATHEMA. In MATHEMA, we have a micro-society of artificial tutoring agents that may interact with the human learner, aiming to involve him in a cooperative learning situation. So, we have two types of interaction: one among the agents of the micro-society, and another between a

---

* The first author is a Ph.D student in Electrical Engineering at the Universidade Federal da Paraíba. Mail should be sent to the second author.

human learner and a tutoring agent. In this paper we are mainly interested in the first interaction type.

In this paper our major objective is to model the communication protocol involved in the interaction among the multi-agents in the environment of MATHEMA. Indeed as argued by in [6], the name communication protocol is not completely adequate because besides sending and receiving messages, as in a distributed communication, each agent has to be able to infer the intent of a partner in a communication. Based on this consideration, an *interaction protocol is defined*. This interaction protocol provides both communication in the sense of sending and receiving messages as well as means by which the intent of the sender can be clearly defined. We apply a Petri net based formalism to model the higher level abstraction of this protocol. Petri nets have been extensively used to model communication protocols, we apply a modified object oriented Petri net named *G-Nets* [3] and *Colored Petri Nets* [5] to model this high level protocol.

In this work, we present some characteristics of MATHEMA, focusing on its micro-society. We begin, in Section 2, presenting MATHEMA's environment. In Section 3, we introduces details of the micro-society of artificial tutoring agents. In Section 4, we focus on the interaction model, mainly the interactions among micro-society's agents. Conclusions are presented in Section 5.

2 Environment of MATHEMA

MATHEMA is an interactive environment oriented to a teacher/learning situation. Its structure was designed to support functionalities and techniques of Distributed Artificial Intelligence (DAI), through a Multi-Agent Systems (MAS) based approach [2]. One of the our main interests in the framework of MAS is in the cooperation process among different tutoring agents to perform a complex problem solving activities. By complex activity we mean a situation in which an agent tutor cannot solve a given goal by itself. Our idea is to integrate a human learner in a micro-society of artificial tutoring agents, aiming to involve him in a learning situation. The architecture of MATHEMA is shown in Figure 1. It consists essentially of the six following components:

1. a motivator (representing human external entities that can motivate the learner to work in MATHEMA, for example, his teacher, his colleagues, etc.)
2. a human learner
3. a Micro-society of Artificial Tutoring Agents (MARTA), that may cooperate among themselves to achieve problem solving activities;
4. a Human Experts Society (HES), working as sources of knowledge to the MARTA;
5. an Interface Agent between a human learner and MARTA, which is responsible by the role of communication and a mechanism of selection to the choose a tutor agent (his supervisor), and

6. a Communication Agent which provides the interaction between MARTA and HES, offering the necessary means for the communication and maintenance of MARTA, including a language for agents descriptions.

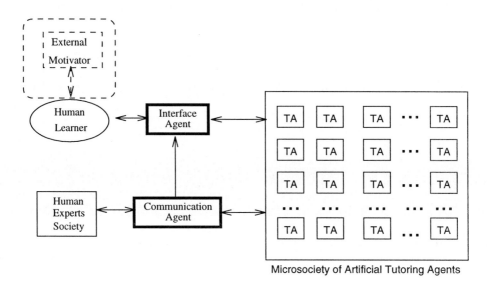

Fig. 1. Architecture of MATHEMA

The general idea of MATHEMA's functionality is as follows. First, a certain human learner, motivated by a motivator, starts working with the system. In this case, he dialogs with the interface agent about the tutoring environment. After this, the interface agent helps the learner to choose his supervisor. From now on, a cooperative interaction process between the learner and the supervisor agent starts. At this moment, situations with different complexities may occur.It is for example when the demand of the learner involves more than the supervisor agent and in some cases involving the HES.

3   Micro-society of MARTA

The micro-society is made up of a set of tutoring agents that may cooperate among themselves to promote the learning of a certain human learner. These agents work in a specific, formal, sufficiently rich, and well structured knowledge domain, as for instance the classical logic domain. This knowledge domain is divided in different micro-domains, each one covering micro-specialities, distributed in three different knowledge dimensions: one is the deep, the other is the breadth, and the last one is composed by different viewpoints(in order to implement the idea of viewpoints [8]), in the subject domain. Our objective with these dimensions is to have an environment larger than a specific knowledge.

Therefore, having an environment more adequate to promote cooperative learning and so, more adaptable to a student, considering his peculiarities and his personality.

Each one of the agent is an intelligent entity in some micro-domain, having the necessary knowledge to solve problem in this micro-domain.

To each agent are associated the capabilities of:

1. problem solving: the system should not only propose the problem to the learner with respect to inherent interactive process, but also should solve or help to solve it.
2. learning: it is required from an agent, that it should learn about others agents (a kind of social learning), and also with the possibility of the agent to learn with the human learner and about him. Moreover, the possibility of an agent learns with the HES.
3. disagreements resolution: this situation is concerned with the situation where there are disagreements which can emerge between the agent knowledge and the learner.
4. communication and cooperation: with the others agents, with the learner, and with HES.

In this paper we will not discuss all these capabilities, our focus is on the last one, more specifically communication and cooperation among tutoring agents. Further discussions of the other capabilities can be found in [1].

3.1 Agent Model

The agent model which we are adopting is based on a cognitive agent model [9], in the sense that it is inspired in a kind of social organization, characterized by means of its interactions. More specifically, we are interested in the cooperative interactions among tutoring agents during a teaching/learning interaction aiming the learning of a given student. Moreover, we are also interested, in the cooperative interaction process between a human learner and a Tutoring agent. To achieve this model, we divide a tutoring agent into two main layers: its cooperation layer and its tutoring layer.

The Cooperation Layer This layer reflects the social behavior of an agent. It is responsible for the coordination of the cooperative activities and internal activities of the agent. In order to cooperate with each other, each tutoring agent has five main components, namely:

Communication Module which is responsible to exchange messages with other agents;

Cooperation Module which manages the agents social and cooperative activity, namely negotiation and conflict resolution, through protocols for exchanging relevant information;

Monitor or control module which controls local activity by performing scheduling of local tasks;

Self Knowledge is the structure is made up of a collection of capabilities representing what the agent is able to do, that is, the knowledge about his own knowledge. It is used when an agent has to decide whether it has knowledge to solve a problem (a kind of reflexive act). As soon as a problem is available the agent verifies whether it has or not the knowledge to solve it.

Social Knowledge is the structure in which the agent can explicitly represent knowledge about the expertise of the agents of the micro-society. It is a knowledge source suitable for the cooperative process. It is used when an agent cannot solve a problem with its own knowledge, it tries submitting the goal, or a part of it, to other agents. In case that the agent knows who knows an agent able to solve the goal, it sends it to this agent. Otherwise it simply broadcasts the goal, asking someone to solve it.

The Tutoring System Layer This module is responsible for the cooperative interaction between a tutoring agent and a human learner. The teaching/learning process is here viewed as a particular case of this cooperative interaction.

In order to accomplish this model, our tutoring system deals with by three fundamental elements: *Oracle*, *Probe* and *Master*. These elements were inspired in the concepts formal protocol of automatic learning (machine learning) named MOSCA, proposed by Reitz [4]. Application micro-domain knowledge is distributed between the Oracle and the Probe. The Oracle represents the knowledge base considered as correct. The Probe is a noisy knowledge base aiming the cognitive disequilibrium, in the piagetian sense, of the apprentice (traps) plus a bug catalog linked with these traps. The Master is responsible by tutoring properly related to the apprentice, working as a facilitator in a teaching/learning process. For this, it has a cognitive apparatus including a knowledge module about the knowledge (meta-knowledge) into the Oracle and into the Probe. Also, it has a dynamic knowledge module about the student (student model) and another about pedagogical strategies (pedagogical module), increased with a control module. With this apparatus, the Master dialogs with the apprentice through a cooperative interaction mechanism aiming the apprentice learning.

4 Interaction Model

Our work is mainly focused on three types of cooperative interactions:(1) the interaction that occur between human learner and a tutoring agent ; (2) the interaction among tutoring agents; and (3) between MARTA and human experts society.

In this paper, we want to limit our analysis to particular issue: when and how agents decide to achieve a certain goal together.

Considering that in MATHEMA communication among agents may take complex formats, the partners involved in a communication must be able to identify their intentions in the body of a message. In order to provide means for this communication we define a *communication language* and *agent language*, this partition is clearly identified in [6]. The former is directly related to how messages can be delivered in a distributed environment. The latter provides means by which agents can inform its intention in form of an application domain language, as for example first order logic. It should be important to point out that interaction protocols and communication protocols are fundamentally different, mainly because that in the former the information exchanged is knowledge not pieces of information delivered by packets in a communication network, therefore the abstraction level is quite high. And, as pointed out in [6] interaction protocols may describe problem solving strategies in different forms, as for example cooperation or negotiation.

Therefore, in an interaction two well defined parts can be identified, namely: *communication* and *intent* of an agent. Each of these parts are encapsulated together in a unique message that is sent to the receivers.

We define a message as: ⟨message⟩ ::= ⟨communication⟩⟨intent⟩ . A communication is defined by: ⟨communication⟩ ::= ⟨from⟩⟨to⟩ . Where ⟨from⟩ in the sender, ⟨to⟩ can be either an agent identifier or a *broadcast* identifier. In the case of MATHEMA we consider that agents communicate in an asynchronous mode.

As argued in [6] the complexity of the interaction language depends on the complexity of the application language that is used by the agents. The agent language is defined by: ⟨intent⟩ ::= ⟨type⟩⟨message⟩ , ⟨type⟩ is the type of the message expressing the agent intention in the communication that can be ask for a solution (solve), introduce or present itself, ask for cooperation, and ask for opinion, and ⟨message⟩ is the message to the destination agent, or agents, expressed in the agent language.

We have introduced the semantics of a message exchanged among agents in the MARTA. This message format allows each agent to explicitly take parts of the message, allowing the control of the interaction (information exchange) as well as the control of each tutoring agent in the MARTA. Upon receiving a message, the receiver can clearly identify the intent of the sender.

4.1 Modeling the Interaction Protocol

To model the protocol we apply an object oriented class of high level Petri Net, named *G-Nets* together with Colored Petri Nets [3, 5]. *G-Nets* are a Petri net based framework for the modular design and specification of distributed information systems. The framework is an integration of Petri net theory with the object oriented software engineering approach for system design. A *G-Net* G, is composed of two parts: a special place called *Generic Switch Place (GSP)* and an *Internal Structure (IS)*. The *GSP* provides the abstraction of the module, and serves as an interface between the *G-Net* and other modules. The internal structure is a modified Petri net, and represents the detailed internal realization of the modeled application.

The *IS* of the net is enclosed by a rounded corner rectangle, defining the internal structure boundary, please refer to Figure 3. The *GSP* is indicated by the ellipse in the left upper corner of the rectangle defining the *IS* boundary. The inscription $GSP(net\_name)$ defines the name of the net to be referred by other *G-Nets*. The rounded corner rectangle in the upper right corner of

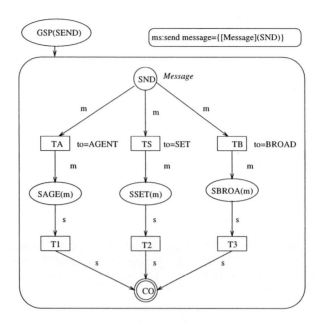

Fig. 2. *G-Net* modeling the sender in the interaction protocol

the IS boundary is used to identify the methods and attributes for the net, where: ⟨*attribute_name*⟩ = {⟨*type*⟩} defines the attribute for the net where: ⟨*attribute_name*⟩ is the name of the attributes, and ⟨*type*⟩ is a type for the attribute. ⟨*method_name*⟩ is the name for a method, ⟨*description*⟩ is a description for the method. ⟨*p1 : description*, · · · , *pn : description*⟩ is a list of arguments for the method. Finally, ⟨*sp*⟩ is the name of the initial place for the method. A circle represents a normal place. An ellipse in the internal structure represents an *instantiated switching place (isp)*. The *isp* is used to provide *inter-G-Net* communication. The inscription *isp(G'.mi)* indicates the invocation of the net *G'* with method *mi*. A rectangle represents a transition, that may have an inscription associated with it. This inscriptions may be either an attribution or a firing restriction. We will use the standard Language C notation for both attributions and firing restrictions. A double circle represents the termination place or *goal place*. Places and transitions are connected through arcs that may carry an expression.

The protocol is modeled as defined by the *G-Nets* shown in Figures 2 and 3, also in Figure 4 we show the variables and colors defined for these two *G-Nets*.

In Figures 2 and 3 we define two *G-Nets* namely, *G(SEND)* modeling a object responsible to start an interaction, and *G(RECEIVE)*, that is the model for the receiver. It should be noted that since the interaction may involve more than two partners, in the case of a interaction with a set of agents or a broadcast, the sender should consider these different cases. In what follows we informally discuss the behavior of each one of these *G-Nets* [3, 5].

G-Net G(SEND) has one method defined, namely *ms* which permits mes-

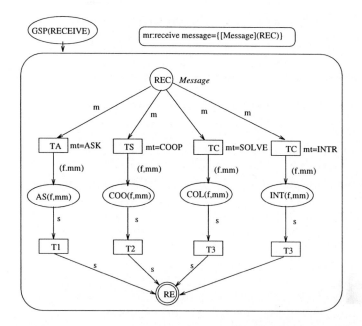

Fig. 3. *G-Net* modeling the receiver in the interaction protocol

sages to be send through this object. This method has only one argument named *Message*, The starting place for the invocation is SND. The semantics of the argument message is defined in Figure 2 by the color set *Message*. The three *isp's* represent the invocation of different objects for each kind of message, that is agent-to-agent, agent-to-set of agents, a broadcast, that are represented by the color set To, with the elements $AGENT$, SET, and $BROAD$, respectively.

G-Net $G(RECEIVE)$ has one method defined, namely mr which permits the receiving of messages to other agents through the invocation of this object. This method has only one argument named *Message*, The starting place for the invocation is SND. The semantics of the argument message is defined in Figure 2 by the color set *Message*. In this figure the four *isp's* represent the invocation of objects responsible for each kind of interaction, namely ask for a solution (solve) , introduce or present itself, ask for cooperation, and ask for opinion, each of each represented in the color set $MessageType$ as either $SOLVE$, $INTR$, ASK, $COOP$, respectively.

5 Conclusion

In this paper we have discussed a computer-based learning environment called MATHEMA. MATHEMA is an intelligent learning environment based on a multi-agent architecture. Its main idea is to integrate a human learning in a micro-society of artificial tutoring agents, with the objective of promoting the his learning.

```
  ┌─────────────── types and variables defined for G-Nets SEND and RECEIVE ───────────────┐
  │ color Message = product of Communication*Agent      color MessageType = with ASK | COOP | SOLVE | INTR
  │ color Communication = product of From*To            color MessageData = string;
  │ color To = with AGENT | SET | BROAD                 color AgentId = with product AgentName*AgentId
  │ color From = string;                                color Status = bool with (ack,nak)
  │ color Agent = product of record mt: MessageType     var m : Message; var t : To; var f: From; var s: Status;
  │                              *md: MessageData;       var mt: MessageType; var md: MessageData;
  └──────────────────────────────────────────────────────────────────────────────────────┘
```

Fig. 4. Color sets and variables for *G-Nets* shown in Figures 2 and 3

Our emphasis in this paper was centered in the cooperative interaction among agents in the micro-society. We discussed languages and protocols related to the interaction process.

Currently we are working on refining the introduced protocol and on the implementation of it in a distributed computer environment.

References

1. E. B. Costa, M.A. Lopes, and E. Ferneda. Mathema: A Learning Environment Based on a Multi-Agent Architecture. In J Wainer and A. Carvalho, editors, *Proc. of 12th Brazilian Symposium on Artificial Intelligence*, volume 991 of *Lecture Notes in Artificial Intelligence*, pages 141–150. Springer-Verlag, Campinas, Brazil, October 1995.

2. Y. Demazeau and J.P. Muller. Decentralized Artiticial Intelligence. In Y. Demazeau and J.P. Muller, editors, *Decentralized A.I.*, pages 3–13. Elsevier Science, 1990.

3. Y. Deng, S.K. Chang, J.C.A. de Figueiredo, and A. Perkusich. Integrating software engineering methods and petri nets for the specification and prototyping of complex software systems. In M. Ajmone Marsan, editor, *Application and Theory of Petri Nets 1993*, volume 691 of *Lecture Notes in Computer Science*, pages 206 – 223. Springer-Verlag, Chicago, USA, June 1993.

4. E. Ferneda, M. Py, P. Reitz, and J. Sallantin. L'agent Rationnel SAID: une Application en Gémeétrie. In *Proc. of IX Brazilian Symposium on Artificial Intelligence*, pages 175–192, Orsay, France, 1992.

5. K. Jensen. *Coloured Petri Nets: Basic Concepts, Analysis, Methods and Practical Use*. EACTS – Monographs on Theoretical Computer Science. Springer-Verlag, 1992.

6. J.-L. Koning and Y. Demazeau. Collaborative Learning Using DAI Interaction Protocols in a Telecommunication Setting. In *Proc. of IT&P'95: Interacting Agents*, Plovdiv, June 1995.

7. F.M. Oliveira, R.M. Viccari, and H. Coelho. A Topological Approach to Equilibrium of Concepts. In *Proc. of the XI Brazilian Symposium on Artificial Intelligence*, Fortaleza, Brazil, 1994.

8. J. Self. Computational Mathetics; the Missing Link in Intelligent Tutoring Systems? In *Proc. of the NATO Advance Research Workshop*, Sintra, Portugal, 1990.

9. J.S. Sichman, Y. Demazeau, and O. Boissier. When Can Knowledge-Based Systems be Called Agents. In *Proc. of IX Brazilian Symposium on Artificial Intelligence*, Rio de Janeiro, Brazil, 1992.

A Case-Based Approach to Collaborative Learning for Systems Analyst Education

Takashi Fuji[1], Takeshi Tanigawa[1], Masahisa Kozeni[1], Masahiro Inui[2] and Takeo Saegusa[3]

[1] Software Research Laboratory, 45 Nishinopporo, Ebetsu-shi, Hokkaido, 069 Japan
[2] OGIS Research Institute Co., LTD, 8-2-12, Nankohigashi Suminoeku, Osaka, 559 Japan
[3] Hokkaido Information University, 59-2 Nishinopporo, Ebetsu-shi, Hokkaido, 069 Japan

Abstract. In the Business Systems Design learning environment, there may be more than one solution to any given problem. We have developed CAMELOT (Collaborative and Multimedia Environment for Learners on Teams)[10] using the Nominal Group Technique for group problem solving. This paper describes the basic framework of the collaborative learning system, the effectiveness of collaborative learning in designing the Data Model, and how to apply AI technologies such as rule-based and case-based reasoning to the system. By using CAMELOT, each learner learns how to analyze through case studies and how to cooperate with a group in problem solving. Learners come to a deeper understanding from using CAMELOT than from studying independently because they can reach better solutions through discussion, tips from other learners, examination of one another's individual works, and pedagogical actions using case-based reasoning.

1 Introduction

A recent trend in information systems education in Japan is that systems analyst education is in higher demand than programmer education. An advisory committee of the Ministry of International Trade and Industry (MITI) has suggested that systems analysis and design is one of the most important skills in the coming advanced information society. The career path of systems analysts is like an apprenticeship, and current computer supported learning and training environment is very limited, making the demand of research and development for ITS in systems analyst education very high.

Systems analysis and design is a particularly appropriate area of application for group learning because more than one solution may exist for any given problem. This means that it is impossible to predefine all solutions. The technology of case-based reasoning is presumably useful in this area. Furthermore, the current focus of intelligent and traditional CAI is to teach each individual learner according to his/her level of understanding while classroom teaching addresses a group of learners. Some CAI systems are connected by a network to gather statistics on learners' achievements in CAI environments. Beyond this, however, group learning systems using computers are important for fields involving collaborative work because learning involves more than the simple transfer of knowledge from a teacher to individual learners.

From the technical point of view, case-based reasoning is one AI technique to search for the most analogous case and to apply it to a new problem. This technology is widely used in expert systems but in which seldom in intelligent CAI. One relevant study is "DICABTU(DIstributed CAse-Based TUtoring)" [1], the major feature is to decide an appropriate decision by case-based reasoning. In our research, the system searches for the most analogous answer of the learners and this paper will show the effectiveness of this approach.

This paper proposes a new framework for collaborative learning without any instructor. Individuals and the whole group are monitored and are offered appropriate remedies using AI techniques, especially, case-based reasoning. The concept of our framework is more organized than anything in the research. The collaborative learning process is introduced in Section 2, the pedagogy of collaborative learning based on case-based reasoning in Section 3, the architecture of CAMELOT in Section 4, and a case study of CAMELOT in Section 5.

2   The Collaborative Learning Process

The Nominal Group Technique [2] has been proposed to make group discussion effective. It is thought that this technique is more fruitful than others in which there is usually only one idea generator and several idea reactors involved in the discussion. It is more effective, however, for all members to generate ideas. The Nominal Group Technique is based on this, and has five steps.

(a) Initial thinking
(b) Presenting ideas
(c) Restructuring ideas
(d) Discussing & integrating ideas
(e) Reaching consensus or ranking solutions

Group members try to reach a consensus on the best solution. If they cannot reach a unanimous conclusion, they agree on a ranking of their ideas. A learning process model has been established for our system based on the Nominal Group Technique. It consists of seven sessions.

Session 1: Posing the Problem through Multimedia
A problem in a subject (e.g., systems analysis) is posed by multimedia, for example video, to learners.
Session 2: Problem Solving (Exercise)
Before cooperative work, each learner answers questions. In the systems analysis example, the answers are by an Entity-Relationship diagram (a Data Model) using a micro-world. Learners' inputs into the micro-world are transformed to an internal data format defined by the classes. The system compares the learner's

data with the right answer. Knowledge bases of the subject matter exist to evaluate what kind of mistakes and how many mistakes learners have made.

Session 3: Presenting Each Individual Work

All the learners are divided into groups. The basic goal for each group is to carry out tasks cooperatively. The system presents each individual's work to all the learners in the group through a computer network, Internet, so that they can evaluate one another's work. They check each other's work and can agree, disagree, query, or give an answer. Through this process, they learn to recognize a good answer or better answers.

Session 4: Selection of the best individual work

After their first discussion, the learners in each group vote on the best work to use for their cooperative work. The system monitors the situation and gives advice if necessary.

Session 5: Group Discussion

Any learner can try to modify the selected work, but only one at a time. They can also discuss modifications. During the modifications, the system evaluates the learners' activities according to functions monitoring the cooperative work.

Session 6: Remedies for mistakes

After the group work is finished, the system provides predefined explanations to the learners about any basic mistakes. It shows the case most analogous to the learners' solution and provides more detailed explanations to deepen their understanding using case-based reasoning.

Session 7: Advice for group discussion

The system also provides comments on the group discussion by collaborative functions (Duration of no discussion by any learner, Duration of no discussion by an individual learner, and Percentage of discussion occupied by a single learner).

3 Pedagogical Strategies for Collaborative Learning

There have been a number of studies on the establishment of pedagogical strategies in individual learning CAI [3][9], but few in collaborative learning CAI [4][5][10]. Here we introduce our pedagogical strategies based on the learning process described in Section 2.

3.1 The Pedagogical Strategies of the Collaborative Work

Four types of group discussion are described in Brightman's study [2]:

(a) Conflict
(b) Avoidance
(c) Adaptation
(d) Collaborative Work

Group learning should aim at (d) rather than (a), (b) or (c). Based on Brightman's study and our hierarchy, some of the functions evaluated in cooperative work are described below.

Selection of the proper number of learners. Basically, the system selects five to seven learners [2]. The minimum number of learners is three, because this is the smallest group in which learners interact with more than one other group member.

Evaluation of individual work. Each individual's work is evaluated by a weighted average of mistakes and then ranked. The system monitors whether the group has selected an appropriate individual work for the starting point of the cooperative work.

Duration of non participation. If no one contributes to the discussion, collaborative learning is impossible. The system measures the duration of lack of discussion and monitors it if it exceeds a given time limit. The system warns all learners.

Duration of non participation by an individual learner. Collaborative learning assumes the participation of all learners. The system monitors the lack of participation by any specific learner. The system warns that learner.

Percentage of discussion occupied by a single learner. The system measures the percentage of discussion dominated by an individual learner. The system warns all learners except the individual learner because every individual should be encouraged to participate actively.

3.2 Remedy with Case-Based Reasoning for a Collaborative Work Solution

Integrating rule-based reasoning and case-based reasoning makes pedagogical strategies more effective in remedying any mistakes in the collaborative work solution. Fig. 1 shows the processes of rule-based reasoning and case-based reasoning. The system remedies basic mistakes such as wrong Entities and wrong Relationships by using Data Modeling Rules. After remedying basic mistakes, the system remedies complex mistakes such as a wrong E-R diagram, for example, from the system's performance point of view by using Systems Development Cases. Learners come to understand better solutions through these pedagogical strategies.

Remedy by Rule-Based Reasoning.
The Basic Concept: In Data Modeling practice, a pedagogical strategy using rule-based reasoning can remedy the mistakes wrong Entity, wrong Relationship, and wrong Normalization. The strategy has Data Modeling Rules based on a correct E-R diagram.
The Structure: There is a rule base which compares any collaborative work solution with a right solution to differentiate the information. The system identifies learners' mistakes, and then the violated rules or principles are shown as a remedy. Learners see the instruction and compare their works and the right solution.

Remedy by Case-Based Reasoning.
The Basic Concept: If the system shows violated rules or principles as a remedy

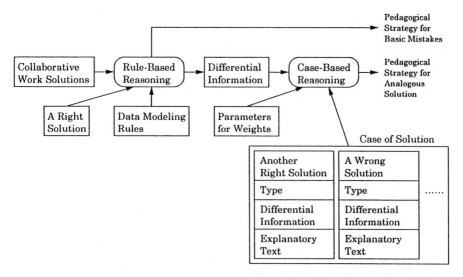

Fig. 1. The process of Rule-Based and Case-Based Reasoning

but the learner does not understand the explanation, seeing analogous examples is helpful, because such analogous examples lead to deeper understanding.

The Structure: Cases are composed of past learners' solutions and past systems development experience. Each solution has three kinds of information as well as the solution itself:

(a) The type of the solution

The type represents the important aspects such as system's performance or discrepancy in interpretation of the scenario for other right solutions and crucial errors for wrong solutions.

(b) Differential information

The difference in information between the right solution and each case is filed by internal forms to calculate an analogy to the current collaborative work solution.

(c) An explanation

Human instructors check the above cases, and then add appropriate detailed explanations for learners to deepen their understanding. Some learners' works may include other right solutions because, as mentioned above, there may be more than one solution in systems analysis domains.

Using case-based reasoning engine, a solution by the current group work and each case are compared and the degree of analogy is calculated. In this calculation, weights differ according to the Data Type (Entity or Relationship) and the Solution Type (another right solution or wrong solution) of the E-R diagrams. When the most analogous case is found, the system shows so that the learner can see the E-R diagram and the explanation (instruction). Therefore s/he finally gets the information on the analogous solutions or mistakes and can understand how and why the working solution is right or wrong.

4 CAMELOT Architecture

4.1 The Client/Server System

In terms of architecture, CAMELOT is a client-server system. The server system administers the information on the learners and controls the learning process for multiple clients. In addition, the server system gives learners groupware functions by sending messages from one client to the other clients according to the message contents. One of the several servers which constitute the system has domain knowledge and pedagogical strategies and plays a central role. When it receives messages from the clients, the server carries out inferences and decides whether to intervene in the learners' activities, what kind of strategies to adopt, what messages to send to the clients, and so on. The domain knowledge is used to create instructions and explanations, solve problems in the domain, and detect learner errors. The pedagogical strategies are utilized to decide more fundamental things, that is, what kind of pedagogical actions to take and when, how, and so on.

The client system provides learners with a user interface to CAMELOT. Learners have access to both individual and collaborative learning activities through this client system. Learners' actions are transformed into messages with a specific format and sent to the servers. The following sections describe the server system and the client system.

4.2 Functional Modeling of CAMELOT

The Server system is used to enable all of the pedagogical functions. The Functional Model of CAMELOT is showed in Fig. 2, using OMT notation [6]. The following functions are included in the Server system.

Managing the Learning Process. Managing the learning process includes commands of remedy for learners' mistakes, positiveness and collaboration of discussion. It is based on a collaborative navigation of "Pedagogical Strategy". The process is controlled by state transition rules.

Managing Pedagogical Strategies for Remedies. The system identifies learners' mistakes in the E-R diagram solutions stored in "Individual Learning Environment" and "Collaborative Learning Environment" in Fig. 2. It utilizes knowledge about the identification of mistakes included in "Domain Knowledge". The results are sent to "Learner Models".

Monitoring Learners' Discussion. The system monitors discussion among learners in a discussion model stored in "Group Discussion Environment". Then the system sends the type of activities (e.g., issue, answer, agree, disagree) and

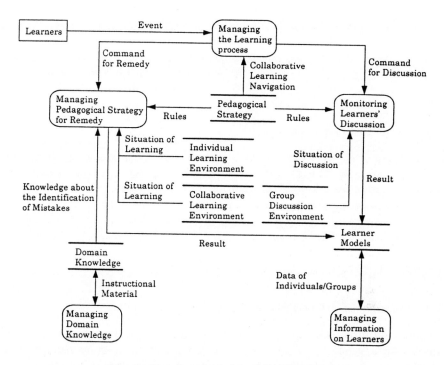

Fig. 2. Functional Model of CAMELOT

the number of each activity to the "Learner Models". The system also advises on the positiveness and collaboration of discussion to each learner, using the rules of "Pedagogical Strategy". The rules are fired if a value is over a threshold, as described in Section 3. The result is sent to "Learner Models".

Managing Domain Knowledge. The system manages instruction materials by domains or levels.

Managing Information on Learners. According to the message sent from "Managing the Learning Process" and "Managing Pedagogical Strategy for Remedy", this function revises "Learner Models" for individuals and groups. The function also keeps each learner's information (ID and his attributes) and authenticates the password.

4.3 The System Environment

CAMELOT is run on Sun Workstations. The software C++, ET++, X-Window, Socks are used for the development. ET++ [7], which is a C++ class library, is an object-oriented framework for user interface building blocks. It provides meta-level information, such as the class structure, which is useful for program debugging.

5   A Case Study of CAMELOT through Internet

After CAMELOT had been developed, several case studies were done. This section describes the procedure and the results through Internet between SRL in the northern part of Japan and OGIS-RI in the western part.

5.1   Case Study Procedure

In this system, learners watch a video provided on a window at the beginning of an individual task. The story in the video is of a systems analyst interviewing a customer about what kind of information system he wants to order. In the Information Engineering process, systems analysts first design an Entity-Relationship diagram of the target system. That is, the learners design the E-R diagram on a micro-world. The CAI monitors keywords, relationships, and the normalization of the diagram. The training follows the process described in Sect. 2 in the CAMELOT system.

5.2   Results of a Case Study

This section describes the results of three learners, because this is the smallest number in a group in which learners can interact with more than one other member and because the environment of the experiment was limited.

Learning Process. The learners reported that the learning process was very natural; the process includes Individual Work, Presenting Each Individual Work, Group Discussion, and Remedy.

Influence from Other Learners.
Advantages: Each individual's understanding is deeper for unclear or inconsistent portions when these points have been clarified by other learners. Each individual's understanding is deeper in some portions, after asking questions, giving or being given explanations. Individuals gain confidence in their answers when the other learners support them.
Issues: If a learner makes a mistake and the others accept it, nobody can point out the mistake. (Of course, the system will give the remedy in later sessions.) If nobody can answer a question, the discussion does not proceed.

Remedies using case-based reasoning for Collaborative Work Solution.
Advantages: By using rule-based reasoning, the learners can understand basic mistakes. Furthermore, the learners' understanding is deepened by the system showing the case most analogous to the learners' solution using case-based reasoning. They can learn to think flexibly about designing E-R diagrams and learn other representations from different perspectives through explanations of another right solution, and its sample screen is showed in Fig. 3. As a whole, the effectiveness of the combination of rule-based reasoning and case-based reasoning was confirmed.

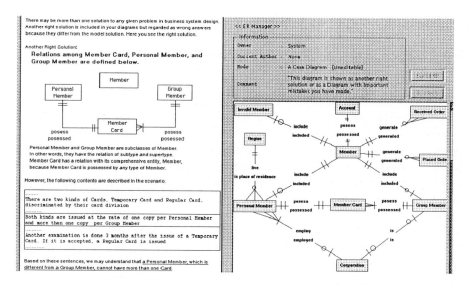

Fig. 3. Sample screen of another right solution

Issues: A learner who understands basic mistakes by using rule-based reasoning, sometimes can not understand the meaning of another right solution which is similar to the learner's solution. This indicates a lack of explanation about the difference between basic mistakes and another right solution. Supplemental explanation is needed.

The Discussion Tool. The browser makes it easy to follow the process and content of the discussion. Furthermore, after a break, it is also easy to review the last discussion. Although it is generally thought that an unexpected form in discussion cannot be handled in a structured discussion format, this does not apply to collaborative learning. A structured discussion form close to gIBIS [8] can cover collaborative learning for a certain domain and it is good for prevents digressions.

Remedies and Warnings in Collaborative Work.
Warning for self-assertion: Duration of non participation and duration of no discussion by an individual learner is set at 5 minutes. The limit of discussion dominated by a single learner is set at more than 50% for every 5 minutes. A warning shown as learners input their messages is not effective. Therefore, it is necessary to reinvestigate the timing of warnings.

Remedies for cooperation: In this case study, more than 50% of agree or disagree opinions were an object of remedies. The group learning was judged to be good because there were no cases below this threshold.

6 Conclusions

We are proposing a new framework, the collaborative learning system for systems analyst education. Based on this framework, a prototype called CAMELOT has been developed. We have evaluated the effectiveness and feasibility of CAMELOT in group learning. It is especially useful in enabling learners to understand their own misunderstandings by examining other learners' work and learning how to cooperate in problem solving. Also, we have made pedagogical strategies using especially case-based reasoning. It is clarified that our system gives more appropriate remedies to learners by using a combination of rule-based and case-based reasoning. We believe that the collaborative learning system described in this paper is appropriate for developing a variety of training systems using group learning and that the technology of case-based reasoning is very useful for the development of learning systems. An experiment was done by connecting SRL and OGIS-RI through Internet, which was very useful in evaluating CAMELOT.

Acknowledgements

We would like to thank Professor Yasutaka Shimizu, Professor Riichiro Mizoguchi and Professor Yoshifumi Masunaga for their valuable comments. We also thank our project members of SRL and OGIS-RI for their cooperation.

References

1. Vergas, J.E. & Kee, C.J.: Improving the Scope of Intelligent Tutoring by Adapting a Case-Based Methodology through a Distributed Architecture. Applied Artificial-Intelligence, USA, 1994.
2. Brightman, H.J.: Group Problem Solving: An Improved Managerial Approach. College of Business Administration, Georgia State University, 1988.
3. Woolf, B.P.: Context Dependent Planning in a Machine Tutor. COINS Technical Report, 84–21. Cambridge, MA: University of Massachusetts, 1984.
4. Katz, S. & Lesgold, A.: The Role of the Tutor in Computer-based Collaborative Learning Situations. The Report of the University of Pittsburgh. Pittsburgh, PA: the Univ. of Pittsburgh, 1992.
5. Koschmann, T.D.: Toward a Theory of Computer Support for Collaborative Learning. The Journal of the Learning Sciences, 3(3), 219–225, NewJersey, 1994.
6. Rumbaugh, J.E., et al.: Object-Oriented Modeling and Design. Englewood Cliffs, NJ: Prentice-Hall International, 1991.
7. Fujikawa, K., Shimojo, S., et al.: Multimedia Presentation System Harmony with Temporal and Active Media. USENIX-Summer91, 75–93, 1991.
8. Conklin, J., Begeman, K.L.: gIBIS: A Hypertext Tool for Exploratory Policy Discussion. ACM Transactions on Office Information Systems (Vol. 6), 4, 303-331, 1988.
9. Fuji, T., et al.: Prototype System of Advanced and Individualized CAI with OMT. IPSJ SIG Notes 93-SE-92, Vol.93. No.44, 17–26, 1993.
10. Fuji, T., et al.: CAMELOT : Collaborative and Multimedia Environment for Learners on Teams. Conference Abstracts sixth IFIP World Conference on Computers in Education, pp.104, 1995.

Design and Development of a Distributed Multi-User Visual Learning Environment

Jia-Sheng Heh[1], Wei-Ting Shu[1], Jihn-Chang J. Jehng[2] and Tak-Wai Chan[3]

[1]Dept. of Info and Comp. Eng. Chung Yuan Christian Univ., Chung-Li , Taiwan
E-Mail: jsheh@cycs01.ice.cycu.edu.tw

[2]Inst. of Human Resources Management, Nationl Central Univ., Chung-Li, Taiwan

[3]Dept. of Comp. Eng. National Central Univ., Chung-Li , Taiwan

Abstract

This paper describes a distributed visual learning environment, TurtleGraph II, that is designed and developed to assist students to acquire understanding and help build their own models of the deep structure of the recursive function. By applying the whiteboard technology, the TurtleGraph II provides a real time on-line interactive environment that allows multi-users to work on the recursive problems collaboratively. In the paper, we first discuss the learning theory and the instructional model that underpin our work to exploit the potential of the computer supported collaborative learning (CSCL) technology. A methodology is then introduced to explain how the system is designed and developed. The purpose in sharing our work is to foster consideration of both instructional and research issues.

Keywords: Computer supported collaborative learning, Distance learning

1. Introduction

The TurtleGraph II is a descendent of the first generation TurtleGraph system which was developed in the Macintosh machine (Jehng *et al.*, 1994). The first generation TurtleGraph distributed visual learning environment allows for on-line synchronous peer-to-peer interaction, but not for real time communication among multi-users. However, the learning environment is so limited that only two collaborators are allowed to work together concurrently, and the system is not powerful and efficient enough to support a community of collaborative group work whose participants are usually geographically separate. Therefore, to equip the system with enough power and function for a community of group work, we plan to extend our research work and attempt to build up a multi-user collaborative learning environment that allows more participants to join the group work and also allows us to organize students into separate collaborative teams. Each team has a leader who can monitor and control the collaborative team work and has the authority to decide the right of utterances among members of the team. The leader and other members in a team can use synchronous "Coeditor" and "Dialog" to help them accomplish their works while interacting and collaborating with other members in a team. "Synchronization" means that when a student inputs something into the "Coeditor" or "Dialog", all other students in the team can see what the student is trying to do from their own screens without any time lag. In addition, we have set up some indicators to show the intensity of collaboration among members in a team to motivate learners to learn to work with their partners and these indicators will make system more attractive and interesting in the process of collaborative learning.

2. Theoretical Framework

The design and development of the TurtleGraph II distributed visual learning environment is based on the idea of social learning environment and the theory of situated learning.

2.1 Social Learning Environment

The introduction of computer into education has long-term been emphasized about its programmability of instructional materials that are fairly suited to individualized learning. However, problems of lack of intrinsic motivation and instructional ineffectiveness have been addressed by many educators for its nature of social isolatedness and incompatibility with the way that human beings always learn as a group. In order to motivate learners to learn and improve the educational effectiveness of the individualized computer-assisted learning (CAL) system, the social learning system, by applying artificial intelligence and computer network technology, provides a multi-user learning environment where individuals can work either at the same computer or across connected machines. Social learning systems can be built up in a centralized or distributed forms and their design approaches can be analyzed into three types: Reciprocal, cooperative or collaborative, and competitive learning.

(1) Reciprocal learning system: The reciprocal learning system is designed in a way that changes the role of system users to be either a teacher or a student. The partners that a students learns with can either be a real student or a virtual learning companion (Chan & Baskin, 1988). For example, the Meta-tutoring-Kid (Kurt VanLehn, 1993) and RTS (Reciprocal Tutoring System) in LISA (Learning IS Active) project (Chan *et al.*, 1996) belong to this type of social learning system.

(2) Cooperative or collaborative learning system: Cooperation is that a learning task is divided into two or more parts to be accomplished by different learners dependent on their individual expertise, and collaboration is that a learning task is accomplished by learners with shared responsibility in each part of the work. Collaboration requires certain degree of coordination between learners, such as TurtleGraph (Jehng *et al.*, 1994).

(3) Competitive learning system: The competitive learning system is created in a way to make the learner to have a strong intention or motivation of learning by comparing their learning performance with others'. Systems, such as the Contest-kid (Chan & Lai, 1995) and Distributed West (Chan 1992), fall into this type of category.

2.2 Theory of Situated Learning

American educator and philosopher John Dewey conceived the idea about the practical aspect of education by advocating the notion of "learning by doing". Due to the rapid development of recent computer technology, more and more educators are interested in issues of the interactive nature of personal cognition in different computer-based learning environment and enhancement of learning by current computer technology. The theory of situated learning is one of the concerns that emphasizes the development of individual skills and knowledge in certain learning activities, and skills and knowledge itself should be contextualized during teaching and should be regarded as tools for future uses (Brown, Collins, & Duguid, 1989).

This theory has several instructional proposals. First, the theory emphasizes the social aspects of learning. Learning is determined not only by the individual pre-stored knowledge and processing capabilities, but also by learners' understanding of each action that they react to the situation. Therefore, learning activities should be arranged in a way that learners need to be informed of what they learned, why they need to learn, and how the learned knowledge can be used. The design of learning activities should relocate cognitive functioning within its social, culture and historical contexts. Second, the theory stresses that knowledge need to be contextualized and practiced in order to make learning more meaningful, and considers learning activities should emphasize not only the part of knowledge acquisition but also the part of knowledge application and transfer. The process of knowledge acquisition need to be integrated with the process knowledge application in any learning activity.

The theory of situated learning regarded learning as a process of enculturation, it has promoted the notion of "learning communities" where knowledge stems from distributed expertise. Particular individual knowledge have ownership of particular knowledge and no one individual has it all. Technology can be used to enrich distributed expertise and social discourse in the community.

3. Instructional Model

Two instructional principles were emphasized in the design of the TurtleGraph II distributed visual learning environment: collaborative learning and problem-based learning principles.

3.1 Collaborative Learning Principle

People naturally tend to gather in groups to learn. Collaborative learning is especially useful for learning a complex domain in which it is difficult to assimilate knowledge through individual efforts. Successful collaboration requires highly shared conception about the nature of the task to be performed and tight coordination in relation to each action initiated among participants in the group. Activities occur in collaborative learning, such as reciprocal tutoring, mutual evaluation, and cognitive scaffolding, can enhance learning by inducing more self-reflection and exploration of multiple perspectives. More capable learners assist their partners to resolve a difficult point, and their partners can help monitor each step taken in the process of learning. Three critical kind of support for collaborative learning can be identified in the TurtleGraph II learning environment.

(1) Support for reflection: The environment provides the "Dialogue Recorder" that can keep track of students verbal conversations, and allows students to reflect and elaborate what they have thought over.

(2) Support for negotiation: Negotiation is important for elaborating individual's ideas. TurtleGraph II is a perceptual learning environment that allows students to examine their argument visually and provides a common space for joint reasoning.

(3) Support for exploration: New ideas can be ready for investigating in the TurtleGraph II environment. This allows for more generative collaborative learning.

3.2 Problem-Based Learning Principle

Problem-based learning (PBL) is a student-centered, context-bound approach to schooling. In this approach, learning begins with a problem to be solved rather than the content to be mastered. This is consistent with new models of teaching and learning that suggest the emphasis of instruction needs to shift from teaching as knowledge transmission to less teach-centered learning. PBL includes among its goals: (1) developing scientific understanding through working on cases, (2) developing reasoning strategies, (3) developing self-directed learning strategies, and (4) developing knowledge application skills.

Collaborative learning is a key part of the PBL approach. As students articulate and reflect upon their knowledge, learning and transfer are facilitated. Group problem solving allows students to tackle more complex problems than they could on their own. In TurtleGraph II distributed learning environment, collaboration is encouraged in problem solving. Students are requested to write recursive programs to design geometric figures. Learning by collaborative problem solving can help students envision how knowledge is used in certain contexts. Presentation of problems is in a sequence based on the complexity of problems, and related examples are provided as support for solving problems. The acquisition and indexing of examples that occur during PBL should allow later problems to be solved by case-based reasoning.

In the TurtleGraph, the problem-based learning environment is designed using CSCW tools, such as real-time coeditor and dialog box to facilitate group collaboration or team work. Students can edit their answers and share their programs by using the coeditor, express and exchange their ideas in text-based conversations by dialog box. All functions encourage and facilitate collaborative problem solving.

4. System Architecture

4.1 Overall Structure

A distributed visual learning environment is a multi-user cooperative working environment, which can be studied through CSCW researches. (Bentley *et al.*, 1994, Ellis *et al.*, 1991) In CSCW research area, Liang *et al.* (1994) points out that the traditional client/server model is not enough for the collaboration within a group and a group server is needed for a groupware. Accordingly, a three-layer model is proposed for the construction of distributed learning environment, as shown in Figure 1.

The first layer is a team server (TS), which is located in a fixed computer and can control the whole process of the environment. The next layer is a set of team managers (TMs), each of which represents a team and serves as a group leader. Finally, the third layer consists of members (Ms), which constitute teams but will never become team leaders. Both TMs and Ms should register in TS, and all their information are obtained from TS. Then, this structure is a distributed learning environment with a hierarchical control structure, where members are controlled by team managers and all TMs get served through TS. The functions of the TS, TMs and Ms have been specified in the following subsections.

4.2 Functions of TS, TM and M

The communication mechanisms of TS, TM and M are displayed in Figure 2. For each module of TS and TMs, there are two kinds of accessing ports: Port-A and Port-B. The former (Port-A) is a public port responsible to accept new client request for new Port-B; whereas, the latter (Port-B) is a private port used by a requesting client to transmit actual data.

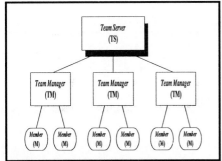

Figure 1 Overall structure of distri-buted visual learning environment

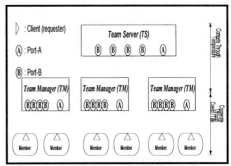

Figure 2 Functions of distributed visual learning environment

In this distributed environment, there is only one TS managing all the teams. Therefore, TS has to keep an eye on the status of every team, including TM's name and its IP (Internet Protocol) address. These information can be accessed by any TMs or Ms through Port-B of TS, then the members in this environment can join any team without knowing the team's location beforehand. Furthermore, all the data about inter-team relationship are placed in TS, such as the starting status and ending condition of the whole environment, knowledge and problem database, the *team competition index*. The team competition index is an index to indicate team's outcome and is defined as the number of finished problems for the time being.

A TM is the representative of a team leader, which manages the joining and leaving of members in this team and keeps a list of all its members and the corresponding IP addresses. It delivers the problems to be solved to the members and notifies TS the finish of a problem through message passing. Meanwhile, the TM assigns who has the right to speak or to edit for cooperation, then dispatches the contents of speech or editing to all Ms. Hence, each TM can calculate his/her *member cooperation index*, defined as the contribution of each member to cooperation.

On the screen of every member, there are several CSCW tools, including Coeditor and Dialog. These utilities support the students to cooperate or compete under the lead of the TM. The current results of each team will be shown in all screens as competition indices and member cooperation indices.

4.3 System Dynamic Behaviors

The system begins to work when the TS is initiated. Then, other participants can enter this environment as a TM or an M. When a participant enters the environment through a TM, he/she will serve as a team manager/leader. The processing steps for this participant to register as a team manager is shown in Figure 3.

ALGORITHM FOR TEAM MANAGER REGISTRATION

1. TS Port-A connection

    1A. TM connects to the Port-A of the TS.

    1B. The TS assigns a new Port-B to the TM.

    1C. The TM disconnects the Port-A of the TS.

2. TS Port-B connection

    2A. The TM connects to the assigned Port-B of the TS.

    2B. The TM sends its name and IP address to the TS.

    2C. The TS disconnects the TM, then the Port-B is released.

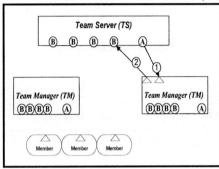

Figure 3 Processing steps for team manager registration

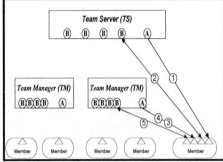

Figure 4 Processing steps for member registration

When the role of a person in this system is only a member of some team, the used module is only M and his/her processing steps will follow Figure 4.

ALGORITHM FOR MEMBER REGISTRATION

1. TS Port-A connection

    1A. M connects to the Port-A of the TS.

    1B. The TS assigns a new Port-B to the M.

    1C. The M disconnects the Port-A of the TS.

2. TS Port-B connection

    2A. The M connects to the assigned Port-B of the TS.

3. Selection for joining a team

    3A. This M requests the list of the names and IP addresses of existent teams.

    3B. The M chooses one team to join in.

4. TM Port-A connection

    4A. This M connects to the Port-A of the TM.

    4B. The M requests to join the team through the Port-A.

    4C. If the request is rejected, go to Step 3.

    4D. The TM assigns a new Port-B to the M.

    4E. The M disconnects both Port-B of TS and Port-A of TM.

5. TM Port-B connection

    5A. The M connects to the assigned Port-B of the TM.

    5B. The M sends its name and IP address to the TM.

After all TMs and Ms enter their positions, the TS can deliver a new job for each team to work collaboratively. Each job includes a set of problems. All teams receive the same problems and begin to work at the same time, hence they work synchronously. After all the work is done, the Ms and TMs can withdraw from this environment. There are totally three conditions for an M / TM to leave this system:

(1) When a job has not yet begun, an M can send a leave-message to its TM, then the TM will delete its registration data from the member list and the members process is closed.

(2) Also, when a job has not yet begun, a TM can send a leave-message to the TS, then the TS will delete its registration data from the team list, the TM's process is closed and the member in this team will leave automatically.

(3) When the time of job is exhausted, the TS sends an stop-message to all TMs, then each TM sends the same message to its members and all the processes of the TM and Ms in this team will be closed.

All the above procedure are divided into six working states: *login, designation, question-selection, cooperation, measurement* and *logout*. The detailed actions of these actions are described in Table 1.

States	TS	TM	M
Login State	(A1): 1. construct database 2. wait requests	(B1): 1. connect TS. 2. wait for members 3. disconnect TS	(C1): 1. connect TS. 2. query teams 3. select a team to join 4. connect TM & TS
Design-ation State	(A2): 1. send job to TMs 2. reject any new user	(B2): 1. reject any new member 2. send message to Ms.	(C2): 1. engage cooperation

Question Selec-tion State	(A3):
	1. wait for query
	2. reply query
		(B3):
		1. select question
		2. Ms confirm through
		   Dialog
			(C3):
			1. discuss with others
			   through Dialog

Coope-ration State	(A4) :
	1. wait for
	   competition-index
	   query
		(B4):
		1. solve question with
		   Coeditor
		2. verify answer with Test
		   button
		3. discuss through Dialog
		4. query competition index
		5. dispatch competition index
		   to Ms
			(C4):
			1. solve question with
			   Coeditor
			2. verify answer with Test
			   button
			3. discuss through Dialog
			4. update competition index

Measure-ment State	(A5): 1. compute competition index	(B5): 1. send leave-message to TS	(C5): no operation
Logout State	(A6): 1. send leave-message to TMs	(B6): 1. send leave-message to Ms 2. close TM	(C6): 1. close M

Table 1. Working states of TurtleGraph II

5. System Implementation

5.1 Implementation Platform

Figure 5 shows the implementation platform of the proposed distributed visual learning environment. In this environment, a team server can connect to unlimited number of TMs and each TM can connect to no more than five Ms. The chosen platform is IBM-compatible PCs, with operating system being Microsoft Windows NT / 95 / 3.1. The communication protocol is TCP/IP with socket interface, then it can be operated through LAN (Local Area Network) or WAN (Wide-Area Network).

With this environment, we build an experimental system, TurtleGraph II, which is a distributed visual learning system. In this system, several teams are assigned to solve a set of recursion problems. Each team has many members, who can cooperate with a coeditor and exchange their opinions through a common dialog box. When a recursion problem is solved, it can be executed by a LISP interpreter and the result is shown as a Turtle graph.

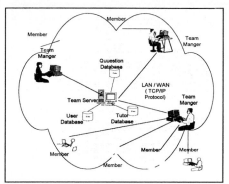

Figure 5 Platform of distributed visual learning environment

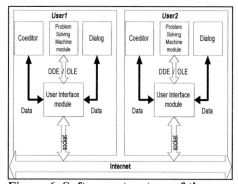

Figure 6 Software structure of the proposed environment

5.2 Software structure design

Figure 6 shows the software structure of the experimental system. The whole system is divided into two modules: User Interface and Problem Solving Machine, the former gives users a friendly interface for group work, such as synchronous Coeditor and Dialog; whereas, the latter provides a execution environment of problem solving, such as LISP interpreter. These two modules communicate in Windows DDE (Dynamic Data Exchange) protocol or OLE (Object Linking and Embedding) protocol, and communication among different machines are accomplished through TCP/IP protocol with Windows socket interface.

There are four parts in User Interface module:

(1) Question: used to show the recursion problem delivered by TM / TS.

(2) Coeditor: used to show the collaboratively editing LISP program or to insert some new editing contents by the operator (team manager or members with the right.

(3) Dialog: used for exchanging the opinions in a team and divided into two parts: Display and Entry. The Display part shows the talking contents to all users in a team and the Entry part accepts what the operator inputs.

(4) Information Display: used to show some information of a team or teams.

On the other hand, Problem Solving Machine module is decomposed into two parts:

(1) LISP Interpreter: used to interpret the program of the assigned problem.

(2) Turtle Graph: used to display the program result of the assigned problem.

5.3 Execution Results

All working states of TurtleGraph II have been listed in Table 1. A full sample with 1 TS, 2 TMs and 2 Ms for each team is used to describe the whole execution flow of this system, as Table 2 shown. Figures 7 and 8 show the screen layouts of User Interface module and Problem Solving module, operated in Step 8 to Step 10.

Step	Role	State Transitions	Action Description
1	TS	(A1)	start TS
2	TM-1	(B1)	start TM-1
3	M-1	(C1)	M-1 joins TM-1
4	TM-2	(B1)	start TM-2
5	M-2	(C1)	M-2 joins TM-1
6	M-3, M-4	(C1)	M-3 and M-4 join TM-2
7	TS, TMs, Ms	(A2)→(B2)→(C2), (A3), (A4)	TS sends job to TMs, then to Ms
8	TMs, Ms	(B3)←→(A3), (B3)←→(C3)	TMs and Ms select one question
9	TMs, Ms	(B4)←→(C4), (B4)←→(A4)	TMs and Ms solve question cooperatively
10	TMs, Ms	(B5)←→(A5)	TMs and Ms solve question cooperatively
11	TS, TMs, Ms	(A4)→(B6), (B6)→(C6)	terminate the system

Table 2 Sample Execution Flow

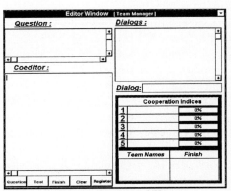

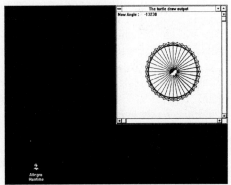

Figure 7 Screen layout of User Interface module (team manager)

Figure 8 Screen layout of Problem Solving module (team manager)

Through the above process, students can learn the concept of recursion in a distributed visual learning environment. For the students in the same team, they can learn collaboratively with Coeditor being a cooperating tool of problem solving and with Dialog being a mean for opinion exchange. On the other hand, each team's problem accomplishment is shown to other's display. This makes the whole system to be a competition environment, which is effective to stimulate learning motivation.

6. Conclusion

This paper presents a distributed multi-user synchronous collaborative learning environment mode via CSCW researches. Within a less restricted and group-based synchronous co-working interface, the system can prompt students to make more kinds of collaboration, being able to know how companions think through, and get other thinking path with a problem. In addition, we add a little competitive factors during the learning processes in order to increase the learning motivation. Furthermore, we try to make a common distributed visualized structure of collaborative learning in self-direction , pair or more learning situation. Today we use it to teach the recursive program skills, but we hope it can be used in other problem-based learning by just changing the knowledge database and the Problem Solving Machine. The technical infrastructure and model of the TurtleGraph II cooperative learning environment will continue to develop.

References

Bentley, R., Rodden, T. Sawyer P., & Sommerville, I. (1994) Architectural Support for Cooperative Multi-user Interfaces, *IEEE Computer*, Vol.27, No.5, pp.37-46.

Bhuiyan, S., J. E., & McCalla, G. I. (1992). Learning Recursion Through the Use of a Mental Model-based Programming Environment, *2nd International Conf. of Intelligent Tutoring Systems, Lectures Notes in Computer Science 608*, Springer-Verlag, pp.50-57.

Brown, J. S., & Burton, R. R. (1978). Diagnostic Models for Procedural Bugs in Basic Mathematical Skills, *Cognitive Science*, Vol.2, pp. 155-191.

Brown, J. S., Collins, A., & Duguid, P. (1989). Situated Cognition and the Culture of Learning. Educational Researcher, *Cognitive Science*, Vol.18, No.1, pp.32-42.

Chan, T. W. & Baskin, A. B. (1988). Learning Companion Systems, In C. Frasson & G. Gauthier (Eds.), *Intelligent Tutoring Systems: At the Crossroads of Artificial Intelligence and Education*, New Jersey: Ablex Pub. Co., pp.6-33.

Chan, T. W. (1996) A tutorial on social learning systems, *Emerging Computer Technologies in Education*, AACE.

Ellis, C., Globs, S. & Reline, G. (1991) Groupware: Some Issues and Experiences, *Comm. ACM*, Vol.34, No.1, pp.39-58.

Jehng, J. C., Shih, Y. F., Liang, S., & Chan, T. W. (1994). TurtleGraph: A Computer Supported Cooperative Learning Environment, *Proc. of World Conference on Educational Multimedia & Hypermedia*, Vancouver, Canada, AACE, pp. 292-298.

Liang, T., Lai, H., Chen N., & Wei, H. (1994) When Client/Server Isn't Enough: Coordinating Multiple Distributed Tasks, *IEEE Computer*, Vol.27, No.5, pp.73-79

Lai, J. A. (1994). *Contest-Kid: A Distributed Competitive Learning Environment.* Ms. thesis, Inst. of Comp. Science and Electronic Eng., National Central Univ., Taiwan.

De la modélisation d'un processus de coopération à la conception de systèmes coopératifs d'apprentissage

Pascal LEROUX, Martial VIVET

Laboratoire d'Informatique de l'Université du Maine
BP 535 - F 72017 LE MANS cedex - FRANCE

Résumé. Nous présentons dans ce texte nos travaux sur des systèmes coopératifs d'apprentissage. Leur spécificité se situe au niveau de l'assistance apportée par le système informatique aux utilisateurs dans un contexte d'apprentissage. L'assistance évolue en terme de degré d'intervention du système et de contenu, ceci de façon à rendre les apprenants plus autonomes au fil des activités. Nous avons défini un modèle de système coopératif d'apprentissage fondé sur la coopération entre des agents informatiques et humains au travers d'un module interface qui est le support de l'activité. Ce modèle a été mis en œuvre dans le cadre du développement d'un assistant pédagogique (ROBOTEACH) en alphabétisation à la technologie de contrôle pour des publics variés (élèves de collège, stagiaires de CAP, adultes en reconversion).

1. Introduction

Le Laboratoire d'Informatique de l'Université du Maine (France) développe des environnements d'apprentissage supports d'une pédagogie de projet dans des activités originales de construction et de conception (par groupes de deux ou trois apprenants) de micro-robots modulaires (Cf. fig. 1) [9]. L'ordinateur est utilisé dans ces situations pour piloter les micro-robots et, au travers du pilotage, pour amener les apprenants à comprendre le fonctionnement des micro-robots. Notre but est de concevoir des environnements permettant l'alphabétisation en direction de la productique. Cette alphabétisation s'adresse tant à la formation initiale dans le domaine de la technologie qu'à la reconversion d'ouvriers susceptibles de travailler dans des milieux robotisés.

Fig. 1. Exemple d'un micro-robot

Un premier environnement d'apprentissage a été créé dans ce contexte, sa mise en œuvre s'appuyant sur le concept de micromonde au sens de Papert [7]. Il est conçu sur la base d'un micromonde à deux facettes : l'une matérielle constituée de micro-robots de type Fischertechnik® et l'autre logicielle (LOGO) pour programmer et piloter les machines [11]. Cet environnement a fait l'objet d'expérimentations menées en partenariat avec des entreprises et les milieux de la formation professionnelle (projets de recherche QUADRATURE [11] et PLUME [12]).

Dans ce premier environnement d'apprentissage, l'ordinateur est l'exécutant des ordres que lui donne un groupe d'apprenants. Les expérimentations ont révélé des difficultés pour certains groupes à programmer les mouvements des micro-robots. Il nous est apparu nécessaire d'enrichir la tâche de l'environnement informatique pour que l'ordinateur ne soit plus uniquement un exécutant mais devienne aussi un assistant logiciel qui coopère avec le groupe afin d'aider les apprenants à piloter correctement les micro-robots. Nous avons développé un tel système : il se nomme ROBOTEACH [5]. Son architecture est fondée sur le principe d'intégration de systèmes coopératifs d'apprentissage coopérant avec un groupe d'apprenants dans le cadre d'activités liées à la programmation de mouvements et au pilotage de micro-robots.

L'objectif de nos travaux n'est pas de réaliser un système permettant la coopération entre des personnes (cas fréquents dans les recherches sur le *"groupware"* ou Computer-Supported Cooperative Work) mais de réaliser un système coopérant avec des hommes. C'est dans ce sens que nous employons par la suite les termes de coopération homme/machine, de système coopératif et système coopérant.

D'un point de vue du maître, ROBOTEACH est un assistant pédagogique logiciel qui permet de préparer et de gérer les activités d'un groupe d'apprenants. Le maître prépare les sessions en planifiant et en paramétrant les activités du groupe. Ces activités se déclinent sous la forme de navigation dans des livres électroniques sur les notions de base en technologie ou sous la forme de projets de conception, de construction et de pilotage de micro-robots. Nous avons conçu ROBOTEACH comme un partenaire du maître notamment au niveau de la gestion de ses interventions pédagogiques avec les apprenants [10]. Ces interventions se produisent dans deux cas distincts : soit le maître les a planifiées lors de la création de la session, soit le système fait appel au maître quand il ne sait plus répondre aux sollicitations du groupe d'apprenants dans les activités de projet (Cf. section 4.1).

Dans cet article, nous présentons d'abord, de notre point de vue, les spécificités des systèmes coopératifs d'apprentissage par rapport aux systèmes de coopération homme/machine traditionnels. Nous détaillons ensuite le modèle de système coopératif d'apprentissage que nous avons élaboré. Dans une troisième section, nous présentons une mise en œuvre de ce modèle dans l'application ROBOTEACH et enfin le paramétrage des systèmes coopératifs d'apprentissage par le maître.

2. Coopération Homme/Machine et Systèmes Coopératifs d'Apprentissage

La coopération abordée dans cet article se déroule dans un contexte particulier : l'apprentissage. Il ne s'agit pas seulement de coopérer pour résoudre une tâche mais aussi d'apprendre en coopérant avec la machine. C'est pourquoi il nous semble nécessaire de situer nos travaux par rapport aux recherches menées sur la coopération homme/machine.

2.1. Recherches en Coopération Homme/Machine

La recherche en coopération homme/machine s'attache principalement à développer des systèmes coopératifs qui font intervenir l'homme et l'ordinateur en prenant en compte les buts de l'homme, les forces et les faiblesses de l'homme et de l'ordinateur, ainsi que la nature et la structure de la tâche [4] (Woods et al. parlent de «*Joint Human-machine Cognitive Systems*» [13]). Ces systèmes ont pour objectif de permettre à l'homme et à la machine de réaliser des tâches que chacun pris séparément ne pourrait pas faire, ou ferait mal ou moins vite. «*La coopération consiste donc à amplifier les capacités des agents pris isolément et à augmenter leurs performances*» [3].

Dans les différents travaux du domaine, nous avons identifié trois types de systèmes coopératifs :
- les systèmes coopératifs de résolution de problèmes (exemples d'applications dans [4] et [6]). Le(s) problème(s) à résoudre est(sont) décomposé(s) en plusieurs tâches, chacune des tâches étant allouée à un des agents participant à la résolution [2]. Le contrôle de la résolution est assuré soit par l'utilisateur, soit par le système, soit par les deux.
- les systèmes de résolution de problèmes avec assistance coopérative (par exemple l'environnement d'aide à la conception architecturale JANUS [4]). Dans cette classe de systèmes, c'est l'utilisateur qui résout le problème et contrôle la coopération. L'assistance est soit demandée par l'utilisateur quand il en ressent le besoin, soit proposée par le système lorsque ce dernier détecte une erreur dans la résolution.
- les systèmes qui combinent les deux types précédents (Cf. [1] sur la conception d'un système coopératif intelligent pour la supervision d'un processus industriel dans le domaine nucléaire).

2.2. Spécificités des Systèmes Coopératifs d'Apprentissage

Les trois classes de systèmes coopératifs identifiées précédemment peuvent être utilisées en formation. Néanmoins nous pensons que les systèmes coopératifs en situation d'apprentissage ont une spécificité propre correspondant à une évolution de l'assistance.

En situation d'apprentissage, l'objectif d'un système coopératif est double. Il s'agit d'amener le ou les apprenant(s) à résoudre son(leur) problème tout en lui(leur) faisant acquérir des savoirs et savoir-faire qui le(les) rendront progressivement autonome(s). L'intérêt d'utiliser un système coopératif destiné à l'apprentissage (nous parlons alors de système coopératif d'apprentissage) est donc d'aider mais surtout de faire progresser les apprenants. Prenons comme exemple, le contexte de la micro-robotique pédagogique. Le groupe d'apprenants qui ne connaît rien aux micro-robots a besoin d'une assistance forte contrairement au groupe qui a manipulé plusieurs fois le matériel et a ainsi été confronté à diverses pannes. Cette assistance diminue au fil des activités (en fonction du comportement et des connaissances des apprenants) jusqu'à être réduite au strict minimum voire à disparaître.

Il est possible de faire évoluer l'assistance en agissant sur le degré d'intervention du système et sur le contenu de l'assistance. Nous avons identifié quatre degrés d'intervention du système sur l'échelle de graduation de l'assistance (Cf. fig. 2).

En modulant le contenu de l'assistance, le type de conseil donné au cours de la session se trouve modifié. Par exemple dans le cas du pilotage de micro-robots, les conseils portent sur l'utilisation de l'environnement de programmation/pilotage, la programmation des mouvements ou sur le diagnostic d'une panne mécanique ou électrique du micro-robot. Il suffit d'intervenir sur les connaissances présentes dans la base de connaissances d'assistance pour agir sur le type de conseil apporté et la part d'autonomie laissée aux apprenants.

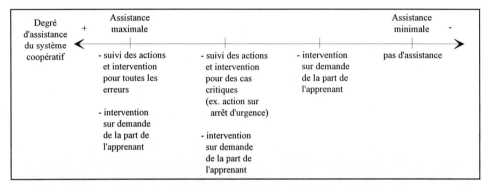

Fig. 2. Échelle des degrés d'assistance dans un système coopératif d'apprentissage

Nous avons envisagé plusieurs possibilités au niveau de la mise en œuvre de l'évolution de l'assistance : soit le système s'adapte aux profils et comportements des apprenants au cours de la séance, soit le maître, le système ou les deux, paramètrent avant la session l'assistance dans le système. Étant données les difficultés qui existent pour construire un modèle de l'élève [8] et le manque de connaissances pédagogiques dans le domaine de la micro-robotique pédagogique, nous avons instauré un paramétrage des systèmes coopératifs d'apprentissage par le maître (Cf. section 5). Cette solution nous a permis de développer un EIAO (Environnement Interactif d'Apprentissage avec Ordinateur) effectivement utilisé en situation d'apprentissage.

3. Modèle de Système Coopératif d'Apprentissage

Le modèle de système coopératif d'apprentissage (Cf. fig. 3) que nous avons élaboré est constitué :
- d'un module interface qui est le support de l'activité (par exemple les pages écran de description ; Cf. section 4.1) ;
- d'agents informatiques spécialisés (par exemple un agent générateur de programmes et un agent d'assistance à la description ; Cf. section 4.2).

Le module interface sert de média de communication entre les agents informatiques et humains (apprenants, maître). Les agents informatiques sont activés par le groupe d'apprenants au travers du module interface, ou en fonction d'événements survenant dans ce module (par exemple un clic sur le bouton d'arrêt d'urgence qui interrompt l'exécution de tous les mouvements du micro-robot). C'est toujours par l'intermédiaire de ce module qu'un agent informatique fait appel au maître quand il ne sait plus répondre aux sollicitations des apprenants. L'appel au maître peut se faire par affichage d'un message ou émission d'un signal.

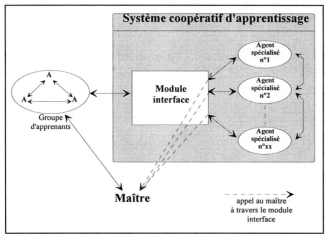

Fig. 3. Modélisation de la coopération dans le système coopératif d'apprentissage

Deux agents de même nature peuvent communiquer sans que les autres agents soient au courant. Par exemple les apprenants et le maître peuvent dialoguer entre eux, deux agents informatiques peuvent se transmettre un message.

Le module interface représente une partie des connaissances partagées entre les différents agents et fait partie du contexte commun aux agents. Dans ce modèle de coopération les actions entre les agents ne sont pas planifiées, mais elles interviennent en fonction des événements : la coopération émerge donc des interactions.

4. Mise en Œuvre du Modèle de Système Coopératif d'Apprentissage dans l'Application ROBOTEACH

L'originalité de ROBOTEACH, du point de vue des activités d'apprentissage, se situe au niveau de l'assistance apportée par le système à un groupe d'apprenants (deux à trois personnes) dans le cadre des activités de projets. Cette assistance est fondée sur une coopération entre ROBOTEACH et les apprenants. Dans cette section, nous présentons d'abord la modélisation de la coopération en projet puis l'environnement de description qui est une mise en œuvre du modèle du système coopératif d'apprentissage.

4.1. Modélisation de la Coopération en Projet

Dans le cadre d'une activité de projet, l'objectif du groupe d'apprenants est de concevoir, de construire et de faire fonctionner un micro-robot exécutant les tâches spécifiées dans un cahier des charges. Du point de vue du système, un projet s'articule autour de deux activités distinctes : la description d'une part et la programmation et le pilotage d'autre part. Voyons en détail la modélisation de la coopération entre le groupe d'apprenants et le système en situation de projet (Cf. fig. 4).

Le groupe d'apprenants connaît du point de vue mécanique le micro-robot qu'il a construit et les actions qu'il veut lui faire faire. Par contre, il ne sait pas créer les programmes qui lui permettent de piloter le micro-robot. Le système a des connaissances sur la génération des programmes et sur le diagnostic de pannes mécaniques et électriques des micro-robots. Par conséquent, le groupe d'apprenants et le système coopèrent afin d'aboutir au pilotage correct du micro-robot conçu.

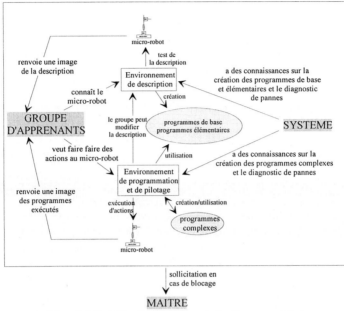

Fig. 4. Modélisation de la coopération en projet

La coopération se traduit par la séparation des tâches à effectuer. Le groupe d'apprenants a pour tâche de décrire le micro-robot au système à travers l'environnement de description et d'élaborer les programmes complexes[1] dans l'environnement de programmation/pilotage à partir des programmes de base[2] et les programmes élémentaires[3] générés par l'environnement de description. Quant au système, il génère, d'une part, les programmes de base et les programmes élémentaires à partir de la description donnée par les apprenants dans l'environnement de description et, d'autre part, assiste le groupe lors de la description ou de la création des programmes complexes.

L'assistance dans la phase de description consiste à apporter des conseils pour déterminer les pannes mécaniques ou électriques du micro-robot ou aider le groupe d'apprenants à retrouver les erreurs dans la description (par exemple un mauvais nom attribué à un moteur). Le diagnostic de pannes fait partie aussi de l'assistance dans

---

[1] Un programme complexe est composé d'une combinaison de programmes élémentaires et éventuellement de structures algorithmiques d'itération et/ou de répétition.

[2] Un programme de base permet d'activer ou d'arrêter une sortie (par exemple un moteur), ou de lire l'état d'une entrée (par exemple un interrupteur, une cellule photo-sensible).

[3] Un programme élémentaire assure l'exécution au niveau du micro-robot d'un mouvement élémentaire (mouvement permettant d'aller d'un interrupteur à un autre interrupteur, les deux interrupteurs étant associés à un même axe) ou d'une action élémentaire (par exemple l'activation d'un aimant, l'ouverture d'une pince).

l'environnement de programmation/pilotage. Un deuxième type d'assistance existe dans l'environnement de programmation/pilotage. Elle intervient lors de la création de programmes complexes pour déboguer les programmes créés par les apprenants ou aider à les construire.

Dans tous les cas de figure, lorsqu'il ne sait plus répondre aux sollicitations des apprenants, le système fait appel au maître pour débloquer la situation. C'est la contribution du maître à la coopération entre le système et les apprenants.

Le micro-robot manipulé est le centre d'intérêt du dispositif mais il n'intervient que d'une façon indirecte dans la coopération. Ce n'est pas un agent coopérant mais son comportement joue un rôle important dans la coopération. En effet, le test d'un élément de la description ou d'un programme se traduit par l'exécution d'une action au niveau du micro-robot. Si le résultat de l'action est positif (l'effet obtenu correspond à l'effet attendu), la partie de la description ou le programme testé est validé. Dans le cas inverse, la description ou le programme est remis en cause, impliquant des modifications voire une assistance de la part du système. Le micro-robot, par ses mouvements, renvoie une «*image*» de la description ou des programmes créés. Il agit en tant que révélateur des dysfonctionnements de la description, de la programmation et du pilotage.

Au niveau de ROBOTEACH, une activité de projet commence d'abord par une activité de description puis une activité de programmation/pilotage. Dans la deuxième phase, il est souvent nécessaire de revenir sur la description, pour corriger les erreurs ou modifier la description par rapport à des changements opérés sur la machine. C'est la raison pour laquelle il est possible de modifier la description à partir de l'environnement de programmation/pilotage. Toutes les modifications effectuées sur les programmes générés par l'environnement de description sont automatiquement répercutées dans l'environnement de programmation/pilotage.

Les environnements de description et de programmation/pilotage ont été développés à partir du modèle de système coopératif présenté dans la section 3. Nous présentons dans la section suivante la mise en œuvre de ce modèle dans le cadre de la réalisation de l'environnement de description.

4.2. Environnement de Description

L'architecture de l'environnement de description est constituée d'un module interface et de deux agents : un agent pour la génération automatique des programmes et un agent d'assistance à la description (Cf. fig. 5).

Le groupe d'apprenants décrit et teste sa description du micro-robot par l'intermédiaire du module interface. L'agent d'assistance à la description intervient à la demande du groupe ou dès la détection d'une erreur. Le degré d'assistance dépend du paramétrage effectué par le maître (Cf. section 5). Il donne des conseils en fonction de la description effectuée par le groupe et de ses connaissances générales en micro-robotique et/ou spécifiques au micro-robot manipulé. Cet agent est constitué d'un système expert utilisant un moteur d'inférences d'ordre 0 fonctionnant en chaînage avant, utilisant une base de règles, une base sur les problèmes que les apprenants peuvent rencontrer et une base de faits correspondant aux objets décrits dans les pages de description [5]. Quant à l'agent générateur de programme, il interagit avec le groupe d'apprenants dès que la description d'un axe ou d'un élément isolé est terminée.

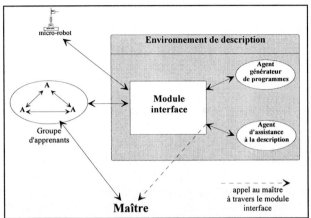

Fig. 5. Architecture de l'environnement de description

5. Paramétrage des Systèmes Coopératifs d'Apprentissage dans ROBOTEACH

Le bon fonctionnement d'un micro-robot passe par la description sans erreur du micro-robot et la création de programmes corrects de pilotage. Ces deux activités s'appuient sur une coopération entre un groupe d'apprenants et le système. Ce sont les diagnostics et les mises à jour des descriptions et des programmes face aux dysfonctionnements du micro-robot qui font évoluer la représentation que le système se construit du micro-robot ainsi que la représentation qu'a le groupe de sa machine.

Par ailleurs, les apprenants n'abordent pas la description et le pilotage de la même façon s'ils découvrent les micro-robots ou s'ils savent parfaitement comment ces machines sont composées. L'analyse du comportement des apprenants, face au micro-robot et à sa modélisation, doit par conséquent permettre la construction de nouvelles situations de remédiation ou de situations plus adaptées aux attentes du groupe. À terme la création de ces situations pourrait être réalisée par ROBOTEACH. Dans la configuration actuelle du système, c'est au maître de mettre en place ces situations.

Pour créer les sessions pédagogiques en adéquation avec ses objectifs, le maître dispose d'un générateur de sessions qui lui permet de planifier les activités et de paramétrer les systèmes coopératifs d'apprentissage que sont les environnements de description et de programmation/pilotage. Ce paramétrage consiste notamment à déterminer le degré d'intervention du système dans les phases d'assistance ainsi que le contenu des bases de connaissances des agents d'assistance.

6. Conclusion

Dans cet article, nous nous sommes attachés à présenter l'intérêt de développer la coopération homme/machine en créant des systèmes coopératifs d'apprentissage. Le paramétrage par le maître de l'évolution de l'assistance permet d'adapter les systèmes utilisés aux situations d'apprentissage en fonction des objectifs pédagogiques et des publics formés.

Le système ROBOTEACH a été développé avec le générateur d'applications ToolBook®. Il a été utilisé en situation réelle de formation pendant plus de 400 heures par des publics différents (Certificat d'Aptitude Professionnelle en Électricité Équipement Industriel, ouvriers en reconversion), et est en cours de test avec des élèves de collèges et d'écoles primaires (Cf. [5] pour une description complète de ROBOTEACH et des expérimentations). L'application a été accueillie avec beaucoup d'enthousiasme tant par les stagiaires que par les formateurs. Une grille d'évaluation a permis de montrer la fiabilité du système et son intérêt dans des contextes de formation distincts.

L'étude présentée dans cet article est orientée vers la réalisation d'un système utilisé dans le contexte d'alphabétisation à la technologie. Néanmoins, les caractéristiques mises en évidence pourraient être transposables pour des applications à d'autres domaines tels que l'électronique, la physique, l'automatisme.

7. Références Bibliographiques

1. Brézillon, P., Cases, E.: Cooperating for assisting intelligently operators. Proceedings of the International Workshop on the Design of Cooperative Systems. Juan Les Pins, France, (january 1995) 370-384
2. De Greef, H. P., Breuker, J. A.: Analysing system-user cooperation in KADS. Knowledge Acquisition 4 (1992) 89-108
3. Ferber, J.: Coopération réactive et émergence. Revue Intellectica n°2 (1994) 19-52
4. Fischer, G.: Communication requirements for cooperative problem solving systems. Informations Systems Vol. 15 n°1 (1990) 21-36
5. Leroux, P.: Conception et réalisation d'un système coopératif d'apprentissage - Étude d'une double coopération : maître/ordinateur et ordinateur/groupe d'apprenants. Thèse de Doctorat de l'Université Paris 6, spécialité Informatique (1995)
6. Oddy, R. N.: Information retrieval through man-machine dialogue. Journal of documentation 33(1) (1977) 1-14
7. Papert, S.: Jaillissement de l'esprit. Editions Flammarion (1981)
8. Self, J. A.: Bypassing the intractable problem of student modelling. Actes du congrès ITS-88 (1988) 18-24
9. Vivet, M.: Pilotage de micro-robots sous LOGO : un outil pour sensibiliser les personnels de l'industrie à la robotique. A l'école des robots (diffusée par la robothèque du Cesta). 5ème symposium canadien sur la technologie pédagogique, Ottawa (1986) 195-210
10. Vivet, M.: Uses of ITS : which role for the teacher ?. New Directions for Intelligent Tutoring Systems. NATO ASI series vol. F91, Springer-Verlag (1990) 171-182
11. Vivet, M., Parmentier, C.: Low qualified adults in computer integrated enterprise : an example of in service training. TRAINING : from Computer Aided Design to Computer Integrated Enterprise. IFIP TC3/WG3.4. Alesund, Norway (1991)
12. Vivet, M., Leroux, P., Hubert, O., Morandeau, J., Parmentier, C.: Teleassistance of Trainees in an SME : A Case Study. Teleteaching (A-29). Elsevier Science Publishers B.V. (North-Holland) (1993) 907-914
13. Woods, D. D., Roth, E. M., Bennett, K.: Explorations in Joint Human-Machine Cognitive Systems. Cognition, Computing and Cooperation. Ablex, Norwood NJ (1990) 123-158

Modelling Dialogue and Beliefs as a Basis for Generating Guidance in a CSCL Environment

Kristine Lund[1], Michael Baker[1] and Monique Baron[2]

[1] C.N.R.S.-GRIC-COAST, ENSL, France. lund@ens-lyon.fr, mbaker@ens-lyon.fr

[2] LAFORIA, Université Pierre et Marie Curie, Paris, France. baron@laforia.ibp.fr

Abstract. Existing approaches to integrating ITS and CSCL environments have not attempted to model the *collaborative interaction* between human learners in order to exploit its pedagogical potential. We present an approach to modelling such interactions and students' underlying beliefs, within the framework of a CSCL environment designed for learning the concept of energy in physics (C-CHENE). The environment is based on *flexible structuring* of the collaborative interaction using a specially designed communication interface, and a dialogue grammar. We propose three types of automatic guidance that could be provided on this basis.

1 Introduction

Although CSCL designers have usually concentrated on designing tools for collaborative interaction, some attempts have been made to integrate aspects of AI and Education research into collaborative educational environments (e.g. [6], [10], [13]). Nevertheless, these systems have not yet attempted to exploit the pedagogical potential of the *interaction* between human learners. The goal of this paper is therefore to describe an approach to modelling the interaction between collaborative human learners and their underlying beliefs, with a view to generating guidance within the framework of an architecture of a CSCL environment called "C-CHENE"[1], designed for teaching the concept of energy in physics.

We view the students' collaborative interaction both as a source from which students' beliefs can be (partially) inferred, and as a 'domain' to be modelled and 'tutored' in its own right. The latter depends on identifying and encouraging the occurrence of interaction forms that favour learning, such as "giving reasons/explanations [7], joint participation and productive resolution of conflicts. Our approach - termed *flexible structuring* - involves constraining the students' interaction by providing a limited set of dialogue moves (in the form of buttons or menu items to be selected), whose design was based on analysis of 'free' network interactions and explicit models of collaborative dialogue ([5], [1]). Use of particular dialogue moves is not however *enforced*, as in approaches based on interaction "scripting" (e.g. [22]), or normative dialogue grammars [18]. This leaves open the question as to *when* a particular form of the interaction should be imposed automatically by the system. More generally, such a communication interface based on graphical interaction lightens students' typing load, thus enabling them to concentrate on a more knowledge-based interaction. From the system's point of view, some natural language understanding problems can be avoided.

After describing the general architecture of C-CHENE, we focus on two of its components : the communication interface, with its underlying dialogue model, and

---

[1] "C-CHENE" = Collaborative "CHaîne ENErgétique"/"Energy Chain".

belief inference mechanisms. In conclusion we describe automatic guidance strategies that could operate on the basis of these components, and describe future work.

2 C-CHENE - a CSCL Environment for Learning Modelling in Physics

C-CHENE was developed as an experimental CSCL environment, within the framework of a long-term research project on teaching and (collaborative) learning of modelling in physics. Previous research has been carried out on analysing and AI modelling of students' modelling processes ([21], [9], [4]).

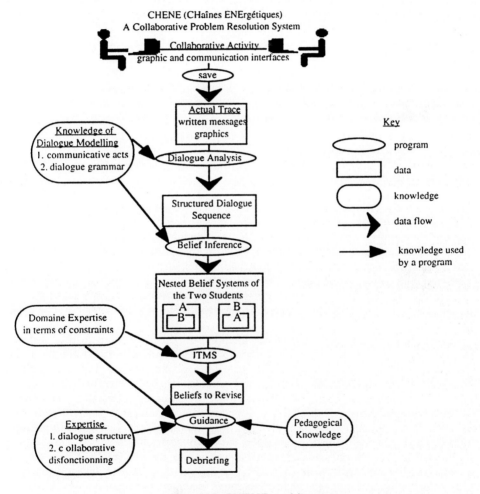

Fig. 1 C-CHENE architecture

The task studied requires students (16-17 years old) to (co-)construct qualitative models for energy storage, transfer and transformation for simple experiments ("energy chains")[2], using a specially designed graphical interface. Students worked in pairs at a distance in a network (SUN / ShowMe), each having their own physics experiment available, a text describing the problems to be solved, as well as the same graphical and specially designed communication interfaces projected simultaneously onto his/her personal computer screen.

The architecture of C-CHENE can be understood by following the data flow from the top to the bottom of Figure 1. Collaborative activity is carried out within the communication and graphic (energy chain construction) interfaces (see Figure 2). The resulting student interaction (communicative acts - "CA"s) and energy chain constructions (graphical interface actions) are written to a file as they occur. The full trace of the collaborative problem-solving activity is then structured according to a normative dialogue grammar (see §3). Dialogue analysis and belief inference is begun *at the end of a problem-solving session*. Beliefs are inferred on the assumption that graphical interface actions imply agents' beliefs in the change of state produced, and on the basis of standard sincerity conditions and effects of CAs, with their relations to the previous interaction.

Students' beliefs spaces are then entered into a JTMS [11]. Any incoherencies with the theory of energy in physics are tagged. Opportunities for providing guidance are then identified based on the structured trace, the dialogue grammar and representations of the students' belief systems (see §5).

3 Designing and Modelling the Collaborative Problem-solving Interaction

Figure 2 shows the communication interface (redrawn - the original is in French). The upper section of the screen shows the area for energy chain construction (with appropriate menus), and the lower the communication area. The lower part of the communication area contains a set of buttons to be used by both students for performing different communicative acts, and the upper part the ongoing interaction history displayed for the students. The interaction history is viewed as an important resource in collaborative dialogue since it provides a common objective reference to previous activity that may encourage reflection and more effective collaboration ([8], [15]).

Providing a limited set of buttons was intended to ease the typing load as well as encourage the students to engage in certain preferred communicative activities (e.g. using the [Because ...] button to give reasons and explanations for intermediary solutions). It was not obvious to us that the students would be able to introspect on and 'classify' their own communicative actions. Analysis of interaction transcripts, however, showed that the [I think that ...] button (a 'catch-all') was used infrequently, and that where students could type free text, the communicative act actually realised corresponded generally to that stipulated by the CA button concerned.

The set of CA buttons provided was designed on the basis of analysis of a corpus of 'chat-box' interactions with C-CHENE using existing models for conversation [16], information dialogues [5] and collaborative problem-solving dialogues [1].

---

[2] See upper part of Figure 2 for an (erroneous) example of an energy chain constructed by two students for a circuit where a bulb is connected to a battery by two wires.

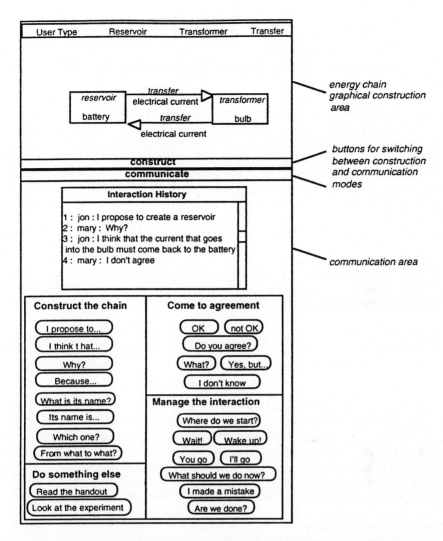

energy chain
graphical construction
area

buttons for switching
between construction
and communication
modes

communication area

Fig. 2 C-CHENE communication and graphics interfaces

Three fundamental distinctions are drawn upon in the design of the interface :

(1) *Task-oriented* CAs, whose primary function is to accomplish the dialogue-external task (e.g. transfer of information, problem-solving), are distinguished from *dialogue control* CAs, whose function is to keep the dialogue itself 'on track' (e.g. attitudinal reactions such as [Ok] or [Not Ok], perception and understanding, dialogue structuring such as opening and closing). This distinction is reflected in the organisation of the two basic columns of buttons in the communication interface (task-oriented = left column ; dialogue control = right column).

(2) *Initiative / reactive* CAs. This distinction is reflected in the different types of *semantic content* of CAs. Initiative acts, such as [I propose to ...], or [Its name is ...] generally introduce a new *propositional* content, determined here by selection on a hierarchical set of menus that are displayed once the CA button is clicked (e.g.

following [I propose to ...], the student can select one of {<create a reservoir>, <create a transformer>, ...}). Other acts refer either to *the dialogue itself* (e.g. [Are we done ?]), or, in the case of *reactive* CAs, to propositions expressed in previous CAs (e.g. [Why?]). Finally, some CAs have a content that is a (presently unanalysed) free text string (e.g. [I think that...]).

(3) We draw on the well-known distinction between different types of *illocutionary acts* (e.g. QUESTION function, REQUEST function, ASSERTION function, etc.), each of which has specific sincerity conditions and effects on the dialogue context.

In terms of these three distinctions, the specific CA "[I propose to ...]<create a reservoir>" is, for example, *task-oriented* (it aims to achieve the problem-solving task), *initiative* (it does not *react* to a previous CA), and has an OFFER communicative function (see [1]). Its most characteristic sincerity condition is : "Speaker believes that if Hearer accepts that Speaker performs action p, then Speaker will perform it".

However, the standard attitudes underlying CAs, considered in isolation from their insertion in the dialogue sequence, are insufficient for inferring all the relevant attitudes, precisely because certain acts *relate* to previous ones. Consider Figure 3, taken from a collaborative problem-solving session involving real students.

```
1: A : [I propose to...] <create a transfer>
2: B : [Why?]
3: A : [ I think that...] "the current that goes into the bulb must come back to the battery"
4: B : [I don't agree]
```

Fig. 3 Example dialogue sequence

Apart from the problem of determining the identity of the transfer mentioned in line 1, should the system assume from line 4 that student B *does not agree* with the *reason* student A gives for the proposed transfer creation, or rather that the student does agree with the reason given, but *not* that it constitutes a justification of the first proposal. This example illustrates the necessity of maintaining a relational if not hierarchical representation of a dialogue ([14], [16]) from which a system can infer beliefs. Awaiting construction of such a complete representation, this necessity can be obviated in part by constraining the *possible* relations using a normative dialogue grammar, as described below.

Although it is highly questionable as to whether there could be a *descriptive* grammar of dialogue (see e.g. [12]), it is nevertheless possible to define a *normative* one, i.e. one to which a given natural dialogue is expected, or constrained, to conform. In our case, such a normative grammar is designed to constrain the students to certain forms of interaction that favour *learning* (in conjunction with the guidance generation module), and to facilitate inference of students' beliefs. We therefore term the grammar "Dialogue For Learning" (DFL).

current CA under analysis	possible relations to previous CA's
ASSERT	ASSERT, OFFER, REQUEST
OFFER	OFFER
REQUEST	ASSERT, OFFER

Fig. 4 Selected examples of relations between communicative acts

DFL is largely based on Sitter & Stein's [20] ATN-network for information-seeking dialogues. The edges in the network are the communicative acts available in C-CHENE's communication interface. Figure 4 shows part of the grammar ; the first column shows the current CA under analysis, and the second a set of CAs produced in the previous dialogue to which it could relate. In traversing the network, the system gathers some of the *relations* between the communicative acts in the dialogue.

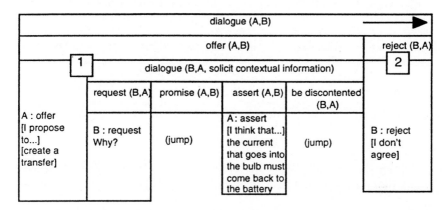

Fig. 5 Representation of dialogue grammar relations shown in Figure 4

Figure 5 shows relations between CAs for the example dialogue sequence of Figure 3, in the formalism of Sitter and Stein (op.cit.). The relevant part of the DFL is, however, insufficient *alone* to establish precisely these relations, since the grammar only defines a *space* of previous CAs to which the current one could relate. Thus, for example, the REQUEST of line 2 (Figure 3) could, according to Figure 4, relate back to either an ASSERT or an OFFER. In this case, given that only *this* sequence is being analysed, the OFFER (line 1) is selected as the only possibility. On other occasions, heuristics must be used to select between alternatives. For example, the ASSERT of line 3 is assumed to be providing the information requested in line 2, rather than being an assertion that elaborates on the offer of 1, since 2 is more *recent*.

4 Inferring and Maintaining Students' Beliefs

The beliefs that could be inferred from the example dialogue sequence in Figure 3 are shown in Figure 6. For example, the last column last line (inferred from line 4 in Figure 3) shows that C-CHENE has no information concerning student B's beliefs about the object "current". In addition, C-CHENE believes that student B *does not* believe that transfer3 should go from the bulb to the battery. The first column and line reflects the fact that student A is aware of student B's beliefs.

C-CHENE represents beliefs attributed to each of the students, including those that the students are held to ascribe to each other. Beliefs are nested in the manner described by Ballim and Wilks [2], each belief being grouped according to the topic of its proposition and the agent who possesses it. Without natural language interpretation, DFL is unable to tag *all* relevant justifications as such. The beliefs and justifications that *are* inferred (propositions or text strings) are placed into a dependency network using a JTMS.

System C-CHENE's beliefs...	
... about student A's beliefs	... about student B's beliefs
1 : B_A((transfer3	1: $B_B(B_A$((transfer3
(is-a-transfer(transfer3))))	(is-a-transfer(transfer3)))))
3: B_A((transfer3	3: $B_B(B_A$((transfer3
(is-object(transfer3,current))	(is-object(transfer3,current))
(goes-from(transfer3,bulb))	(goes-from(transfer3,bulb))
(goes-to(transfer3,battery))))	(goes-to(transfer3,battery)))))
4: $B_A(B_B$((is-object(transfer3,?	4: B_B((is-object(transfer3,?
(~B_B(goes-from(transfer3,bulb))	~B_B(goes-from(transfer3,bulb))
(~B_B(goes-to(transfer3,battery))))))))	~B_B(goes-to(transfer3,battery)))))

Fig. 6 The students' beliefs inferred from the dialogue example

Several problems for students' belief modelling in CSCL, well identified for student modelling in classical ITS systems (see e.g. [3], [19]), must be dealt with, such as :
• modification of a student's belief space after (s)he changes his/her mind ;
• modification of a student's belief space subsequent to different types of guidance ;
• ramifications of the above modifications for the rest of the belief space.

The beliefs inferred by C-CHENE are necessarily incomplete which means that any guidance based on this inference must necessarily be non-directive or negotiative [17].

5 Guidance Strategies

We propose three main bases on which these architectural components could be used for generating guidance :

(1) *domain-related beliefs* - detecting and pointing out "no-goods" between students' beliefs and the domain-rules for modelling energy in physics ;

(2) *collaborative interaction forms* - 'preferring' interactions where for example :
• both partners make relatively equal contributions to problem solving,
• partners propose explanations for intermediary problem solutions (externalisation reflection -> cognitive change),
• domain-related CAs occur to a greater extent than interaction-control CAs.

(3) *communication problems* - helping to resolve 'discrepancies' between students' models of each others' beliefs (miscomprehensions), from the system's point of view.

In addition, the display of the dialogue history provided for students can be exploited here, since failure to take into account previous statements or actions in the ongoing discussion can be pointed out.

6 Conclusions and Further Work

At the present state of our research, the new communication interface, specially adapted to the architecture of C-CHENE, has been implemented and experimented with groups of students. The set of communicative acts has been defined and represented, as has the dialogue grammar. An experimental belief system has been implemented, and appropriate belief inference and maintenance mechanisms are still being specified, in close relation with analysis of the dialogue transcripts produced in the experiments. So far we have nevertheless been able to progress with specification of the complete architecture and to identify some of the major research problems to be addressed, including the identification of relations between dialogue utterances and the implications of this problem for belief inference. These are difficult problems given that most existing work on belief system already assumes beliefs to be derived, and thus concentrates on the internal maintenance mechanisms. Our future research will therefore concentrate on refining the existing belief inference and maintenance techniques, and on developing/evaluating the above mentioned mechanisms for detecting opportunities for providing educational guidance.

Acknowledgements

We would like to thank members of the COAST research team for assistance in carrying out experiments with students, and Andrée Tiberghien for comments on an earlier draft. This research is financed by the C.N.R.S and is based in part on K. Lund's DEA thesis, supervised by M. Baker and M. Baron.

References

1. Baker, M.: A Model for Negotiation in Teaching-Learning Dialogues. *Journal of Artificial Intelligence in Education*, 5 (2), (1994) 199-254.
2. Ballim. A., & Wilks, Y.: *Artificial Believers, The Ascription of Belief*. Hillsdale, New Jersey : Lawrence Erlbaum Associates. (1991)
3. Baron, M.: Quelques problèmes de nonmonotonie en EIAO, *Actes du 1er Colloque Européen Intelligence Artificielle et Formation*. Applica 88, (1988) 143-155.
4. Bental, D., Brna, P.: Enabling Abstractions: Key Steps in Building Physics Models. *The Proceedings of Artificial Intelligence in Education*, August, Washington, D.C. (1995) 162-169.
5. Bunt, H.C.: Information Dialogues as Communicative Action in Relation to Partner Modelling and Information Processing. In M.M. Taylor, F. Néel, D.G. Bouwhuis (Eds.), Human Factors in Information Technology 4, *The Structure of Multimodal Dialogue*. Amsterdam: Elsevier Science Publishers B.V. (1989)
6. Chan, T.W., Chou, C.Y., Lee, M.F., Chang, M.H.: Reciprocal-tutoring-kids: Tutor-tutee role playing systems. *The Proceedings of Artificial Intelligence in Education*, August, Washington, D.C. (1995) 226-233.
7. Chi, M.T.H., Bassok, M., Lewis, M.W., Reimann, P. & Glaser, R.: Self-explanations : How Students Study and Use Examples in Learning to Solve Problems. *Cognitive Science* 13 (2). (1989) 145-182.
8. Collins, A. & Brown, J.S.: The computer as a tool for learning through reflection. In H. Mandl & A. Lesgold (eds.) *Learning Issues for Intelligent Tutoring Systems*, (1988) pp. 1-18, New York : Springer Verlag.
9. Devi, R., Tiberghien, A, Baker, M., & Brna, P.: Modelling students' construction of energy models in physics. *Instructional Science*. (to appear)

10. Dillenbourg, P. & Self, J.: A computational approach to socially distributed cognition. *European Journal of Psychology of Education*, 7 (4), (1992) 353-372.
11. Doyle, J.: A Truth Maintenance System. *Artificial Intelligence* 12. (1979) 231-272.
12. Good, D.A.: The Viability of Conversational Grammars. In M.M. Taylor, F. Néel, D.G. Bouwhuis (Eds.), Human Factors in Information Technology 4, *The Structure of Multimodal Dialogue*. Amsterdam: Elsevier Science Publishers B.V. (1989)
13. Hoppe, H.U.: The Use of Multiple Student Modeling to Parametrize Group Learning. *The Proceedings of Artificial Intelligence in Education*, August, Washington, D.C. (1995) 234-249.
14. Joab, M.: Modélisation d'un dialogue pédagogique en langage naturel. (Thése de Doctorat, Université de Paris VI, Paris) (1990).
15. Katz, S. & Lesgold, A.: The role of the tutor in computer-based collaborative learning situations. In S. Lajoie & S. Derry (eds.) *Computers as Cognitive Tools*. Hillsdale NJ : Lawrence Erlbaum Associates (1993).
16. Moeschler, J.: *Argumentation et Conversation : Eléments pour une analyse pragmatique du discours*. Paris : Crédif-Hatier (1985).
17. Moyse, R. & Elsom-Cook, M.T.: *Knowledge Negotiation*. London : Academic Press. (1992)
18. Okamoto, T., Inaba, A., Hasaba, Y.: The Intelligent Learning Support System on the Distributed Cooperative Environment. *Proceedings of Artificial Intelligence in Education*, August, Washington, D.C. (1995) 588.
19. Paiva, A., Self, J., Hartley, R.: On the Dynamics of Learner Models. *Proceedings of ECAI*. (1994) 178-182.
20. Sitter, S., & Stein, A.: Modeling the illocutionary aspects of information-seeking dialogues. *Information Processing & Management*. 28 (2) (1992) 165-180.
21. Tiberghien, A. & Megalakaki, O.: Contribution to a characterisation of a modelling activity case of a first qualitative approach of energy concept. *European Journal of Psychology of Education*. (to appear)
22. Webb, N.M.: Task Related Verbal Interaction and Mathematical Learning in Small Groups. *Research in Mathematics Education*. 22 (5) (1991) 366-389.

MONACO_T:
Un MOdèle à NAture COopérative pour la représentation de Tâches coopératives dans un STI

Serge Tadié Guepfu[1], Bernard Lefebvre[2], Claude Frasson[1]

[1]Université de Montréal, Case postale 6128, succursale Centre-Ville, Montréal (Québec), H3C 3J7, CANADA

[2]Université du Québec à Montréal, Case postale 8888, succursale Centre-Ville, Montréal (Québec), H3C 3P8, CANADA

tadie@iro.umontreal.ca, lefebvre.bernard@uqam.ca, frasson@iro.umontreal

Résumé

MONACO_T utilise un ensemble de moyens de structuration et de représentation des connaissances (règles, graphes, couches) pour permettre une modélisation des tâches coopératives de conception qui soit utilisable pour un système tuteur intelligent. Dans ce modèle, une tâche est constituée d'une dimension statique et d'une dimension dynamique. La dimension statique représente les liens de composition existants entre tâches et sous-tâches. La dimension dynamique quant à elle représente la description du comportement général de la tâche. La dimension statique est représentée par une structure de graphe classique, alors que la dynamique de la tâche est représentée grâce à l'introduction de bases de règles dans chaque noeud d'un graphe qui est isomorphe au graphe de la statique.

Mots clés: STI, représentation des connaissances, modélisation de la tâche coopérative.

1. Introduction

Lorsqu'on construit un modèle de tâche coopérative destiné à être enseigné par un Système Tutoriel Intelligent (STI), on doit s'organiser pour que ce modèle permette de garder la structure cognitive de la tâche coopérative, soit capable de présenter une vue globale de la tâche coopérative et facilite la génération d'explications pouvant être utilisées par un conseiller, un critique, ou toutes autres stratégies d'apprentissage.

Les travaux coopératifs sur lesquels nous nous penchons sont des travaux d'équipe. Dans ce contexte, chaque membre de l'équipe de travail doit maîtriser d'une part les actions à faire au niveau du poste qu'il occupe dans l'équipe et d'autre part l'intégration de ses actions dans le processus de la tâche collective. Un STI orienté dans l'enseignement du travail coopératif doit répondre à ces deux objectifs.

Dans les STI classiques qui sont consacrés à l'enseignement de tâches individuelles, plusieurs modèles de tâches ont été proposés. Il s'agit en l'occurrence de GUIDON [3], des tâches génériques [2], du modèle de Kieras [1], de la couche tâche dans le modèle KADS [8] ou encore du graphe de tâche utilisé dans le projet SAFARI [4]. Ces modèles sont efficaces dans les STI, mais ne sont pas adaptés pour les tâches coopératives.

L'univers des systèmes multi-agents, a donné naissance à des modèles de tâches coopératives [7], [5]. Ces modèles de tâches sont orientés agent, car ils donnent la priorité de la modélisation à la structure de l'agent. Avec cette approche, la structure cognitive de toute la tâche coopérative est dispersée dans les différents agents chargés de réaliser la tâche. Ces modèles sont donc orientés vers la simulation et la réalisation de tâche coopérative. Ils sont en général structurés sous la forme de boîte de verre ou de boîte noire. Dans le premier cas, les explications peuvent être données mais la structure cognitive de la tâche n'est pas conservée. Dans le second cas, les explications ne peuvent même pas être générées.

Dans le cadre de cet article, nous proposons un modèle de représentation de tâches coopératives utilisable dans un STI. Les tâches que nous modélisons sont des tâches de manipulation de concepts par opposition aux tâches de manipulation de systèmes sur lesquelles ont travaillé Kieras et Djamen. Ce sont des tâches abstraites, comme la prise de décision en fonction d'un certain nombre de paramètres, qui n'exigent pas la modélisation d'un système physique doté d'un comportement propre.

Nous allons d'abord décrire le modèle MONACO_T et ensuite, nous verrons comment il prend en considération la dimension coopérative de la tâche.

2.   Spécification d'une modélisation de la tâche

Dans le domaine des tâches coopératives, deux approches de modélisation sont possibles: modélisation orientée agent (utilisée dans les systèmes multi-agents) et modélisation orientée tâche (utilisée dans les STI classiques). Cette dernière donne la priorité à l'analyse cognitive de la tâche avant d'y greffer les différents agents chargés de réaliser la tâche.

La structure cognitive de la tâche est largement utilisée dans le cadre des STI pour contrôler l'activité, donner des conseils, répondre aux questions relatives à la tâche ou évaluer la performance. Pour cette raison, nous allons utiliser une approche orientée tâche dans notre modèle (Figure 1).

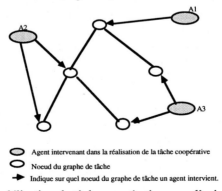

⬭ Agent intervenant dans la réalisation de la tâche coopérative
⬮ Noeud du graphe de tâche
➤ Indique sur quel noeud du graphe de tâche un agent intervient.

Figure 1: Modélisation de tâche coopérative avec l'orientation tâche

Dans MONACO_T, décrire une tâche coopérative consiste donc dans un premier temps à modéliser la tâche en se souciant uniquement de la structure cognitive de la tâche sans s'intéresser aux interactions entre les acteurs de la coopération et par la suite à spécifier la ressource qui doit effectuer chaque action.

Notre approche de modélisation considère deux couches qui distinguent, d'une part les propriétés d'une tâche coopérative qui constituent ses caractéristiques intrinsèques, et d'autre part le comportement de cette tâche lors de son exécution. Ces deux couches sont respectivement la statique et la dynamique de la tâche (Figure 2):

∘ la statique représente la structure arborescente de la décomposition de la tâche en sous-tâches; on parle de décomposition statique ou physique,

• la dynamique représente le comportement de la tâche en phase d'exécution avec la génération et l'utilisation d'événements se produisant au niveau de chaque sous-tâche.

Nous précisons dans ce qui suit les caractéristiques de ces deux couches.

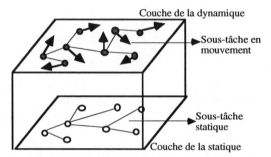

Figure 2: Modélisation d'une tâche sous forme de deux couches

2.1. Description de la statique

La plupart des modèles qui permettent de générer des explications sont des cas particuliers du modèle GOMS (Goals, Operators, Methods, and Selection Rules). Nous citerons par exemple la structuration des tâches dans SHERLOCK [6], le modèle de tâche de Kieras ou encore le graphe de tâche dans le projet SAFARI. Au niveau de la statique, cette approche considère que:

• une tâche est décomposée en sous-tâches,

• le résultat de la décomposition est une arborescence,

• seules les feuilles de cette arborescence sont les opérations de la tâche (sous-tâches opérationnelles), les autres noeuds de l'arborescence représentent des tâches abstraites (buts ou sous-tâches abstraites)

Dans MONACO_T nous empruntons au modèle GOMS la décomposition d'une tâche en une arborescence de sous tâches. Les différences que notre approche a avec le modèle GOMS sont les suivantes:

• Une tâche n'est pas un but abstrait à atteindre, mais représente une action à réaliser. Lorsque cette tâche est décomposable, son action consiste en la composition des résultats produits par ses sous-tâches.

• Il n'y a pas de notion de sous-tâches abstraites et de sous-tâches opérationnelles (toutes les sous-tâches sont opérationnelles car représentent une action).

- Il y a une prise en considération de la possibilité d'une exécution coopérative de la tâche (par l'introduction de postes de travail au niveau de chaque sous-tâche).

La notion de composition telle que nous l'entendons est une notion vaste et complexe qui peut aller de la simple juxtaposition des résultats produits par les sous-tâches composantes, à une combinaison complexe des résultats produits par ces sous-tâches.

Si nous voulons comparer les modèles de type GOMS avec le modèle MONACO_T, nous dirons qu'un modèle GOMS est un modèle MONACO_T où toutes les sous-tâches abstraites ont comme action de composition la juxtaposition des résultats produits par leurs sous-tâches. Dans le cas d'une tâche de manipulation de système, les modèles GOMS suffisent pour représenter l'analyse cognitive de la tâche, alors que dans les tâches de manipulation de concepts, l'analyse cognitive de la tâche est difficilement représentable en GOMS.

Un exemple de tâche coopérative décomposable dans le milieu est représenté ci-dessous (Figure 3).

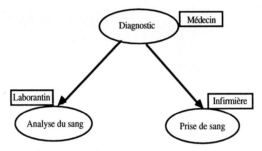

Figure 3: Exemple de tâche coopérative

Cette décomposition hiérarchique se lit: pour faire un diagnostic, on a besoin des résultats de l'analyse du sang et de la prise de sang.

Chaque noeud au niveau de la statique possède un ensemble de propriétés: *nom*, *description*, *méthode de réalisation* (qui décrit comment réaliser l'action de la sous-tâches), *liste de résultats* possibles (utile pour spécifier la dynamique), *méthode d'évaluation* (permet d'évaluer les apprenants), *poste de travail* (ressource).

Définition formelle de la statique.

Une tâche à la norme MONACO_T est structurée sous forme de trois ensembles: un ensemble de postes de travail (E_{pt}), un ensemble de sous-tâches (E_{st}), et un ensemble d'actions (E_a). Dans l'exemple de la Figure 3, E_{pt}={Médecin, Laborantin, Infirmière}, E_{st}={Diagnostic, PriseDeSang, AnalyseDeSang}, E_a={Diagnostiquer, PréleverLeSang, AnalyserLeSang}.

Cardinalité de E_a = cardinalité de E_{st}

1:Relation Propriétaire d'action: P_a

Cette relation permet de désigner pour chaque action, la sous-tâche où elle va évoluer.

$\forall x \in E_{st}, \forall y \in E_a$, $x\, P_a\, y \Leftrightarrow$ y est l'action à réaliser dans la sous-tâche x.

La relation (P_a, E_{st}, E_a) définit une fonction bijective.

2:Relation de composition: Ω

Cette relation permet de construire l'arborescence des sous-tâches par une méthode de décomposition basée sur le fait que pour s'exécuter, une sous-tâche a besoin des résultats produits par d'autres sous-tâches.

$\forall x, y \in E_{st}, \quad x\Omega y \Leftrightarrow$: y entre dans la composition de x .

Exemple: Diagnostic Ω AnalyseDeSang

La relation (Ω, E_{st}, E_{st}) définit une arborescence de sous-tâches.

3:Relation Propriétaire de sous-tâches: P_{st}

Cette relation permet de distribuer les différentes actions ou sous-tâches à l'ensemble des postes de travail chargés de réaliser la tâche coopérative.

$\forall x \in E_{pt}, \forall y \in E_{st}, x P_{st} y \Leftrightarrow$ y est est une sous-tâche du poste de travail x.

Exemple: Médecin P_{st} Diagnostic.

À partir de la relation (P_{st}, E_{pt}, E_{st}) on définit une fonction surjective $\Phi: E_{st} \rightarrow E_{pt} / \Phi(x) = y \ ssi \ y P_{st} x$.

Contraintes de constructions:

1: $\forall x, y \in E_{st}, \quad si \ \exists a \in E_{st} / x\Omega a \ et \ y\Omega a$ alors a est dupliqué en

$$a_1 \ et \ a_2, et \ on \ a: x\Omega a_1 \ et \ y\Omega a_2$$

Si deux sous-tâches x et y dépendent d'une sous-tâche a, x et y doivent avoir chacune une copie de la sous-tâche a. Ceci est utile pour la construction de la relation de composition qui doit avoir une structure arborescente.

2: $\forall x, y, z \in E_{st}, \quad si \ x\Omega y \ et \ y\Omega z \ et \ x\Omega z \quad alors$ on supprime $x\Omega z$. Ceci veut dire que MONACO_T ne prend en considération que les dépendances directes.

3: $\forall x \in E_{st}, \quad \exists! \ a \in E_a / x P_a a$. En d'autres termes, chaque sous-tâche est propriétaire d'une et une seule action.

4: $\forall a \in E_a, si \ \exists x, y \in E_{st} / \quad x P_a a \ et \ y P_a a \Leftrightarrow x = y$. En d'autres termes, une action est la propriété d'une et une seule sous-tâche.

Pour construire cette couche de la statique, nous avons créé un éditeur de base de tâche coopérative. L'interface de cet éditeur se présente sous la forme d'un fouineur, il permet de lancer aussi bien les modules de saisie de la dynamique que ceux de la statique (Figure 4).

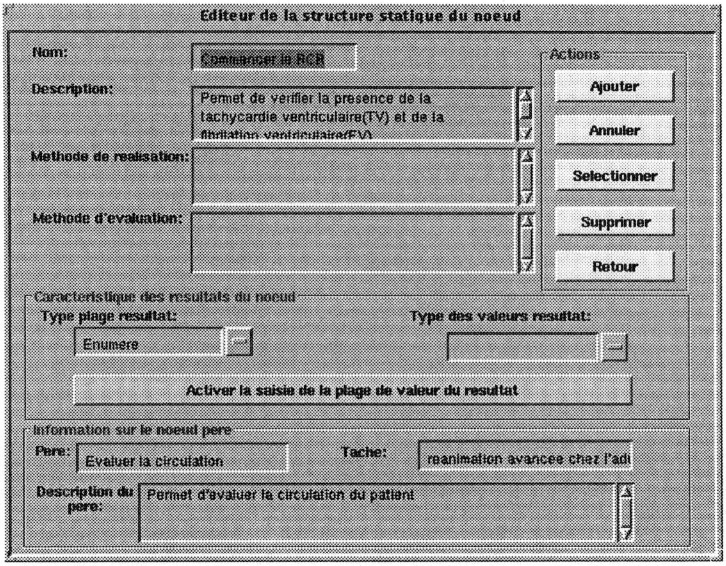

Figure 4: Éditeur des informations de la statique.

2.2. Description de la dynamique d'une tâche.

La dynamique d'une tâche représente la manière dont la tâche évolue en phase d'exécution. Dans les modèles proches de GOMS, cette dynamique est représentée par les règles de sélection. Dans MONACO_T cette dynamique est construite au-dessus de la statique de la tâche et définit les conditions dans lesquelles l'action de chaque sous-tâche est réalisée.

Chaque action dans MONACO_T est divisée en trois étapes:

- une étape de *DÉCLENCHEMENT* qui permet de commencer la réalisation de l'action de la tâche,

- une étape de *COMPOSITION (synthèse de résultats)* qui permet d'exécuter l'action proprement dite de la tâche en mettant en oeuvre la méthode de réalisation de la tâche,

- Une étape de *TERMINAISON* qui permet de clore l'exécution de l'action de la tâche.

Pour définir la dynamique, trois bases de règles ont été implantées au niveau de chaque sous-tâche de l'arbre de décomposition de la tâche. Une base spécifiant les conditions de déclenchement, une base les conditions de composition et une base les conditions de terminaison. Ces trois bases ressemblent aux préconditions, invariants et postconditions qu'on trouve dans le domaine des preuves de programmes. Ces conditions utilisent des termes qui sont des tests sur les états caractéristiques des sous-tâches de la tâche. Les variables définissant l'état caractéristique d'une sous-tâche sont les suivantes: *état* de la sous-tâche, *résultat* de la sous-tâche, *conditions de déclenchement, conditions de composition, conditions de terminaison*. Les différentes bases de règles intégrées dans les sous-tâches de l'arborescence de la tâche forment une base complète modélisant le comportement de la tâche coopérative.

Dans cette approche, exécuter une tâche consiste à exécuter l'étape de terminaison (donner la valeur de vérité vraie à sa condition de terminaison) de la racine de l'arborescence de la tâche, alors que pour des modèles de type GOMS, exécuter une tâche revient à trouver une succession d'opérations acceptables selon les règles de sélection.

Définition formelle de la dynamique

Si (Ω, E_{st}, E_{st}) est une arborescence de sous-tâches alors:

E_{vc} désigne l'ensemble des variables caractéristiques des sous-tâches. Exemple E_{vc}= {état, résultat, note}.

E_r est l'ensemble des règles qui définissent le comportement des sous-tâches.

E_t est l'ensemble des termes utilisés dans les règles.

1:Définition de l'ensemble des valeurs.

$\forall x \in E_{vc}, \forall y \in E_{st}, E_{vp}(x,y)$ représente l'ensemble des valeurs possibles de la variable x pour la sous-tâche y. Exemple: $E_{vp}(etat, diagnostic)$={Initial, Déclenché, EnComposition, Terminé}; $E_{vp}(résultat, diagnostic)$={SIDA, Angine, grippe, paludisme}

2:Définition des opérateurs de comparaison.

$\forall x \in E_{vc}, \forall y \in E_{st}, E_{oc}(x,y)$ représente l'ensemble des opérateurs de comparaison de la variable x de la sous-tâche y. Exemple: $E_{oc}(résultat, Diagnostic)$ = {Égal, Différent, ProbablementÉgal, ProbablementDifférent}

3:Définition d'un terme.

$\forall x \in E_{vc}, \forall y \in E_{st}, \forall op \in E_{oc}(x,y), \forall v \in E_{vp}(x,y),$ *y.x op v* est un terme où *y.x* représente la variable x de la sous-tâche y. Exemple: Diagnostic.Résultat *ProbablementÉgal* SIDA.

4:Définition d'une règle.

$$x \in E_r \Leftrightarrow x \text{ est de la forme } (t_1 \cap t_2 \cap ... \cap t_n)$$

Avec t_k pour $k = 1...n$ des éléments de E_t

En d'autres termes, une règle est une conjonction de termes.

5: *Définition d'une base de règles*: Une base de règles est une disjonction de règles

Chaque élément de E_{st} contient trois bases de règles. Ces trois bases représentent les conditions de déclenchement, de composition, et de terminaison de l'action intégrée dans la sous-tâche.

Le graphe de la dynamique ainsi construit est isomorphe au graphe de la statique. En pratique les deux graphes théoriques sont réunis en un seul graphe où les sous-tâches contiennent les informations de la statique et les règles qui définissent la dynamique. Cette modélisation de la dynamique fait ressortir plusieurs avantages tels que:

- La flexibilité dans la définition du comportement de chaque sous-tâche, qui est due au fait que chaque sous-tâche ne définit que son comportement propre et non celui de ses fils ou de ses descendants.

- On peut spécifier de façon assez complète par les conditions de déclenchement de composition et de terminaison, l'interface qu'une sous-tâche a avec les autres sous-tâches. Cette spécification joue un rôle important dans le cadre du travail coopératif.

- L'intervention possible de toutes les sous-tâches de l'arbre de tâche dans la définition des conditions d'une sous-tâche quelconque, permet de représenter la plupart des contraintes se produisant dans le monde réel.

- L'utilisation de toute la puissance expressive de la logique propositionnelle pour spécifier le comportement de la tâche, permet à MONACO_T d'être particulièrement adapté à la représentation des dépendances entre les sous-tâches de la tâche.

L'un des problèmes que pose la modélisation de tâche avec des règles est que la saisie est relativement compliquée mais surtout difficile à contrôler. Pour pouvoir résoudre ce problème, nous avons construit le module de saisie interactive de règles (figure 5), qui permet à tout utilisateur d'entrer les règles qui régissent le comportement d'une tâche en phase d'exécution avec une interface conviviale produisant des règles sûres dans la mesure où le choix des noeuds, des états, des opérateurs est contrôlé par le module de saisie de règles.

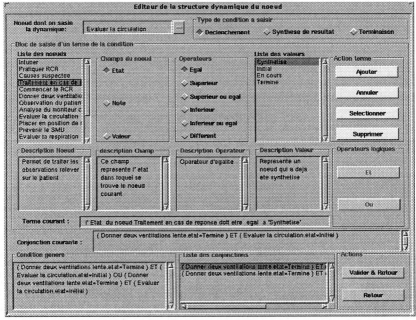

Figure 5: Ecran de création des règles définissant la dynamique d'une sous-tâche

3. Caractéristiques coopératives de MONACO_T

Lorsqu'on parle d'un modèle, ou d'un système coopératif, il est bon de faire ressortir les points suivants: présence de plusieurs agents, objectif commun, mode de coopération, système de communication, gestion du dialogue, synchronisation des activités. Parler des caractéristiques coopératives de MONACO_T, c'est expliquer comment il intègre ces aspects majeurs de la coopération.

Dans MONACO_T, l'introduction des acteurs se fait au niveau de la définition de la statique. Les différents acteurs devant réaliser la tâche sont introduits au niveau des sous-tâches de l'arbre de tâche.

La définition d'un objectif commun par les acteurs chargés de réaliser une tâche coopérative à la norme MONACO_T est déduite du fait que tous les agents sont chargés de réaliser la même tâche.

Le mode de coopération désigne la manière dont les acteurs se répartissent la tâche afin de la résoudre. Trois modes de répartitions sont possibles: figé (fixé à l'avance), dynamique (précisé lors de l'exécution), hybride (fixé au début et modifié lors de l'exécution). Dans MONACO_T la répartition se fait d'une facon figée à la définition de la statique, par l'attribution de sous-tâches aux acteurs. Ce choix correspond bien à la réalité des tâches coopératives où les différents postes de travail sont prédéfinis.

MONACO_T implante le modèle de communication par tableau noir. Le tableau noir est constitué de l'ensemble des valeurs contenues dans les noeuds de la tâche. Chaque cellule du tableau noir à un propriétaire (un des acteurs de la tâche) et seul ce propriétaire peut mettre à jour l'information dans la cellule, les autres n'ont que la possibilité de lecture. Avec ce choix, les problèmes d'accès concurrents sont éliminés.

Dans MONACO_T, le dialogue entre les acteurs se fait par l'intermédiaire des modifications que les actions entraînent dans l'environnement de travail et par la prise en considération de ces modifications par les bases de règles.

La synchronisation dans MONACO_T est régie par le modèle de la dynamique. La puissance expressive qu'offre le modèle de la dynamique de MONACO fait en sorte que toutes les contraintes possibles sur la synchronisation peuvent être modélisées.

4. Conclusion

La modélisation que nous proposons est structurée en couches (statique et dynamique). Chaque couche a une structure arborescente. Les noeuds de la dynamique possèdent des règles qui permettent de définir le comportement global de la tâche. Contrairement aux autres modèles de tâche, qui exploitent uniquement les avantages d'une seule technique de représentation de connaissances ou au maximum deux comme le modèle PIF [4], MONACO_T tire les avantages de ces trois techniques: puissance expressive de la logique, mise en valeur des niveaux d'abstractions par le découpage en couches, bonne représentation cognitive de la tâche par les graphes.

Les sous-tâches internes ou abstraites sont le siège d'actions et peuvent être exécutées contrairement à certains modèles qui font la différence entre les sous-tâches abstraites et les sous-tâches opérationnelles. Ainsi dans MONACO_T lorsqu'un apprenant veut réaliser une tâche, il doit maîtriser la structure abstraite de la tâche alors que dans une structure où les actions se situent dans les noeuds opérationnels, l'apprenant peut exécuter une suite d'actions permettant de réaliser la tâche sans pour autant en connaître la structure abstraite.

La structure coopérative de la tâche est représentée d'une manière assez simple par l'attribution de sous-tâches à des postes de travail. Ainsi lorsqu'on a plus de deux postes de travail dans le modèle d'une tâche, on est réellement en présence d'une tâche coopérative.

Monaco_T s'est avéré assez robuste dans la construction d'un conseiller coopératif pour tâche coopérative [9]. Il nous a permis de générer des agents conseillers coopératifs et des agents simulateurs de tâches.

Dans la suite nous allons étudier l'intégration des contraintes temporelles dans MONACO_T, et la prise en compte des tâches de manipulation de systèmes.

Remerciement: Ce travail est un volet du projet SAFARI et est financé par le Ministère de l'Industrie de la Science du Commerce et de la Technologie du QUEBEC.

Bibliographie.

1   Bovair, S., Kieras, D.E., & Polson, P.G. The acquisition and performance of text-editing skill: A cognitive complexity analysis. *Human Computer Interaction*, (1990) 5, 1-48.

2   Chandrasekaran, B. Towards a functional architecture for intelligence based on generic information processing tasks. *Proceedings of the Tenth International Joint Conference on Artificial Intelligence,* (1987) pages 1183-1192, Milan, Italy .

3   Clancey, W. J.*Knowledge-Based Tutoring: The GUIDON Program*, (1987) The MIT Press, Cambridge

4   Djamen J. Y., B Lefebvre, and Kengne A. Spécification pour la représentation des connaissances, *Rapp. Tech. document interne,* (1994).*SAFARI, DIRO*, Université de Montréal.

5   Ferbert, J. Des systèmes multi-agents pour simuler le vivant. *In Actes du 2e colloques africain sur la recherche en informatique* 12-18 octobre (1994). Edition ORSTOM.

6   Lesgold, A., Lajoie, S., Bunzo, M., et Eggan, G. A coached practice environment for an electronics troubleshooting job. In Larkin, J. et Chabay, R., Editeur, *Computer-Assisted Instruction and Intelligent Tutoring System: Shared Goals and Complementary Approaches*, (1992) pages 201-238. Lawrence Erbaum Associates.

7   Péninou, A., (1993). MACT: un modèle d'agents centrés tâches pour la production de systèmes tuteurs intelligents par l'atelier de génie didacticiel intégré. Thèse de doctorat de l'université paul Sabatier Toulouse. France.

8   Schreiber, A.T., Wielinga, B.J., Breuker, J.A., - KADS : A Principled approach to knowledge-Based System Development, Acamic Press Harcourt Brace Jovanovich, Publishers (1993)

9   Tadié, G.S., Frasson, C., Lefebvre, B.,. Coopération entre agents conseillers pour la génération d'explications dans un environnement coopératif. Journées EXPLICATION96 (1996) (Soumis)

Intelligent Guide: Combining User Knowledge Assessment with Pedagogical Guidance

Ramzan Khuwaja[1], Michel Desmarais[2], Richard Cheng[2]

[1]Cognologic Software Inc.,
3620 Lorne Crescent, #216, Montreal, Qc, H2X 2B1
Phone: (514) 842-1527
Email: khuwaja@steve.iit.edu

[2]Computer Research Institute of Montreal,
1801 McGill College Avenue, #800, Montreal, Qc, H3A 2N4
Phone: (514) 398-1234; Fax: (514) 398-1244
Email: desmar@crim.ca, rcheng@crim.ca

Abstract. Despite their many successes, Intelligent Tutoring Systems (ITS) are not yet practical enough to be employed in the real world educational/training environments. We argue that this undesirable scenario can be changed by focusing on developing an ITS development methodology that transforms current ITS research to consider practical issues that are part of the main causes of underemployment of ITSs. Here we describe an ambitious research project to develop an ITS that has recently completed its first phase of development at the Computer Research Institute of Montreal. This project aims to address issues, such as, making ITS handle multiple domains, developing cost-effective knowledge assessment methodologies, organizing and structuring domains around curriculum views and addressing the needs of users by considering their immediate goals and educational/training settings. This paper concentrates on the outcomes of the first phase of our project that includes the architecture and functionality (specially user knowledge assessment and pedagogical guidance) of the Intelligent Guide.

1 Introduction

The field of Intelligent Tutoring System (ITS) is almost three decades old but only a handful of ITSs built so far made their way into real educational environment [12; 7]. ITS community is beginning to aware of this concern and a number of researchers have already started to suggest different way outs for this situation (see for example, [7]). The field of ITS has great promise and potential to be effective in both educational and training worlds but these two worlds have their own unique demands and requirements. One important step forward for ITSs, to be more practical, can be achieved by identifying and addressing issues that are common to these two worlds.

One of the important issue that the field of ITS is currently facing is the "system problem," [12], i.e., "the design of ITS needs to be done with consideration for how it will be used within an educational [or training] system, rather than just developing it as a stand-alone entity" (p. 53).

The second issue is of making ITS capable of handling multiple domains at the same time. Most of ITSs developed so far deal with only single domain of knowledge. On the contrary, many potential educational and training applications demand knowledge in multiple domains of expertise.

Only cost-effective computer-based systems are capable of justifying their acceptance in real world situations. This is specially true for ITSs that make their way into training domains. These systems are still expensive to build, mainly as a consequence that the development of an ITS still starts from scratch. There is no ready-to-use methodology and technology available that a developer can use to start with.

Two other issues that are very closely related to the "system problem" are the effectiveness of an ITS and its acceptability by the user. An effective ITS should produce a high gain in the user's knowledge/skills. This can only happen if the system provides enough motivation for the user and justify its usage in the pursuit of the user's goal(s).

This paper describes an ambitious research project to develop an ITS that has recently completed its first phase of development at the Computer Research Institute of Montreal (CRIM). This project addresses some of the important issues discussed above.

2 Background

A solution to issues, described above, lies on the development of a generic methodology to design an ITS. This methodology should have power to handle knowledge from multiple domains. Many ITSs developed so far concentrated on a single domain. In general, this resulted in a powerful model of expertise but the methodology used to develop that model becomes restricted to that specific domain. A flexible and generic methodology can result in cost-effective systems for real world educational/training environments. Developing one such generic methodology require detailed understanding of the functioning and architecture of ITSs.

ITSs are complex systems. A common trend in the ITS community is to organize the development of a tutoring system around four functional components [13]: diagnostic, (domain) expert, pedagogy, and communication modules. In order for an ITS development methodology to be flexible and generic it needs to prescribe the development of each of these modules. The nature of these modules depends upon the consideration for the overall architecture for an ITS. Wenger in [13] has characterized ITSs as consisting of either model-based or curriculum-based architectures. A model-based ITS emphasizes the model view of the domain expertise. Some example ITSs in this class are: Lisp Tutor [1], QUEST [14], CIRCSIM-Tutor [8]. The curriculum-based ITSs, on the other hand, emphasize the curriculum view of the domain expertise, example ITSs in this class are: BIP [2], WUSOR [6], MHO [9]. In Wenger's [13] term the curriculum-based architectures "emphasize the notion of *lesson* rather than that of *model* as a reservoir of domain knowledge (p. 149). We believe that the knowledge domains required for many real world educational/training applications land well for curriculum-based ITSs. Another advantage of this approach is that, due to its very nature, it emphasizes the body of knowledge that specifies the goal structure for the system [9]. As noted by Lesgold in [9] a vast majority of courses developed in the educational world use explicit curriculum. A use of explicit curriculum in an ITS, it is hoped, will facilitate its integration in an educational setting.

2.1 Intelligent Guide: An ITS that facilitates acquiring mastery level competence in a domain

This paper describes a computer-based educational system, Intelligent Guide (IG), that is currently under development at the Computer Research Institute of Montreal (CRIM). The first phase of development for this system has recently completed. This paper concentrates on the outcomes of the initial phase of this project.

The long term goal of Intelligent Guide is to develop a generic Intelligent Tutoring System (ITS) that could provide user knowledge assessment and pedagogy guidance for a number of domains that require the user to master a number of concepts or skills to achieve a satisfactory level of competence in the domain. Our research has this definite objective of bringing this system into real world educational/training environment.

Intelligent Guide has a generic curriculum-based architecture. It is designed to operate with a general knowledge assessment method [3]. This method uses a kind of overlay type user model. One of the advantage of this method is that it has power to be effective in multiple domains. We are currently experimenting the Intelligent Guide with a specific domain, the Graduate Management Admissions Test (GMAT).

3 Architecture of Intelligent Guide

The typical knowledge domains we are envisioning for the Intelligent Guide will consists of a large body of concepts and/or skills that a student needs to master. Learning of a concept /skill will be tested by asking one or more questions to the student. All the concepts and skills can be arranged in a network of nodes that are connected by several relationships (e.g., part of, prerequisite, analogy, co-topic). In other words, knowledge in our domains can be represented by a type of curriculum structure.

The major objective of Intelligent Guide is to provide guidance to the user in the pursuit of achieving satisfactory level of competence in a domain. Intelligent Guide is like a tutoring assistance that assesses the knowledge state of the student for a domain. Based upon this assessment it points out areas in the knowledge domain that require attention from the user. Unlike the currently available software products (see Sec. 2.1), the degree of attention required by the user for these areas is part of the feedback provided by Intelligent Guide. Further, depending upon the user's choice this tutoring assistance can invoke a tutorial session for a domain concept/skill that needs to be learned/mastered by the user. Intelligent Guide is not designed to provide a full delivery of contents for each domain topic but rather a brief but comprehensive overview of major concepts required. We assume that the users in our case know the basics of the knowledge domains. These users are mainly looking for assessment of their knowledge level and an individualized (active) review of the different domains. We do not attempt to restrict the user to learn domain contents from only Intelligent Guide, in fact this system provides pointers to commonly available books and other forms of resources for the user to acquire advance knowledge of the domain.

An ultimate goal of Intelligent Guide is to encourage the user to periodically use this system while participating in a preparatory course or preparing for a test like GMAT. In this way the user would have an opportunity to keep track of his/her progress in learning the domain material. Considering this goal of our system it is imperative to continuously evaluate the knowledge state of the student to individualize feedback/guidance.

Fig. 1 shows a scenario for Intelligent Guide. In this scenario the Intelligent Guide is like a shell, missing the domain knowledge. In order for this system to be functional in a domain, the knowledge for that domain needs to be fed into it. We assume that this knowledge comes from a course designer in that domain. Currently we are developing a software tool, course development environment, that allows a course designer to structure and organize his/her view of the domain knowledge. This tool then automatically transforms this knowledge into an intermediate form recognizable by Intelligent Guide. When Intelligent Guide is invoked by the user, it reads this intermediate form of domain knowledge to create a knowledge base which is used to perform reasoning in the domain.

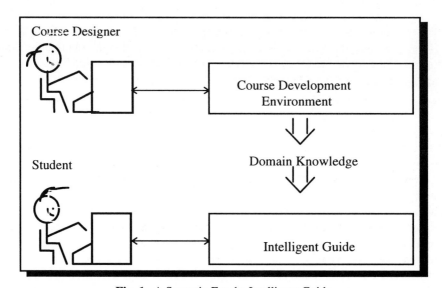

Fig. 1. A Scenario For the Intelligent Guide

Fig. 2 shows the internal architecture of Intelligent Guide. The arrows in this figure represent the data flow paths between components of this system. As it is shown in this figure, this system consists of six major components. Intelligent Guide is designed using an object-oriented methodology and is implemented using the C++ programming language.

The architecture of Intelligent Guide is influenced by Lesgols's research (see [9]). Besides this formalism two very practical issues influenced this architecture, these are: making Intelligent Guide available on multiple platforms and plugging it with multiple user interfaces. Currently Intelligent Guide runs on UNIX and Windows environments and uses a Web-based user interface.

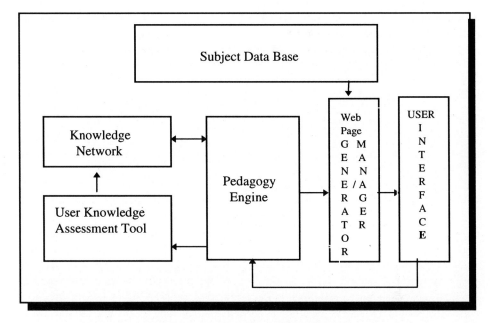

Fig. 2. Architecture of Intelligent Guide

The knowledge network of Fig. 2 contains Knowledge Units (KU) or domain entities (e.g., domain concepts) that are connected via multiple domain relationships (e.g., prerequisite). This network is created from an intermediate form of domain knowledge provided by the curriculum development environment (see Fig. 1). This knowledge network is basis for the domain intelligence in the system.

The subject data base is the second component that uses output from the course development environment. This data base consists of actual content of domain entities that is communicated to the user, for example, content for various GMAT questions is kept in various files of this data base. When the pedagogy engine selects a question that needs to be asked to the user, an appropriate file(s) containing this question is accessed from the subject data base.

The user knowledge assessment tool is responsible for assessing the knowledge state of the user. It uses a specific technique to keep track of the changing state of the user's knowledge. Sec. 4 describes in detail the theoretical background and working of this component.

The pedagogy engine is the heart of Intelligent Guide. It is responsible for interpreting the knowledge state of the student and, depending upon the currently selected goals and the state of interaction with the user, it determines "what to do next" in a session. Within the architecture of Intelligent Guide this component is also responsible for coordinating the communication between other components of the system. Sec. 5 describes the theoretical background and functioning of this component in detail.

Once the pedagogy engine has decided about what and how to present contents to the user, it sends messages to the web page generator and manager (see Fig. 2) to compose a HTML (Hyper Text Markup Language) page for the user. It is this component that queries the subject data base to develop a HTML page. Once a page is generated, it is sent to the user interface (see Fig. 2), the component that handles communication with a HTML server.

4 Knowledge Assessment in the Intelligent Guide: A Generic User Model

One of the fundamental component of the Intelligent Guide is the user knowledge assessment module (see [3; 4]). This module is responsible for providing a user profile of the knowledge network's state of mastery. Based upon the information it receives from the pedagogy engine about what knowledge unit (KU) is mastered by the user, the knowledge assessment module will infer the likelihood that every other KU is mastered.

The knowledge assessment module adopts the overlay approach to defining the whole domain knowledge. It uses a view of the knowledge network that organizes fine-grained Knowledge Units (KU), or nodes, into a *knowledge structure* [5] that represents the order in which KU are learned. An individual's knowledge about the domain, i.e., a knowledge state, is modeled by a collection of numerical attribute values attached to the nodes. Each value indicates the likelihood (i.e., probability) of a user's knowing a specific KU. In the knowledge structure, KU are connected by implication (precedence) relations. An implication relation is, in fact, a gradation constraint which expresses whether a certain concept has to be understood before another difficult one, or whether a certain skill is acquired prior to an advanced one. It is these implication relations that enables the inferences about the mastery of KU.

In contrast to other work that also adopted similar approaches to knowledge assessment (see in particular [6]), the knowledge structure is induced entirely from empirical data composed of samples of knowledge states. Because the knowledge structure induction process is automatic, it allows a much larger number of KUs to be included than other approaches which "manually" build the structure with the help of domain experts. A more detailed treatment of the knowledge structure construction method is given in [3].

Once a knowledge structure is obtained, it can be used as a basis for knowledge assessment. The knowledge state of a user is built and updated as soon as some observations are made (e.g., questions and exercises are answered). Each observation can be viewed as a piece of evidence. This new information may be propagated to other nodes in compliance with the gradation constraints (inference structure). Standard evidence propagation techniques can be used to perform this process (a number of such techniques can be found in [11]). Again the reader is referred to [3] for further details.

5 Pedagogy Guidance

This section describes the design and functioning of the pedagogy engine (see Fig. 2). The major function of this component is to provide pedagogy guidance to the user. Its behavior depends upon (1) the domain knowledge in the knowledge network, (2) user's actions, (3) an assessment of the user's knowledge state, and (4) the pedagogy knowledge represented as rules in this component.

Like Lesgold (see [9]) we also make distinction between the domain knowledge and curriculum (or goal structure) in our system. The domain knowledge provides the domain intelligence that the pedagogy engine tries to impart to the user but it is the curriculum knowledge that provides a mean of planning a session and making moment-to-moment decisions while communicating with the user.

Before we further describe the pedagogy engine, let us briefly sketch the organization of the knowledge network. This network consists of domain entities (Knowledge Units - KU - or nodes) and relationships between these entities. There are two major sections of this network, we call them, subject-matter hierarchy and question hierarchy. The subject-matter hierarchy is organized into four layers: course layer, section layer, topic layer, and concept layer. The question hierarchy consists of nodes for questions, solutions to questions, and problem-solving strategies to solve a question. Questions in this hierarchy test knowledge for various domain entities in the subject-matter hierarchy. These two hierarchies intersect at nodes (e.g., real number division) representing the domain entities that need to be tested to evaluate the user's competence in the domain.

This type of break down of subject-matter contents is very important from our point of view because (1) this is a common way of organizing domain knowledge by the instructional system designers, (2) it also provides a view of curriculum that the system needs to consider before engaging the user in a session, (3) it provides a vehicle for generating system goals for the Intelligent Guide.

It is one of the important goal of our research that the Intelligent Guide be designed quickly and efficiently for a domain by minimally restructuring the contents of a book to develop a domain knowledge network for our system. We believe that the domain knowledge organization used in our system provides a generic framework that can be used to transform pre-organized knowledge in a book into a knowledge network for the Intelligent Guide. Using this framework we have transformed the math (review) section of the book *The Official Guide for GMAT Review* by the Graduate Management Admission Council to develop the current network for the Intelligent Guide.

The pedagogy engine is a hierarchical, incremental instructional planner [10]. It uses the subject matter classification of the knowledge network to develop plan at four different levels: course, section, topic, and concept (notice the similarity of these levels with the layers in the knowledge network). Because of this multiple-level organization it is possible for the pedagogy engine to develop plan at the global level to consider the overall objective of a session and at the interaction level where moment-to-moment decisions are made to continue a form of dialogue with the user.

The decision making process within the pedagogy engine is fueled by the pedagogy rules. These rules reside in a rule base. The interpretation and execution of these rules is carried by a rule base engine. We have classified these rules as: meta-rule, session management rule, goal refinement rule, goal execution rule, and the student initiative handling rule. Most of these categories are self explanatory. Meta-rules are rules that decide which rule category to consider in view of the current state of the system. The student initiative handling rules decide how to respond to the user's actions (e.g., questions, requests). An English version of an example goal refinement rule is as follows.

IF   current goal is to guide-the-student, and
  current planning level is topic-level
THEN   create sub-goals:
         * *sequence currently focused topics*
         * *select a focused topic, and*
         * *present (to the student) the selected topic*

The behavior of the pedagogy engine can also be viewed as setting and execution of goals at four different decision making levels. This multi-level planning model is based on the decision making process commonly used by the instructional designers. Intelligent Guide provides option for the user to set some of the goals at each level. This means that the user can select a course, a section, a topic, and/or a concept to pursue with. This, we hope, will provide enough motivation to the user to take change of the system to achieve his/her goals.

The organization of the pedagogy engine is very generic (i.e., domain independent). We believe that Intelligent Guide can handle most of the domains whose contents can be organized into a curriculum-type structure described above.

6 Conclusion

One of the major objective of our current research and development track is to bridge the gap between research and practical application of intelligent computer-based teaching/training systems. We are striving to develop a methodology and technology for ITS that could facilitate to develop effective and economical systems that could be easily integrated in a real world teaching/training environments. Unlike the current trend in the ITS community we are aiming for techniques that may not be very sophisticated but effective enough to achieve our goals. This require us to adopt and transform currently available ITS research and also to develop new techniques for our purposes.

Most of ITS developed so far were oriented towards developing methodologies for single domains. In order to achieve our goals we believe that we need to take the next logical step towards ITS research, i.e., to orient our methodology towards a group of domains and educational/training situations. Our group oriented methodology, we hope, will be a good candidate to effectively address the issues raised in the introduction (see Sec.1).

We have selected knowledge/skill evaluation tests like GMAT and preparatory courses as our target domains for our research and development. Moreover, we are currently focusing on knowledge evaluation and pedagogical guidance as the main functions for our system. Considering our target educational situation we have observed that our domains could be organized to explicit their curriculum structures. These structures provide a very fertile ground for our knowledge assessment methodology which already, theoretically and practically, have been proved to be generic and effective (see for example [3]). We have adopted current ITS research for developing curriculum-based ITS to provide pedagogical guidance for Intelligent Guide.

Our journey towards our goals has just started. In our first phase of development we have started to address some of our theoretical and practical issues. In our second phase we are aiming to develop a set of tools that could help course designers to develop contents for our system. We are also aiming to test our system in a variety of educational settings that are originally intended for our project. We do realize that we are aiming for an ambitious project but with our clear, cautious, and practical approach we hope to succeed in our goals.

References

1. Anderson, J. R., Boyle, C. F., Corbett, A. T. & Lewis, M. W. (1990). Cognitive modeling and intelligent tutoring. In Clancey, W. J. & Soloway, E. (Eds.). *Artificial intelligence and learning environment* (pp. 7-49). Cambridge, MA: The MIT Press.
2. Barr, A., Beard, M. & Alkinson, R. C. (1976). The computer as a tutorial laboratory: The Stanford BIP project. *International Journal of Man-Machine Studies*, 8, 567-596.
3. Desmarais, M. C., Maluf, A. & Liu, J. (to appear). User-expertise modeling with empirically derived probabilistic implication networks. *User-Modeling and User Adaptive Interaction.*
4. Desmarais, M., Giroux, L., Larochelle, S. & Leclerc, S. (1988). Assessing the structure of knowledge in a procedural domain. In *Proceedings of the Tenth Annual Conference of the Cognitive Science Society* (pp. 475-481).
5. Falmagne, J., Doignon, J., Koppen, M., Villano, M. & Johannesen, L. (1990). Introduction to knowledge spaces: how to build, test and search them. *Psychological Review*, 97, 201-224.
6. Goldstein, I. P. (1982). The genetic graph: A representation for the evolution of procedural knowledge. In Sleeman, D. & Brown, J. S. (Eds.), *Intelligent tutoring systems* (pp. 51-77). London: Academic Press, Inc.
7. Jones M. (1992). Instructional systems need instructional theory: Comments on a truism. In Scanlon, E & O'Shea, T. (Eds.), *New directions in educational technology* (pp. 1-13). Berlin, Germany: Springer-Verlag.
8. Khuwaja, R. A. (1994). *A model of tutoring: Facilitating knowledge integration using multiple models of the domain.* Ph.D. Thesis, Computer Science Department, Illinois Institute of Technology, Chicago, Illinois.
9. Lesgold, A. (1988). Towards a theory of curriculum for use in designing intelligent instructional systems. In Mandl, H. & Lesgold, A. (Eds.), *Learning issues for intelligent tutoring systems* (pp. 114-137). New York: Springer-Verlag.
10. Murray, W. R. (1988). *Control for intelligent tutoring systems: A comparison of blackboard architecture and discourse management networks.* Technical Report R-6267, FMC corporation.
11. Pearl , J. (1988). *Probabilistic Reasoning in Intelligent Systems: Networks of Plausible Inference.* San Mateo, CA: Morgan Kaufmann.
12. Reigeluth, C.M. (1992). New directions for educational technology. In Scanlon, E & O'Shea, T. (Eds.), *New directions in educational technology* (pp. 51-59). Berlin, Germany: Springer-Verlag.
13. Wenger, E. (1987). *Artificial intelligence and tutoring systems.* Los Altos, CA: Morgan Kaufman.
14. White, B. Y. & Frederiksen, J. R. (1990). Causal model progressions as a foundation for intelligent learning environments. In Clancey, W. J. & Soloway, E. (Eds.). *Artificial intelligence and learning environment* (pp. 7-49). Cambridge, MA: The MIT Press.

Parallel Computing Model for Problem Solver Towards ITSs
– Epistemological Articulation of Human Problem Solving –

Noboru MATSUDA *and* Toshio OKAMOTO

Graduate School of Information Systems,
The University of Electro-Communications
1-5-1, Chofugaoka, Chofu, Tokyo, 182 JAPAN
Email: {mazda,okamoto}@ai.is.uec.ac.jp

Abstract. *Study on building powerful and robust problem solver for ITSs is described. The proposed problem solver is based on parallel computing technology to simulate some of the intelligent characteristics of human problem solving including the concurrency of thought, the case based reasoning, and the awareness of the key to problem solving. We propose the multiagent problem solver which divides a given problem into several small sub-problems and solves them concurrently. This system is especially useful for ITS which teaches procedural problem solving to novice students, because it is capable of showing the reason of achieving an idea for solution by thinking aloud by the "trial-and-error" method.*

1 Introduction

The purpose of this study is to build powerful and robust problem solver for Intelligent Tutoring Systems (ITSs). Previous problem solvers which have been used for ITSs are typically based on the framework of production systems which invokes linear searching method[2, 7]. However such problem solvers have serious limitations on their performances which would decline the educational capability of ITS itself.

In this study, the development of a problem solver which has the ability to solve problems from thinking many plausible situations simultaneously is described, and then we discuss the system's ability to explain the reason of *why* the computer finds out solutions, rather shows how to solve problems. This problem solver is base on the super parallel computing technology[4], and is built with several workstations connected by local area network (LAN).

The paper has three major sections. Section 2 describes desired problem solver for ITSs from the educational point of view. Section 3 describes a model of human problem solving and its symbolic implementation issues compared to traditional production systems. Section 4 describes a basic configuration of our problem solver and the mechanism of problem solving based on parallel computing technologies.

2 Problem Solver for ITSs

ITSs consist of many complicated components. Nearly all available systems depend on a domain knowledge base. This means that typical ITS fundamentally consists of (i) the *problem solver with domain knowledge base*, (ii) the student model diagnosing system which uses diagnostic knowledge as well as *domain knowledge*, (iii) the tutoring module which basically transfers the content of *domain knowledge* to students, and (iv) the other modules (e.g., the human interface, etc).

The component to which domain knowledge is deeply related is the problem solver. Therefore, the efficiency of ITS is greatly influenced by the performance of problem solver. This effect is more evident when constructing an ITS desired to teach problem solving to novice students since greater degree in detail of explanation is required. One of the greatest issues to construct a system which efficiently accomplishes such task is that it must be capable of solving much more problems in details over broader base, even within a given domain, so as to make novice students understand solution processes sufficiently. That is, ITS has to explain how to solve problems in terms of situation based operational decisions. Those explanations have to point out specifically the *reason* (i.e., why) for the application of each operation as well as the *situation* (i.e., when) students apply particular type of operations.

Typically, during an explanation on how operations are being applied in solving a specific problem, the system uses the "demonstration – explanation" procedure utilizing the process of the problem solving itself. What this means is that the system first solves a problem and then shows the sequence of operations that was applied in solving the problem. With the current AI technologies, implementation of this explanation method in ITSs is not so hard; but there are number of considerable problems with this approach:

- *Grain size of knowledge* : If the goal of the problem solver is simply to solve problems efficiently, then it is possible to allocate various elements of procedural knowledge to the system. It is also possible, in algebra for example, that the system has a set of formulae to answer the questions by simply matching a given question against those formulae. However, in order to show the details of each formula, or for ITSs to be flexible in handling various tutoring situations in the multiple degree of difficulties, it is necessary to break down the formula into pieces of knowledge which are at more primitive level. [1]
- *Set of terms used in explanations – the issues of ontology – :* The inference procedure of typical production systems (explained in the following section) is essentially based on pattern matching. That is, the system merely replaces expressions according to the patterns written in inference rules. In this case, the record of problem solving is just a collection of patterns translated toward the goal from an initial state. In order to teach students how to apply operations, the process of problem solving must be described in the multiple level of details and difficulties with well understandable terms.

Disclosing the reason of why particular operation is applied to a specific situation is even more difficult. Usually, the novice students can hardly recognize *"how the system (or a human teacher as well) thought of or selected such a good solution?"* just from observing a resulted solution process. In other words; even though the system is surely able to tell the applicability of operations, the students tend not

---

[1] The degree of granularity of the knowledge is defined in terms of the flexibility of its use here. The more the knowledge is primitive, the more it would be re-usable for many different situations.

to know *"why the system selects a particular operation most suited in solving the problem among the other similarly suitable ones?"* There has been no ITS research reported so far which proposes a beneficial technique in accommodating to this issue. Although even human teachers find it hard to answer such questions, of course. They often *think aloud* and such a "trial-and-error" utterance seems to be beneficial for students and feasible for the teacher.

In conclusion, the problem solver for ITSs to teach problem solving has following requirements and issues;

- Ideally, the system should have as much knowledge which are spread over the various degree of granularity as possible. This requirement has been leading to serious trade-off between "the scale of knowledge base and the efficiency of inference".
- To generate well understandable explanations, the domain knowledge base has to be exceedingly rich in its description. That is, some sort of concept description language would be required to construct domain knowledge base.
- A practical nor theoretical method to show the reason of achieving an idea for the solution has not been proposed so far. The system should show students its labouring process not only in the succeeded story but also in the failed attempts as well.

Above requests are somewhat outside of the aim of AI expert systems. However, from the educational point of view, they are crucial elements in creating an effective tutoring system for various domains and for multiple level of students. For this reason, it is of an importance and necessity to incorporate above issues into the study of superior ITSs.

3 Model of Problem Solving

3.1 Architecture of Production System

Ordinary production systems, which consists of a set of productions (*production memory – PM*), a database of assertions (*working memory – WM*), and an inference engine (*interpreter*), has been regarded as a model of human problem solving[1]. This is because (1) WM is a model of the real world; each of its element (called *working memory element –WME*) is an assertion on a state of the given problem and WM is continuously changed throughout the process of problem solving, (2) PM is the model of a domain knowledge; each of its element is a rule (fragmentation of knowledge) which represents how to change a state of the problem, and (3) process of problem solving (made by *inference procedure*) is divided into three different steps, i.e., (i) matching step where the interpreter checks an applicability of each rule, (ii) selecting step where one of the applicable rules is chosen as an appropriate one for current situation, and (iii) acting step where the selected rule is applied to change the state of WM.

The inference procedure depends on the linear search. That is, it searches a solution path between initial and goal state in the problem space. This linearity of the search possesses considerably problems like *explosion of the search* and the *utility problem*[6]. This is one of the serious problems of production systems.

Production system is capable of explaining *a track of problem solving* in terms of a sequence of rules that translates initial problem state into a desired one (i.e., goal state). This explanation is useful to show, for example, the validity of the solution or how to solve problems with given operations. However, just providing a sequence of applied rules is not effective enough for educational systems, especially when explanation is given to novice students who are just beginning to learn problem solving, because such a prefabricated sequence of rules does not imply *the thought process of finding a solution* i.e., the selective reasoning of rules and operations. This is another considerable problem in utilizing production systems for ITSs.

Beyond the above disabilities of ordinaly production systems, the remaining section discusses the nature of human problem solving and then propose an extended production system, which is based on multiagent systems, toward ITSs.

3.2   Concurrences of Human Problem Solving

When humans solve problems, they tend to consider several different possibilities not just one by one (as in finding an alternative path or method for the solution when one fails) but also in a simultaneous way. Although this diverse ability seems redundant and rather time consuming in the precise logical world of the computer based applications, it is to be the foundation of the human intelligence because such diversified thought process eventually derives a solution even from the chaos of tangled information.

This advanced thinking is organized by a collection of relatively small problem solving tasks that are rationally derived from the original problem, and each of them yields further tasks. Such recurrent task yielding seems to get an explosion of thought. Nevertheless, human power of problem solving actually relies on this concurrent activity of collaborative tasks. *Why?* One of the advantages of concurrent thinking is that every plausible tasks considered are acting to give / get effects to / from others. The most basic and important influence among the collaborative task processing appears to be derived from the propagation of possibility of success and failure at an incredible rate. As a task successfully completes, it can propagate some information on how to solve given subproblem. It can also know whether a certain situation can be solved with the current knowledge, because when a task fails to solve a problem it propagates information on failure. In this way, the maximization of problem solving is accomplished by eliminating such unnecessary process as duplication or repetition.

One of the notable characteristics of human behaviour is to memorize the experiences of problem solving and utilize them to solve other problems. This facility, case based reasoning, prevents humans from doing the resemble inference over again.

The humans also do not take into account any situations which have no relation to the current problem being solved. This is somewhat of a trivial matter, but is quite a special ability. That is the continuous focussing on the proper situation useful to keep track of the ways toward a solution is one of the most important nature of human problem solving. The computational model of such navigation mechanisms have not been uncovered so far, while some epistemological models have. We do not believe humans *select* only useful information out of indescribably large problem solving space. Instead, we assume that they have the ability to formulate a sort of key indexing system from a given problem itself. This is what we call humans *awareness of key* to problem solving. The keys, depend on the problem, can spread out diversely to guide them successfully solving the giving problem including the process of excluding unrelated situations and information.

3.3 Next Problem Solver for ITSs

Model of human problem solving realized by traditional production systems is formalized as a cyclic process of matching knowledge against the situation, selecting the best one, and applying it. This model has limitations on its performance with educational systems as described the previous section, and then a new powerful problem solver which is designed based on some characteristics of human intelligence on problem solving including the concurrency of thought, the case based reasoning, and the awareness of the key to problem solving is desired.

We propose the distributed problem solver (*DPS*) with multiagent system which is based on parallel computing technology[5]. The system divides a given problem into several small sub-problems (linked by goal - subgoal relation) and solves them concurrently with multiple extended production systems. They are extended so that they can passively get some information from working environment. Each of them is similar to ordinary production systems except (1) it has a third agent which passes information about the environment, and (2) when it is encountered number of plausible suitable operations at a particular situation, it might request another production system for each operation to resolve individually. The details of the multiagent problem solver is described in the next section.

4 Distributed Problem Solver

4.1 Structure of DPS

DPS consists of search space management system and multiple production system agents (*PSAs*). Figure 1 shows basic structure of DPS. DPS solves a problem by searching problem space like ordinal AI problem solvers except the search is carried out in a parallel method. When more than two plausible instructions are available for a certain situation, parallel search facility is invoked to handle all of the instructions simultaneously. Each search, fulfilled by PSA, may successfully return usable results on some or all of instructions. DPS relies on a simple conflict resolution strategy that only the first successful result is adopted as a solution. All searches by PSA are sound (while not necessarily complete), so that the final answer from DPS is always valid.

Figure 2 shows a parallel search of the DPS. The concurrent search is accomplished by multiple autonomous PSAs. They are basically the production systems, so they have the initial and goal states as well as individual production memories and working memories. [2] They are working collaborative by exchanging the informa-

---

[2] The production system agents in the current DPS system all share the same production memories. Ideally, every production system agents have their own production memories; and each of them acting as a specialized agents in solving specific sub-domain of the problem solving process. This topic needs future work.

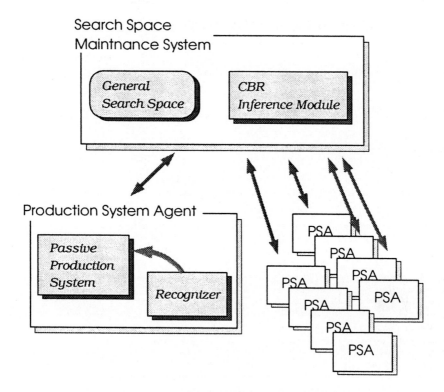

Fig. 1. The basic configuration of a distributed production system.

tion about the result of the search. Since they don't know what agents are working where, they give and take the message through the mediator, called Search Space Maintenance System, which keeps track of search activities of a problem space.

4.2 Search Space Maintenance System

Each of PSA handles only a small problem, so that none of them knows general search space. This lack of global view over the search space might cause several problems of the search operation such as the fruitless search or impossibility of propagating the result of search.

Search Space Maintenance System manages all of the situations which have once been explored by PSAs. Since Search Space Maintenance System (and no other agents) knows the whole aspect of search space, PSAs make inquiries to the maintenance system about the status of other situations when necessary. They might request the maintenance system, for example, to propagate the results of inference, or want to know the answer of the current goal state if it had once been resolved.

Search Space Maintenance System creates a database of situations as being reported by PSAs. The database is just a collection of the combination of goals and

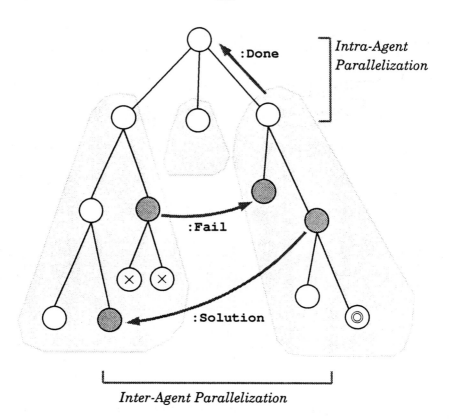

Fig. 2. A parallel search of the DPS.

results; i.e., the maintenance system mainains the case base of problem solving. The first thing a PSA inquires upon contacting the maintenance system is achievement status of a specific goal. If there is an instance in the case base which matches the inquired goal, then the PSA knows a result (not only the succeeded solution, but also the information about failure) without having to spend unnecessary time searching for the same result.

Search Space Maintenance System also produces a list, called the *goal queue*, of PSAs which are working on a particular problem. As soon as one agent finds a solution or fails to find it for a particular problem, then the agent reports the result to the maintenance system. Search Space Management System propagates the reported result to the agents in the goal queue which were working on the same problem.

4.3 Autonomous Production System Agent

Each PSA is comprised of ordinal production system (PS) and a special device, called the *recogniser*. The recogniser is not a part of PS, instead it actually works independently of PS and gives some information to PS (therefore, we refer to PSs invoked by PSAs as passive). PSAs have the following knowledge of prescribing its own performance;

- *Goal* : The desired state of problem solving.
- *Preconditions* : The necessary condition for doing action.
- *Action* : Instructions which should be taken place to change current situation towards the goal state.
- *Working Memory* : A list of assertions for current situation same as traditional production systems.
- *Production Memory* : A set of rules for problem solving. Each of them consists of the condition and action part.

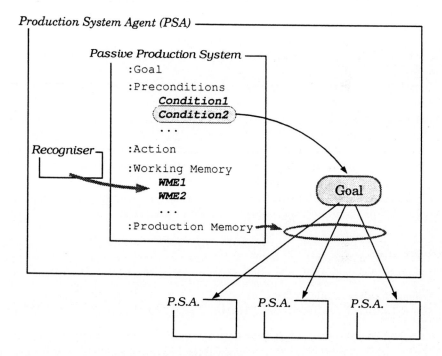

Fig. 3. Configuration of production system agent.

Figure 3 shows the structure of production system agents and the framework for problem solving (hence force, we would use the word "agent" as the abridgment of the passive production system agent, as long as there is no confusion). An agent tends to satisfy all of the conditions specified in *preconditions*. A condition is satisfied if (1) there is an assertion in WM which matches a condition, or (2) there is an instance in the case base at Search Space Maintenance System which demonstrates a validity of a condition. When a condition of the current situation is not satisfied, then the agent selects all of the plausible rules form production memory. The plausible rules are the ones which conditions are all satisfied or unknown (i.e., the agent can not prove its negation as well as its validity). If more than two plausible rules are selected, then the agent invokes a number of PSAs to resolve them. In this way, multiple PSAs are working collaborative to solve a problem. This concurrence of the search avoids an explosion of the search as well as a decline of the search efficiency like the utility problem.

The search fails when there is no applicable rule in production memory, or the depth of search exceeds the predetermined limitation.

5 Conclusion

The multiagent problem solving system with parallel computing capability has a great power far exceeding that of other problem solvers developed in the past.

We have developed the system over several UNIX workstations connected with LAN. Multiple production systems are working on those computers all over the network, and they are communicating through Parallel Virtual Machine (PVM) libraries[3].

The model of problem solving described here is useful for educational systems. The followings are primary contributions of this model;

- The system would be able to show thought process, while not perfect, through trial and error method.
- The system would be able to solve much more problems than traditional linear search based problem solvers, due to its ability to accumulate greater number of knowledge without any decline of search power.

Building an ITS which involves this problem solver to evaluate robustness of the model is one of the important subjects for further research.

References

1. Avron Barr and Edward A. Feigenbaum. *The Handook of Artificial Intelligence.* William Kaufmann, Inc., 1981.
2. W.J. Clancey. *Knowledge-Based Tutoring: The GUIDON Program.* The MIT Press, 1987.
3. Al Geist, Adam Beguelin, Jack Dongarra, and Weicheng Jiang. *PVM: Parallel Virtual Machine.* MIT Press, 1994. http://www.netlib.org/pvm3/book/pvm-book.html.
4. Anoop Gupta. *Parallelism in Production Systems.* Morgan Kaufmann Pub., Inc., 1987.
5. Toru Ishida. *Parallel, Distributed and Multiagent Production System.* Springer-Verlag, 1991.
6. Steven Minton. *Learning Search Control Knowledge: An Explanation Based Approach.* Kluwer Academic Publishers, Boston, 1988.
7. E. Wenger. *Artificial Intelligence and Tutoring Systems.* Morgan Kaufmann, Los Altos, CA, 1987.

Approche qualitative de la ré-ingéniérie d'un système tuteur intelligent à partir d'une méthodologie d'evaluation

Sophie MILLET[1et2] et Guy GOUARDERES

[1]IUT de Bayonne - Dépt. Informatique - Château neuf - Place Paul Bert -64100 Bayonne -
[2]Laboratoire API - IUT Paul Sabatier - 50, chemin des maraîchers - 31077 Toulouse -
FRANCE - Tél. : (33) 59-46-32-11 - Fax : (33) 59-46-32-29
Email : millet@iutbay.univ-pau.fr

Résumé : Cet article décrit les phases d'analyse et d'évaluation du projet "Agent Réviseur" qui vise à embarquer dans un système tuteur intelligent, la révision des connaissances comme un agent intelligent agissant en temps réel. Les expertises nécessaires à l'acquisition des connaissances pour cet agent réviseur ont été réalisées dans le laboratoire d'évaluation spécialisé du CNRS/SOSI à Toulouse avec la participation de chercheurs réunissant différentes compétences pour le projet européen Delta-Value.

Sont plus précisément détaillées les phases préalables de définition et de mise au point de la démarche d'analyse, de conception et d'évaluation de la méthode de révision et de ré-ingéniérie des connaissances utilisées. On précise également les protocoles de diagnostic, d'analyse et de synthèse sur le prototype. On en déduit les principes de base de l'agent réviseur et on réalise en parallèle un prototype de cet agent pour tester son fonctionnement.

On se propose de porter l'ensemble système tuteur intelligent et agent réviseur sur une plate-forme multi-agents déjà opérationnelle dans le laboratoire, le Modèle d'Agent Centré Tâche - MACT.

1 Introduction

La révision des connaissances dans les STI fait souvent référence aux méthodes et techniques éprouvées dites d'acquisition de connaissances [1, 2]. Certaines de ces approches combinent l'extension des connaissances avec celle de l'évolution des stratégies par adaptation à l'apprenant [3] ou encore par apprentissage symbolique automatique [4].

La démarche que nous avons adoptée consiste à voir la révision comme une procédure globale agissant en temps réel. Ce processus est embarqué dans le système tuteur comme un agent intelligent, fonctionnant initialement avec des connaissances ontologiques. Il enrichit ensuite ses propres connaissances par apprentissage tout au long du cycle de vie du tuteur, c'est à dire depuis son premier prototypage rapide jusqu'à l'abandon définitif de l'application.

Pour définir l'architecture et le fonctionnement de cet agent réviseur de connaissances, nous avons choisi d'expertiser tous les aspects de sa conception et de son usage en essayant d'intégrer au mieux les facteurs humains selon des techniques proches des représentations formelles [5] et plus précisément inspirées des méthodes d'évaluation des interfaces usagers telles que les scripts-scénarios "papiers" [6] ou bien le prototypage d'agents intelligents par la méthode du Magicien d'Oz [7].

Le projet "Agent réviseur" fait suite aux travaux entrepris en 1993 au laboratoire API sur les architectures multi-agents des STI [8] et notamment sur : (1) l'étude du diagnostic, du contrôle et de la réutilisabilité de tâches définies sous MACT; (2) l'étude d'un langage de spécification abstraite des raisonnements mis en œuvre par les agents[9]. L'agent réviseur utilise (1) pour détecter en temps réel les dysfonctionnements et (2) pour proposer des révisions ou inférer des corrections.

L'objectif principal de cet article est de définir une méthode globale d'analyse et de conception d'un STI embarquant cet agent réviseur. Cette méthode doit permettre, dans un premier temps, la conception et le prototypage rapide du système tuteur envisagé. Dans les étapes suivantes, elle assure le développement incrémental des prototypes successifs par des évaluations selon différents points de vue. Lors de l'étape ultime de ce travail, le processus de révision doit être intégré dans le tuteur par l'intermédiaire d'un système à base de connaissances d'aide à la mise au point d'une part, et de ré-ingéniérie des connaissances et de l'architecture du tuteur, d'autre part. (Cf. Annexe 1).

Dans une première partie, nous étudions la spécification et le prototypage du TI pour lequel nous justifions dans la seconde partie, la nécessité d'une évaluation intégrant différentes expertises. Dans une troisième partie, nous décrivons l'évaluation que nous avons menée. La partie suivante est une mise en place de la méthode à partir de cette évaluation. Enfin la dernière partie est une conclusion sur ces recherches.

2 Démarche de Spécification et Prototypage de SIERA:

SIERA (Système Intelligent pour l'Etude des Ressources Agricoles) a été réalisé pour fournir un exemple de révision des connaissances. Il a été développé dans le cadre d'une collaboration internationale (France, Canada, Gabon) pour le projet Aupelf.

2.1 Le Projet

Il s'agit d'un système d'aide aux développeurs et aux aménageurs travaillant dans le domaine de l'économie rurale sur les agro-systèmes villageois en Afrique de l'ouest francophone. Les objectifs du projet étaient de promouvoir l'intérêt des systèmes éducatifs intelligents pour la formation dans les pays en voie de développement. Pour cela, nous avons réalisé un premier prototype de tuteur intelligent sur les agro-systèmes villageois au Niger, dans la région du Maradi [11].

2.2 Architecture du Tuteur

Trois parties composent le système : le simulateur, le système tuteur intelligent, le système d'évaluation.

Le simulateur modélise le domaine avec la méthode orientée objets de S. Shlaer et S. Mellor [12] qui présente l'avantage de dégager une méthodologie cohérente, réutilisable et surtout validable par simulation. Le modèle qui en a résulté caractérise l'évolution d'un agro-système villageois en fonction du climat, de la population et de la terre. Ces connaissances sont exploités par un moteur qui utilise une base de règles qui fait fonctionner le cas.

Le STI repose sur un modèle d'interaction pédagogique qui prend en compte le profil de l'apprenant en interaction avec le système. Cette interaction de l'apprenant peut être séparée en trois parties : le module profil qui détermine le niveau de l'apprenant, le module visite guidée qui est la partie analyse d'un cas sélectionné et le module améliorations où l'apprenant doit trouver les améliorations possibles pour le cas étudié.

Le TI tel que nous l'avons décrit dans la phase 1 ne comprend que le simulateur et le STI; il faut alors ajouter dès le début du processus de conception un élément supplémentaire : l'évaluation. L'évaluation porte sur trois problèmes : le contrôle de l'apprenant, la validation du domaine et l'évaluation du produit. Le contrôle de l'apprenant détermine son score par une analyse de ses réponses à des QCM et des paramètres qu'il a donnés pour la simulation. La validation du domaine est réalisée par prototypage rapide afin de contrôler l'analyse. Les tests qui doivent être réalisés par des spécialistes du domaine afin de valider les contenus sont mis en place en même temps que l'évaluation finale du produit. Cette évaluation devra donc faire intervenir diverses compétences : du domaine, ergonome, informaticien, psychologue, pédagogue... Nous réduirons ici notre problème aux aspects ergonomiques, pédagogiques et informatiques de l'évaluation.

3 Nécessité de l'Evaluation par une Méthode d'Intégration

Le projet SIERA a été réalisé à partir d'une étude du CIRAD dont nous avons extrait l'expertise du domaine. L'évaluation permet alors de vérifier si les données sont justes pour les experts et si le produit correspond bien aux besoins des pédagogues. En effet, il se peut que l'informaticien, lors de la réalisation, dérive par rapport à ce que demande le pédagogue. Pour résoudre ce problème, T. Nodenot [13] préconise un travail interactif entre l'informaticien et le pédagogue. Ceci est une méthode coûteuse car elle implique un travail de groupe qui devient souvent fastidieux. Nous proposons donc de pallier ce problème par une évaluation automatique, embarquée dans le produit, à partir d'un système à base de connaissances. Pour obtenir les règles d'évaluation du logiciel, nous avons réalisé une évaluation de SIERA en dégageant une première méthodologie.

3.1 Pourquoi Evaluer et Comment le Faire ?

Aujourd'hui l'évaluation est souvent réalisée trop tard et les informaticiens, confrontés aux contraintes de temps, ne peuvent alors entreprendre que des modifications de surface. L'évaluation doit donc être un processus dynamique, itératif et synchrone en temps réel, c'est à dire un processus devant intervenir très tôt dans la démarche de l'informaticien afin qu'il ait le temps nécessaire pour prendre en compte toutes les remarques.

Pour que cette méthode d'évaluation s'intègre dans le cycle de vie du logiciel, il faut d'abord, selon Faveaux [14], choisir une méthode parmi : les interviews, les observations et les questionnaires d'enquêtes. Or, il est rare qu'une seule de ces méthodes suffise à réaliser une évaluation. L'évaluateur choisit d'abord une méthode prioritaire qu'il accompagne d'une ou deux autres méthodes secondaires. Ceci est confirmé par Patesson [14] et par Spérandio renforce cette idée : "il n'existe pas une méthode ergonomique, mais un choix de méthodes adaptées à des objets d'études particuliers". Notre démarche adapte différentes méthodes aux outils mis à notre disposition dans la salle d'évaluation du CNRS/SOSI à Toulouse (Cf. Annexe 2).

Lors de l'évaluation, différents acteurs interviendront afin d'évaluer le produit selon divers critères.

3.2 Différents Acteurs

La méthode d'évaluation va permettre l'enregistrement en temps réel de tous les événements internes et externes des différents points de vue qui sont :

• *L'ergonome :* Pour garantir l'adéquation du logiciel aux caractéristiques de l'utilisateur et aux besoins relatifs à sa tâche, il faut dans un premier temps identifier et définir les principaux critères ergonomiques auxquels les interfaces utilisateurs doivent répondre. Ces critères sont au nombre de sept dans la norme AFNOR Z67-133-1 et huit dans les travaux de Scapin [15]. Nous nous sommes basés sur ces travaux et nous les avons complétés pour obtenir la grille donnée en annexe 3.

• *L'informaticien :* Du point de vue informatique, ce sont les critères du génie logiciel sur la qualité du logiciel qui priment. Lehman [16] recense sept critères d'évaluation pour les logiciels : correction, satisfiabilité, fiabilité, modifiabilité, reconfigurabilité, sûreté et efficacité.

• *Le pédagogue :* Lors de la spécification, les pédagogues doivent exprimer les objectifs et les contraintes liées aux tuteurs intelligents. Ils modélisent les objets constituant l'environnement du tuteur et définissent le rôle du système par rapport à ces objets. Lors de l'évaluation, on doit pouvoir retrouver ces spécifications. Ils vont donc observer les attitudes de l'apprenant et la façon dont le système va contrôler et orienter son suivi.

Pour cela, T. Nodenot [17] propose d'utiliser trois bibliothèques :

      - la bibliothèque de définition des objectifs du curriculum qui définit la situation-problème de départ (notions à enseigner, tâches des apprennants, critères de réussite, consignes, matériel) et les objectifs mentalistes. Les pédagogues doivent donc retrouver les connaissances déclaratives enseignées, le registre de conceptualisation que les élèves doivent atteindre, les caractéristiques du champ notionnel, les objectifs fixés et les obstacles, la situation-problème.

      - la bibliothèque de définition de la structure du curriculum et de contrôle des éléments du curriculum. En observant les tâches demandées à l'apprenant, le pédagogue remonte et déduit les objectifs concrets, puis abstraits et enfin les objectifs cognitifs.

      - la bibliothèque des tâches appartenant au curriculum. Chaque tâche est caractérisée par le contexte d'exécution (langage de commande utilisable par l'élève et langage de description, ensemble des symboles utilisés par la machine), la formalisation des buts à atteindre en terme de concepts-buts, la formalisation de la solution à cette tâche, la référence à une leçon associée à la tâche proposée.

4 Descriptif de l'Evaluation

Toutes les phases de la méthode ont donc été dirigées par les besoins du laboratoire d'évaluation et ont été réalisées dans le cadre d'un projet européen [18]. L'objectif de cette salle est de proposer des outils pour l'observation, l'analyse et la synthèse des résultats d'une évaluation. Elle permet l'intervention de plusieurs personnes : le responsable de l'évaluation, l'expert, l'ergonome, le script... et facilite la mise en commun de leurs compétences.

4.1 La Phase de Préparation

Lors de cette phase, il faut choisir les intervenants : les observateurs et les utilisateurs. Dans ce projet, sont intervenus en tant qu'observateurs : un responsable d'évaluation (chef de projet), le responsable du laboratoire (ingénieur), un ergonome spécialiste des interfaces, un ergonome spécialisé dans la conduite d'évaluation, un didacticien, un développeur informaticien (expert). Les utilisateurs étaient des cadres moyens choisis par rapport à leur connaissance du sujet. Le responsable de l'évaluation doit préparer l'évaluation en remplissant une fiche, produit METANE[19], sur les caractéristiques techniques du produit. Cette se décompose en trois parties : l'identification du produit, l'analyse de ce produit et le contexte de formation.

      Il essaie alors de réaliser sa cartographie des connaissances du produit. Cette cartographie résume les diverses composantes de l'architecture générale du tuteur : les connaissances du domaine données par l'expert, les connaissances sur les situations, les stratégies pédagogiques données par le pédagogue et les connaissances sur l'évaluation qui sont à établir au fur et à mesure avec la méthode. La cartographie des connaissances du domaine est découpée en : terre, population, climat. La cartographie des interactions pédagogiques est celle qui met en scène le tuteur (stratégies par rapport aux connaissances). La cartographie de l'évaluation peut être décomposée soit par spécialité, soit en suivant le type de travail à faire lors de la ré-ingéniérie (en fonction de l'architecture du TI).

4.2 La Phase d'Observation

Le laboratoire d'évaluation se compose de deux salles séparées par une vitre sans tain et insonorisées l'une de l'autre : le studio et la régie. Dans le studio, se trouve une personne dont le rôle est d'utiliser un logiciel mis à sa disposition. Dans la régie, se trouvent les observateurs, c'est-à-dire les ergonomes, les pédagogues, les informaticiens... Leur rôle est de noter tous les problèmes rencontrés par les utilisateurs lors de la manipulation du logiciel, de manière synchrone, selon un temps codé (système de référence temporelle des images; c'est à dire qu'à chaque image est associé un code en heures, minutes, secondes et images pour la situer dans le temps). Pour cela, un magnétoscope enregistre l'attitude de l'utilisateur et les documents qu'il utilise. Un second magnétoscope enregistre un suivi des écrans informatiques. Ces enregistrements se font selon le temps codé.

A la fin de cette phase d'observation, on réalise une interview semi-dirigée sur des points ayant posé problèmes aux observateurs. Il s'agit aussi ici de laisser parler l'apprenant afin de connaître son appréciation du produit.

4.3 La Phase d'Analyse

Durant cette phase, on revoit en régie, sur les bandes enregistrées, les passages qui ont été annotés par différents intervenants. Tous les points qui ont posé problèmes dans la phase d'observation sont analysés et classés selon les différents critères.

Grâce au temps codé, on a un accès direct sur des points précis de l'évaluation, ce qui permet un gain de temps très important et une grande facilité de manipulation. Ces points forts visionnés, le groupe de travail peut les discuter et affiner les commentaires. Si la séquence semble importante pour la synthèse, elle est numérisée en animation QuickTime et stockée pour une réutilisation en phase finale.

4.4 La Phase de Synthèse

Cette phase est réalisée par le responsable de l'évaluation. C'est un récapitulatif de toutes les phases d'observation et d'analyse. Elle est réalisée soit sous forme d'un rapport, soit sous forme d'un tableau synthétisant tous les problèmes rencontrés lors de l'utilisation du produit classés par type ainsi que les recommandations associées. Cette synthèse est donnée au demandeur de l'évaluation et, pour aider à la compréhension des problèmes, on y joint les séquences QuickTime afin que les personnes qui réalisent les modifications aient une représentation concrète des problèmes. Ces séquences vidéos serviront aussi de preuves.

5 Utilisation de l'Evaluation et Mise en Place de la Méthode

Après avoir décrit l'évaluation, intéressons nous à la méthode mise en œuvre.

5.1 L'Evaluation dans le Cycle de vie du Logiciel

Le cycle de vie d'un logiciel éducatif suit un modèle en spirale bouclant sur quatre phases : détermination des objectifs, analyse des risques / résolution, développement / vérification du produit, planification des phases suivantes. L'évaluation que nous avons décrite est intervenue lors de la phase de développement/vérification du produit.

Elle permet la ré-ingéniérie par affinage du logiciel au cours des reprototypages. A terme, l'évaluation interviendra plus tôt sous forme d'un système multi-agents embarqué dans le TI.

5.2 Les Objets de la Ré-ingéniérie et la Synchronisation

La méthode repose sur deux concepts : les objets de l'évaluation 'réifiant' les observateurs d'une séance d'évaluation et l'intégration des différents points de vue des spécialités.

Ces objets sont des objets dynamiques car leur cycle de vie est représenté par un modèle d'états qui permet de repérer aisément leur interaction et leur synchronisation grâce aux événements. Dans le § 3, nous avons vu l'intérêt d'un modèle événementiel. On vérifié ici qu'il permet de synchroniser et de faire interagir les différents points de vue de l'évaluation. Ainsi, on peut imaginer qu'un vecteur d'événements représentera dans le temps, de façon synchrone, tous les positionnements de tous les évaluateurs. Le modèle d'événements sert de base de connaissances à l'agent réviseur. Il interprète le comportement réel des autres agents de l'application (objets dynamiques) et c'est à partir de cette interprétation qu'il va pouvoir réviser les connaissances. Ce vecteur intégrera le point de vue de tous les évaluateurs ayant spécifié un problème, instant par instant. L'objet de référence sur lequel ils travaillent sera le même pour tous; mais la façon de traiter cet objet sera différente selon les points de vue.

On peut imaginer un dysfonctionnement détecté par l'ergonome, celui-ci diagnostique le problème puis donne les recommandations pour le résoudre. Ceci peut alerter le pédagogue. Si le problème est adidactique, aucune action ne se déclenche; si il est didactique, c'est alors son point d'ancrage (événement de départ). Il va à son tour réaliser un diagnostic et une remédiation. Eventuellement, le pédagogue peut avoir besoin du point de vue du psychologue pour identifier le problème (didactique ou adidactique). Une fois que le pédagogue et l'ergonome auront terminé leur analyse, l'informaticien peut spécifier le problème et reprototyper le produit. Voici un exemple typique des interactions entre les différents observateurs. On voit bien ici que la synchronisation entre les acteurs est très importante; et donc nous utilisons la méthode de Shlaer et Mellor pour exprimer formellement notre méthode d'évaluation. Elle recense les relations synchrones et asynchrones entre les objets en fonction de leur modèle d'états et les modèles des processus nous ont permis de générer directement des règles telles que : Si erreur

Alors enregistrer Temps-codé et Description de Interactions
Et générer P2-Analyse(Temps-codé)

6 Conclusion

Dans cet article nous avons présenté l'étude préalable du projet Agent Réviseur et les premiers résultats obtenus avec une méthode d'analyse et de conception objets permettant d'évaluer et de réviser en temps réel les dysfonctionnements d'un TI. Ces résultats sont encourageants et on a pu ainsi établir une cartographie des connaissances nécessaires à la conception d'un agent réviseur.

A partir de cette cartographie, il a été procédé à l'analyse et à la synthèse des connaissances de surfaces (environ 100 items révisés par l'évaluation) et leur mise en relation avec les connaissances profondes et les paramètres d'architecture du tuteur.

En parallèle, un prototype d'agent réviseur a été réalisé pour tester son opérabilité sur une partie de la base des connaissances de surfaces et profondes.

Il reste maintenant à intégrer l'ensemble pour obtenir une première réalisation d'un TI révisable en temps réel par cet agent embarqué.

Les perspectives envisagées consistent, dans un premier temps à étendre le fonctionnement de l'agent réviseur à l'ensemble des connaissances collectées et analysées dans l'étape d'évaluation, dans un deuxième temps à enrichir les connaissances de cet agent par des évaluations plus ciblées et plus affinées sur les nouveaux prototypes.

Références

[1] B.J. Wielinga, A.T. Shreiber, J. Breuker
KADS : A modelling approach to knowledge engineering.
Revue Knowledge Acquisition - 1992

[2] P. Dillenbourg
Un modèle d'acquisition de connaissances par les tutoriels intelligents.
International Conference of ITS'88 - Montreal (Canada) - 1988

[3] C. Frasson, D. Ramanzani
Prédiction du niveau d'acquisition des connaissances dans la modélisation de l'apprenant.
International Conference of ITS92 - Montreal(Canada) - 1992

[4] J.G. Ganascia
CHARADE : apprentissage de bases de connaissances.,
in Y. Kodratoff et E. Diday - Apprentissage symbolique et numérique - 1990

[5] G. De Hann, G.C. Van De Veer, J.C. Van Vliet
Formal modelling techniques in Human-Computer Interaction.
Acta Psychologica - 78 - pp. 26-76 - 1991

[6] D.E. Rowley, D.G. Rhoads
The cognitive Jogthrought ; A fast-paced user interface evaluation procedure.
ACM SigCHI - 1992

[7] D. Maulsby, S. Greenberg, R.D.G. Mander
Prototyping an intelligent agent through Wizard of Oz.
ACM SigCHI - Amsterdam (The Nederlands) - 1993 - pp. 277-284

[8] A. Péninou
MACT : un Modèle d'Agents Centrés Tâches pour la production de Systèmes Tuteurs Intelligents pour l'Atelier de Génie Didacticiel Intégré.
Thèse de doctorat de l'université Paul Sabatier - Toulouse III - 1993

[9] T. Mengelle
Etude d'une architecture d'environnements d'apprentissage basés sur le concept de préceptorat avisé
Thèse de doctorat de l'université Paul Sabatier - Toulouse III - 1995

[10] H. Lieberman
Attaching Interface Agent Software to Applications.
http://lcs.www.media.mit.edu/people/lieber/Lieberary/Lieberary.html

[11] S. Millet, G. Gouardères, C. Frasson
Adapting CASE tools to produce vocational training systems (Agriculture).
Sixième conférence internationale WCCE'95 - Birmingham (UK) - Juillet 1995

[12] S. Shlaer, S. Mellor
Object lifecycles : modeling the world in states.
Prentice Hall - 1992.

[13] T. Nodenot
M.A.G.E. : un Méta-Atelier de Génie Educatif.
Thèse de doctorat de l'université Paul Sabatier - Toulouse III - Novembre 1992

250

[14]Institut Des Logiciels et des Systèmes
Actes du colloque quatrième ERGO-IA'94 - Ergonomie et Informatique avancée.
Bayonne - Octobre 1994
[15]D. L. Scapin et J.M.C. Bastien
Ergonomic criteria for the evaluation of human-computer interfaces.
INRIA Rocquencourt - Technical Report N° 156 - May 1993.
[16]M.M. Lehman
Les propriétés souhaitées des produits logiciels et du processus de développement des systèmes logiciels.
Revue Génie Logiciel et Système Expert - N° 14 - Mars 1989
[17]T. Nodenot
What if pedagogues specified educational software ?
Sixième conférence internationale WCCE'95 - Birmingham (UK) - Juillet 1995
[18]S. Millet, G. Gouardères
Rapport d'évaluation sur l'interactivité de CD-ROM d'espagnol.
Projet Delta-Value AC-143/93-F'SEPARTI - IUT de Bayonne - Septembre 1995
[19] J. Cabanat, V. Richard, B. Baruk, S. Veaux, S. Chakroun, G. Goéré
METANE : Méthode d'analyse des multimédias pour la formation des adultes.
ORAVEP - Juillet 1992.

Annexe 1 : Etat final du prototype SIERA intégrant l'agent réviseur

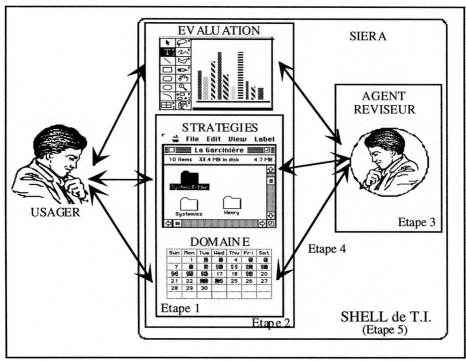

Annexe 2 : Salle d'évaluation

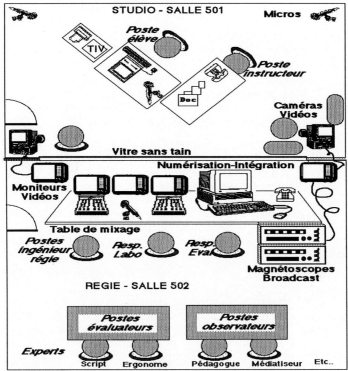

Laboratoire d'évaluation multimédia du CNRS/SOSI – TOULOUSE –

Annexe 3 Grilles Ergonomiques

Critères	Sous-critères
1- GUIDAGE *** Incitation**	Navigation / Conservation-contexte / Historique-de-consultation / Aide-en-ligne / Consigne / ...
* Groupement / Distinction entre items	Organisation-écran / Format-objets (couleur/souligné...)
* Feedback immédiat	Qualité-feedback / Rapidité-feedback /...
* Lisibilité	Gestion-couleur / Chevauchement-fenêtre / ...
2- CHARGE DE TRAVAIL *** Brièveté**	Suite-actions / Combinaison-clavier / Raccourcis-clavier
* Densité informationnelle	Surcharge-cognitive / Objet-inutile / ...
3- CONTROLE EXPLICITE *** Actions explicites**	Validation-utilisateur
* Contrôle utilisateur	Contrôle-dialogue / Interruption-commande / ...
4- ADAPTABILITE *** Flexibilité**	Personnalisation-affichage / Personnalisation-valeur-défaut
* Prise en compte expérience utilisateur	Niveau-apprenant / Annuler-guidage
5- GESTION DES ERREURS *** Protection contre les erreurs**	Actions-imprévues / Validation-provisoire
* Qualité des messages d'erreur	Pertinence-message / Exactitude-message / ...
* Correction des erreurs	Correction-partielle / Auto-correction / ...
6- HOMOGENEITE	Code / Libellé-bouton / Localisation-item / ...
7- SIGNIFIANCE DES CODES	Mnémonique / Abréviations-significatives / ...
8 - COMPATIBILITE	Organisation-données / Termes-familiers / ...
9- MULTIMEDIA *** Qualité**	Qualité-image / Qualité-vidéo / Qualité-son / Qualité-icône / Esthétique-générale
* Synchronisation	Vidéo / Son / Image / Bouton
* Gestion	Fonction-inopérante

Issues in Computerizing the Inquiry Dialogue Planning Process

Lung-Hsiang Wong*; Chee-Kit Looi**; Hiok-Chai Quek*

(e-mail: lhw@uranus.sas.ntu.ac.sg; cheekit@iti.gov.sg; ashcquek@ntuix.ntu.ac.sg)

* Intelligent Systems Laboratory, School of Applied Science,
Nanyang Technological University, Singapore 639798
** Information Technology Institute, 11 Science Park Road,
Singapore Science Park II, Singapore 117685

Abstract. The TAP (Tutoring Agenda Planner) project studies the feasibility of implementing the inquiry teaching method of Collins & Stevens [4] as an ITS shell. Inquiry teaching is a case- as well as dialogue-based teaching style. It has the objective of training scientific reasoning skills while at the same time can be used to teach subject domain knowledge. Collins and Stevens [5] proposed four sets of rules for the delivery of inquiry dialogue. This paper reports on the tackling of some of the major issues that arise in our effort to computerize the rules, particularly in the following aspects: (1) the reorganization of the rules; (2) the role of case selection in the rule selection process.

1. Introduction

Inquiry teaching is a dialogue- and case-based teaching style that forces students to articulate theory that is critical for an in-depth understanding of a domain. This paper describes the second phase of the TAP (Tutoring Agenda Planner) project with the aim of studying the feasibility of developing a computational framework for the inquiry teaching method of Collins and Stevens [4]. The first phase of this project, which has been completed, produced TAP-1 [6, 8, 9], a simple inquiry tutor. The work reported here is a revised inquiry teaching planner (ITP) using the proposed framework of the TAP-2 architecture [10]. The design of the ITP is based on Collins and Stevens' 59 planning strategies [5] (in the form of condition-action pairs, i.e., rules), with certain adaptations in order to fulfill the new constraints as well as Collins' other viewpoint [3].

2. Inquiry Teaching Planner

Collins and Stevens [4] proposed a cognitive theory to formalize the inquiry teaching style. This theory has been developed inductively by observing human teachers [2]. Teachers typically pursue several subgoals (different steps in scientific reasoning, e.g., "form a hypothesis", "test a hypothesis", "debug a hypothesis", "make novel predictions") simultaneously. Each subgoal is associated with a set of strategies for selecting cases, asking questions and giving comments. In pursuing subgoals, teachers maintain an agenda that allows them to deliver various goals efficiently. Given a set of teaching goals, they select cases that optimize the ability of the student to master the goals. Then teachers question students about the cases and the rules interrelating them. The answers reveal what the student does or does not know, which will modify the student model. When the students' specific misconceptions are identified, new subgoals are created to correct the bugs. If the questions reveal multiple bugs, then there will be an agenda that orders the subgoals.

Collins and Stevens [5] described 59 strategies for delivering inquiry dialogues. These production rules are divided into 4 categories:

(1) Case Selection Strategies (denoted as CSS*)
(2) Entrapment Strategies (ENS*)
(3) Hypothesis Identification Strategies (IS*)
(4) Hypothesis Evaluation Strategies (ES*)

A dissection of the dialogue between PADI-2, a TAP-based ITS for teaching rice growing factors, and a student is shown in Figure 1. This serves as an illustration of an inquiry dialogue. PADI-2 is planned to facilitate a formative evaluation of TAP-2. Two of the inquiry rules which are used in the dialogue are elaborated in Figure 2 [5].

(T = Tutor; S = Student)
(Session 1:   Goal - teach the rule of "Water supply is a necessary factor for rice growing";
　　　　　　　Subgoal - form a hypothesis)

(Student Model: blank)

01 T:　Consider Yangtze Plain and Nigeria. Do you know why Yangtze Plain produces rice while Nigeria does not? **[CSS6: Differentiation exemplar of factors (minimal pair)]**
02 S:　Because Nigeria is short of fertile soil.
03 T:　You think fertile soil is necessary for rice growing. **[ES2: Ask if a rule is correct or incorrect]**
04 S:　Yes.
05 T:　You are right. Fertile soil is necessary for rice growing.
　　　　However, Nigeria actually has fertile soil. **[IS7c: Suggest values of factors]** Please think about other possibility. **[IS3: Ask for formulation of an alternative rule]**

(Student Model: add - understood "fertile soil as a necessary factor")

06 S:　Because Nigeria lacks rainfall.
07 T:　Do you think heavy rainfall is a necessary factor for rice growing? **[ENS2: Rule based on unnecessary factors] [ES2: (see above)] [ES5: Ask if factors are necessary or unnecessary]**
08 S:　Yes.

(Student Model: add - bug "water supply as a necessary factor")
(Note: Water can be obtained from rainfall OR irrigation, so rainfall is NOT necessary for rice growing.)

(Session 2:   **Goal** - same with Session 1;
　　　　　　　Change **subgoal** to: debug a wrong hypothesis)

09 T:　Okay. You have made a guess. Let us test it to see whether it is correct. Now, back to the case of Yangtze Plain. Suppose Yangtze Plain doesn't have heavy rainfall, do you think it still grows rice? **[CSS14: Construct a hypothetical case for unnecessary factors]**
10 S:　Yes.
11 T:　Why? **[IS6: Ask for relevant factors]**
12 S:　Because Yangtze Plain has irrigation facilities.
13 T:　So you think either heavy rainfall or irrigation facilities supplies water for rice. **[ES2: (see above)]**
14 S:　Yes.

(Student Model: remove - bug "water supply as a necessary factor"; add - understood "water supply as a necessary factor")

15 T:　Bravo. Water supply, which can either be obtained from heavy rainfall or irrigation, is necessary for rice growing.

(proceed to teach other goals, e.g., "flat terrain as a necessary factor for rice growing" ...)

Fig 1. A sample dialogue of PADI-2

CSS6: Differentiation exemplar for factors (Minimal Pair)

IF   (1)   a student has not identified one or more factors that are relevant to a particular value on the dependent variable, *(for sentence 01 in Figure 1: relevant factor - water supply; dependent variable - rice growing)* **AND**

        (2)   there is a case identified that is a positive or negative exemplar of those factors, *(for sentence 01: case I - Yangtze Plain -- as a positive exemplar)*

THEN (3)   pick a case that has a different value from the previous case on the given factor, that has the same or similar values on other factors, and that has a different value on the dependent variable. *(for sentence (01): case II - Nigeria - as a negative exemplar)*

IS6: Ask for relevant factors

IF   (1)   there are either necessary or sufficient factors that have not been identified, *(for sentence 11; also refer to 09 and 10: unidentified factor: irrigation)*

THEN (2)   ask the student for any relevant factors. *(for sentence 11: "Why?")*

Fig 2. Condition-action pairs of CSS6, ENS2 and IS6

An important observation made by Collins from his inspection of inquiry dialogues is that good inquiry teachers tend to stick to a case and make sure that they have used it in all possible ways to deliver the dialogue before they switch to another case. "Drill a case (that the student is familiar with) to death" will free the student from finding out the unfamiliar background in new cases. Hence, he will be able to focus his attention on the conceptual knowledge and the scientific reasoning skill. This aspect of inquiry teaching has not been mentioned in any of Collins or Stevens' papers [3].

Note that Collins and Stevens' theory is basically a human theory. Although certain parts of the theory have yet to be formalized or seem incomplete, human teachers are expected to be able to "fill in the gaps" by perceptions and experience. However, a systematic approach is needed for converting the theory into a computational model in order to preserve the functionality of the original framework. This is probably a common challenge that general AI researchers and programmers face.

3. The TAP-2 Architecture

A complete TAP-based ITS consists of two major parts: the TAP kernel and the domain-specific module. The TAP kernel is a domain-independent ITS shell that functions as the tutoring module. It consists of three software modules: a control module, a planner and a student modeler; and maintains three databases: an agenda, teaching history (TH) and a student model (SM). In particular, the tutoring module has also adapted Peachey and McCalla's "globalized" curriculum planning technique [7] to complement Collins and Stevens' cognitive theory that focuses on the delivery planning of inquiry teaching. The Global Curriculum Planner (GCP) essentially sequences the "top-level goals" to be taught (e.g., the goal of teaching "water supply is necessary for rice growing"). For more details of how GCP is integrated into TAP-2, please refer to [10].

The domain-specific module represents the domain-specific part of the system. It contains a domain knowledge base, a curriculum knowledge base, an executor and a user-interface manager. TAP is intended to be an ITS shell so that "*domain programmers*" (or domain developers) can design and code their own domain-specific modules and integrate them with the TAP kernel.

The full planning-execution cycle of TAP-2 is somewhat complicated. For the purpose of this paper, the inquiry planning and execution procedure are summarized for discussion:

STEP 0: (Assuming that GCP has selected a goal and passed it to the ITP.)

STEP 1: The top goal is broken into several subgoals. These subgoals are added onto the agenda.

STEP 2: Given the first item on the agenda (a combination of goal+subgoal), ITP selects an inquiry rule (strategy) and a case(s) needed to execute the rule.

STEP 3: ITP passes goal+subgoal+rule+case combination to the executor.

STEP 4: The executor interprets the delivery plan and starts the execution. The executor frequently passes control to the UI manager for the user-interface.

STEP 5: The UI manager passes the student's responses to the executor for diagnosis. The diagnosis is in turn passed to the student modeler for student modeling.

STEP 6: When the student modeler reveals bug(s) of the students, the system would create subgoals to correct it(them). These debugging subgoals will be ordered, based on some priority rules [4], and appended to the agenda.

STEP 7: If a debugging subgoal has failed, then loop back to step (0) to select other goals; else loop back to step (2) to execute the next item on the agenda.

The rest of this paper will focus on the computerization of step (2) which is the rule and case selection process.

4. The Delivery Rules and the Dialogue Sessions

One significant amendment to the TAP architecture that departs from Collins and Stevens' theory is to treat the dialogue session of each goal+subgoal combination (e.g., Session 1 & 2 in Figure 1) as the most basic unit for performing instructional planning. This differs from Collin's work where the planning and replanning are performed at the lowest level - which occurs each time after the student has "spoken" something and before the system responds (e.g., in Figure 1, every statement made by the tutor is an application of one or several inquiry rules).

Such an amendment is made because of two considerations. Firstly, the context switching between the planner and the executor poses significant computational overhead. Thus, it is not worthwhile to replan the dialogue at the lowest level (that is, high frequency of replanning). Secondly (and more importantly), the modified policy is expected to produce more systematic and modularized dialogue. In this case, the student will have a better idea of the dialogue flow (that is, what are the goals that he has gone through and what is the current goal) and less likely to be put off by the dialogue.

Through analysis of the excerpts of inquiry dialogue in various sources [1, 2, 4, 5], we induce a phenomenon: the first rule that is applied to each dialogue session is always the pre-dominant rule of that session. The choice of "the first rule" decides the general content of the session. We refer to such rules as *"Dialogue Session Rules"* (DSR). For example, in Session 1 of Figure 1, the system chooses CSS6 (Minimal Pair) as the DSR of the session. Hence, the entire session is focused on the discussion of the positive (Yangtze Plain) and negative (Nigeria) exemplar pair.

Once the DSR has been applied to the session, the choice of subsequent rules will depend on the student's responses. Generally, these rules are "small" and could be re-used by more than one dialogue session. ENS2, IS3, IS6, IS7c, ES2 and ES5 in Figure 1 illustrate such rules. Among them, ES2 has been applied in both sessions 1 and 2. We refer to this type of rules as "*Dialogue Micro-Rules*" (DMR).

Hence, we could divide Collins and Stevens' 59 inquiry rules into two groups: DSR and DMR, on the basis of the nature of each rule. Figure 3 shows the categorization of these the rules (please refer to [5] for the descriptions of the rules).

	CSS	ENS	IS	ES
DSRs	1-16	-NA-	4-6; 11-14	11-14
DMRs	-NA-	1-12	1-3; 7-10; 15-16	1-10

Fig 3. DSRs and DMRs

This re-grouping classifies the entire set of ENS (Entrapment Strategies or Rules 1-12) as DMRs. The basic function of entrapment is to reveal the student's misconceptions (bugs). When the system suspects that the student's response to an inquiry is due to a misconception, it may want to entrap the student in order to confirm the suspicion and then decides on what to do next. If a bug of the student has been diagnosed "with high confidence", then no entrapment is needed - the system will simply create a new debugging subgoal. We recommend the domain programmers to encode the DMRs implicitly in the dialogue flow while they are programming the UI manager.

The conditions and the actions of DMRs are generally quite simple. They are essentially the immediate responses to the student's latest input. Simple software switches or IF-THEN-ELSE constructs (with the student's responses as the conditions) can be used to implement these rules.

5. Re-selecting previous case(s)

As a case-based teaching method, the selection of the cases for the dialogue is a significant issue in inquiry teaching. Collins advises the avoidance of changes of cases. This is a primary concern in case selection. Even with old cases, there should not be too much switching.

Most of the DSRs require the selection of cases (only IS4-6 do not require that). For IS11-14 and ES11-14, the required cases are restricted to previously chosen ones (e.g., IS12 in Figure 4). On the other hand, there are two kinds of rules in the CSS* group. The first kind of the rules (CSS5-8) requires a previous case and the selection of another case (e.g., CSS6 in Figure 1). Whether to choose an "old" case or a new case as the second case is not explicitly stated in [5]. The second type of rules (the rest of the CSS*) requires only one case (e.g., CSS10 in Figure 4). Again this can be either an "old" or new case.

In implementing CSS*, two important points have to be discussed. Firstly, although we prefer "old" cases, some of them may not suit *all* of new cases if the need arises. A suitable way of executing the actions is: to find a suitable "old" case first; if such "old" case is not available, then look for an unused one.

IS12: Ask for differences in factors between similar cases

IF   (1)   two or more cases have been identified that have similar values on the dependent variable,

THEN (2)   ask the student to identify any other factor on which the cases have different values.

CSS10: Counterexample for an unnecessary factor

IF   (1)   a student proposes a rule or makes a prediction based on one or more factors that are unnecessary, **OR**

      (2)   is entrapped by a rule (ENS2 or ENS10) based on one or more factors that are unnecessary,

THEN (3)   pick a case that does not have the values specified on the unnecessary factors, but does have the value specified on the dependent variable.

Fig 4. Condition-action pairs of IS12 and CSS10

This leads us to the second concern: what happens if the domain knowledge base does not store any case that is suitable for the rule? Under this situation, the system is unable to execute the rule since no case can be discussed. In TAP-1, the strategy selection (similar to the inquiry rule in the context of TAP-2) and the case selection processes are interleaved - the planner decides the strategy first and then selects suitable cases for the strategy. Therefore, the planner must "backtrack" to the strategy selection process if no suitable case is found for the selected strategy. This is again another overhead. Our solution in TAP-2 is to promote the actions of "THEN: pick a case ..." to be new conditions for the relevant rules, and leave the actual dialogue discussions of the cases as the actions. Although conceptually the actions of CSS* are case selection (as the name "Case Selection Strategies" suggests), we implement the "case selection actions" of these rules as conditions in order to improve the performance. For instance, the modified version of CSS6 is:

IF   (1)   a student has not identified one or more factors that are relevant to a particular value on the dependent variable, **AND**

      (2)   there is a case identified that is a positive or negative exemplar of those factors, **AND**

      (3)   a case is available that has a different value from the previous case on the given factor, that has the same or similar values on other factors, and that has a different value on the dependent variable,

THEN (4)   discuss with the student about the differences of the given factors of the two cases and how they affect the dependent variable.

LISTS (global; non-volatile memory)
Unused_Cases := all the cases stored in the domain knowledge base [initially]
Used_Cases := (blank) [initially]

STRUCTURE (local)
Rule_List (eligible rules with their suitable cases)

VARIABLE (local)
Boolean   NeedNewCase

PROCEDURE FireDSRs

NeedNewCase := TRUE
Rule_List := (blank)

Fig 5. DSR Firing Algorithm

```
FOR all the inquiry rules

        IF the goal+subgoal+rule combination has been used in the dialogue before
            THEN continue with next iteration of the FOR loop (check next rule)
        ENDIF

        check other conditions (i.e., NOT conditions about cases)
        IF other conditions are unsatisfied
            THEN continue with next iteration of the FOR loop
        ENDIF
        IF the rule is CSS* with the requirement of TWO cases
            THEN  select the first case from the Used_Cases ---- (B)
                    IF no case is found
                        THEN   continue with next iteration of the FOR loop
                        ELSE   select the second case from the Used_Cases ---- (B)
                                IF a case is found
                                    THEN   NeedNewCase := FALSE
                                ELSE IF   NeedNewCase := TRUE ---- (A)
                                    THEN   select the second case from the Unused_Cases ---- (B)
                                ENDIF

                                IF a case is found in either Used_Cases or Unused_Cases
                                    THEN   add the rule and the cases into Rule_List
                    ENDIF
        ENDIF
        ELSE IF the rule is CSS* with the requirement of ONE case
            THEN select the case from the Used_Cases ---- (B)
                    IF a case is found
                        THEN   NeedNewCase := FALSE
                    ELSE IF NeedNewCase := TRUE ---- (A)
                        THEN   select the case from the Unused_Cases ---- (B)
                    ENDIF

                    IF a case is found in either Used_Cases or Unused_Cases
                        THEN   add the rule and the case into Rule_List
                    ENDIF
        ELSE                    (IS* or ES*)
                    select cases from the Used_Cases ---- (B)
                    IF cases are found
                        THEN   NeedNewCase := FALSE
                                add the rule and the case into Rule_List
                    ENDIF
        ENDIF

        IF Rule_List has more than one rule
            THEN pick a rule with the most preferred case(s) being attached to ---- (C)
        ENDIF

ENDFOR

END PROCEDURE
```

Fig 5. DSR Firing Algorithm *(cont.)*

The ideas being discussed in the current section can be summarized in two points: (1) minimize the case switching and the introduction of new cases; (2) promote the "case selection actions" of CSS* to be new conditions and if no suitable previous case can be found for these "action-turned-condition" then select a case from the unused ones. A DSR firing algorithm (see Figure 5) is proposed to realize these.

In the algorithm, the first IF condition in the FOR loop is a criterion inherited from TAP-1. The reason behind is that it is better to select another inquiry rule to teach the same goal and subgoal, rather than keep repeating the same goal+subgoal+rule combination.

The boolean flag NeedNewCase is another means of rule filtering. This is first initialized with the value "TRUE", and will toggle to "FALSE" only if an eligible rule, when all its attached cases are re-used ones, has been identified. Hence, all the subsequently identified rules with new cases will be de-selected. This occurs in the two lines labeled (A) in the algorithm. This filtering process will reduce the execution time of the procedure.

Another important step appears at line (C) whereby "the most preferred case" is to be decided there. We have worked out a set of criteria that is also applicable to all the lines labeled as (B) in the algorithm (if more than one case is eligible for the current rule). The criteria, listed in the order of checking, are given below:

(1) the most recently used cases first (cases that have just been used in the latest dialogue session; this ensures minimal switching of cases)
(2) more frequently used cases first (in term of the number of previous sessions that have chosen the cases)
(3) previously selected cases first
(4) more common or popular cases first (choose from a set of unused cases)

6. Refinements of the rule conditions

Further analysis of the application of the rules to the inquiry dialogue reveals that the conditions of many of the 59 rules are loosely specified in [5]. In actual dialogue, some rules are applicable to certain situations but not others. We have revised all the DSRs and added in some new conditions. Take for example IS12 (whose description is in Figure 4), the only condition specified in IS12 is fairly simple and only involves the required cases. However, from the following example (adapted from [5; pg. 112]) one may conclude that such rule is only applicable to teaching unnecessary factors:

"Supposing that both Japan and Java have been identified as producing rice, the teacher could ask the student for any difference in factors between the two cases. In fact Japan is much more mountainous. This indicates that flat land is not a necessary factor."
(Note: Japan applies terracing technology to overcome the problem.)

Also, such rule is more suitable for pursuing the subgoals: "test a hypothesis" and "debug a wrong hypothesis", but is less suitable for pursuing the subgoal "form a hypothesis". Therefore, a modified version of IS12 is proposed as follows,

IF   (1)   the top goal is to teach an unnecessary factor, **AND**
        (2)   the subgoal is either "test a hypothesis" or "debug a wrong hypothesis", **AND**
        (3)   two or more cases have been identified that have similar values on the dependent variable,
THEN (4)   ask the student to identify any other factor on which the cases have different values.

The increase in the conditions is not only necessary, but also provides additional filtering criteria for rule firing. Since the bottleneck of the condition checking is at the case selection process, the additional conditions (which are simply value checking of a few individual global variables like top goal and subgoal) allow possible early rejection of more rules before the case selection is executed, hence providing an improvement in the performance.

7. Conclusion

TAP is intended to demonstrate the basic integrated architecture of ITP and GCP. The major contribution is the consideration of what it takes to implement a theory of inquiry teaching. In this paper, we discuss some major issues in computerizing Collins and Stevens' 59 inquiry rules (strategies). Methods are proposed to make the ITP in TAP-2 fulfill the following requirements:

- take "drilling a case to its death" as the main concern of not only the case selection, but also the inquiry rule selection;

- inherit TAP-1's policy of taking each dialogue session as a "planning unit", while at the same time adopt the 59 inquiry rules which, in contrast, takes each statement of the tutor as a planning unit;

- reduce the considerable computational effort in rule firing (especially the bottleneck in the case selection process) without the expense of simplifying the specifications of the inquiry rules.

The TAP-2 kernel and the PADI-2 tutor are currently being written using Visual C under Microsoft Windows 3.1. A formative evaluation of the system is also being planned.

References:

[1] Collins, A. [1987], A sample dialogue based on a theory of inquiry teaching, in C.M. Reigeluth (Ed), *Instructional Theories in Action: Lessons Illustrating Selected Theories and Models*, Hillsdale, N.J.: Erlbaum, 1987, 181-199.

[2] Collins, A. [1988], Different goals of inquiry teaching, in Questioning Exchange, 1988, **2**(1), 39-45.

[3] Collins, A. [1995], personal conversation.

[4] Collins, A., & Stevens, A.L. [1982a], A cognitive theory for inquiry teaching, in P. Goodyear (Ed.), *Teaching knowledge and Intelligent Tutoring*, Norwood, N.J.: Ablex, 1991, 203-230.

[5] Collins, A., & Stevens, A.L. [1982b], Goals and strategies of inquiry teachers, in R. Glaser (Ed.), *Advances in Instructional Psychology II*, Hillsdale, N.J.: Erlbaum, 1982.

[6] Looi, C.K., Wong, L.H., & Quek, H.C. [1994], An agenda planner for inquiry teaching, *Proceedings of PRICAI-94*, Beijing: International Academic Publishers, 1994, 1021-1027.

[7] Peachey, D.R., & McCalla, G.I. [1986], Using Planning Techniques in Intelligent Tutoring Systems, in *Int. Journal of M-M Studies*, 1986, **24**(1-6).

[8] Wong, L.H. [1995], *An Intelligent Tutoring System Based on Inquiry Teaching Approach*, Technical Report ISL-TR 05/95, Singapore: Nanyang Technological University, 1995.

[9] Wong, L.H., Looi, C.K., & Quek, H.C. [1995a], An ITS to plan inquiry dialogue, *Proceedings of the 7th World Conference on Artificial Intelligence in Education, AI-ED '95*, Washington D.C., U.S.A., 1995, 461 to 468.

[10] Wong, L.H., Looi, C.K., & Quek, H.C. [1995b], Design of an ITS for inquiry teaching, *Proceedings of the Third World Congress on Expert Systems* (WCES3), Seoul, South Korea, 1996, **1**, 421-428.

ELM-ART: An Intelligent Tutoring System on World Wide Web

Peter Brusilovsky, Elmar Schwarz, and Gerhard Weber

Department of Psychology, University of Trier
Trier, Germany
E-mail: {plb | schwarz | weber } @cogpsy.uni-trier.de

Abstract: Making ITS available on the World Wide Web (WWW) is a way to integrate the flexibility and intelligence of ITS with world-wide availability of WWW applications. This paper discusses the problems of developing WWW-available ITS and, in particular, the problem of porting existing ITS to a WWW platform. We present the system ELM-ART which is a WWW-based ITS to support learning programming in Lisp. ELM-ART demonstrates how several known ITS technologies can be implemented in WWW context.

1   ITS Technologies and WWW Context

WWW opens new ways of learning for many people. However, most of the existing educational WWW applications use simplest solutions and are much more weak and restricted than existing 'on-site' educational systems and tools. In particular, most WWW educational systems do not use powerful ITS technologies. A promising direction of research is to port these technologies to a WWW platform, thus joining the flexibility and intelligence of ITS with world-wide availability of WWW applications.

Most of traditional intelligent techniques applied in ITS can be roughly classified into three groups which we will name as technologies: curriculum sequencing, interactive problem solving support, and intelligent analysis of student solutions. All these technologies are aimed at supporting the "intelligent" duties of the human teacher which can not be supported by traditional non-intelligent tutoring systems. Curriculum sequencing and intelligent analysis of student solutions are the oldest and best-studied technologies in the domain of ITS. Most ITS developed during the first 10 years of ITS history belong to these groups. The technology of interactive problem solving support is a newer one, but it is more "intelligent" and supportive (it helps the student in the most difficult part of the learning process and provides the most valuable support for the teacher in the classroom). It is not surprising that it became a dominating technology during the last 15 years. The WWW context changes the attitudes to traditional ITS techniques [Brusilovsky, 1995]. For example, interactive problem solving support currently seems to be a less suitable technology for WWW-based ITS. Vice versa, the two older technologies seem to be very usable and helpful in the WWW context. Intelligent analysis of solutions needs only one interaction between browser and server for a complete solution. It can provide intelligent feedback and perform student modeling when interactive problem solving support is impossible. Curriculum sequencing becomes very important to guide the student through the hyperspace of available information. In addition to traditional ITS technologies, some of more recent (and much less used) ITS technologies become important. Two examples are adaptive hypermedia [Beaumont & Brusilovsky, 1995] and example-based problem solving [Weber, 1995].

This paper discusses the problems of developing WWW-based ITS and, in particular, the problem of porting existing ITS to a WWW platform. We present the system ELM-ART which is an ITS to support learning programming in Lisp. ELM-ART is developed on the base of the system ELM-PE [Weber & Möllenberg, 1994] specially to be used on WWW. The presentation is centered around intelligent features of ELM-ART (a number of interesting non-intelligent features of ELM-ART are described elsewhere [Schwarz, Brusilovsky & Weber, 1996]). The goal of the paper is to demonstrate how several known ITS technologies can be implemented on WWW and what has to be added when porting a traditional ITS to WWW.

2   ELM-ART

ELM-ART (ELM Adaptive Remote Tutor) is a WWW based ITS to support learning programming in Lisp. ELM-ART is based on ELM-PE [Weber & Möllenberg, 1994], an Intelligent Learning Environment that support example-based programming, intelligent analysis of problem solutions, and advanced testing and debugging facilities. For several years, ELM-PE was used in introductory Lisp courses at the University of Trier. The course materials were presented to students in lecture form (complemented with printed material) and ELM-PE was used to practice the obtained knowledge by problem-solving. ELM-ART, which is expected to be used for distance learning, provides on-line both the course materials and the problem solving support.

ELM-ART can be considered as an on-line intelligent textbook with an integrated problem solving environment (we call it I^3 textbook, or intelligent interactive integrated textbook). It provides all the course materials (presentations of new concepts, test, examples, and problems) in hypermedia form. ELM-ART differs from simple WWW "hyperbooks" in two major aspects. First, ELM-ART "knows" the material it presents to the students and supports them in learning and navigating the course material. Second, all examples and problems (which are important components of any textbook) in ELM-ART are not just a text as in other textbooks, but "live experience". Using ELM-ART, the student can investigate all examples and solve all problems on-line. For any textbook problem, ELM-ART provides the student with almost the same level of intelligent problem solving support as the original ELM-PE. All these features of ELM-ART are presented below in more detail.

2.1 On-line Course Material

The course material in ELM-ART is provided on WWW in hypertext form. It consists of two main components: the textbook and the reference manual. The textbook (which is an on-line version of the normal printed Lisp textbook used in the courses during the last years) is hierarchically structured into units of different level: chapters, sections, and subsections. Each of these units can be presented to the student as a WWW "page" which shows the content of this unit (text and pictures) and various kinds of links from this unit to related elements of the course. All problem solving examples and problems are presented on separate "interactive" pages which use the possibilities of WWW fill-out forms. The reference manual provides the reference access to the course material. Each "page" of the manual contains a brief explanation of one of the course concepts and the links to the related course units and to related manual pages. Thus, the manual in ELM-ART performs also the role of glossary and index of traditional textbooks.

Two kinds of links are used in the course: normal hierarchy links and content-based links. The hierarchy links connect a higher level unit (like a chapter) with all its subunits (like sections in this chapter) and in other direction - each unit with its parent unit. Content-based links can be provided by ELM-ART because the system "knows" what is presented on each page of the course material, i.e., which concepts are introduced, presented, or summarized in each subsection, which concepts are demonstrated by each example, and which concepts are required to solve each problem. As a result, the system can provide references from each textbook page (including example and problem pages) to corresponding manual pages for each involved concept. Vice versa, from each manual page describing a concept (for example, a Lisp-function) the system can provide references to all textbook pages where this concept is introduced, explained, or summarized, to all example pages where it is demonstrated, and to all problem pages which can be used to master this concept. The links within the manual are also content-based links. The system "knows" the pedagogical structure of the Lisp domain and the relationships between various concepts. All these relationships are shown as links on the manual pages. Finally, the system "knows" the structure of any problem solving example. Thus, it can provide "similarity" links from each example to other most similar examples. This feature is based on the EBR method [Weber, 1995].

2.2 Adaptive Navigation Support

ELM-ART provides many more opportunities for browsing the course materials than traditional on-line textbooks. The negative side of it is that there is a higher risk for the student to get lost in this complex hyperspace. To support the student navigating through the course, the system uses two adaptive hypermedia techniques - adaptive annotation and adaptive sorting of links. *Adaptive annotation* means that the system uses visual cues (icons, fonts, colors) to show the type and the educational state of each link. Using the student model (an individual permanent student model is maintained for each registered student), ELM-ART can distinguish several educational states for each page of material (including problem, example, and manual pages): the content of the page can be known to the student, ready to be learned, or not ready to be learned (the latter case means that some prerequisite knowledge is not yet learned). The icon and the font of each link presented to the student are computed dynamically from the individual student model (Figure 1). They always inform the student about the type and the educational state of the node behind the link. *Adaptive sorting* is used to present similarity links between cases. Since the system can measure the similarity between each two cases, it can also sort all cases related to the current one according to the similarity values. Links are presented in sorted order - the most relevant first - so the student always knows what the most similar cases are.

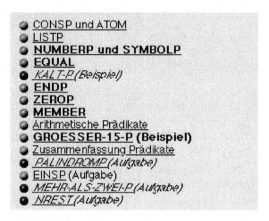

Fig. 1. Example of adaptive annotation of links at the beginning of the course.
The metaphor is traffic lights. Red (italic typeface) means not ready to be learned, green (bold) means ready and recommended, yellow means ready but not recommended.

2.3   Prerequisite-based Help

The system knowledge about the course material comprises knowledge about what the prerequisite concepts are for any page of course material including example and problem pages. As a rule, the prerequisites are not shown directly. But, they can be shown to the students in the following two cases. First, when a student enters a page which is not yet ready to be learned, the system warns the student that this material has unlearned prerequisites and shows additional links to textbook and manual pages where the unlearned prerequisite concepts are presented. This feature adds intelligent help and implicit guidance to hypermedia freedom of navigation. Second, when the student has problems with understanding some explanation or example or solving a problem, he or she can request help (using a special button) and, as an answer to help request, the system will show the links to all pages where the prerequisite knowledge is presented.

2.4   Intelligent Problem Solving Support

As ELM-ART is a system that supports example-based programming, it encourages the students to re-use the code of previously analyzed examples when solving a new problem. The hypermedia form of the course and, especially, similarity links between examples help the student to find the relevant example from his or her previous experience. An important feature of ELM-ART is that the system can predict the student way of solving a particular problem and find the most relevant example from the individual learning history. This kind of problem solving support is very important for students who have problems with finding relevant examples. Answering the help request ("show example" on Figure 2), ELM-ART selects the most helpful examples, sorts them according to their relevance, and presents them to the student as an ordered list of hypertext links. The most relevant example is always presented first, but, if the student is not happy with this example for some reasons, he or she can try the second and the following suggested examples.

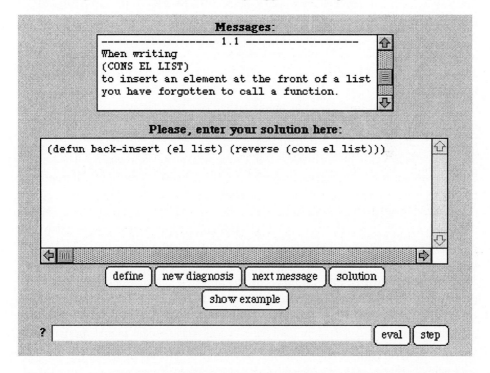

Fig. 2. Form-based interface for problem solving support

If the student failed to complete the solution of the problem, or if the student can not find an error which was reported by the testing component, he or she can ask the system to diagnose the code of the solution in its current state. As an answer, the system provides a sequence of help messages with more and more detailed explanation of an error (Figure 2). The sequence starts with a very vague hint what is wrong and ends with a code-level suggestion of how to correct the error or how to complete the solution. In many cases, the student can understand where the error is or what can be the next step from the very first messages and do not need more explanations. The solution can be corrected or completed, checked again, and so forth. The student can use this kind of help as many times as required to solve the problem correctly. In this context, the possibility to provide the code-level suggestion is a very important feature of ELM-ART as a distance learning system. It ensures that all students will finally solve the problem without the help of a human teacher.

3   Implementation of ELM-ART

3.1   Knowledge

The key to the intelligent behavior performance of ELM-ART is the knowledge about the subject domain and about the student which is represented in the system in several forms. The major part of the ELM-ART knowledge base consists of the knowledge about problem solving in Lisp which is represented as a network of concepts, plans, and rules. Most of this knowledge, as well as tools to work with it were inherited by ELM-ART from its mother, ELM-PE [Weber, 1996].

To support all intelligent techniques that are used to work with the course material we have enhanced ELM-ART knowledge base with the conceptual knowledge about Lisp and with the knowledge about the course. We have applied an approach described in [Brusilovsky, 1992] to represent this knowledge. The core of this knowledge is the Lisp conceptual network (LCN) which represents all important concepts used in the course and all relationships between them. The kinds of represented concepts include several kinds of Lisp objects (functions, data objects, data types) and several kinds of high level concepts related with Lisp and programming. Each represented concept has a corresponding page in the ELM-ART reference manual. Two main types of relationships in LCN are the traditional "part-of" and "is-a". The prerequisite relationships between concepts are not represented directly, but the system is able to compute them from part-or and is-a relationships using several heuristics. To represent the conceptual knowledge of individual students the system uses a traditional weighted overlay student model. In particular, this model is used by ELM-ART to compute the current educational state for each concept that are shown to the student by adaptive visual cues.

To represent the knowledge about the course, all terminal units of the learning material (explanations, examples, and problems) were indexed by LCN concepts. It means that for each unit we have provided a list of concepts related with this unit (we call this list *spectrum* of the unit). For each involved concept, the spectrum of the unit represents also the kind of the relationships or the role of the concept. For example, a concept can be *introduced, presented, summarized* in an explanation unit, or be a *prerequisite* concept for this unit.

3.2 Platform

The WWW implementation of ELM-ART[1] is based on the Common Lisp Hypermedia Server CL-HTTP [Mallery, 1994]. CL-HTTP[2] is a fully featured HTTP server completely implemented in Common LISP. Since the original ELM-PE system was also implemented in Common LISP, CL-HTTP appears to be an optimal platform for our purposes. CL-HTTP offers a Common Gateway Interface[3] to handle incoming URLs from all over the world via the Internet. To enable the server to respond to a particular URL, this URL has to be associated to a response function implemented in LISP. Answering an incoming request, the server recognizes a URL, calls an associated function, and returns an HTML page which is generated by this function. The received URL and enclosed form values that may contain an arbitrary amount of incoming data are submitted as function parameters. The function generates an HTML page as an adaptive response. To do that, the function can use a special set of HTML-generating functions. With such an architecture, CL-HTTP is a very flexible and powerful tool for implementing intelligent applications on WWW. Since a LISP function is called to handle the request, any interactive or intelligent tool written in LISP can be connected to WWW with the help of CL-HTTP.

3.3 Functionality

Adapting Pages. An important feature of the system is that all pages presented to the user are generated adaptively on the fly when the user requests them. To generate pages, the system uses the text of the course which is stored as an annotated HTML file, and knowledge about the structure of the course. When assembling a page of the course, ELM-ART extracts the text of the requested unit from the HTML file and generates the rest of the page (header, footer, hierarchy links and content based links) from the knowledge base. The situation with reference manual pages is even more flexible, because for most of them not only links, but also the content itself is generated from the knowledge base. With this approach, all adaptive features of ELM-ART presented above such as additional headers for not-ready-to-be-learned pages or adaptive annotation of links according to their educational state can be easily implemented. An information about methods applied for adaptive annotation of links can be found elsewhere [Beaumont & Brusilovsky, 1995].

---

[1]ELM-ART URL: http://www.psychologie.uni-trier.de:8000/elmart
[2]http://www.ai.mit.edu/projects/iiip/doc/cl-http/home-page.html
[3]http://hoohoo.ncsa.uiuc.edu/cgi/

Problem solving support. To integrate various forms of problem solving support, we provide a form-based interface by which the user can send a LISP expression to ELM-ART for evaluation or send a problem solution for analysis. A page with a problem to solve is implemented as a HTML fill-out-form[4] with slots to be filled with LISP code and several buttons to request different feedback from the system (Figure 2). For example, the slot "solution" has to be filled with the code of the problem solution and the associated buttons are used for defining, testing, and diagnosing the inserted solution. When the user "pushes" one of these buttons, a HTTP request with an attached content of the form is sent to the server. The server calls the responsible LISP function to process the solution. The processing functions provide the interface to different components of ELM-ART inherited from ELM-PE (evaluator, tester, diagnoser, etc.): they prepare the data for these components and transform their output into HTML form. The functionality of all these components is described elsewhere [Weber & Möllenberg, 1994]. The most advanced case here is an interface to the diagnoser. As we mentioned above, the diagnoser generates several levels of help on from hints to the code-level suggestions and this help should be presented to the user not in one shoot, but step by step. Currently, this functionality is implemented by presenting the diagnostic feedback in a scrollable window of the fill-out form so that only one message is visible at once. The user can browse these messages step by step until he or she understands the problem.

4   Conclusion

The system ELM-ART described in this paper is an example of an ITS implemented on WWW. ELM-ART provides remote access to a hypermedia-structured learning material which includes explanations, tests, examples, and problems. Unlike traditional electronic textbooks, ELM-ART provides the learner with intelligent navigation support and possibilities to play with examples, to solve the problems, and to get intelligent problem-solving support which usually can be provided only by a human teacher. ELM-ART integrates the features of an electronic textbook, of a learning environment, and of an intelligent tutoring system.

ELM-ART can also serve as a good example to discusses the problems of implementing and porting ITS systems on WWW. It demonstrates that some ITS technologies, such as intelligent analysis of solutions and example-based problem solving can be ported relatively easily to a WWW context. It shows the importance of on-line course material and the technologies of adaptive hypermedia and curriculum sequencing which help students to navigate through this material. From the practical side, ELM-ART demonstrates an effective way of implementing ITS on WWW using the Common Lisp Hypermedia Server CL-HTTP.

---

[4]http://www.ncsa.uiuc.edu/SDG/Software/Mosaic/Docs/fill-out-forms/overview.html

We consider the problems of implementing ITS on WWW as an important direction of ITS research. WWW can help ITS to move from laboratories to real classrooms. In the WWW context, ITS can be located on HTTP servers in the research laboratories which have powerful equipment to run intelligent systems and ITS professionals to support and update the systems. At the same time, learners from over the world can access these ITS using any WWW browser. These browsers require relatively cheap hardware and can run on almost any platform. It gives ITS really world-wide audience and unlimited source of data for testing and improving their functionality.

Acknowledgments

Part of this work is supported by a Grant from "Alexander von Humboldt - Stiftung " to the first author and by a Grant from "Stiftung Rheinland-Pfalz für Innovation" to the third author.

References

Beaumont, I. and Brusilovsky, P. (1995) 'Educational applications of adaptive hypermedia'. In: K. Nordby, P. Helmersen, D. J. Gilmore and S. A. Arnesen (eds.): *Human-Computer Interaction*. London: Chapman & Hall, pp. 410-414.

Brusilovsky, P. (1995) 'Intelligent tutoring systems for World-Wide Web'. *Proceedings of Third International WWW Conference*, Darmstadt, pp. 42-45.

Brusilovsky, P. L. (1992) 'A framework for intelligent knowledge sequencing and task sequencing'. In: C. Frasson, G. Gauthier and G. I. McCalla (eds.): *Intelligent Tutoring Systems*. Lecture Notes in Computer Science, Berlin: Springer-Verlag, pp. 499-506.

Mallery, J. C. (1994) 'A Common LISP hypermedia server'. *Proceedings of the First International Conference on the World-Wide Web*.

Schwarz, E., Brusilovsky, P., and Weber, G. (1996) 'World-wide intelligent textbooks'. *Proceedings of ED-MEDIA'95 - World conference on educational multimedia and hypermedia*, Boston, MA.

Weber, G. (1995) 'Examples and remindings in a case-based help system'. In: J.-P. Haton, M. Keane and M. Manago (eds.): *Topics in case-based reasoning. Selected Papers of the Second European Workshop, EWCBR-94, Chantilly, France*. Berlin: Springer-Verlag, pp. 165-177.

Weber, G. (1996) 'Episodic learner modeling'. *Cognitive Science* .

Weber, G. and Möllenberg, A. (1994) 'ELM-PE: A knowledge-based programming environment for learning LISP'. *Proceedings of ED-MEDIA '94*, Vancouver, Canada, pp. 557-562.

Intelligent Agent-Based Virtual Education using the Java Technology

Enrique Espinosa, Alejandro Brito and Fernando Ramos

{eespinos,abrito}@campus.ccm.itesm.mx, framos@campus.mor.itesm.mx

ITESM-CCM Computer Science Department ; ITESM-Mor, Graduate School

México D.F. & Cuernavaca, Morelos ; México

Abstract : This paper presents preliminary results of two [complimentary] research projects in progress at ITESM : Intelligent Multiagent Systems, and the Virtual University Definition. The implementation of the latter [Espinosa95b] [Espinosa95c] requires the merger of the former, plus an Implementation Technology : Java. A practical, but theoretically sound approach to the implementation of the skill acquisition and learning measurement model described in [Boumedine96a] [Espinosa96a] is thus presented. A multiplatform programming project shows us how multidisciplinary research may allow us to merge [traditionally] incompatible fields of study such as Psychology, Cognition and Artificial Intelligence, by placing Agents within the realm of a Higher Education context, describing the epistemological implications of such an Agent characterization, by identifying particular behavior patterns which may be measured qualitatively and quantitatively, and by making a case study out of a Virtualized Datastructures course.

1. Introduction

It is our intention to characterize new ways in which humans can learn with the aid of machine (ie. software) *agents*, given that we are situated within a *college-level reengineering* [Masi95] effort called the *Virtualization of the University* [Espinosa95b] [Espinosa95c]. Given this approach, a student will be placed in a situation which confronts him/her with an intellectual challenge. This implies that he/she is expected to use criteria, power of decision and common sense beside skills, experience, and data. Non-monotonic reasoning [Post90] takes place within that universe. We emphasize the need for autonomous, creative and discovery-rich action by the student, which directly conflicts with current educational practices [Ramos96a] [Espinosa96a]. However, in traditional teaching practices, it is assumed set of [pedagogical and structured] plans must be executed by a student if credit is to be achieved. In order for creative independence to occur, we propose that we must first identify a set of epistemological problems (sections 1.1-1.3), and then distinguish between human and machine agents as described in section 1.4. We may then start the characterization process by placing our agents in the correct context, using a model we call ALOPY (described in section 1.5). Java-based agents then make sense making a suitabe implementation of the EMI Model [Boumedine96a] [Espinosa96a]. Finally, we explain future research lines, and work, so we may validate and mature our effort.

1.1.The Closed World Assumption and the Learning Process

The first, and probably the most popular of the closed world assumptions in education lies within the realm of the evaluation of the student. Consider the inference problem in Figure 1[1].

$$\forall y \left(student(y), \frac{\xrightarrow{\ /\ } learnedTheSubject(y)}{\neg learnedTheSubject(y)} \right), where$$

$$learnedTheSubject(y) \leftrightarrow traversedAllNodesInGUIas(y) \wedge passedAllMidterms(y) \wedge$$

$$passedFinalExam(y)$$

Figure 1: Closed World Assumption in Student Evaluation

Where the $\xrightarrow{\ /\ }$ symbol represents the idea of a clause not being deductible from a given knowledge base, and is taken from Deiter's treatment of the *Closed World Assumption* in [Deiter78]. In Figure 1, we may,

---

[1] All the following examples assume that the student is using the hypermedia system currently under development here at ITESM [Espinosa95a].

therefore, infer that the student (y) does not have "enough knowledge" about the subject, given that it was unable to deduce that he/she actually learned about it. This deduction is proved true or false by assigning a series of declarative rules. Such rules constitute a conjunctive equation, where each term occurs in an interval of time within a predefined educational plan to be followed by the student. This means that *all the goals must be met* in order for the student to be considered as knowledgeable in the current subject. As we use the Closed World Default, we conclude that we must explicitly state all possible actions in the current educational world. This is done by generalizing Figure 1 as shown Figure2.

$$\tau_1(x_1), \tau_2(x_2), \tau_3(x_3), \dots, \tau_k(x_k) \xrightarrow{\quad\prime\quad} \frac{P(x_1, x_2, x_3, \dots, x_k)}{\neg P(x_1, x_2, x_3, \dots, x_k)}$$

Figure 2: Default Assumptions

This schema signifies that reasoning is conducted under a closed set of parameters, which do not consider negative knowledge. That is, we are not considering the possible ways in which some $\tau_1(x_1)$ may be coinsidered as false, and we resort to simply stating that if one of the terms in the conjunctive equation (B) fails, the default will be that student (y) failed to learn. That is, *negative information is inferred by default* [Deiter78]. We may apply this type of reasoning to *machine agents,* but is hardly adecuate for *human agents* [Ramos96a]. In other words, we cannot simply *impose* the lack of knowledge to a student (human agent) based on a set of defaults (ie. lack of declarative knowledge). The traditional education paradigm [Espinosa94a] has done so for almost two centuries. The *Virtuality of the Educational Process* [Espinosa95a] demands, however, a *systemic change in the academy and the lecturing processes it executes* [Peters94].

1.2. The Qualification Problem and the Learning Process

This problem, as reported by Shoham and McDermott in [Shoham88], may be summarized as the problem of making sound predictions about the future without taking into account everything about the past. It is based on the need for making inferences of the form "if *this* is true now, then *that* is true later". As in the previous section, the issue of inference making appears again. We now exemplify with respect to the educational activity which we embarked in: a Datastructures Course. Take, for example, the case in Figure 3.

$$\forall s \exists t \begin{pmatrix} student(s) \wedge GUIas(t), where: \\ isAbleToCode(s, CLanguage) \rightarrow \rho_1 \wedge \rho_2 \wedge \dots \wedge \rho_k \end{pmatrix}$$

Figure 3: Qualification Problem

Let $\rho_1, \rho_2, \rho_3, \dots, \rho_k$ be requisites for course credt, such as :
- traversedAllNodesInGUIas(s, Ctutorial, part1)
- passedExam(s, t.midterm1)

In order for the teacher to predict that the student (s) will be fluent in C, a large number of assumptions would need to be taken for granted in order that the final inference be valid, as shown in Figure 4. Furthermore, what if the student resists using the hypermedia system and resorts to lecture notes or books alone [Moore1]? This would change a previously defined status to a new, possibly undefined one. There simpy are too many factors affecting the outcome of the inference, including *cognitive* ones [Ramos96a]. Their *qualification* is impossible, given our non-deterministic problem space and its non-monotonic reasoning. We might then fall upon a Closed World Assumption of what the student is *supposed to do,* a closed educational plan to be executed without regard to the *external* or *internal* factors which may affect the human being during his/her semester period. It is important to make a difference between external and internal factors. The former are institutional ones, and must be dealt with in a *systemic manner* [Peters94] [Press94]. They are not in direct contact with the *cognitive state of the human being,* although they will probably affect it. The latter are factors which the student carries with him/herself throughout his/her life, and are not directly caused by the state of the educational system they dwell in.

$$\rho_1 = traversedAllNodesInGUIas\big(s, CTutorial, chapter1\big), and$$

$$traversedAllNodesInGUias(s, CT, ch1) \Rightarrow \begin{cases} \forall t \in time \wedge t \subseteq semester \wedge \\ \left\langle \begin{matrix} t \geq start(semester) \wedge \\ t \leq end(semester) \end{matrix} \right\rangle, \\ \therefore \\ wasOpen(t, CompCtr) \wedge \\ available(t, CompCtr, PC) \wedge \\ available(GUias, PC) \end{cases}$$

Figure 4: SampleEvents leading to Qualification Problems

The resolution of both problems cannot be solved by a single discipline. It requires a multidisciplinary effort to take place, and is the main reason why this article presents merging research : an Intelligent Multiagent System Project being conducted at the Morelos Campus of ITESM, by Dr. Fernando Ramos Quintana and MS Enrique David Espinosa, and the Virtual University Definition Project, at the Mexico City Campus of ITESM, conducted by Enrique David Espinosa, Alejandro Brito, and the Educational Technology Center staff.

1.3 The Frame Problem and the Learning Process

It is hard for an ITS to keep track of the preconditions and posconditions in each of the intervals in time as the semester continues. The interval progress requires that a temporal reasoning engine keep track of the preconditions and postconditions between each one of them. In other words, it is hard to explicitly indicate which *Educational States* [Espinosa96a] change between time intervals. Moreover, the human being being subject to the plan *is never consulted by any of the computational processes.* The declarative knowledge is kept in the [closed] world base, *even though the actions are emitted by the student.* It is this knowledge base which is consulted on the state of the human being - his/her opinion could be extremely important, if considered. The *traditional educational paradigm is hereby shown.* The reasons for these phenomena are a direct result of the Closed World Assumption and Qualification problems described in sections 1.1 and 1.2. The only sources of information are the *World Itself* as well as the current state of the hymerpedia system: the path traversed by the student, which might be an indication of what is the learning strategy being followed by him/her. It all depends on the human´s personal *Cognitive State* [Ramos96a], a departure from the *Commonality Assumption* [Ramos96a].

1.4 Enclosed but Open Worlds

The three problems just presented pose a question : how can such a *Cognitive State* be considered within an ITS ? We now present a small portion of a research work focused on such a computational characterization for Intelligent Agents set for Higher Education modelling. Consult [Ramos96a] for a more in depth treatment of the subject. As noted before, it is reasonable to expect the human to participate in his/her own educational process. This imples that the communication channel between an ITS and its user must be tightened. Consider the change to Figure 3 presented in Figure 5. The Cognitive State is a whole world by itself, since the Commonality Assumption, which tends to generalize people´s minds, no longer holds as we take into account all opinions. We then have a combinatory explosion of possible Internal [Cognitive] States. Now, the Closed World Assumption depends on external factors, taken for granted, about the world. We therefore have three worlds to deal with. An External and Open world, a Closed World, and an Enclosed and also Open World. If we complement the Closed World Assumptions with the Enclosed World´s individual facts, we reach a model as shown in Figure 5. The closed world allows us to restrict the knowledge domain being characterized to that of Higher Education within Datastructures, thus making the study a feasible one.. Such a merger is already being deployed in various educational institutions around the world as the need for students to become responsible for their educational process [Peters94] [Press94].

$$\forall s \exists t \begin{cases} student(s) \wedge GUIas(t), where: \\ isAbleToCode(s, CLanguage) \rightarrow \rho_1 \wedge \rho_2 \wedge ... \wedge \rho_k, \\ where: \\ \rho_m = likes(s, CLanguage) \wedge \\ likes(s, CLanguage) \rightarrow CognitiveState(s) \wedge \\ CognitiveState(s) \rightarrow Memory \wedge Desires \wedge Symbols \wedge imagination \\ \therefore \\ \langle CognitiveState(s) \subset ClosedWorld \subset OpenWorld \rangle \wedge \\ \langle CognitiveState(s) \supset ClosedWorld \supset OpenWorld \rangle \end{cases}$$

Figure 5: The Enclosed but Open World Concept

1.5 Imposed vs. Autonomous Educational Planning : The ALOPY Model

We realize, however, that not all multiagent systems are required to handle the three worlds just described. Machine agents are a reality, and they are not intended to have a common sense [Minsky91]. Machine agents are suitable for a wide range of real-world tasks while being unconditional workers. Many researchers, such as Minsky, Selfridge, Kay, Negroponte, Brooks and Maes [Riecken94] [King95] [Goodwin93] have defined such agents.In order to situate our work, we present a model that forces us to rethink our current development context. The model is called *Agent Location Pyramid (ALOPY) Model*, shown in Figure 6.

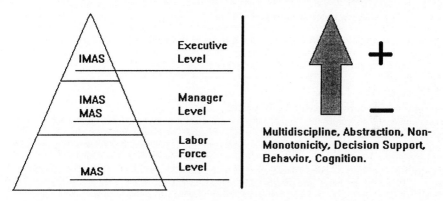

Figure 6: The ALOPY Model

The ALOPY Model recognizes three levels of activity for any multiagent system. The bottom level, called *Labor Force Level*, is where we might place the robotic agent systems which make efficient use of a planner and executing mechanisms. No criteria is required of these agents, and may be regarded as slave entities with no problems deriving from this nature. No decisions are expected from these agents, and thus their cognitive characteristics are not relevant. The middle level, called *Manager Level*, requires that the agent display a more complex set of traits, in which the multidisciplinary work begins to appear. An agent on this level needs to perform some set of managerial tasks, which imply the use of criteria for decision-making. A predefined plan is therefore not suitable. The *non-monotonicity* [Post90] of the environment in which this agent moves may not be too great, however, just as it happens in real life to a middle-level manager. Consider Figure 7.

$$\forall x \begin{pmatrix} manager(x) \supset strictManager(x), \\ strictManager(x) \supset strictprojectLeader(x) \end{pmatrix}, and$$

$$\exists a, p \begin{pmatrix} strictprojectLeader(p), analyst(a), \\ fires(p,a) \to considersAsNotCapable(p,a) \end{pmatrix}$$

Figure 7: Manager Level Example

In order to deduce that the leader is strict, we might need to infer that he/she considers programmer (y) as not capable. However, this information depends on behavioral features and [sometimes subjective] criteria. The upper level, called *Executive Level*, requires the agent to display a full set of behavioral characteristics, such as criteria, experience, personality, data-based knowledge, compromise, skills etc. An expanded set of Enclosed but Open Worlds is thus required at this stage. Examining Figure 8, we find out that the Qualification problem takes control of the outcome of the critical budget meeting since for it to succeed we would need to be able to not deduce that there is a discrepancy among its participants. None of the clauses in the DiscrepancyAmong clause would need to be deduced as false, but we are semantically unable to express that truth relationship from the clauses themselves. But that information cannot be imposed on the agents, since it depends on the behavioral state of the managers, something which depends on many complex, human, factors, such as language(ie. [lack of] communication). Once again, and more than ever, the agent *must show its own plan*, so further inferences may be made. It the location on either levell of the ALOPY model that determines Agenthood (Multiagent Systems : MAS) vs. *Intelligent* Agenthood (Intelligent Multiagent Systems : IMAS).

$$\forall y \big(meeting(y) \supset budgetmeeting(y) \supset criticalbudgetmeeting(y) \big)$$

$$\exists m, s, i, b \begin{pmatrix} marketingMgr(m), salesMgr(s), ISManager(i), \\ discrepancyAmong(m, s, i, on(y)) \to \\ conflictingInterests(m, s) \land conflictingInterests(s, i) \land dislikes(i, m) \end{pmatrix}$$

Figure 8: Executive Level Example

2. Java : An Agent Language for EMIspectors

Our current production system for the Visual Guides for Datastructures II is a PC-Based implementation of a hypermedia educational tool [Espinosa95a]. It is used by the students in stand-alone PC´s. The software allows them to learn at their own pace. We have also built a student profile engine using Microsoft´s Mediaview Help Compiler. Such an engine scans the student's activity in a per-session fashion. The output of this scan is a recursive structure depicting the Educational State (ES) the student chose to visit that day. The ES structure is presented in Figure 9. It makes use of the following Taxonomical Units : *Topic Description* (TD), *Taxonomical Units* (TU), and *Taxonomical Weight* (TW). A modified *Knowledge Corpus* (K) is depicted as the result of traversing a given ES. For a full tutorial to the ES and the Educational Measurement Instrument (EMI) model it belongs to, consult [Espinosa96a]. We have worked with standalone PC EMI data recollection for one semester. The basic model works fine, but lacks virtuality, since the instructor needs to be present in order to gather de data. The next logical step is to network the PC´s. The problem is that many of our students work at the campus´ computer center, where they access IBM RS6000 Workstations, and Power Macintosh machines. If we were to satisfy every platform, the programming effort would then have to triple, and adjust to every hardware and operating system change the Academic Computing Staff members performed on their machines. A change in computing paradigm is a must.

$$ES = \left[\left\{ \prod_{j=1}^{k} \left(TD_j \times TU_j \times TW_j \right) \right\} \rightarrow K_i \right]$$

Figure 9: EMI Recursive Structure

We now refer to the ALOPY Model. Our project is located in an area intersecting the Managerial and Executive levels. This is consistent with our goals, since we intend to overcome the shortcoming of an imposed planning requirement on the student. As said on the introduction to this paper, a student will be placed in a *situation* which confronts him/her with an intellectual challenge. This implies that he/she is expected to use criteria, power of decision and common sense beside skills, experience, and data. This implies that the TD´s in each ES must resemble real-life situations, and the TU´s must impose analysis, synthesis and evaluation requirements on the student. Such an *Instructional Design* is to be performed in a multidisciplinary teamwork, and is a key element in the Virtual University definition scheme depicted in [Espinosa95c]. We now move towards eliminating the barriers imposed by the Closed World Assumption and Qualification Problem. We therefore need to implement machine agents that resemble our students (ie. their human counterparts) in such a way that they will help the human student have a birds-eye view of him/herself as he/she applies criteria common sense. Only with the constant feedback from the human will a Software Agent, hereby called EMIspector, be able to maintain a consistent internal [cognitive] state. It is a requirement that the Qualification data come from the Enclosed but Open world described in Figure 5. This model is depicted in Figure 10.

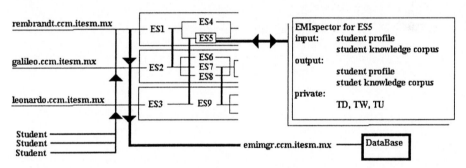

Figure 10: EMIspectors inside the EMI Network

Programming the EMI model, and at the same time requiring the system to perform cognitive-style functions as shown in Figures 3,4,5,7, and 8 is a steady evolution to *Agent-Oriented-.Programming* (AOP), something our current programing scheme is unable to accomplish. Clearly, we need an agent-bound production language and media. We chose Java because it is a swift change from the C++ implementation we now have. Java is also partially compatible with Mayfields´s Desiderata for Agent Communication Languages [Mayfield95] : Java is sintactically simple, is concise, and is linear, as well as reliable, and capable of working in a highly distributed, heterogeneous, and dynamic environment - the Internet. For this last purpose, it fits well with modern networking technology. On the other hand, it still is not well suited for high bandwidth communications, and is not expressive enough, which means there is no solid merger between its *communication* and *content* languages. We expect Java to become the starting point of an evolution towards such an expressive content language. Finally, some work will have to be performed before Java exhibits a *canonical form*, although it is predictable that this will happen, given the enormous commercial and industrial interest currently set on SUN´s Technology.

2.1 EMIspectors : Case Study in a Datastructures Virtual Course
As can be seen in Figure 10. Our community of agents reside within the EMI network, one agent per ES plus one central agent, located outside the network, for data integration. We now refer to these agents as

EMIspectors. The Datastructures course as of this writing is made of 215 ES´s within 9 course topics (or EM's according to the EMI terminology). The ES´s range from theory to design and codification activities, but always centered upon a situation to be solved. That is, we force the students to follow a Top-Down approach in all activities. If creative independence to occur, we must let them work at their own pace. That is what the software agents monitor.

Each EMIspector is an invisible Applet, whose only purpose is to monitor the student´s activity. We only added a small Trademark tag for legal purposes.

```
public void init() {
        resize(xSize,ySize);
        textFont1 = new Font("Arial", Font.BOLD, 16);
        backColor = Color.black;
        textColor = Color.green;
}
public void paint(Graphics g) {
        g.setFont(textFont1);
        g.setColor(textColor);
        g.drawString("EMIspector™",xCoord1,yCoord1);
}
```

Each of the network-centric EMIspectors is required to gather information from the student as he/she traverses its home ES. The student must be identified so that his/her student profile can be accessed and modified. Given that the student has logged on to the Visual GUIdes homepages, using an enhanced password protection scheme, each time a monitored page (eg. an ES given the EMI model) is entered, the EMIspector will request information about the student. This is done by invoking a CGI script which can easily obtain the user ID and mail it back to the account where the central database (see Figure 10) is located.

```
URL doc = null;
    try {
    doc = new URL("http://www.emimgr.ccm.itesm.mx/cgibin/Student?Myparam="getID");
    } catch (MalformedURLException e) {
    doc = null;
    }
```

Once this process is complete, the EMIspector may access the student database where the current student profile and knowledge corpus are stored. The profile is a set of predetermined indicators regarding field dependence/independence as defined in [Boumedine96a] and [Espinosa96a]. The knowledge corpus currently is a set of data items supposedly of the student´s domain once each ES is traversed. How many times will such a traversal be required depends on the taxonomical data determining the student profile. It is important to note here that all the data has been fed by the student him/herself. There has been no expert imposition. Such data is relevant for the construction of the EMI recursive model. As each page is left behind, the agent makes an access to the central database, adding its portion of the recursion. The information required for the agent to access the correct databases is located in the HTML <applet> tag :

```
<applet code="emimgr.class" width=10 height=10>
<param name="station" value="emimgr.ccm.itesm.mx">
<param name="matricula" value="matricula.mdb">
<param name="perfiles" value="perfiles.mdb">
<param name="emichain" value="emichain.mdb">
</applet>
```

The names of the correct database files are placed here, so that the EMIspector will have full acces to the right files. Once all the agents are placed in the Web Pages containing the course material, the traversal information is mailed to the central repository. This is done concurrently for all logged in users :

1. Log on to the Course Material account.
2. Validate Student Identity.
3. Establish profile and knowledge corpus.
4. For each traversal of a given EMI-monitored Web Page :
    5. Locate user ID.
    6. Mail traversal info (time, date, profile, new knowledge) to repository.
    7. Update repository, profile and knowledge corpus.
8. Register logoff times for each logged-on student.

Finally, at a place, time and date disjoint to that of the student access, the instructor may enter the repository using a Manager EMIspector, whose task is that of allowing the statistical analysis of the data in store. Statistical data review is one of our primary concerns at the time of this writing, since it is the vehicle for educational, cognitive and pedagogical evaluation.

3. Conclusions and Further Work

Therefore, the purpose of our study is to find ways to extract information from this enclosed (internal) but open world, as a resource to compensate for the Frame and Qualification problems. We emphasize this is valid only for IMAS's located in the Manager and Executive levels of the ALOPY Model. How to do such extraction is still a research line. The EMI Model will be upgraded so that it may capture not only information relevant to the Bloom Taxonomy, but also to the *RSI-TTT Cognitive Model* [Ramos96a]. This will be performed as part of the Intelligent Multiagent System Group work[2]. At the same time, the Instructional Design Methodology will be fully validated, so that the classroom impact of the EMI Model is optimized. This is being conducted by the Virtual University Group[3]. Finally, the Java effort will continue to grow as we expolore the evolution of such a technology within the ITESM-CCM *Java User´s Group*[4], a joint venture between SUN Microsystems and ITESM.

4. Bibliography

[Banks95a]   Banks, David. Why SUN thinks HotJava will give you a lift...
                San Jose Mercury News, March 23, 1995. http://www.sjmercury.com/archives/hotjava.htm
[Boumedine96a] Towards the Definition of a General Model for the Transfer of Knwledge in Multimedia-
                Based Learning Systems. Boumedine, Marc; Chirino, Ivonne; Espinosa, Enrique
                Proceedings of ED-Media96. AACE. 1996.
[CBS95]   Java Isn´t Just Coffee Anymore ; CBS News up to the Minute Update Online
                Digital Drive: Excursions in Cyberspace. June 2, 1995.
                http://uttm.com/drive/june_1995/june2.html
[Colouris88]   Distributed Systems: Concepts and Design G.Colouris; J. Dollimore
                Addison-Wesley, Reading, Mass., 1988.
[Deiter78a]   On Reasoning by Default ; Reiter, Raymond
                Proceedings of TINLAP-2, Theoretical issues in Natural Language Processing
                University of Illinois at Urbana Champaign, 1978, pp. 210-218.
[Director95]   Internet Multimedia W/ Director
                Electronically published at: http://www.net101.com/dir.html
[Espinosa94a]   GUIas Visuales para Estructuras de Datos 1 y 2. Espinosa, Enrique David
                XII Reunión de Intercambio de Experiencias en la Educación, Sistema ITESM
                Monterrey, Nuevo Leon, México. August 1994.pp. 45-49.
[Espinosa95a]   Intelligent Classroom information Agent Multimedia Lab and Visual GUIdes
                for Datastructures II. Espinosa, Enrique David
                Proceedings of the 2nd IEEE Intl. Conference on Multimedia Computing and Systems
                Washington DC, May 1995. pp. 302-305.
[Espinosa95b]   Modelo Universitario Virtual a Través del Transporte Situacional
                Espinosa, Enrique David; Medina-Mora, Teresa; Vallejo, Isabel
                V Reunión de Intercambio de Experiencias Docentes
                ITESM - Campus Ciudad de México .July 1995.

---

[2] Http ://www.ccm.itesm.mx/~enrique/EECDOCS/SMAS/SMASMain.html
[3] Virtual University link at http ://www.ccm.itesm.mx/~enrique/EECDOCS/Main.html
[4] http ://www.ccm.itesm.mx/~jug/itesm-ccm.html

[Espinosa95c]   The Virtual University: A Definitional Approach and Methodology
                Espinosa , Enrique David; Medina-Mora, Teresa; Vallejo, Isabel
                Journal of the Learning Sciences (under revision) 1995.
[Espinosa96a]   A Formal Approach to the EMI Model and Case Study
                Espinosa, Enrique; Boumedine, Marc; Chirino, Ivonne
                Proceedings of ED-Media96. AACE. 1996
[Goodwin93]   Formalizing Properties of Agents. Goodwin, Richard
                Carnegie Mellon Computer Science Dept. Technical Report CMU-CS-93-159
[Kaplan95]   New Directions for Intelligent Tutoring. Kaplan, Randy; Rock, Denny
                AI Expert, February 1995, pp 31-40.
[Karpinski95]   Karpinski, Richard
                HotJava arrives: SUN aims to revolutionize the Web. Interactive Age, May 22, 1995.
                http://techweb.cmp.com/ia/15issue/15hotjava.html
[King95]   Intelligent Agents: Bringing Good Things to Life. King, James A.
                AI Expert, February 1995. pp 17-19.
[Macromedia95] Macromedia
                Electronically published at: http://www.macromedia.com/
[Mayfield95]   Desiderata for Agent Communication Languages ; Mayfield, James ; Labrou, Yannis ; Finin, Tim
                Electronically published : Univ of Maryland-Baltimore Agents HomePage, 1995.
[Masi95]   Re-Engineering Engineering Education : Masi, C.G.
                IEEE Spectrum, September 1995. pp. 45-47.
[Minsky91]   Logical vs. Analogical or Symbolic vs. Connectionist or Neat vs. Scruffy
                Minsky, Marvin. AI Magazine, Summer 1991, pp35-51.
[Oconnel95]   Java: The Inside Story ; O´Connell, Michael
                SunWorld Online, July 1995.
                http://www.sun.com/sunworldonline/swol-07-1995/swol-07-java.html
[Peters94]   Technos Interview: Tom Peters ; Technos, Vol.3, No. 3, Fall 1994. 23-31.
[Post90]   An Overview of Automated Reasoning ; Post, Stephen; Sage, Andrew
                IEEE Transactions on Systems, Man and Cybernetics Vol 20, No1. Jan/Feb 1990, 202-224.
[Press94]   Tomorrow´s Campus ; Press, Larry. Communications of the ACM, July 1994.13-17.
[Ramos96a]   A Study for Modeling Creativity and Discovery in Intelligent Agents inspired
                on the Human Unconscious ; Ramos, Fernando ; Espinosa, Enrique
                Proceedings of the 2nd Intl. Conference on Creativity and Cognition. LUTCHI Research Centre. Loughborough
                University. Loughborough, UK. 1996
[Riecken94]   M: An Architecture of Integrated Agents. Riecken, Doug
                Communications of the ACM, July 1994, Vol37. pp. 106-116
[Shoham88]   Problems in Formal Temporal Reasoning ; Shoham, Yoav; McDemottt, Drew
                Artificial Intelligence, 36 (1988), pp. 49-61.
[VanHoff95a]   JAVA and Internet Programming: Similar to C and C++ but much Simpler
                Van Hoff, Arthur. Dr. Dobbs Journal. August 1995, pp

The Use of a Semantic Network Activation Language in an ITS Project

Adil KABBAJ, Khalid ROUANE, Claude FRASSON

Université de Montréal, Département d'informatique
et de recherche opérationnelle
C.P. 6128, Succ. Centre-Ville, Montréal, H3C 3J7

fax : 514 343 5834
E-mail : kabbajad@iro.umontreal.ca

Abstract We report the use of a graphical multi-paradigm language in SAFARI ; an environment for the development of ITSs. The language, called *Synergy* uses "active semantic networks" to manipulate both declarative and procedural knowledge.
After an overview of the language, we present its use in some modules of SAFARI, especially for a visual agent-oriented modeling of the Intensive Care Unit and for course generation from a curriculum. The first application illustrates the use of Synergy as a tool for task cognitive analysis.
Synergy could be used in other modules of SAFARI, in other ITS' projects and in other artificial intelligence and computer domains.

Key words Programming models integration, semantic networks activation, intelligent tutoring systems, intensive care unit, course generation.

1 Introduction

Several kinds of knowledge are used in intelligent tutoring system (ITS) and to deal with, different processing paradigms are often used in one intelligent tutoring system (ITS). Communication and share of knowledge, intra and inter ITSs become difficult.
In an attempt to solve this problem, we have developed a graphical multi-paradigm language, called *Synergy*. The language uses semantic network formalism to represent both declarative and procedural knowledge and to integrate many programming models (sequential/parallel procedural, functional, object-oriented and graph-activation models).
Synergy and its environment have been implemented in Visual C++ and used in SAFARI [Gecsei and Frasson, 94], an ITS' development project underway at the University of Montreal.
The language, i.e. the PC executable code, the examples' directory and the User' manual, will be available in summer 1996 at the following address :
        ftp.iro.umontreal.ca   /pub/its/pub_safari/kabbaj/Synergy .

The paper is organized as follows : after a brief overview of Synergy (§ 2), we present two applications, visual agent-oriented modeling of the Intensive Care Unit (§ 3) and course generation from a curriculum, taking into account the student model (§ 4). The two applications are taken from SAFARI project. We then report some related and future works (§ 5 and 6) and terminate with a conclusion (§ 7).

2 An overview of Synergy

This section introduces basic elements of Synergy: the conceptual environment of the language, the semantic network (SN) structure and the activation of a SN.

2.1 The conceptual environment of Synergy

The conceptual environment of Synergy is composed of a *long-term memory* (LTM) and of a *working memory* (WM). Synergy' WM provides the working space where the user specifies his requests. Requests can be evaluated in parallel.

Synergy' LTM represents the base where the knowledge about a domain (or some related domains) is stored. As in object-oriented languages, Synergy' LTM is represented as a generalization graph. When a new application is created, Synergy provides its built-in generalization graph composed of primitive types (types not defined in Synergy) and some predefined types (defined in Synergy but provided to the user as predefined). A user can define new types and add them to the generalization graph. He can also specify instances of types.

Primitive/predefined types "Data" primitive types are Number, String, Boolean, List, Window and Semantic network. Among "operation" primitive types, Synergy provides affectation (:=), arithmetic, relational, boolean, I/O, list, and SN operations (unification, fusion, generalization, subsumption, contraction, etc.).

Among "operation" predefined types, Synergy provides communication operations (AcceptMessage, Send, SendAck, Receive, WaitMessage, MethodMgr). Communication operations are used in sequential/concurrent object-oriented and/or agent-oriented applications.

Defined types A user can define a new type as a specialization of existing types (primitive, predefined or defined types). Of interest here the four primitive types : ProcedureActivity, ProcessActivity, StrictActivity and LazyActivity. They are sub-types of the primitive type Activity. ProcedureActivity and ProcessActivity reflect the difference in the life-time of an activity while StrictActivity and LazyActivity reflect the difference in the evaluation mode of the arguments of an activity (if it has). A new type can have some of those primitives as super-types and so, it will be interpreted according to their semantics.

Figure 1.a gives the definition of a new type IsAdult. "sp" link represents the specialization relation. Type "IsAdult" is a procedure with a strict evaluation. In the definition of "IsAdult", the concepts [Age :in/] and [Boolean :out/] represent input and output parameters respectively. Figure 1.b illustrates how the user can specify instances of types, either by giving a specific description of the instance (as for

MyTable in figure 1.b) or just by specifying that the individual is an instance of a type (as for Tble34). For the later case, Synergy will create, when necessary, the description of the instance by an instanciation of its type's definition.

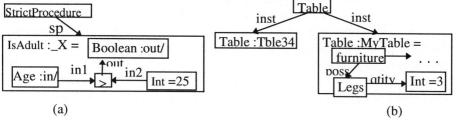

(a)   (b)

Figure 1: Definition of a type and description of instances

2.2 Synergy's semantic network structure

Semantic network (SN) is the basic structure in Synergy : the LTM, a request in the WM, the body of a concept type definition and of an instance description are SN.

Our SN structure is derived from conceptual graphs formalism [Sowa, 84] which is proposed as a synthesis of many SNs formalisms.

In Synergy, a *semantic network* is a labeled directed graph where nodes represent *concepts* and arcs *relations*.

Concept A concept specifies a referent with its type, value (or description) and state. A general form of a concept is : [Type :Referent =Value #State]. In general, when one concept' component isn't specified, a default is taken.

Concept' type can be primitive or defined. *Concept' referent* can be an instance identifier, a variable (that could have a referent as a value) or a co-reference, i.e. a reference to another concept. For instance, the concept [Man :Daniel.eyes.canOpen] is a co-reference to a concept with referent "canOpen" which is in the description of "eyes" which is itself in the description of "Daniel" (Figure 2).

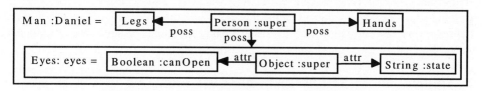

Figure 2: Co-reference to an embeeded concept

Concept' value can be a number, a boolean, a string, a list or a SN. *Concept' state* specifies the state of the concept. Basic states of a concept are "steady", "trigger", "wait-for-value", "wait-for-preconditions", "in-execution" and "wait-for-postconditions". The activation (execution) of a SN depends on the state of its concepts. Also, the state of a concept could change during the activity of the SN.

Relation Synergy provides a finite set of "procedural" relations subdivided in : 1) data relations (in/out) which connect concepts that are input/output arguments to a concept that represents a parametric activity (as a function, a procedure, ...), 2) control relations (condition "cond" and succession "succ"), and 3) memory relations (specializationOf "sp", instanceOf "inst" and schemaOf "scm").

The above set of relations is special because each relation of the set has a procedural meaning and so, can have an effect on the activation of a SN.

Beside this set, a Synergy programmer can use any identifier as the name of a relation between two concepts, the relation will have, however, no "procedural" effect on Synergy interpreter.

2.3 Semantic network's activation

An execution of a Synergy "program" will correspond, in general, to a parallel activation of many SNs. SN' activation begins with the parallel activation of some concepts, then procedural relations spread, in parallel, the activity through the network. Procedural relations serve also to express conditions and constraints on concepts' activation and so, on the spreading of the activation.

Concept' activation corresponds to the determination and then the activation (execution) of its value. If the concept' type corresponds to a primitive operation, the operation will be activated, if the concept has a value which is a SN then it will be activated, if the concept has no value but its type is defined, the value is then created (by instanciation of the type' definition) and activated.

The graphical environment of Synergy helps the user to navigate in (and explore) such a dynamic space, composed of active SNs.

Due to space limitation, we can't go further in the description of Synergy, but the documentation and the language (reachable via the ftp address provided in the introduction) can be consulted for a complete presentation.

Graphical environment of Synergy The graphical environment of Synergy is basically a SN editor, it enables the management of : files of SNs, SN (creation, destruction, modification of concepts and relations, etc.), contexts (like putting in focus the LTM or other active contexts), execution and windows. A browser is provided to locate a concept into the LTM. Semantic network' activation is expressed as SN animation due to visual change of concept' state and of concept value. Each state has a graphical representation.

3 Application 1: Visual agent-oriented modeling of the Intensive Care Unit

Synergy has been used for a visual agent-oriented modeling of the Intensive Care Unit (ICU). ICU modelization is an important module in the SAFARI project. The goal of the ICU' module is to support tutorial sessions for nurses and physicians trainees. We focused on patient' assessment task performed by a nurse, and on the interaction between the two agents. During the modeling process, we became more and more aware of the potential role of Synergy as a tool for task cognitive analysis. Indeed, during the formulation and the simulation with Synergy, corrections, refinements and extensions have been added to the initial model.

Figure 3 shows a part of the LTM for the ICU application : the definitions of Agent, Nurse, Patient and some related types. The definition of the type Agent is part of the built-in generalization graph provided by Synergy upon a creation of a new application (i.e. a new LTM). An Agent (Figure 3, window Agent:_Agt) has a messageQueue, a name, a dialog' window and an agent' manager . The types Nurse and Patient are specializations of the type Agent. Nurse (Figure 3, window Nurse:_n) is an agent with a spacial position and is responsible of patient' assessment which corresponds to five system evaluations (nervous, respiratory, circulatory, digestive and urinary). Two instances of Nurse have been specified : Magy and Susan.

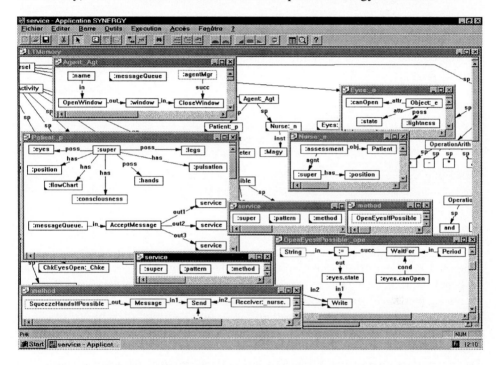

Figure 3 : Definitions of some types of the ICU' application

Patient (Figure 3, window Patient:_p) is an agent with attributes relevants to our modelization. Patient' behavior is to respond to three types of message' patterns : "open eyes", "move legs" and "squeeze hands". A method is associated to each pattern (Figure 3, window service). When the patient receives a message that can be matched with a pattern, the associated method will be activated. For instance, if the patient receives the message "open eyes", the method "OpenEyesIfPossible" will be activated. The definition of OpenEyesIfPossible (Figure 3) specifies that if the patient can open his eyes, a delay will occur that simulates the time for the patient to open his eyes, and then the state of his eyes will be set to "open".

Once the ICU' model has been defined, many scenarios (or situations) can be specified and simulated, depending on the states of the patient and the nurse.

Let us consider now the scenario sc_icu1 (Figure 4, window sc_icu1) where a nurse has to evaluate the patient' nervous system. In another scenario (not specified in this paper), the nurse has to evaluate both the nervous and the circulatory systems. For this later, she has to use the Multi Channel Monitor to check several parameters.

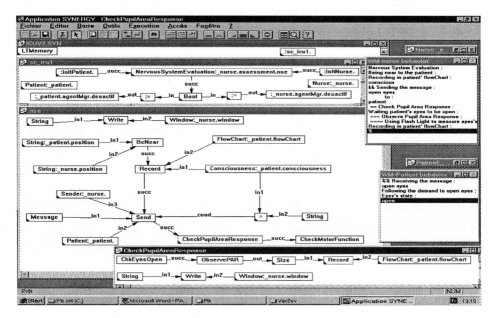

Figure 4 : Execution of the specific scenario sc_icu1 (part 1)

Scenario sc_icu1 (Figure 4, window sc_icu1) specifies the activation of a patient, a nurse and a request to the nurse to evaluate the patient' nervous system. The two concepts "initPatient" and "initNurse" (Figure 4, window sc_icu1) put the two agents in particular states (with specific values to some of their attributes). For instance, initPatient specifies that patient' eyes can be opened (canOpen = true) and their state is "close", patient' consciousness is "conscious", he can move legs, he can squeeze hands, etc.

The activation of the scenario sc_icu1 is done by putting the concept [Scenario :sc_icu1. #trigger] in the working memory (Figure 4, window ICUV2.SYN). Once the scenario sc_icu1 is activated, the patient Daniel (i.e. _patient = Daniel) and the nurse Magy (i.e. _nurse = Magy) will be created, initialized to a specific state and activated. For the two agents, the first action is to create a dialog' window (Figure 4, windows "WM-patient behavior" and "WM-nurse behavior") where comments are written as the agent' behavior proceed. Next, the nurse is asked to evaluate the patient' nervous system (NSE): the concept [NervousSystemEvaluation :_nurse.assessment.nse] in sc_icu1 is now "in-execution" state. Figure 4 shows the definition of this concept and the two dialog windows that give a "trace" of the concept' activation.

The simulation can be done step-by-step under the control of the user, so he can navigate in the active semantic networks and follow the execution in deeper detail.

According to the definition of the nervous system evaluation (Figure 4, window :nse), the nurse has to stand near the patient and record patient' consciousness in patient' flowChart. Hence, if the nurse' position is different from the patient' position, the nurse must move toward the patient (this is basically the definition of BeNear procedure, used in NSE). In our case, the nurse and the patient have the same position "center", and the patient is conscious.

Next, the nurse has to ask the patient to open his eyes in order to check the patient' pupil area response. Note that the nurse will ask the patient only if he is conscious, otherwise the nurse won't send a message to him and so, the next two checking tasks won't be executed.

The task "CheckPupilAreaResponse" is now in activation (Figure 4) : in order to observe patient' pupil area response, the nurse has to wait until the patient opens his eyes (this is done by the sub-task "ChkEyesOpen" in "CheckPupilAreaResponse"). Next, the nurse has to observe the patient' pupil area with a flash light and then record the result in the patient' flowChart. After the termination of CheckPupilAreaResponse, the nurse has to check patient' motor function. To do that, she first asks the patient to move his legs, waits for the response from the patient and then, records the result in patient' flowChart. The nurse will repeat the same behavior for the message "squeeze hands". With the termination of the task "CheckMotorFunction", the nervous system evaluation, as well as the activation of the whole scenario are terminated.

4 Application 2: Course generation from a curriculum

We have used Synergy to simulate the generation of a course from a curriculum, taking into account the student model. Our Synergy' formulation of this application is based on [Nkambou et al., 96]. Course generation process operates on the Curriculum Knowledge Transition Network (CKTN), a network of capabilities, instructional objectives and learning resources. If many objectives contribute to the acquisition of a capability, an heuristic is used to select a subset of objectives from the initial set. One such an heuristic is to consider "one strong objective", or "two moderate objectives " or "one moderate objective and one weak objective" or "three weak objectives".

The generation of a course takes into account the student model: the first step in the generation process is to mark each capability of the CKTN by "known", "partially known" or "unknown" (by the student). The definition of heuristics like the above one considers in fact the mark of the capability. For instance, the above heuristic is for an unknown capability, a different definition of the heuristic is given for a partially known capability. The generation process is activated by expressing the objective of the course : the set of the capabilities to be acquired by the student. With this initial set, a *selective* backward activation is done to determine for each unknown or partially known capability, the objectives that must be satisfied to acquire the capability. The backward activation is selective because the determination of the objectives to activate is done by an heuristic which selects a subset of objectives from the initial set. Next, for each activated objective, a selective backward activation is done to determine the capabilities that are mandatory for the objective. Each of these capabilities must be acquired too.

Figure 5 shows our reformulation of this application in Synergy : Capabilities and Objectives are "active" concepts ; when a capability is activated, the function

ComputeObjectiveContr (Figure 5, window Capability) will identify all the objectives that contribute to the acquisition of the capability. The result will be taken by the function HeuristicObjective which returns a list of selected objectives. The primitive operation "Map" will then apply the operation "TriggerConc" on each element of the list ("TriggerConc" is the value of the second argument of Map). TriggerConc puts its argument (which is a concept' referent) in a trigger state.

The type Objective is defined in the same way but in addition, we specify that the referent of the objective (once it is active, and so required !) will be added to the course structure.

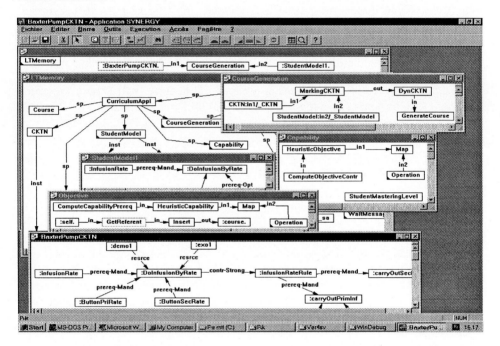

Figure 5 : Generation of a course from a curriculum

5 Related works

Graph-oriented formulation of procedural knowledge is used in programming languages (for instance, Petri nets and data flow graphs), in software engineering and modelization methods where data flow diagrams and transition diagrams are used and in ITS and learning environments ([Psotka et al., 88], [Larkin and Chabay, 92]) where some of the above graphs are used as well as other graphs : task graphs, action graphs, genetic graphs, structural graphs, etc.

Graph-based formalism was used also for declarative knowledge, as the case for semantic networks families [Lehmann, 92].

We attempt to integrate in one graph-based language many graph-oriented models.

6 Future works

Some extensions to our visual agent-oriented modeling of ICU are in order : to consider for instance the physician role, the simulation of some devices used in the ICU and the addition, to the simulation/demonstration mode, of a critic system.
We plan to use Synergy in the student modeling module and for a multi-agents modeling of SAFARI as whole. Also, a visual-multi-media general-purpose simulation environment for Synergy is in progress [Kabbaj and Frasson, 95].

7 Conclusion

We introduced a graphical multi-paradigm language, based on active semantic networks. The language, called Synergy is useful for many complex systems, as ITS. Indeed and as this paper attempts to illustrate, an integration-based language can be used in many modules of an ITS, where different types of knowledge are treated by different processes.

In the User' manual of Synergy we illustrate its use with many examples taken from procedural, functional, object-oriented and agent oriented programmings. Other examples are taken from specific domains as causal networks, project management, real-time temporal knowledge based systems, etc.

Acknowledgment

This research is part of SAFARI project which is supported by the MICST (Ministère de l'Industrie, du Commerce, des Sciences et de la Technologie).

Bibliography

Gecsei J., and Frasson C., SAFARI: an Environment for Creating Tutoring Systems in Industrial Training, EdMedia, World Conference on Educational Multimedia and Hypermedia, Vancouver, June 1994.

Kabbaj A. et C. Frasson, CAL : When education influences the design of an AI language, in Proc. of AI-ED'95, 7th World Conference on AI in Education, pp. 343-350, Washington, Aug. 1995.

Larkin J. H. et R. W. Chabay (eds.), Computer-Assisted instruction and intelligent tutoring systems: Shared goals and complementary approaches, Lawrence Erlbaum Associates, 1992.

Lehmann F. (ed), Special Issue on Semantic Networks in AI, in Computers and Mathematics with Applications, 23:2-9, 1992.

Nkambou R., M. C. Frasson and C. Frasson, Generating Courses in an Intelligent Tutoring System, aie-eai'96, 9th Intern. Conf. on Industrial & Engineering applications of AI & Expert Systems, Japon, June 1996.

Psotka J., L. Dan Massey et S. A. Mutter (Eds.), Intelligent Tutoring Systems, Lessons Learned, Lawrence Erlbaum Ass. Pub., 1988.

Sowa J. F., Conceptual Structures : Information Processing in Mind and Machine, Addison-Wesley, 1984.

Combining General and Domain-Specific Strategic Support for Biological Inquiry

Iris Tabak, Brian K. Smith, William A. Sandoval, Brian J. Reiser
School of Education and Social Policy
and Institute for the Learning Sciences
Northwestern University

Abstract. BGuILE is a learning environment in which students explore rich problem contexts in evolutionary biology and behavioral ecology. BGuILE uses domain-specific *investigation models* to scaffold students for the particular strategies experts use in these domains. These investigation models focus students on the relevant aspects of each domain, and support productive investigation strategies within the domain. BGuILE's explanation construction tools encourage students to bridge from their problem-specific explanations to broader domain theories and a more general understanding of scientific inquiry and theory-building. BGuILE is situated within classroom activities which encourage students to inquire into complex problems and discuss their research with their teachers and peers.

1. The Need for Strategic Support in Science Learning

Modern goals for science education stress the active nature of students learning about science through their own investigations (NRC, 1996). Interactive learning environments have been argued as one way to support this type of learning, providing students simulated microworlds in which they can manipulate variables and explore phenomena (Shute, Glaser, & Raghavan, 1989; White, 1993). Yet, studies of students' exploration and hypothesis testing reveal differences in strategies that can affect how well students can learn through inquiry (Schauble, Glaser, Raghavan, & Reiner, 1991). An interactive learning environment for science must do more than provide a world for students to explore, it must provide strategic support. In this paper, we explore the types of strategic support required in rich scientific environments and describe a learning environment designed to provide such support for biological inquiry.

Our goal is to support student-directed investigations in science. We are focusing on topics in evolution and behavioral ecology, in which students can ask questions about how and why organisms behave as they do. The goals for this environment concern both biological phenomena in particular, and a better understanding of science in general. Many students develop a view of science as a method for discovering static facts about the world, and see learning science as simply learning those facts (Lederman, 1992). Instead, we wish to foster a view of science as a process of building and revising models to better explain observed phenomena. Thus, a learning environment for science must combine facilities allowing students to conduct experiments or collect observations with specific scaffolding for scientific inquiry and explanation processes. Encouraging students to articulate explanations and be systematic about tying results back to candidate hypotheses is important. Yet, while this general type of scaffolding is promising, we do not believe it will be sufficient strategic support for students' investigations in rich complex environments. Additional domain-specific support to help students understand what makes reasonable explanations in this domain is also needed.

1.1. Domain-General Support for Hypothesis Testing

A learning environment can support inquiry by making explicit the strategies needed for problem solving that are at best implicit in most instruction (Collins, 1990). Providing support for investigative strategies is particularly critical if students are developing explanations for themselves. One method of providing strategic support is to focus on the process of hypothesis testing itself. Students with more sophisticated prior knowledge and with more effective hypothesis generation, experimentation, and data organization skills learn more from their experimentation (Schauble, et al., 1991). Supporting students in articulating and organizing their questions, hypotheses, and evidence should help them plan and monitor their investigations. General tools for communicating and reflecting on students' research are now being explored (O'Neill & Gomez, 1994; Scardamalia & Bereiter, 1993/1994). Directly incorporating such support into a scientific investigation environment can more strongly guide students' investigations. By helping students articulate relevant questions and hypotheses, making explicit the hypotheses and goals underlying an experiment, such support could help students better understand the goals and processes of experimentation.

1.2. Investigation Models and Explanation

Experts implicitly use domain principles and assumptions to focus their attention on situations requiring explanation and the forms those explanations can take. This implicit knowledge constrains explanation by providing a context for interpretation and evaluation of new findings. Such knowledge is used to assess the testability of hypotheses, the relevance of data to hypotheses, and the soundness of inferences concluded from data.

Consulting with behavioral ecologists, we outlined a set of strategies that focus biological inquiry we call an *investigation model*. Evolutionary biology and behavioral ecology share the basic investigation model below, although each domain will specialize some of the constituents.

Observe: Look for structural or behavioral variation between/within species and for environmental dependencies that could lead to a selection pressure.

Compare: Compare variation in structural or behavioral characteristics to identify differences in survival or reproduction abilities.

Relate: Relate structure to function.

Explain: Explain the adaptive value of characteristics in terms of selection pressures and genetic fitness.

The investigation model is not a psychological model, although it makes explicit the implicit strategies used by biologists. It specifies reasoning strategies that may prove effective for students approaching novel biological problems. The components of the model propose ways to recognize and interpret patterns. For instance, when a variation between closely related species is observed, it is useful to look for selection pressures underlying the variation through further comparisons of traits and behaviors. The investigation model can also be used to validate hypotheses and explanations by assessing the relevance of supporting data in terms of these strategies.

1.3. BGuILE

BGuILE (*Biology Guided Inquiry Learning Environment*) presents puzzling natural phenomena and offers a set of analytical and explanatory tools allowing students to investigate and explain them. BGuILE's complex problem contexts enable students to consider a number of competing, yet plausible, hypotheses. Students work in groups to construct, evaluate, iteratively refine, and communicate explanations. The learning environment couples domain-specific strategic support from investigation models with more general support for scientific investigation and explanation. The following sections present an overview of the types of investigations supported in BGuILE and how the investigation models are reflected in the environment.

2. Investigations of Natural Selection in BGuILE

One set of scenarios in BGuILE concern problems in evolution. One of these is based on studies of the finch population on the Galapagos island Daphne Major (Grant, 1986). This scenario focuses on 1977, when the finch population dropped considerably. Students are asked to explain why some of the finches are surviving while others are dying and the implications for future generations. In the investigation environment students can make observations of animals, plant life, and climate. For example, students can explore structural measurements of plants and animals (e.g., weight, beak size, seed rigidity), eating behaviors, and mating behaviors. BGuILE couples investigation tools that help students interpret the data in a way that reflects the investigation model of evolutionary biologists with an explanation construction tool that supports the process of explanation by providing domain-specific structures which reflect general criteria for scientific explanations.

2.1. Support for Evolutionary Investigations

Evolutionary biologists have tacit knowledge of evolutionary investigation models and explanation structures, as well as a rich base of content knowledge, all of which combine to facilitate their investigations. In contrast, students are in the process of acquiring content knowledge, strategies and explanation structures, in addition to attempting to explain the problem phenomenon. BGuILE provides scaffolding that bridges these gaps in content knowledge and strategic knowledge. The investigation tools are designed to reflect the following evolutionary investigation model: *observe* organisms, looking for variation within species; *compare* variation in structural characteristics or behaviors that affect an organism's genetic fitness; *relate* structural characteristics to behavior; and *explain* the adaptive value of characteristics in terms of selection pressures.

Evolutionary biologists observing organisms in situ use their knowledge of biological principles to direct their attention to features of the situation that will help them relate how a structural characteristic enables an advantageous behavior under a particular pressure. We encourage students to use similar principles, making *structure* and *function* objects of observation, by separating structural information from behavioral information. For each species depicted in the environment, we provide both a population view, containing aggregate data, and an individual view (Figure 1), containing measurements and observations for a unique, tagged animal. The individual view targets the observe component of the task model, helping students identify variability of traits within a population, while the population view contributes to the compare component, enabling students to track changes in proportions of individuals with a particular trait.

In order to identify environmental pressures, variability of traits in a population and changing proportions of traits in a population, biologists compare observations across time, individuals and populations, noting changes and trends. This facet of the investigation model is supported through the *compare tool*. In earlier versions of this tool, students selected items from a list of their observations to contrast side by side (Figure 1). A revised *compare tool,* designed to provide more structured support, allows students to choose the type of comparison they want to make (e.g., across time, across populations). Students choose variables to compare according to a template. For example, the template for comparison across time involves choosing dimension, time 1, and time 2. The dimension could be any characteristic available for observation in the investigation environment, e.g., rainfall or beak size. We expect the comparison template will foster the general strategy of varying only one variable at a time, that is, time varies while dimension stays constant.

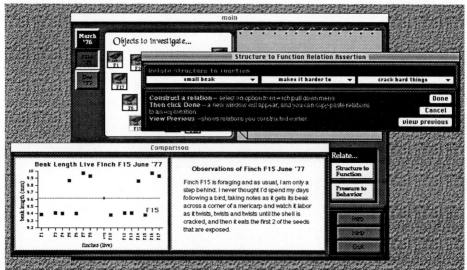

Fig. 1. A comparison and relate window overlaid on an individual live finches view.

Constructing an explanation involves moving from a description of temporal trends to articulating causal relationships. Biologists constructing evolutionary explanations draw "structure to function" relationships, and "pressure to adaptive trait" relationships. These relationships combine to tell a causal story of how a trait enables a behavior that can withstand a particular pressure. The investigation environment provides a *relate tool* to help students articulate these types of relationships. Students choose words from menus to construct a sentence according to a template. The general templates state the types of claims that are part of an evolutionary explanation, while the menu choices provide specific examples from the scenario. For example, the template for the "structure to function" relationship is [characteristic] [affects] [behavior]. An example sentence, shown in Figure 1, would be [small beak] [makes it harder to] [crack hard things]. The assertions created in the relate tool can be imported into the explanations that students construct through the explanation construction tool. Each assertion created by the relate tool can be supported by, and linked to, observations students have made in the environment (including comparisons).

2.2. Scaffolding Explanation Construction

BGuILE's explanation constructor supports explanation at both the general and domain-specific levels, reflecting the fact that scientific explanations have both general and domain-specific requirements. At a general level, students should understand what constitutes a legitimate scientific explanation: it should be primarily based on observable data, account for as much of that data as possible, and justifiably reject alternative explanations. At the domain level, explanations must account for observed data in the domain, according to known principles of this domain. An explanation based upon the theory of natural selection, for example, should identify an environmental pressure affecting the organism under study and account for how that pressure selects for a trait, or set of traits, belonging to that organism.

The explanation constructor (Figure 2) provides students with a structured framework to write their explanations. At the highest level, students organize their inquiry around a set of questions. In the finch scenario, students are prompted with two overarching questions to answer: Why are so many of the finches dying? and Why are some of the finches surviving? They are able to decompose these questions into smaller, more manageable ones, or attack them head on. For each question students pose, they can create new candidate explanations, revise an existing one, or spin off a new explanation based upon one of their existing ones. This design visually encourages students to maintain multiple, potentially competing, hypotheses and supports the development of the idea that science is a process of iteratively refining explanations to account for more and more data.

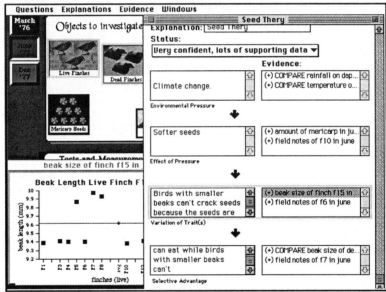

Fig. 2. A "selective pressure" explanation template, showing a group's partial explanation from a recent pilot study.

We designed the explanation constructor to encourage students to make their causal reasoning explicit. Students construct explanations in causally related pieces. Each piece can contain free text or statements constructed using the relate tool. These components are linked to define a causal chain representing the students' explanation. Further, students can attach data obtained from the scenario as supporting or refuting evidence for each piece of their explanation. Thus, at a domain-general level, students are encouraged to articulate causal relations within their explanations, and to support each of the parts of these relations with data.

The explanation constructor provides an intermediate level of support bridging specific domain problems to scientific explanations more generally by providing students with domain-specific explanation templates. These templates are essentially theoretical frameworks students can use to build their explanations, much like Collins' and Ferguson's (1993) epistemic forms. Different templates suggest different types of explanations. In the finch scenario, for example, students might choose a predator-prey or natural catastrophe template to explain the cause of the finches death. Figure 2 shows an explanation based upon the selective pressure template. The template labels each component of the explanation and indicates how they are related. The students' task remains to produce a convincing story within the framework provided by the template.

Explanation templates indicate causal structure at a theoretical level, a more abstract level than the causal relations embodied in the relate tool. This theoretical structure can help students abstract from the specific explanation they are constructing for this problem to a larger explanatory theory. By providing domain-based templates, the explanation constructor focuses students on the important aspects (e.g., identifying environmental pressures and their effects) of explanations within a domain.

The compare, relate and explanation construction tools work in concert to foster expert strategies. Comparing data can help identify causal relationships that can be articulated in the relate tool, while the collection of components in the relate tool menus point students toward potential observations and comparisons. Intermediate relation assertions combine to form a broader causal explanation. In turn, the components of the explanation templates suggest intermediate relationships that can be explored in the investigation environment. The overall structure of the task, flexibly moving between the investigation environment and the explanation constructor, encourages students to go through an iterative process of continually refining their explanations, while the explanation constructor itself organizes the history of students' model building.

3. Investigations in Behavioral Ecology in BGuILE

We explore issues in behavioral ecology through an examination of the Serengeti lion's hunting behaviors. Only 15-30% of all hunts attempted by lions result in the successful capture of prey (Schaller, 1972), and we ask students to explore and explain the behavioral factors contributing to this result.

3.1. Supporting Descriptive Analysis

Students begin by watching video clips of lions obtaining food. The films vary across a number of features (e.g., number of lions/prey, prey species) to illustrate a range of variables influencing hunting success. The observe and compare components of the investigation model are prominent in this exercise. Students make observations of the video and annotate frames with descriptive information and/or explanations. The types of variation become more evident when films are compared. We are refining our current annotation tool to explicitly support comparison by allowing frames from different films to be linked and labeled with a variation type (e.g., trait, behavior), the variable being compared (e.g., amount of ground cover), and the result of the variation (e.g., less ground cover led to a failed hunt). The video activity is also used to connect discussions of scientific abstractions to real world specifics, and the initial annotations generated here form the basis for future elaboration of causal features.

3.2. Identifying Salient Events

Video does not highlight salient events or allow for interactive inspection and manipulation, so as students begin forming questions for investigation, we introduce a computer simulation of the lion hunt. The simulation portrays an aerial view of animated agents behaving in a two-dimensional world. Students conduct experiments by manipulating aspects of the world and its inhabitants (e.g., prey species, time of day) and observing the results. For example, if students decide that the number of lions is an important factor, they could vary this number across a series of experiments to see the effects on prey capture. Qualitative and quantitative information about the creatures and the world can also be obtained during execution (i.e., speed, climate).

After each hunt, a timeline can be accessed showing the relationship between each agent's actions and the time they occurred (Figure 3). This timeline provides a static representation of the hunt dynamics emphasizing sites for investigation. General information about creatures, their actions, and the Serengeti environment can also be accessed through this timeline.

Agents in the timeline can explain their decisions for taking an action, for example, "Lion-102 began chasing Zebra-103 after stalking close to it." Students can trace through the timeline using these explanations to determine interactions between creatures. Again, these features help students with observation and comparison by highlighting salient events. The timeline display resembles the annotations produced earlier by the students, as both capture important "frames" of the hunt. Students can compare their work to the timelines to elaborate their explanations. We will also allow students to save and compare multiple timelines to view differences across multiple runs of the simulation.

3.3. Decomposing the Experiment Space

In addition to highlighting events, we want to assist students in forming subgoals for investigation. Our investigation model prescribes methods for detecting behavioral patterns, and these are instantiated as strategic prompts. When students query agents or request background information from the timeline, prompts relevant to the current simulation context are provided (Figure 3), for example:

- *Behavioral variation*: Look for differences in behavior across individuals and/or species (Are there times when the lion doesn't need to stalk?).
- *Environmental pressures*: Look for effects on behavior across varying environmental conditions (How much vegetation is in the area?).
- *Limits*: Look for critical bounds on variables (How far is the lion from the prey when it begins its chase?).

This classification of comparisons is instantiated as situation-specific subquestions for students to consider investigating. Using information collected while pursuing these subquestions, students can elaborate the explanations developed earlier in the annotation tool. As students progress from these descriptive annotations to the simulation, we hope to see students elaborating their explanations with the assistance of these strategic prompts.

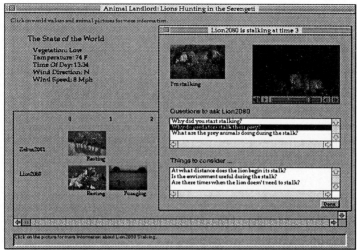

Fig. 3. The lion scenario's agent timeline and explanation window.

4. BGuILE in a Classroom Context

We wish to foster a view of science as a process of building and revising explanations rather than a search for "the right answer." The goal is to make explanation an explicit part of the task and to have students report on the history of their investigation, rather than just the final answer. We envision classroom use of BGuILE for deep investigation of problems through iterated cycles of investigation, discussion, and reflection.

Classroom discussions create a context where students communicate and receive feedback on the specific content of their explanations, as well as the history of their investigations. The investigation history describes how they arrived at their explanation, what questions they raised, and what strategies they used to answer these questions. These classroom discussions help students identify places where they relied more on plausibility than data in supporting claims, or places where they could have explored alternative hypotheses and interpretations. It is important that discussions occur in the midst of investigations to provide students with opportunities to refine their use of investigation strategies and revise their explanations. We expect that constructing and critiquing detailed explanations will not only deepen students understanding of evolution and behavioral ecology, but also foster new conceptions of the process and goals of science.

5. Conclusion

We have described BGuILE, a learning environment situated within classroom activities, where students investigate problems in evolutionary biology and behavioral ecology, and discuss their research with their teachers and peers. BGuILE uses domain-specific investigation models to focus students on the relevant aspects of each domain, and support productive investigation strategies within the domain. BGuILE's explanation construction tools encourage students to bridge from their problem-specific explanations to broader domain theories and a more general understanding of scientific inquiry and theory-building. We have used BGuILE in two classroom trials and are in the process of analyzing the data from these trials.

Acknowledgments

This research is supported by a grant from the James S. McDonnell Foundation and by graduate traineeships from the National Science Foundation and the Patricia Roberts Harris Fellowship Program. We are grateful to Tammy Porter for background research, and to Jeff Hoyer, Robert Motsko, and Martin Esgar for discussions of the environment and activities design. We also thank Hans Landel for discussions of biological content and investigation strategies.

References

Collins, A. (1990). Cognitive apprenticeship and instructional technology. In B. F. Jones & L. Idol (Eds.), *Dimensions of thinking and cognitive instruction* (pp. 121-138). Hillsdale, NJ: Erlbaum.

Collins, A. M., & Ferguson, W. (1993). Epistemic forms and epistemic games: Structures and strategies to guide inquiry. *Educational Psychologist, 28,* 25-42.

Grant, P. (1986). *Ecology and evolution of Darwin's finches.* Princeton, NJ: Princeton University Press.

Lederman, N. G. (1992). Students' and teachers' conceptions of the nature of science: A review of the research. *Journal of Research in Science Teaching, 29,* 331-359.

NRC (1996). *National science education standards.* Washington, DC: National Research Council.

O'Neill, D. K., & Gomez, L. (1994). The Collaboratory Notebook: A distributed knowledge-building environment for project-enhanced learning. In T. Ottmann & I. Tomek (Eds.), *Educational Multimedia and Hypermedia, 1994: Proceeedings of Ed-Media 94* (pp. 416-423). Charlottesville, VA: AACE.

Scardamalia, M., & Bereiter, C. (1993/1994). Computer support for knowledge-building communities. *The Journal of the Learning Sciences, 3,* 265-283.

Schaller, G. B. (1972). *The Serengeti Lion: A Study of Predator-Prey Relations.* Chicago, IL: University of Chicago Press.

Schauble, L., Glaser, R., Raghavan, K., & Reiner, M. (1991). Causal models and experimentation strategies in scientific reasoning. *The Journal of the Learning Sciences, 1,* 201-238.

Shute, V. J., Glaser, R., & Raghavan, K. (1989). Inference and discovery in an exploratory laboratory. In P. L. Ackerman, R. J. Sternberg, & R. Glaser (Eds.), *Learning and Individual Differences* (pp. 279-326). New York: W. H. Freeman and Company.

White, B. Y. (1993). Intermediate causal models: A missing link for science education? In R. Glaser (Ed.), *Advances in instructional psychology* (pp. 177-252). Hillsdale, NJ: Erlbaum.

Using Cognition of Programming Literature in the Design of a Tool for Learning a Second Programming Language

Vikki Fix[1] and Susan Wiedenbeck[2]

[1]Computer Science Dept., Univ. of South Dakota, Vermillion, SD 57069 USA

[2]Computer Science Dept., University of Nebraska, Lincoln, NE 68588, USA

Abstract. This paper reports on the design rationale and early evaluation of an intelligent tool to aid student programmers, who already have knowledge of one programming language, in acquiring a working knowledge of key parts of the Ada language. Research on transfer between programming languages has shown that previous programming experience helps students learn subsequent languages, but is also a source of negative transfer. Our tool ADAPT addresses the pedagogical problem of transfer between programming languages, emphasizing the problem of developing programming plans which are appropriate to the Ada language. ADAPT was designed based on the findings of research in the cognition of programming, and one of our goals was to evaluate how much guidance the literature gives to design. The results of empirical studies provided appropriate general guidance but tended to be underspecified for use in design.

1 Introduction

Research on the cognition of programming often suggests the relevance of its findings to pedagogy and tool building (e.g., Kitchenham & Carn, 1990, Scholtz & Wiedenbeck, 1992a). However, the step of actually designing curricula and tools based directly on the results of research is less often taken. In this paper we report on the design rationale and early evaluation of a pedagogical tool to aid in learning programming. The design rationale rests largely on research results in the cognition of programming. We implemented a prototype of the tool and carried out a formative evaluation. From this we are able to make judgments about the value of our empirically-based design decisions.

We are interested particularly in the problem of aiding intermediate to advanced students, who already know how to program in one language, to learn a second or subsequent language. In contrast to learning a first language, there is often little support for the student learning a second or subsequent language. An implicit assumption is made that the student possesses the basic concepts and skills of programming and that those will be sufficient for learning a new language rapidly and without much formal training. There is a growing body of literature on transfer of skills between programming languages. While this literature does show that transfer occurs in learning programming, it also suggests that students encounter difficulties, which may result in using the new language suboptimally.

We began with the premise that existing programming tutors meant for novices do not provide precisely the kind of help that a more experienced student needs in learning another language. This led us to the empirical literature for design guidance. The result was our prototype tool, ADAPT (ADA Packages Tool), which helps students who know a procedural language, such as Pascal or C, learn to use Ada packages to create reusable software components.

2 ADAPT

ADAPT concentrates on helping students choose solution plans that are appropriate to Ada when using packages to implement abstract data types. It does not give extensive tutoring on syntactic issues. Users of ADAPT learn about packages and the plans necessary for using them by completing exercises. In an exercise, the learner is given a problem and must write a procedure, function, or package that solves it. Figure 1 shows the ADAPT screen at the start of problem solving. The screen is divided into four tiled windows: 1) a problem window in the upper right containing the statement of the problem to solve, 2) a package window in the lower right containing the specification of an Ada package to be used in the solution, 3) a solution window in the upper left which contains the current state of the student's solution, and 4) a dialog window in the lower left in which the student inputs Ada code and receives tutorial guidance.

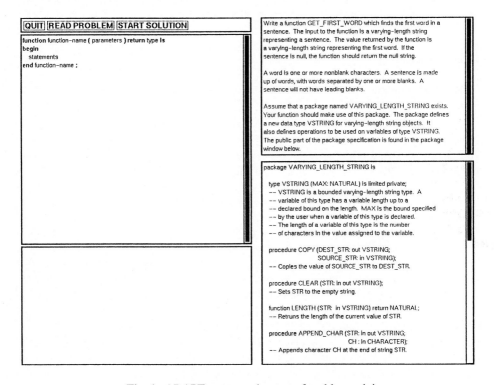

Fig. 1. ADAPT screen at the start of problem solving

At the beginning of problem solving, the solution window contains Ada code (e.g., keywords such as "function" and "return") and code templates (such as "parameters" and "type"). The code templates must be expanded in creating a solution. The user expands a code template by clicking on it. If the template can be replaced by a few lines of Ada code, control is passed to the dialog window where the student inputs the code and receives feedback if errors are made.

The solution window can also contain plans. For example, "Return first word in sentence" is the high-level plan for the function in Figure 1. When the learner chooses to replace a high-level plan by a more detailed plan, a menu of possible replacement plans pops up to the right of the solution window. The menus contain brief natural language phrases describing alternative plans for solution. These plans represent steroetypical solution approaches for the problem (Ehrlich & Soloway, 1984). When the student chooses a more detailed plan from the menu, it replaces the high-level plan in the solution window. Plans must be elaborated by stepwise refinement until they can be replaced by a small segment of Ada code. The user carries out this elaboration through a series of menu choices, which gradually make the plan more detailed and explicit, up to the point where the user can implement the lowest level plans by typing code. The user has a good deal of flexibility in building the solution. Plans appearing simultaneously in the solution window can be expanded in any order, and the user can temporarily leave a partially expanded plan to work on another one. ADAPT tutors negative transfer from other languages by representing plans that are inappropriate in Ada in the menus and tutoring why they are incorrect. The architecture of ADAPT uses several existing tutoring technologies and is described elsewhere (Fix & Wiedenbeck, 1995).

3 Design Rationale

Carroll and Moran (1991, p. 198) describe a design rationale as articulating and representing "the reasons and reasoning processes behind the design and specification of artifacts." We developed an explicit design rationale for ADAPT working from results in the literature of the cognition of progamming. ADAPT's design rationale rests on 3 principles:

1) emphasis on planning combined with deemphasis of syntactic issues of coding,
2) a top-down approach to plan development within any given plan, but flexibility to expand different plans in any order,
3) explicit tutoring of negative transfer from other programming languages.

Planning is the focus of ADAPT, rather than coding, because of cognitive studies which document planning problems of experienced programmers learning new languages (Wu & Anderson, 1991; Katz, 1991; Scholtz & Wiedenbeck, 1992a, 1992b; Siddiqi et al., 1996; Wiedenbeck & Scholtz, 1996). In particular, these studies suggest that programmers have a tendency to continue to use known plans even when they are clearly suboptimal in the new language. This indicates a need for a tool to emphasize the planning of appropriate solutions in Ada. In ADAPT, coding is seen as simply a language-dependent way to represent a plan and is thus an extension of planning at a lower-level. The steps of planning and coding really form one continuous process of building a solution.

In keeping with its strong focus on planning, ADAPT minimizes interactions about syntax. The justification for the lack of emphasis on syntax is the studies of transfer in programming which showed that programers had little difficulty with syntax when learning a new language (Wu & Anderson, 1991; Scholtz & Wiedenbeck, 1992a; 1992b). When the user inputs code that is syntactically incorrect, a message is displayed telling the user that a syntax error has been found in the code and where. The user is asked to reinput the code. It is assumed that an experienced programmer will quickly see the error and correct it without further detailed tutorial interactions.

The literature of the cognition of programming shows that people design in many ways. A strongly top-down approach to design was observed by Jeffries, Turner, Polson, and Atwood (1981). They also observed a depth-first approach by novices and a breadth-first approach by experts. Design methodologies encourage a top-down approach to program development, so Davies (1993) suggests that programmers with exposure to these methodologies are more likely to adopt a top-down strategy. Visser (1987) observed a programmer using an opportunistic approach. The "parsing/gnisrap" model of Green et al. (1987) suggests that the programmer writes down code fragments when working memory is loaded or when another task is given higher priority than the current goal. While the works described above have viewed design as either a top-down or an opportunistic process, Davies (1991) tries to integrate the two views by characterizing design as "broadly top-down with local opportunistic episodes" (p. 176).

Rist (1989) showed that the first time a programmer develops a particular schema, or plan, which has never been encountered before there is a tendency to develop the focus of the plan first. The focus is the key part of the plan for accomplishing its goal, for example, the swap in a sort. After the focus is developed, the programmer goes on to add the surrounding code needed to flesh out the plan to work correctly. However, when a programmer retrieves a known plan, the plan is expanded in schema order. Rist also found that in creating a whole program, consisting of multiple plans, for the first time the programmer tends first to elaborate the program focus, i.e., the plan or part of a plan that is most central to accomplishment of the goals of the whole program.

In ADAPT a top-down approach is followed in the development of a plan. The student starts with the specification of a very high-level plan, refines it and makes it more detailed through several iterations, then creates the implementation plan consisting of the actual Ada code. Learners specify plans with a menu-based planning language. While ADAPT constrains the learner to using the menus for higher-level planning, and thus to a top-down approach in elaborating a given plan, it is quite open-ended otherwise. In creating a solution, several plans and subplans are normally involved, and the user of ADAPT may expand them in any order. Also, a learner may temporarily suspend work on a partially elaborated plan in order to work on another. As the learner moves more deeply through the menus making choices, higher-level plans are replaced by more specific ones in the solution window. If a higher-level plan is replaced by two or more lower-level plans, the learner still has the freedom to work on those lower-level plans in any order. Only when the stage is reached where the lowest-level plan must be replaced by Ada code is the learner forced to work in a strict top-to-bottom, left-to-right order.

Students using ADAPT are thus required to develop a plan top-down. A completely opportunistic process is not possible, but the students have flexibility in exanding plans. They can develop a plan either breadth-first or depth-first. We believe that the situation of our students using ADAPT is much like Rist's schema creation. The students are creating a program consisting of multiple plans for the first time in a new language. While they know plans for how to write the program in other languages, they do not know whether those plans are appropriate in Ada. Thus, we reasoned that the students might tend to prefer a strategy of focal plan expansion, as did Rist's subjects.

ADAPT constrains the learner's style of problem solving because the learner must use the menus for higher-level planning until the point where the plan can be completed in a few lines of code. Menus have been used previously in tools for novice programmers (Bonar & Cunningham, 1988), but their acceptability to experienced programmers was a question in the design of ADAPT. We believed they would be acceptable only if they were not perceived as placing an undue burden on the learner. In order to keep the planning menus manageable, plan choices were restricted to those we had seen used by subjects in an earlier empirical study. Normally, the learner can reach the stage of entering code for any plan by traversing two to four menu levels. There are usually three or four alternative plan choices on any given menu. The menu language expresses the plan choices using about five to eight words. The terminology used in the menu language was developed from several sources: the terminology used in the cognition of programming to describe plans, examples in pedagogical materials, and the advice of Ada experts.

Buggy plans appear in the menus along with correct plans. These plans are appropriate in Pascal or C but are incorrect or very suboptimal in Ada. We chose to represent these plans in the menus because they are natural solution approaches for our target users to take. In cognitive studies of transfer between programming languages, use of such incorrect and suboptiomal plans was observed (Scholtz & Wiedenbeck, 1992a, 1992b; Siddiqi et al., 1996; Wiedenbeck & Scholtz, 1996). Putting the buggy choices in the menus and tutoring why they are inappropriate when the learner chooses them allows ADAPT to deal explicitly with negative transfer at the key moment when it occurs. This is in accord with Anderson and Skwarecki's (1986) arguments that feedback is most useful if it is immediate. Indicating that a plan is inappropriate implicitly by its absence from the menus would be much weaker pedagogically because it would rely on the learner making inferences that the plan was wrong and why, without any explicit discussion of it.

4 Evaluation

The ADAPT prototype fully tutors one problem concerning the access and use of Ada packages. We carried out a formative evaluation (Carroll and Rosson, 1995) of the prototype. The evaluation did not attempt to compare learners using ADAPT to others learning without it. That would be a summative evaluation, and, because learning is a long-term cumulative process, it would be premature until a full problem set is implemented. The formative evaluation carried out at this early point was designed to allow us to make inferences about our design rationale and to draw conclusions about the guidance given by the empirical literature to design.

The subjects in our evaluation fit the profile for which ADAPT was intended: student programmers who were proficient in Pascal or C but did not know Ada. Subjects read a three-page introduction to abstract data types and how Ada packages are used to implement them. An Ada textbook and reference manual were available. As subjects worked, they thought aloud, and a videotape recorded the session. Subsequently, the subjects were interviewed about using the tool.

The first principle for ADAPT's design rationale emphasized a focus on learning plans and deemphasized syntactic issues. Our subjects were familiar with the concept of stereotypical code sequences for solving common programming subproblems. In their protocols they often verbalized such stereotypical plans. The subjects were accustomed to expressing plans in pseudocode, consisting of natural language descriptions intermixed with code. It is not surprising then that subjects found ADAPT's plans emphasis both understandable and natural. In the interview after using the tool, all 6 subjects were positive about the mixture of Ada code and plan descriptions in the solution window. In the protocols one subject said that the solution window looked like a cleaner version of the pseudocode he normally wrote.

Syntax only becomes an issue in ADAPT at the implementation level where the learner enters lines of Ada code. The tutoring given for syntactic errors is minimal. We observed in the videotapes and protocols that subjects often made guesses about the syntax of Ada, based on knowledge of Pascal and C. These guesses were frequently correct because in most ways the syntax of Ada is similar. We also observed instances of negative transfer, in which Pascal or C-inspired syntax was wrong in Ada, and a few instances of wrong Ada syntax in which the inspiration for the error was not at all clear. In over 80 percent of the cases of wrong syntax, ADAPT's simple error message, which indicated that an error had occurred and marked the point of the error, was sufficient to lead to a correct input on the next try.

The second principle of top-down development of plans appeared to be readily accepted by subjects. No one wanted simply to begin typing code to elaborate a higher-level plan. Our subjects accepted the guidance of the tool and were pleased that, by the time they reached Ada coding, the plan was so specific that only one or a few lines of code needed to be entered. Three subjects expressed in the interviews that the guidance provided by increasingly specific plans in the menus saved them from becoming deeply immersed in the details of the language, to the exclusion of a broader understanding of Ada package concepts.

ADAPT allows plans appearing simultaneously in the solution window to be expanded in any order. We expected that we would see a large number of instances of focal plans being elaborated first, rather than the elaboration of plans from top-to-bottom in the order they occurred in the solution window. This would happen if the plan was a new one, not used in Pascal or C, or it might happen with a plan already known from a previous language, if the subject felt unsure working in the transfer language. We observed only 6 instances of subjects choosing to elaborate plans in any order other than their sequence in the solution window, and these instances were usually the result of difficulties in elaborating a previously attempted plan. Most of the plans in the menus were ones known to users of Pascal or C, often with slight modifications. It may be that the top-to-bottom expansion reflected the fact that programmers perceived their activity as plan retrieval, i.e., they saw their Pascal and C plans translating quite directly to Ada. Even so, we expected more expansion of plans in other than top-to-bottom order than we actually observed. A possible reason might be that the guidance of the tutor, which visually lays out the plans in the solution window in the order in which they occur in the solution, creates a bias toward elaborating them in sequential order. At present, we cannot answer this question about the use and value of flexibility in the order of plan expansion, except to say that our protocols suggest a preference for top-to-bottom order, as observed by Corbett et al. (1988).

The evaluation showed that the natural language descriptions used to represent the plans in the menus were a source of some difficulty for the subjects. Few subjects explicitly expressed that they were having difficulty understanding the meaning of a plan choice. However, other aspects of their behavior visible in the videotapes led us to believe that there was some general difficulty understanding plan choices. We found that subjects almost always took the first plan choice on a menu. All of the plans in the menus were used by one or more subject in an earlier study done to create the knowledge base. We expected subjects using the tool to choose a variety of these plans. The fact that they favored the first may be a sign that they did not understand the plan choices well, and took the first one by default. In our interviews, one subject suggested another window to show an elaboration of the plan choices and an example to explain them.

It appears that the subjects did not perceive the restriction to certain plan choices in the menus as a source of constraint or annoyance. In the interviews, all the subjects said that they liked having the guidance of the menus, and none wished for a redesign of the tool so that all interaction would be through entering code. In the protocols we identified only one instance in which a subject verbalized that he was searching for a plan that was not in the menus. It is possible that other plans would have been used by subjects if they had not been constrained by the tool. However, there was no hard evidence of it other than this one instance. From this we have reason to believe that a tool such as ADAPT, which knows about a relatively small number of plans for a given purpose, is usable. It may be the case that subjects saw the tool as a kind of structure editor that helped them avoid the language details and were willing to live with planning menus and restricted plan choices in order to get this help.

Explicit tutoring of negative transfer was the third principle in ADAPT's design rationale. The subjects' protocols gave us some early insights on negative transfer from known languages. At the higher levels of planning, we did not observe negative transfer. Buggy plans occurred in the menus; but, as described above, the subjects had a strong tendency to choose the first plan listed. Since by chance the buggy plans were not at the top of our menus, subjects did not choose them. At the implementation stage, i.e., the coding stage, subjects did make a considerable number of plan errors. In these plan errors, subjects typed in code that was syntactically correct but did not represent a correct Ada implementation of the plan they were attempting to replace. In about half the cases these implementation errors were classified by the investigators as errors arising from knowledge of Pascal or C. In almost all cases, subjects were able to use the messages which they received in response to incorrect plans to correct their work. Thus, from this early evaluation we do know at least that subjects make errors that come from their past experience in other languages and that they are able to correct them when they are identified, although with varying degrees of effort.

5 Conclusions

ADAPT applies existing artificial intelligence techniques to the solution of a pedagogical problem that has gained prominence over the past few years: the acquisition of new programming languages by learners who already have programming experience. Our goal was to apply results from the field of cognition of programming to the pedagogical problem. The tool is still incomplete, but from the work to date, how well has the literature of the cognition of programming informed our design choices? Our formative evaluation gives some insights into the question. The answer is mixed. The protocols of our subjects suggest that some of the cognitively based design choices were successful. These include the focus on planning activities, the deemphasis of the syntax of the new language, and the explicit instruction about negative transfer at the level of implementation of a plan in Ada. Other design choices which we made based on the literature of the cognition of programming are less certain. In particular, we do not know whether the flexibility to allow learners to expand plans in any order is necessary. We also did not have the opportunity to observe users choosing buggy tactical plans from the menus, and thus do not have any sense of whether explicit interactions about negative transfer at this level will aid acquisition of the new language.

The literature was most helpful in developing the design rationale for high-level decisions, e.g., the emphasis on plans or the top-down approach to planning. It was less helpful in making decisions about lower-level details of the tool. For example, we found little guidance in the literature on the development of our menu language describing programming plans. Although this can be considered a detail rather than a fundamental design decision, it is of extreme importance in the pedagogical success of the tool. In fact, our formative evaluation suggested that the language describing plans was the weakest point of the prototype.

Acknowledgements. Dee Christenson wrote the user interface toolkit and Russell Moseman wrote the parser. The first author was supported during this work through a Bush Leadership Fellowship and a grant from Sigma Xi.

References

1. Anderson, J.R., & Skwarecki, E. (1986). The automated tutoring of introductory computer programming. *CACM, 29*, 842-849.
2. Bonar, J., & Cunningham, R. (1988). Bridge: An intelligent tutor for thinking about programming. In J. Self (Ed.), *Artificial Intelligence and Human Learning: Intelligent Computer-Aided Instruction*. London: Chapman and Hall.
3. Carroll, J.M. & Moran, T.P. (1991). Introduction to this special issue on design rationale. *Human-Computer Interaction, 6*(3 & 4), 197-200.
4. Carroll, J.M. & Rosson, M.B. (1995). Managing evaluation goals for training. *CACM, 38*(7), 40-48.

5. Corbett, A.T., Anderson, J.R., & Patterson, E.J. (1988). Problem compilation and tutoring flexibility in the LISP tutor. *Proceedings of the Conference on Intelligent Tutoring Systems*, 423-429.

6. Davies, S.P. (1991). Characterizing the program design activity: neither strictly top-down nor globally opportunistic. *Behaviour and Information Technology, 10*(3), 173-190.

7. Davies, S.P. (1993). Models and theories of programming strategy. *IJMMS 39*, 237-267.

8. Ehrlich, K. & Soloway, E. (1984). An empirical investigation of the tacit plan knowledge in programming. In J.C. Thomas and M.L. Schneider (Eds.*), Human Factors and Computer Systems*. Norwood, NJ: Ablex.

9. Fix, V. & Wiedenbeck, S. (1995). ADAPT: An Intelligent Tool for Experienced Programmers Learning Ada. *Technical Report*, CSE Department, University of Nebraska.

10. Green, T.R.G., Bellamy, R.K.E., & Parker, J.M. (1987). Parsing and gnisrap: a model of device use. In H.J. Bullinger & B. Shackel (Eds.), *Proceedings INTERACT '87*. Amsterdam: Elsevier/North Holland.

11. Jeffries, R., Turner, A.A., Polson, P.G, & Atwood, M.E. (1981). The processes involved in designing software. In J. R. Anderson (Ed.), *Cognitive Skills and Their Acquisition*. Hillsdale, NJ: Erlbaum.

12. Katz, I.R. (1991). Assessing transfer of a complex skill. *Proceedings of the Fourteenth Annual Conference of the Cognitive Science Society*.

13. Kitchenham, B. & Carn, R. (1990). Research and practice: Software design methods and tools. In J.-M. Hoc, T.R.G. Green, R. Samurçay and D. J. Gilmore (Eds.), *Psychology of Programming*. Academic, pp. 271-284.

14. Rist, R.S. (1989). Schema creation in programming. *Cognitive Science, 13*, 389-414.

15. Scholtz, J. & Wiedenbeck, S. (1992a). Learning new programming languages: an analysis of the process and problems encountered. *Behaviour and Information Technology, 11*(4), 199-215.

16. Scholtz, J. & Wiedenbeck, S. (1992b). The role of planning in learning a new programming language. *IJMMS, 37*, 191-217.

17. Siddiqi J., Khazaei, B., Osborn, R., & Roast, C. (1996). The pitfalls of changing programming paradigms. In W.D. Gray & D. Boehm-Davis (Eds.), *Empirical Studies of Programmers: Sixth Workshop*. Norwood, NJ: Ablex.

18. Visser, W. (1987). Strategies in programming programmable controllers: A field study on a professional programmer. In G.M. Olson, S. Sheppard, & E. Soloway (Eds.), *Empirical Studies of Programmers: Second Workshop*. Norwood, NJ: Ablex, pp 217-230.

19. Wiedenbeck, S. & Scholtz, J. (1996). Adaptation of programming plans in transfer between programming languages: a developmental approach. In W.D. Gray and D. Boehm-Davis (Eds.), *Empirical Studies of Programmers: Sixth Workshop*. Norwood, NJ: Ablex.

20. Wu, Q. & Anderson, J.R. (1991). Knowledge transfer among programming languages. *Proceedings of the Fourteenth Annual Conference of the Cognitive Science Society*, 376-381.

A Content-Balanced Adaptive Testing Algorithm for Computer-Based Training Systems

Sherman X. Huang

Alberta Research Council
6815, 8th Street, Calgary, Alberta, Canada T2E 7H7

Abstract. There are two main obstacles that make use of adaptive testing in computer-based training difficult. One is the requirement of conducting a large-scale empirical study for item calibration. The other is the difficulty of generating content-balanced tests that meet the goal of the test administrators. In this research, we have developed a new adaptive testing algorithm, CBAT-2, to provide a solution for these problems and some other practical problems in adaptive testing. CBAT-2 generates questions based on the portion of the course curriculum that meets the goals of a test. It uses a simple machine learning procedure to determine the item parameter values.

1. Introduction

Testing is an important component of training. It is important for a computer-based educational system to contain a high-quality on-line testing component. An *adaptive test* is a computer-administered test in which the presentation of each test item and the decision to stop the test are dynamically adapted to the student's performance in the test.

Research in adaptive testing is usually oriented to large-scaled standardized tests designed by testing centres such as Educational Testing Service (ETS). The algorithms developed require a major empirical study in order to calibrate the test item pool (Wainer, 1990). Such an empirical study is rarely affordable for smaller schools or industrial organizations that offer on-line training for their students or employees. This difficulty prohibits adaptive testing algorithms from being used in computer-based learning environments.

Another major difficulty for applying adaptive testing algorithms is the content-balancing problem. Most adaptive testing algorithms are content-blind. Their question selection strategy does not take into account from which content areas in the curriculum the questions come. However, a test designer or instructor usually has a plan for the test to cover certain content areas. If the testing algorithm does not address the content-balancing problem, the test would not be able to meet the goals of the plan.

The goal of this research is to develop a *content-balanced adaptive testing* algorithm for computer-based training systems. The algorithm, called *CBAT-2,* is aimed at meeting the growing demand of computer-based education and just-in-time training provided by schools and industrial organizations. In particular, it generates tests that cover content areas in the test designer's plan, and eliminates the requirement for an empirical study to calibrate test items. From our experience in developing commercial adaptive learning software, we have seen the great potential of incorporating CBAT-2 into computer-based learning environments.

2. How an Adaptive Testing Algorithm Work

In general, the goal of an adaptive testing algorithm is to increase the efficiency and assessment precision of the test by selecting items that provide the most information about the student and terminating the test as the assessment reaches a precision criterion. An adaptive testing algorithm usually has three important components: a test item pool, an item selector and a proficiency estimator.

The test item pool contains items that may be selected for the test. Each item is characterized by a number of parameters. Three commonly used parameters, as described in the item response theory (IRT), are: the *difficulty level*, the *discriminatory power* and the *guessing factor* (Wainer, 1990). The difficulty level describes how difficult the question is. The discriminatory power describes how well the question can discriminate students of different proficiency. The guessing factor is the probability that a student can answer the question correctly by guessing.

At any time during a test, the algorithm has a temporary estimation for the student's proficiency (usually denoted θ). The item selector selects an item from the test item pool. The selected item is aimed at providing the most information about the student's proficiency. The selection is based on the item's three parameters and the temporary proficiency θ'. An ideal item should have a difficulty level close to the temporary θ', a high discriminatory power and a low guessing factor.

Once the student provides an answer for the selected item, the proficiency estimator calculates a new θ' and its confidence level, based on whether the student's answer is correct or incorrect, the old θ' and the item parameters. If the confidence level of the θ' reaches a designated level, then the test terminates. Otherwise the item selector selects another item for the student, and the test continues.

3. CBAT-2

CBAT-2 is aimed at providing a solution for the following problems in applying adaptive testing to computer-based training environments.

- *Content-balanced:* Ensure that the items selected for the test cover all content areas in the test plan. No content area is over-tested or under-tested.
- *Test item pool calibration:* Remove the requirement for a major empirical study to calibrate a test item pool.
- *Intelligent selection of test items:* Select test items that will provide the most assessment information to increase the efficiency and precision of the test.
- *Security:* Selected test items do not form a pattern. Having a selection pattern may increase the chance of guessing and cheating.
- *Questions in multiple content areas:* Allow a question to be associated with multiple content areas.
- *Two-level assessment:* Provide assessment information for each content area as well as for the global test.

3.1 Content Areas in a Curriculum and in a Test

A content-balanced testing system must be able to associate questions with content areas. This requires a representation of content areas. In CBAT-2, content areas in a course curriculum is represented by a directed acyclic graph called a *curriculum hierarchy*, as shown in Figure 1.

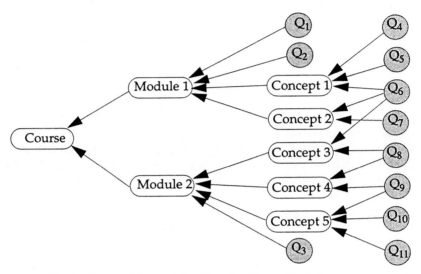

Fig. 1. Content Areas and Questions in a Course Curriculum

Each rectangle in the hierarchy, called a *component* in general, represents a content area at a certain level. Each component in the hierarchy has exactly one parent, except for the root that has no parent. The root of the hierarchy is the course. A component may have zero or many child components which represent its content sub-areas. For example, in Figure 1, a module is a sub-area of the course; and a concept is a sub-area of a module.

A question, represented in Figure 1 by a solid circle, may be associated with one or many components at any level of the curriculum. Questions associated with components at higher levels are those that require general knowledge. Questions associated with components at lower levels, in particular at the lowest level, are those that require knowledge of specific concepts and skills.

In CBAT-2, a test assesses a student's knowledge at two content area levels. For example, a module test covers a module, and does assessment for the concepts under the module. Only questions associated with this module or its concepts may be selected for the test. A course test covers the course, and does assessment for the modules under the course. All questions in the course may be selected for the test. However, the algorithm is sensitive to only the course-ship and the module-ship of the questions, it is not sensitive to the concept-ship of the questions. Questions associated with different concepts under a module are treated in the same way. They are also treated as the same as questions associated with general knowledge of the module. Figure 2 shows the system's two views of the curriculum in Figure 1. One view is in a module test for Module 1, and the other in a course test.

One might wonder why we don't do the assessment for content areas at all levels in one test. This is because such an overall test is usually too long. In practice, two-level information is usually sufficient. If assessment at every level is needed, then the student should take tests at all levels.

Thus, as a part of the initialization, CBAT-2 generates a *sub-curriculum* for each specific test. CBAT-2 also consults the test designer for the weight of each content area in the test. For example, in Figure 2-(a), general knowledge of the module weighs 1/10, Concept 1 weighs 6/10, and Concept 2 weighs 3/10. By default, all content areas in the test that have questions have the same weight.

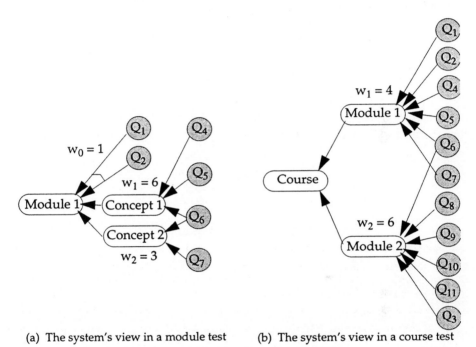

(a) The system's view in a module test   (b) The system's view in a course test

Fig. 2. Different views of the curriculum in different tests

3.2 Questions

Questions are located at the lowest level of the curriculum hierarchy. They have no children. Unlike a component which has only one parent, a question may have one or many parents. This reflects the fact that a question may require knowledge/skills from several content areas to answer. A question may have parents at any levels in the curriculum hierarchy. This allows general questions to be in a test. However, in practice, most questions' parents are components at the lowest level of the curriculum (e.g., concepts in Figure 1).

Questions in CBAT-2 are indexed by two parameters: a *difficulty level* and a *guessing factor*. The difficulty level describes how difficult a question is. It is comparable to the parameter b in IRT. The guessing factor describes the likelihood that a question is correctly answered by guessing. It is comparable to the parameter c in IRT. The *discriminatory power*, parameter a in IRT, is not used in the current CBAT-2 because its values are usually difficult to calibrate and its meaning is difficult to be understood by test designers.

The guessing factor of a question is determined by the rate of the number of correct answers and the number of answers that the student may choose. For example, it is 0.5 for a True-Or-False question, 0.25 for a Multiple-Choices question with four mutual exclusive choices, and 0 for an Written-Answer question.

The value of the difficulty level ranges from 0 to 1. It is obtained by combining a designated initial value and historical information, using the following formula:

$$\text{diff}_i = \frac{20 \cdot \text{init}_i + \Phi_i}{20 + R_i + W_i}$$

where init_i is the *initial difficulty* of question; the constant 20 is a normalization factor; R_i and W_i are the numbers of times that Q_i was correctly answered and incorrectly answered in the past, respectively. Φ_i is a difficulty accumulator for question Q_i such that every time a student incorrectly answers Q_i, the difficulty level equivalent to the student's temporary proficiency θ' is accumulated. Thus,

$$\Phi_i = \sum_{j=1}^{n} k_j \cdot f(\theta_j')$$

where n is the number of answers for Q_i in the past (i.e., $n = R_i + W_i$); θ_j' was the temporary proficiency of the student who gave the jth answer for Q_i; $k_j = 0$ if the jth answer is correct, and $k_j = 2$ if the jth answer is incorrect; $f(\theta_j')$ converts a θ value (-4 to 4) to a difficulty level (0 to 1). In the current implementation of CBAT-2, f is a linear function.

The initial difficulty has a value from 0 to 1. It is assigned by the test designer, based on his/her knowledge about the question. With the initial difficulty, it is no longer necessary to conduct an empirical study or to have historical information before adding questions to a pool. At the beginning, if there is no historical data, the initial difficulty determines the difficulty level. As the question is used in the tests, R_i and W_i become larger, and the difficulty level converges to $\Phi_i/(R_i + W_i)$. Thus, in some sense, CBAT-2 has a learning ability.

3.3 The Testing Algorithm

For each specific test, the test algorithm operates on the sub-curriculum of the test (see Figure 2) that is generated in the initialization of the test.

The algorithm consists of three procedures: a *question selector*, a *proficiency estimator*, and a *score and mastery decider*. Initially, there is an initial proficiency, θ_I, for a student, based on the test designer's knowledge about the student or a default value. The question selector selects a question based on θ_I. Once the student answers the question, and the correctness of the answer is determined, the proficiency estimator calculates a new temporary proficiency, θ', for the student. It also calculates the confidence degree, v', for θ'. If v' has not reached a pre-designate confidence criterion v_0, then the question selector selects another question for the student. This goes on until v' passes the confidence level of v_0. Then the test stops. The temporary proficiency θ' becomes the proficiency θ. The score and mastery decider converts θ to a score that is comparable to the raw score in a conventional paper-and-pencil test, and determines whether the student is a master or a non-master.

This three-procedures approach is similar to the approach of Kingsbury and Weiss' (1979) Adaptive Mastery Testing (AMT), but each procedure is designed to meet the goals of CBAT-2. In the following subsections, we discuss these procedures in details.

Question Selection

The question selection procedure contains two steps. The first step is to decide which component (content area) the question comes from. This *working component* is randomly selected among a set of candidate components. A *candidate component* is a component under the sub-curriculum of the test such that the student's proficiency in this component has not been decided. However, the candidate components don't have an equal chance of being selected. The probability for a candidate component to be selected depends on its weight. The following formula is used to calculate the selection probability P_i for component C_i, where W_i is the weight of C_i.

$$P_i = \frac{W_i}{\sum_j W_j \mid C_j \text{ is a candidate component}}$$

The second step is to select a question among those associated with the chosen component. The question is selected based on the amount of information that a question may provide for the student's assessment. The information available, $I_i(\theta)$, from question Q_i, is calculated based on Birnbaum's (1968) logistic ICC (item characteristic curve) model. In this model, $I_i(\theta)$ is decided by the three IRT parameters (a, b and c) of the question and the student's temporary proficiency θ'.[1]

Questions in CBAT-2 does not have the parameter a. We use a constant, 1.2, for the parameter in the model because 1.2 is near the mean of the parameters in the question pools in Kingsbury and Weiss' (1979) study. For the parameter b, we use function $g(\text{diff}_i)$ to convert the value of the difficulty level, 0 to 1, of each question to a b value, -4 to 4. The function g is the reverse function of f (see section 3.2). It is currently a linear function. The parameter c directly uses the guessing factor of the question.

Once the $I_i(\theta)$ for each question is calculated, a set of questions with the highest $I_i(\theta)$ becomes the *candidate questions* among which a question is randomly selected for the

---

1. Due to the size restriction of the submission, we do not explore the details of the logistic ICC model. Interested readers may refer to the publication by Birnbaum (1968) and Kingsbury and Weiss (1979).

test. (The size of the candidate question set may vary with different applications.) This is different from AMT where the question that has the highest $I_i(\theta)$ is selected for the test. Our approach does not have the deterministic property that may cause a security problem.

Proficiency Estimation and Test Termination

Once the student has provided an answer for the selected question, and the system determined the correctness of the answer, the proficiency estimator is invoked to update the temporary proficiency, of the student. In CBAT-2, besides a temporary proficiency, θ', for the test (which is also the temporary proficiency of the parent component in the sub-curriculum of the test), there is a temporary proficiency, θ_i', for each child component C_i in the sub-curriculum of the test. Also, if there are questions directly associated with the parent component, CBAT-2 would create a component to represent the general knowledge of the parent component. This created component is treated in the same way as other child component of the parent component. It also has its temporary proficiency. For example, in the module test in Figure 2a, there are θ' for the module, θ_1' and θ_2' for Concept 1 and Concept 2, and θ_0' for the general knowledge of the module. In the course test in Figure 2b, there are θ' for the course, θ_1' and θ_2' for Module 1 and Module 2.

The proficiency estimator updates the temporary proficiency of the test and the components associated with the question that the student just answered. It also calculates the confidence level of each updated temporary proficiency. The proficiency estimator uses Owen's (1975) Bayesian updating procedure.[2] (This procedure is also used in AMT.)

There are two parameters that a test designer may set values to decide when a test terminates. One is the confidence level criterion for the proficiency estimation (say, 95%). We call it the *confidence criterion*. The other is the minimum number of questions that must be selected from each child component in the sub-curriculum (say, 2). We call this number the *MNQ*. Normally, the test terminates when two conditions are met: (1) the temporary proficiency of the parent component (or the test), θ', has passed the confidence criterion; (2) every child component has at least MNQ associated questions selected for the test.

Once a test terminates, the temporary proficiency of each component becomes its proficiency. However, the administrator must use with caution the assessment information for the child components because their proficiency may not have passed the confidence criterion. If the assessment of a child component, say C_i, is critical and must be precise, then a test on the sub-curriculum where C_i is the parent component may need to be conducted.

---

2. Again, due to the size restriction, we do not explore the Bayesian updating procedure here. Interested readers may refer to the publications by Owen (1975) and Kingsbury and Weiss (1979).

Scoring and Mastery Decision

The proficiency of each component in the sub-curriculum, in particular the proficiency of the parent component (or the test), may be converted to a percentage score that is commonly used in conventional paper-and-pencil tests. The conversion is based on the test characteristic curve (TCC) of a three-parameter logistic ogive used in AMT (Kingsbury and Weiss, 1979). We use the same conversion method as that in our question selection procedure (see section 3.3.1) to obtain the three parameters of each question.

If the test is a mastery test, then the score is used to compare with a master level set by the course administrator. A score above the master level classifies the student a master of the corresponding component or the test. A score below the master level classifies the student a non-master of the component.

4. Related Work

Much of the algorithm of CBAT-2 is based on IRT. Some techniques that we use come directly from AMT (Kingsbury and Weiss, 1979). However, like other IRT-based algorithms, AMT requires an expensive item calibration process to develop an item pool. This approach may work for large-scale institutional testing, but it doesn't seem to be appropriate for computer-based industrial training and local school education where the budget is normally small and the courses are diverse. CBAT-2 uses a simple machine learning approach to item calibration which requires no empirical study. It removes a main obstacle which prohibits small organizations from using adaptive testing.

AMT does not address the issue of content balancing, but Kingsbury and Zara (1989) recently developed a simple content-balanced testing algorithm. CBAT-2 is alike to their algorithm in that both deal with two-level content areas. However, rather than viewing a test as a stand alone activity, we place a test in the context of a course curriculum, which allows a test at the high-level of the curriculum to use questions in low-level content areas, and frees the test designer from having to develop a different pool for every test.

Wainer and Kiely (1987) has proposed the *testlet* approach for the content-balancing problem and the context effect problem. "A testlet is a group of items related to a single content area that is developed as a unit and contains a fixed number of predetermined paths that an examinee may follow. (P.190)" If an adaptive testing algorithm selects a testlet and a particular path of the testlet, then all items on the path will be presented in the test in the same order as they are in the testlet. The testlet approach relies on the test designer to ensure that the content areas are covered. This actually degrades adaptive testing to a mix of conventional fixed-item testing and adaptive testing. One may view a fixed-item test as a big linear testlet that contains all items in the test. Kingsbury and Zara (1989) have criticized the testlet approach, for it reduces the measurement accuracy and efficiency of adaptive testing.

To address the problem of requiring a demanding item calibration process in IRT-based algorithms, Welch and Frick (1993) have used an expert system approach to develop a series of *EXSPRT*'s. They showed a study of EXSPRT where a group of 38 student subjects were used for item calibration. Comparing to IRT-based algorithms that require 200 to 1,000 student subjects for item calibration, EXSPRT has made a significant advance. However, a study of 38 subjects may still be too difficult for most small organizations, especially when the knowledge and experience of educational empirical study is required. Also, like most other algorithms, EXSPRT's do not address the content-balancing problem.

An EXSPRT is a mastery testing algorithm. A vital hidden problem in an EXSPRT is that the master level is decided in the empirical study that collects the historical data for its rules. Once the study is done, the test designers and administrators cannot change this master level freely. This is hardly acceptable for most organizations that live in a dynamic world.

5. Future Directions

Several things are in our future research agenda. We are planning to do an empirical study on real testing data provided by Alberta Education to compare the results of CBAT-2 and other adaptive testing algorithms as well as the conventional paper-and-pencil testing. We are doing research on student modelling (Collins et al., 1995). We intend to use the adaptive testing results as a source of input for our student modelling system that will provide assessment on the student's knowledge. We also intend to integrate CBAT-2 into a commercial learning environment, using it in real-world training.

Acknowledgment

Special thanks to Jason Collins, Jim Greer and Mike Dobson for their contribution in developing CBAT, an earlier version of CBAT-2, Gage Kingsbury for his valuable inputs to this research. Thanks to Janet McCracken and Chris Hughes for their comments on an early draft of the paper, and the Alberta Research Council for providing research funding.

References

1. Birnbaum, A. (1968): Some latent trait models and their use in inferring an examinee's ability. In F. M. Lord and M. R. Novick, Statistical Theories of Mental Test Scores. Reading, MA: Addison-Wesley.
2. Collins, J. A., Greer, J. E. and Huang, S. X. (1996): Adaptive testing using granularity hierarchies and Bayesian nets. Proceedings of ITS '96.
3. Kingsbury, G. G. and Weiss, D. J. (1979): An Adaptive Testing Strategy for Mastery Decision. Research Report 79-5, Psychometric Method Program, Department of Psychology, University of Minnesota.
4. Kingsbury, G. G. and Zara, A. R. (1989): Procedures for selecting items for computerized adaptive tests. Applied Measurement in Education 2, 359-375.
5. Owen, R. J. (1975): A Bayesian sequential procedure for quantal response in the context of adaptive mental testing. Journal of the American Statistical Association 70, 351-356.
6. Wainer, H. (1990): Computerized Adaptive Testing: A Primer. Lawrence Erlbaum Associates, Inc., Publishers.
7. Wainer, H. and Kiely, G. L. (1987): Item clusters and computerized adaptive testing: A case for testlets. Journal of Educational Measurement 24, 189-205.
8. Welch, R. E. and Frick, T. W. (1993): Computerized adaptive testing in instructional settings. ETR&D 41, 47-62.

Un modèle de situation d'évaluation pour le suivi de formation en langue étrangère

Philippe TEUTSCH

LIUM - Université du Maine
B.P. 535 - 72017 LE MANS Cedex - FRANCE
Tel : (33) 43 83 33 76 - Fax : (33) 43 83 35 65
E-mail : Philippe.Teutsch@lium.univ-lemans.fr

Résumé. La conception d'un environnement d'évaluation en langues est un domaine difficile à appréhender : la modélisation du domaine linguistique et le traitement automatique du langage sont encore mal dominés, l'apprentissage d'une langue est relativement contextuel. De plus, l'ordinateur crée une situation didactique particulière que l'on connaît mal.

Ce texte montre l'intérêt de décrire dans ce cas un modèle de "Situation d'Évaluation" et de mettre en œuvre une méthodologie de conception itérative pour parvenir à produire des prototypes qui tiennent compte des objectifs et des contraintes de chacun. Notre propos est illustré par la présentation de l'environnement MARPLE, système d'auto-évaluation des connaissances en anglais. La question fondamentale de ce projet est de garantir la qualité de la formation individualisée : un suivi complet et cohérent du parcours de l'apprenant. Nous présentons MARPLE à travers l'environnement d'interaction proposé à l'utilisateur, l'architecture logicielle du système, ainsi que le module d'analyse de réponse.

1. Introduction

Les Systèmes Tuteurs Intelligents (STI) intéressent les enseignants en langues pour leur capacité à créer des environnements interactifs d'apprentissage. L'intégration de techniques d'Intelligence Artificielle (IA) et de supports multimédias permettent la création d'une interaction riche avec l'élève (Yazdani 1989). Chanier (1991) affirme de plus que l'ordinateur est aujourd'hui considéré comme un partenaire à part entière du processus d'acquisition des langues, et qu'il est nécessaire de rechercher de nouveaux modèles pour son utilisation dans l'apprentissage des langues.

À travers une démarche d'individualisation de la formation, les formateurs en langues cherchent, quant à eux, à mettre l'apprenant en situation réelle de communication et à lui permettre d'analyser sa propre production (Narcy 1990). Les outils d'auto-évaluation et d'auto-orientation assistés deviennent dans ce cadre aussi importants que les supports d'apprentissage proprement dits.

Mais on ne doit pas oublier que l'on ne peut pas connaître a priori l'usage qui sera fait d'un système informatique. L'usage de l'ordinateur comme support de communication influence profondément la situation d'apprentissage vécue par l'apprenant (Vivet 1991).

C'est dans ce contexte que nous avons conçu un système d'évaluation des connaissances en langue étrangère dont le nom est MARPLE. Ce texte se propose de définir une méthode de conception basée sur des descriptions de la situation d'évaluation et sur un ensemble d'expertises dédiées à l'analyse des compétences. Notre propos sera illustré par la présentation du système MARPLE.

2. Projet MARPLE

Le projet MARPLE (acronyme de Modélisation de l'Apprenant et Repérage des Performances en Langue Étrangère) est issu d'un constat d'insuffisance des ressources humaines disponibles pour assurer la tâche de validation de compétences en langues étrangères dans un centre de formation. Le projet est mené par une équipe d'informaticiens, de didacticiens, d'enseignants en université et de formateurs en entreprise. Son objectif est de compléter les outils de formation déjà disponibles pour assurer un suivi complet et cohérent du parcours de l'apprenant tout en maintenant la qualité de la formation individualisée.

2.1. Objectifs

Le projet MARPLE s'intéresse à la construction d'un système d'évaluation des compétences pour la formation en langues étrangères. Les fonctions attendues du système sont de deux types : premièrement, valider certaines compétences individuelles en langue, en compréhension, aussi bien écrite qu'orale, et en expression écrite; deuxièmement, permettre l'apprenant de faire le point sur ses connaissances à la fin de chaque séquence de cours. Le rôle du système n'est pas simplement de valider le niveau de l'apprenant et de souligner ses erreurs. L'objectif est de rendre l'apprenant conscient de ses capacités, des situations qui lui sont accessibles, et de celles qui lui posent encore des difficultés.

2.2. Problématique

Nous nous sommes intéressés aux difficultés que rencontrent les concepteurs pour produire des STI dédiés à l'apprentissage des langues qui soient réellement exploitables. Il semble que les systèmes actuellement proposés souffrent principalement d'un manque d'expertise sur la situation didactique créée par l'usage de l'ordinateur.

L'usage de l'ordinateur impose de formaliser et d'implémenter des concepts et connaissances pour lui permettre d'interagir avec l'utilisateur (Pitrat 1990). Mais les difficultés qui apparaissent en cherchant à appréhender la langue et son enseignement posent des problèmes de modélisation des connaissances insurmontables au premier abord. Le domaine d'enseignement ciblé se limite souvent à quelques exercices structuraux et l'analyse des réponses est relativement appauvrie. La plupart des recherches ont visé l'apprentissage de compétences grammaticales et linguistiques pures (Yazdani 1989), la conception d'exercices très ciblés (Cf. Swartz & Yazdani 1991), ou encore l'emploi de techniques multimédias, mais en dehors de toute étude sur l'usage réel du logiciel.

Seuls quelques projets s'intéressent aux aspects conversationnels. Au Québec, le système PILÉFACE de Lelouche (1991) propose à l'apprenant une situation de dialogue dans laquelle les relations socio-culturelles entre interlocuteurs sont explicitement fixées. En terme d'évaluation, le système E.T. (pour "English Tutor", Fum et al 1991) présente l'avantage d'appliquer une stratégie d'analyse et de suivi des erreurs. Une réponse erronée de l'élève déclenche l'émission d'un certain nombre d'hypothèses sur les connaissances précises de l'apprenant. Ces hypothèses sont prises en compte dans le choix des exercices ultérieurs.

Rares sont donc les environnements proposant une réelle situation communicative. Th. Chanier (1991) a bien montré que "le degré d'individualisation offert par les logiciels s'appuyant sur les acquis théoriques de l'Intelligence Artificielle (I.A.) et de la linguistique informatique reste très limité". L'appel aux techniques d'I.A. est donc certainement nécessaire à la construction d'un environnement linguistique mais pas suffisant en terme d'analyse de l'usage d'un système interactif.

La problématique fédératrice du projet MARPLE est celle de la méthodologie de conception d'un système fortement interactif et ayant une fonction d'aide à l'apprentissage. Les recherches aboutissant à la spécification d'un tel système (besoins des enseignants, représentation des concepts et des connaissances du domaine, modèle d'architecture logicielle) doivent être complétées par une analyse sur les caractéristiques de l'usage du logiciel dans un cadre d'enseignement. L'objectif de ce type de recherches est d'aboutir à la spécification d'une méthodologie de conception généralisable et réutilisable dans d'autres domaines. Il s'agit alors de s'interroger sur ce que les ordinateurs apportent à l'apprentissage, et en quoi leur usage peut compléter le travail de l'enseignant.

La conception de l'environnement MARPLE a permis d'apporter des réponses à ces questions par la mise en œuvre d'une démarche de conception associant la création d'un prototype à l'observation de sa mise en œuvre par les usagers (Teutsch 1994).

3.   Méthodologie de conception

Le travail en équipe pluridisciplinaire mis en place autour du projet MARPLE a permis de définir un outil de conception de situation d'interaction avec ordinateur : la "Situation d'Évaluation". Ce modèle est le point de rencontre entre la spécification informatique d'un système et l'analyse d'une situation didactique. Il est issu du modèle d'interaction proposé au LIUM (Dubourg 1995) en tenant compte des caractéristiques propres à un environnement de tests.

3.1.   Situation d'Évaluation

Le modèle de situation d'évaluation se décompose en trois grandes classes d'éléments décrivant chacune des caractéristiques intervenant dans le mode d'interaction.

-    Une description de la formation à travers le contenu d'enseignement (séquences de cours, points de grammaire abordés, listes de vocabulaire et surtout tâches d'entraînement proposées à l'apprenant) ainsi que les différents thèmes culturels abordés pendant cet enseignement.

-    Une description du support d'évaluation à travers les objectifs d'évaluation, l'activité proposée à travers la consigne donnée à l'apprenant, et la référence précise de la question ou de l'élément à travailler. Chaque question est accompagnée d'un "Modèle d'Analyse" permettant de définir les productions attendues des apprenants, ainsi que les commentaires associés aux erreurs.

-    Une description du mode d'interaction lié au support de présentation (texte, son, image) et au mode de réponse proposé à l'utilisateur. Ce mode d'interaction doit également être pris en compte par l'évaluation dans la mesure où il guide plus ou moins fortement la réponse de l'apprenant.

Ce modèle de situation d'évaluation permet à la fois de s'adapter aux principes d'architecture logicielle modulaire et à un processus de conception itératif : un dialogue s'instaure entre informaticiens, didacticiens et formateurs autour de maquettes et de tests auprès des utilisateurs-apprenants.

3.2.   Processus de Conception Itératif

Le manque d'expériences concernant la modélisation d'environnements de formation linguistique impose d'adopter une démarche de conception itérative. Le principe est de pouvoir s'adapter au comportement de l'apprenant et du formateur mis en présence du matériau pédagogique en tenant compte, au fur et à mesure des expérimentations, de leurs réactions et de leurs initiatives.

Cumming & Self (1990) ont montré que "l'approche frontale" de conception des STI impose des représentations extrêmement détaillées des connaissances mises en jeu et que, en conséquence, les difficultés rencontrées apparaissent être insurmontables et empêchent la réalisation de systèmes réellement exploitables. Cumming et Sussex (1991) proposent en conséquence d'adopter une stratégie de développement qui s'appuie sur la mise en place d'activités d'apprentissage à base d'outils informatiques et sur l'observation des échanges provoqués par ces activités entre les enseignants et les apprenants.

Pour MARPLE, l'approche incrémentale que nous avons mis en œuvre a associé la création de prototypes à l'observation de leur mise en œuvre par les usagers (Teutsch & Vivet, 1993). Une première phase a consisté à définir et concevoir l'environnement interactif proposé à l'apprenant à partir des spécifications de situation d'évaluation. La seconde phase concerne l'étude et la conception du contenu linguistique et des tâches d'évaluation.

Nous nous sommes donc attachés à respecter, cycliquement, les étapes suivantes :

Analyses préalables. Les premières spécifications de situation d'évaluation sont accompagnées de propositions de squelettes d'architecture logicielle et d'une étude sur les usages envisageables du logiciel.

1° Conception expérimentale de l'environnement interactif à partir de l'interface. Cette étape s'intéresse aux phénomènes d'interaction que crée la situation d'évaluation. Elle permet de conclure sur les spécifications de situations d'interaction relativement indépendantes de la langue cible.

2° Étude et conception du contenu linguistique ainsi que des tâches d'évaluation. Cette étape permet de décrire les spécifications des connaissances linguistiques et diagnostiques nécessaires à la construction du système. La définition des tâches d'évaluation et la prise en compte des difficultés usuelles rencontrées par les apprenants ont pour conséquence d'identifier et de modéliser les connaissances utiles à l'analyse de réponses.

3° Validation de l'environnement en tenant compte des nécessités d'interaction en terme d'interface et de traitement des réponses. Cette étape a pour objectif de vérifier la pertinence des tâches d'évaluation proposées et de connaître le comportement linguistique des apprenants en situation réelle de production.

D'un point de vue informatique, la mise en œuvre de cette méthode de conception cyclique permet de proposer un squelette d'architecture initial puis d'affiner progressivement les aspects fonctionnels et communicationnels du système. Pour MARPLE, les modules initiaux (module d'interface et module de diagnostic) se sont ainsi transformés en agents devant échanger des messages. Il a donc fallu spécifier le protocole de communication.

3.3.   Environnement d'Évaluation

L'environnement de test MARPLE propose à l'apprenant un ensemble de situations d'évaluation liées à son cursus et aux objectifs de formation du niveau qu'il doit atteindre. Chacune des situations invite l'apprenant à se trouver dans un lieu particulier ou dans une activité originale tels que, pour le premier niveau de formation : téléphoner, aller à la banque, prendre l'avion, chercher du travail.

Les figures 1 et 2 présentent respectivement la copie d'une page de situation d'évaluation avec production écrite de l'utilisateur et un extrait des analyses de réponses correspondantes. Le thème de travail concerne l'étude de l'emploi du temps de "Janet", la saisie des réponses est entièrement libre, et la validation grammaticale s'intéresse principalement à la place de l'adverbe dans la phrase.

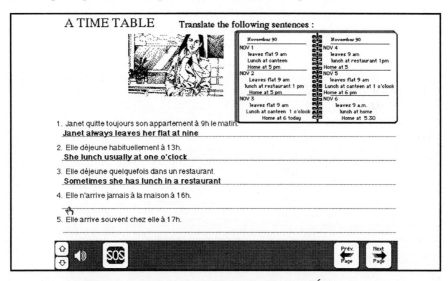

Fig. 1 Productions écrites dans une Situation d'Évaluation

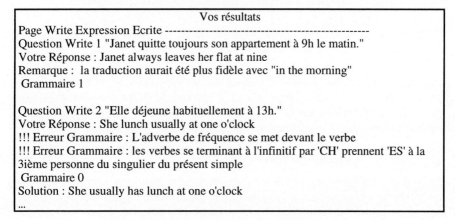

Fig. 2 Commentaires issus de l'analyse de réponse

3.4. Structure Logicielle

L'architecture logicielle retenue pour MARPLE (Fig. 3) s'appuie essentiellement sur :

- Un module d'interface (Agent d'interaction) dédié aux interactions de surface avec l'usager (son, images, texte et boutons de commande). Ce module présente la page d'accueil et visualise les situations d'évaluation.
- Un ensemble de modules experts intervenants sur la gestion de la session d'évaluation, l'analyse des productions de l'utilisateur, la synthèse des connaissances.
- Une base de données Apprenants. La modélisation de l'apprenant se limite pour l'instant à ses objectifs de formation, son niveau initial et l'historique des sessions précédentes. Ces informations sont mises à jour par le système.
- Une base de données Formation qui définit le contenu du cours étudié à travers le vocabulaire, les règles de grammaire, les erreurs classiques liées à cette grammaire, et les ressources de formation.

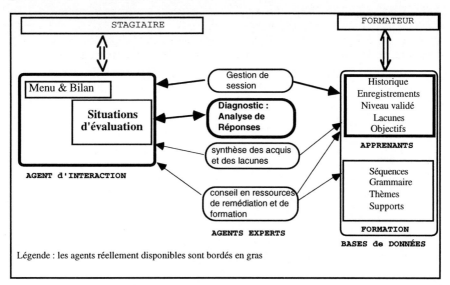

Fig. 3 Structure du système MARPLE

Les agents communiquent entre eux par envoi de messages. Par exemple, à chaque nouvelle réponse de l'utilisateur, au clavier ou par QCM, l'agent d'Interaction demande à l'agent de Diagnostic d'analyser cette réponse en lui précisant le contexte d'évaluation ainsi que le modèle d'analyse pour la question concernée.

4. Expertise de Diagnostic

Les psychocogniticiens modélisent l'apprentissage à travers la notion d'Interlangue (Ellis 1985) qui suggère que l'apprenant commet des erreurs à partir d'hypothèses qu'il élabore sur la nature de la langue. L'erreur est donc le signe de l'activité cognitive de l'apprenant. Il paraît alors important de repérer et d'inventorier ces erreurs afin d'établir le modèle des connaissances justes et erronées de l'apprenant.

4.1. Représentation de Connaissances

La méthode d'analyse de réponse actuellement retenue pour MARPLE assure une comparaison "mot à mot". Elle s'intéresse essentiellement à la syntaxe de la phrase produite et fait référence à des modèles de réponse complets.

Chaque question est liée à un Modèle d'Analyse permettant au système de diagnostic d'analyser les réponses de l'apprenant. Ce Modèle d'Analyse est défini par un ensemble de modèles de réponse, d'équivalences et de commentaires (Fig. 4) dont nous récapitulons ici le contenu :

- Modèle syntaxique de réponse. Chaque modèle de réponse correspond à une production complète, relativement correcte syntaxiquement, et utilise des équivalences de termes pour certains mots ou expressions. Les erreurs sont intégrées aux modèles de réponses par l'ajout d'équivalents erronés ou de syntaxes incorrectes. Chaque erreur fait référence à un commentaire répertorié.

- Équivalence. À une expression correspond un ensemble de synonymes ou d'expressions équivalentes.

- Code et Commentaire d'erreurs. À chaque type d'erreur correspond un commentaire permettant d'informer l'apprenant de cette erreur. Le commentaire tient compte du type d'erreur et du contexte de la phrase et de l'exercice.

```
Question :      Janet quitte toujours son appartement à 9h le matin.
Solution :      Janet always leaves her flat at nine in the morning
Grammaire:
        AdvFreq --Les adverbes de fréquence font partie de la séquence de cours
-- Modèles de syntaxes possibles :
Janet %always %leaves %HerFlat %prepATheure %9am
...
! Janet %leaves %always %HerFlat %prepATheure %9am
                                            EAdvFreqAlwaysPlace !!
...
-- Avec les équivalences suivantes :
%Janet      [ Janet / %she ]
%always     [ always / ! # EAdvFreqAlwaysPlace !! ]
%leaves     [ leaves / ! leave EPresSimpS3PS !! ]
%HerFlat    [ %Her %flat / home ]
...
-- Avec les commentaires suivants
EAdvFreqAlwaysPlace :
    l'adverbe de fréquence 'Always' se met toujours devant le verbe
EPresSimpS3PS :
    il faut un 'S' à la 3ième pers. du singulier d'un verbe au présent simple
...
```

Fig. 4 Modèle d'Analyse dans MARPLE

4.2. Analyse de Réponse

Le principe de l'analyse de réponse est de pouvoir reconnaître, dans la réponse donnée par l'apprenant, une des formes issues du modèle d'analyse. Ce problème de reconnaissance de formes a été traité par un parcours d'arbre. Chaque noeud de l'arbre correspond à un mot ou à une alternative sur un ensemble d'expressions équivalentes.

La fonction du module d'analyse de réponse est de valider la réponse de l'apprenant tout en y décelant les erreurs éventuelles. L'algorithme retenu compare récursivement, et mot à mot, la réponse de l'apprenant avec l'ensemble des modèles de réponse (formes syntaxiques) issus du modèle d'analyse associé à la question. Les erreurs décelées génèrent un commentaire *ad hoc* et complètent le modèle des lacunes de l'apprenant.

4.3. Perspectives

Une première perspective d'amélioration de ce système d'analyse de productions de l'apprenant est de distinguer les deux fonctions : analyse d'erreurs d'une part (activité purement linguistique), et analyse de réponses proprement dite d'autre part (évaluation pédagogique et personnalisée). La première fonction pourrait être assurée par un correcteur automatique, ce qui soulagerait le travail de description de modèles d'analyse syntaxique actuellement demandée aux auteurs. Il leur resterait "simplement" à définir le commentaire associé à chaque type d'erreur.

D'autre part, les fonctionnalités attendues d'un système de suivi de formation en langues étrangères tel que MARPLE font émerger un ensemble d'expertises complémentaires au diagnostic d'erreur : planification d'agenda pour gérer la session d'évaluation, validation des acquis en référence aux objectifs de formation, conseil en support de formation.

L'acceuil et le guidage de l'apprenant en "consultation" reviennent à gérer un agenda des différents contrôles à effectuer d'une session à l'autre. Les décisions de l'agent dédié à cette tâche sont guidées par les objectifs de formation et les résultats intermédiaires.

Dans MARPLE, la validation des compétences concernent l'expression et la compréhension, écrites et orales. Celles-ci sont validées séparément par un pourcentage de réussite sur la base des notes attribuées à chaque question. Cette fonctionnalité devrait être complétée par un suivi à longue échéance de l'apprenant en formation. Le principe est de doter le système de connaissances permettant de définir des classes d'erreurs et de donner des priorités dans l'analyse des erreurs répertoriées pour un apprenant donné. Seul un corpus conséquent d'une centaine de sessions permettrait une classification complète et stable des erreurs liées à chaque type d'utilisateur.

L'objectif du conseil en formation est d'informer l'apprenant sur la suite à donner à sa formation en fonction des lacunes décelées. Le conseil fait le lien entre les acquis, les lacunes et les objectifs de formation d'une part et les ressources de formation d'autre part. Il porte sur la suite à donner à l'enseignement et sur les moyens de remédiation à travailler.

La mise en place de cette compétence devrait de plus permettre au système de s'auto-évaluer. L'observation de l'évolution des compétences sur des domaines précis pris en considération lors des sessions les plus récentes doit permettre de comparer les niveaux théoriquement accessibles grâce aux conseils, et les niveaux réellement atteints.

5. Conclusion

L'environnement MARPLE est disponible sur Macintosh sous système 7. Il a été développé en HyperCard pour l'agent d'interaction et les bases de données, et en langage C pour l'agent de diagnostic. Le système MARPLE dispose actuellement d'une vingtaine de situations d'évaluation intéressant une formation de remise à niveau en anglais. Cet environnement de tests a été validé en milieu professionnel et universitaire. Nous cherchons maintenant à générer un corpus de réponses assez conséquent afin de développer les agents de suivi de formation.

Ce texte nous a permis de montrer qu'à travers la conception pluridisciplinaire et la réalisation du système MARPLE, nous avons conçu un environnement d'évaluation à base d'architecture multi-agents et avons défini un ensemble d'expertises liées à l'évaluation de connaissances en langue.

Ce travail a été l'occasion d'une étude sur l'évaluation, la gestion des erreurs, et le suivi des apprenants en langues étrangères. Nous avons proposé un modèle général de description d'une situation d'évaluation. Ce modèle tient compte des aspects liés au contenu de la formation, à l'évaluation elle-même, ainsi qu'au mode d'interaction proposé par la situation. La conception de l'agent de diagnostic a posé de nombreuses questions sur les objectifs de l'analyse de réponse, sur les moyens dont on dispose pour déceler les erreurs, les répertorier et les gérer. Notre analyseur assure une double fonction de repérage des erreurs et d'explications sur ces erreurs. La transformation de ce module d'analyse de réponses en plusieurs agents aux compétences bien définies (correcteur linguistique et analyseur pédagogique de production) représente une intéressante perspective de recherche pour le projet MARPLE.

6. Bibliographie

Chanier Th. (1991) : "Perspectives de l'apport de l'EIAO dans l'apprentissage des langues étrangères ", *4ème Assises de l'IA et de la Formation,* Paris.

Cumming G., Self J. (1990) : "Intelligent Educational Systems: Identifying and decoupling the conversational levels", *Instructional Science, n° 19*, pp. 1-17.

Cumming G., Sussex R. (1991) : "Intelligent educational systems to support second langauge learning", *Sixth International PEG Conference*, Rapallo (Genova) Italie, p. 271-277.

Dubourg X. (1995) "Modélisation de l'interaction en EIAO, une approche événementielle pour la réalisation du système REPÈRES ", Thèse de l'Université du Maine, Le Mans.

Ellis R. (1985) "Understanding Second language Acquisition", Oxford University Press.

Fum D., Giandgrandi P., Tasso C. (1991) "The Use of Explanation-based Learning for Modelling Student Behavior in Foreign Language Tutoring", *in Swartz & Yazdani 91.*

Lelouche R. (1991) : "Using Multiple Knowledge Bases to Help Teach some Pragmatic Aspects of French", *CALL,* Intellect Books, Oxford, vol.4 n°1, p. 29-40.

Narcy J.P. (1990) : "Apprendre une Langue Étrangère", Les Editions d'Organisation, Paris.

Pitrat J. (1990) : "Métaconnaissance, avenir de l'Intelligence Artificielle", Eds Hermes, Paris.

Swartz & Yazdani Eds (1991) : "Intelligent Tutoring Systems for Second-Language learning, the Bridge to International Communication", Springer Verlag.

Teutsch Ph & Vivet M. (1993) : "Interaction Issues in Computer Assisted Language Learning Systems", *International Conference on Computers in Education*, Taiwan, p. 144-149.

Teutsch Ph. (1994) : "Environnements Interactifs et Langues Étrangères, MARPLE : système d'évaluation et de suivi de formation", Thèse de l'Université du Maine, Le Mans.

Vivet M. (1991) : "Usage des tuteurs intelligents : prise en compte du contexte, rôle du maître.", *2ième Journées EIAO* Cachan, p. 239-246.

Yazdani M. (1989) : "An Artificial Intelligence Approach to Second Language Teaching", *2nd ICCAL*, Dallas USA, Springer Verlag Eds.

On the Formal Evaluation of Learning Systems

Albert K W Wu

Department of Computing
Hong Kong Polytechnic University, Hong Kong
Email: csalbert@comp.polyu.edu.hk

Abstract. In this paper, we present an attempt towards formal evaluation of learning systems (LSs) based on a LS description framework. Moreover, the central issues of completeness and efficiency pertinent to evaluation are elicited with the problem complexity also shown.

1   Introduction

Conventional work in the field of LSs (here a LS refers to any type of system for instructional and/or learning purpose such as CAI or ITS, etc.) in general, and ITS (intelligent tutoring system) in particular, is more on probing the potentials of LSs and the investigation of implementation issues involved in its actual construction, see [3,12] for example. However, as more systems are developed, evaluation becomes more prominent for claims to be made.

Yet, until now, there is no standard set of evaluation methods within the community for addressing the problem with most relying on empirical endeavors [7,8]. While empircal experimentation is unavoidable and even necessary, such an orientation also carries with it shortcomings of ambiguity and being subjective in the process with the result difficult to be translated into solid proposal for exploring alternative design choices. Indeed, a pure empiricist approach may also run into the danger of failing to take into account all relevant aspects of the experimental tasks at different levels of abstraction, thus leading to inconclusive and conflicting research findings as frequently exhibited in the literature.

Can learning systems be formally evaluated? If a learning system can be formally described, perhaps, its properties can be better inspected and evaluated.

2   On Describing Learning Systems

In general the following components constituting a LS can be identified.

The LS components:
- the curriculum, the addressed domain topics and the overall course organization imposed on them [5; p.80];
- the system goals, also called the ILOs (intended learning outcomes) in some literature [9];

- the instructional materials, the actual manifestation of the curriculum as an ensemble of instructional instances and presentations/interaction sessions (called transactions);
- the pedagogic strategy, the strategy based on which the instructional instances and interactions are organized and sequenced;
- the assessment, by assessment it means the measure through which the mastery or understanding of the learner is evaluated; an example is a set of assessment questions inter-related by their underlying examined topics, precedence structures and related goals.

Moreover, in order to carry out evaluation, some additional components, the evaluation components, are needed to bring to the scenario. Depending on needs, these components may include a reference teaching domain, a reference expert teacher and even a model student. In fact, these components may also serve as the reference components used during the design and development of a LS.

A Description Framework. Below we propose a context-free description framework for describing a LS.

The basic tenet of the framework follows that of formal grammar with a LS represented in a 10-tuple format. Assume we have:

i) D_T, the set of domain-related terminal symbols (names) denoting the elementary, undefined or most primitive terms of the domain; these terminal names thus signify the most elementary topics of the domain

ii) G_T, the set of teaching goal oriented terminal predicate symbols (names) denoting the elementary, undefined or most primitive terms for describing pedagogic goals; it is also assumed that a goal statement is some predicated statement on the curriculum topic(s)

iii) M_T, the set of instruction-presentation oriented terminal function symbols (names) denoting the elementary, undefined or most primitive terms for describing a basic instructional operation or function; it is assumed that these primitives operate on the curriculum topics and it also has some bearing with the elements of G_T

iv) A_T, the set of assessment oriented terminal function symbols (names) denoting the elementary, undefined or most primitives terms for describing a basic assessment method or function; it is assumed that these primitives operate on the curriculum topics and it also has some bearing with G_T elements

v) **Inst**, an instance function which can return a set of domain-related terminal symbols (names) its operand is associated;

vi) **CP**, the set of composition operators derived from the following set of relations: {aggregation/decomposition, generalization/specialization, classification/ instantiation, more/less-difficult, causal-precedence}

Then a LS can be described as

Definition 1: $LS = < C, G, M, T, I, A, P_C, P_G, P_M, P_A >$

where C, the set of curriculum associated domain topics

G, the set of system goals

M, the set of instructional materials including the relevant instructional modules and transactions

T, the tutorial heuristics; in a sense it is the LS encoded pedagogic knowledge

I, the set of interface mechanisms

A, the set of assessments,

$\mathbf{P_C}$, the set of productions or rewrite rules for elaborating **C** in terms of its element(s) and element(s) of $\mathbf{D_T}$ joined together by some operator(s) from CP

$\mathbf{P_G}$, the set of productions or rewrite rules for elaborating **G** in terms of its element(s) and element(s) of $\mathbf{G_T}$ joined together by some operator(s) from CP

$\mathbf{P_M}$, the set of productions or rewrite rules for elaborating **M** in terms of its element(s) and element(s) of $\mathbf{M_T}$ with these functions joined together by some operator(s) from CP

$\mathbf{P_A}$, the set of productions or rewrite rules for elaborating **A** in terms of its element(s) and element(s) of $\mathbf{A_T}$ with these functions joined together by some operator(s) from CP

For the productions, they basically take the form B::=α with B$\in$Q where Q is some complex component such as **C**, **G**, **M** or **A**; and α is a string of symbols either from the elements of the correponding complex component or its constituent primitives with them joined together by some composition operator(s) from CP. Thus it is always possible for these productions to assume a recursive enumeration until the primitive or terminal terms are used in the final elaboration.

For example, suppose we are working in the domain of computer architecture with the set of domain primitives being: {SINGLE_PROCESSOR, MULTIPLE_PROCESSOR, ..., SHARED_MEMORY, PRIVATE_MEMORY, ...} and C: {<operating_principle>, <hardware structure>, ... }. A few of the rules of $\mathbf{P_C}$, the set of productions or rewrite rules for elaborating **C**, may take the form

    <operational_principle>::= <information_structure>,<control_structure>

    ......

    <processor allocation>::=SINGLE_PROCESSOR| MULTIPLE_ROCESSOR
    <memory allocation>::=SHARED_MEMORY,PRIVATE_MEMORY

    ......

where "|" and "," denote the "or" - composition derived from the relation "classification", and the "and" - composition derived from the relation "aggregation" respectively; with the notation <....> also denotes a non-terminal symbol.

Whilst a detailed primer of the framework together with a knowledge acquisition front-end are under preparation, the above should suffice for the time being.

About the evaluation components. Basically all the three components of reference domain, expert teacher and model student are knowledge oriented. With the many problems yet to be solved in machine learning [13], we only concentrate on the first two components at the moment.

For describing them, let's first adopt a well-known high level concept for knowledge that *Knowledge* = *KnowThat* (includes the declarative and causal knowledges) + *KnowHow* (includes the procedural and reasoning knowledges) [10]. Second, by viewing the reference teaching domain D as containing a finite set of knowledge elements, it can thus be described as: $D = \{ d_1, d_2, ..., d_n \}$. Here an element d_i does not have to be atomic or a singleton, ie. $d_i \in D$ can be some condition or action or may include both condition and action. That is, it may consist of declarative or procedural knowledge or both. The teaching domain universe D is therefore a symbolic representation of *KnowThat* and *KnowHow* about a domain.

As for representing the reference teacher, first let's assume that a knowledge of the domain D is there. Thus, by describing the reference teacher pedagogic knowledge, it means the encoding of her pedagogic KnowHow - some reasoning knowledge concerning pedagogic presentation forms and sequence of the domain elements. As such, some form of relational table would cater as it is always regarded as the universal form transformable from/to all other representations. Nonetheless, such a relational table distinguishes from the conventional relational model in database theory [2] in the sense that the table elements do not have to be atomic. The pedagogy relational table, denoted as P, is thus assumed containing a finite set of tuples and is represented as $P = \{ p_1, p_2, ..., p_s \}$, with each tuple $p_i \in P$ bearing some condition elements and some action elements. And p_i can be further decomposed to consist of sub-elements as follows.

$$p_i = \{p_{i,1}, p_{i,2}, ..., p_{i,x}\} \qquad \text{where } p_{i,j} = d \text{ or } p_{i,j} \in d \text{ and } d \in D$$

3   The Evaluation

In general, it's agreed that the ultimate goal of LS evaluation rests on its "effectiveness" measure. By "effectiveness" three main aspects are generally considered: correctness, completeness and efficiency. By undertaking a formal approach, the following three aspects of evaluating an artefact (as a system) are facilitated: i) correctness - whether there exists no inconsistencies in the system; ii) soundness - whether there always consists a reliable chain of deductions in producing solutions; and iii) completeness - whether all intended solutions are covered. Translated into the context of LS, in very broad terms they are the three concerns of i) whether the knowledge contained in the LS is consistent; ii) whether the LS can always be able to aid its prospective learners to reach a certain knowledge state, and iii) whether all intended learning goals are covered by the LS respectively. Amongst the three concerns, given the current status of technology it is obvious that the second one is best tested out via experimentation. Provided the construction of the LS is based on correct knowledge, the issue of completeness then becomes our major concern and will be the theme pertained throughout the rest of the paper. As the issue of efficiency would best be elicited after completeness, it is presented at the end of the discussion.

The Completenss Problem. Classically, the completeness problem is defined as follows. A system is complete if any well formed formula (wff), represented by ω say, that logically follows (or implied) from any set of axioms and/or wffs represented by Γ, is also a theorem which can be derived from Γ. Mathematically, this is represented as: if $\Gamma \Rightarrow \omega$ then $\Gamma \rightarrow \omega$. However, such a classical definition for completeness check of formal systems may not be directly applicable to LS. The reason being that i) LS in general is not a rigorous formal system; ii) many inferences used in LS are not modus ponens nor resolution-based; and iii) the frequently used representations for inferencing in LS are often not depicted in exactly well formed formulae. Thus we need some transformation and contextualization of the problem to make it suitable to the LS realm.

We state that a LS is complete when it has all the information necesary to deal with any instruction (or any teaching goal) demanded of the specific teaching domain. Here, "all information" includes the common sense, structural, exceptional, meta, and heuristic knowledges. Obviously, this is a sufficient condition for the completeness of any learning system.

Sufficient Completeness. If the LS can do all that the expert domain teacher can do, the LS is *sufficiently complete*.

However, such sufficient completeness is too strong to be realized in most cases given the problems of the field [1]. Instead, we can impose some other conditions and consider the LS completeness problem from a different perspective:

Curriculum Completeness. If a LS curriculum addresses all the system goals related topics, then the LS is *curriculum-wise (or curriculum) complete*, denoted C_complete.

Further, there can have multiple curricula working on a certain knowledge domain and multiple instruction (materials) for the same curriculum. As a basic check, we may need to know if a reference domain covers the curriculum knowledge requirement and the available instruction also covers the total curriculum of the LS. Thus we have

Domain Completeness. If the domain knowledge covers all the knowledge content of a curriculum, then the reference domain of the LS is *domain complete*, denoted D_complete.

Instruction Completeness. If the instruction (materials) of a LS covers all the knowledge topics/concepts prescribed of the curriculum, then the LS is *instructionally complete*, denoted **Instr**_complete.

Another viewpoint for LS completeness can be defined from yet another perspective, the covering of the teacher's pedagogic knowledge.

Pedagogical Completeness. If the teacher's pedagogy can be described with some relational table(s), and the LS tutoring heuristics can cover all tuples in these tables, then the LS is *pedagogically complete*, denoted **P**_complete.

More specifically, they are

Definition 2: A LS is **C_complete** with respect to the system goals set **G** if Inst(**G**) and the curriculum **C** satisfy the condition: **C**⊇Inst(**G**).

Definition 3: The domain of a LS is **D_complete** with respect to the domain instances of **C** if **D**⊇ **C**.

Definition 4: The instruction of a LS is **Instr_complete** if Inst(**M**)⊇ **C**.

Further, we introduce the following concept:

Exactly covered. A pedagogic table **P** is *exactly covered* by the rule set **T** if and only if (1) each tuple $p_i \in$ **P** is covered by some rule $t_j \in$ **T**;

(2) for any rule t∈ **T**, if some tuple p∈ **Ins**(t), then p∈ **P**; here **Ins** is the instance-tuple set function for returning all instance tuples of the argument t, t∈ **T**;

(3) the intersection of any pair of rules t_i and t_j, $t_i, t_j \in$ **T** s.t. **Ins**(t_i)∩**Ins**(t_j) =∅

We are now ready to refine the P_completeness definition.

Definition 5: A LS is **P_complete** with respect to the pedagogy table **P** if the rule set **T** of the LS *exactly covers* **P**.

In the next section we discuss the evaluation of LSs based on the issue of completeness check by giving an illustration.

5 A Sample Illustration

5.1 A LS on Bagging Groceries

Suppose we have a LS for teaching how to bag groceries (basically it's a simplified version of [13;p.132-137]) in the manner of a grocery-store checkout clerk. We do not expect optimal packing, but we do want our system learners to be able to *grasp the principles and apply* them for grocery bagging. That is, place some large items into the bottom of the bag first; bag some medium items when enough room is left, bag some small items last, putting them wherever there is room; and start with a fresh bag when needed.

The domain and curriculum.

Suppose we have   B: represents a big item

M: represents a medium item

S: represents a small item

then any bagging instance can be represented as $B^n M^m S^k$ where m,n,k≥0. As the expression is "recursively enumerable" [6], thus we can always produce the domain and curriculum instances by Enum($B^n M^m S^k$), the enumeration function applied to the expression inside the parentheses.

The goals specification. Basically it can be indirectly represented by a set of assertions about the domain subjects, which is summarized informally by the following statement:

G = apply_bagging_principles (bagging all combination of items)

The above can be further partitioned into the following assertions:

g_1: apply_bagging_principles (bagging small items)
g_2: apply_bagging_principles (bagging medium items)
g_3: apply_bagging_principles (bagging big items)
g_4: apply_bagging_principles (bagging any two types of items together)
g_5: apply_bagging_principles (bagging any three types of items together)

The instructional materials, pedagogy and tutorial heuristics. Assume we have the following instructional instances in the LS:

m_1: teach_with_application (bagging small items)
m_2: teach_with_application (bagging medium items)
....
m_6: teach_with_application (bagging all three types of items)

Therefore the instructional materials for the bagging LS is **M** = $\{m_1, m_2,..., m_6\}$.

Further, assume the teacher's pedagogy table **P** is available with a segment of the table look like

Condition(s)	Action
$\sim L_s \wedge \sim L_m \wedge \sim L_b$	teach_with_application(bagging small items)
.....	
$L_s \wedge L_m \wedge \sim L_b$	teach_with_application(bagging big items)
$L_s \wedge L_m \wedge L_b$	teach_with_application(bagging small and medium items)
....	

where L_s , L_m , L_b stand for the learner_knows_how_to_bag small, medium and big items respectively.

And we have the tutorial heuristics in the form of rule, look like

.....
t_3: IF the learner does not know of bagging medium items THEN start M_2
t_4: IF the learner does not know of bagging big items THEN start M_3
.....

Checking for C_, D_ , Instr_ and P_Completeness. Based on the above, it can easily be shown that all the completeness checks are safisfied as C⊇Inst(G), D⊇C, Inst(M) ⊇C, and T exactly covers P.

6 A Note on Efficiency

In general the concept of efficiency means the measured output against certain inputs. Translated back to our theme of evaluating LSs, to achieve for efficiency might imply the following:

- The designation of the least number of instructional instances of **M** such that the course goal **G** is met.

- The designation of a minimum number of rules for **T** such that the reference pedagogic knowledge **P** is still completely covered.

While the first of the above is more directly related to instructional planning - planning for *instructional efficiency*, the second is a direct indication of the *pedagogic efficiency* of the LS - covering the teacher's pedagogy with the minimum of heuristic rules. Thus, in principle, pursuing for pedagogic efficiency is a further step beyond achieving pedagogic completeness. Due to space reason, only the issue of *pedagogic efficiency* is discussed.

Assume for the time being, the pedagogic table **P** and the set of rules **T** are provided (as the LS author would always be able to create the set of rules **T** based on the pedagogic relational table **P**). Then the issue of pursuing for *pedagogic efficiency* is transformed into the following two steps:
(1) First check whether the given set of rules **T** does exactly cover **P**, i.e. a **P**_completeness check.
(2) If there are several sets of rules, $T_1, T_2,...,T_h$, with $h > 1$, and all of them do exactly cover the given relational table **P**, then look for the best, i.e. the most efficient or "optimal" set of rules from $T_1, T_2,...,T_h$.

For the 1st step, its worst case complexity is $O(K^2 \times L^3)$ with L, the common factor for **P**'s tuple size, **T**'s rule size and number of elements in a rule of **T**; and K, the common factor for the cardinality of **P** and the cardinality of **T**.

For the 2nd step, it can be shown that the problem depicted has a one-to-one correspondence transformation with the more general minimum coverage problem [4]. It is therefore NP-complete.

More detailed working and derivation of results for these steps can be found in [14].

Thus, to have the teacher's knowledge acquired optimally into a computer is an NP-complete problem and is therefore very difficult. Instead, we should be satisfied if the pedagogic knowledge is covered by the system heuristics. (Discerning readers would notice that this is just the formal illustration of the celebrated intractable student modelling problem [11].)

7. Conclusion
In this paper, we have presented and demonstrated a modest attempt towards formal evaluation of learning systems via a description framework. The problem is then elicited from the completeness and efficiency viewpoints. Four different aspects of the completeness problem are defined: the *curriculum completeness* (**C**_complete) concerns the functional aspect; the *domain completeness* (**D**_complete) checks whether the domain can circumvent the needed curriculum; the *instruction completeness* (**Inst**_complete) ensures instruction coverage of the curriculum knowledge; the *pedagogical completeness* (**P**_complete) probes into the inherent pedagogic capability of the system. With an example illustration shown, the

theoretical results on the complexity for checking for **P_completeness** and pedagogic efficiency are also given. Although the problem and example presented here may seem somewhat contrived with many issues such as the process of learning, explicit student model, etc. not discussed, the presentation nevertheless should be able to shed light on the long-ignored issue of LS formalization. It is also hoped that the work may stimulate and initiate the long-awaited efforts towards the direction. Hopefully the goal of carrying out evaluation of LSs in an elegant and comprehensive manner can be achieved some day as we have long been suffered from the fact that: "current techniques of external evalution cannot really determine whether an ITS is effective" [7; p.233-234].

References

1. Clancey, W. J.: Guidon-Manage Revisited: A Socio-Technical Systems Approach. In: *Proc of ITS '92*, Montreal, Canada, June 1992, 21-36.
2. Codd, E. F. Relational Database: A Practical Foundation for Productivity. *CACM* 25 (2) (1982 Feb), 109-117.
3. Frasson, C., Gauthier G. & G.I. McCalla (Eds.): Proc of ITS '92. (also appeared as LNCS No.608, Intelligent Tutoring Systems, Springer-Verlag)
4. Garey, M. R. and D. S. Johnson: *Computers and Intractability A Guide to ihe Theory of NP-Completeness,* NY: W. H. Freeman and Company (1979).
5. Halff, H. M.: Curriculum and Instruction in Automated Tutors. In Polson, M.C. and Richardson, J.J. (eds.) *Foundations of Intelligent Tutoring Systems.* NJ:Lawrence Erlbaum Asso. (1988), 79-108.
6. Hopcroft, J. E. and J. D. Ullman: *Formal Languages and Their Relation to Automata.* Addison Wesley (1976).
7. Littman D. and E. Soloway: Evaluating ITSs: The Cognitive Science Perspective. In Polson, M.C. and Richardson, J.J. (eds.): *Foundations of Intelligent Tutoring Systems.* NJ:Lawrence Erlbaum Asso. (1988), 209-242.
8. Mark, M. and J. Greer *J. of AI in Ed.*, Vol.4 (1993), 129-153.
9. Posner, G. J. and A. N. Rudnitsky (1985). *Curriculum Design.* NY: Longman.
10. Reichgelt, H.: *Knowledge Representation: An AI Perspective* Norwood, NJ: Ablex (1990).
11. Self, J. A. Bypassing the Intractable of Student Modeling. In Frasson, C. and G. Gauthier (eds.) Intelligent Tutoring Systems: at the Crossroads of Artificial Intelligence and Education. Norwood, NJ: Ablex Publishing (1990), 107-123.
12 Wenger, E.: *Artificial Intelligence and Tutoring Systems: Computational and Cognitive Approaches to the Communication of Knowledge.* Los Altos: Morgan Kaufmann (1987).
13. Winston, P. H.: *Artificial Intelligence (3rd ed.).* AddisonWesley (1992).
14. Wu, A. K. W.: The Intractable Problem of Pedagogic Modelling in ITS. *Proc of the 19th ACSC Conf.* Jan 31 - Feb 2, 1996, Melbourne, Australia, 116-121.

La programmation logique par contraintes pour l'aide à l'enseignant

Denis Bouhineau et Stéphane Channac

Laboratoire IMAG - LSR
BP 53 X, 38041 Grenoble Cedex 9
FRANCE

Abstract. Cet article soutient le point de vue que les Environnements Informatisés d'Apprentissage Humain (EIAH) ne considèrent pas assez l'enseignant comme un utilisateur potentiel distinct de l'apprenant. Aussi, le néologisme "préceptoriel" est introduit pour décrire des EIAH ayant une approche centrée sur le professeur.
Le domaine des logiciels de construction de figures géométriques est ensuite pris comme exemple. Une analyse des aides que l'on peut apporter au professeur dans ces logiciels est menée. Elle conduit au problème de la validation des constructions de l'apprenant et de la production de contre-exemples. La notion de contre-exemple est étudiée en vue de son intégration dans un préceptoriel de géométrie à l'aide de la programmation logique par contraintes. Une mise en œuvre informatique est présentée ainsi qu'un exemple d'utilisation.

Mots clés : Spécifications logiques de figures de géométrie, Préceptoriel, Production de contre-exemples, Calculs sur intervalles.

Introduction

Dans leur très grande diversité, les environnements informatisés d'apprentissage humain, dont l'acronyme EIAH est utilisé dans la suite, ont un point commun : ils sont principalement centrés sur l'apprenant. L'enseignant n'est pas toujours oublié, mais un rôle secondaire lui est réservé : celui d'alimenter l'EIAH en situations pédagogiques. Eventuellement, il peut paramétrer la configuration des menus, cf Cabri [Lab95], ou la définition de la théorie de la géométrie utilisée, cf TALC [Des94]. De même, il est symptomatique de constater qu'une très faible partie de l'intelligence des EIAH lui est dévolue. Notre démarche est originale dans la mesure où elle considère que la place de l'enseignant est distincte de celle de l'élève et qu'une partie du système doit être développée à son intention.

Dans la suite, nous nous intéressons aux EIAH de géométrie, et principalement à ceux qui mettent en œuvre des problèmes de constructions géométriques.

Un préceptoriel de géométrie. La liste des termes utilisés pour nommer les EIAH de géométrie est longue : Le terme *tutoriel*, qui a dérivé en *didacticiel*, désigne le plus souvent des EIAH où une situation d'apprentissage dirigiste est proposée à l'apprenant. Des exemples de tuteurs sont donnés en géométrie par Mentoniezh

[Py90], TALC. La notion d'*imagiciel* est plus récente. Elle concerne des systèmes d'exploration de phénomènes réels via une visualisation/modélisation informatique. Le champ d'investigation se situe entre le didactique et l'a-didactique. Enfin la notion de *micro-monde* concerne les environnements où le savoir exploré n'est pas défini au départ. C'est le domaine de l'exploration pure ; celui des situations a-didactiques. Dans ces EIAH, la tâche du système n'est pas de diriger l'élève vers tel ou tel savoir, mais seulement de lui garantir un soutien logistique. Un exemple de micro-monde est donné en géométrie par Cabri.

Nous constatons que la place du professeur n'est pas prise en compte dans cette taxinomie des EIAH. Pour fonder notre approche nous introduisons donc un nouveau terme faisant référence à notre volonté d'introduire le professeur dans notre démarche : le néologisme "*préceptoriel*". La classe des EIAH désignée par ce terme est celle des didacticiels centrés sur l'enseignant.

Un préceptoriel pour qui et pour quoi faire ? L'aide que l'on peut apporter à l'enseignant dans un préceptoriel peut se situer : - en amont, pour la préparation d'une situation de classe, - au cours de sa mise en œuvre, - ou en aval pour analyser les résultats. Nous nous intéressons ici au moment où l'apprenant interpelle l'enseignant au cours de l'expérimentation d'une situation d'enseignement. Dans un intervalle de temps le plus court possible, car c'est un espace critique, l'enseignant doit - comprendre l'historique des opérations de l'élève, - le point où celui-ci est arrivé, - les problèmes qu'il rencontre, - et enfin, après une courte réflexion, il doit donner à l'élève une direction pour résoudre ses problèmes.

Le facteur temps est encore plus crucial dans le cadre d'un télé-enseignement où un enseignant supervise le travail d'un ensemble d'élèves isolés les uns des autres. Dans un tel cadre, la disponibilité du professeur est primordiale, et la mise en place d'une machine partenaire souhaitée cf [Bal95]. Par ailleurs, dans ce même cadre, mais cette fois pour des raisons économiques, la réduction du temps de télé-présence du professeur est d'un intérêt non négligeable.

L'aide qu'un préceptoriel peut proposer au professeur est double : diagnostiquer la production de l'apprenant, et seconder le professeur dans sa recherche de contre-exemples des plus expressifs. Ce dernier point est le but que nous nous sommes fixé en considérant d'une part que la production de contre-exemples doit être effectuée selon un processus où intervient le professeur, et d'autre part qu'il ne s'agit pas de produire un contre-exemple mais un ensemble parmi lequelle le professeur doit pouvoir exercer son choix.

Exemple. Afin de comprendre divers problèmes intervenant dans l'analyse d'une figure et la production de contre-exemples, considérons la situation qui suit. L'exercice soumis à l'élève est la construction d'un carré. Il répond avec la construction :

```
Créer deux points A, et B quelconques, une droite (d) passant
par A, et un point C sur (d). Construire la droite (d') passant
par C parallèle à (AB), (d'') parallèle à (d) passant par B, D
l'intersection de (d') et (d''), et les segments [A, B], [A, C],
[C, D], [D, B]. Effacer les droites (d), (d') et (d'').
```

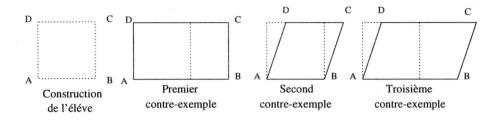

Fig. 1. Construction et contre-exemples

L'élève a construit un parallélogramme à la place du carré demandé, cf figure 1. Visuellement il semble avoir répondu à l'exercice, mais l'analyse du dessin et de sa construction montre que la figure produite ne réalise pas deux propriétés géométriques du carré : la perpendicularité et l'égalité des longueurs de deux côtés consécutifs. Sur le dessin, la perpendicularité est obtenue astucieusement grâce à la pixélisation de l'écran. L'égalité des longueurs est obtenue au jugé. Trois types de contre-exemples peuvent être produits : l'animation horizontale de B met en évidence l'inégalité des longueurs, la rotation de (d) autour de A montre le manque de perpendicularité, et les animations composées de B et de (d) permet de voir la véritable classe des figures construites.

Dans ce qui suit, nous abordons la notion de contre-exemple en géométrie. Dans une seconde partie nous tentons de mettre en lumière les outils, et en particulier la programmation logique par contraintes (PLC) [JM94], qui nous apparaissent adéquats pour produire des contre-exemples. Enfin, nous présentons le prototype que nous avons mis en œuvre et les perspectives de ce travail.

1   Les contre-exemples en géométrie

Tout d'abord, situons notre domaine d'étude, et observons les praticiens.

Définition et analyse de la situation. Notre travail concerne les situations en géométrie où l'élève doit construire, avec un environnement informatisé de construction de figures géométriques, une figure correspondant à un énoncé donné par le professeur. Les bénéfices recherchés par cette construction sont doubles, cf [All90] : - la vérification que l'élève a bien compris les hypothèses et les conclusions du problème, - l'appropriation de la situation géométrique par l'élève. Pour renforcer ce point, l'élève est invité à explorer les déformations de sa figure.

Pour assurer que ces animations parcourent l'ensemble de la classe des figures dont la figure initiale est un exemple, tous les systèmes informatisés de constructions géométriques imposent de nouvelles règles aux utilisateurs. Celles-ci sont reprises par les praticiens de Cabri et enseignées aux élèves. Par exemple, Colette Laborde écrit dans [Act93], "le tracé à l'écran d'un dessin attaché à un objet géométrique doit garder au cours du déplacement ses propriétés spatiales rendant compte des propriétés géométriques de cet objet, il nécessite donc d'être produit par les primitives géométriques.". Comme le remarque Bernard Capponi dans [Act93], "Cet aspect [...] change la nature du travail proposé aux élèves. Ce n'est plus un simple dessin qui doit être réalisé mais ils [les élèves] doivent fournir une description de la construction".

Par conséquent, la production de l'élève est double, elle est visuelle avec le dessin présenté à l'écran, et géométrique avec le procédé de construction proposé. Ces deux aspects doivent être pris en compte dans la suite.

Sur la validité d'une construction. Se pose naturellement le problème de la validation de la construction de l'élève. Dans la très grande majorité des cas, ce travail incombe au professeur. Certains systèmes inscrivent explicitement dans la résolution de l'exercice un appel au professeur pour l'effectuer cf [Ler95].

Pour citer les cas positifs où la vérification d'une production est effectuée par le système on peut parler du prototype TALC, de Cyrille Desmoulins. Ce travail permet de cerner les difficultés et limitations de l'informatisation du pocessus de validation de constructions géométriques. Consciente de l'importance de la tâche de validation, Colette Laborde propose une solution partielle pour Cabri : une validation pragmatique de la construction de l'élève. Celle-ci s'effectue à l'aide d'une macro-construction dont les arguments sont les données du problème et le résultat, la solution du problème. La construction de l'élève est validée si elle se superpose à la construction obtenue par la macro-construction de validation.

En l'absence de vérification automatique, quels sont les outils du professeurs pour détecter une erreur ? On peut reprendre Jean-François Bonnet qui relève dans Cabri trois outils pour le professeur, cf [Act93]: " - la manipulation de tous les objets de base de la figure, - l'utilisation de l'historique, - l'affichage de tous les éléments de la figure". Un préceptoriel peut reposer sur ces trois outils pour diagnostiquer la validité du dessin et produire un contre-exemple.

Qu'est-ce qu'un contre-exemple et comment l'utiliser ? D'une manière générale le contre-exemple est un dessin en relation avec celui de l'élève qui montre l'inadéquation entre la construction géométrique proposée par l'élève et la spécification géométrique attendue par le professeur. Le contre-exemple est visuel.

Le cas le plus courant, celui de la production par l'élève de figures sous-contraintes[1], un contre-exemple peut être obtenu grâce à une animation du dessin de l'élève qui mène à un dessin qui montre visuellement qu'une propriété manque. Plus radicalement, le dessin contre-exemple peut posséder une propriété incompatible avec celle qui manque.

Enfin il convient de relier le contre-exemple au dessin initial de l'apprenant, car comme le remarque Jean-Marie Laborde [Lab95] "...une figure n'est acceptée comme un contre-exemple que si l'utilisateur perçoit le chemin qui conduit de "sa" configuration à celle proposée comme contre-exemple par l'environnement".

---

[1] Une figure est sous-contrainte si une propriété géométrique manque.

Ce propos s'applique aussi bien au professeur, à qui l'on veut faire des propositions de contre-exemples comme il est décrit dans cet article, qu'à l'élève qui est le bénéficiaire final de la production de contre-exemples. Pour assurer ce lien, un préceptoriel doit pouvoir déformer le dessin de l'apprenant pour atteindre celui du contre-exemple.

2 Outils informatiques disponibles

Cette partie concerne les problèmes de type informatique liés aux propositions d'automatisation du diagnostic et de recherche de contre-exemples.

Comment diagnostiquer une construction ? Le problème de la validité d'une construction vis à vis d'une spécification peut être abordé avec des méthodes géométriques, heuristiques, et combinatoires comme dans TALC, algébriques avec des algorithmes tirés des travaux de Wu, cf [Wu94], numériques exactes en prenant la figure comme modèle minimal, ou numériques approchées correctes. Il s'agit avec chaque méthode d'observer si les propriétés de la spécification sont respectées par la construction proposée et vice-versa.

Le choix le plus immédiat est en faveur des méthodes numériques approchées à base d'arithmétiques sur les intervalles comme le propose la PLC sur intervalles [Ben94], vient ensuite le calcul numérique exact car ces deux méthodes sont correctes, prennent en compte le dessin et sont rapides.

Sur la construction de contre-exemples. La méthode que nous proposons pour mettre en évidence une lacune dans une construction, par rapport à une spécification, consiste, à partir de la spécification de la figure de l'apprenant, à construire un contre-exemple où une propriété antagoniste à celle manquante est ajoutée. Ceci assure la possibilité future de déformer la figure de l'apprenant pour atteindre le contre-exemple.

Deux questions apparaissent naturellement sur le plan informatique, celle du choix de la propriété antagoniste et celle de la construction automatique. En ce qui concerne le choix de la propriété de remplacement, il semble le plus simple de laisser le choix au professeur, le mieux étant de lui proposer une correspondance entre propriété manquante et propriété antagoniste. En ce qui concerne la construction automatique de la figure, c'est un problème plus difficile encore que celui de la validation. Il peut être abordé par les mêmes méthodes : algébriques, géométriques, ou numériques mais les coûts en complexités sont encore pires. Aussi il semble que le seul choix pratique soit les constructions avec des méthodes numériques. La PLC sur les intervalles semble pour ce faire le meilleur candidat sinon le seul.

3 Réalisation

Nous avons développé un prototype, en PrologIII [Col90] et BNR-Prolog [OB94], répondant aux concepts proposés précédemment. Ce prototype, opérationnel, fonctionne sur MacIntosh.

3.1 Architecture générale

Pour concevoir l'architecture de notre prototype, nous avons répondu aux interrogations suivantes :

- Quel outil utiliser pour acquérir et animer les figures ? S'agissant d'enseignement de la géométrie, le logiciel qui s'est imposé naturellement à nous est Cabri-Géomètre, projet IMAG interdisciplinaire informatique et didactique dont nous faisons partie. Ce choix est motivé par l'usage répandu de ce micro-monde de géométrie.
- Quel outil utiliser pour le diagnostic de la construction de l'élève ? Le dessin d'une figure étant fourni avec Cabri-Géomètre, il importe d'obtenir une spécification logique de ce dernier afin d'une part de pouvoir construire le cas échéant une figure basée sur la construction de l'élève mettant clairement en évidence ses erreurs, et d'autre part de faciliter un diagnostic formel. Notre choix s'est porté sur le logiciel GéoSpécif [Bou95], le micro-monde de géométrie déclaratif que nous développons en PrologIII, qui intègre un module de communication avec Cabri-Géomètre.
- Quel outil utiliser pour la construction des contre-exemples ? Pour construire automatiquement une figure géométrique à partir d'une spécification logique de celle-ci, nous avons opté pour UniGéom [Cha96]. Ce prototype, développé en BNR-Prolog, aborde le problème de la construction automatique de figures géométriques de manière algébrique. La résolution des systèmes d'équations obtenus est réalisée en usant du paradigme de la programmation logique avec contraintes sur intervalles.

3.2 Réalisation du prototype

Nous explicitons d'une part les phases de l'analyse d'une construction, et d'autre part les choix effectués lors de la réalisation du prototype, en référence à l'architecture que nous venons d'exposer.

Phases d'analyse d'une construction On retrouve numérotées sur la figure 2 les phases de l'analyse d'une construction. Après une phase préliminaire au cours de laquelle le professeur donne une spécification logique du problème, les phases de l'analyse d'une construction sont les suivantes :

1. L'élève construit une figure, à l'aide du logiciel Cabri-Géomètre, supposée répondre à un problème posé.
2. La figure construite est récupérée par le logiciel GéoSpécif, afin d'en obtenir une spécification logique issue de la construction.
3. Le diagnostic de la figure est opéré conformément aux spécifications logiques du problème données par le professeur.
4. Si une erreur est détectée, la spécification logique d'une figure mettant en évidence l'erreur commise est déterminée à partir de la spécification issue de la construction de l'élève.

5. La spécification logique d'un contre-exemple est transmise à UniGéom.
6. UniGéom construit les figures répondant à la spécification logique donnée.
7. GéoSpécif récupère les constructions des contre-exemples proposés.
8. Le professeur commande les animations déterminées à Cabri-Géomètre.

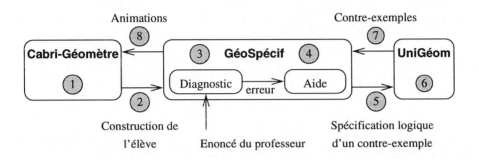

Fig. 2. Architecture générale du système.

Un scénario exemple est présenté au paragraphe 3.3.

Choix retenus pour la conception des composants Pour le composant de diagnostic, les choix concernent :

- La validité de la construction : Les cas d'erreurs détectés sont les cas des sous-spécifications, c'est-à-dire les dessins semblant visuellement corrects mais géométriquement incorrects.
- Le cas des erreurs multiples : Dans la situation où plusieurs erreurs auraient été commises par l'élève, seule la première erreur détectée est mise en évidence.
- Le diagnostic de la construction : L'approche du diagnostic que nous avons choisie est l'approche numérique approchée pour sa simplicité de mise en œuvre et sa rapidité.

Pour le composant d'aide à la construction de contre-exemples, les choix concernent :

- La manière de montrer qu'une propriété n'est pas vérifiée : Le choix de la contrainte antagoniste imposée aux éléments sous-spécifiés pour la construction de contre-exemples est codée dans le système.
- L'animation de la figure : Parmi les différents types d'animations (translation, rotation, homothétie), nous avons considéré de manière implicite que les animations orchestrées sur les éléments de la figure de l'apprenant menant aux contre-exemples sont des translations.

3.3 Exemple de scénario

Enoncé *Construire la médiane du triangle ABC issue du sommet A.*

La spécification logique de ce problème est :

```
point(A), point(B), point(C), point(H),
droite(A, B), droite(A, C), droite(B, C), droite(A, H),
H ∈ (B, C), |BH| = |CH|.
```

1. La construction fournie par l'élève est illustrée en pointillé sur la figure 3. L'erreur commise par l'élève réside dans la confusion entre la notion de hauteur et la notion de médiane dans un triangle.

2. Si le dessin semble répondre au problème, le point H étant proche du milieu du segment *[B, C]*, c'est parce qu'il s'agit d'un dessin ou le triangle ABC semble isocèle en A. La construction de l'élève correspond à la spécification logique suivante :

```
point(A), point(B), point(C), point(H),
droite(A, B), droite(A, C), droite(B, C), droite(A, H),
H ∈ (B, C), (A, H) ⊥ (B, C).
```

Cette spécification ne répond pas au problème posé. En effet, cette figure est incorrecte d'une part parce qu'elle n'implique pas que le point H soit le milieu du segment *[B, C]*, et d'autre part parce qu'elle implique que la droite *(A, H)* est perpendiculaire à la droite *(B, C)*.

3. L'étape de diagnostic consiste à déterminer que le point H n'est pas le milieu du segment *[B, C]*.

4. Une fois le diagnostic effectué, il s'agit de mettre en évidence l'erreur commise à l'aide d'une animation des éléments de la figure. Afin de montrer clairement l'erreur de l'élève, le système choisit de contraindre le point H à être au dixième de la distance du segment *[B, C]*.

5. La spécification logique obtenue du contre-exemple est la suivante :

```
point(A), point(B), point(C), point(H),
droite(A, B), droite(A, C), droite(B, C), droite(A, H),
H ∈ (B, C), (A, H) ⊥ (B, C), |BH| = 1/10 |BC|.
```

6. L'ajout d'une contrainte à un élément de la figure impliquant la libération d'une autre, le système libère successivement les points de base de la figure afin de permettre la construction des contre-exemples.

7-8. Ainsi, le point A, ou le point B, ou encore le point C sont déplacés suivant l'axe des abscisses ou l'axe des ordonnées, donnant lieu aux constructions rapportées par la figure 3.

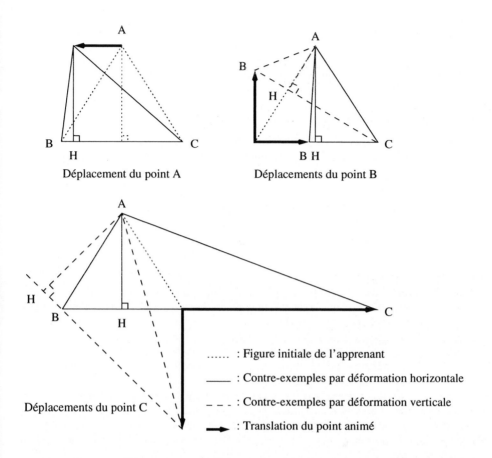

Fig. 3. Animations menant aux contre-exemples.

4   Conclusions et perspectives

Dans cet article, nous avons proposé d'aborder un nouveau concept, celui de préceptoriel. Du constat des insuffisances des différents systèmes tutoriels intelligents, trop centrés sur l'apprenant, nous avons dégagé une approche singulière d'aide à un professeur qui face à la construction d'un élève, cherche à diagnostiquer et éventuellement mettre en évidence les erreurs commises dans la résolution de problèmes géométriques. De l'analyse des différentes notions liées au concept de préceptoriel, nous avons bâti un prototype opérationnel. L'apport des notions de contre-exemples et de déformations de la figure de l'apprenant conclut notre travail avec succès en enrichissant qualitativement le diagnostic textuel.

Les travaux futurs ou amorcés pour améliorer notre prototype concernent :

− **La validité de la construction** : Gérer le cas des dessins sur-spécifiés, c'est-à-dire montrer qu'un carré est un exemple particulier de rectangle.

- **Le diagnostic** : Combiner à la fois l'approche géométrique formelle et l'approche numérique approchée pour éviter les problèmes de la détermination de l'intervalle de validité du diagnostic.
- **La manière de montrer qu'une propriété n'est pas vérifiée** : Laisser au professeur le soin de définir la contrainte à imposer aux éléments de la construction pour la détermination des contre-exemples selon le type d'erreurs rencontrées pour gagner en paramétrisation.
- **La manière de construire les contre-exemples** : Définir un langage permettant au professeur de spécifier prioritairement les objets d'une construction devant subir une animation.
- **La manière d'animer la figure** : Définir un langage d'animation permettant au professeur de spécifier le type d'animations qu'il souhaite afin d'accroître le caractère cognitif de notre système.

References

[Act93] Acte de l'université d'été : Apprentissage et enseignement de la géométrie avec ordinateur. Utilisation du logiciel Cabri-Géomètre en classe Édition Lsd2-IMAG, IREM/IUFM de Grenoble . Juillet 1993.

[All90] Richard Allen, Pierrick Nicolas et Laurent Trilling, *Figure Correctness in an expert System for Teaching Geometry*, Proceedings of the eight biennial conference of the Canadian society for computer studies of intelligence, Ottawa, 1990.

[Bal95] Nicolas Balacheff, *TéléCabri : principe d'une machine partenaire du formateur dans un contexte d'apprentissage distant utilisant la téléprésence*, 1995.

[Ben94] Frédéric Benhamou. Interval Constraint Logic Programming. *Constraint Programming : Basics and Trends*, pages 1–21, May 1994.

[Bou95] Denis Bouhineau. *Vers une approche déclarative pour les logiciels de dessins géométriques.* IVèmes journées EIAO de Cachan, ed Eyrolles, 1995.

[Cha96] Stéphane Channac. *Techniques d'Intelligence Artificielle pour l'Exécution de Programmes Logiques Géométriques.* IIèmes Journées 3IA de Limoges, 1996.

[Col90] Alain Colmerauer. An Introduction to PrologIII. *Communication of the ACM*, 33(7):69–90, July 1990.

[Des94] Cyrille Desmoulins, *Étude et réalisation d'un système tuteur pour la construction de figures géométrique*, Thèse de Doctorat, Université Joseph Fourier, 1994.

[JM94] Joxan Jaffar and Michael J. Maher. Constraint Logic Programming : a Survey. *The Journal of Logic Programming*, 19/20:503–581, 1994.

[Lab95] J.M. Laborde, *Des connaissances abstraites aux réalités artificielles, le concept de micromonde Cabri*, IVèmes journées EIAO de Cachan, ed Eyrolles, 1995.

[Ler95] P. Leroux, *Conception et réalisation d'un système coopératif d'apprentissage* , Thèse de L'Université Paris VI, 1995.

[OB94] William J. Older and Frédéric Benhamou. Programming in CLP(BNR). *PPCP'94, Newport*, 1994.

[Py90] Dominique Py, *Reconnaissance de plan pour l'aide à la démonstration dans un tuteur intelligent de la géométrie*, Thèse de Doctorat, Université de Rennes, 1990.

[Wu94] W. Wu, *Mechanical Theorem Proving in Geometries*, Springer-Verlag, 1994.

Computational Mathetics Tool Kit: Architectures for Modelling Dialogues

Stefano A. Cerri

Dipartimento di Scienze dell'Informazione; Università di Milano
Via Comelico, 39; 20135 MILANO, Italy
http://www.dsi.unimi.it/home.html
email cerri@hermes.mc.dsi.unimi.it

Abstract. The paper presents the results of an attempt to find fundamental computational concepts for the description of abstract agent - to - agent dialogues, with applications to specific teacher-student dialogues. Using as a description language Scheme, we outline a software architecture for dialogue modelling that is based on three notions: a. the notion of stream, modelling infinite sets and delayed evaluation, such as a stream of utterances or "dialogue acts" by a single agent in a dialogue; b. the notion of object as a function generated by evaluating another function, such as a model of an agent able to react to messages with a partner agent, and c. the notion of environment, modelling bindings between names and values, i.e. a context, to be interpreted as a model of an agent's private knowledge or belief about a partner's knowledge.

1   Introduction

The problem of representing dialogues - including user models - is certainly one with a high priority in Computer Science and related disciplines. Its priority is testimonied by the rapid increase of the communication component in complex problem solving (cf. the WWW and the trend to asynchronous, distributed, event driven computing), with respect to the more traditional control components modelled by algorithms, as well as by concrete considerations about the most studied human-computer dialogues, e.g. those managed by learning environments and tutoring systems (see [12], [2], [10] and, for the author: [5], [6], [8]).

In order to contribute to the progressive accumulation of knowledge about learning processes and about systems aimed at facilitating learning, John Self proposed to go back to the fundamental, theoretically based attitude of theory formation in AI and Ed research [16,18]. Other researchers [3] identify as crucial the contributions of the pragmatics of dialogue for building realistic tutoring systems. That pragmatic component is basically made of a. a pragmatic classification of messages exchanged by the partners, and their influence on beliefs, goals and plans represented in memory ; b. a planner for the next move in dialogues based on that classification ; c. a cognitive diagnosis and therapy .

Within traditional studies of the pragmatics of communication one may find specific studies on real teacher-pupil interactions (e.g. [20]). More recent studies (e.g. [22], [15]) focus on the computer-based dynamic construction of dialogues. The first group of linguistic studies was not mainly concerned with computable models. The second group, uses programs implemented with available languages as a running proof of the discourse theory, that is the kernel of the work. Concerning user modelling and their related shells (see [13] for a review) the idea is to build on top of an existing language a set of modules that implement reasoning strategies about either the system's or the user's beliefs, goals and plans.

In this paper we will try to go further in the search for fundamental description primitives and present preliminary results. Using as a description language Scheme, we show an architecture for dialogue modelling that is based on three computational notions, building blocks for dialogue systems in general and tutoring systems in particular : streams, objects as functions and environments [1] . The advantages of the architecture are mainly to be found in its simplicity with respect to the primitives of the language. It is hoped that this simplicity helps in the comprehension of fundamental phenomena of dialogues by facilitating concrete experiments to be performed.

2   Foundations

Each of these dialogues is basically a set of message exchanges E among two agents each with a private memory. The constraint that memory as a whole is necessarily not shared (though it may be partially shared) is a realistic one in concrete human-computer [17] and human-human dialogues [9]. It is also the case in computer-computer dialogues, because sharing the memory may be computationally inefficient, for instance in distributed computing.

Each message exchange may be considered as one or more pair of moves M, sometimes called acts. Each move is performed by one agent in turn, that accepts a message, executes a set of internal actions and sends a message to the partner in the dialogue. In each pair of moves, we may distinguish an agent that takes an initiative, and an agent that reacts to the other agent's initiative. Agents may take the initiative when they wish, but we assume to respect the turn-taking rule[2] even if a swap of the "initiative" role among partners is - in principle - allowed during the dialogue process.

In computational terms, each agent's operation in a single move may therefore be modelled by a REPL: *"read - eval - print - listen* " loop, similar to the cycle of an interpreter. Assuming the above outlined simplification, the question that arises is whether it is possible and simple to model two agents communicating as two autonomous interpreters of a programming language augmented by a pragmatic component that is - in a first approximation - independent from the syntax and semantics of the language. The consequence is that qualified candidates for expressions in the dialogue will be - essentially - valid expressions in the programming language interpreted by the agents.

We will classify the messages into three pragmatic classes: <u>declarative messages</u> - such as an assertion -; <u>query messages</u> - such as a question or an order - and <u>reply messages</u> - such as an acknowledgement or an answer - In this simplification of the pragmatics of dialogues, assuming the REPL loop operated by an agent during a move, we may associate to each agent the *read* phase to the input operation of the partner's move, the *eval* phase transforming the input move to produce the output move, the *print* phase transmitting the output move to the partner in the dialogue and the *listen* phase awaiting for the partner's next move, or either generating an initiating move, swapping the initiative. Within a pure interpreter, this REPL cycle operates on expressions of the language. In order to account at least for a minimal pragmatic level

---

[1] Environments are not part of the Scheme standard description, as outlined in the Revised Report on the Algorithmic Language Scheme [7] and therefore their structure is left to the implementation. A list-based implementation of environments is described extensively on chapter 4 of [1]; the same is used here.

[2] with the exception of the very first move.

in our dialogues, our programming language expressions are embedded into moves that are explicitly typed. Therefore, while the "pure interpreter REPL cycle" operates on the programming language expressions, our "full agent's REPL cycle" operates on moves, including a minimal pragmatic theory.

Among the various classes of programming languages, functional languages reflect better as other ones the basic REPL cycle of interaction among agents, because the evaluation model of a functional language is cognitively quite simple. It is not argued here that this evaluation model has any cognitive value, only that it is simpler than other ones, so that it is not too hard to understand a model of dialogue based on a functional architecture [3]. It is also argued that most if not all the requirements put forward in [4] will find an adequate answer within the architecture presented here. In the following, therefore, we will concentrate on examining one of the most popular and simple functional languages, Scheme, that is taken as a description language for identifying models of dialogues that respect essential properties of real dialogues [4].

3   General conventions

In case the input move is an assertion, it is reasonable to assume that the expected result is the extension of the receiver's environment by a new binding that reflects the assertion's content. If the assertion states that a variable has a value, then the partner will store the binding variable-name variable-value in his private environment and acknowledge the other partner so that he knows that the operation has been successful. If the assertion states that a variable has a procedural value, i.e. is the variable name should be bound to a procedure, then the new binding will be as well stored in the receiver's private environment. Therefore, when the input message is an assertion, the expected behaviour of the receiver will be to <u>define</u> a new name-value binding, that extends the receiver's environment, and to acknowledge the partner of the success of the operation.

When the input move is a query, the expected reaction of the partner will be either a search for a value in the private memory or the execution of a procedure, according to the nature of the query. Any query either is a request for a value associated in the environment or is a request for the application of a procedure to arguments, provided both are meaningful for the queried agent. In the latter case, the query is in fact an order. A search in the environment is performed in Scheme by calling the <u>eval</u> on the expression included in the move: if that is a variable, a search in the private environment will find the corresponding value, if that is an expression indicating functional application, the <u>apply</u> is invoked on the value of the first sub-expression after the evaluation of each parameter .

The querying agent may predict the answer from his partner (in case he is able to make hypotheses about the partner's private environment, i.e. the partner's knowledge or beliefs). If the partner's answer does not match the predicted answer then the agent may

---

[3] Though the evaluation model chosen here is the environment or applicative order model [1] , other models may be used, such as the substitution model or the normal order evaluation model. Further: as it is quite simple to embed another language in Scheme, by writing an interpreter for it, other higher level languages may be chosen for the expressions that are part of the moves. For instance, a logic programming language or a query language may be the language of expressions.

[4] As we cannot expand here into a tutorial , we admit that a working experience with Scheme, or with a functional language will help understanding. Experiments were performed using EdScheme for Macintosh 4.0, © Schemers Inc, 1993. For a complete information, consult the FAQ : Frequently Asked Questions about Scheme available in the WWW.

attribute the cause to a mismatch of the environments or either to a mismatch of the evaluation models. In the current presentation, we will assume that at least the semantics of the communication language - i.e. Scheme's evaluation mechanism - is common to both partners, but this is not a limitation in principle. Therefore a mismatch may only occur if there are inconsistencies between the environment available to the queried partner and the model-environment available to the querying partner.

In dialogues involving humans (e.g. students learning by means of an ITS) this search for a cause of mismatch constitutes the traditional issue of cognitive diagnosis. Cognitive diagnosis must cope with the problem that one cannot make a closed-world assumption in a human and therefore one should identify strategies for the testing of hypotheses empirically selected. The same, unfortunately, occurs also when the assumption may be considered valid, as it is the case of dialogues among artificial agents, because an exhaustive search of the inconsistencies may become intractable.

Finally we assume the availability of an agent of a different type as the communicating agents, that plays the role of "co-ordinator", giving the first initiative to one of the communicating agents, solving conflicts, interfacing the communicating agents with the user / experimenter [5].

4   Lexical conventions

Let us call P the agent initiating the dialogue, and Q the partner. Let's look at the sequence of messages: i_0 , ... i_n , ... of agent P . This sequence of messages is usually modelled - as an abstract data type - by a file. However, the traditional file abstraction assumes that items in the file are stored in the file itself before the file is used. In dialogues, any input i_n, instead, is the result of a computation performed by P on the result of the previous interaction with Q: a partner in a real dialogue does not have but the initiating move available because the second one, the third one, and so on will depend on the other partner's reactions to his first, second etc.

Table 1 : the dialogue process

Exchanges   **Moves**

E0 :	i_0		->	$(g_0\ i_0)=>$	o_0	M0P
	i_1	$<=(f_0\ o_0)$	<-		o_0	M0Q
E1 :	i_1		->	$(g_1\ i_1)=>$	o_1	M1P
	i_2	$<=(f_1\ o_1)$	<-		o_1	M1Q
E2 :	i_2		->	$(g_2\ i_2)=>$	o_2	M2P
	i_3	$<= (f_2\ o_2)$	<-		o_2	M2Q
....						
En :	i_n		->	$(g_n\ i_n)=>$	o_n	MnP
	i_{n+1}	$<= (f_n\ o_n)$	<-		o_n	MnQ

Let us call:
o_0 , ... o_n , ... the sequence of outputs of agent Q, each corresponding to an input;

---

[5] The current "coordinator" is quite unspecified, even if in principle it may be assigned various important roles. At the moment it represents "anything we did not wish to include in the full agents", such as, for instance, the interface with the external "experimenter" to allow the dynamic inspection of the agent's beliefs, the practical input of the moves considered to be "invented" by the experimenter and attributed to an agent or the assignement of the initiative role to one or another partner. The current experiments on the architecture have been carried out with two partner agents, but their extension to more agents is straightforward, though we foresee an unavoidable increase of complexity for the belief structures, i.e. the environments.

g_0 , ... g_n , ... the sequence of procedures applied by Q and
f_0 , ... f_n , ... the sequence of procedures applied by P, respectively to its inputs o_0 , ... o_n , ..., evaluating to i_1 , ... i_{n+1} ...

Adopting a syntactic notation for the application of a function to its argument that consists in simple juxtaposition, we may assume that:

$$o_n = (g_n \ i_n) \text{ and } i_{n+1} = (f_n \ o_n).$$

In table 1 there is an overview of the lexicon concerning the dialogue process, assuming that each exchange consists of a single pair of moves and agent P keeps the initiative all the times.

5 Streams for modelling the message exchange

According to this model , the set I is build dynamically during the process of message exchange. A data structure that captures this idea requires two properties:

a. it must be indefinitely extensible (i.e. it must be dynamic as a list);

b. the first element i_0 is known; the rest is dynamically computed.

In particular, the first of the rest - called i_1 - is the result of the application of a function to the partner's message generated previously $i_1 = (f_0 \ o_0)$. Therefore, the evaluation of i_1 should be *delayed* until o_0 is known and P has made a decision about what f_0 to apply to o_0 . This decision constitutes the result of a dynamic planning process that has been studied in many occasions. The planner is basically a function of o_0 (and, in general, of the history) that evaluates to a function f_0 as a value: f_0 is applied then to o_0 in order to generate the next move i_1 .

An abstract data type that represents this mechanism of delayed evaluation is the stream. We model therefore P's messages to Q as a stream I ; and Q's messages to P as a stream O. Streams may be combined to form other streams: for instance one may form a stream of pairs from two streams. According to this interpretation, the external appearance of a dialogue may be represented by a stream R of input-output pairs.

In the model, each element i of I may take the form of a move that is an explicitly typed Scheme expression to be evaluated by Q by applying (g i) , while each element o of O is the move resulting from that evaluation. In turn : the functions f represent the evaluations of P performed on the o expressions giving as a result : (f o), i.e. the next element of the I stream .

6 Environments for modelling state mutation

We said that the major problem in modelling real dialogues is the constraint that one cannot assume a completely shared memory.

In the environment model of evaluation, the environment is responsible for what usually is called the memory. In many Scheme interpreters the environment may be constructed and selected at run time. It is in fact a kind of user-defined abstract data type. One may define as many environments as one wishes, and evaluate expressions within any of those environments. This allows to have a potential availability of any "context" for evaluating expressions in the language.

Therefore, in our architecture, we have chosen to represent explicitly four such contexts, to be interpreted as the private environment and the partner's model for each of the two agents. The private environment is used for the evaluation of the partner's moves, the partner's model - by now - is only used for activating a (primitive) diagnosis. Environments are modified during the dialogue process, according to the pragmatic principles governing the agent's behaviour reacting to the partner's moves.

Table 2 : the dialogue process with explicit environments

Exchanges					Moves
E0 :	i0	->	$((g0\ i0)eQ0)=>$	o0	M0P
	i1	$<=((f0\ o0)eP0)$ <-		o0	M0Q
E1 :	i1	->	$((g1\ i1)eQ1)=>$	o1	M1P
	i2	$<=((f1\ o1)eP1)$ <-		o1	M1Q
E2 :	i2	->	$((g2\ i2)eQ2)=>$	o2	M2P
	i3	$<=((f2\ o2)eP2)$ <-		o2	M2Q
....					
En :	in	->	$((gn\ in)eQn)=>$	on	MnP
	in+1	$<=((fn\ on)ePn)$ <-		on	MnQ

We will call eQ_0 ... eQ_n the private environments of Q and eP_0 ... eP_n the private environments of P. Each environment includes a set of local frames - modelling a private, non shared memory - and possibly other higher level frames modelling a memory shared with the partner, up to the global environment that is supposed to be shared. This shared environment models the agreement among agents about the syntax and semantics of the Scheme expressions that are part of the moves. As we will see shortly, because agents are instances of the same object class, they share also the functionality reacting to moves, i.e. they share the pragmatic rules of the dialogue - but this may be modified easily - .

We may rewrite the dialogue process by referring explicitly to the environments, as in table 2 .

7   Objects for modelling private memory and control

The notions of <u>private memory</u> and private control are crucial in generic dialogues. Some knowledge may be shared, other knowledge is necessarily private. Encapsulation of variables and methods, among other features of objects in object-oriented programming (OOP), make them attractive for modelling private knowledge in dialogue agents.

Functional languages with procedures as first class objects (therefore, e.g. Scheme but not Common Lisp) allow procedures to have a procedure as a (first class) value. This has the consequence that one may define a derived procedure - say instance - as the value of another derived procedure - say class, thus obtained at run time. The consequence is that instance objects may be obtained from classes as a result of functional abstractions (the classes) and application (the instances). The advantage is that both the syntax and the semantics of the Object Oriented Programming extension may be reconstructed by simulation tailored to the user's needs. Therefore, we will model our agents in the dialogue as objects with private memory and we consider objects as variants of functions [6] .

8   Accessibility of environments

The stream of messages R seen from an observer of the dialogue process after the dialogue has terminated may belong to four different types:

---

[6] In order to keep the architecture simple, we will not include here any in-depth consideration about objects, such as multiple inheritance, meta-object protocol and the like. These - more advanced - opportunities offered by objects may all be modelled by using the standard primitives of the language (see [14] for an introduction).

Expression type A : P and Q's environments are inaccessible

$$R = (\quad\quad (i_0 \quad\quad o_0)$$
$$\quad\quad\quad\quad (i_1 \quad\quad o_1) \quad\quad\quad\quad ....)$$

But: $o_n = ((g_n \ i_n) \ eQ_n)$; therefore

Expression type B: P's environment inaccessible; Q's environment accessible

$$R = (\quad\quad (i_0 \quad\quad ((g_0 \ i_0) \ eQ_0) \ )$$
$$\quad\quad\quad\quad (i_1 \quad\quad ((g_1 \ i_1) \ eQ_1) \ ) \quad\quad\quad\quad ...)$$

Alternatively, from expression type A; since $i_{n+1} = ((f_n \ o_n) \ eP_n)$

Expression type C: P's environment accessible; Q's environment inaccessible

$$R = (\quad\quad (i_0 \quad\quad\quad\quad o_0)$$
$$\quad\quad\quad\quad (((f_0 \ o_0) \ eP_0) \quad o_1) \quad\quad\quad\quad\quad ....)$$

Finally, combining B and C:

Expression type D: P and Q's environments are accessible

$$R = (\quad\quad (i_0 \quad\quad\quad\quad ((g_0 \ i_0) \quad\quad\quad\quad eQ_0))$$
$$\quad\quad\quad (((f_0 \ ((g_0 \ i_0) \ eQ_0)) \ eP_0) \quad ((g_1 \ ((f_0 \ ((g_0 \ i_0) \ eQ_0)) \ eP_0) \ eQ_1)) \ ....)$$

9   Informal classification of moves and applicative scenarios

Table 3 : Move classification and interpretation; single initiative

move type	move subtype	initiating move: examples	effect on receiver	reacting move: examples
assertion	definition of a variable	(define a 3)	env modified	ok (ack)
assertion	definition of a procedure	(define (square x)(* x x))	env modified	ok (ack)
request	value of a variable	a	(eval a)in env	3 (answer)
request	value of a procedure	square	(eval square) in env	(λ (x) (* x x) in <def env>) (answer)
order	application of a procedure to arguments	(square a)	(apply(eval square)(eval a))	9 (executed)
ack	acknowledge positive	ok	update partner's model	generate next move
ack	acknowledge unknown	don't know	update partner's model	generate next move
ack	acknowledge negative	error	update partner's model	generate next move
answer	value	3	start diagnosis	generate next move
answer	procedural value	(λ (x) (* x x) in <def env>)	start diagnosis	generate next move
executed	value (plus potential side effect)	9	start diagnosis	generate next move

The advantages of the above described model should be visible once we produce an interpretation of it in a set of typical dialogues. We will discuss five typical scenarios of interactions of interest for building tutoring systems and for modelling human learning.

Scenario #1: Human teacher P - human student Q dialogues

This is the most commonly studied, but also "obscure" dialogue. One has no "formal" access to any of the two evolving environments (modelling memories of the two agents) and the sole available information about the processes activated within agents is provided by the stream of moves. R may be modelled as in Expression type A. Looking at R one may try to formulate hypotheses about all other components (environments, i.e. knowledge, beliefs, ...) that have influenced the process. This scenario is the one typical of linguistic studies of the pragmatic aspects of dialogues.

Scenario #2: System teacher P - human student Q dialogues

In this case, we have access to the functions f and the environments e_P of our agent P, as described in Expression type C. The situation is that of a traditional tutoring system or learning environment: at each move P has to decide what function f to apply in order to let Q learn. The decision depends on the dialogue strategy that is followed by P and on the assumptions about Q's environment . The available knowledge is necessarily incomplete, because Q's environment should be "estimated" from stream O, i.e. the stream of Q's messages.

Scenario #3: System teacher P - system student Q dialogues

This is a situation useful for simulating / experimenting on potential dialogues under the assumption of a complete availability of knowledge, i.e. a suitable model for R is the expanded one represented by Expression type D. This scenario is the one we propose with our architecture as an experimental laboratory for dialogues.

Scenario #4: Human teacher P - system student Q dialogues

In this case, we have access to the functions g and the environments e_Q of our agent Q. Dialogues may serve to perform experiments that verify P's behaviour in order to discover P's strategies in a controlled setting. The outcomes of the experiments are represented by a stream R as in Expression type B. This is a typical situation in programming: the human programmer "teaches" the system about how to solve a problem. Finally :

Scenario #5: Mixed role dialogues

The flow of exchanges may be such that during the dialogue P and Q exchange their roles. This role exchange has been described in [6] and also, independently in [11], together with several properties of one or the other role-exchange methodology. Role exchange may occur in combination with any of the previously described scenarios. The proposed architecture supports experiments about role exchange under the assumption of complete availability of knowledge, but other scenarios may easily be conceived.

A "classical" example of dialogue and dialogue management

Let us now try to expand - at least - with one concrete example, borrowed from [19] referring to [21]. The example concerns a system **c** mediating an interaction between two medical students **a** and **b** such that: **c** believes that thalassemia is a genetic disorder; and that any person medically informed believes that thalassemia is a genetic disorder, while the average person believes that thalassemia is a disease, and finally **c** believes that for any genetic disorder the child of two parents suffering from that disorder suffers also from the same disorder; **a** is a medically informed person that believes that Fred and Mary suffer from thalassemia; **b** believes that Fred and Mary suffer from thalassemia. Such a system may reason that **a** will believe that a child of Fred and Mary will suffer from thalassemia, but **b** will not. Consequently, **c** will << carry out independent dialogues with the two students, but neither such dialogue will be of much interest to the other student. Instead, the system could take account of what one student believes the other student believes. For example, the system might consider that **a** believes **b** is also medically informed (making the default assumption that **b** is the same as **a** unless **a** has evidence otherwise) and thus that **a** believes that **b** also believes that a child of Fred and Mary would suffer from thalassemia. In general the point is that in any interaction between two or more agents it may help (or be essential) for an agent to hold beliefs about what may be believed by the other agent(s). >>

Our scenario # 3 would allow a simulation of the situation described above, with **a**, **b** and **c** modelled as our full agents, and with Self's "beliefs" modelled as environments; "reasoners" modelled as functions from [beliefs] to [beliefs] and "monitors" as functions from [beliefs X reasoners] to [beliefs X reasoners] ; X being the Cartesian product in the Domain equations. As Scheme (differently e.g., from Common Lisp) considers functions to be first class, a meta function such as a monitor would be a natural abstraction from the Domain of [environments X functions] to [environments X functions], i.e. controlling the application of reasoning strategies on beliefs , such as the strategic choice described for **c** when it decides what dialogue strategy to follow for interacting with student **a** (cf. above : considering only **c**'s beliefs about **a**, or "instead" **c**'s beliefs about **a**'s beliefs about **b**).

10   Conclusions

The goal of the work was to show that a functional language with first class procedures such as Scheme is an adequate description language for generic dialogues; specifically for dialogues occurring in teaching and learning. Communicating agents are described as objects that perform a Read-Eval-Print-Listen interpretation cycle over the partner's moves. The interpretation occurs on the basis of a minimal pragmatic level denoted by move types, and a semantic and syntactic level offered by the underlying language.

The advantages of choosing a formal description language that is also a real programming language over choosing a purely theoretical language (such as Logic) are evident in experimental research: the model build is runnable on a machine, even if a successful run does not ensure the generality of the deduced results. In order to reach the goal, we have taken three fundamental architectural notions in computation : delayed evaluation (streams) ; functional abstraction (objects) and environments. Each of these notions, and their combination shows that they nicely model aspects of dialogues that are otherwise difficult to describe and to simulate. We have outlined a software architecture embodying these notions and called it: computational mathetics tool kit, as we agree with the current efforts [19] aiming at a better foundation of the discipline.

The purpose and the results reflect also a quite general request from most research areas in Computing, i.e. providing fundamental notions for describing and constructing complex problem solvers, by exploiting more and more the communication processes among independent, autonomous and distributed agents - human and artificial - better as extending the power of single algorithms, that may become intractable, if not for a computer to execute, at least for a human to design and comprehend.

11   References

1.   Abelson, H.;Sussman,G.J.: Structure and Interpretation of Computer Programs. The MIT Press, Cambridge, Mass. (1985)
2.   Beun,R.J.; Baker,M.; Reiner,M. (eds.): Dialogue and Instruction. Modelling Interaction in Intelligent Tutoring Systems. NATO ASI Series F,Vol.142, Springer (1995)
3.   Bunt, H.C.: Dialogue Control Functions and Interaction Design. In: Beun, R.J.; Baker, M.; Reiner, M. (eds.): Dialogue and Instruction. Modelling Interaction in Intelligent Tutoring Systems; NATO ASI Series F,Vol.142, Springer (1995) 197-214
4.   Cerri,S.A.: The requirements of conceptual modelling systems. In: Self,J. (ed.): Artificial Intelligence and Human Learning. Chapman and Hall (1988) 88-108
5.   Cerri,S.A.; McIntyre,A. : Knowledge Communication Systems. Invited Paper at the 8ème Congrés Reconnaissance des formes et Intelligence Artificielle, Lyon - Villeurbanne; 25-29 Novembre 1991; Proceedings, AFCET; AFIA-ARC-IRIA (eds.) (1991)
6.   Cerri,S.A.: The "Natural Laboratory" Methodology Supporting Computer Mediated Generic Dialogues. In: Verdejo, M.F.; Cerri,S.A. (eds.): Collaborative Dialogue Technologies in Distance Learning; NATO ASI Series F,Vol.133, Springer (1994)181-201
7.   Clinger,W. ; Rees, J. (eds.) R^{4}RS : Revised-4 Report on the Algorithmic Language Scheme. ACM Lisp pointer IV, July-September 1991
8.   Fabiano, A.; Cerri, S.A.: Conceptual Driven Search among Distributed Knowledge Sources. In: Proc. 6th IEEE Int. Conf. on Tools with Artificial Intelligence, New Orleans, USA, Nov. 1994. IEEE Computer Society Press: 594-600. To appear in: Applied Artificial Intelligence (1996).
9.   Garrod,S.C. ; Doherty, G.: Conversation, co-ordination and convention: an empirical investigation of how groups establish linguistic conventions. Cognition 53(1994)181-215
10.   Gisolfi, A.; Loia, V.: Designing Complex Systems within Distributed Architectures: an Intelligent Tutoring Systems Perspective. Applied Artificial Intelligence 8,3(1994)393-412
11.   Guin, D.: Towards Models of Interaction Between an Artificial Agent and a Human one. In: Verdejo, M.F.; Cerri,S.A. (eds.): Collaborative Dialogue Technologies in Distance Learning. NATO ASI Series F, Vol.13, Springer (1994)170-180
12.   Kobsa, A.; Wahlster, W. (eds.): User Models in Dialogue Systems. Springer (1989)
13.   Kobsa, A.; Pohl, W.: The User Modelling Shell System BGP-MS. User Modelling and User-Adapted Interaction 4 (1995) 59-106
14.   Noermark,K.: Simulation of Object-Oriented Concepts and Mechanisms in Scheme. Inst. of Electronic Systems, Aalborg University, Strandvejen 8, DK-9000 Aalborg (1991)
15.   Pinkilton, R.M. ; Hartley, R.J.; Hintze, D.; Moore, D.J.: Learning to argue and arguing to learn: an interface for computer-based dialogue games. Journal of Artificial Intelligence in Education 3,3 (1992) 275-297
16.   Self, J.A.: Computational mathetics: the missing link in intelligent tutoring systems research. In: E. Costa, (ed.): New Directions in Intelligent Tutoring Systems. NATO ASI Series F, Vol.91, Springer (1992) 38-56,
17.   Self, J.: Model-Based Cognitive Diagnosis. User modelling and user-adapted interaction 3,1 (1993) 87-106
18.   Self, J.A.: Formal Approaches to Student Modelling. In: Greer,J.E., McCalla,G. I. (eds.): Student Modelling: the Key to Individualised Knowledge-Based Instruction. NATO ASI Series F, Vol.125, Springer (1994) 295-352
19.   Self,J.: Artificial Intelligence in Education: Towards Computational Mathetics. Unpublished draft manuscript, CBLU, The University of Leeds (1996)
20.   Sinclair, J McH.; Coulthard, R.M.: Towards an analysis of discourse: the English used by teachers and pupils. Oxford University Press (1975)
21.   Wilks,Y.; Ballim,A.: Multiple agents and the heuristic ascription of beliefs. In: Proc. of the Int. Joint Conf. on Artificial Intelligence (1987) 118-124
22.   Winkels, R.: Explorations in Intelligent Tutoring and Help. IOS Press, Amsterdam. (1992)

An Intelligent Problem Solving Environment for Designing Explanation Models and for Diagnostic Reasoning in Probabilistic Domains

Jörg Folckers, Claus Möbus, Olaf Schröder, Heinz-Jürgen Thole[1]

OFFIS Institute, Escherweg 2, D - 26121 Oldenburg, Germany

E-Mail: {folckers, moebus, schroeder, thole}@informatik.uni-oldenburg.de

Abstract. MEDICUS[2] is an Intelligent Problem Solving Environment (IPSE) currently under development. It is designed to support i) the construction of explanation models, and ii) the training of diagnostic reasoning and hypotheses testing in domains of complex, fragile, and uncertain knowledge. MEDICUS is currently developed and applied in the epidemiological fields of environmentally caused diseases and human genetics. Uncertainty is handled by the Bayesian network approach. Thus the *modelling task* for the learner consists of creating a Bayesian network for the problem at hand. He / she may test hypotheses about the model, and the system provides help. This differs from existing reasoning systems based on Bayesian networks, i.e. in medical domains, which contain a built-in knowledge base that may be used but not created or modified by the learner. For supporting *diagnostic reasoning*, MEDICUS proposes diagnostic hypotheses and examinations. This will be extended to support learners' acquisition and training of diagnostic strategies.

1 Introduction

Diagnosis is a reasoning and problem solving task that can be quite difficult. This is especially true in medical domains (Barrows & Tamblyn, 1980; Boshuizen & Schmidt, 1992; Elstein et al., 1978; Elstein & Bordage, 1980; Patel & Groen, 1986) where the knowledge is particularly complex, interrelated, fragile, and uncertain. Two examples of such domains are the epidemiology of diseases caused by environmental influences, like pollution, and of diseases caused by genetic defects. In these domains, a clear-cut taxonomy of diseases, or syndromes, has not been developed yet. Still these domains are getting increasingly important. This is reflected by the fact that these fields receive increasing attention in medical science at university as well as in further education training courses and postqualification courses for physicians.

Computer-based support of medical reasoning started more than twenty years ago. From the beginning, the problem of uncertainty received central attention. Since there were no efficient algorithms for processing probabilities, early systems like MYCIN

---

[1] We thank Karsten Rommerskirchen for assisting in the implementation and in the mathematical work.

[2] **M**odelling, **e**xplanation, and **di**agnostic support for **c**omplex, **u**ncertain **s**ubject matters

(Shortliffe, 1976), CASNET (Weiss et al., 1978), PIP (Szolovits & Pauker, 1978; 1993), or INTERNIST (Miller et al., 1982) used heuristic approaches. This situation changed in the 1980's, enabling the development of normative probability-based medical expert systems (i.e., NESTOR, Cooper, 1984; MUNIN, Andreassen et al., 1987; PATHFINDER, Heckerman, 1991). The main aim of these systems is to provide the user with diagnostic hypotheses, given the available evidence, and to suggest further diagnostic evidence gathering steps, for example, for differential diagnosis. Some systems, like CASNET, also generate therapeutic recommendations. But in spite of some capability to explain their reasoning steps, the reasoning and knowledge structures of these systems remain largely hidden to the user.

For the purpose of medical training, the recommendation of diagnostic hypotheses and investigations is important but not sufficient. Since hypothetical model building and diagnostic reasoning are problem solving tasks, there is a need for students of medicine to *train* these two skills (Barrows & Tamblyn, 1980):

Firstly, apart from diagnosis the learner should have an opportunity to *actively construct* models of diseases, their possible causes, and the symptoms associated with them, and to evaluate the consequences of these models. In this way the learner acquires and uses the knowledge necessary for diagnostic reasoning.

Secondly, the learner should be given the opportunity to *actively perform* diagnostic reasoning and to apply diagnostic strategies.

Currently we develop MEDICUS, an Intelligent Problem Solving Environment (IPSE, Möbus, 1995), in collaboration with several medical institutions (Health Authority of Oldenburg, Documentation and Information Center for Environmental Issues, Osnabrück, Medical Institute for Environmental Hygiene, Düsseldorf, Robert-Koch Institute, Berlin). MEDICUS differs from existing medical expert systems by being designed to support the two activities mentioned:

• *Model construction* is supported by a model editor based on a simplified natural language. After creating an initial model of the domain of interest, the learner may further specify, evaluate, and revise the model at a qualitative and quantitative level.

• *Training of diagnostic strategies* will also be supported qualitatively (i.e., what information is necessary in order to support or differentiate between what hypotheses?) and quantitatively (i.e., how does information gathered affect my diagnostic hypotheses? What is the most important information to acquire next?)

Though MEDICUS is developed for fields of medicine, our intention is that it will be applicable to diagnosing and modelling problems in other domains of uncertain and complex knowledge as well. The next section gives an overview of the design decisions for the system. Then the implementation state is described. Conclusions and directions of further work will be sketched in the closing section.

2 Design Decisions for MEDICUS

In order to create a system designed to support problem solving in a knowledge domain, a set of design principles is required that is based on a theory of problem solving and knowledge acquisition. We call our approach an *Intelligent Problem Solving Environment* (IPSE, Möbus, 1995): The learner acquires knowledge by actively *testing hypotheses*. This means that the learner creates solution proposals for

problems, tests hypotheses about their correctness, and the system analyzes the proposals making use of an oracle or an expert knowledge base, and provides help and explanations. The psychological foundation of our IPSE approach is the ISP-DL Theory of knowledge acquisition and problem solving (Möbus, 1995) which is influenced by theoretical positions of van Lehn (1988), Newell (1990), and Anderson (1993), and Gollwitzer (1990). Briefly, it states that new knowledge is acquired as a result of problem solving: applying weak heuristics in response to impasses. In contrast, existing knowledge is optimized if applied successfully. Furthermore there are four distinct problem solving phases: deliberating, resulting in setting a goal, planning how to reach the goal, executing the plan, and evaluating the result. The ISP-DL Theory leads to several design principles for IPSE's. Some of them are (Möbus, 1995; Möbus et al., 1992):
• According to the theory the learner will look for and appreciate help at an impasse. So the system should not interrupt the learner but offer help on demand.
• Feedback and help information should be available any time, aiming at the actual problem solving phase of the learner.
• At an impasse, the learner should be prevented from trapping into follow-up impasses. Thus help should refer to the learner's pre-knowledge as much as possible.
MEDICUS is designed according to these criteria. Help information is or will be always available on demand. Planning a model is facilitated by the simplified-natural-language model editor which allows the learner to state her or his ideas in an informal way. The evaluation of models is supported qualitatively and quantitatively. Close correspondence to the learner's knowledge will be achieved by giving help that changes the learner's proposal as little as possible (minimal modifications).
Besides general design criteria for IPSE's, each domain has special features. In this case, it is the uncertainty of knowledge, which we chose to handle by the Bayesian network approach. A Bayesian network (e.g., Neapolitan, 1990; Pearl, 1988) represents knowledge as a set of propositional variables and probabilistic interrelationships between them by a directed acyclic graph. The variables are represented by the nodes of the graph, and the relations by directed arcs. The relations are conditional probabilities (each variable conditioned on its parents in the network). They define a joint probability distribution that can be used to compute desired aposteriori distributions. Figure 1 shows a simple Bayesian network for the joint distribution p(injury, space requirement, haemodynamic irritation, vomiting, dislocation of vessels, infection of meninges, permanent headache). The conditional distributions needed to compute this joint distribution can be simplified by independence assumptions. In the graph, independencies between variables are represented by omitting arcs. For example, in Figure 1 the variables "vomiting" and "dislocation of vessels" are independent given knowledge about "space requirement". This means that information about "vomiting" is not relevant for the hypothesis "dislocation of vessels" (and vice versa) if it is already known whether the patient suffers from a space requirement process: p(dislocation of vessels I space requirement, vomiting) = p(dislocation of vessels I space requirement).
An important reason for choosing the Bayesian network approach is that the system is designed to support qualitative reasoning. A physician engaged in medical diagnosis proceeds in a highly selective manner (i.e., Elstein et al., 1978). We pursue

the hypothesis that this selectivity corresponds to the kind of (in)dependencies present in Bayesian networks. Reviews of published case studies in the domain of environmental medicine support this hypothesis. More generally, there is empirical evidence that qualitative reasoning by (in)dependencies as supported by Bayesian networks (like for example "explaining away") corresponds closely to human reasoning patterns (Henrion, 1987; Pearl, 1993; Waldmann & Holyoak, 1992).

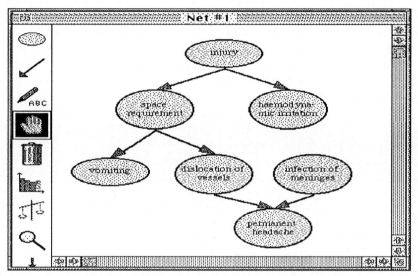

Fig. 1. A simple Bayesian network for a medical problem

Alternative approaches. The Dempster-Shafer Theory of evidential reasoning is an extension of probability theory. Uncertainty is represented by belief intervals limited by the positive belief in an event and its plausibility. This requires additional knowledge acquisition and explanation facilities. So at the current stage we consider the probability-based approach sufficient for our aims, which is not meant to preclude other methods at later stages. Fuzzy-Set Theory reasons with propositions that have vague meaning. In our application domain, there are many vaguely specified concepts, like "severe headache" or "typical symptom" (see also the examples below). Therefore we work on integrating fuzzy concept descriptions into the Bayesian network approach, that is, to generate conditional distributions for fuzzy relations.

3 The Implementation State of MEDICUS

This section is organized according to the two functions of MEDICUS: supporting the construction of explanation models, and training diagnostic reasoning.

3.1 Supporting Model Construction
Model construction is supported in three steps:

Initial Model Formulation

One of the main goals of MEDICUS is the assistance of the learner in developing a model of perceived causes, effects, and other relationships in a domain of interest with a formal tool, Bayesian networks. The reason to use a formal tool is to be able to derive consequences (dependencies, independencies, aposteriori distributions) that can be used for proposing recommendations and modifications. But at the same time it is necessary that a mathematically untrained learner is able to state his ideas in an informal way which he is used to. Therefore, we developed a simplified-natural-language model editor. After stating his model in this editor, the system can generate an initial graph automatically.

Figure 2 shows a small example with four sentences. Each sentence is placed in a sentence field. In order to create sentences, the learner may use variable categories (like state, event, action, object, substance), relations, modifier, and logical junctions. After placing a variable category in a sentence field, it can be named.

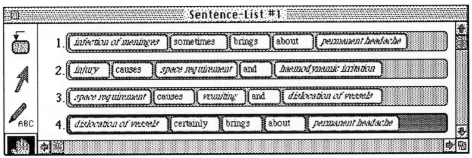

Fig. 2. Four sentences created in the simplified-natural-language model editor

For the relations there is a taxonomy based on i) probabilistic concepts of causality (Schurz, 1988; Suppes, 1970) organized according to the two dimensions "kind of influence" (positive / negative) and "direction of influence" (forward, backward, or undirected), and ii) has-part / is-a hierarchies. Table 1 shows the taxonomy. Relations currently available in the model editor are marked by asterisks. They were selected initially as a result of two sessions of discussing a topic of environmental medicine with an expert, but the user of MEDICUS may specify additional relations.

The sentences created by the learner are checked by a definite clause grammar. Besides syntactical correctness, semantic restrictions between variable categories and relations are checked. (For example, a state cannot cause a substance.) The learner receives feedback if the grammar finds errors.

The learner may ask the system to create a graph representation for the model specified. For the sentences in Figure 2, MEDICUS proposes the graph shown in Figure 1. The graph is an initial heuristic proposal that may have to be refined by the learner qualitatively, getting assistance from the system (see below). The graph is created in the following way:

• *Generating nodes.* Nouns, that is, variable categories named by the user, are represented by nodes (propositional variables). A proposition is assigned to each possible node instantiation. For example, if "injury" in Figure 2 has been categorized as an "event" by the user, then the node "injury" is created (Figure 1) as a binary-valued node (unless specified otherwise by the user), and the propositions "Person experiences the event 'injury'" and "Person does not experience the event 'injury'" are assigned to it. The propositions can be inspected by the user.

• *Generating edges.* The relations between nouns are represented by links as depicted in the rightmost column of Table 1. For relations describing undirected relations (like "corresponds to"), a dialog is called where the learner is asked to specify the direction of influence, or to specify a third variable as the common cause or effect of the two variables in question.

In order to facilitate understanding of the graph representation further, natural-language expressions of the conditional distributions for each node (resp. apriori distributions for root nodes) are generated. Furthermore, the learner may ask for an explanation of the relationship between the sentences in the model editor and the net. Alternatively, a net can be created directly by editing and naming nodes and edges.

direction of influence		Directed and undirected relations:		Representation in the graph:
		kind of influence		
		positive	negative	
forward tA ≤ tB		A causes B* A brings about B* A triggers B* $p(B \mid A) > p(B)$	A counteracts B* A prevents B $p(B \mid A) < p(B)$	A B
backward tA ≥ tB		A follows B A is consequence of B ... $p(A \mid B) > p(A)$	A does not follow B ... $p(A \mid B) < p(A)$	B A
undirected		A corresponds to B* A occurs with B*	A and B are mutually exclusive	Dialog required
		Is-a and Part-of hierarchies:		Representation in the graph:
		A is example for B* A contains B* $p(B \mid A) = 1$ A is exemplified by B A is part of B $p(B \mid \neg A) = 0$		A B

Table 1. Taxonomy of relations used in the model editor

Qualitative Model Revision

After the initial formulation of the model, it has to be analyzed and revised on a qualitative level. In particular, it has to be verified that the dependencies and independencies implied by the graph correspond to the assertions stated by the modeller. For example, the graph in Figure 1 states that space requirement and haemodynamic irritation are independent, given injury, that is, p(space requirement | injury) = p(space requirement | injury, haemodynamic irritation). This means that knowledge about a haemodynamic irritation is not relevant for the hypothesis "space requirement", if it is known that an injury took place or not. Information about a haemodynamic irritation is useless for the hypothesis "space requirement", given knowledge about injury. In contrast, if nothing is known about injury, information about a haemodynamic irritation is useful for the hypothesis "space requirement": p(space requirement) ≠ p(space requirement | haemodynamic irritation). Similarly, vomiting and dislocation of vessels are independent, given space requirement. In contrast, dislocation of vessels and infection of meninges are dependent, given permanent headache. For example, if it is known that a patient suffers from permanent headache, then if new evidence arrives that weakens the hypothesis "dislocation of vessels", the hypothesis "infection of meninges" will be strengthened, and vice versa: Weakening one explanation for "permanent headache" strengthens the other one, and vice versa. Formally, conditional independence is described by the d-separation criterion (Pearl, 1988).

The knowledge of the modeller has to be acquired by the system in a way that is at the same time comfortable to the modeller and informative for generating independence assertions. Therefore, a second variant of knowledge acquisition (besides the model and net editor) is needed that can be used for model *construction* or for model *validation*, that is, for verifying or rejecting the independencies inherent in the graph. The system will offer a diagnostic dialog that proceeds in three steps. The current, yet to-be-improved dialog is described here:

1. For a case, the modeller specifies the initially known data and symptoms (left window in Figure 3: for example, "injury" and "dislocation of vessels"). Next, he specifies a diagnostic hypothesis (middle window in Figure 3, for example "space requirement"). Thirdly, he specifies what information he would look for next, that is, what information he considers relevant for his hypothesis (right window in Figure 3: for example "haemodynamic irritation" and "vomiting"). Independencies are constructed from this dialog in the following way: Information not considered relevant to the hypothesis by the modeller, given the case data and symptoms, is independent of the hypothesis. In Figure 3, "permanent headache" was *not* selected by the user in the right window, so "permanent headache" and "space requirement" are considered independent, given "injury" and "dislocation of vessels": p(space requirement | injury, dislocation of vessels, permanent headache) = p(space requirement | injury, dislocation of vessels).

2. The modeller states the hypothesis that the graph is consistent with the information specified by her or him in the diagnostic dialog. The system analyzes this hypothesis using the d-separation criterion. If differences are found, a graph is constructed internally (using the algorithm of Srinivas et al., 1990) from the dependence and independence assertions acquired in the diagnostic dialog (provided they are consistent). This internal graph is compared to the modeller's graph. This may lead to the result that i) graph and in-/ dependencies are consistent, or ii) edges have to be removed from the graph in order to be consistent with the in-/ dependencies, or iii) edges have to be added to the graph (this is the feedback for the

net in Figure 1 after the dialog in Figure 3 has taken place), or iv) edges have to be removed from as well as added to the graph in order to be consistent with the in-/dependencies.

3. On further request, the modeller may ask the system for modification proposals and their explanation. For example, for the net in Figure 1 and the dialog in Figure 3, MEDICUS recommends to add an edge from "space requirement" to "haemodynamic irritation" because in the dialog the user considered "haemodynamic irritation" informative for "space requirement" given "injury" and "dislocation of vessels".

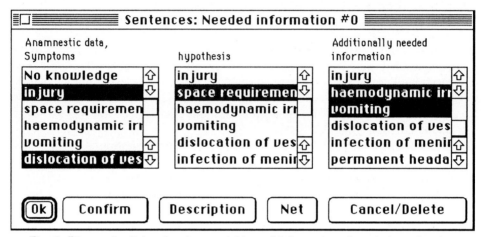

Fig. 3. Diagnostic dialog for the acquisition of information about independencies

Quantitative Model Specification
After the qualitative model revision, the modeller may quantify the net with apriori and conditional probabilities and let MEDICUS generate marginal distributions. Additionally, the user may enter evidences and let MEDICUS generate posterior distributions. Like for example in ERGO and HUGIN, evidence propagation is implemented according to the Lauritzen & Spiegelhalter (1988) algorithm.

3.2 Training Diagnostic Reasoning
The second purpose of MEDICUS is to assist in training diagnostic reasoning and strategies. Training of diagnostic strategies will also be supported qualitatively (i.e.: What information is necessary in order to support or differentiate between what hypotheses? How does information gathered affect my diagnostic hypotheses? What do I have to do in order to diagnose for example "space requirement"? What is the most important information to acquire next? When is it appropriate to consider an environmental etiology of the patient's complaints, and when is it not?) and quantitatively (i.e.: How much does a certain piece of evidence contribute to the currently best hypothesis? What evidence would be necessary in order to achieve a certain probability level for a diagnostic hypothesis?).

Currently MEDICUS is able to generate qualitative recommendations. For this purpose, the user has to specify whether propositional variables refer to syndromes, symptoms, external influences, or the general living and working environment. The most probable syndromes in the light of the available evidence are presented to the learner. For example, in Figure 1, "injury" might have been specified as available evidence. After this evidence, the most probable syndrome hypotheses (i.e. the syndromes with the highest a posteriori probabilities) are "space requirement" and "infection of meninges". The system now recommends to examine those symptoms that are yet unknown and that depend on these syndromes directly, namely, "vomiting" and "permanent headache". These qualitative recommendations have been successfully demonstrated with a multiply connected net containing about fifty variables to a community of environmental medicinal professionals.

4 Conclusions and Further Work

The intelligent problem solving environment, MEDICUS is designed to support the construction of explanatory models in complex, uncertain domains, and to support diagnostic reasoning. Our example application domains stem from medicine. Unlike most existing systems based on the Bayesian network approach, MEDICUS is designed as a problem solving tool. The learner may construct explanatory models, evaluate their consequences qualitatively and quantitatively, and revise the models, getting support from the system. Secondly, the learner may state diagnostic hypotheses and receive feedback about the usefulness of diagnostic investigations.

Concerning the *modelling component*, our near future plans are i) to develop a component for the acquisition of conceptual domain knowledge that can be used for generating explanations for relations between variables, and ii) to be able to acquire distributions from verbal descriptions of relations between variables (phrases like e.g. "sometimes brings about" in Figure 2). We are pursuing a Bayesian and a fuzzy approach in this respect. Concerning the *diagnostic support component*, we plan to implement a dialog that supports the learner's generation and revision of diagnostic hypotheses as well as diagnostic reasoning steps, and that provides feedback and explanations.

Concerning *applications* of MEDICUS, one of our cooperations is aimed at generating realistic models with the help of case data. These models will serve for health consulting as well as for diagnostic training. Some of the other cooperations are aimed at applying MEDICUS to assist in planning, executing, and evaluating environmental exposition analyses ("environmental monitoring"). MEDICUS is seen as a promising contribution to quality ensurance and improvement in this subdomain.

5 References

Anderson, J.R. (1993). *Rules of Mind*. Hillsdale: Erlbaum.

Andreassen, S., Woldbye, M., Falck, B., Andersen, S.K. (1987). *MUNIN - A Causal Probabilistic Network for Interpretation of Electromyographic Findings*. Proceedings 10th IJCAI 87, 366-372.

Barrows, H.S., Tamblyn, R.M. (1980). *Problem-Based Learning: An Approach to Medical Education*. New York: Springer.

Boshuizen, H.P.A., Schmidt, H.G. (1992). On the Role of Biochemical Knowledge in Clinical Reasoning by Experts, Intermediates, and Novices, *Cog. Science*, 16, 153-184.

Cooper, G.F. (1984). *NESTOR: A Computer-Based Medical Diagnostic Aid that Integrates Causal and Probabilistic Knowledge*, PhD Thesis, Medical Computer Science Group, Stanford University, Stanford, CA (Report HPP-84-48).

Elstein, A.S., Bordage, G. (1980). Psychology of Clinical Reasoning., in G.C. Stone, F. Cohen, N.E. Adler, and Associates (eds), *Health Psychology - A Handbook*. San Francisco: Jossey-Bass Publ., 333-367.

Elstein, A.L., Shulman, L.S., Sprafka, S.A. (1978). *Medical Problem Solving - An Analysis of Clinical Reasoning*, Cambridge: Harvard University Press.

Gollwitzer, P.M. (1990). Action Phases and Mind-Sets. In E.T. Higgins, R.M. Sorrentino (eds): *Handbook of Motivation and Cognition: Foundations of Social Behavior*, 2, 53-92.

Heckerman, D.E. (1991). *Probabilistic Similarity Networks*, Cambridge: MIT Press.

Henrion, M. (1987). Uncertainty in Artificial Intelligence: Is Probability Epistemologically and Heuristically Adequate? In J.L. Mumpower, L.D. Philipps, O. Renn, V.R.R. Uppuluri (eds), *Expert Judgements and Expert Systems*. Berlin: Springer (NATO ASI Series F: Computer and Systems Science), 106-129.

Lauritzen, S.L., Spiegelhalter, D.J. (1988). Local Computations with Probabilities on Graphical Structures and their Application to Expert Systems, *Journal of the Royal Statistical Society*, B50(2), 157-224.

Miller, R.A., Pople, H.E., Myers, J.D. (1982). INTERNIST-I, an Experimental Computer-Based Diagnostic Consultant for General Internal Medicine, *The New England Journal of Medicine*, 307(8), 468-476.

Möbus, C. (1995). Towards an Epistemology of Intelligent Problem Solving Environments: The Hypothesis Testing Approach, in J. Greer (ed), *Proc. of the World Conf. on Artificial Intelligence and Education AI-ED 95*, 138-145.

Möbus, C., Pitschke, K., Schröder, O. (1992). Towards the Theory-Guided Design of Help Systems for Programming and Modelling Tasks. In C. Frasson, G. Gauthier, G.I. McCalla (eds): *Intelligent Tutoring Systems, Proc. ITS 92*. Berlin: Springer, LNCS 608, 294-301.

Neapolitan, R.E. (1990). *Probabilistic Reasoning in Expert Systems*, New York: Wiley.

Newell, A. (1990). *Unified theories of cognition*. Cambridge: Harward University Press.

Patel, V.L., Groen, G.J. (1986). Knowledge Based Solution Strategies in Medical Reasoning, *Cognitive Science*, 10, 91-116.

Pearl, J. (1988). *Probabilistic Reasoning in Intelligent Systems: Networks of Plausible Inference*, San Mateo: Morgan Kaufman (2nd ed.).

Pearl, J. (1993). Belief Networks Revisited. *Artificial Intelligence*, 59, 49-56.

Schurz, G. (1988). *Erklären und Verstehen in der Wissenschaft (Explanation and Understanding in Science)*, München: Oldenbourg.

Shortliffe, E.H. (1976). *Computer-Based Medical Consultations: MYCIN*, New York: North-Holland.

Srinivas, S., Russell, S., Agogino, A. (1990). Automated Construction of Sparse Bayesian Networks from Unstructured Probabilistic Models and Domain Information. In M. Henrion, R.D. Shachter, L.N. Kanal, J.F. Lemmer (eds): *Uncertainty in Artificial Intelligence 5*, Amsterdam: North-Holland, 295-307.

Suppes, P. (1970). *A Probabilistic Theory of Causality*, Amsterdam: North-Holland.

Szolovits, P., Pauker, S.G. (1978). Categorical and Probabilistic Reasoning in Medical Diagnosis, *Artificial Intelligence*, 11, 115-144.

Szolovits, P., Pauker, S.G. (1993). Categorical and Probabilistic Reasoning in Medicine Revisited, *Artificial Intelligence*, 59, 167-180.

Van Lehn, K. (1988). Toward a Theory of Impasse-Driven Learning. In H. Mandl, A. Lesgold (eds): *Learning Issues for Intelligent Tutoring Systems*. Springer, 19-41.

Waldmann, M.R., Holyoak, K.J. (1992). Predictive and Diagnostic Learning Within Causal Models: Asymmetries of Cue Competition, *Journal of Experimental Psychology: General*, 121, 222-236.

Weiss, S.M., Kulikowski, C.A., Amarel, S. (1978). A Model-Based Method for Computer-Aided Medical Decision Making, *Artificial Intelligence*, 11, 145-172.

EpiTalk
A Platform for Epiphyte Advisor Systems Dedicated to Both Individual and Collaborative Learning

Sylvain Giroux[1], Gilbert Paquette[1], François Pachet[2] and Jean Girard[1]

[1]LICEF/UER Science et Technologie, Télé-Université, 1001 Sherbrooke est, Montréal, P.Q., H2L 4L5 Canada, sgiroux@teluq.uquebec.ca
[2]LAFORIA, Université Paris VI, 4, place Jussieu, 75252 Paris Cedex 05, France, pachet@laforia.ibp.fr

Abstract. In distance learning environments, advisors can start off again a stalled learning process. EpiTalk is a platform enabling to develop advisors for individual and collaborative learning. EpiTalk advisors rely on agents, organizations and hierarchical graphs. Hierarchical graphs describe advisors. At run-time, agents provide autonomy to each advisor's components, while organizations link and co-ordinate agents. Since advisors are grafted onto existing arbitrary information systems, we say that they are *epiphyte* .

1 Introduction

To support distance learning, Télé-université supplies learners with information systems either needed for tasks, or managing on-going learning processes [1]. Besides there are human tutors [13]. But tutors are not *on-line*. So when a learner gets into trouble, accurate help may not be at hand. Advisor information systems can provide a just-in-time and ever available individualized first-line help. As communication technologies are integrated into modern distance learning environment [26], collaborative learning activities can take place at distance [3] [13] [2]. So advising isolated activities is not sufficient, distributed advice to groups must also be provided.

The EpiTalk project [27, 29] addresses the complex issue of advising individuals and groups using the existing home-made or commercial applications. Our solution is to consider advisors as *epiphytes*[1] information systems, that is as information systems growing onto other information systems, their *hosts*, without perturbing them whatsoever [8]. Exploiting this metaphor, we devised and implemented EpiTalk, a platform dedicated to epiphyte advisor information systems (EAIS). EpiTalk provides the means for describing EAIS: pattern/plan recognition algorithm based on information spied from host information systems [20], distributed student modeling [19] [15] [16], and advice contents and strategies [21]. At that time EpiTalk generates a multi-agent EAIS using descriptions of hosts, of content and task structures, and of pieces of advice [10]. Next EpiTalk grafts the EAIS onto learning environments [22]. Finally EpiTalk provides tools to monitor and debug EAIS [9].

This paper presents EpiTalk's main features and commitments. First we present our goals and constraints (§2-3). Then we show how EpiTalk enables to design, launch and monitor EAIS dedicated to individual (§4-7) and collaborative learning (§8). Next we sketch advice strategies (§9). Finally current works are outlined (§10).

---

[1]An epiphyte plant grows on the surfaces of other plants, its host, without damaging it. It lives on its own, but needs other plants. Ivy, and most orchids are typical examples.

2 A Generic Architecture for Advisor Systems

2.1 EAIS for Individualized and Collaborative Learning

Several applications can run concurrently on today's multi-window operating systems. Networks enable distributed collaborative work. Therefrom a learner may pursue as many goals as there are on-going individual and collaborative learning processes intertwined on its workstation. Thus advisors on distinct on-going processes must be distinct while still be able to cooperate, and prevent inconsistent pieces of advice. Moreover advisors must express advice that span across different levels of abstraction [21] and pieces of advice related to either an application —how to perform a task more effectively with the application? [14]—, a production —how to improve the design of a course [28]?—, a process —what is the next step to perform? [21] [23].

EpiTalk solutions to these issues bear on agents [4], organizational reflection [18], and knowledge graphs [25]. Agents are used to disentangle threads of concurrent learning processes. Each EAIS is an agent which focuses on one object —process, production, or application. Agents also bring concurrency between EAIS, and within an EAIS. Organizational reflection permits to easily shift viewpoints on agents and groups: "an agent can be viewed as an organization of agents" and vice-versa [5]. These shifts allow to treat uniformly both individual and collaborative learning. The same mechanisms for communication, cooperation and negotiation apply uniformly inside and outside EAIS. The knowledge graph expresses the designer's viewpoint on the object of advice. The part-of relations are used as a *template* to generate the multi-agent EAIS. Each node provides information used to generate and link EAIS agents, to graft the EAIS on the host, and to adapt the EAIS to the host evolution.

2.2 Capitalizing on Existing Applications

Most advisor systems are designed and developed either as self-contained systems, or as components of top-down designed, integrated learning environments [33]. As a result, the design of an advisor is buried into the design of large systems, which makes transposing the advisor to different contexts a difficult task. Besides it precludes to build learning environment by integrating existing home-made or commercial applications. An advisor too closely coupled to a platform, an operating system or an application version must be thrown away whenever it changes, even if in most cases, advice relative to a task would not. Our approach to advisor systems has been to consider them not as parts of a self-contained system, but as independent extensions of applications, not necessarily designed to be parts of a learning environment. EpiTalk uses organizational reflection to graft the advisor on hosts. The hierarchical structure of knowledge graphs is then exploited to complete the separation of advisors from applications, providing a complete independence from a sufficiently abstract level.

2.3 Reusable Advisors

Advisors are one of the cornerstone of the virtual campus designed at Télé-université [30]. Since programming resources are limited, as many tasks as possible should be automated, and advisor designers must be autonomous. With respect to design, EpiTalk is based on graphs, a formalism pedagogues feel comfortable with. Using a palette of behaviors, the designer can assembled them with a simple graph based interface. When a brand-new behavior is designed, it is automatically integrated in the palette. At run-time, continuations [11] are used to linked the behaviors.

3 Advisor Systems as Epiphyte Systems

The very nature of advisor is to observe the behaviors of other systems and to reason upon observed actions as soon as they are performed. By analogy, we consider advisors as *epiphyte* information systems (Fig.1). EpiTalk provides a precise framework to design advisor systems in a way that reflects the characteristics of advice (viewpoints-dependency and hierarchical nature), while providing satisfactory solutions to our needs (§2). EpiTalk organizes the reasoning of the EAIS according to a hierarchical knowledge graph that models the object aimed at by the advice. EpiTalk also supplies models to represent the knowledge needed to build an EAIS: structure of the object, advice contents, advising strategies... At run-time, EpiTalk enables an EAIS to follow the evolution of its host. In the next sections we describe how EpiTalk allows advisor systems to be specified as epiphyte systems.

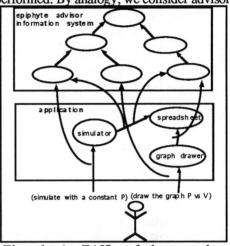

Fig. 1. An EAIS grafted onto a law induction system developed at Télé-université.

4 EpiTalk at One Glance

Within EpiTalk, description and run-time are distinct phases (Fig. 2). First the host and the EAIS are described. The host description is twofold: code (Smalltalk code, events...), and a description which gathers various information in one Smalltalk class. This information give the means to track the host evolution (user actions, new objects, new windows...) and provide the primitive actions an EAIS will have to interpret [20]. The EAIS descriptions are gathered in the knowledge graph: agents, communication network, and agent structure and reasoning process. Once descriptions are sufficiently precise, the run-time phase may proceed. The host is launched. A reflective description of the host is created and a causal link[2] is established. Then the multi-agent EAIS is generated and linked to its host through spies [22]. From then on, the EAIS agents receive spied information, analyze it and provide pieces of advice.

5 Describing an EAIS

A knowledge graph expresses the designer's point of view on the object the pieces of advice are on. There are as many knowledge graphs as there are points of view. A knowledge graph contains three kinds of nodes: non-terminal nodes, star nodes, and leaves. Star nodes are special non-terminal nodes; they express the notion of "0 to n" occurrences. For instance, the knowledge graph on courses designed with a knowledge-based didactic and generic workbench [28] (Fig. 3) specifies that a course is made of 0 to n objectives, and 0 to n learning units; a learning unit is made of...

---

[2] This link is causal because any modification in the host (for instance, a new window) is reflected in the description and conversely, any modification of the description is reflected in the host (for instance, deleting the object representing a window, close thewindow).

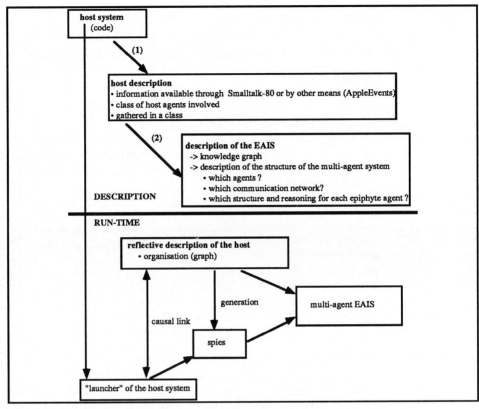

Fig. 2. EpiTalk uses descriptions to produce run-time EAIS.

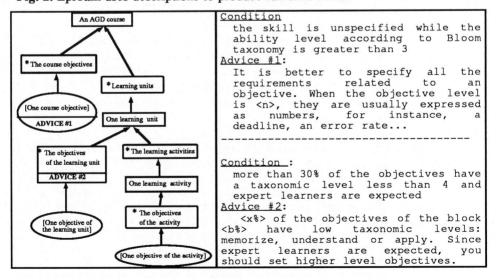

Fig. 3. A knowledge graph for a production.

Pieces of advice are assigned to any nodes. Leaves correspond to local points of view. As we goes up in the graph, the perspective on the course structure enlarges. Specific pieces of advice are placed at the bottom of the graph (advice #1 deals with one single course objective) while general ones require a larger perspective, and appear upper in the hierarchy (advice #2 deals with all the objectives of the learning unit). Pieces of advice can be contextualized.

The knowledge graph hierarchical structure fixes the multi-agent EAIS structure to generate (§7). Each node is used to generate either statically (leaves and non-terminal nodes) or dynamically (star nodes and their subnodes) one epiphyte agent implemented as a concurrent continuation. An epiphyte agent is itself a multi-agent system described by a behavior graph. Behavior nodes are predefined: memory, advisor... They are used to generate concurrent continuation behavior agents. Edges in knowledge (behavior) graphs define the communication net of the multi-agent EAIS (epiphyte agents). Because continuations obey to a uniform protocol, epiphyte (behavior) agents can be easily mixed. Thanks to the hierarchical nature of knowledge graphs, plan recognition and advising are performed in a single walk through at run-time. Since in EAIS, information sift up from leaves to roots, primitive host actions to observe are specified only for leaves. The nature of information to observe depends on hosts and platforms, e.g. selectors and classes for hosts coded in Smalltalk-80. This information is used to generate, graft, and link spies to EAIS' leaf epiphyte agents.

6 EAIS Generic with Respect to Hosts

The hierarchical nature of knowledge graph provides the right handles to achieve EAIS generic with respect to hosts, operating systems, and platforms. Such genericity shelters EAIS from rapid software evolution. The basic idea is to partition the knowledge graph into spies, trace analyzer and advisor layers (Fig. 4). The spies layer collects primitive events (e.g. ⌘-C). The trace analyszer layer combines primitive events into higher level ones (e.g. replacements). The advisor layer processes higher level events to produce pieces of advice. The advisor layer depicted in Figure 4 was reused for two different word processors: Microsoft Word for Windows 3.1 and a homemade word processor implemented in Smalltalk on a MacIntosh. For the latter host application, the trace analyzer is a multi-agent system (Fig. 4). For the former, it is implemented as a syntactic analyzer for DDE based on a grammar[3]. As EAIS are designed, libraries of high-level events and translators are defined and enriched.

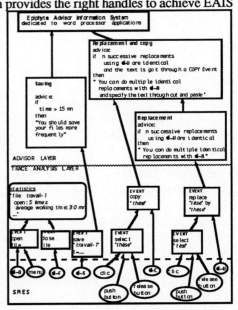

Fig. 4. A knowledge graph on word processing.

---

[3] [Ritter and Koedinger, 95] proposes an approach similar to this solution.

graph describes the activities and the knowledge the learner must master to perform them. When an homework is issued, as many contract nets as it is necessary to give work to all registered learners are instantiated. Then learners divide work amongst themselves using the contract net protocol. A learner can bid on tasks he does not know how to achieve. In this case, he must learn how to do it. For instance, the simulation presented on Fig. 6 involves 4 learners (Etudiant), 2 tutors (Professeur), and 1 administrative agent (Registraire). Two homework contract net (ContratDevoir) were instantiated. Learner 4 is learning the knowledge required to perform its task.

Then a knowledge graph models collaborative work in the simulated campus (Fig. 6b). 0 to n learners evolve in a virtual classroom. Tutors and teams are involved in teaching and support. A team is composed of contract net agents. At run -time, the EAIS is able to identify and model groups and interactions according to membership, team structure, leadership, division of the tasks among learners. The EAIS is also able to use these models to give pieces of advice to a member or to the group on balancing a team workload, directing a learner towrds appropriate teaching resources (teammates, other learners in the classroom, tutors.

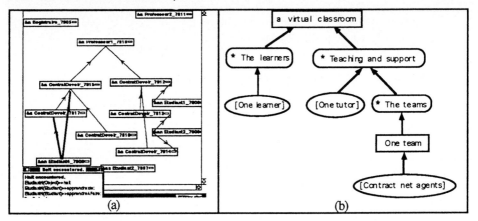

Fig. 6. A simulation run and a knowledge graph on collaborative learning.

9 Advice Strategy

EpiTalk supplies various means to provide pieces of advice. The designer sets a global advice strategy, but can also define local advice strategies on a per piece of advice basis. A piece of advice can be given an unlimited number of time or a limited one, only on request or at the full initiative of the advisor, using a dedicated passive window or a pop-up window, to specific individuals or to the whole group.

10 Current and Future works

A lot of work is still on progress. We are exploring the integratation of multiple perspectives on a problem solving process, cooperation among several EAIS having different focusses, modelling erratic processes, detecting and modelling expertisation [17], exploiting new kinds of relations in knowledge graphs (e.g. precedence relation) in the production of generic advice module [23], teleconference analysis [12] in EAIS for collaborative learning, the articulation between individual and collaborative EAIS in a distributed Web-oriented virtual colloquium, the management of the physical

7 EAIS: Generation, Graft, and Evolution

The generation of an EAIS from the knowledge graph is straightforward. When the host is launched, the EAIS is generated following a top-down traversal of the graph (Fig. 5a). First roots of the knowledge graph are put in the set of nodes to instantiate. Next for each node in the set, an epiphyte agent is created, then the epiphyte agent's internal behavior agents are instantiated (§5, finally the epiphye agent is linked to its hierarchical superiors with respect to the `part-of` relations. The instantiation process is then repeated with the sons of the instantiated nodes that are not star nodes. Sons of star nodes are excluded to delay the instantiation of their subnodes since there is no existing instance of the concepts they model. For instance, the host editor (Fig. 5a) shows that the AGD host has been launched. Three EAIS agents `a1, a2, a3` have been generated. The creation of agents stops there because epiphyte agents `a2` and `a3` correspond to star nodes: there is no objective and learning unit yet defined. Once created, the brand-new EAIS is grafted onto its host and begins to observe its behavior. As the host evolves, the EAIS evolves accordingly: each time a new object is created within the host, relevant star nodes are instantiated, and a spy is installed on the new host object and linked to epiphyte leaf agents interested in the new host object. For instance, opening the `course objectives editor` and defining one course objective triggers the lazy instantiation of the star node `*The objectives of the course` (Fig. 3) and the epiphyte agent `a4` is created (Fig. 5b).

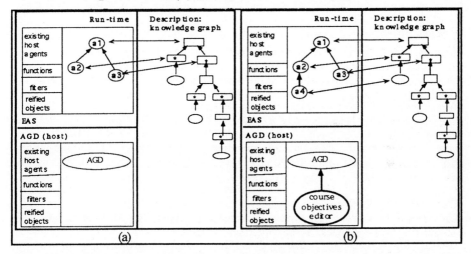

Fig. 5. The symbiotic evolution between the AGD host and an EAIS (cf Fig. 3).

8 EAIS for Collaborative Learning

First to investigate EpiTalk with respect to collaborative learning, we built up a simulation of a virtual campus based on Télé-université everyday practice, namely the learning and administrative procedures. A simulation involves administrative agents, tutor agents, learner agents and contract agents (Fig. 6a). Administrative agents register courses, learners and tutors. Tutor agents teach, give homeworks, and manage grades. Learner agents register to courses and do homework. They have a limited working capacity and limited knowledge. Contract agents manage homeworks according to the contract net protocol [32]. A homework is equivalent to a scenario. A distribution of EAIS epiphyte agents (for instance, local knowledge can be ascribed to leaves and thus the corresponding agents will be resident on the learners' workstation).

11 Conclusion

Télé-université supplies learners with information systems that either help them to manage their on-going learning processes or that enable them to perform their tasks. Furthermore distance learning asks for resources capable to start off again a stalled learning process. That is where advisors take up their duties. In distance education, advisors have to address both individualized and collaborative learning. In this paper, we have shown how EpiTalk helps to design, generate, launch, graft and monitor advisor information systems for both individual and collaborative learning processes. Advisors produced by EpiTalk rely on agents, organizational reflection and hierarchical knowledge graphs. Hierarchical graphs help to design and structure descriptions of an advisor. Using a hierarchical knowledge graph enabled to combine at run-time plan recognition and the production of advice into a single walk through. At run-time, agents provide autonomy, an essential feature, to each component of an advisor, and organizations link and co-ordinate agents. So EpiTalk addresses the design and description of advisors as well as their generation and unfolding at run-time. We have also shown how advisors could be designed in such a way to become platform, operating systems and applications independent. Since advisors were grafted onto existing arbitrary applications, we say that they are *epiphyte* by analogy with botany.

12 References

1. Bergeron, G., Paquette, G., Bourdeau, J.: *HyperGuide: An interactive student guide for a virtual classroom*, ED-MEDIA-93, Orlando, USA, June 23-26, 1993.
2. Christiansen, E.,Dirckinck-Holmfeld,L.:*Making Distance Learning Collaborative*, in3.
3. *CSCL '95, Computer Support for Collaborative Learning*, October 17-20, 1995, Bloomington, IN, USA, Lawrence Erlbaum Associates, Inc.
4. Gasser, L.: *Social Conceptions of Knowledge and Action: DAI Foundations and Open Systems Semantics*, Artificial Intelligence, 1991, vol. 47, no 1-3, pp. 107-138.
5. Giroux, S., Senteni, A., Lapalme, G.: *Adaptation in Open Systems*, First International Conference on Intelligent and Cooperative Information Systems (ICICIS), IEEE Computer Society Press, May 11-14, 1993, Rotterdam, Hollande, pp. 114-123.
6. Giroux, S.: *Agents et systèmes, une nécessaire unité*, Ph. D. thesis in computer science, DIRO, Université de Montréal, August 1993, Publication #883, 246 p.
7. Giroux, S.: *Open Reflective Agents*, in Intelligent Agents II, M. Wooldridge, J.-P. Müller and M. Tambe, eds, Springer-Verlag, LNAI-1037, 1996.
8. Giroux, S., Pachet, F., Paquette, G.: *Des systèmes d'information multi-agents épiphytes*, Deuxièmes Journées Francophones Intelligence Artificielle Distribuée et Systèmes Multi-Agents, Voiron, France, May 9-11, 1994, pp. 211-222.
9. Giroux, S., Pachet, F., Desbiens, J.: *Debugging Multi-Agent Systems: a Distributed Approach to Events Collection and Analysis*, CWDAI'94, Canadian Workshop on Distributed Artificial Intelligence, Banff, Canada, May 16, 1994.
10. Giroux, S., Pachet, F., Paquette, G., Girard, J.: *Des systèmes conseillers épiphytes*, Revue d'intelligence artificielle, Afcet/Hermès, vol. 9, no 2, 1995, pp. 165-190.
11. Hewitt, C.: *Viewing control structures as patterns of passing messages*, Artificial Intelligence, 1977, vol. 8, pp. 323-364.
12. Henri, F., Ricciardi-Rigault, C.: *Collaborative Learning and Computer Conferencing*. NATO Advanced Research Workshop, Grenoble, Sept. 1993. In Liao, T.T. ed. Advanced Educational Technology: Research Issues and Future Potential, Springer-Verlag, 1994.

13. Hotte, R.: *Encadrement assisté par ordinateur et formation à distance*, Revue de l'éducation à distance, vol. VIII, no 2, Fall 1993, pp. 37-53.

14. Karsenty, S., Pachet, F.: *Un mécanisme hiérarchique de répétition et de prédiction de tâches*, in Conférence IHM'95, 7e Journées sur l'Interaction Homme-Machine, Toulouse, France, October, 11-13, 1995.

15. Leman, S., Giroux, S., Marcenac, P.: *A Generic Distributed Method for Cognitive Modelling*, 7th Australian Joint Conference on Artificial Intelligence, Nov. 94.

16. Leman, S., Giroux, S., Marcenac, P., *A Multi-Agent Approach to ModellingStudent REAISoning Process*, AI-ED 95, Aug. 16-19, 95, Washington DC, USA, pp. 258-265.

17. Leman, S., Marcenac, P., Giroux, S.: *When the student surpasses the master*, 3rd International Conference on Computer Aided Engineering Education, CAEE'95, Bratislava, Slovakia, September 13-15, 1995, pp. 22-27.

18. Maes, P.: *Concepts and Experiments in Computational Reflection*, OOPSLA '87 Proceedings, Orlando, Florida, October 4-8, 1987, pp. 147-155.

19. Marcenac, P., Giroux, S., Leman, S.: *A Multi-Agent Approach to Student Modelling*, EW-ED'94: Third East-West Conference on Computer Technologies in Education, 19th-23rd Sept. 1994, Yalta, Crimea, Ukraine, pp. 148-153.

20. Pachet, F., Giroux, S.: *Building plan recognition systems on arbitrary applications: the spying technique*, IJCAI-95 Workshop on The Next Generation of Plan Recognition Systems: Challenges for and Insight from Related Areas of AI, Aug. 20, 95, Canada.

21. Pachet, F., Giroux, S., Paquette, G.: *Pluggable Advisors as Epiphyte Systems*, CALISCE '94, August 31, September 1-2, 1994, Paris, France, pp. 167-174.

22. Pachet, F., Wolinski, F., Giroux, S.: *Spying as an object-oriented programming paradigm*, TOOLS Europe '95, France, March 6-9, 1995, Prentice-Hall, pp. 109-118

23. Pachet, F., Djamen, J.-Y., Frasson, C., Kaltenbach, M.: *Un mécanisme deproduction de conseils pertinents exploitant les relations de décomposition et précédence dans un arbre de tâches*, to appear in Sciences et Techniques Educatives, Hermès.

24. Paquette, G.: *Metaknowledge in the LOUTI development system*. Proc. of CSCSI-92, Canadian Society for Computational Study of Intelligence, Vancouver, Canada, May 92

25. Paquette, G.: *La modélisation par objets typés: une méthode de représentation pour les systèmes d'apprentissage et d'aide a la tâche*. to appear in Sciences et techniques éducatives, Hermès.

26. Paquette, G., Bergeron, G., Bourdeau, J.: *The Virtual Classroom revisited*, Conference TeleTeaching'93, Trondheim, Norway, August 1993.

27. Paquette, G., Pachet, F., Giroux, S.: *ÉpiTalk, un outil générique pour la construction de systèmes conseillers*, Sciences et Techniques Educatives, Hermès, vol. 1, no 3, 1994.

28. Paquette, G., et al., *Design of a Knowledge-based Didactic and Generic Workbench*, CALISCE '94, August 31, September 1-2 1994, Paris, France, pp. 303-311.

29. Paquette, G., Pachet, F., Giroux, S., Girard, J.: *EpiTalk, a generic tool for the development of advisor systems*, to appear in J. of AI in Education.

30. Paquette, G., Ricciardi-Rigault, C., Bourdeau, J., Paquin, C., Liégeois, S.: *Modeling a Virtual Campus Environment for Interactive Distance Learning*, ED-Media International Conference, Graatz, Austria, June 1995.

31. Ritter, S., Koedinger, K. R.: *Towards lightweight tutoring agents*, AI-ED 95, August 16-19, 1995, Washington DC, USA, pp. 91-98.

32. Smith, R. G.: *The Contract Net Protocol: High-Level Communication and Control in a Disptributed Problem Solver*, IEEE Trans. on Computers, vol. C-29, no 12, 1980.

33. Wilson, B.G., Jonassen, D.H.: *Automated instructional systems design: A review of prototype systems*. J. of AI in Education, vol. 2, no 2, 1990, pp. 17-30.

Automated Advice-Giving Strategies for Scientific Inquiry

M. Paolucci[†], D. Suthers[‡], and A. Weiner[‡]

† ISP, University of Pittsburgh, Pittsburgh, PA 15260
‡ LRDC, University of Pittsburgh, Pittsburgh, PA 15260
E-Mail: paolucci\suthers\arlene+@pitt.edu

Abstract

We describe a prototype advisor for students using Belvedere, an environment for conducting discussions about scientific controversies. The advisor has two strategic components, syntactic and consistency-based. Syntactic strategies are based on structural and categorical patterns in argument representations constructed by the students, and suggest ways in which students can continue their inquiry. Consistency-based strategies check student-made links between pairs of statements against the pairwise relations specified between corresponding units in a knowledge base constructed by a teacher or expert, and identify information that may challenge or corroborate relationships proposed by the students.

1. Introduction

Consistent with research that shows that students learn better when they actively pursue understanding rather than passively receiving knowledge [3, 8, 15] the classroom teacher is now being urged to become a "guide on the side" rather than "the sage on the stage." New roles have been recommended for ITS that parallel the teacher's new role in "decentered" classrooms [2, 5, 9]. Our work is addressed towards ITS that augment the learning processes of students engaged in collaborative critical inquiry [7, 10].

With others in our group,[1] we have developed a computer environment that supports students in conducting discussions of problems of scientific knowledge. In this environment, called "Belvedere" [13, 12], students can explore problematic situations by searching on-line information and by producing and manipulating graphical representations of arguments called "inquiry diagrams."

We have now prototyped an automated advisor that gives advice on demand concerning ways in which an argument in this environment can be extended or revised. Rather than supplying oracular advice whenever the student missteps, the advisor is on-demand, avoiding inappropriate intrusion into student discussion that may be taking place external to the computer environment. Advice is phrased as suggestions and questions because we cannot presume that an automated advisor has sufficient information to be imperative, and we want students to think about the advice, not just execute it.

In this paper we discuss two methods of advice generation that we have implemented. Syntactic advice strategies make suggestions based solely on the syntactic structure of students' inquiry diagrams. Consistency-based advice strategies use a simple knowledge base of consistency relations between information units to identify information that may

---

[1] Violetta Cavalli-Sforza, John Connelly, Alan Lesgold, and Arthur Nunes; recently joined by Kim Harrigal, Dan Jones, Eva Toth, and Joe Toth.

challenge or corroborate relationships postulated by the students. Before describing these advice giving methods, we first briefly describe the activity that the students are engaged in.

2. The Scientific Inquiry Tasks

The Belvedere interface affords students the means to readily produce symbolic diagrams, by assembling graphical shapes and connecting them with a variety of links, typing in text, and searching an index of online documents to cut and paste text from them into the diagrams. The students select the shapes and links they want from a column of icons labeled with the names of argument components (see figure 1). In order to focus the students' attention on the argument relations, some of the work of drawing and layout is automated, such as sizing shapes to fit text and positioning of links.

In a typical session in lab studies, pairs of students worked side by side on individual monitors, close enough to see and point to each other's displays. Working together in a shared drawing space, they were asked to find information to resolve an actual scientific problem, and to use Belvedere graphics to express the work that they did together. Problems that we have used hinge on conflicts between scientific theories or between a theory and discrepant data. For example, in the "iguanas problem," the students begin with a text explaining an anomaly for evolutionary theory: the two species of iguanas native to the Galapagos islands would appear to have separated more than 12 million years ago, but the Galapagos islands are dated at only 2-3 million years of age, conflicting with the theory that the species diverged on the islands [1]. In the studies, the students were given a 3-node graphical representation of the problem, the tools for extending the representation, and access to brief on-line texts relevant to the problem (as well as some that were not relevant). They were asked to work together to try to resolve the anomaly. Results of our formative evaluations are described in [13, 12].

3. Pedagogical Constraints on Advice

Our design of the advisors to be discussed were guided in part by the following constraints.

Maintain the student-initiated character of Belvedere's environment. Belvedere encourages reflection by allowing students to see their argumentation as an object. They can point to different parts of it and focus on areas that need attention. They can engage in a process of construction and revision, reciprocally explaining and confronting each other. An advisor should not intervene prematurely in their thinking process. It should be discreet, offering advice on request. Students should feel free to discard an advisor's suggestions when they believe them to be irrelevant or inappropriate.

Address certain parts of the task that are critical to the desired cognitive skill. Research on "confirmation bias" and hypothesis driven search suggests that students are likely to be concerned with the process of constructing an argument for a favored theory they

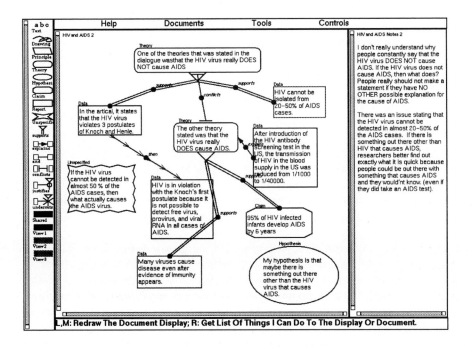

Figure 1: Diagram by Students on HIV/AIDS Issue.

are supporting, sometimes overlooking or discounting discrepant data [6, 4]. Also, they may not consider alternate explanations of the data they are using. An advisor should address these problems. For example, it should offer information that the student may not have sought, including information that is discrepant with the student's theory.

Be applicable to problems constructed by outside experts and teachers. The advisor should be able to give useful advice based on a simple knowledge base that an expert or a teacher might construct. So far Belvedere has been used to construct arguments in domains as different as theory of evolution, contrasting theories of mountain formation, cause of the Cretaceous extinctions, whether HIV causes AIDS, and theories in social psychology. It is not feasible to develop for each a representation of the knowledge needed to deal with the argumentation students potentially could engage in. We are instead interested in a general approach, applicable to all the cases, in which the knowledge base can be constructed by a teacher.

4. Syntactic Advice Strategies

The first approach we implemented gives advice in response to situations that can be defined on a purely syntactic basis, using only the structural and categorical features of the students' argument graphs. (The students' text is not interpreted.) Types of advice are defined in terms of patterns to be matched to the diagram, and textual advice to be given if there is a match. Example advice patterns are given in Table 1.

```
(def-advice circular-support
    :advice "This looks like a circular argument. Is there a statement in this group of
            statements that doesn't depend on accepting the rest of them?"
    :arguments (?x)
    :test (:and (statement ?x) (support-or-explain* ?x ?x))
    :type :incoherence)
(def-advice support-competitor
    :advice "Could the empirical data that supports one theory also support the other?"
    :arguments (?t1 ?t2 ?d)
    :test (:and (theory ?t1) (theory ?t2) (empirical ?d) (:not (:same-as ?t1 ?t2))
            (supports* ?d ?t1) (:not (supports* ?d ?t2)))
    :type :open-world)
```

Table 1: Examples of Syntactic Advice Patterns

The advice applicable to a given inquiry diagram is often more than a student can be expected to absorb and respond to at one time. When more than one instance of advice is applicable, a preference-based quicksort algorithm is used, following a mechanism used by Suthers [11] for selecting between alternate explanations. Advice instances are sorted in priority order, and the highest priority advice is given. Objects that bind to variables in the patterns are highlighted in yellow when the advice is given, so the user can easily identify what the advice is about. If further advice is requested before the diagram changes, subsequent advice instances on the sorted list are used without reanalysis. We are investigating preferences that take into account factors such as prior advice that has been given, how that advice has been responded to, how recently the object of advice was constructed, and various categorical attributes of the applicable advice.

We believe that the most important kind of advice is that which stimulates and scaffolds constructive activity on the part of the students. To give this kind of "open world" advice, our first step was to identify partial argument patterns in the inquiry diagram the students had constructed so far and indicate how the student could complete these patterns. For example, the advisor might find theoretical claims that have no empirical support and suggest that support be sought, or it might find competing theories where one theory is supported by some empirical observation and ask if the same observation can support the other theory (support-competitor in Table 1).

The syntactic advisor also responds to illegal and incoherent constructions. "Illegal" constructions are those that use elements of the diagrammatic language in a manner inconsistent with their intended semantics. For example, a "support" link should not be used between data. "Incoherent" constructions are those in which the elements are each used legally, but in combinations that are semantically problematic. Examples include a loop of "support" links (circular-support in Table 1), or a datum that both supports and undermines the same claim.

Consider the inquiry diagram shown in Figure 1, constructed by two students during formative evaluations at a public school site. The following advice is given (one by one and in this order) by our syntactic advisor when applied to that diagram:

1. Highlights the unconnected hypothesis (lower right); asks whether the students can say how this part relates to the rest of the diagram.

2. Highlights the same hypothesis and asks whether the students can find a way to support it, or show that it predicts or explains an observed phenomenon.

3. Highlights the two theories and one of the "Data" boxes that supports one of them and asks whether it is possible that the same data supports the other theory. ("Data" is a kind of "Empirical Observation." This is an instance of support-competitor.)

4. Highlights the "explains" link (right of center), points out that ideas such as theories and hypotheses explain empirical observations, not the other way around, and tells the student an easy way to reverse the link.

In addition to those mentioned above, other kinds of advice that we have implemented include suggesting that a theory or hypothesis be formulated when none is present in the inquiry diagram; asking whether there is another theory that provides an alternate explanation for the empirical data when only one theory or hypothesis is involved in the inquiry diagram; and asking whether data can be found to discriminate between two theories that have identical support.

5. Consistency-Based Advice Strategies

Ideally, we would like to have an advisor that understands the students' text as well as the domain under discussion, and provides fully knowledge-based advice. This is not currently possible due to the difficulty of constructing domain knowledge bases and of understanding students' texts. Instead, we have adopted the strategy of investigating how much useful advice we can get out of a minimal semantic annotation before we move on to more complex approaches. In this manner we hope to better understand the cost/benefit tradeoff between knowledge engineering and added functionality.

The consistency-based advisor is our first step in this direction. It is intended to offer specific information that the student may not discover on her own. It makes two assumptions: students construct their inquiry diagrams from existing units of text, and these units are annotated with relationships recording whether they are consistent or inconsistent with each other, based on expert judgment. The advisor searches the latter "consistency graph" to find paths between units that students have used in their inquiry diagrams, and selects other units found along those paths which are brought to the students' attention. Our claim is that this enables us to point out information that is relevant at a given point in the inquiry process without needing to pay the cost of a more complete semantic model of that information.

5.1 The Consistency Graph and Algorithm

The algorithm for the consistency-based advisor is based on a comparison of the student's inquiry diagram with information derived from a teacher's or expert's inquiry diagram. For the purposes of advice-giving, Belvedere's various relations between argument components are classified simply as relations of inconsistency or consistency and are

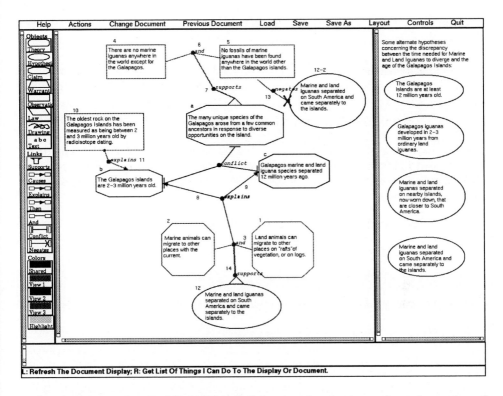

Figure 2: Diagram by "Emin" and "Mo," Galapagos Iguana Anomaly, early version of Belvedere

assumed to be symmetrical. Thus a "consistency" link means that the information in the connected nodes is at least compatible, and preferably one can be offered as evidence for the other. If a theory explains some datum, then the theory and the datum are "consistent." If a datum conflicts with a theory, then they are "inconsistent." In the diagram displayed in figure 2, the links "support," "causes," "explains" and "then" are interpreted as consistency relations. Links like "conflict" and "negates" are interpreted as inconsistency relations. The link "and" is a concept-forming link: it defines an implicit node that is consistent with the conjuncts, and inconsistent with nodes that are inconsistent with either conjunct. More precisely, the consistency relation of and-links is based on the following rules:

1. $(A \land B)$ is consistent with each of A and B individually.

2. If C is inconsistent with A or inconsistent with B, then C is inconsistent with $(A \land B)$.

The converse of rule 2 does not hold: $(A \land B)$ can be inconsistent with C while both A and B are individually consistent with C.

When the teacher or domain expert defines the task and the information needed, she can draw an inquiry diagram in Belvedere. The diagram is easily transformed into a set of consistency relations between pairs of texts, following the rules described above. These relations become the "expert model" or knowledge base for the consistency-based advisor.

During a student session, students can drag texts authored by the expert into their diagrams, and express argumentation relationships between them. The links in the student diagram are interpreted as consistency relationships in the manner described above. The advisor can then compare consistency relations defined by the students with consistency relations defined by the expert, and look for inconsistencies and other possible advice. The comparison is based on a graph-search algorithm, which has been implemented and tested as reported below. It searches in the *expert's* consistency graph for paths between nodes that have been related in the *students'* graph, constrained by the following rules:

1. Only the shortest path between two nodes is considered.

2. A "positive path" crosses only consistency links.

3. A "negative path" ends with an inconsistency link.

4. A path can cross only one inconsistency link. An inconsistency link ends a path.

5. Conflicts between positive and negative paths are resolved in favor of the negative path.

The advisor can then select an item on the path found in the expert's graph that is not present in the students' graph, and present this to the student for consideration. If the path is of a different polarity than the students' link, the information presented could possibly contradict the relationship claimed by the students; if the polarity is the same the information would presumably support the relationship claimed by the students. (See figure 3 for an example.)

The five rules presented above define a non-monotonic logic similar to Thomason's skeptical reasoning [14]. Rule 1 is used to control the search and control the length of meaningless paths. The "consistency relation" is weaker than logical implication. It can easily be the case that inconsistent statements are at the ends of a long chain of consistency links. Although limiting the search to the shortest path does not solve this problem, it greatly reduces the effect of long and meaningless paths.

Rules 2 to 4 are used to maintain the consistency of the path. Once a negative link is crossed, it is plausible that the two nodes at the end of the path are inconsistent. We cannot extend the path any farther, because whatever conclusion is drawn from there is quite arbitrary. For example, suppose that A is inconsistent with B, and B is inconsistent with C. We can't conclude that A is inconsistent with C: they could be consistent components of an argument against B. On the other hand, we can't assume that A is consistent with C: they could be arguing against B based on incompatible assumptions. Thus, Rule 4 forces the search to stop when a conflict is reached. Rule 5 is introduced to address the confirmation bias.

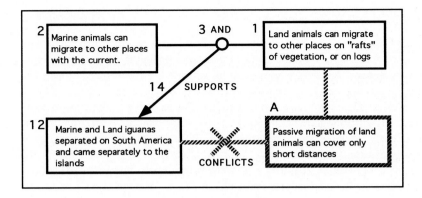

Figure 3: Example consistency path identifying information to be used in advice

5.2 Preliminary Evaluation

We have conducted two preliminary experiments with the consistency-based advisor. In the first experiment we were interested in testing consistency relations that we expected to be difficult or that required some inferential power. We used a subset of the "iguana problem" knowledge base used in some of the studies with the students comprised 19 nodes, 14 consistent and inconsistent relations, and 2 and-links. The three authors made judgments of consistency between pairs of statements corresponding to the nodes. Then we compared our judgments with the advisor's judgments. In all the relations about which all three authors agreed, the advisor made the same judgment. The only disagreements were on relations about which the authors disagreed. These cases were all characterized by the lack of a connecting path between the tested nodes. Either the search process was blocked by an inconsistency link, or a critical link was missing in an intermediate step of the process.

In the second experiment, we were concerned with the advice that would be given in a real interaction with students. We constructed a consistency graph of 90 statements and 73 relations from the materials used in one of the sessions with students, and performed consistency analysis on each link from two student sessions (see diagram in figure 2 for one of the sessions). The performance was similar to the previous experiment. We always agreed with the system's judgement, and the intermediate steps were sequences of coherent proofs. On most of the links the advisor agreed with the students (these were among our best students). In one case only, link 14, the advisor gave a different judgement: see figure 3. The path the advisor constructed starts at node 3, crosses node 1 and node A (not displayed in the students' graph), and ends at node 12. The advisor recognizes that this path (shaded) crosses an inconsistency link, so conflicts with the students' link 14. If the students would ask the advisor for a critique of their argument, the advisor would highlight link 14 and it would display Node A (the only information on the path that they have not seen), confronting them with the conditions for land animals' migration which they overlooked.

6. Conclusions

The syntax-based advisor can make suggestions to stimulate students' thinking with no knowledge engineering required on the part of the teacher or domain expert. However, the advice is very general and does not adequately address the confirmation bias. The consistency-based advisor can provide students with assistance in identifying relevant information which students may have not considered (perhaps due to the confirmation bias), and which may challenge their thinking. This advice cannot be provided by the syntax-based advisor, because the advice depends on knowledge of certain semantic relationships between the textual units involved. The level of "understanding" of the texts on the part of the system required is extremely minimal: this is an advantage, as it reduces the knowledge engineering demands on educators preparing materials for students. Clearly, a minimal semantic approach have limitations. For example it cannot infer the goals of the student, in particular which theory she is trying to build or support. The advisor described in this paper cannot help the student in the construction of an argumentation or find a counter argument that attacks her theory or engage the student in a scientific discussion. However, by investigating the utility of advice obtained from these minimal semantic annotations we hope to gain interesting insights that will help us to move toward more complex approaches, also we can better understand the cost-benefit tradeoff between knowledge engineering and added functionality.

References

[1] M. W. Browne. Galapagos mystery solved: Fauna evolved on vanished isles. *Science Times, the NY Times*, January 21 1992.

[2] T.W. Chan and A.B. Baskin. Studying with the prince: The computer as a learning companion. In *Proceedings of the International Conference on Intelligent Tutoring Systems*, pages 194–200, 1988.

[3] M.T.H. Chi, M. Bassok, M. Lewis, P. Reimann, and R. Glaser. Self-explanations: How students study and use examples in learning to solve problems. *Cognitive Science*, 13:145–182, 1989.

[4] C. Chinn and W. Brewer. Factors that influence how people respond to anomalous data. In *Proc. 15th Annual Conf. of the Cognitive Science Society*, pages 318–323, Hillsdale, NJ: Lawrence Erlbaum, 1993.

[5] W. J. Clancey. Guidon-manage revised: A socio-technical systems approach. In *Intelligent Tutoring Systems*, pages 21–36, 1992.

[6] J. Klayman and Y.-W. Ha. Confirmation, disconfirmation, and information in hypothesis testing. *Psychological Review*, 94:211–228, 1987.

[7] D. K. O'Neill and L. M. Gomez. The collaboratory notebook: A distributed knowledge-building environment for project-enhanced learning. In *Proceedings of Ed-Media '94*, pages 416–423, Vancouver, BC, June 1994. Charlottesville, VA: Association for the Advancement of Computing in Education.

[8] L. Resnick and M.T.H. Chi. Cognitive psychology and science learning. In M. Druger, editor, *Science for the Fun of it: A Guide to Informal Science Education*, pages 24–31. National Science Teachers Association, 1988.

[9] J. Roschell. Designing for cognitive communication: Epistemic fidelity or mediating collaborative inquiry? *The Arachnet Electronic Journal on Virtual Culture*, 2(2), 1994.

[10] R. E. Slavin. *Cooperative Learning: Theory, Research, and Practice*. Prentice-Hall, Englewood Cliffs, NJ, 1990.

[11] D. Suthers. Preferences for model selection in explanation. In *Proc. 13th International Joint Conference on Artificial Intelligence (IJCAI-93)*, pages 1208–1213, Chambery, France, August 1993.

[12] D. Suthers and A. Weiner. Groupware for developing critical discussion skills. In *CSCL '95, Computer Supported Collaborative Learning*, pages 341–348, Bloomington, Indiana, October 1995.

[13] D. Suthers, A. Weiner, J. Connelly, and M. Paolucci. Belvedere: Engaging students in critical discussion of science and public policy issues. In *AI-Ed 95, the 7th World Conference on Artificial Intelligence in Education*, pages 266–273, Washington, D.C., August 1995.

[14] R. H. Thomason. Netl and subsequent path-based inheritance theories. *Computers Math. Applic.*, 23(2-5):179–204, 1992.

[15] Noreen Webb. Peer interaction and learning in small groups. *International Journal of Education Research*, 13:21–40, 1989.

Acknowledgments

This research was conducted while supported by grant MDR-9155715 from the NSF Applications of Advanced Technology program and grant N66001-95-C-8621 from the ARPA Computer Aided Education and Training Initiative. We also thank Violetta Cavalli-Sforza, John Connelly, Alan Lesgold, and Arthur Nunes for their valuable input and support as members of the LRDC Belvedere project, and Richmond Thomason for his knowledge-based advice.

AGD: A Course Engineering Support System

Gilbert Paquette and Jean Girard

Centre de recherche LICEF

Télé-université, 1001 Sherbrooke est, Montréal, Qc, H2L 4L5
Tél: (514) 522-4046 ; Fax: (514) 522-3608
E-Mail: licef @ teluq.uquebec.ca

Abstract

AGD is a performance support system for content expert involved in educational design. It puts a strong emphasis on strategic Instructional design knowledge that help in the decisions that the designers must make to achieve a learning system. This knowledge is embedded in an advisor system, while the conceptual (design objects to produce) and the procedural (how to produce it) ID knowledge is embedded in a comprehensive and integrated task support system.

We will first describe briefly the task support system (AGD). Then we will concentrate on its companion advisor system, presenting the methodology we have developed to add an advisor to the AGD task support system. We will also give an overview of some generic tools that were developed to facilitate the development of such an advisor. Finally, we will discuss different aspects of the approach such as level the of abstraction in the advisor system, the diversity of point of views made possible, generality and productivity issues and finally future developments that we intend to achieve .

Keywords

Instructional Design Tools, Advisors systems, Task support systems

Introduction

The new learning environments must integrate a large array of methods and tools in a way that breaks with traditional linear instructional design. With the rapid evolution of Technology based learning, the question of support to designers becomes critical. As one leading researcher in the field writes: « while there have been moderate additions to the tool set and some changing of perspective from a behaviorist to a cognitive psychological orientation, to date they do not represent a fundamental change in the tool set » [Gustafson, 1993] Also, the productivity issue is not well addressed: « traditional ID practices are too slow and costly for many situations, and should be replaced by electronic performance support systems (EPSS)» [Gery , 1991]

Four categories of instructional design tools are now used

- Authoring systems aim at the production of computer assisted courseware; but each represent only a small component among a diversified array of media and learning activities one can expect in a mature learning system; furthermore they do not embed explicit educational knowledge to support the designer.

- A designer can also use a set of independent task support tools, for example one for needs analysis, another one for content modeling and still other tools to state learning objectives or chose instructional tactics and media. Used in combination, these tools do not provide the integration required to ensure the consistency of a learning system, its maintenance and the reusability of its components.

- ID-expert systems aim at replacing, at least partially, the designer by automating the design process. The few existing systems [Merrill, 1992; Spector, 1993] are certainly useful for small applications to structured domains, but they cannot solve yet the more global design problems involved in building comprehensive learning scenarios and systems.

- Some comprehensive support systems can help designers by providing forms, tables, or database elements for different design tasks. Most of them, except for a few experimental systems [Pirolli, 1990] , are based on traditional procedural design and do not embed any strategic ID knowledge.

The AGD project, starting at the end of 1992, aims to address these issues. A first version of the AGD support system has been completed by the end of 1994 and validated within 7 organizations throughout 1995. AGD is a performance support system for content expert involved in educational design. It puts a strong emphasis on strategic ID knowledge. This knowledge is embedded in an advisor system, while the conceptual (design objects to produce) and the procedural (how to produce them) ID knowledge is embedded in a comprehensive and integrated task support system.

The first section of this paper describe briefly the task support system (AGD) while the other sections concentrate on its companion advisor system. The second section presents the methodology we have developed to add an advisor to the AGD task support system. The third one gives an overview of some generic tools that were developed to ease the development of such an advisor. Finally, the last section discusses different aspects of the approach such as level of abstraction and the diversity of point of views, generality and productivity issues and finally future developments that will be needed.

1. Overview of the AGD task support system

We will first focus on conceptual and procedural ID knowledge, which forms the basis of AGD task support system.

1.1 Conceptual ID knowledge: components of a learning system

From a product's point a view, the goal of AGD is to build what we can call a *Learning system*. There are of course many ways to define such a concept. Because we have to build a computer support system, we try to be both comprehensive and parsimonious. Comprehensive so the concept of a Learning system can include all the essential elements; from problem definition, to a precise description of each of the subsystems the learner will use. Parsimonious in the sense that all components that cannot be related in any operational way to other essential components will have to be discarded.

After two years of discussion on these grounds, we have build the following concept of a Learning System, composed of three main components:

1. A definition of the learning situation: description of the context of learning and learning needs of target populations;

2. A structured knowledge model composed of different types of knowledge units and links between them, and a distribution of this model within a pedagogical structure possibly composed of a curriculum, courses, course modules and learning activities;

3. A design of the Learning System:
   - the description of each learning event or activity:
     — learning objectives based on the local knowledge model;
     — strategies, tactics, media and delivery mode for the learning event;

— learning scenarios, graphs of learning events for each target audience;

— didactic instruments and tools;

- definition of each didactic instrument: name, plan, type, media, component of the knowledge model covered;

- definition of both the didactic support system (how students are grouped and supported by trainers or training agents) and the technological support system.

Because we were in the process of building a computer support system, each of these concept had to be defined very precisely using an object-oriented methodology. These concept definitions gave us the structure of the storage module of AGD system, all the concepts components forming a large graph called « a project ». They also helped define the user interface. Finally, they were used to build a contextual on-line help system for the subject matter expert unfamiliar with ID terminology.

1.2 Procedural ID knowledge: tools of the task support system

The definition of the essential components of a learning system lead us to define the procedural ID knowledge needed to support a user in the design of each of these components. Globally, we have identified 156 sub-tasks to the global task « Building the Learning system »: 25 of them are sub-tasks of « Define the learning situation »; 24 of « Build and distribute the knowledge models » and 68 of « Design the learning system ». Other tasks (16) concern project management such as saving intermediate designs, printing reports or importing components from other projects. Still others (13) concern planning the development of the learning system.

Each higher level process or task in the hierarchy gives birth to design tools , while the lower level tasks and operations correspond to possible operations within these tools.

Figure 1 shows a first example of such a high level tool: the Knowledge Model Editor. In the model being constructed by a user, a procedure (oval shape) is broken down into five sub-procedures linked together by precedence (P) links. Two concepts are linked to the main procedure by IE links, representing the fact that they are input or output to the procedure. A "fact" is shown as an instance (I) link from a concept. A principle (diamond-shape) rules (R link) one of the procedures. In the lower right corner of the figure a tool bar allows for editing and linking the knowledge units. These knowledge units are objects that can be selected, moved, deleted, grouped and/or renamed.

Our validation results have shown that the knowledge model is a powerful tool, not only for structuring a knowledge domain, but also as a communication tool to collect data and validate it with a subject matter expert. Knowledge modeling offers the possibility to structure a knowledge domain without giving immediate attention to instructional processing. It also allows for quick verification of the consistency and completeness of the instructional content. The impacts of knowledge modeling on instructional design/engineering are two fold:

1) Knowledge types provide important clues for selecting the appropriate learning objectives level and for selecting adequate learning strategies and tactics. For example, to teach principles, one would often target high level learning objectives and select problem solving tactics.

2) Links between knowledge units prevent from fragmenting a coherent group of knowledge units into various learning activities. Links between knowledge units also have a direct impact on the development of learning scenarios, the most important component of a learning system.

The knowledge model is also central to the definition of learning needs. Figure 2 illustrates another tool in AGD where learning needs have been attached to some knowledge unit, defining the actual and the desired states of competency for the knowledge unit. In foreground of the model, a competency level scale and a ruler are provided to that effect.

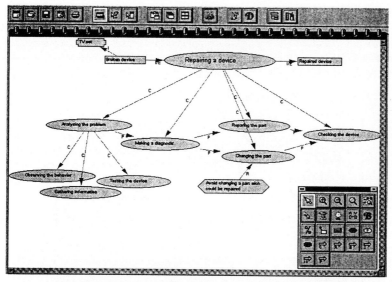

Figure 1 - View of the Knowledge Modeling Editor in AGD

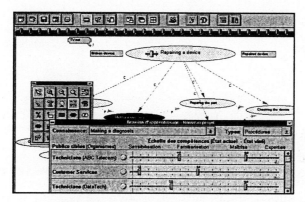

Figure 2 - Learning needs definition

The knowledge model is also central to define the pedagogical structure that can expand on four (4) levels of learning events: curriculum, course, learning unit or learning activity. Using another of AGD's tools, one can transfer a selected group of knowledge units from an existing model, by a simple drag&drop operation. These transferred units are automatically marked, thus allowing for quick verification of which units have been distributed and which have not.

Yet other tools have been implemented to define graphically learning scenarios using another graphical tool, as a network of learning events, didactic instruments and evaluation activities. In the network, learning components can be linked with optional or mandatory precedence links to form a suggested learning path. Didactic instruments are also iconized and linked to corresponding learning events by a link "is used by..." . They can be opened to proceed with the description of their main attributes.

2. From strategic ID knowledge to the definition of the advisor on AGD

We will now turn our attention to strategic ID knowledge, that is the control knowledge that helps a designer decide WHEN a task is completed to a reasonable degree and other tasks can be started or WHEN a task in progress should be left aside to revisit a task that has not been achieved with sufficient details.

2.1 The Tasks tree and the Advisors tree

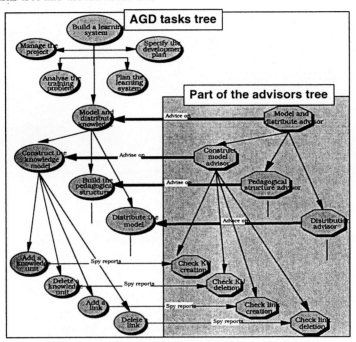

Figure 3 - Tasks tree and corespondent advisor agents

The left part of figure 3 presents the AGD tasks tree. The main task has been decomposed into subtasks such as "Model and distribute knowledge (into courses, modules and activities)". Then the "model and distribute" task is further decomposed and associated to the corresponding agents of the advisors tree. Finally, a third level task like "Construct the knowledge model" is decomposed into terminal tasks like create or delete a knowledge unit or a link. These correspond to direct user actions or set of actions with the AGD host system. One can notice that the Advisors tree has the same structure than the Tasks tree. This is the basis of the a methodology we are developing in this project and others [Paquette et al, 1994] to support the development of advisor components on an existing application.

Adding context for advising

We can define progress levels to add contextual information to each task that will enable the advisor to build a structured memory of the user's actions relative to the task. The following table shows an ordered list of such progress levels for the task "Construct the model". The second column gives the informal definition of each level; in the actual implementation of the advisor, this definition is formalized in SmallTalk code using the class methods in the application. The third column gives the general meaning of a set of associated advises. Each advice will be fired if the user is at or further then the corresponding progress level, but has not reached the following level.

"Construct the model"

Progress level	Definition	Associated advice
Not started	Default value at start	"Please start using the model editor....."
Model started	"Knowledge unit list in the user defined model is not empty "	"Try to complete an initial model containing at least 10 knowledge units" "Specify the learning needs for all client groups"
Initial model sufficient	"The model has at least 10 knowledge units for which the learning needs have been specified for all the client groups"	"The following knowledge units are not linked to the rest of model: (list) " "The model is not well balanced for this reason: (too many or too few facts, concepts, procedures or principles" "There is not enough knowledge units because you have too many (courses, modules or learning activities)......."
Model completed and well-balanced	Model contains enough knowledge units to "cover" each learning event already defined) & Model is well balanced between facts, concepts, procedures and principles according to the learning needs & All the knowledge units in the model are linked to others.	"This task is completed for now, you should turn to the development of the pedagogical structure and add some new learning events"
Mainly achieved	Always false value	

Table 1 - Progress levels and advice on the task "Construct the model"

Notice that the second and third progress levels refer to another task "specify learning needs" that is related to "construct the model". This is an example of a progression relationship between two different tasks. The present task with its level "initial model sufficient", should be preceded by the task "specify learning needs" at the progress level where it is "Mainly achieved", that is learning needs are specified for all the knowledge units.

Structure of an advisor agent

Each advisor agent on a task uses information from its user model. This memory component stores the progress level that the user has reached in the corresponding task, and also the values of useful variables compiled from the user's productions related to the task. Table 2 gives an example of the state of an advisor when a rule is ready to fire:

PROGRESS LEVEL IN THE TASK: « CONSTRUCT THE MODEL»
"Initial model completed" ² USER < "Model completed and well balanced"
USER PRODUCTIONS
USER has produced learning needs that are at the SENSIBILIZATION level
USER actual knowledge model contains: Facts = 10%; Concepts = 30%; Procedures 35%; Principles = 30%.
EXAMPLE FROM THE ADVISOR'S RULE BASE:
Advice name: "Model-05"

- *Advice*: "Increase the proportion of facts and concepts in your knowledge model by adding new facts or concepts or deleting some procedures or principles.
- *Additional explanation:* Usually, learning needs at the SENSIBILIZATION level entail mainly facts (more than 30%) or concepts (more than 40%)
- *Progress position:* between "initial model completed" and "model complete and well balanced"
- *Additional condition:* Maximum target for learning needs ² 2.5 and (Facts% < 30 or Concepts% < 40)

Table 2 - State of some components of an advisor

Mode abstract advisors

If we go a step higher in the hierarchy, the advices on the "model and distribute" task will be more abstract. As shown in table 3, the progress levels of this task are defined in terms of

"Model and distribute" task

Progress level	Definition	Associated advice
Not started	Default value at start	"Start building an initial model and create a first learning event"
Model-distribute ready to start	Model started & Create pedagogical structure started	"Start developing sub-events of the main learning event and distribute knowledge units in these events...."
Model-distribute started	Model started & Distribution started	"The knowledge model is inadequate for some of first-level sub-events ..."
Model-distribute completed on level 1	Model completed and well-balanced & Pedagogical structure completed on level 1 & Distribution completed on level 1	"Due to the number of knowledge units in your model, you should consider developing a second-level layer of sub-events"
Model-distribute adequate	Model completed and well-balanced & Pedagogical structure completed & Distribution complete	"You should proceed with the "state learning objectives" task"
Mainly achieved	Always false value	

Table 3 - Progress levels and advises on the "model and distribute" task in AGD

progress levels of its immediate subtasks, and advices are more focused on the general progress in the task.

3. Development tools for Advisors systems.

In this section, we will present a generic editor that was developed by our team and used to program the advisor for the AGD system. These tools support most of the steps in the method presented in the previous section. The main goal here is to facilitate the design of the advisor component without too much intervention from a programmer.

3.1 Task specification

First, the designer opens a task definition tool. Sub-tasks at any depth can be defined using the menus and the up and down buttons showing three levels of the tasks tree at any time. Tasks and sub-tasks can be added, deleted, modified or reordered. Buttons give access to other tools, mainly to define structure within the selected task or between it and other tasks.

3.2 Specifying progress levels within a task

For each task (and sub-tasks), the user can then define an ordered set of stability levels, each interval between subsequent progress levels representsing a natural phase within a task. The tool offers also two comment fields and a « condition » field, programmed as Smalltalk code, that provides a definition for that level.

3.3 Specification the advises associated to each task

Using progress levels in a task, the designer of the advisor can define a set of advises for this using the advice definition tool displayed in figure 4.

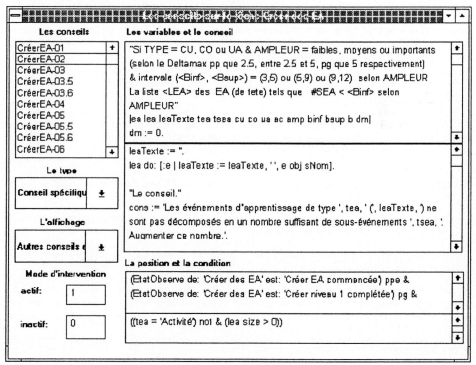

Figure 4 - Advice definition screen

The upper left sub-window lists the advises already defined on a certain task, while the lower left menus provide the possibility to define display parameters, such as the number of repetition of the advice or if more than one advice will be made available.

On the right, the first scrolling sub-window contains SmallTalk code to define any variable that will be used in the complementary condition of the selected advice. The second sub-window contains the code for an action to be displayed, here a text message, when the firing conditions will be met.

The third sub-window defines the interval between progress levels in which the advice is positioned, while the last contains Smalltalk code describing the supplementary condition.

4. Validation results and discussion

Section 2 and 3 have shown two main aspects of the advisor system that provide a lot of flexibility. First, the advisors being organized in a hierarchy isomorphic to the task tree, they can provide advice at different levels of abstraction. The lower advisors in the tree are only informed on the user actions related to a small terminal or near terminal task, so they can only give advice on such concrete tasks. On the contrary, advisors near the roots of the advisors tree have a broader view, being informed by all their descendants; they will be able to give more abstract and general advice, for example on the coherence of the user actions. At this level questions like « are the learning scenarios coherent with the types of knowledge in the domain model? » can be addressed.

Second, the Tasks tree serving as the backbone of the Advisor system is one of many possible point of view on the application. Not all of the 168 tasks in the AGD application need to be selected in the Tasks tree. Only the one critical to the intended users will be retained for Advice. This approach opens the way for multi-advisors system where more than one tasks tree is defined on the application, leading to many advisors that can cooperate in the assistance process. For example, an advisor could be called if the user is found to belong to a certain category, while another could be activated if he/she belongs to another category. Also, in AGD, an advisor can check the coherence of the user's actions, while another is sensible to the adequate use of the tools in the application. Even though this possibility has not been used in AGD, another application on the teaching of geometry has explored this possibility.

4.1 Positive validation results

The AGD system has been field tested since the beginning of 1995 to assess these potentialities. It has been used at Télé-université to design two university courses, and also in industry to design training in the following companies: DMR Group Inc., Éduplus (Tecsult), Teledac, Transit Resources, Bank of Montreal (Institute for Learning) and Sidoci.

A careful experimentation plan has provided us with lots of tracing and interview data. Many comments show promising results:

- One user says "I was able to use AGD with minimal guidance and training and generate an initial course plan and analysis in three days(...)".

- Another experimenter states that "AGD enabled the layout of the design framework in probably one-tenth the time our process usually requires and was also more thorough."

- One experimenter says "The system of linkages requires you to document each step, whereas a designer may keep the same thing in her/his head, believing it to be self-evident (...)" Other users have also strongly supported the use of knowledge modeling as a way to ensure coherence between the different components of the learning system.

4.2 Limitations

On the other hand, only a small number of ID strategic knowledge has been implemented in AGD, so the advisor does not yet provide support on all of the tasks where it would be useful.

Also, user's demands on the Advisor has been less important than expected. We attribute this result to the fact that we have not given enough attention to the way the advisor manifest itself in the interface. The display of advises in textual form is not very interesting while the user is generally coping with difficult design problems. Also, in this first version, the advisor is very discrete since it has to be called by the advisor to act. We find here similar result that are encountered with most contextual help systems, and we are looking forward for a more active advisor. Finally the fact that not all areas were covered by the first version of the advisor might have had a role on the motivation to use it.

Most Subject Matter Experts experimenting AGD have expressed satisfaction with the instructional knowledge they have gained while designing their learning events. Results of pre-tests and post-tests have also shown considerable progress in ID knowledge acquisition. This impact could be greatly enhanced as new strategic ID knowledge units are embedded in the Advisor System, and as the Advisor is made more present and easily accessed.

References

[Gery , 1991] Gery G. *Electronic Performance Support Systems,* Weingarten, Boston, 1991.

[Gustafson, 1993] Gustafson K.L. *Instructional Transaction Fundamentals: Clouds on the Horizon,* Educational Technology, February 1993, pp 27-32

[Merrill 1994] D. Merrill. Principles of Instructional Design. Educational Technology Publications, Englewood Cliffs, New Jersey, 465 pages.

[Merrill, 1992] Merrill M.D., Li Z., Jones M.K., *Instructional Transaction Shells: Responsibilities, Methods, and Parameters,* Educational Technology, February 1992, pp 5-26 [Minsky, 1975]

[Paquette,1994] G. Paquette, F. Crevier et C. Aubin *ID Knowledge in a Course Design Workbench.* Educational Technology, USA, volume 34, n. 9, pp. 50-57, November 1994

[Paquette, 1993] Paquette , G. *Un système de modélisation cognitive et métacognitive. pour l'ingénierie didacttique* Notes de recherches du LICEF, Novembre 1993.

[Paris, 1983] S. Paris, M.Y. Lipson, & K.K. Wixson. *Becoming a strategic reader.* Contemporary Educational Psychology, 8, 293-316

[Pirolli, 1990] Pirolli P., Russell D.M., *The Instructional Design Environment: Technology to support design problem solving.* Instructional Science 19, 1990, pp 121-144.

[Reigeluth, 1987] Reigeluth, C. *Instructional Theories in Action: Lessons Illustrating Selected Theories and Models.* Hillsdale, NJ: Lawrence Earlbaum.

[Romizowski, 1981] Romizowski, A.J. *Designing Instructional Systems.* Nichols Publ., NY: Kogan Page.

[Spector, 1993] Spector, M. Polson, M. Muraida, D. *Automating Instructional Design.* Educational Technology Publications, Englewood Cliffs, New Jerseay, 1993.

[Tennyson, 1988] Tennyson, R. *Linking cognitive learning theory to instructional prescriptions,* Instructional Science, vol. 17, 369-385.

[Winograd 1985] T. Winograd. *Beyond the declarative/procedural controversy,* in R. J. Brachman & H. J. Lévesque (Eds), Readings in Knowledge Representation. Morgan Kaufmann Publishers

A Knowledge–Based Framework for Learning, Applying and Consulting Engineering Procedures

Pablo Roberto de Buen–Rodríguez[1], Eduardo F. Morales[2] and Sunil Vadera[3]

[1] Instituto de Investigaciones Eléctricas, Cuernavaca, Morelos, 62420, México, Fax: +52 (73) 18–25–38, email: debuen@iie.org.mx
[2] ITESM - Campus Morelos, Cuernavaca, Morelos, 62050, México
[3] University of Salford, Salford, M5 4WT, United Kingdom

Abstract. A knowledge–based framework called LACEPRO where civil engineers are able to learn, consult and apply established procedures is presented. LACEPRO's knowledge base was designed to be used by three different knowledge operators: the Tutor, the Consultor, and the Expert. Each of these knowledge operators has its own mechanisms to perform their functions over the shared knowledge base. The core of the knowledge base is a set of networks which represent the steps of the engineering procedures. They function as a platform for: teaching procedures, automatic problem generation, diagnosis of user's misunderstandings, problem solving, consultation, and user's navigation through the domain knowledge.

1 Introduction

Many domains imply the use of procedures. For instances: (i) in mathematics there are procedures or methods to solve systems of equations, integrals and derivatives; (ii) in chemistry, there are procedures to obtain or separate substances; (iii) almost all industrial activities are based on procedures of different kinds; and (iv) many administrative tasks must follow a set of steps. Particularly, civil engineering is a domain in which procedures play an important role. In this domain, there are procedures for the design of each of the different elements of distinct materials (foundations of several types, columns, slabs, beams, pipes, etc.) that are found in all kinds of constructions. There are also methods to obtain the loads that a construction as a whole, and each of their structural elements, have to resist under different types of circumstances (e.g., every day loads, seismic loads, and wind loads).

This paper presents the architecture of LACEPRO, which is a novel multifunctional knowledge–based system that provides civil engineers a computer environment in which they can learn, consult, and apply engineering procedures. These three activities are conducted respectively by the following three knowledge operators: the Tutor, the Consultor, and the Expert. LACEPRO's knowledge base provides all the information that the knowledge operators require to perform their specific activities. It includes: (i) the general tasks that the specific area of the domain implies (e.g., conditions to be revised in a design), (ii) the procedures to perform those tasks, (iii) requirements for the use of these procedures, (iv) the factors (variables) and facts involved in the procedures, (v) information that procedures need to consult (e.g., tables and graphs), (vi) engineering fundamentals behind the procedures, (vii) models that describe constructions, their structural components and other concepts of the domain (e.g., material properties), (viii) tutoring knowledge, and (ix) knowledge about the user.

The paper is organised as follows. Section 2 describes the characteristics of LACEPRO's architecture. A summary of related work is given in Section 3. Finally, section 4 presents some final comments.

2 LACEPRO's Architecture

LACEPRO's architecture was designed to enable the user to perform the following three main activities:

- The first is to learn the procedures used to solve the problems of an engineering domain (e.g., those found in manuals and design codes), and the theoretical knowledge behind those procedures.
- The second is to consult specific information related with the procedures mentioned above. This consultation is done by navigating within the system's knowledge or using searching mechanisms to access the information related with specific domain topics.
- The third is to solve problems using the procedures.

The core of the architecture is a set of networks that represent all the procedures of the domain. These networks are organized around a hierarchy of knowledge *units* called IONs (Issues Of Knowledge). Each level of this hierarchy corresponds to an abstraction level of the domain. At the highest level of the hierarchy, an ION represents the view of a procedure from the highest abstraction level (see the example of Fig. 1). The steps of this procedure are represented by a network of IONs of a lower abstraction level. One or more of these new IONs can correspond as well to procedures involving networks of IONs. At the lowest level, an ION represents a single step of a procedure (e.g., the value assignment of a parameter, a simple or complex calculation, or the application of some rules). In this way, the system architecture enables the use of different abstraction levels during consultation and tutoring.

In addition, LACEPRO has a working memory with information of the domain objects (i.e., constructions, structural elements, materials, construction sites, etc.) required by the procedures. The results obtained by the procedures are also part of this working memory. Finally, there is a hypertex network that provides basic theoretical domain information only available for inspection.

The links among IONs indicate the order in which the steps are performed to obtain the procedure's results. For example, in Fig. 1 the links (represented by arrows) indicate that to obtain Vd, first, Fa, Ft and Vr have to be calculated.

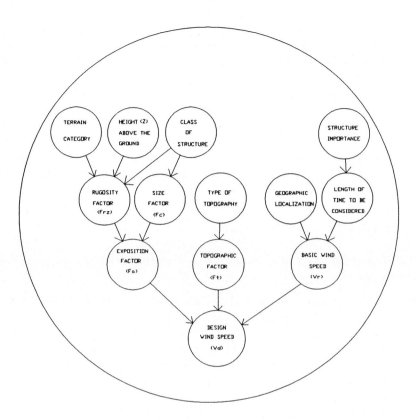

Fig. 1. Procedure for the determination of the design wind speed.

The links also denote the dependencies between the concepts participating in the procedures. For example, as shown in Fig. 1, the upper IONs of the network (i.e., terrain category, height above ground, class of structure, type of topography, geographic localization, and structure importance), define the value of the design wind speed since the values of all the other parameters in the network depend on them. However, if the values of Fa, Ft and Vr are known, the value of Vd is independent of the rest of the concepts. A similar notion is used in causal or Bayesian networks [1]. This feature is exploited during tutoring, problem and example generation, diagnosis of user's errors, and problem solving.

Engineering procedures, often involved similar steps. In LACEPRO, similar procedures can share a network of IONs.

Each of the three main LACEPROS's activities described above are carried on by the three knowledge operators: the Tutor, the Consultor, and the Expert. A top level user interface transfers the control to these operators (see Fig.2).

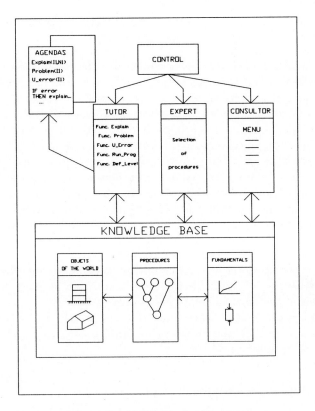

Fig. 2. LACEPRO's Architecture.

2.1 ION's structure

An ION has a frame like structure. Its components are divided into two groups. The first group is formed by those components that are used to identify the function of the ION, and by those components that are active when the ION is one that does not represent a procedure by itself. These components are the following:

- an identification name,
- a general description of the contents and functions of the ION,
- a list of keywords about the function of the ION,
- the material for tutoring and consultation,
- the material for the application of the procedure's step (provides the formulas, rules and/or functions required to solve examples and problems),
- the information for the generation examples and problems,
- a list of the input links (links to those IONs above the ION),
- a list of the output links (links to those IONs below the ION),
- a flag that indicates if the ION has been seen by the user and under which mode (consultation or tutoring) and level of knowledge (e.g., novice),

- an index indicating the user's mastery of the IONs' subject based on his or her performance during the solution of problems.

Information of the level (novice/intermediate/expert) and the user's evaluation on each ION that has been consulted/taught, is stored in a file for each user. This constitutes the user model which is loaded and updated on each session.

The material for tutoring and consultation includes the information for the explanation of the contents of the ION. It considers different presentation formats to take into account diverse user's knowledge level and requirements. This can involve one or more of the following: (i) theory about the topic, (ii) a detailed description of the corresponding procedure's step and factors involved, (iii) examples and/or simulations in which the user can experiment.

The second group of components of an ION are those that are active only when the ION represents a procedure. These are the following three:

- The first is a pointer to its network of IONs.
- The second are the criteria to define during tutoring: (i) the way the network will be perused (i.e., depth first, breadth first, etc.), (ii) how to generate problems, and (iii) how to locate user's errors.
- The third are the control statements that specify the loops (i.e., runs with different data through the network) required during the application of the procedure on specific problems.

2.2 The Commands Language

LACEPRO has a simple command language which has different operators to traverse the network in different ways (e.g., depth–first). In addition each knowledge operator has its own functions which can be called through the command language.

2.3 The Tutor

The Tutor is in charge of the tutoring activity. It defines the following concepts: (i) the topics to be taught, (ii) the user's knowledge level to be considered when explaining a topic, and (iii) the abstraction level of the explanations. After an evaluation of the user, based on the user model, it decides which of the three concepts listed above have to be changed in order to adapt the tutoring to the user's requirements. To perform its activities, the Tutor possesses the following functions:

- a function to explain the domain topics,
- a function for the generation of problems,
- a function for the localization of user's errors,
- a function to run specialized programs (i.e., to call simulations or didactic programs about the topic in question), and
- a function to define the user knowledge level from the user model.

All the information required by these functions is located within the ION networks.

The general functioning of the Tutor is defined within a set of agendas which contain all the steps the Tutor has to go through in order to teach the contents of the domain. These agendas are specified by the knowledge engineer utilizing the command language (see Fig. 2). The topics to be taught are defined using the names of the networks (i.e., the name of the corresponding high level IONs) that have to be followed when teaching a topic.

In general, a tutoring lesson consists of the following four main stages:

- The first is material presentation. In this stage, the tutor navigates through an ION network presenting the material contained in each ION. This includes the steps of the procedure and (if the user is a beginner) the conceptual knowledge behind it. If the subject allows it, graphical simulations complement this stage. In these simulations, the user can experiment with the values of those variables involved in the procedures and observe their influence. By default, the network is navigated following a depth first mechanisms from left to right. The navigation can be easily modified to another traversing strategy with different commands in the agenda, allowing great flexibility during tutoring.
- The second is to present one or more examples to the user. Using the automatic generator of examples, the Tutor generates the data of these problems and explains the steps followed to solve them. For instance, the problem and example generator could set the values of all the upper parameters of the network in Fig. 1 and explain how the value of Vd is obtained following the network from its upper IONs to the bottom or target IONs (Vd in this case). These examples can be generated by assigning values to the parameters of intermediate IONs (i.e., those located between upper IONs and lower IONs) as well.
- The third is the problem generation for the user's evaluation. As in the example generation, the problem generator produces the data of a problem. Afterwards, the user's solution to the problem is evaluated. These mechanisms help to ensure the user's correct understanding of the procedures.
- The fourth is the diagnosis and correction of the user's misunderstandings. If the user gives an incorrect answer, the system navigates through the knowledge network and traces the steps followed by the user, comparing them against those followed by the Expert. For example, if when obtaining Vd (see Fig. 1) the user defines a wrong value for Fc, the diagnosis mechanism would try to find this error. First it will look for an error in the IONs that are above Vd. As an error can be the result of other errors, the values of Fa, Ft and Vr will be compared against those obtained by the system. In this example, only the value of Fa will be found to be wrong, eliminating the two other branches from the analysis. The next step will consist of the inspection of Frz and Fc. It will be found that Fc is wrong. Afterwards, the value of the "class of structure" will be inspected. In this case it will have a correct value. Thus, the mistake will be located at Fc. Then, the Tutor will recommend a remedy (e.g., teach the subject again using other approach).

2.4 The Consultor

The Consultor is in charge of the consultation activities. It contains the following elements:

- a graphical interface that allows the user to: (i) navigate through the knowledge base (the ION's networks) consulting the topics (s)he wants, (ii) ask for an explanation about a specific topic, (iii) request examples showing the way to obtain a particular factor, and (iv) request problems to evaluate his or her understanding about a topic,
- a function that automatically generates tables of contents from the key words of the IONs,
- a function that generates plans for performing calculations about a specific topic following the corresponding ION network (the plans specify the data that must be collected and how the data should be combined to achieve the desired goal), and
- a function that suggests to the user the knowledge level to choose, and the abstraction level of the explanations, taking into account his or her performance during his/her solution of problems.

To perform its functions, the Consultor accesses the explanation materials located in the IONs.

2.5 The Expert

The Expert is in charge of the application of the procedures in the solution of problems. It selects the procedures that are used to solve the different problems that can be formulated by the user or the Tutor. To solve the problems, the Expert follows the corresponding ION network and uses the formulae and procedures included in the IONs.

It has two functioning modes. In the first, it only solves problems. In the second, it solves the problems and explains the steps of the solution. The Expert plays an important role during the user's evaluation and diagnosis (its results are compared against the user's answers).

3 Related Work

Networks have been used to represent: dependencies among concepts as in SCHOLAR [2]; relations between skills and tasks to exercise them as in BIP [3]; the evolutionary nature of knowledge as in WURSOR–III [4]; a curriculum as in MHO [5]; different levels of abstraction about concepts as in the Bite–Sized Tutor [6]; and relations among concepts, and among concepts and tools as in ICADT [7]. Procedures for solving problems have also been represented using networks. In BUGGY [8], for example, procedural networks were utilised to model skills and the buggy variants (or bugs) of these skills. However, these representations have not been used to explain the steps of procedures and the knowledge that supports them.

In many ITS current implementations, information is spread apart. ITS are usually conceived as semi–independent components (e.g., tutor, diagnoser, explainer), without sharing diverse pieces of closely related knowledge. More recently, Bonar et al.[6] used an object–oriented architecture where the information and all the components are viewed as generic classes. This allows sharing information and components. In LACEPRO, different knowledge operators use the same domain knowledge to perform various functions. LACEPRO is not restricted to teaching and, in principle, new knowledge operators (e.g., design) could be used over the same network of knowledge.

The multifunctionality of knowledge bases has been exploited from the perspective of retrieving information from a knowledge base considering different viewpoints [9]. Now a days, at the Systems Laboratory at Stanford University a group of researches led by Richard Fikes [10] is working in the development of knowledge–based technology for representing knowledge about engineering devices in a form that enables the knowledge to be used in multiple systems for multiple reasoning tasks. We are not aware that it will allow tutoring functions.

4   Final Comments

The proposed architecture has the following interesting and important features:

- It provides a way to represent, through a single structure, the knowledge and information required for tutoring, consulting and problem solving.
- Its functionality is given by the information in the IONs and the ways the network is navigated to perform the different tasks.
- The hierarchy of IONs, provides different levels of abstraction during tutoring and consulting.
- Through the use of different views of the knowledge network, it allows the use of the same network to represent several procedures.
- Its structure and modularity favours optimization, maintenance and documentation of the code. In case of modifications in the procedures, only the IONs and links involved have to be changed. Afterwards, the indexes of lessons, topics and concepts are automatically generated by retrieving the information from the knowledge networks.
- It provides a very detailed view of the user's state of knowledge. Each ION has an index of the user's knowledge about the IONs topic. Through these indexes, the Tutor can know what has been taught to the user, what (s)he has consulted, and what (s)he has not used properly during his or her evaluation. Based on this information and on its agenda, the Tutor defines what to do next.
- It provides great flexibility during tutoring and consulting. Each topic can be explained using a different approach. It allows both guided tutoring and user's free navigation and experimentation.

– From the practical point of view it has the following advantages:
  (a) The user can have access to both (i) the steps followed by the system to solve a problem and (ii) the knowledge that is behind those steps.
  (b) A flexible framework is also provided with the capacity to adapt to the user's specific requirements and knowledge level during their work with procedures. In this framework: (i) novice users can learn, experiment and be evaluated and corrected in their misunderstandings about a procedure, before they apply it in real problems; (ii) intermediate users can consult and experiment with those procedures with which they are not familiar, and; (iii) experienced users can apply the procedures to specific problems.

A prototype of the LACEPRO framework has been tested on the procedures recommended by a Wind Design Manual [11]. So far, we have obtained very encouraging results. Further tests will be carried out with another two different sources of engineering procedures.

References

1. Pearl, J.: Probabilistic Reasoning in Intelligent Systems: Networks of Plausible Inference. Morgan Kaufmann, San Mateo, CA (1988).
2. Carbonell, J.R.: AI in CAI: an artificial intelligence approach to computer-assisted instruction. IEEE Transactions of Man-Machine Systems **11(4)** (1970) 190–202.
3. Barr, A., Beard, M., Atkinson, R.C.: The computer as a tutorial laboratory: the Stanford BIP Project. International Journal of Man–Machine Studies **8** (1976) 567–596.
4. Goldstein, I.P.: The genetic graph: a representation for the evolution of procedural knowledge, in Proceedings of the Second Annual Conference of the Canadian Society for Computational Studies of Intelligence, Toronto, (1978) 100–106.
5. Lesgold, A.M., Bonar, J.G., Bowen, A.: An intelligent tutoring system for electronics troubleshooting: DC-circuit understanding. Technical Report. Learning Research and Development Center, University of Pittsburgh, Pennsylvania (1987).
6. Bonar, J.G., Cunningham R., Schultz, J: An object–oriented architecture for intelligent tutoring systems, in Proceedings of the ACM Conference on Object–oriented Programming systems, Languages and Applications, New York, USA (1986).
7. Scott, P., Ryu, J.: An Intelligent tutorial system for computer aided architectural design, in Proceedings of Artificial Intelligence in Design'91, Edinburgh, UK, Butterworth–Heinemann, (1991) 331-46.
8. Brown, J.S., Burton, R.R.: Diagnostic models for procedural bugs in basic mathematical skills, Cognitive Science **3** (1978) 155–191.
9. Acker, L., Porter, B.: Extracting viewpoints from knowledge bases. In Proceedings of AAAI–94 (1994).
10. Fikes R., Gruber T., Iwasaki Y., Levy A., Nayak, P.: How things work project overview, Knowledge Systems Laboratory Technical Report KSL-91-70, Computer science Department, Stanford University, USA, November (1991).
11. López, A., Vilar, I., Muñoz, C., Alanís, A., De Buen P.: Manual de diseño por viento, Comisión Federal de Electricidad, CFE-IIE, México (1993).

The HSIIP Approach.
An Extension for a Teacher's Apprentice

Jon A. Elorriaga and Isabel Fernández-Castro

University of the Basque Country - Dep. of Computer Languages and Systems
649 Postakutxa, E-20080 Donostia, Spain.
e-mail: jibelarj@si.ehu.es

Abstract. This paper presents a new approach for the development of self-improving Intelligent Tutoring Systems (ITSs) based on the Case-Based Reasoning technique. In addition, a knowledge acquisition system for pedagogical expertise is defined on the same basis. On the one hand, the proposal integrates a Case-Based Instructional Planner inside an existing ITS, provided it follows a planning approach, to enhance it with learning capabilities. Thus, the enhanced tutor couples the Case-Based Instructional Planner with a more conventional one in order to obtain a robust hybrid instructional planner. On the other hand, the knowledge acquisition system allows the teacher to create new instructional plans on his/her own, as well as supervise and modify the plans already generated and used by the tutor.

1 Introduction

The field of Intelligent Tutoring Systems (ITSs) uses techniques from Artificial Intelligence to provide effective instruction. Furthermore, some ITSs and educational programs profit from Machine Learning techniques in order to achieve two different goals [6]: to model the student knowledge and behaviour, and to build self-improving ITSs. Although it seems to be a promising area, only a few self-improving ITSs have been built and [10], [4], [12], [11] and [14] are some of them. Most of them were rule-based systems and the self-improving characteristic consisted of the alteration of the pedagogic decision rules. Indeed in the past, most of the ITSs were designed as rule-based expert systems, though it is really difficult to encode the pedagogical expertise by means of a set of rules. We propose a different approach for instructional planning based on the record and recovery of previous plans (cases). So, the first aspect of the research presented here is to build a self-improving ITS on the basis of the Case-Based Reasoning paradigm (CBR). The second aspect pointed out is based on the capability of the teacher to define its own instructional plans (lessons), provided the suitable, friendly and informative interface.

CBR technique has already been used in the tutoring field for different purposes [3] [5] [16], but none of them has profited from the learning capability of CBR to develop self-improving ITSs. We propose to apply this problem solving technique to build instructional plans for ITSs. A Case-Based Instructional Planner coupled with a more conventional rule-based one forms a robust hybrid instructional planner with self-improving capabilities [7]. Moreover, it has been proved empirically that the case-base representation schema fits the usual way that human teachers plan their lessons.

In this paper we introduce the main characteristics of the Hybrid Self-Improving Instructional Planner and present a new extension which addresses the task of acquiring the pedagogical expertise from the human instructor. Even in the ITS field, in which the tutor is able to adapt the instruction to the characteristics and needs of the particular students and can react (with limitations) to unforeseen situations, we feel that it should be supervised by the actual teacher in such a way that s/he can adapt by him/herself the instruction for certain students, (e.g. students with special needs). In order to overcome the lack of participation of teachers in intelligent computer-aided learning, we propose a knowledge acquisition system to be used by teachers for supervising and/or modifying the lessons that the ITS plans as well as for adding new lessons. Thus, a *Pedagogical Expertise Acquisition System* (PEAS) is integrated within the Case-Based Instructional Planner.

The rest of this paper is structured as follows. The next section presents the Hybrid Self-Improving Instructional Planner. Section 3 describes the extension of the planner with a Pedagogical Expertise Acquisition System. Finally, in section 4 the advantages of our approach and the perspectives for future work are pointed out.

2 The Hybrid Self-Improving Instructional Planner

Instructional planning is a complex task for ITSs. So far, ITS methods for planning require an explicit expert model on instructional planning. Generally, they have been implemented as production systems and are difficult to build and maintain. Therefore, a self-improving planner is an interesting choice to overcome these difficulties. Moreover, it is also suitable to incorporate the ability of learning from the experience into ITSs that already exist. The Hybrid Self-Improving Instructional Planner (HSIIP) applies Case-Based Reasoning to enhance the process of generation of instructional plans in ITSs by adding a self-improving capability. This is accomplished by integrating a Case-Based Instructional Planner into the corresponding module of the ITS. Next we present a brief description of the case-based reasoning paradigm, the application of this approach to the instructional planning and finally the HSIIP.

2.1 Case-Based Reasoning

Case-based reasoning (CBR) [1] [19] [15] is a relatively recent problem solving and learning paradigm that seems to alleviate some of the problems of knowledge-based systems (i.e. knowledge elicitation, implementation of expertise in production systems, maintenance, and difficulties in handling large volume of data). The basic idea underlying case-based problem solving is to solve new problems by adapting solutions that were used to solve previous problems. Furthermore, learning is inherent to the case-based problem solving process as it is directly performed by storing the solved problems in new cases. A *case* is the representation of a previous experience; it is composed of three elements: the description of the problem, the applied solving method and its outcome. The set of cases is stored in the case memory (CM).

The basic CBR cycle is performed in four phases. First, the current problem is analysed and the relevant features of the situation are used to search the CM through the indices in order to find a set of similar cases (*Retrieve*). Once the case is chosen the case-based reasoner must adapt it to fit the characteristics of the current situation (*Reuse*).The adapted solving method is then applied to the problem. After applying the recovered method, the next CBR phase consists of revising the outcome in order to check whether the proposed solving method really solves the problem or not (*Revise*). If the outcome is not valid the failure is explained and the solution is repaired. Finally, the current problem, the proposed solving method and the results are stored in the CM and the indices updated (*Retain*). If the outcome was correct the new case will help in future problem solving activity. Otherwise, the failure and its remedy are stored in order to avoid similar failures.

2.2 Case-Based Instructional Planner

The Case-Based Instructional Planner (CBIP) distributes its functions into two active modules: the Generation Component is responsible for performing the plan generation phases, and the Learning Component is responsible for analysing the results of the plan and for inserting the plan into the Case Memory. The last component of the CBIP is the structure that stores the cases: the Case Memory, it is based on Schank's *dynamic memory model* [17]. A case defines a previous instructional plan and contains the context in which it was applied, the instructional plan itself (or a part of it if the plan is layered) and the results that it achieved.

Instructional Objectives	Didactic Strategies	Operative Strategies
Knowledge (Sum-rule)		
		Summarise last session
		Present lesson's topics (KN (Sum-rule), AP (Sum-rule))
	Introduce (Sum-rule)	
	Explain (Sum-rule)	
Application (Sum-rule)		
	Example (Sum-rule)	
	Exercise (Sum-rule)	
		Summarise session

Fig. 1. Example of instructional plan for the symbolic differentiation based on [7].

Instructional plans are complex objects with different structures. For instance figure 1 shows an instructional plan, applied to the domain of symbolic differentiation, that is organised in three levels: instructional objectives (i.e. *cognitive skills that the tutor wants the student to achieve along the training session*), didactic strategies (i.e. *teaching activities that the tutor programs for the session)* and operative strategies (i.e. *link activities between Didactic Strategies for guiding and motivating the trainee during the accomplishment of an Instructional Objective).*

Figure 2 shows the case pattern at the level of instructional objectives. The application context contains: a set of condition elements related to the student features, basically the level of acquisition of the skills (KN: knowledge and AP: application) of each concept (C_i), session features and domain features.

```
Application     Context
Student Related Features
    Learning Characteristics:
          Type = (OR Weak, Average, Good)
          Speed of learning = (OR Low, Medium, High)
    Knowledge:  ∀ j, j = 1,..., n
          Level [KN (Cj)] = (OR Low, Medium, Required, null)
          Level [AP (Cj)] = (OR Low, Medium, Required, null)
Session Related Features
    Duration = n minutes
    Type = (OR Free, Guided)
Domain Related Features
    Difficulty [KN (Ci)] = (OR Low, Medium, High)
    Difficulty [AP (Ci)] = (OR Low, Medium, High)
    Type (Ci) = (OR Declarative, Procedural)
Plan
    (KN (Ci), AP (Ci))
Results  of  the  application
    Level [KN (Ci)]
    Level [AP (Ci)]
```

Fig. 2. Case pattern at the level of Instructional Objectives.

The CBIP results from an adaptation of the general CBR mechanism (see figure 3) to fit the special characteristics of the instructional planning task, and more concretely the structure of the instructional plan of the ITS. Some of the current ITSs used to be guided by a complex instructional plan organised in several levels [9] [2]. Taking this characteristic into account the case-based generation process is divided into a number of stages, and each of them builds a level of the instructional plan. These stages are performed in cascade by the Generation Component, in such a way that each stage uses information obtained in previous stages. Each stage is carried out by performing the same CBR phases: *retrieval* of old cases from the case memory and *adaptation* to the current situation. Once the instructional plan is completed, it is applied to develop an instructional session whose results (changes in the Student Model) are *revised* by the Learning Component to check whether the student achieved the expected instructional objectives and whether the didactic actions were successful. Finally, the Learning Component creates a new case to be *retained* in the case memory. Thus, the Case-Based Instructional Planning process is distributed among the Generation and the Learning components: the former builds the plan (retrieve and reuse) and the later evaluates and stores it (revise and retain).

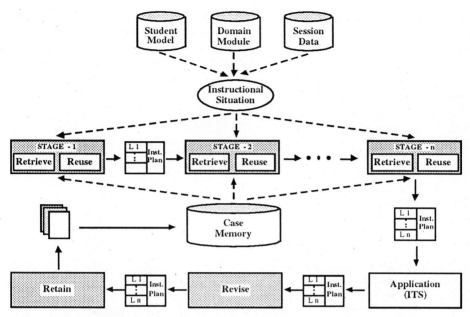

Fig. 3. CBR cycle adapted to a generic Instructional Planning task.

2.3 The Hybrid Approach

The hybrid approach for enhancing ITSs with learning abilities consists of the integration of the CBIP into an existing ITS. It is assumed an ITS with the classical architecture: Tutor Module, Domain Module, Student Model and Interface. Concretely, the CBIP is included into the Tutor Module which initially is composed of a *Didactic Instructor* and a *Didactic Dispatcher* (the former plans the teaching session and the later executes it). This basic structure is extended with the components of the CBIP which are introduced taking into account their functionality as it is shown in figure 4.

An ITS extended with the CBIP works as follows. The Didactic Instructor plans the session supported by both the Classical Instructional Planner (CIP) and the Generation Component, besides it is responsible for deciding which plan of those proposed by both planners will be developed. The Didactic Dispatcher carries out the session, so that it refines the plan until basic actions and executes them. The Learning Component monitors the development of the session and evaluates and stores the new cases into the case memory. So, this module treats plans built both by the Generation Component of CBIP and the CIP.

Initially the case memory of the CBIP is empty, so planning is performed by the CIP of the ITS (e.g. a dynamic opportunistic planner). In this first stage (training phase), the Learning Component monitors the input and output of the CIP and creates new cases representing each new instructional session. When the case memory contains enough cases for the CBIP to work, it will reuse them to generate the instructional plan. However, if the CBIP fails in building an appropriate plan, the ITS can use the plan proposed by the CIP (co-operation phase). Combining both planners we get a sound system that is able to learn from its experience and overcomes the eventual lacks in the case memory.

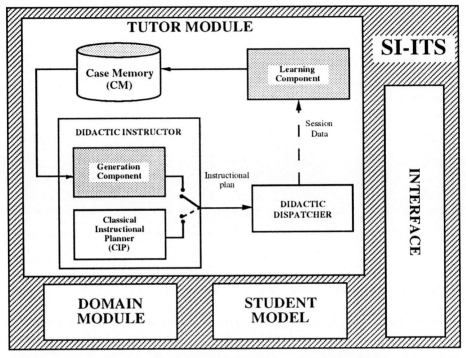

Fig. 4. Architecture of an ITS enhanced with the CBIP.

During the development of a session the original Tutor monitors the performance of the student in order both to update the Student Model and to check if the plan is still appropriate. The tutor uses certain didactic actions (e.g. *to propose an exercise, to propose a test* , and so forth) to get feedback from the student in order to infer changes in the Student Model. Moreover, the information gathered during the session about the student's performance and the inferred level of acquisition of the instructional objectives are used to evaluate the suitability of the plan. At this point, the need to dynamically modify the instructional plan (re-planning) is clear. If the tutor decides that the current plan is not valid for the rest of the session (e.g. when the student makes a serious error while performing an exercise) then the instructional planner must consider the current situation and modify the plan in order to take into account the new conditions. These conditions are treated by means of local instructional plans also generated following the same hybrid instructional planning approach.

At the moment, we have designed and implemented a prototype of the kernel of the CBIP that must be adapted to the particular characteristics of each ITS in order to integrate learning capabilities by means of this hybrid approach.

The method for carrying out the integration of the CBIP into the ITS is performed in three steps. First we must analyse the original ITS in order to extract information about the structure and items composing the instructional plan, the features taken into account in the Student Model (e.g.: knowledge of the learner, preferences, etc.) and also other objects used to represent the instructional context, such as duration of the lesson or type of the lesson. In the second step the CBIP kernel must be adapted to the characteristics obtained in the previous phase. The information about the structure of the instructional plan will determine the number of stages of the cycle of plan generation while the knowledge that the ITS is able to extract from the interaction with the student will be used as the condition elements to describe the instructional context attached to the cases. The last phase consist of connecting both planners in the Didactic Instructor.

This approach is applicable for the particular class of ITSs that separates the pedagogical decision from the session dispatching (e.g. [8] [18] [13] [12]). HSIIP can be applied to a large number of instructional planners, but how it is applied depends on the particular characteristics of each ITS concerning its instructional plan. Depending on the complexity of the plan the building process is split into a number of sequential stages. Concretely [7] shows an application of this idea to the INTZA system [9], an ITS for training. The didactic component of this ITS generates a three-layered instructional plan, thus the planning activity is performed in cascade trough three stages.

3 Pedagogical Expertise Acquisition System

The HSIIP presented above is general enough to be integrated into any ITSs which follows a planning approach. In this section we propose to amplify the enhanced planner with a knowledge acquisition system. This will serve the human instructor to transfer instructional planning knowledge to the HSIIP and also to supervise and modify the contents of the CM in order to check the plans and their results.

Most of the shells and environments for automatic generation of ITSs include a knowledge acquisition module for gathering the domain knowledge, while few of them are also able to acquire the pedagogical expertise. These last systems elicitate the pedagogical decision rules that the human teacher uses for planning the lessons. As the teachers must specify the rules in a quite direct way, a great effort in creating the production system is required, even more if they are not used to program. Some of these shells provide a menu-driven interface that facilitates the knowledge transfer but it is not easy enough. So, if a successful knowledge acquisition system is desired it is important to make the knowledge transfer work more understandable for the user. We claim that a case-based system provides an environment for pedagogical knowledge representation closer to that the human teachers have because such systems are more intuitive and resemble the human way of planning the lessons. In fact, common patterns can be easily inferred from real teaching protocols.

Since using cases is a good way of representing the instructional planning knowledge and can provide an easier tool for the teachers, we propose an extension of HSIIP in order to acquire the instructional planning knowledge directly from the teacher. The new system, Pedagogical Expertise Acquisition System (PEAS) facilitates the supervision of the planning behaviour and also the acquisition of pedagogical expertise .

The schema and objects needed for the interaction between PEAS and the teacher is mainly determined by the structure of both the instructional plan and the case which represents it. Therefore, PEAS should provide the teacher with an interface that facilitates the management of all of the resources of the instructional planner, meanwhile the system should infer all the information it can in order to alleviate the teacher's work. In order to help the teacher, the PEAS translates the instructional plan from the internal representation that manages the ITS to a more comprehensible *instructional lesson*. This structure contains the activities to perform during the session. Next we will describe briefly the underlying structure of the instructional planner.

The new knowledge acquisition system is composed of two main modules: the *Teacher's Interface* and the *Converter*. The *Teacher's Interface* facilitates the design of instructional lessons using the Case Memory and the resource libraries of the tutoring system (i.e. libraries of instructional strategies). The acquisition system provides a menu-driven interface that is used to create and/or modify the lessons. The PEAS carries out a knowledge elicitation process in which the tool requests to the teacher the structure of the lessons that s/he prepares for a particular domain and the conditions under which that lesson should be applied (these conditions are a fixed set related to the application context of the cases of HSIIP). This process is assisted by a set of support libraries which identify the possible choices.

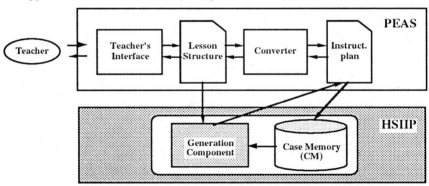

Fig. 5. Structure of PEAS and data flow.

The PEAS contains also a *Converter* that translates the instructional lesson specified by the teacher to a complete instructional plan by performing inferences when it is necessary. Therefore, the teacher does not specify all the contents of the instructional plan, but PEAS does infer as much knowledge as possible from the input data in order to obtain a complete instructional plan.

Besides, the process of creating lessons is aided by the CBIP: when the teacher specifies the application conditions of the lesson plan, the CBIP searches the case memory using this information as indices in order to generate automatically and offer the teacher a candidate plan; this plan is translated in a reverse direction to generate an instructional lesson. This offered lesson can be modified in a part or in a whole. The teacher can remove items from the offered lesson and add other items selected from the support libraries in order to generate the final instructional lesson. Once the teacher finishes the design of the lesson, PEAS translates it to an instructional plan and generates a new case representing it. Next, the case is integrated into the Case Memory.

Figure 5 shows the data flow of the enhanced HSIIP, the Case Memory is the source of cases of the Generation Component and is fostered by both planners with the cases revised by the Learning Component and directly with the cases that the teachers defines using the PEAS.

4 Conclusions

In this paper we have described the Hybrid Self-Improving Instructional Planner (HSIIP) and a new extension of this approach: a Pedagogical Expertise Acquisition System (PEAS). The HSIIP is a new approach to enhance ITS with learning abilities. PEAS is used by teachers for supervising and/or modifying the lessons that an ITS extended with HSIIP plans as well as for adding new lessons. This tool will increment the participation of the teachers in the Intelligent Tutoring Systems and will also enhance the adaptation ability of the tutoring system by acquiring lessons from the teacher for students with special needs.

Human teachers are used to formulating the instruction into lessons This way of organising instruction fits very well with a case-based instructional planner. Therefore, such a system can provide a suitable mean to acquire the instructional planning expertise of a teacher. This system requires from the teacher the application context of the lesson and its structure and infers the instructional plan.

The use of Case-Based Reasoning in the ITS field can solve some of the problems of developing such complex knowledge-based systems. The Case-Based Instructional Planner (CBIP) does not require an explicit model of tutoring, as the knowledge elicitation becomes a task of gathering cases. The implementation of the CBIP is reduced to identifying significant features that describe the instructional sessions. Finally, as the CBIP is able to learn, the maintenance of the system is an easy task.

The behaviour of this hybrid instructional planner is sound because it is supported by two planners (CBIP and a 'classical' planner) and also supervised by the teacher. So, when the CBIP is not able to generate a suitable plan, the tutor can use the original planner, furthermore the teacher can supervise and add new lessons to the planner. Therefore, the proposed self-improving tutor module performs three kinds of learning: the CBIP learns by observing the behaviour of the traditional planner, it also learns from its own experience, and finally it learns by memorising the teacher's lessons.

At the moment the first prototype of the kernel of the CBIP is implemented, and it has been used in an ITS on the domain of the symbolic differentiation. We are currently working on this prototype and the PEAS.

References

1. Aamodt, A. & Plaza, E.: Case-Based Reasoning: Foundational Issues, Methodological Variations, and System Approaches. AI Communications **7** (1994) 39-59
2. Arruarte, A., Fernández-Castro, I., Ferrero, B.: A requirement-based proposal for a general ITS shell. Proc. Int. Conf. on Computers in Education ICCE'95 Singapore (1995) 348-355
3. Coulman, R.: Combining Case-Based Reasoning and Granularity for Educational Diagnosis in an Intelligent Tutoring System. Research report 91-9, ARIES laboratory, Department of Computational Science, University of Saskatchewan, Canada (1991)
4. Dillenbourg, P.: Designing a self-improving tutor: PROTO-TEG. Instructional Science **18** (1989) 193-216
5. Du, Z. & McCalla, G.I.: A Case-Based Mathematics Instructional Planner. Proc. of the Int. Conference on the Learning Sciences, Northwest Univ. (1991) 122-129
6. Elorriaga, J.A., Fernández-Castro, I. & Gutiérrez, J.: Sistemas Tutores Inteligentes y Aprendizaje Artificial. Technical Report UPV/EHU/LSI/TR-295 (1995)
7. Elorriaga, J.A., Fernández-Castro, I. & Gutiérrez, J.: Case-Based Reasoning for Self-Improving Intelligent Tutoring Systems. Proc. Int. Conf. on Computers in Education (ICCE'95) Singapore (1995) 259-266
8. Fernández-Castro, I., Díaz de Ilarraza, A., Verdejo, F.: Architectural and Planning Issues in Intelligent Tutoring Systems. Jl. of Artificial Intelligence in Education **4** (1993) 357-395
9. Gutiérrez, J.: INTZA: un Sistema Tutor Inteligente para Entrenamiento en Entornos Industriales. PhD Thesis. Facultad de Informática, EHU-UPV, Donostia (1994)
10. Gutstein, E.: Using Expert Tutor Knowledge to Design a Self-Improving Intelligent Tutoring System. Intelligent Tutoring Systems, 2nd Int. Conference ITS'92, Frasson, C., Gauthier C., McCalla, G.I. (Eds.), LNCS Springer-Verlag (1992) 625-632
11. Kimball, R.: A self improving tutor for symbolic integration. Intelligent Tutoring Systems, Sleeman, D., Brown, J.S. (Eds.), Academic Press. (1982) 283-307
12. MacMillan, S.A. & Sleeman, D.H.: An architecture for a self-improving instructional planner for intelligent tutoring systems. Computational Intelligence **3** (1987) 17-27
13. Murray, W.R.: A Blackboard-Based Dynamic Instructional Planner. Research Report R-6376, Artificial Intelligence Centre, FMC Corporation, Santa Clara. USA. (1990)
14. O'Shea, T.: A self improving quadratic tutor. Intelligent Tutoring Systems, D. Sleeman & J.S. Brown (Eds.), Academic Press, (1982) 309-336
15. Riesbeck, C.K. & Schank, R.C.: Inside Case-Based Reasoning. Hillsdale, NJ: Lawrence Erlbaum Associates. (1989)
16. Riesbeck, C.K. & Schank, R.C.. From Training to Teaching: Techniques for Case-Based ITS. Intelligent Tutoring Systems: Evolutions in Design, Burns, H., Parlett, J.W. & Redfield, C.L. (Eds.), Lawrence Erlbaum Associates Pub. (1991) 177-193
17. Schank, R.C.: Dynamic Memory: a Theory of Reminding and Learning in Computers and People. Cambridge University Press. (1982)
18. Wasson, B.: Determining the Focus of Instruction: Content Planning on ITSs. PhD Thesis. University of Saskatchewan. Canada. (1990).
19. Watson, I. & Marir, F.: Case-Based Reasoning: A Review. The Knowledge Engineering Review **9** (1994) 327-354

Acknowledgements: This work is partly supported by the Department of Education, Universities and Research of the Basque Country Government (Eusko Jaurlaritza) and the University of the Basque Country. The authors also want to thank all the members of the GTI research group of the Computer Science Faculty at the University of the Basque Country.

The Program Tutoring Text Model

Hiroyuki OHNUMA and Toyohide WATANABE

Department of Information Engineering,
Graduate School of Engineering, Nagoya University
Furo-cho, Chikusa-ku, Nagoya 464-01, JAPAN

Abstract. This paper describes a program tutoring text model which is an improved version of multi-layers network authoring-text model. Our model focuses on a flexible ability to analyze various kinds of algorithms or different program descriptions, which are coded by students in accordance with a given exercise, and a systematic ability to reuse the existing exercises compositively, using the prepared solutions when a given exercise can be partly solved. To achieve these objectives, we introduce a relationship ISA-link between the learning items when one learning item can be produced successively from another. And, we use a relationship REF-link with a view to representing that one procedure item is composed of other exercise items collectively. Also, we refer to how the diagnosis strategies are constructed by means of relationships ISA-link and REF-link according to students' errors.

1   Introduction

The domain knowledge is one of important knowledge resources in ITS (Intelligent Tutoring System)[1][2] and its systematic structure has not been investigated fully. The authoring-text model based on multi-layers network has already been proposed to make it clear that the domain knowledge does not only include the professional knowledge resources, but also can be organized together with the instruction knowledge systematically [3][4]. The authoring-text model supports a systematic construction/management facility of domain knowledge and also provides a reconstruction facility of the existing domain knowledge so as to be apt to the tutoring/learning processes of individual students. In the multi-layers network authoring-text model the learning unit in the upper layer is composed of several learning units in the lower layers. The learning units in the bottom layer are distinct learning items which are classified into the explanation item, example item, exercise item and so on in order to make the tutoring process effective, and also several kinds of links such as necessary knowledge link (N-link), similar knowledge link (S-link) and so on, are introduced to indicate the connective relationships among these different learning items.

However, this model is not successful to manage the domain knowledge about program algorithms concretely though the concepts of programs and programmings are handled successfully. It is necessary to manage the practical programs directly when we deal with the technical problems of programmings, composition problems of program or diagnosis problems of program errors. In this paper, we focus on the composition problem of programs to be adaptable to various program descriptions from a viewpoint of program diagnosis.

2 Framework

We must pay attentions to the representation issue of domain knowledge:

1. to support the diagnosis process of students' programs;
2. to analyze various kinds of algorithms or different program descriptions, which are coded by students;
3. to reuse the existing domain knowledge systematically when a given exercise is definitely composed of the existing exercises as partial knowledge.

Thus, we propose a program tutoring text model for supporting the diagnosis process of students' programs as an improved version of the multi-layers network authoring-text model. When we intend to develop a tutoring system for the instruction of programming, we must, first of all, investigate a successful text model to be applicable to various program descriptions.

In this model, the procedure item introduced newly as one of learning items is an extensive version of exercise item so that one of practically applied algorithms or coded programs could be specified directly. In Fig.1 the procedure item can deal with algorithms or programs directly. Here, ISA-link indicates that the lower item is derived from the upper item and that the lower item can inherit its own properties from the upper item, like the class hierarchy mechanism in the traditional object-oriented paradigm. Additionally, we introduce another link to point out the composite relationship between procedure (or exercise) items. In many cases, a program may be composed of interrelated/independent subprograms with the module structure. REF-link indicates that the relationship of aggregation among 2 or more procedure (or exercise) items can be derived: one item is a compound item; and another is a part item. We show an example of REF-link in Fig.1. In Fig.1, we observe that the procedure item "Selection sorting" is composed partly by making up the exercise item "Minimum" as one subprogram.

3 Declarative Description of Program

In case of program tutoring systems, it is very difficult to prepare the domain knowledge (e.g. programs themselves) so as to be independent of the diagnosis strategies or interpretation mechanisms. Practically, the researches about program tutors always focused on the procedure-like module organization in addition to the tutoring scopes of grammatical knowledge or diagnosis ranges of predefined knowledge.

In our model, the procedure item, introduced newly as an improved version of exercise item, makes it possible to specify such programs directly. The procedure item is composed of four different slots: problem, I/O-type, classification and program slots. The values in the problem slot and I/O-type slot are inherited from the corresponding exercise item, while the values in the classification

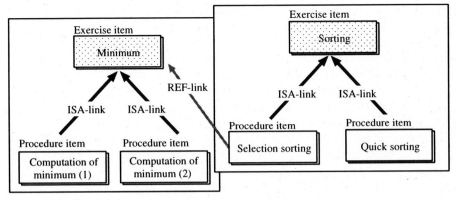

Fig. 1. ISA-link and REF-link on program tutoring text model

slot and program slot are self-defined. This program description in the program slot is translated automatically from the LISP program of selection sorting. The correspondence between program description in the procedure item and LISP source program is interpretatively illustrated in Fig.2. As shown in Fig.2 the translation is very easily done on the basis of LISP functions. So, the program description in the procedure item is composed of the sequence of primitive operations. The basic operation form in the program description is as follows:

```
(Seq-No Block-No (Operation Argument-1) Argument-2)
```

Seq-No indicates the sequence number of each element: the initial value is "0". *Block-No* is the level of each program block. The program block is defined according to the control structure of program, like the concept of block division applied by the traditional compiling techniques. *Operation* is a function and returns the evaluation result to *Argument-2* by applying to *Argument-1*.

Operation is divided into six classes.

```
Case-1 (set parameter)
Case-2 (branch condition block-1 block-2)
Case-3 (repeat condition block)
Case-4 (return parameter)
Case-5 (call exercise-item parameter-list)
Case-6 (apply operator parameter-list)
```

The case-1 indicates an assignment statement. The case-2 represents a conditional branch: "block-1" is evaluated when "condition" is TRUE; otherwise, "block-2" is done. The case-3 corresponds to the traditional do-while statement: "block" is repeatedly evaluated while "condition" is TRUE. The case-4 represents a return value of the block which the program description belongs to. The case-5 indicates to call the subprogram, pointed out by the exercise item: this is connected to the exercise item by REF-link. If the exercise item is "self", this represents the recursive call. The case-6 points out to apply the functional

LISP operations, such as list processing function or predicate function, to the parameter list.

In the program slot of Fig.2, in Step 0 the first argument is substituted for data1, and in Step 1 the conditional branch structure is represented: namely, if data1 is NIL, block1 is evaluated; otherwise, block2 is done. Step 2 represents to return the value NIL in the block1 and Step 3 indicates to compute the minimal element of data1, substitute the return value for data2 and assign it to data3. Step 4 represents to remove data2 from data1. Step 5 shows that the return value of recursive call is substituted for data4. Step 6 indicates to return the list whose car part is data1 and whose cdr part is data4, and assign it to data5. In Step 6 the operator "make-list" is an operator to return the list which is composed of elements indicated by the parameter list. Finally, Step 7 represents to return data5. In the algorithm of selection sorting, Step 1 and Step 5 represent the recursive stop condition and the recursive call, respectively.

In Fig.3, we show the correspondence among individual learning items/units, related to the exercise item "Sorting". Also, the program description is abstractly specified in Fig.3. ISA-links, REF-links and N-links are derived among several learning items.

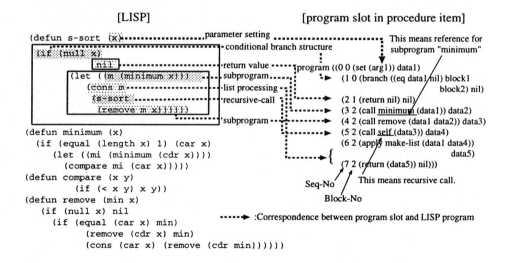

Fig. 2. Correspondence between program slot and LISP program

4 Relationships in Program Description

4.1 ISA-link

The procedure item introduced to represent program descriptions directly is derived from the existing exercise item. ISA-link indicates that a procedure item is derived from the exercise item and includes the program description

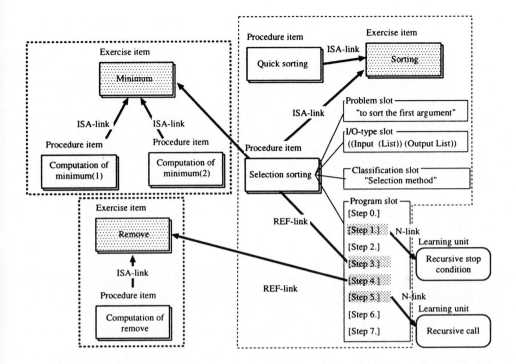

Fig. 3. Relationships among individual items

related to the content of the corresponding exercise item. Namely, ISA-link supports the concepts of generalization and specialization in the traditional object-oriented paradigm. Thus, the procedure item inherits the properties from the corresponded exercise item.

Also, ISA-link is applied to the explanation items. In this case, ISA-link is available between two different explanation items: program-dependent knowledge and program-independent knowledge. The program-independent explanation item is located as a parent through ISA-link and the program-dependent explanation item is specified as a child.

4.2　REF-link

REF-link in the procedure item indicates to refer to another exercise item. For example, when we consider the program of selection sorting, the processes to compute the minimum number and remove some number from a number set are always included in the program body. Since these processes may be predefined as a self-contained program or described as another independent program, it is better and effective to compose the program of selection sorting by aggregating these other programs as composite elements. Fig.3 shows such a relationship between procedure item and exercise item by REF-link. Step 3 in the program slot of the procedure item "Selection sorting" connects to the exercise item "Minimum" by REF-link. Similarly, Step 4 does to "Remove". This reference mechanism is a kind of abstraction in the object-oriented paradigm. In Step 3, this task is to compare the minimum number from "data1" but the computation way is not important for the sorting problem. When the minimum computation ways are different user by user, if REF-link is not supported as our framework then this program slot cannot define the program steps smartly: its structure must be complex. The separation of program parts which may generate various program descriptions from the critical program sequence does not only make the representation of program structure simple but also makes the composition process of professional domain knowledge easy.

5 Diagnosis Strategy

Our diagnosis process as the off-line processing is begun after students have finished to code the answer programs. The diagnosis process is executed according to the following steps approximately: First, check the student program syntactically by the grammatical knowledge; Second, transform the student program into the corresponding program form with a view to reducing the variation of program descriptions; Third,compare the transformed student program with the teacher program and identify the erroneous description.

In this section, we address the logical program diagnosis. Namely, we assume that the student program is correct in point of the program syntax.

5.1 Program Diagnosis

The basic processing in the program diagnosis is to compare the student program, translated from the original LISP program to the corresponding primitive sequence, with the teacher program, stored into the program slot of procedure item in advance, and then to judge whether the correspondence between them can be distinguished or not without depending on the variation of program descriptions. In case of comparing the student program with the predefined teacher program, the algorithm adapted in the student program may be not always consistent to the instruction of exercise. It is often that students code the exercise program, using their own well-known algorithms/methods. In this case, our text model is adaptable.

The diagnosis process is as follows:

Step 1. Set their sequence indicators to individual primitives between teacher program description in the program slot of procedure item and the primitive sequence of transformed student program;

Step 2. Compare these primitives indicated individually;

Step 3. If they are consistent, set the indicators to the next ones, respectively; Otherwise, goto Step 6.

Step 4. If the term pointed respectively out by each indicator is not the primitive, and if their individually indicated terms are not the primitive at once, then check up whether the student program is analytically described by using the corresponding algorithms represented in the procedure items when the exercise item as a parent contains several procedure items as children.

If the corresponded primitives satisfy at least one of the following conditions, the student program is described by using the appropriate algorithm represented in the procedure item:

Condition 1 All the primitives on the program slot as a subprogram are corresponded to the primitives of transformed student program;

Condition 2 All the primitives which are members of control function are corresponded to the primitives of transformed student program.

Step 5. Finish. Otherwise, the student does not understand either the exercise or the algorithm. Thus, ask first to the student whether he could understand the exercise or not. If he could, then the algorithm or the description method must be studied. If he could not, then the explanation for understanding the current exercise should be done. After, finish this process in order to instruct each operation.

Step 6. If the primitive of transformed student program is a member of control function, then goto Step 6-1, else goto Step 6-2;

Step 6-1. The student program contains either a logical error or is described by the different algorithm;

Step 6-2. The student program contains a logical error.

After setting the indicators to the next ones, in order to compare successively the primitives on both the lower blocks of teacher program description and transformed student program. Goto Step 2.

5.2 Example

We address an example of the diagnosis process described in the previous subsection. We consider the diagnosis process for the exercise which returns a medium value of input list. Fig.4 is an example of student program which is described by selection method as the subprogram "Sorting" and includes two logical errors on the conditional branch structure and function "mod". Fig.5 illustrates the transformed student programs shown in Fig.4 and the correspondence relationships between the primitives which are distinguished with each other by the identifiers.

This diagnosis sequence is as follows:

Phase 1. Check up primitives in the main function "mymedian" of transformed student program and primitives in the program slot of procedure item "Median". First, the indicators are set to individual primitives "(0 0 (set (arg1)) data1)" whose step numbers are "0", respectively. Their primitives correspond to each other by means of the correspondence (1). Second, the primitive "(1 0 (apply length (data1)) data2)" in the program slot is corresponded by the correspondence (2). Third, the indicator is set to the next primitive "(2 0 (apply mod (data2 '2')) data3)" in the student program. All the primitives in the program slot are not equivalent to the indicated primitive on both *operator* and *parameter-list*. The indicated element is erroneous. Fourth, the primitive "(3 0 (apply floor (data3)) data4)" is corresponded though the parameter "data3" of the indicated primitive is not corresponded (by the correspondences (1), (2) and (3) in Fig.5).

Phase 2. When the indicator is set to the next primitive "(4 0 (call sorting (data1)) data5)",the next indicated primitive is corresponded to the primitives of procedure items which are children of exercise item "Sorting". After then, check up the primitives in the transformed student program and the primitives in the program slot of procedure items "Quick-sorting" and "Selection-sorting", respectively. Correspondence result of "Selection-sorting" is shown from (4a) to (9a) in Fig.5.

Phase 3(Selection-sorting). After the correspondence process for the sub-program "mysort", since the primitives "(1 0 (branch ((eq data1 nil) block1 block2)) nil)" and "(2 1 (return nil) nil)" in the procedure item do not correspond to any primitives of transformed student program, the student program is judged as an erroneous program logically. The primitives "(1 0 (branch ((eq data1 nil) block1 block2)) nil)" and "(2 1 (return nil) nil)" are connected to the learning unit "Recursive stop condition" by N-link as illustrated in Fig.3. Thus, the knowledge of learning unit must be instructed in the next instruction step.

```
(defun mymedian (x)
    (nth (floor (mod (length x) 2)) (mysort  x)))

(defun mysort (unsorted) ; to sort the list "unsorted"
      (cons (mymin unsorted)
            (mysort (remove (mymin unsorted) unsorted)))))
(defun mymin (select-min) ; to select minimum of the list "select-min"
    (if (= (length select-min) 1) (car select-min)
      (let ((m (mymin (cdr select-min))))
       (if (> (car select-min) m) m
                           (car select-min))))))
```

Fig. 4. Student program

6   Conclusion

This paper described a program tutoring text model which is an improved version of multi-layers network authoring-text model. We introduced ISA-link to make the relationship between the learning units/items clear when one learning item can be produced successively from another. Also, we used the relationship REF-link with a view to representing that one procedure item is composed of other exercise items collectively.

Our future work is as follows:

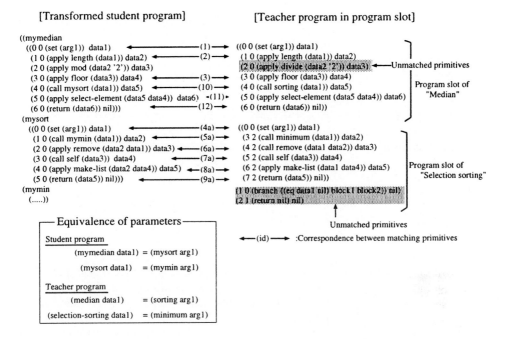

Fig. 5. Diagnosis process for procedure item "Selection-sorting"

- Verification of our model;
- Development of successful instruction strategy.

Acknowledgements

We are very grateful to Prof. T. Fukumura of Chukyo University, and Prof. Y. Inagaki and Prof. J. Toriwaki of Nagoya University, for their perspective remarks, and also wish to thank Dr. Y. Sagawa, Mr. K. Asakura and our research members for their many suggestions, discussions and cooperations.

References

1. D. Kopec and R. Brent: " *Artificial Intelligence and Intelligent Tutoring Systems* ", Elice Horwood Limited, pp.111-151 (1992).
2. P.L. Brusilovsky: "A Frame for Intelligent Knowledge Sequencing and Task Sequencing ", *Proc. of ITS-92*, pp.499-506 (1992).
3. T. Watanabe, A. Tanaka and N. Sugie: "A Tutoring-text Model Based on a Multi-layers Network", *Proc. of ED-MEDIA'93*, pp.622 (1993).
4. T. Watanabe, A. Tanaka and N. Sugie: "A Composition Method of Tutoring Plans, Using the Multi-layers Network Authoring-text Model", *Proc. of ICCE'93*, pp.402-404 (1993).

Un modèle de représentation du curriculum dans un STI

Roger Nkambou[1] and Gilles Gauthier[2]

[1] Université de Montréal, Département d'Informatique et de R.O.,
Montréal (Québec) H3C 3J7, Canada
[2] Université du Québec à Montréal, Département d'Informatique,
Montréal (Québec) H3C 3P8, Canada

Résumé. Nous présentons dans cet article une approche de modélisation de la connaissance de la matière à enseigner, dans un système tutoriel intelligent (STI) à grande échelle. Cette approche nommée CREAM (*Curriculum REpresentation and Acquisition Model*) permet d'organiser la matière sur trois aspects: domaine, pédagogie et didactique. L'aspect relié au domaine est mise en oeuvre par un modèle des capacités (CREAM-C) qui représente et organise les connaissances du domaine suivant des liens logiques existant entre elles. Le volet pédagogique crée un cadre de définition et d'organisation des objectifs d'enseignement (CREAM-O et CKTN). L'organisation des objectifs consiste notamment à modéliser les prédispositions nécessaires à leur réalisation et à étudier l'impact que peut avoir l'atteinte d'un objectif sur les connaissances du domaine. Enfin, la dimension didactique revient à produire un modèle qui définit et organise les différents moyens nécessaires pour l'enseignement de la matière considérée (CREAM-R).

1 Introduction

Dans le domaine de l'éducation, le développement d'un curriculum est considéré comme une étape importante dans le processus de conception de l'enseignement. En effet, le curriculum est souvent considéré comme une donnée en entrée d'un système d'enseignement [3]. Dans les systèmes tutoriels intelligents, l'aspect curriculum reste fort implicite: très peu de recherches se sont préoccupées de la nécessité d'un curriculum dans un STI. Un des problèmes qui se posent est celui de trouver une définition et une représentation du curriculum dans le cadre d'un STI. Quelques travaux ont été fait dans ce sens [10, 6, 12, 7, 2]. Halff dans [6] considère que le but du curriculum dans les STI est de formuler une représentation du matériel d'enseignement, et de sélectionner et ordonner les activités de formation à partir de cette représentation. Ainsi, Halff oriente la représentation du curriculum sur le matériel.

S'il est vrai que l'accent doit être mis sur les connaissances que le STI veut faire acquérir à un apprenant, il n'en demeure pas moins que l'acquisition de ces connaissances se fait à travers une variété d'activités d'apprentissage et d'enseignement véhiculées par le matériel d'enseignement (ressources didactiques). Ainsi, nous considérons que le curriculum, tout en se focalisant sur les connaissances relatives à une matière donnée, doit aussi se préoccuper des ressources didactiques nécessaires à l'acquisition par l'apprenant de ces connaissances dans des situations d'enseignement ou d'apprentissage. Par exemple, l'acquisition d'une connaissance concernant la résolution d'un système d'équations linéaires nécessite la réalisation d'un certain nombre d'activités (enseignement de concepts associés aux notions impliquées, résolution de problèmes ou d'exercices sur les systèmes d'équations linéaires...). Cette réalisation n'est possible que si les ressources didactiques concernées sont disponibles.

Nous définissons un curriculum dans un STI comme étant une représentation structurée de la matière à enseigner en terme de capacités (*capabilities*) au sens de Gagné [5], d'objectifs dont l'atteinte contribue à l'acquisition des capacités, et de ressources didactiques (exercices, problèmes, démonstrations, vidéos, simulations, etc.), le tout organisé dans des structures de connaissances pour soutenir l'enseignement d'une matière. Notre idée est de créer et d'organiser un environnement riche et varié pouvant supporter la génération de cours [13], la planification et le déroulement de l'enseignement et certains aspects liés à la modélisation de l'apprenant [15]. Nous présentons dans ce papier, les différents aspects de CREAM.

2 Architecture de CREAM

Le modèle de représentation que nous proposons (figure 1) fait ressortir une représentation de la matière à enseigner à travers une organisation de capacités (CREAM-C), une organisation d'objectifs d'enseignement (CREAM-O) et une organisation de ressources didactiques (CREAM-R). Sur ces trois organisations (modèles) nous construisons une structure représentant le modèle pédagogique de la matière. Cette structure appelée CKTN (*Curriculum Knowledge Transition Network*) contient des liens particuliers entre des éléments provenant des trois modèles (capacités, objectifs et ressources). Un curriculum de modèle CREAM offre une interface d'accès contenant des protocoles permettant aux autres composants du STI ou à des utilisateurs humains (professeurs, formateurs...) d'accéder aux informations qu'il renferme. Le module d'acquisition, constitué de méthodologies et d'une boîte à outils (atelier), représente le module chargé de supporter la construction d'un curriculum selon l'approche proposée, en interaction avec les sources de connaissances (experts du contenu, experts du domaine, analystes de la formation, concepteurs d'enseignement...). Dans ce papier nous décrivons uniquement les quatres modèles représentant la structure d'un curriculum. Le protocole d'accès (interface) et le module d'acquisition ne sont pas décrits ici (voir [14]).

2.1 Modélisation des capacités

Une capacité est une connaissance, acquise ou développée, permettant à une personne de réussir dans l'exercice d'une activité physique ou intellectuelle. Il s'agit d'une information (connaissance ou unité cognitive) qui est emmagasinée dans la mémoire à long terme de l'apprenant et qui rend possible un comportement.

422

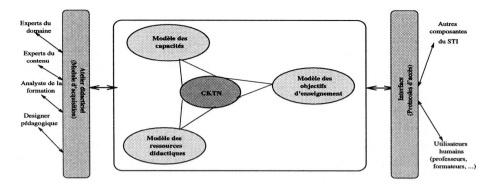

Fig. 1. Architecture de CREAM

Classification et représentation des capacités. Selon Gagné [5] cinq grandes catégories de capacités peuvent produire la plupart des activités humaines: les informations verbales, les habiletés intellectuelles, les stratégies cognitives, les habiletés motrices et les attitudes. Certaines de ces catégories comprennent plusieurs types de capacités. Un des intérêts de cette taxinomie est que les conditions particulières à respecter pour favoriser l'acquisition de chacun des types de connaissances ont été définies par Gagné [4]. Cet aspect nous semble important pour la planification des leçons (composante planificateur) et le choix des tactiques d'enseignement (composante tuteur) par le STI. Dans le cadre de CREAM, nous n'avons considéré que les trois premières catégories de capacités, les deux.

La représentation d'une capacité dépend de sa nature. De manière générale, une capacité se définit comme dans la figure 2(a). *ÉlémentDeLaMatière* représente l'objet du domaine sur lequel la capacité est définie. Pour un même élément de la matière, on peut définir plusieurs capacités. Par exemple, les capacités perfusion(concept) et perfusion(règle) sont définies sur un même élément de la matière qui est *perfusion*.

Les attributs d'une capacité varient suivant le type de capacité considéré. Par exemple, pour une règle, les procédures doivent être représentées; pour un concept, les facteurs discriminants (attributs intrinsèques et fonctionnels du concept) et les règles de reconnaissance doivent être représentés (figure 2(a)). La figure 2(b) montre quelques exemples de réprésentation de capacités (tels qu'implémentés en Smalltalk).

Organisation des capacités. Nous avons identifié cinq types de relations entre les capacités: les relations d'analogie $(\mathcal{A})$, de généralisation $(\mathcal{G})$, d'abstraction $(\mathcal{A})$, d'aggrégation $(\mathcal{A}_{\}})$ et de déviation $(\mathcal{D})$.

Relation d'analogie entre capacités. L'analogie entre deux capacités peut être du point de vue de leur fonctionnalité, des résultats ou de leur définition (dans les deux derniers cas, on parlera d'analogie structurelle). Considérons k1

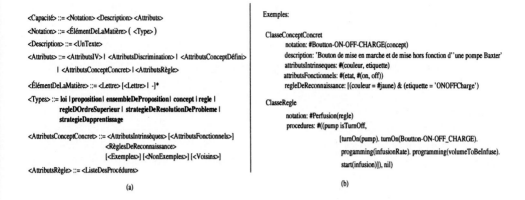

Fig. 2. Définition d'une capacité

= *perfusion-primaire(règle)* et k2 = *perfusion-secondaire(règle)*, deux capacités sur l'utilisation de la pompe Baxter. Il existe une analogie du point de vue de la fonctionnalité, notée $\mathcal{A}$(k1, k2, fonctionnel) entre k1 et k2.

Relation de généralisation. Certaines capacités sont plus générales que d'autres. Deux capacités liées par ce type de relation partagent les attributs de la capacité la plus générale mais la capacité la plus spécifique possède des attributs supplémentaires. Considérons k1 = *perfusion-primaire(règle)* et k2 = *perfusion-primaire-avec-taux-et-volume(règle)*. La capacité k1 est plus générale que le capacité k2, ceci est noté $\mathcal{G}$(k1, k2).

Relation d'abstraction. Cette relation existe entre deux capacités lorsque l'une hérite de certains attributs de l'autre. Une capacité k1 est dite plus abstraite qu'une capacité k2, si k2 hérite de certains attributs et comportements de k1.

Relation d'agrégation. Cette relation traduit le fait qu'une connaissance est une composante d'une autre. Considérons les capacités k1= *taux(loi)*, k2 = *volume(loi)* et k3 = *temps(loi)*; les capacités k2 et k3 sont des constituantes de k1, ce qui est noté par $\mathcal{A}_]$(k1, k2) et $\mathcal{A}_]$(k1, k3).

Relation de déviation (mal-capacité). Cette relation traduit le fait qu'une capacité est une malformation de l'autre. Par exemple, *perfusion-primaire-avec-temps-et-volume(concept)* peut être une déviation de *perfusion-primaire-avec-temps-et-taux(concept)*.

Modèle des capacités. Chaque relation définit un ensemble de liens entre les capacités. Ces liens peuvent porter des informations décrivant la nature du lien. Le sous-ensemble défini par chaque relation est un graphe étiqueté correspondant à l'organisation des capacités par rapport à cette relation. Le modèle de capacités (CREAM-C) est représenté par le multi-graphe $(\mathcal{E}, \mathcal{A}, \mathcal{G}, \mathcal{A}_., \mathcal{A}_], \mathcal{D})$ où $\mathcal{E}$ est l'ensemble des capacités et où $\mathcal{A}, \mathcal{G}, \mathcal{A}_., \mathcal{A}_]$ et $\mathcal{D}$ sont les graphes (étiquetés) définis par les relations décrites plus haut. Ce modèle reste extensible à d'autres type de relations.

2.2 Modélisation des objectifs pédagogiques

Un objectif d'enseignement est une description d'un ensemble de comportements (ou performances) qu'un apprenant doit être capable de démontrer suite à un apprentissage. Il peut aussi décrire l'ensemble des capacités que doit posséder un étudiant après une activité pédagogique. Ainsi, il décrit le résultat que doit atteindre l'enseignement plutôt que le processus d'enseignement ou les moyens à mettre en oeuvre. Plusieurs travaux ont démontré la nécessité de spécifier les objectifs dans un système d'enseignement [10, 16]. Nous avons pris cette dimension en compte dans notre approche de représentation, en introduisant un modèle des objectifs pédagogiques (CREAM-O) dans lequel les objectifs pédagogiques sont représentés et organisés entre eux par des liens didactiques.

Classification et représentation des objectifs. Nous avons opté pour la classification de Bloom [1] en ce qui concerne le niveau d'un objectif. Ainsi, six catégories d'objectifs sont disponibles: acquisition, compréhension, application, analyse, synthèse et évaluation. À chaque catégorie est associée une liste de verbes d'action décrivant le comportement rendu possible par l'atteinte de l'objectif. La figure 3(a) donne la définition d'un objectif. *Habileté* décrit le comportement impliqué dans l'objectif. Cet attribut est représenté par un verbe d'action appartenant à un niveau de la taxinomie de Bloom, qui exprime le comportement ou la performance exigée par l'objectif. *ÉlémentDeLaMatière* décrit l'élément du domaine sur lequel porte l'objectif. *Description* est la description textuelle détaillée de l'objectif. *Niveau* indique la catégorie de Bloom à laquelle appartient l'objectif. Normalement, cette catégorie peut être déduite à partir de l'habileté. *Contexte* décrit les conditions dans lesquelles va se dérouler la performance de l'étudiant [11]. Cette condition précise les données, les contraintes, ou les deux. *CritèreDeRéussite* représente la règle qui permettra de déterminer si l'objectif est atteint. Un exemple d'objectif du curriculum "code de la route au Québec" est présenté dans la figure 3(b).

Organisation des objectifs. Comme pour les capacités, nous disposons dans CREAM d'une organisation des objectifs dans laquelle les objectifs sont reliés entre eux par plusieurs types de relations: prérequis ($\mathcal{P}$), prétexte ($\mathcal{P}_*$) et constitution ($\mathcal{C}$).

Un objectif O est dit *prérequis obligatoire* à l'objectif O', si l'étudiant doit avoir atteint O pour espérer réaliser O'; on note ce fait par $\mathcal{P}$(O,O',obligatoire). Une forme plus faible de prérequis est le *prérequis souhaitable*. L'objectif O est un prérequis souhaitable à l'objectif O' et on écrit $\mathcal{P}$(O,O',souhaitable), si l'atteinte de O favorise la réalisation de O'. Les relations de prérequis entre objectifs peuvent être générées ou déduites automatiquement à l'aide d'un raisonnement

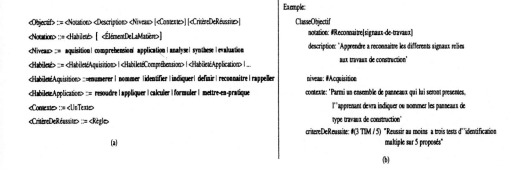

Fig. 3. Définition d'un objectif d'enseignement

sur le modèle résultant du couplage des modèles (voir la notion de CKTN plus loin).

Un objectif O' est *prétexte* à un objectif O, et on écrit $\mathcal{P}_*(O,O')$ si O' peut servir de support au développement d'habiletés spécifiées par O. Par exemple, si l'objectif est de développer des habiletés de manipulation d'un appareil physique chez un apprenant, l'apprentissage de la manipulation de la pompe Baxter pourrait être considérer comme un objectif prétexte.

Un *objectif constitutif* (sous-objectifs) représente certains des éléments formant un objectif. Un objectif peut comprendre plusieurs sous-objectifs. On écrit $\mathcal{C}(O,O')$ si O est un objectif constitutif de O'. Dans le curriculum, des liens de constitution entre objectifs peuvent être générés automatiquement à partir d'une analyse de la structure d'aggrégation des capacités.

Modèle des objectifs. Le modèle des objectifs (CREAM-O) est représenté par le multi-graphe $(\mathcal{O},\mathcal{P},\mathcal{P}_*,\mathcal{C})$ où $\mathcal{O}$ est l'ensemble des objectifs et où $\mathcal{P},\mathcal{P}_*$ et $\mathcal{C}$ sont les graphes (étiquetés) définis par les relations décrites ci-dessus.

2.3 Modélisation des ressources didactiques

Nous définissons une ressource didactique comme étant un moyen tactique (exercice, problème, test, simulation, démonstration, document HTML...) utilisé par le système d'enseignement pour supporter l'acquisition ou le renforcement, par un apprenant, de capacités le rendant capable des performances définies par les objectifs.

Classification et représentation des ressources didactiques. Les ressources didactiques jouent un rôle important dans un processus d'apprentissage. En effet c'est à travers l'interaction avec une ressource didactique qu'un étudiant acquiert des connaissances et est évalué. Il est important d'étudier les différentes catégories de ressources et leur nature afin de mieux cerner leur impact dans le processus d'enseignement-apprentissage.

L'analyse des différentes ressources nous a permis de produire une typologie des ressources didactiques. Cette typologie fait ressortir trois catégories de ressources didactiques: les *ressources intelligentes* qui sont utilisées dans le processus d'enseignement-apprentissage pour l'acquisition des connaissances (problèmes, tests, exercices...), les *ressources de tutorielles* qui oeuvrent comme des experts pouvant intervenir dans le processus d'enseignement-apprentissage pour aider, conseiller ou critiquer l'apprenant dans une activité précise (systèmes critiques, systèmes conseillers...), les *ressources "dumb"* représentant du matériel d'enseignement (simulateurs, images, vidéos...).

Organisation des ressources didactiques. Une fois les ressources didactiques identifiées et représentées, il est important de procéder à leur organisation. Nous avons retenu six relations sur les ressources au vu de leur intérêt pédagogique: similarité (analogie), abstraction, cas particulier, utilisation, *auxiliariat* et équivalence.

Le modèle des ressources (CREAM-R) est le multi-graphe défini par les relations précédentes. Ce modèle peut servir pour conseiller un étudiant pendant l'utilisation d'une ressource didactique. Par exemple, l'étudiant peut avoir des difficultés avec un problème alors qu'il en a déjà résolu un cas particulier; dans ce cas, le système devrait, si cela est nécessaire, lui donner de l'information concernant le fait qu'il a déjà eu à traiter un cas particulier du problème qu'il est en train de résoudre et si possible, le contexte dans lequel ceci avait été fait.

2.4 Couplages des modèles précédents: un modèle pédagogique du curriculum

Le couplage des modèles précédents se traduit par des liens intermodèles. Nous avons identifié trois classes de liens entre les connaissances des différents modèles: les liens entre objectifs et capacités (couplage(CREAM-O, CREAM-C)), les liens entre ressources didactiques et objectifs (couplage(CREAM-O, CREAM-R)) et les liens entre ressources didactiques et capacités (couplage (CREAM-C, CREAM-R)). De plus nous avons identifié des liens entre ressources didactiques et les liens des divers modèles.

Liens entre objectifs et capacités. Des liens entre objectifs et capacités existent dans les deux sens: capacités-objectif (*lien de prélable*), et objectif-capacités (*lien de contribution*).

Lien de préalable. L'existence d'un lien d'une capacité C à un objectif O traduit le fait que la capacité C est préalable à la réalisation de l'objectif O. Un préalable peut être *obligatoire* ou *souhaitable*. Une autre caractéristique d'un lien de préalable est le niveau à partir duquel ce lien peut être considéré comme franchissable: on parle de niveau d'entrée. Le niveau d'entrée correspond au niveau de maîtrise exigé sur une capacité pour qu'elle soit considérée comme suffisante au franchissement du lien de préalable dont elle est la source. Nous l'exprimons par une valeur qualificative appartenant à un alphabet d'évaluation. Chaque alphabet d'évaluation est un ensemble ordonné. Un exemple d'alphabet pour l'évaluation de l'acquisition d'un concept est celui de Klausmeier [8] qui comprend quatre niveaux d'acquisition: *identifie, reconnaît, classifie* et *généralise*. Plusieurs alphabets peuvent exister pour la qualification d'un même type de capacité. Le concepteur du curriculum devra toutefois faire son choix au début de la conception.

Lien de contribution. L'existence d'un lien d'un objectif O à une capacité C traduit le fait que l'objectif O contribue à l'acquisition de la capacité C. La contribution de la réalisation d'un objectif à l'acquisition d'une capacité peut être *forte, moyenne* ou *faible*. Plusieurs objectifs peuvent contribuer à l'acquisition d'une même capacité. Ainsi, la sélection des objectifs pertinents à réaliser dans le cadre d'un enseignement nécessite un raisonnement sur cette organisation.

Association de ressources didactiques aux objectifs, capacités et liens.

Les liens entre ressources didactiques et objectifs associent à un objectif des ressources didactiques utiles pour sa réalisation. Une ressource didactique peut être *critique* ou *accessoire* à la réalisation d'un objectif. Une ressource est dite accessoire à la réalisation d'un objectif, si l'objectif peut être atteint sans qu'elle soit activée. Par contre, une ressource sera dite critique, lorsque son activation et la réussite à son utilisation sont indispensables à l'atteinte de l'objectif auquel elle est associée. L'affectation des ressources aux objectifs tient compte des conditions d'apprentissage [4].

On peut aussi associer des resources didactiques aux capacités. Des resources génériques peuvent être associées à certains types de capacités. Par exemple on peut associer à un concept des ressources illustrant des exemples du concept, des non-exemples ou des concepts voisins.

Enfin, du matériel pédagogique assez particulier peut être associer à certains types de liens. En pédagogie, ce type de ressource est utilisé pour l'enseignement correctif [9] qui est un enseignement portant sur les connaissances mal acquises. Par exemple, des ressources didactiques peuvent être associées à un lien de type déviation entre capacités et pourront être activées pour la correction de cette déviation chez un apprenant.

Un modèle pédagogique résultant du couplage précédent.

Dans l'espace résultant du couplage des trois modèles (CREAM-O, CREAM-C, et CREAM-R), nous regroupons chaque objectif et les ressources didactiques associées en un élément que nous appelons *transition*. Le résultat de ce regroupement est une structure de réseau appelée CKTN (Curriculum Knowledge Transition Network). La figure 4 (tirée de [15]) montre une portion du CKTN du curriculum de l'enseignement de l'utilisation d'une pompe Baxter. Cette structure, conjointement avec la spécification d'un public cible, permet la génération automatique de cours [13].

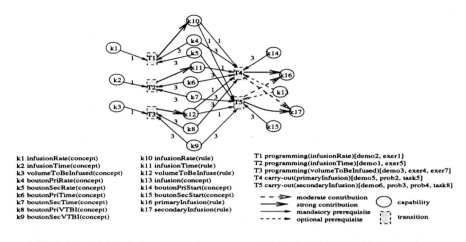

k1 infusionRate(concept)
k2 infusionTime(concept)
k3 volumeToBeInfused(concept)
k4 boutonPriRate(concept)
k5 boutonSecRate(concept)
k6 boutonPriTime(concept)
k7 boutonSecTime(concept)
k8 boutonPriVTBI(concept)
k9 boutonSecVTBI(concept)

k10 infusionRate(rule)
k11 infusionTime(rule)
k12 volumeToBeInfuse(rule)
k13 infusion(concept)
k14 boutonPriStart(concept)
k15 boutonSecStart(concept)
k16 primaryInfusion(rule)
k17 secondaryInfusion(rule)

T1 programming(infusionRate)[demo2, exer1]
T2 programming(infusionTime)[demo1, exer5]
T3 programming(volumeToBeInfused)[demo3, exer4, exer7]
T4 carry-out(primaryInfusion)[demo5, prob2, task5]
T5 carry-out(secondaryInfusion)[demo6, prob3, prob4, task8]

- - -► moderate contribution
——► strong contribution
———► mandatory prerequisite
- - - -► optional prerequisite

◯ capability

⬚ transition

Fig. 4. Une portion du CKTN sur la manipulation d'une pompe Baxter

2.5   Implémentation

Nous avons utilisé une approche objet pour l'implémentation de CREAM. Chaque élément du curriculum (objectif, capacité et ressource) est représenté comme un objet ayant des attributs tels que spécifiés dans la représentation, et répondant à des messages. Les liens entre ces éléments sont aussi implémentés comme des objets. De la même façon, chaque modèle (CREAM-O, CREAM-C, CREAM-R et CKTN) est implémenté comme un objet. Ces quatres modèles représentent l'état privé d'un curriculum construit selon l'approche CREAM.

Le modèle CREAM a été implémenté en VisualWorks, version 2 et expérimenté pour le développement de plusieurs curriculums (curriculum pour l'enseignement de l'utilisation d'une pompe de perfusion intraveineuse, curriculum pour l'enseignement du code de la route, curriculum pour la pratique de l'examen clinique dans une salle de soins intensifs).

3   Conclusion

CREAM est un modèle de représentation du curriculum pouvant supporter l'enseignement d'un cours complet dans un STI. Il a permi de répondre aux attentes de la phase 3 du projet SAFARI [3], concernant le support d'un cours complet. Le modèle CREAM facilite l'exploitation d'un curriculum par un STI pour la génération de cours, la planification de l'enseignement et pour supporter le déroulement d'un cours complet. Nous avons expérimenté l'intégration de ce modèle dans un STI en assurant l'interaction avec les autres composantes du STI.

---

[3] Ce travail a été supporté par le programme SYNERGIE du Ministère de l'Industrie, du Commerce, des Sciences et de la Technologie du Québec

Le modèle CREAM répond à deux caractéristiques fondamentales dans la théorie du design pédagogique: la représentation du contenu de la matière à enseigner et son organisation.

Références

1. B.S. Bloom, *Taxonomy od educational objectives, Handbook I: Cognitive domaine*, David McKay, New York, NY, 1956.
2. S. J. Derry, 'Learning strategies for acquiring useful knowledge', in *Dimensions of thinking and cognitive instruction*, eds., B.F. Jones and L. Idol, 15–51, LEA, (1990).
3. C. R. Finch and J. R. Crukilton, *Curriculum development in vocational and technical education: Planning, content and implementation*, Allyn and Bacon, Inc., 2 edn., 1986.
4. R.M. Gagné, *The conditions of learning and the theory of instruction*, CBS College Publishing, 4 edn., 1985.
5. R.M. Gagné, L. Briggs, and W. Wager, *Principles of instructional design*, Harcourt Brace Jovanovich, Orlando, FL, 4 edn., 1992.
6. H. Halff, 'Curriculum and instruction in its', in *Foundations of intelligent tutoring systems*, 19–108, Hillsdale, NJ:LEA, (1988).
7. R. Hartley, 'The curriculum and instructional tasks: Goals strategies, and tactics for interactive learning', in *Adaptive learning environments: Foundation and frontiers*, pp. 123–146, Berlin, (1990). Springer-Verlag.
8. H.J. Klausmeier, 'Conceptualizing', in *Dimensions of Thinking and Cognitive Instruction*, pp. 93–138, NJ: LEA, (1990). Hillsdale.
9. R. Legendre, *Dictionnaire actuel de l'éducation*, Librairies Guérin et Eska, Montreal, QC, 1993.
10. Alan Lesgold, 'Toward a theory of curriculum for use in designing intelligent instructional systems', in *Learning issues for Intelligent Tutoring Systems*, 114–137, Springer-Verlag, Berlin, (1988).
11. G. Mager, *Comment définir les objectifs pédagogiques*, Bordas, 1990.
12. Gordon I. McCalla, 'The search for adaptability, flexibility, and individualization: Approaches to curriculum in intelligent tutoring systems', in *Adaptive learning environments: Foundation and frontiers*, pp. 91–112, Berlin, (1990). Springer-Verlag.
13. R. Nkambou, M.C. Frasson, and C. Frasson, 'Generating courses in an intelligent tutoring system', in *Proceedings of the 9th International Conference on Industrial and Engineering Applications of Artificial Intelligence and Expert Systems*, pp. 261–267, New York, NY, (1996). Gordon and Breach Science.
14. R. Nkambou, G. Gauthier, C. Frasson, and M. Antaki, 'Integrating expert system in authoring systems for curriculum and course building', in *Proceedings of the 7th International Conference on Artificial Intelligent and Expert Systems Applications*, pp. 485–490, San Francisco, CA, (1995).
15. R. Nkambou, B. Lefebvre, and G. Gauthier, 'A curriculum-based student model for intelligent tutoring systems', in *Proceedings of the 5th International Conference on User Modeling*, pp. 91–98, Hawaii, (1996).
16. J.G. Webster, 'Instructional objectives and bench examinations in circuits laboratories', *IEEE Transactions On Education*, **37**(1), 111–113, (1994).

A Process-Sensitive Learning Environment Architecture

Fabio N. Akhras[*] and John A. Self

Computer Based Learning Unit, University of Leeds, Leeds, LS2 9JT, England
{fabio, jas}@cbl.leeds.ac.uk

Abstract. In this paper we describe an architecture for intelligent learning environments that provides means to analyse the process rather than the product of learning, in order to support the development of individualised learning experiences in environments oriented by a more open and constructivist philosophy of learning. The architecture is described in terms of the conceptual structure and functionality required to support the representation and analysis of processes of learner-environment interaction and the adaptation of the environment according to the state of the learning process revealed by the analysis. An application in which a simple learning environment was implemented using the architecture exemplifies the approach.

1 Introduction

Intelligent systems to support learning share the view that the learning experiences to be developed in the interaction between the learner and the system must be in some way adapted to suit the learner's needs. This means that the system should be informed about the learner, the environment, and the interaction between the learner and the environment, and use this information to enable changes in the course of the learning process that could be beneficial to the learners at each time, according to the underlying educational philosophy of the system.

A typical instance of this general idea is an intelligent tutoring system (ITS) which bases its instructional interventions on a model of the knowledge to be learned and on a learner model that informs the ITS about the correct or wrong knowledge that the learner has about the subject.

For interactive learning environments (ILEs), that emphasise an active and autonomous role for the learner to interact with an environment in which the focus is on the process of constructing knowledge rather than on having an explicitly defined target domain knowledge to be acquired by the learner, we may need informative models of a different nature and assuming different roles.

As an example, a recent study reviewing a number of projects that explored the role of learner models in ILEs has concluded that many of the deeper problems of learner modelling (e.g.: that learner modelling should serve more subtle goals than just the repair of wrong knowledge) may not disappear within ILEs but may become more central [4]. Similarly, a review of the function of student modelling in various instructional paradigms has pointed out that there is a need for more than analysing the learner's performance in terms of procedural knowledge and mistakes [2].

Exploring the shift in focus that ILEs emphasise, from the product to the process of learning, we are developing an approach by which processes of learner-environment interaction are formally analysed to inform the decisions of a learning

---

[*] Scholar of the National Council of Scientific and Technological Development (CNPq), Brasilia - Brazil.

environment concerning the promotion of individualised learning in the more open and constructivist context that characterises ILEs.

The general idea is to consider the interaction between the learner and the environment as a process in time, and formalise the conceptual and temporal aspects of this process in terms of a set of entities that can be used to define certain regularities found in this process. Being attuned to these regularities the system can analyse these processes in terms of certain desired properties to obtain, for example, the information that a process has been constructive in certain locations and with respect to certain items of knowledge, but not in others. Based on this information the system could then act to create open opportunities of interaction to the learner which can enable the desired properties to happen in the following process of learner-environment interaction.

To support the development of ILEs capable of such a deep sensing of the learning process we are developing a learning environment architecture that is characterised by the following functions:

• *Extract information from the process of learner-environment interaction.* This requires the explicit representation of several kinds of entities involved in processes of learner-environment interaction that are relevant for the analysis of the process.

• *Analyse the process of learner-environment interaction.* This requires the formalisation of several regularities of processes of learner-environment interaction that are meaningful to determine how the learning process is developing.

• *Determine the state of the learning process.* This requires the formal definition of several properties of learning processes.

• *Change the environment to enable changes in the state of the learning process.* This requires the identification of the process needs and the search for possibilities in the environment to the development of interactions that can meet these needs.

2 Extracting Information from the Process of Learner-Environment interaction

To explicitly represent the process of learner-environment interaction, two kinds of entities were defined: *environment entities,* which represent all the concepts, actions, physical objects, tools and information related to the subject matter, and *process entities,* which represent information about the occurrence of environment entities in the process of interaction.

In the next two sections we present an informal description of these entities, illustrating with examples taken from an application in which a simple ILE in the domain of salad design was implemented. The ILE, named SAMPLE (SAlad-Making Process-sensitive Learning Environment), allows the interaction of a learner with situations in which she or he has a set of ingredients and a set of tools to operate on these ingredients transforming their states or adding them to the salad or dressing.

2.1 Environment Entities

Essentially, modelling an environment corresponds to specifying the types of situations that the learner may encounter at some time during the course of her or his interactions with the environment.

Each *situation type* represents an open context for learner-environment interactions. It is defined in terms of a set of entities that represent how things stand in the type of situation and how a learner can interact with that type of situation.

The way things stand in a situation type is represented by sets of *objects, relations* between objects, *properties* of objects or relations, *states* of objects, and types of *transitions* between states. Additionally, we can represent types of *objects, relations, properties*, and *states*, and relations of *abstraction* or *aggregation*. Some examples taken from SAMPLE are:

sit_type (salad_lab_A1)   state (ingredient(lettuce), unwashed)
obj (ingredient(lettuce))   part (salad, ingredient(lettuce))

The way learners can interact with a situation type is represented by sets of *event types*, *preconditions* and *effects* of event types, and *events*. Some examples are:

ev_type (wash)   pre (wash, state(ingredient(X), unwashed), 1)
ev (wash, learner)   eff (add_to_salad, part(salad, ingredient(X)), 1)

To represent that an environment entity is a member of a situation type we *define* the entity in the situation type using the following notation:

def (obj_type(salad), salad_lab_A1)

In SAMPLE, six situation types were modelled. As an example, figure 1 shows some of the entities defined for the situation type "salad_lab_A1". These entities are: events (e. g.: wash, chop), objects (e. g.: lettuce, watercress), states of objects (e. g.: unwashed, whole), and the property "taste" of objects (e. g.: light, strong).

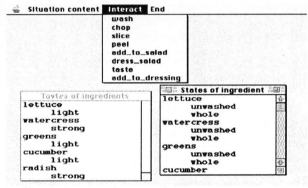

Fig. 1. Interaction with situation type "salad_lab_A1".

2.2 Process Entities

Situation types are abstract entities in the sense that they are not located in a particular time. They are just possibilities for learner-environment interactions resting in the environment. However, when a situation type is by some means chained in the current process of interaction, a temporal dimension is opened, making possible the development of *situations*, which are defined by the pair:

< situation type, time >

Situations are developed by the occurrence of events. Some of these events can be initiated by the learner, others by the system, depending on how they are defined in the situation type. The way situations develop in a process of interaction between a learner and a situation type is represented by the following process entities:

occurs (event, situation_type, time),

which specifies the occurrence of events in situations.

in (environment entity, situation_type, time),

which specifies the presence of environment entities in situations.

Some examples from SAMPLE are:

occurs (wash, salad_lab_A1, 4)

in (state(ingredient(lettuce), washed), salad_lab_A1, 5)

The sequences in which situations develop in a process of learner-environment interaction determine *courses of interaction*, which are represented by the following process entity, which specifies a sequence of developed situations:

course (situation 1, situation 2),

The set of situation types available to the learner to interact with, at each time, constitute the *space of interaction* at that time.

In the next section, we show how the entities defined so far, to model the environment and the process of interaction, are used in the definition of a set of regularities of processes of learner-environment interaction, which constitute the basis for the analysis of these processes.

3 Analysing the Process of Learner-Environment Interaction

The first step to analyse anything is to identify the units of analysis, i. e., the entities to which the analyser needs to be attuned. In the case of processes of learner-environment interaction we have identified three types of units of analysis:

• *Units of analysis located in situations,* which characterise patterns of how situations develop.

• *Units of analysis located in cognitive states,* which characterises patterns of how cognitive states develop.

• *Units of analysis located in courses of interaction,* which characterises patterns of how courses of interaction develop.

3.1 Units of Analysis Located in Situations

Some simple patterns of situation development can be captured by the process entities "occurs" and "in", and the environment entity "def". Being attuned to these patterns, a system can recognise, for example, the presence of a certain object in a situation, the occurrence of a certain event in a situation, the definition of a certain entity in a situation type, etc.. However, for the purposes of our analysis we need to explore patterns of a higher level, that can be obtained by combining these basic patterns. In particular, we need patterns associated with the development of interactions that are meaningful to the learner.

According to [3], two aspects that characterise the meaning of an object are: "what can be done" with the object and "what it is made of". In both cases the meaning of objects is subordinated to action, which can be utilitarian or constructive. Thus, to learn the meaning of an object corresponds to the assimilation of schemas of actions of utilising or constructing objects.

Based on these ideas we have defined two *patterns of meaningful interaction* which are represented by the following entities:

> *utilises (learner, event, environment entity, situation type, time),*
>> which specifies the occurrence of a meaningful interaction in which a learner's event utilises an environment entity in a situation.

> *generates (learner, event, environment entity, situation type, time),*
>> which specifies the occurrence of a meaningful interaction in which a learner's event generates an environment entity in a situation.

Some examples from SAMPLE are:

> utilises (learner, wash, state(ingredient(lettuce), unwashed), salad_lab_A1, 4)
> generates (learner, wash, state(ingredient(lettuce), washed), salad_lab_A1, 4)

To illustrate how these patterns are formally defined in terms of the more basic patterns discussed before, we show the definition of the utilises pattern:

Definition: *utilises*

$$\text{def}(\text{ev}(e, a), s) \wedge \text{occurs}(e, s, t) \wedge \text{in}(\text{pre}(e, x, p), s, t)$$
$$\Leftrightarrow \text{utilises}(a, e, x, s, t)$$

I.e. "if *e* is an event defined in situation type *s* to be initiated by a learner *a*, and *e* occurs in *s* at time *t*, and *x* is a precondition of *e*, then we say that the learner *a* utilises the entity *x* through the event *e* in situation *(s, t)*."

3.2 Units of Analysis Located in Cognitive States

According to the above discussion, the consequence of learner's behaviours that match to the defined patterns of meaningful interaction is that schemas of actions of utilising or constructing entities may be assimilated by the learner. These schemas will carry information about the meanings associated by the learner to the entities she or he has been interacting with, in situations.

These schemas will also be the basis for the learner's actions in situations. Therefore, it is relevant for our analysis to consider patterns involving relations between previously formed schemas and situations in which the learner is presently interacting. Being attuned to these patterns a system can recognise, for example, whether an entity in a situation is new or old to the learner.

To represent regularities involving relations between cognitive states and situations of the environment we have defined *patterns of cognitive situation*. Some of these patterns are:

> *new (learner, environment entity, situation type, time),*
>> which specifies that an entity present in a situation is new to a learner.
> *old (learner, environment entity, situation type, time),*
>> which specifies that an entity present in a situation is old to a learner.
> *newold (learner, environment entity, situation type, time),*
>> which specifies that an entity passes from new to old to a learner in a situation.
> *ev_oldnew (learner, event, old environment entity, new environment entity, situation type, time),*
>> which specifies that an old entity to a learner is related to a new entity to the learner through an event in a situation.

Some examples are:

new (learner, state(ingredient(lettuce), washed), salad_lab_A1, 4)
old (learner, state(ingredient(lettuce), washed), salad_lab_A1, 5)
newold (learner, state(ingredient(lettuce), washed), salad_lab_A1, 5)
ev_oldnew (learner, chop, state(ingredient(cheese), whole),
state(ingredient(cheese), chopped), salad_lab_A1, 8)

The formal definition of the last of these patterns is:

Definition: *ev_oldnew*

$$def(ev(e, a), s) \wedge occurs(e, s, t) \wedge in(pre(e, xo, po), s, t) \wedge$$
$$old(a, xo, s, t) \wedge in(eff(e, xn, pn), s, t+1) \wedge new(a, xn, s, t+1)$$
$$\Leftrightarrow ev\_oldnew(a, e, xo, xn, s, t)$$

I.e. "if *e* is an event defined in situation type *s* to be initiated by a learner *a*, and *e* occurs in *s* at time *t*, and *xo* is a precondition of *e*, and *xo* is old to the learner *a* at *t*, and *xn* is an effect of *e* at time *t+1*, and *xn* is new to the learner *a* at *t+1*, then we say that the event *e* of a learner *a* in situation *s* at time *t* relates an entity *xo* that is old to the learner *a* at time *t* to an entity *xn* that is new to the learner *a* at time *t+1*."

3.3 Units of Analysis Located in Courses of Interaction

Courses of interaction are developed as a consequence of successive interactions between a learner and one or more situation types that are available in the space of interaction at each time. According to the designed characteristics of these situations and the way they end up being arranged in the course of interaction (either by the learner's choices and actions or by influence of the system), certain patterns of courses of interaction will be developed. For example, if two situations have an entity in common (e.g.: the object type "salad"), we can say that the course of interaction eventually developed from the sequencing of these two situations will have the pattern of two situations sharing an entity.

Some of the patterns of the way courses of interaction develop that we have identified involve: sharing of entities between situations, linking of situations through entities, situations that specialise other situations with respect to an entity, situations that elaborate on entities of other situations, etc..

To represent a *pattern of course of interaction* relative to the sharing of environment entities between situations we have defined the following entity:

> *share (situation type 1, time 1, situation type 2, time 2, environment entity),*
> > which specifies that an environment entity is present in (or shared by)
> > two situations that constitute a course of interaction.

An example from SAMPLE is:

> share (salad_lab_A1, 1, salad_lab_A2, 4, state(ingredient(lettuce), washed))

The formal definition of this pattern is:

Definition: *share*

$$in(x, s1, t1) \wedge in(x, s2, t2) \wedge t1<t2$$
$$\Leftrightarrow share(s1, t1, s2, t2, x)$$

I.e. "if an entity *x* is in situation *(s1, t1)* and in situation *(s2, t2)*, for t1<t2, then we say that the two situations share the entity *x*."

In SAMPLE, after the end of the interaction of the learner with a situation type, the system determines, based on the units of analysis defined above, the patterns of meaningful interaction, cognitive situation, and course of interaction developed in consequence of the learner's interaction with that situation type. As an example, figure 2a shows some of these patterns determined by the system after an interaction between the learner and the situation type "salad_lab_A1".

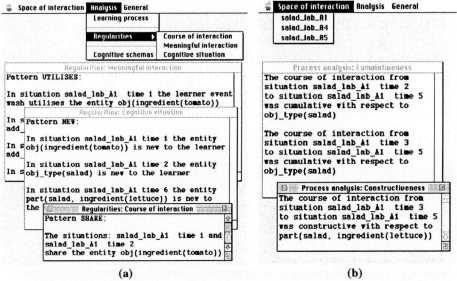

Fig. 2. a) Regularities identified after interaction with situation type "salad_lab_A1".
b) Process state after interaction with situation type "salad_lab_A1", and next space of interaction determined.

4 Determining the State of the Learning Process

There is a general agreement in the educational literature that learning processes that result in meaningful knowledge construction exhibit certain properties. For example, it is often said that meaningful learning is cumulative and constructive (among other things). It is cumulative in the sense that the learner's prior knowledge determines the new knowledge that is learned, and it is constructive in the sense that the new information must be elaborated and related to old information in order that it can be learned [5] [1].

In our approach we have defined the entity "course of interaction" to denote a sequence of interactions between a learner and an environment that may not necessarily result in learning. On the other hand, a learning course of interaction, i. e., a course of interaction in which some sort of learning occurs, will develop certain properties, like the two above, that denote the nature of what is learned in a given course of interaction and how it is learned.

Combining the previously defined units of analysis, we have defined the properties of *cumulativeness* and *constructiveness* of courses of interaction, which are represented by the following entities:

cumulative (situation type 1, time 1, situation type 2, time 2, environment entity),
> which specifies that a course of interaction from situation 1 to situation 2 is cumulative with respect to an environment entity.

constructive (situation type 1, time 1, situation type 2, time 2, environment entity),
> which specifies that a course of interaction from situation 1 to situation 2 is constructive with respect to an environment entity.

Some examples from SAMPLE are:

cumulative (salad_lab_A1, 1, salad_lab_A2, 8, state(ingredient(lettuce), washed))

constructive(salad_lab_A1, 3, salad_lab_A1, 4, part(salad, ingredient(lettuce)))

The formal definition of one possible way in which a course can be constructive is:

Definition: *constructive*

> share(s1, t1, s2, t2, xo) $\wedge$ newold(a, xo, s1, t1) $\wedge$
> ev_oldnew(a, e, xo, x, s2, t2) $\wedge$ generates(a, e, x, s2, t2)
>> $\Rightarrow$ constructive(s1, t1, s2, t2, x)

I.e. "if two situations *(s1, t1)* and *(s2, t2)* that are part of a course of interaction, share an entity *xo*, and *xo* pass from new to old for a learner *a* in *(s1, t1)*, and the learner's event *e* generates an entity *x* in *(s2, t2)* and also relates the old entity *xo* to the new entity *x*, then we say that the course of interaction, *course(s1, t1, s2, t2)*, is constructive with respect to the entity *x*."

The principle behind this definition is that, if in the first situation the entity *xo* becomes old to the learner, probably she or he gathered part of the meaning of *xo*. Furthermore, if later in another situation the learner generates a new entity *x* relating it to *xo*, the previously gathered meaning for *xo* may have been related in some way to the meaning gathered for *x*, in the learner's action, thus indicating a sort of constructiveness.

In SAMPLE, when the system determines the regularities developed in a process of interaction after the end of the interaction between the learner and a situation type (fig. 2a), it also determines the properties of cumulativeness and constructiveness relative to the additional courses of interaction created in consequence of that interaction. The set of properties of cumulativeness and constructiveness developed in the process of interaction up to a certain time characterise the state of the learning process at that time. Figure 2b shows these properties determined for courses of interaction between the learner and the situation type "salad_lab_A1".

5 Changing the Environment to Enable Changes in the State of the Learning Process

The state of the learning process, at a certain time, carries the information about whether courses of interaction in a process of learner-environment interaction have been cumulative or constructive, and with respect to which environment entities.

After determining the state of the learning process, the feedback of the system to the learner is manifested in the space of interaction. This space is generated by the system from the set of existent situation types. It is a matter of determining the set of situation types that are able to offer the kind of interaction that can enable the following process to be cumulative or constructive with respect to certain entities.

Two concepts are involved in changing the environment to enable courses of interaction that change the state of the learning process:

• *Environment regularities*, which represent the possibilities existent in the situation types available in the environment for the development of the learning courses of interaction that are beneficial to the learner at each time.

• *Space of interaction generation*, which is the procedure carried out by the system to select from the situation types available in the environment those that, according to the state of the learning process and according to the possibilities offered by the environment regularities, can be beneficial to the learner at each time.

5.1 Environment Regularities

According to the designed characteristics of situation types, certain regularities that are abstractions of the patterns previously defined (in the sense that they are not located in any particular time like the patterns), can be identified.

For example, a situation type S in which the following entities were defined:
ev (slice, learner) and *pre (slice, state(ingredient(cheese), whole), 1)*
has the potential for the development of the pattern of meaningful interaction:
utilises (learner, slice, state(ingredient(cheese), whole), S, T) at a certain time T.

Therefore, it is possible to analyse the environment (i. e. the set of situation types) to find regularities of this sort which will denote possibilities in situation types for the development of patterns of meaningful interaction, cognitive situation, and course of interaction, and even find, through more complex analysis of combinations of these regularities, possibilities in situation types for the development of properties of cumulativeness and constructiveness, given a certain state of the learning process.

5.2 Space of Interaction Generation

From the state of the learning process it is possible to infer the learner needs at a certain time which will be to learn the meaning of a certain set of environment entities. According to some principles of meaningful learning, this implies certain requirements for the process, for example, to be cumulative and constructive with respect to certain environment entities.

Some examples of these requirements in SAMPLE are:
to be *cumulative with respect to* the notion of a salad.
to be *constructive with respect to* the notion of washing a lettuce.

To generate the space of interaction, the system has to infer, from the environment regularities (which correspond to possibilities of the environment) and from the state of the learning process (which correspond to necessities of the learning process), the situation types in which the possibilities offered by the environment can meet the necessities of the learning process at that time.

The situation types determined in this way are the situation types that can enable the occurrence of patterns that change the state of the learning process, in the sense that the process may then be cumulative or constructive with respect to a set of other environment entities.

Figure 2b shows the space of interaction generated after the learner has interacted with the situation type "salad_lab_A1". From the six situation types available, the system has concluded that the three situation types put in the space ("salad_lab_A1", "salad_lab_A4" and "salad_lab_A5") are the most likely to enable the interactions that suit the learner's needs at the present time.

6 Conclusion

The general idea explored in this paper is that the interaction of a learner with a learning environment, considered as a process in time, may be very rich in patterns that a system can be attuned, in order to get information about how and what is learned in a process of interaction between the learner and the environment.

As a first step to explore this idea, a conceptual structure for a learning environment architecture has been defined in terms of three kinds of concepts: basic entities of processes of learner-environment interaction, various kinds of regularities defined in terms of the basic entities, and properties of learning courses of interaction defined in terms of the regularities.

These definitions allowed us to develop computational mechanisms to cope with the four main functions of the proposed architecture: extract information of a fine granularity from a process of learner-environment interaction, recognise patterns in this process, interpret these patterns to infer how the learning process is going on, and determine the possible changes in the environment that can be beneficial to the learning process.

An implementation of this architecture is illustrated by SAMPLE, an intelligent learning environment for salad design. The SAMPLE implementation of the architecture operates in two levels: the domain-dependent level of interaction between the learner and the types of situations in the domain of salad design, and the domain-independent level of recording the process of interaction, analysing courses of interaction, determining the state of the learning process and generating the space of interaction.

The whole approach has been characterised as a process-sensitive learning environment architecture that can provide learning environments with means to enable individualised constructivist learning by sensing the process and making adequate changes in the environment based on a formal analysis of process information.

References

1. Duffy, T. M., Lowyck, J. and Jonassen, D. H., eds.: Designing Environments for Constructive Learning. Springer-Verlag (1993).
2. Holt, P., Dubs, S., Jones, M. and Greer, J.: The state of student modelling. In: Greer, J. E. and McCalla, G. I. (eds.) Student Modelling: The key to Individualised Knowledge-based Instruction, Springer-Verlag (1994) 3-35.
3. Piaget, J. and Garcia, R.: Toward a logic of meanings. Lawrence Erlbaum (1991).
4. Self, J.: The role of student models in learning environments. Transactions of the Institute of Electronics, Information and Communication Engineers, E77-D(1) (1994) 3-8.
5. Shuell, T. J.: Designing instructional computing systems for meaningful learning. In: Jones, M. and Winnie, P. H. (eds.) Adaptive Learning Environments, Springer-Verlag (1992) 19-54.

A Learning Environment for the Surgical Intensive Care Unit

Carmen Alexe   Jan Gecsei

Université de Montréal
Département d'informatique et de recherche opérationnelle
2920 Chemin de la Tour, Montréal, H3C 3J7, Québec, Canada
E-mail : {alexe, gecsei} @iro.umontreal.ca
Tel : 1-514-343 3505   Fax : 1-514-343 5834

Abstract: We present a learning environment aimed at the formation of nurses in a surgical intensive care unit. As a prototype within the SAFARI project, the main objectives are to combine within a single application different learning modes enriched with multimedia presentations and knowledge representations based on task graphs.

Keywords: simulation based training, knowledge representation , medical education, multimedia.

1. Introduction

The Surgical Intensive Care Unit Learning Environment (SICULE) project is one of a number of prototypes under development within the SAFARI project [4]. SAFARI focuses on the development of training and learning environments for professional applications. The motivation behind SICULE is to extend previous prototypes towards more complex, more dynamic and cognitively richer environments.

In choosing the Surgical Intensive Care Unit (SICU) context we responded to a request from the Montreal General Hospital for such a development. This also went along with our wish to define a learning enviroment that could potentially accommodate very different types of learners such as nurses, technicians, residents and specialist physicians. At the present we concentrate on the formation of nurses; the next group of users targeted are resident physicians. In the SICU the main activity consists in assisting a patient after a surgical intervention. In order to monitor and maintain a patient's condition, a team of qualified personnel cooperate and share knowledge during the patient's assessment, and subsequent therapeutic interventions. The SICU is rich in events that may require rapid reaction and reorganization of task priorities; we saw here a good opportunity to expand the task control structures and to improve task graphs defined in the previous versions of the SAFARI prototype.

Systems similar to ours have been reported, e.g. [1,3]. Compared to these, the main novelty of our approach lies in adapting the environment to different learning modes such as exploration, demonstration, and task resolution. By doing this, we loosely follow Gagné's theory [5] and the findings in [6] which establish the correspondence between the cognitive process and learning levels.

2. SICU Workflow

The time spent in the SICU as well as the procedures and observations applied vary considerably according to the initial diagnostic and the patient's evolution while in the SICU. Nevertheless, there is a common typical workflow observed for all patients, described below in Fig. 1. The patient arrives after surgery to the SICU with a case description indicating his diagnostic, condition and therapy prescription. Upon arrival, the patient is examined by a specialized nurse in order to assess the patient's actual condition in terms of vital signs, haemodynamic state, etc. If the observed signs are within the expected norm, the nurse proceeds with a the prescribed therapy and with periodic checking (observations). If, at any time, the state of the patient is observed to be outside of the norm, (i.e. unstable) then the nurse notifies the physician who examines the patient and recommends the appropriate interventions (the new therapy plan). The nurse is again in charge of executing this plan. The patient is released from the SICU once his state is out of the critical range.

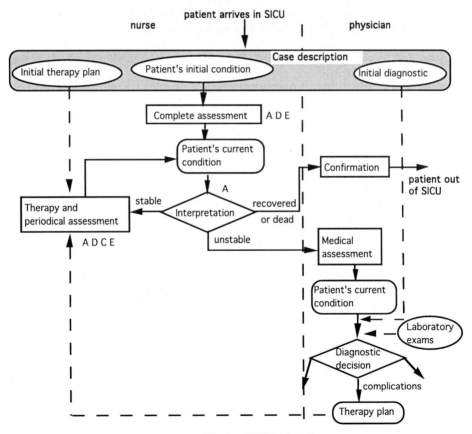

Fig.1. SICU workflow

The preceding scenario is somewhat simplified, e.g. it does not take into account the fact that several activities may be going on in parallel.

3. System Conceptual Architecture

The overall purpose of SICULE is to facilitate the transfer of knowledge towards two types of users who frequently cooperate in the SICU environment: nurses and physicians (Fig. 2).

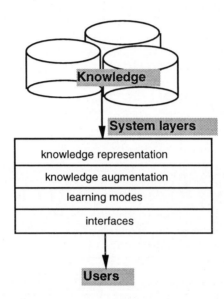

Fig.2. Block diagram of SICU learning environment

The architecture of SICU application, involves three types of knowledge: environmental, medical and pedagogical [2] (Fig.3). Knowledge categories marked by A, B, C, D and E are required by the activities illustrated in Fig. 1.

Environmental knowledge concerns biomedical equipment and tools required when applying the therapy protocols. Categories of this knowledge are: structural, functional and operational. The first two are represented implicitly in the simulation models, while operational knowledge (D) is represented as task graphs.

Medical knowledge is essential for the appropriate assessment of patients arriving in the SICU, for interpreting this information, and for deciding on the necessary interventions. Two categories can be distinguished: general and case-specific knowledge.

General knowledge includes protocols for patient assessment (A) and for therapeutic interventions (C). This is needed by nurses to execute periodic evaluations of the patient and perform the therapy protocols. These protocols are represented as dynamic task graphs. Diagnostic and treatment expertise are used by the physician if the assessment results indicate some abnormal condition (with regard to his initially stable condition). This expertise is not yet implemented in our system.

Case-specific knowledge covers two aspects: the case description presenting the patient's initial condition and diagnostic, and the therapy plan. (These items have been established before the patient's entry in the SICU). The case description is presented as text to the student as background information. Strategic expertise (E) is represented as rules; its purpose is to adapt general knowledge to the case on hand. For example, the order of examinations during the assessment will be different for a patient with a cranial trauma and a patient with stomach surgery.

Pedagogical knowledge is involved in tutoring strategies and organization of the subject matter (curriculum) [7]. Course knowledge groups together the learning objectives and resources needed for a complete learning session.

Knowledge to be taught by SICULE includes items (A), (C) (D) and (E) above. All other types of knowledge serve as background information at different stages of the learning process.

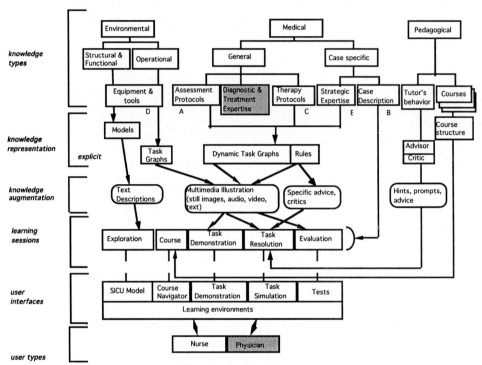

Fig. 3. System layers

3.1 Knowledge Representation - Dynamic Task Graphs

We use dynamic task graphs (DTG) to represent procedural knowledge such as the medical protocols for patient assessment and treatment. Our method is a refinement of a widely used way of representing knowledge [1]. The graph is based upon the decomposition of a task through several abstraction levels, toward basic actions . Figure 4 presents an object-oriented model of the DTG [9]. The graph is made by nodes related by decomposition and constraint links. Non-terminals nodes are decomposable abstract task of different degrees of complexity, and leaves are atomic actions. A task defines the execution sequence of its subtasks by an aspect called behavior. The most common behaviors are "and successive - execute all sub-tasks in a prescribed order", "and - execute all sub-tasks with no order", "or - execute only one of all sub-tasks", etc. [8].

An aspect named result is associated to each node. While the result of a concrete action is a fact directly obtained by doing that action (for example the result of checking the body temperature of a person is that temperature), the result of a task is obtained by reasoning about the results of its subtasks. Thus, the results become more and more synthetic as the graph is covered bottom up. A current set of results together with time events define the current execution context The DTG may be considered as a structure with finite states which correspond to current execution contexts. A state of the DTG maps the values of membership and priority parameters embedded in each decomposition link. After each action the task graph is dynamically reconfigured to take into account the new results, i.e. the execution context This is made possible by a set of rules, embedded in the constraint links, which constitute the strategic expertise (E), shown in Fig. 3. The constraint links also implement an inference mechanism.

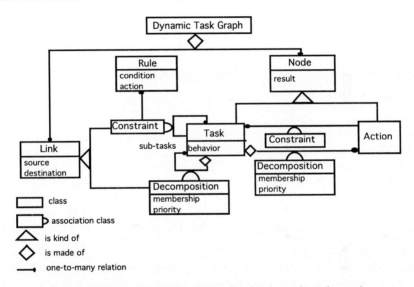

Fig. 4. An object oriented model for the dynamic task graph

As an example, Figure 5 presents a partial view of the patient's assessment task.
The assessment task consists of the initial assessment of the patient upon arrival in SICU and periodic checking. Usualy the initial assessment begins with the respiratory system. .As the patient is already ventilated, the nurse will start by checking the if the patient is correctly intubated by the E.T tube. The results of checking the far out and far in marks on the tube induce a qualitative result with regard to the E.T. tube position. If found incorrect the constraint link (a) will enable the action "Fix the E.T. position", while the the constraint link (b) will change the priority of the action "Listen to breath sounds" from 2 to 3. Another constraint link (c) implements the time dependency of certain actions, such as periodic checkings.

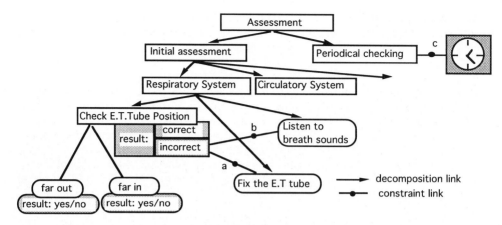

Fig. 5. An example of task decomposition

4. Learning Session and Tutoring Modes

Learning sessions are based on the natural cycle in which most people acquire skills, and on the observation that learning is facilitated when the learner is given an active role. First the learner must get familiar with the SICU by freely examining the artifacts found in the environment. Information is available about the patient (such as case history and records) and the biomedical equipment and auxiliary tools. Each equipment is individually modeled in terms of its input and output parameters and basic functionalities.

In order to best accommodate the particular needs of the learner the SICU learning sessions are configured according to the following "dimensions":

- Subject granularity: This determines whether the learning goal is situated at the course or task level. We remind that (somewhat simplifying) a course may contain several tasks and that a given task can be part of several courses. The structure of a course, its objectives, the pre-requisites and pedagogical resources attached to each objective are presented in the course environment. The course structure is imported from the Curriculum module developed within the Safari project [7].

- Site of control: The two possibilities available are system-controlled and learner-controlled session. The former applies to the course level only, the latter to both granularity levels. That is, the system (using feedback from the student model) may control the sequencing of the tasks within a course according to the student cognitive profile and to the learning goals. By learner-controlled we mean that the student is free to chose the sequencing of the tasks and the tutoring modes.

- *Tutoring modes:* These apply at the task level; a task can be accessed in three basic modes: (a) free exploration (using a simulation or a model), (b) demonstration (interactive and non-interactive), and (c) problem resolution with different kinds of coach.

In *demonstration* mode the user can follow the execution of a task together with multimedia illustrations of the basic actions. Demonstrations are available for both assessment and equipment operational tasks. The user can choose between two demonstration styles: a non-interactive demonstration follows a predefined plan, while the interactive demonstration gives the user the possibility to select the action (and its associated illustrations) to be shown. Figure 6 shows a part of the assessment task, while the highlighted action (check pulse rate) is being demonstrated.

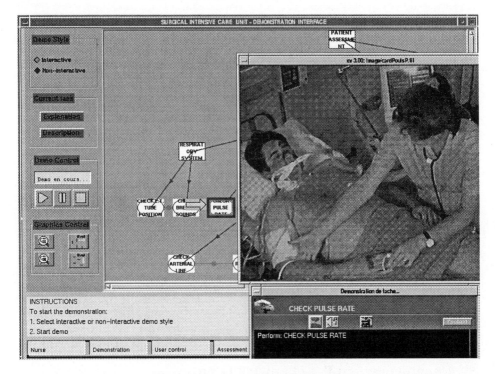

Fig. 6. Demonstration environment

The *task resolution* mode gives access to the principal learning tool of our system. Here, the learner is asked to simulate the execution of a task. Two kinds of coaching are available here: *advisor* and *critic*. Both coaching modules evaluate the student input by matching it into the current state of the DTG. While the advisor module evaluates the timeliness of an action and the accomplishment of a subtask according to its behavior, the critic module qualifies the appropriateness of an action with regard to the current execution context (see § 3.1). Figures 7 shows the task resolution.

The advisor detects an incorrect action and gives positive answers to several questions such as "What next ?", "What I did wrong ?", "What is the expert's solution ?", etc. The resolution of a task is interactively guided by the learner who is asked about the results of his actions, as shown by the dialog in figure 7. For the tasks concerning equipment manipulation real simulations in VAPS are available [10]. One can notice the central role of task graphs, which control both the demonstration and task resolution modes.

At the present development stage our application does not integrate a student model, but provides the user with simple, self evaluation tests based on multiple choice questions with cumulative counting of the good answers.

446

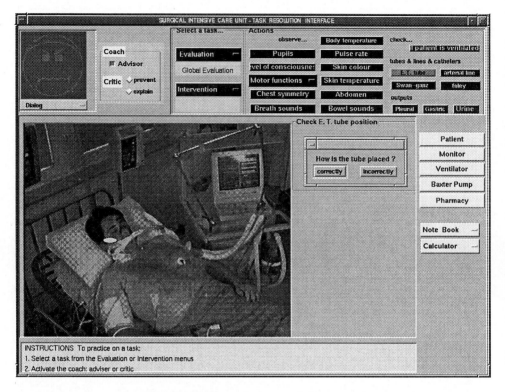

Fig. 7. Task resolution environment

5. Conclusions and Acknowledgments

We outlined the present state of an environment designed to teach skills required for nurses to work in a surgical intensive care unit, developed within the SAFARI project. We have developed dynamic task graphs as flexible structures able to model complex knowledge such as medical protocols. SICULE combines within a single application different learning modes enriched with multimedia presentations and tutoring strategies. The application is implemented on Unix/Solaris platform using VisualWorks version 2.0 and Smalltalk 80.

Work on the project continues in several directions which obviously need enhancements: (a) extension of the system's knowledge base, (b) development of a student model, (c) implementation of realistic dynamic scenarios where patient's state can evolve in response to therapy, and (d) extensive testing with target users.

We wish to acknowledge the cooperation of the Surgical Intensive Care Unit of the Montreal General Hospital, and the continuing contributions of Dr. S. Lajoie and R. Bouchard from McGill University, and Dr. M. Kaltenbach from Bishop's University. This work has been supported by the Ministry of Industry, Trade, Science and Technology (MICST) under the Synergy program of the Government of Québec.

References

[1] C. Eliot and B.P. Woolf, "An Adaptive Student Centered Curriculum for an Intelligent Training System", User Modeling and User-Adapted Interaction, 5:67-86, 1995.

[2] C. Alexe, J. Gecsei and M. Kaltenbach, "The Surgical Intensive Care Unit Application, a Learning Environment", Université de Montréal DIRO-Safari Internal Report, 1995.

[3] "Emergency Room", CD-ROM, Legacy Software, 1995, IBM multimedia software source code # 4775.

[4] J. Gecsei and C. Frasson, "SAFARI: an Environment for Creating Tutoring Systems in Industrial Training", Edmedia'94, Vancouver, July 1994, pp. 15-20.

[5] R. Gagné, The conditions of learning, 4 ed, Les éditions HRW Ltée, Montréal, 1985.

[6] C, Frasson, and M. Kaltenbach, "Strengthening the Novice-Expert shift using the self-explanation effect" Journal of Artificial Intelligence in Education, special issue on student modelling, vol 3(4), 1993

[7] R. Nkambou, G. Gauthier, "Un modèle de représentation du curriculum dans un STI", Proceedings of ITS'96, 12-14 June 1996, Montréal

[8] F. Pachet, J-Y Djamen,., C. Frasson,.M. Kaltenbach, (1995) "Production de conseils pertinents exploitant les relations de composition et de précédence dans un arbre de tâches" Technique des Sciences Educatives 1995 (to appear).

[9] J. Rumbaugh, M. Blaha, W. Premerlani, F. Eddy, W. Lorensen, (1991), Object-Oriented Modeling and Design, Prentice-Hall, Inc.

[10] "VAPS: Conceptual Overview", Virtual Prototypes, Montreal, 1993.

A New Way for Visual Reasoning in Geometry Education

Philippe Bernat
Josette Morinet-Lambert

Centre de Recherche en Informatique de Nancy/CNRS
Université Henri Poincaré - Nancy I, B.P. 239
54506. Vandoeuvre les Nancy Cedex - FRANCE

Abstract. In this paper, we describe two open learning environments for geometry problem solving: CALQUES which is widely used in French secondary schools for mathematical courses, then CHYPRE which is an experimental improvement with reasoning tools. Our aim is not to imitate an expert method nor to implement an existing pedagogical approach but to give freedom to explore a problem in any way and to test any plan of problem-solving. Visual reasoning plays an important role in geometry and provides a far different approach of problem-solving than standard formal proofs. We will explain that a student using CHYPRE focuses only on the main statements that could be observed on the problem diagram and has the opportunity to skip the less important ones. To students, as well as to mathematicians, mathematical concepts are not mere definitions, but they consist of individuals' intuitions. These intuitions are formed by imagination and understanding.

Keywords: visual reasoning, direct manipulation, problem solving, geometry

1. Introduction

Problem-solving in geometry is an excellent tool for learning general problem-solving. Constructing proofs in geometry is often considered as a difficult task for the students. The final written proof is only a part of a complex process which mainly relies on visual reasoning. For D. Guin [6], problem-solving is formed by many phases: reading and understanding the terms of the problem, drawing a diagram, imagining a plan of resolution, testing this plan , if necessary, modifying it, and finally, writing the proof. To imagine and test a plan, the student has to be able to develop strategic skills: by using the problem diagram as a model, he induces possible statements from it and a possible path from the givens to the goal. This activity is a non-formal activity of reasoning. In fact, reasoning and proving are often confused in pedagogical practices. When teaching problem-solving, the teachers present a model of a proof (the best of course) and hope that students are able to reproduce it in other cases, perhaps by analogy. The methods used to find the proof are rarely taught. Students are evaluated on the final writing of the proof and we never see anything of their reasoning skills.

The superiority of graphical representations over written representations has been largely highlighted [10], [3]. Visualization is generally considered helpful in mathematical reasoning. T. Dreyfus [4] shows how visual reasoning plays a far more important role in the work of today's mathematicians than is generally known.

Moreover, geometry is a powerful field for testing visual reasoning ability. However, Dreyfus notices the low status given to visual aspects of mathematics in the classroom. Visual reasoning is considered as a learning aid but not as real mathematics. Computers make it possible to represent visual mathematics. Nevertheless, a dynamic geometry software is not dedicated to problem-solving. It is the role of the teacher to lead to the adequate didactic situation.

For the specific domain of problem-solving, several projects have developed Intelligent Tutoring Systems (ITSs). Examples of ITSs in geometry are the Geometry Tutor [1 developed in USA, Mentoniezh [11] developed in France. But these projects are not centered on (visual) reasoning. Moreover, when using these products, the student is generally constrained in a "step by step" model of problem-solving. He has to find out each rule necessary to the proof and apply it on existing statements to construct a correct inference. Then the proof is complete when the givens are connected to the goal. Nevertheless, like Koedinger and Anderson[8], we observe that experts do not go through all the steps of a proof. They focus on the key steps and skip the less important ones.

Our aim is not to imitate an expert (teacher or professional mathematician), but we observe that the use of a "step by step model" leads students to forget a plan that they have eventually imagined. Accordingly, our work is based on the relevance of basic (or prototypical) configurations (e.g. a parallelogram) in a figure because basic configurations are closed to chunks of knowledge. We believe that planning could be formulated in terms of basic configurations.

2. From Calques to Chypre

Creating geometry proofs requires a spatial understanding of the concepts and abilities in recognizing basic geometry configurations. Then, the first part of our project was to create a tool which helps student in diagram construction and shapes recognition. With this tool, it is relatively easy to visualize a problem diagram and to see how some elements are invariable when moving the basic objects of a construction but it is more difficult to see the main statements of a proof and the links between these statements. For this reason, we completed this software and built Chypre to clarify the process of visual reasoning.

2.1 Drawing a diagram with Calques

Calques Géométriques[1] [2] allows the user to create any Euclidian construction (i.e. any construction which can be constructed with a compass and a straight-edge). The problem diagram is drawn in a menu-driven environment. This interface is similar to many dynamic geometry environments (Cabri Géomètre [9], Geometer's Sketchpad [7]).

---

[1] Calques Géométriques is distributed by Topiques Editions (Pont A Mousson - France). The last version of Calques Géométriques is supported by a "licence mixte" contract from the French Ministry of Education

Calques Géométriques is widely used by French teachers. It is used in a way similar to the Geometric Supposer [14]: with the aid of Calques, students construct a problem diagram and explore the problem to generate conjectures and to verify some properties. Students usually work in pairs in a computer laboratory, guided by a worksheet prepared by the teacher.

In another way, Calques is commonly used by teachers for proof-reading. The screen of a computer is projected overhead and Calques is used as a super blackboard. The teacher explains proofs to the whole class, using visual justifications (see fig. 1).

Let C1, C2, C3 be three circles with same radius and respective centers a, b, c. K is a point common to the three circles. The circles intersect by pair on A, B, C. Proof that AK and ab are perpendicular

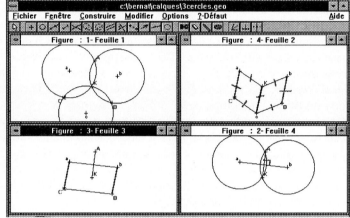

Figure 1: A visual proof as it appears in Calques Géométriques. Sheet #1: terms of the problem. Sheet #2: from circles to rhombuses. Sheet #3: from rhombuses to a parallelogram. Sheet #4: proof of the goal.

This problem is difficult because a complete diagram becomes very unmanageable. With Calques, the diagram could be separated into several diagrams and the sequence of these diagrams may be considered as an obvious visual proof (fig.1). A pencil is also available with which the teacher can mark some signs on the diagram. Nevertheless, Calques doesn't contain expert knowledge for problem-solving. It was necessary to add a specific component dedicated to proof-constructions.

2.2 Problem-solving with Chypre

A diagram could be drawn with Calques and reused in Chypre or it could be drawn directly in Chypre in a Calques-like window. By observing the problem diagram, the student "conjectures" that something in the diagram seems true. This observation corresponds to a basic configuration and can be entered as a statement. The student declares this statement by pointing out the elements of the statement on the diagram. He doesn't have to justify an entered statement. This is the major difference with another software like Angle [8], or Mentoniezh [11]. A statement corresponds to a concept which is mentally imagined. The complex structure of a geometrical concept is cued by a diagrammatic representation. For Larkin and Simon [10], diagrams allow inferences. They consider that it is possible to "see" an inference, and that this "perceptually seeing" could be very efficient. For Fischbein [5], a geometrical figure has intrinsically conceptual properties, but it is not a mere concept. It is an image, a visual image. All geometrical figures represent mental constructions which possess, simultaneously, conceptual and figural properties. When we solve a problem, we notice a parallelogram on the problem diagram. This parallelogram is particular, it is an instance of the concept *parallelogram*. We imagine then a mental parallelogram. It thought to be ideally perfect and has all the properties of the concept. We can easily imagine the links between this concept and other concepts closed to it. Pointing out these links is not necessary, because we estimate that they are obvious.

To create a statement, the user indicates where in the diagram this statement appears. For instance, to conjecture *ABCD is a parallelogram*, it is necessary to click on the points A, B, C and D. After checking the accuracy of this statement, the system creates "implicit statements", i.e. statements which can be inferred naturally from the fact designated by the student. For instance, an implicit of "*ABCD is a parallelogram*" is "*AB and CD are parallel*". The whole statement is added to the solving graph window of Chypre. The statement conjectured by the student is eventually connected to other existing statements. These connections are shown on a graph. The problem is solved when the givens and the goal are connected.

The student is absolutely free to explore the problem. He may begin with inferences either from givens or from goal. He may also develop a set of statements detached from the givens and the goal. Because of the use of implicit statements, the student is not constrained to declare all statements, but only the main ones.

2.3 A sample use of Chypre

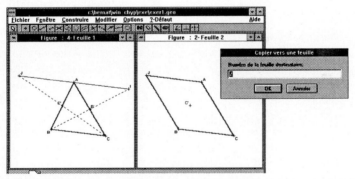

Figure 2: The complete diagram is visible on sheet #1 (feuille 1) in window #4. Some elements of this diagram have been copied on sheet #2, and have been completed, it may be a hint for the student.

Chypre allows teachers to propose any problem which can be solved with the theorems and concepts, which are implemented in the system. The system reproduces actually the geometry in relation with parallelograms, perpendicular bisectors and the configurations nicknamed 'triangle of the midpoints'[2]. The teacher can propose most geometry exercises offered in the orientation cycle of the junior high school curriculum.

> **Exercise** : ABC is a triangle. C' and B' are midpoints of AB and AC.
> I is the symmetric of B by B'. J is the symmetric of C by C'.
> Prove that A is midpoint of IJ.

Drawing a problem diagram

The first task is to draw the problem diagram. Usually, this task is carried out by the student but some teachers prefer to prepare the diagram themselves. They copy some elements of the diagram on separate "sheets" (fig. 2). When typing in the key F2, the diagram visible on the window changes into the diagram of a parallelogram.

Specifying the problem

First, to solve the problem, the student creates the given and the goal statements. To create a new statement, the student uses the menu item "*Solve/New statement*". He gives the type of the statement (example: midpoint), and the value of the statement, which is *hypothesis* (except for the goal: the value of the goal is *conjecture*). On the diagram, the student indicates an instance of the chosen statement by directly designing the elements of the statement (example: to enter *B' is midpoint of CA*, he chooses the type "*midpoint*" and clicks on the three points C, A and B').

Solving the problem

To solve the problem, the student enters any statement corresponding to basic configurations observed on the diagram. He uses the same method to enter these statements than to enter the givens (fig.3). The only difference concerns the values[3] of the statements which can be : *Hypothesis* for the givens, *Conjecture* for the other statements, *Proved* if the fact can be inferred from givens. The two first values are allocated by the student. The third is calculated by Chypre. Notice that the initial value of the goal is *conjecture* obtained automatically when turning on the goal check box. At the end of the proof, the value would be *proved*.

Suppose that the student enters the two following givens: *B' is midpoint of AB, B' is midpoint of BI*. He could see on the diagram the parallelogram AICB and imagine the link between the two givens and this prototypical figure. He creates the statement "*AICB is a parallelogram*", with the value "conjecture". Chypre finishes by adding a link between these statements. Because it is linked with two givens, the value of "*AICB is a parallelogram*" changes from "conjecture" to "proved". All these results are shown on the interface in the solving-graph window (fig.3). The value of each statement is coded by a color: blue for given, red for conjecture and black for proved. Moreover, proved statements and givens are written in bold characters.

---

[2] The configuration said "triangle of the midpoints" is made up with a triangle ABC and the midpoints of the sides AB and AC.

[3] These three values are the reason of Chypre acronym (Conjecture, Hypothese, Preuve). Chypre is also the French name for Cyprus.

The student has worked forward, from the givens, and was beginning to work backward from the goal. Notice that Chypre has also added a link from the goal to a conjecture although this link is useless for the proof.

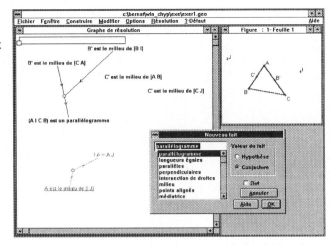

Figure 3: The Chypre interface in the middle of the problem.

The link between statements is not necessarily a single instance of a theorem. It may be more complex. For instance, suppose that the student has entered "*AICB is a parallelogram*" and "*JACB is a parallelogram*". He now enters "*IA and AJ are parallel*". Because the concept of parallelogram contains many properties, particularly the parallelism of the opposite sides, Chypre can infer a link between these statements (bolded link in fig. 4, left).

More generally, Chypre creates a link between statements when this link can be imagined easily. This was possible by way of an adequate knowledge representation which includes in the same shell all implicit properties of a geometrical concept. Because Chypre doesn't know whether a goal is the unique and final goal (it is possible to declare multiple goals), Chypre creates all possible links from existing statements to a new statement. So Chypre could create links which are useless for a specific proof. Nevertheless, useless links (i.e. links from a goal or to a given) are drawn with dotted lines (fig.3).

Chypre accepts all statements which look correct on the diagram. It only rejects the statements which are too distant from a graphical representation. For instance, Chypre rejects the statement *AIBC is a parallelogram*, which doesn't correspond with the sequence of the points.

2.4 Additional features and aids

The aim of the additional features is to help the student to understand the solution and to write the proof.

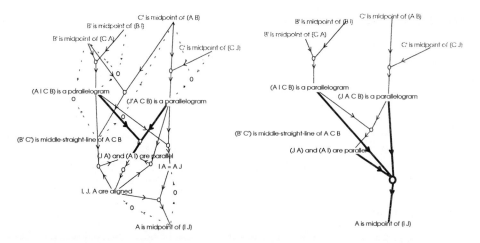

Figure 4: Filtering the graph: implicit statements have been hidden. The result is a tree: the goal is the root and the givens are the leaves.

Filtering the graph

The state of the problem is illustrated by a graphical representation. Like Wertheimer [13], we think that a solving graph is a clear and logical way of representing a proof. The use of a graphical representation facilitates the observation and improves the understanding and reasoning process. This representation is the reduction of a more complex solving graph which has a whole internal representation. Nevertheless, this graph can appear very jammed for many reasons (fig. 4, left). With Chypre, the student is free to conjecture all statements which are plausible and then, during the reasoning phase, it is very common to create statements which are finally useless. Naturally, it is easy to delete these statements, but the problem for the student is to decide which ones are useless.

Another reason for the possible complexity of the graph, is the detailed level of the proof. Chypre allows to work at several proof levels. Sometimes, the student is content with main statements and sometimes he enters many detailed statements, according to his ability. The graph can be filtered as shown in figure 4, right. First, it is possible to filter "from the givens". The result is a graph with no loop. More precisely, this graph is a tree. A tree denotes a final proof, whereas the solving graph denotes the problem state, including all useless statements which result from student indecision. It is also possible to hide dead-end paths (paths which don't lead to a goal): in figure 4, the path which goes from the givens to the statement *"B'C' is middle-straight-line of ACB"* has been automatically hidden. Eventually, the student would delete this statement.

The statements have different levels of importance. A statement which is an implicit of another existing statement could be considered less important because it is easy to recover it mentally. We can ask Chypre to hide these statements (see figure 4, right). Hiding these statements leads to a decrease in cognitive load and points out the relevant information, without increasing the difficulty of understanding.

Understanding and writing the proof

Even if it is often easy to understand each link on the graph, the student would probably see more details of some links. This would be necessary particularly if the graph had been filtered. An example is the last link in the right graph in figure 4. This link does not correspond to a theorem. It is not very difficult to understand it. However, if the student double-clicks on this link, he obtains a dialog box which provides a detailed text of proof (fig.5). This text could also be used for writing the formal proof which is often required.

(AICB) is a parallelogram
so AI = BC
(JACB) is a parallelogram
so JA = BC
(JA) is parallel to (AI)
then
IA = AJ
I,J,A are aligned

then A is midpoint of IJ

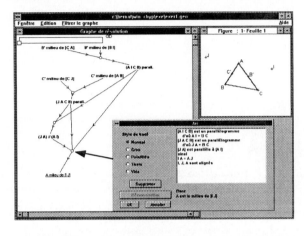

Figure 5: Chypre at the end of the problem. The proof of a step is detailed.

In fact, we are personally convinced that a proof obtained by the way of Chypre and presented as a solving tree is sufficient from mathematical and pedagogical points of view. This proof is obviously mathematically complete. From a pedagogical point of view, it reveals that the student has understood the problem, because he has been able to visually extract the main statements from the problem diagram. But, unfortunately, this kind of visual reasoning is considered by many teachers only as an aid. The teachers don't give full credit for visual solutions because they estimate that visual reasoning is fuzzy reasoning and cannot be well formalized. Such an attitude may be justified by what is usually considered. The slow speed of educational change may be one reason for this. Nevertheless, we have to take the teachers' opinion into account. We must offer the possibility to the student to present his work in a form adapted to the teacher's preferences.

3. Conclusion

We argue that Calques and Chypre are tools for visual reasoning. The construction component, Calques Géométriques, is a very helpful aid for teachers. With this environment, it is easy to show visual proofs. Nevertheless, Calques alone is not sufficient to help unaccompanied students to verify the accuracy of the proofs they conjecture. For that reason, we built Chypre. Chypre respects the main principles of Calques: an encouragement for visual reasoning by direct designation of objects, an understandable level of knowledge, and a clear interface representation. Of course, Chypre doesn't permit all kinds of visual reasoning. Reasoning related to geometric transformations (rotation, translation, ...) or moving points around a figure are not possible with Chypre· Yet, because Chypre supports non-formal proofs, it should help teachers to emphasize reasoning skills.

On the other hand, Chypre reveals didactic problems. The use of Chypre introduces another way of teaching geometry. It is important that teachers accept non formal proofs. They must accept that the student focuses on the key steps and skips the less important ones. They must accept explanations which are not highly formalized. The teachers must understand that, when teaching problem-solving, the main things to teach first is how to reason, how to find the solution and not how to write a formal proof (although this is easier to teach).

References

[1] **ANDERSON, J.R. - BOYLE, C.F. - YOST, G. :** *The Geometry Tutor*. Proceedings of IJCAI 85, Los Angeles, pp. 1-7, 1985

[2] **BERNAT, P. :** *CALQUES2,* Topiques Edition, 1994

[3] **CUNNINGHAM,S. - HUBBOLD R.J.:** *Interactive Learning Through Vizualisation*, IFIP Series on Computer graphics, Springer-Verlag 1992.

[4] **DREYFUS, T. :** *Imagery and Reasoning in Mathematics and Mathematics Education*, Selected Lectures from the 7th International Congress on Mathematical Education, Les Presses de l'Université Laval, Sainte-Foy, pp. 107-122, 1994

[5] **FISCHBEIN, E. :** *The Theory of Figural Concepts*, Educational Studies in mathematics 24, pp. 139-162, 1993

[6]**GUIN, D. :** *Modélisation des connaissances pour un système d'aide à la démonstration géométrique,* Université d'été Informatique et Enseignement de la Géométrie, IREM de Toulouse, pp. 61-72, 1990

[7] **JACKIW, N. :** *The Geometer's Sketchpad (version 3.0),* Visual Geometry Project, Key curriculum Press, 1995

[8] **KOEDINGER, K.R. - ANDERSON, J.R.** : *Effective Use of Intelligent Software in High School Math Classrooms*, Proceedings of AI-ED 93, P.Brna, S. Ohlsson, H. Pain (Ed), pp. 241-248, 1993

[9] **LABORDE, J.M. - BELLEMAIN, F. :** *Cabri 2* - Texas Instruments

[10] **LARKIN, J.H. - SIMON, H.A. :***Why a Diagram is (Sometimes) Worth Ten Thousand Words*, Cognitive Science 11, pp. 65-99, 1987[BP1]

[11] **PY, D. :** *Geometry problem solving with Mentoniezh*, Computers in Education, vol. 20 n°1, Pergamon Press, pp. 141-146, 1993

[12] **TAURISSON, A. :** *Pensée mathématique et gestion mentale, Pour une pédagogie de l'intuition mathématique*. Bayard Editions, 1993

[13] **WERTHEIMER, R. :** *The Geometry Proof Tutor : An Intelligent Computer-based Tutor in the Classroom,* Mathematics Teacher, pp. 308-317, April 1990

[14] **YERUSHALMY, M. - CHAZAN, D. :** *Overcoming Visual Obstacles with the Aid of the Supposer*. Educational Studies in Mathematics n°21, pp. 199-219, 1990

Example Explanation in Learning Environments

Robert Burow and Gerhard Weber

Department of Psychology, University of Trier, D-54286 Trier, Germany
E-Mail: {robbu | weber }@cogpsy.uni-trier.de

Abstract. This paper describes the design and use of an example explanation module embedded in an ITS that teaches the programming language LISP to novices. When examples are provided to support a learning process it is likely that students find it difficult to understand or to interpret them. By explaining examples these problems are reduced and give the students better insights into the problem solving domain as the explanation also serves as a positive instance to self-explanations. Problems, possible solutions, and advantages of providing examples with explanations are described to point out the importance of providing examples added with explanations in an intelligent learning environment.

1 Introduction

In education, examples are a common phenomenon. It is almost impossible to find one textbook that does not have any examples. Teachers use examples to introduce new concepts by explaining the structural similarities of the example and the problem. In Intelligent Tutoring Systems (ITS), however, examples only play a minor role. Although there have been many discussions about the use of examples, like how many examples should accompany a task (e.g., Reed & Bolstad, 1991), whether it is useful to force students to create self-explanations (e.g., Chi, Bassok, Lewis, Reimann, & Glaser, 1989), and in which way examples should be presented to the students (e.g., Linn, 1992), the number of ITSs and intelligent learning environments using examples explicitly remains small.

In this paper we want to discuss the explanation of examples from a student's point of view. An example should help a student to learn how similar solution strategies apply to different problem situations. But, what if the student does not understand the example? What if the student who is learning a new task interprets an example in a wrong way? Or, if the selected examples are everything but optimal for the student? These questions will be addressed in the context of the case-based learning environment ELM-PE (Weber & Möllenberg, 1994) that supports learning LISP.

2 Example Use in Programming Environments

Programming is a typical domain where examples are used very often. Therefore, most tutoring systems and learning environments that use and provide examples are systems that support learning to program. The function of examples in such systems can be divided into three classes:

- *Programming support*
  Programming environments (e.g., Turbo Pascal, C++, or Visual Basic) usually provide examples as add-ons to help providing topics so the user can see how a certain construct or function could be used.
- *Teaching operations*
  Tutoring systems and CAI (e.g., CLEM (Boyle, Gray, Wendl, & Davies, 1994), ITEM/IP (Brusilovsky, 1992)) present examples as important part of the course to demonstrate some useful problem solving techniques in parallel with introducing new concepts to give some practical reference to the use of these concepts.
- *Problem solving*
  Some intelligent tutoring systems, (e.g., DISCOVER (Ramadhan & du Boulay, 1993) and ELM-PE (Weber & Möllenberg, 1994)), use examples to support students in the process of problem solving. That is, the system provides one or more examples to help the student to solve the problem that he/she is working on.

The use of examples in the first two categories may be very useful to provide syntactical insights, but in the process of problem solving, the example as a whole, structurally as well as syntactically, should be similar to the problem the user is working on. We will concentrate on the last category in this paper, as it is a challenging feature of systems that support problem solving.

2.1 Examples as Problem Solving Support

As there are hardly any programming environments that provide examples to support problem solving, experts use their own solutions to previously solved problems. Experienced programmers are able to retrieve remindings from previously solved tasks and are able to adapt them to solve a current problem (Novick & Holyoak, 1991). The fact that they not only have this ability but also use it very often indicates that using examples in programming tasks is very useful.

When a teacher uses examples, whether from a textbook or self-made, to explain the practical use of concepts in solving problems, the teacher will point out the similarities of the example to the situation that he/she is trying to explain. The most important reason for explaining examples is the simple fact that if the students do not understand the example, or misunderstand it, the example will only confuse them and will actually be an obstacle to the integration of the new concepts into the knowledge structure the student has of the domain. Therefore, two main goals exist in an educational situation where examples are used. First, examples have to be chosen carefully to be helpful in a given learning or problem solving situation. Second, examples have to be explained to be really useful, as explanation will provide an optimal problem solving and learning transfer.

2.2 Example Explanation

Examples are most useful when they are not only provided by a textbook or by a tutorial system, but additionally are accompanied by self-explanations (Chi et al., 1989; Pirolli, 1991). Chi et al. (1989) found that students who produced more self-explanations during the first stages of learning physics were more successful in solving physics problems in subsequent lessons. In addition, they observed qualitative differences in the kinds of self-explanations produced by good and poor learners. Perhaps most importantly, students performing better generated significantly more explanations relevant to subsequent phases of problem solving. Pirolli and Bielaczyc (1989) found that good learners show more evidence of monitoring themselves that can be interpreted as higher amounts of metacognition. Additionally, they could show that good learners produce more domain-specific elaborations and that these explanations are more semantics-oriented compared to explanations made by poor learners that are more often syntax-oriented. Thus, using examples may be improved by either forcing learners to build self-explanations, or by an intelligent system which provides explanations so that the system can serve as a positive instance of how examples can be explained.

When a system provides an explanation for an example, we claim that it is most useful when it is based on the similarities in the example on the one side, and the problem the student is trying to solve on the other side.

3 Example Explanation in ELM-PE

As the student is working on a task, he or she can ask for an example by pressing the example button. The system then either provides an example that it selected as the best one or the student can select an example from the pool of examples using a browsing tool. After the example is selected, the system will look for conceptual similarities between the task and the example. Conceptual similarity, in contrast to syntactical similarity, means that the goal-/subgoal tree is analyzed rather than the surface structure (more about this in the next section). After that, the explanation is generated on the basis of these similarities. Now, the student can select pieces of code that will be explained, or just let the system explain the most important similarities step by step. So, the user can actually navigate in the explanation space and look at the explanations that he/she requires.

Stepping through the explanations of the similarities, the student can discover step by step why the explanation is useful and how particular pieces of code realize particular higher level goals when applied in a certain context. As a side-effect, the student learns why this example was selected by the system. This latter effect becomes even more apparent when the student selects another example that is not an optimal one. When looking at the explanation, he or she can observe that there are much less things to explain and thus much less similarities exist.

The explanation module can also be employed for re-using earlier coded functions or pieces of them in the current task because the explanation module points out useful pieces of code that the student can copy into the program window of the current task. This does not mean the student is limited by the system to copy code that is explained by the system, the student is free to copy any piece of code provided in the examples.

To give an impression of how the system presents an example annotated with explanations to the user, we will provide a short example. The student is trying to

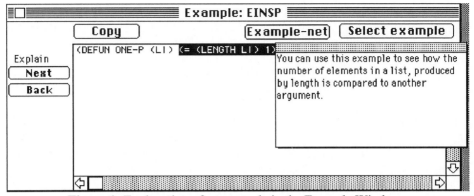

Figure 1: Explanation of an example in the Example Window.

code the function *MORE-THAN-TWO-P* that checks if a list contains more than two elements. A solution to this problem is generated by the code generation module:

```
(DEFUN MORE-THAN-TWO-P (LI)
      (> (LENGTH LI) 2))
```

The student asks for an example and the system selects the function *ONE-P* which is a function the same user defined earlier in the course. *ONE-P* tests whether a list contains exactly one element. The presentation of the example with its explanation to the student is shown in Figure 1.

The explanation points out the similarity between the task and the example by using "compare" as a generalization of "=" and ">." So, the user can see that the selected code could be used in the current task by changing the equal ("=") function to another function that compares two arguments. This also increases the students ability to identify similarities between programs as the system's explanation serves as a positive instance of retrieving and mapping structural and syntactical similarities.

3.1 Implementation of Example Explanation in ELM-PE

When a student starts a new task, the system performs a preanalysis of this task, generating an expected solution code together with an interpretation. This is done by the code generation module in ELM-PE. The code generation module starts from a plan description of the task that describes on a conceptual level how to solve this task. The expected solution could be different for any particular student because the code generation module generates this expected solution by translating the concepts of the plan into code the student has used before to code the same concept. If the concept was not coded by the student then it takes the default code. After the preanalysis, the code generation module produces a task/goal tree (Figure 2) where the task as a whole is the root that splits into concepts (subgoals). Subgoals are split up again until only basic concepts remain in the leaves that directly match the code (Weber, 1996).

The explanation module takes this tree as input and breaks it down into a Task Table. Each row of the Task Table consists of a concept and its subconcepts in the first and the second column, respectively.

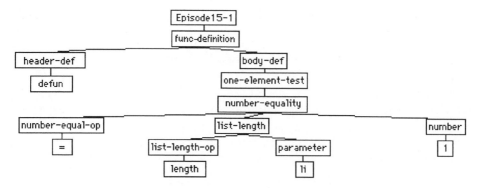

Figure 2: The Task/goal tree for the function One-element-P.

When the student asks for an example, the EBR algorithm compares the expected solution to the examples in the example pool and makes a list of the best examples to the current problem. These examples have all been diagnosed in the past. Therefore, they also have a task/goal tree that is stored in the episodic learner model. The best example determined by the EBR algorithm (Weber, in press) is directly shown to the student. If the student asks for an explanation of the current task, the explanation module takes the task/goal tree and breaks it down into an Example Table that has the same kind of entries as the Task Table. Now, the example explanation works in two steps. First, according parts of the derivation tree are matched. Second, matches (and mismatches) are annotated with explanation texts. These texts are generated from templates.

3.2 Matching

The matching procedure is actually the heart of the example explanation module, as it embodies the 'intelligence' of the module. The matcher analyses the example and the task, and decides which parts should be explained by making a link between similar concepts in the task and in the example. This link is given a similarity value which is based on the following similarity features:

- *Concept/subconcept similarity*, which is determined by either a direct match (they are the same), or a generalized match (they are strongly related), or no match, (according to semantic similarity (Holyoak & Thagard, 1989)).
- *Structural-relatedness*, when certain concepts/subconcepts are grouped in a similar way in the example and in the task (according to structural consistency (Holyoak & Thagard, 1989)).
- *Syntactical similarity*, the fact that functions/concepts have the same number of arguments will result in a small increase in the similarity value. This is important to distinguish large cond-cases from small ones, for instance.
- *Hierarchical value*, the higher a concept is in the task/goal tree, (which gives a strong indication of the importance of the concept in a function), the higher its similarity value will be (according to the systematicity principle (Gentner, 1983)).

The matching module will try to find the similarities between the entries of the Task Table and the Example Table. The matcher starts by comparing the top-concept of the

Example Table with the concepts of the Task Table. The similarity of two table entries is calculated by a two-pass matching process. First, the main concepts will be compared, and, if they are not the same, they will be generalized. After the generalization, the concepts are matched again. If there is still no match, the matcher will abort this match and will try to match this concept to the next entry in the Task Table. If the main concepts did match, directly or generalized, the matcher goes into the second pass. The second pass determines a structural similarity value by matching the subconcepts. The procedure is the same as with the main concept. First, the matcher tries to find two similar subconcepts, and, if this fails, it tries to find two similar generalized subconcepts. If there are no similar subconcepts, the structural similarity value will be zero, and the entry in the Match Table for this match will contain the matched main concept and 'NOSUBS.' The matched concepts and the matched subconcepts are stored into the Match Table together with a goodness of fit value.

3.3 Text Generation

The text generation module gets three tables from the matching module: the Task Table, that contains subtree entries of the task, the Example Table, that contains subtree entries of the example, and the Match Table, that contains similar subtrees of the task and Example Table. As the text generation module can explain an entry in any of the three tables, it is possible to provide an explanation of the function as it should be coded (task), or provide an explanation of the example as it is. Although explanations based on entries in the Task and Example Table are possible without much extra effort, the system currently only explains entries in the Match Table, that is, it explains the similarities of the task and the example. This is done by filling up a text generation template that contains slots for concepts, subconcepts, high concepts and generalizations. These slots are filled with text, stored in the frames of the concept. The text generator gets from the tables what role the concept plays in the explanation; a high concept, a concept, or a subconcept, and it gets from the tables if it is generalized or not. Then, based upon these criteria, it retrieves the appropriate texts from the frames and fills the slots.

4 An Example of the Explanation Process

For an example of the explanation process, we will take the same example as presented earlier where the student is working on the task *MORE-THAN-TWO-P* and gets the function *ONE-P* as an example. After the selection of this example by the system, the example module starts generating the Task and Example Table by analyzing the derivation trees of the task and of the example (Table 1 and Table 2, respectively). Then the matcher generates the Match Table by analyzing and comparing both the Task and the Example Table.

In the first column of the Match Table (Table 3), one can see that the matcher has generalized More-than-two-elements-test and One-element-test both to a high-list-predicate, and equal-number and greater to compare-operator. Compare-operator with

Table 1: Task Table

CONCEPT	SUBCONCEPTS
More-than-two-elements-test (High-concept)	Greater
Greater	Number, List-length
Number	Nosubs
List-length	Nosubs

Table 2: Example Table

CONCEPT	SUBCONCEPTS
One-element-test (High-concept)	Equal-number
Equal-number	Number, List-length
List-length	Nosubs
Number	Nosubs

Table 3: Match Table

CONCEPT	SUBCONCEPTS	Match-value
Compare-operator (gen)	List-length	1.5
High-list-predicate(gen)	Compare-operator (gen)	1.45
List-length	Nosubs	0.7
Number	Nosubs	0.7

subconcept list-length receives the highest value because it has a generalized match in the concept-slot and a direct match (list-length) in the subconcepts-slot. The second entry in the Match Table has almost the same value, although it contains no direct match. This is due to the fact that the concept in this entry, High-list-predicate (a generalization of More-than-two-elements-test and One-element-test), is placed higher in the derivation tree than List-length (see Figure 2).

The text generation module fills the template with the texts found in the frames of Compare-operator and List-length. For Compare-operator it selects the slot main-concept, and for List-length the slot subconcept. The presentation of the example with its explanation to the student is shown in Figure 1.

When the student presses the 'next' button (Figure 1), the explanation module will explain the next entry in the Match Table and the explanation window will switch to the piece of code to which the explanation refers. If the student does not like the example that the system has selected or wants to see another one, the student can select another one by pressing the button 'select example.' If the student just wants to browse through the example space and look at how different examples are related, then the student can press the 'Example-net' button. The student can copy the selected part of code into the programming window to use and to modify it in the task at hand.

5 Discussion

We think we can show that the obstacles described earlier are strongly reduced: The extra load on the student's working memory caused by introducing an example is minimized because of the following reasons. First of all, students are familiar with the examples because they have already seen them in the text of the course, or, because it are self coded functions as in our example. So, there will be not so much extra memory load in figuring out what this example function does. Second, because of the explanation of similarities, the students do not have to look at the whole function to search for relevant parts, but concentrate on the parts that are explained because they are important to the task. This also reduces the extra workload because the student does not have to understand the example in all details on all levels. And it is not necessary to search it completely for related concepts as the explainer does that for the student. Additionally, the process of identifying higher concepts and generalizations is done by the system and works as an example of how to find, to use, and to explain similarities.

This kind of example explanation also reduces the chance that a student will not understand the example in the context of the task, as the example explanation module guides the students interpretation by selecting and explaining the important parts of the example in such a way that the student understands why the system has selected this example. There is always a risk however, that the student will not use the explanations or does not understand them. This brings about the quality of the explanation which is very hard to determine as there is not much reference material to this subject.

We assume, that by getting explanations based on similarity the student will learn to identify structural similarities. An empirical investigation of this question has just started. The part of the explanation module that basically is responsible for this effect would probably be the ability of the explanation module to generalize and to explain concepts. By learning that certain concepts are related and that a particular piece of code can realize different concepts in different contexts, the student will acquire structural knowledge about the domain. As stated earlier, this is a kind of expert knowledge that is not learned easily and, thus, often is used inappropriately by novices. Most of the time, they only look directly at the code, not at the context it is used in. They re-use it on a superficial basis and find out later that it was not appropriate in the new context.

6 Future Research

This paper introduces a first step into example explanation. One of the most important things that is missing at the moment is a smart, flexible template selection module that should be placed *between* the matching module and the text generation module. This module should be able to select the most appropriate template out of a number of different templates. These different templates should have slots that refer to the Task and to the Example Table. So, not only the similarities between example and task can be explained, but also specific task or example concepts.

We also are working on a mechanism that explains a piece of code in the example that was selected by the student. As it is possible to generate explanation texts from the Example Table (which means that the explanation is based only on the example without considering similarities), we can choose between two kinds of explanation. First, one can have an explanation that is based only on the example. Second, one can have an example that tries to explain similarities in the selected code and only gives the example based explanation if that fails. This last one is not always better as it might confuse the student to get different kinds of explanation.

Acknowledgments

This work was supported by a Grant from "Stiftung Rheinland-Pfalz für Innovation" to the second author.

References

Boyle, T., Gray, J., Wendl, B., & Davies, M. (1994). Taking the plunge with CLEM: the design and evaluation of a large scale CAL system. *Computers and Education*, *22*, 19-26.

Brusilovsky, P. (1992). Intelligent tutor, environment, and manual for introductory programming. *Educational and Training Technology International*, *29*, 26-34.

Chi, M. T. H., Bassok, M., Lewis, M., Reimann, P., & Glaser, R. (1989). Self-explanations: How students study and use examples in learning to solve problems. *Cognitive Science*, *13*, 145-182.

Gentner, D. (1983). Structure mapping: A theoretical framework for analogy. *Cognitive Science*, *7*, 155-170.

Holyoak, K. J. & Thagard, P. (1989). Analogical mapping by constraint satisfaction. *Cognitive Science*, *13*, 295-356.

Linn, M. C. (1992). How can hypermedia tools help teaching programming. *Learning and Instruction*, *2*, 119-139.

Novick, L. R. & Holyoak, K. J. (1991). Mathematical problem solving by analogy. *Journal of Experimental Psychology: Learning, Memory, and Cognition*, *17*, 398-415.

Pirolli, P. (1991). Effects of examples and their explanations in a lesson on recursion: A production system analysis. *Cognition and Instruction*, *8*, 207-259.

Pirolli, P. & Bielaczyc, K. (1989). Empirical analyses of self-explanation and transfer in learning to program. *Proceedings of the Eleventh Annual Conference of the Cognitive Science Society* (pp. 450-457). Hillsdale, NJ: Lawrence Erlbaum Associates.

Ramadhan, H. & du Boulay, B. (1993). Programming environments for novices. In E. Lemut, B. du Boulay, & G. Dettori (Ed.), *Cognitive models and intelligent environments for learning programming* (pp. 125-134). Berlin: Springer-Verlag.

Reed, S. K. & Bolstad, C. A. (1991). Use of examples and procedures in problem solving. *Journal of Experimental Psychology: Learning, Memory, and Cognition*, *17*, 753-766.

Weber, G. (1996). Episodic learner modeling. *Cognitive Science*, *20*, (in press).

Weber, G. (in press). Individual selection of examples in an intelligent programming environment. *Journal of Artificial Intelligence in Education*.

Weber, G. & Möllenberg, A. (1994). ELM-PE: A knowledge-based programming environment for learning LISP. In T. Ottmann & I. Tomek (Eds.), *Proceedings of ED-MEDIA '94* (pp. 557-562). Charlottesville, VA: AACE.

Toward a Learning Environment Allowing Learner-Directed Problem Practice

— Helping Problem-Solving by Using Problem Simplification —

Tsukasa Hirashima   **Akihiro Kashihara**   **Jun'ichi Toyoda**

The Institute of Scientific and Industrial Research, Osaka University
8-1, Mihogaoka, Ibaraki, Osaka, 567 JAPAN
TEL: +81-6-879-8426, FAX: +81-6-875-4344
E-mail: tsukasa@ai.sanken.osaka-u.ac.jp

ABSTRACT: A promising way to foster learners' motivation in problem practice is to allow learners to freely select problems. However, in such a learner-directed problem practice, it becomes difficult to design the methods to help the learners who cannot solve the problems. In this paper, a method which helps the learners solve the problems by themselves by using simplified problems is proposed. This paper describes (1) a definition of the problem simplification, (2) a facility to simplify problems and (3) a method to help learners to solve problems by using the simplified problems. In this help, a learner who cannot solve the original problem is provided a problem which is generated by simplifying the original problem. To solve the simplified problem is useful to make clear what the learner needs to solve the original problem. When the learner cannot solve the simplified problem, the simplified problem is further simplified.

1. Introduction

Problem practice plays a crucial role in enhancing the learners' problem-solving capabilities. Therefore, developing an advanced and elaborate form of problem practice is one of the most important issues in the ITS (Intelligent Tutoring System) research [1-4]. In problem practice, learners are usually required to solve problems in a given order, since each problem is designed to prepare for the next problem. However, such constraint often reduces learners' motivation to solve the problems and to learn from the problem-solving. A promising resolution to keep learners' motivation is to allow learners to freely select problems [5]. (In this paper, such problem practice is called "learner-directed problem practice.") This resolution is easy and effective when the learners are able to solve the problems. However, it becomes very difficult to design the methods to help the learners who cannot solve the problems. A resolution is to provide the learners with correct solutions which can be prepared for each problem independently of problem sequences in problem practice. Although providing correct solutions is useful to let the learners escape from the failures of problem-solving, the learners often accept the solutions without trying to check or to regenerate the solutions [6]. Therefore, a method is required to help the learners solve problems by themselves.

Providing problems which are simplified from the original problem is the most promising method to help learners solve the original problem by themselves [7]. A problem which a learner cannot solve should include difficult elements for the learner but these elements should be only part of the problem. Therefore, the learner can solve a problem from which the difficult elements are taken. The simplified problem manifests the easy part of the original problem, and the difference of the two problems manifests the difficult part for the learner. The learner who could solve such a simplified problem can recognize the difficulties of the original problem and focus his/her efforts on those difficulties. Sometimes the learner can solve the original problem only by the focusing. Even if the learner cannot solve the original problem by him/herself, the learner can recognize what he/she should learn to solve the original problem. This recognition is very important for effective learning.

Because simplified problems can be prepared for each original problem independently of problem sequences, the problem simplification is a promising method for the learning environment allowing learner-directed problem practice. However, in order to prepare necessary and sufficient simplified problems for every problem, the problem simplification should be defined. The definition should not only be useful in preparing simplified problems but also be useful in developing a facility which generates simplified problems from the original problems.

This paper describes (1) a definition of the problem simplification, (2) a facility to simplify problems and (3) a method to help learners to solve problems by using simplified problems. Here, the target domain is problem practice of mechanical problems taught in high school. In the definition, a simplified problem is viewed as a problem which can be solved by (i) a few subprocesses from the original problem-solving process only or (ii) a specialized problem-solving process from the original problem-solving process. The simplified problems defined in section 2 of this paper are called auxiliary problems. In section 3, a facility is described which can generate or retrieve the auxiliary problems by using characteristic descriptions of the original problems based on the definition in section 2. Currently, to facilitate automatic generation of the auxiliary problems from sentences of the original problems is future work. Section 4 describes a method to use auxiliary problems in a learning environment allowing learner-directed problem practice. Currently, this environment is still being developed.

2. Definition of Auxiliary Problems

2.1 Characterization of Problems

The problem-solving process can be divided into three phases [8]: (1) statement-understanding process, (2) formulation process and (3) calculation process, which are

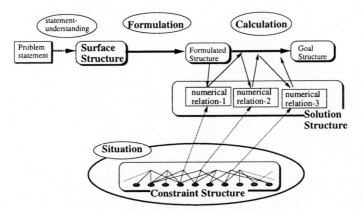

Fig. 1. A Scheme of Problem Solving Process.

shown in Fig. 1. The task of the formulation process is to reduce and remove differences between the surface structure which is a description of surface features of the problem, and the formulated structure to which numerical relations can be applied. The surface structure is used to characterize the formulation process. The task of the calculation process is to derive the answer of the problem by applying a series of numerical relations. The series of numerical relations is called a "solution structure" and the solution structure is used to characterize the calculation process. Currently, the statement-understanding process isn't dealt with.

Numerical relations which don't contribute to solving a problem but which exist in the situation set up by the problem are also important to characterize problems. For example, numerical relations according to kinetic energy aren't necessary to solve Problem-1 shown in Fig. 2, but the numerical relations are necessary to solve Problem-2 which requires the kinetic energy of the block after T minutes in the same situation. Therefore, numerical relations included in the situation are indispensable to characterize the problem. The situation is characterized by a network composed of numerical relations among attributes included in the situation. The network is called a "constraint structure" and the constraint structure is used to characterize the situation.

2.2 Categorization of Auxiliary Problems

In this paper, a problem is characterized by a surface structure, a solution structure and a constraint structure. The reduction of problem-solving process is carried out by formalizing

---

[Problem-1] A block of mass M is put on a smooth incline quietly. The angle of the incline is ϕ and the gravity acceleration value is G. Find the force of the block in parallel direction to the incline.

[Problem-2] A block of mass M is put on a smooth incline quietly. The angle of the incline is ϕ and the gravity acceleration value is G. Find the kinetic energy of the block after T minutes.

[Problem-3] A person who is going up in an elevator moving with velocity: V0, releases a ball. Find the velocity of the ball after T minutes. The gravity acceleration value is G.

[Problem-4] The ball is thrown with initial velocity V0 to the upper vertical direction. Find the velocity of the ball after T minutes. The gravity acceleration value is G.

[Problem-5] A block of mass M is put on a smooth incline quietly. The angle of the incline is ϕ and the gravity acceleration value is G.

(5a) Find the acceleration of the block in parallel direction to the incline.

(5b) Find the velocity of the block when it moved for a distance of S on the incline.

[Problem-6] A block of mass M is put on a coarse incline. The angle of the incline is ϕ and the gravity acceleration value is G. The coefficient of friction between the block and the incline is μ. Find the acceleration of the block in parallel direction to the incline when its initial velocity is zero.

[Problem-7] A block of mass M is put on a coarse incline. The angle of the incline is ϕ and the gravity acceleration value is G. The coefficient of friction between the block and the incline is μ. Find the acceleration of the block in parallel direction to the incline when its initial velocity is V to the upper parallel direction on the incline.

[Problem-8] A block of mass M is put on a smooth incline. The angle of the incline is ϕ and the gravity acceleration value is G. Find the longest moved distance to the upper parallel direction on the incline when the initial velocity of the block is V to the upper parallel direction on the incline.

Fig. 2 Examples of Mechanical Problems.

of the surface structure and partitioning of the solution structure. Formalizing of the surface structure means reducing of the formulation process. A problem which can be generated by formalizing the surface structure of the original problem is called an "equivalent problem." Partitioning of the solution structure means reducing of the calculation process. A problem which can be generated by partitioning the solution structure of the original problem is called a "partial problem." Specializing of the problem-solving process is carried out by specializing the constraint structure. A problem which can be generated by specializing the constraint structure of the original problem is called a "specialized problem."

Problem-4 is an equivalent problem for Problem-3, which are shown in Fig. 2. The surface structure of Problem-3 is Structure-A shown in Fig. 3. To solve Problem-3, Structure-A should be changed to Structure-B where "elevator" is omitted and "velocity of the elevator" is transformed to "initial velocity of the ball." Structure-B corresponds to the surface structure of Problem-4. Because Problem-4 has the more refined surface structure than Problem-3, Problem-4 is easier than Problem-3 in the formulation process.

Problem-5a is a partial problem of Problem-5b, which are shown in Fig. 2. Fig. 4 shows the solution structure of Problem-5b. "Derived" denotes the attribute whose value is derived in the calculation process but isn't an answer of the problem. By changing several derived attributes to given attributes or required attribute, a partial solution structure of the original solution structure can be generated. The problem with such a partial solution structure is simpler than the original problem in the calculation process. In the solution structure of Problem-5b, by changing "acceleration of the block in parallel direction" to the required attribute, a partial solution structure is generated. Therefore, Problem-5a, characterized by the partial solution structure, is a partial problem of Problem-5b.

Problem-5a is a specialized problem of Problem-6, which are shown in Fig. 2. Fig. 5 shows the constraint structure of Problem-6. Simplification of a constraint structure is achieved by changing values of attributes to values which make it possible to omit the attribute in the constraint structure. For example, when the value of the frictional coefficient becomes zero, the frictional coefficient can be omitted in numerical relations. As a result, some numerical relations can be simplified or omitted in the constraint structure. When the value of the frictional coefficient becomes zero in the constraint structure shown in

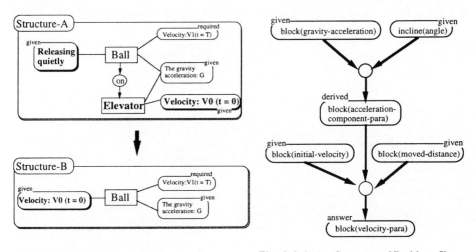

Fig. 3. Simplification of Surface Structure.   **Fig. 4.** Solution Structure of Problem-5b.

Fig. 5, the equation of motion is simplified from "$ma = mg \sin\emptyset - \mu mg \cos\emptyset$" to "$ma = mg \sin\emptyset$." Such specialized numerical relations can be used only in the specialized situation where the frictional coefficient is zero. Then, the original numerical relations can also be used in the specialized situation. Therefore, Problem-5a, characterized by the specialized constraint structure, is a specialized problem of Problem-6.

2.3 Evaluations of the Definition [9]

First, problem pairs of the original problem and a problem which is supposed to help learners solve the original problem were collected. Then, the relations of the two problems in the pairs were examined whether or not the relations could be explained by the definition of auxiliary problems. The problem pairs were collected in two ways as follows: (1) problem simplification by human tutors and (2) analysis of practice books. The problem pairs were examined by the authors of this paper with the following conditions;

When the two problems have the same solution and constraint structures, one of the two might be an equivalent problem. When the surface structure of one problem can be generated by formalizing the surface structure of the other problem, the former problem is an equivalent problem for the latter problem. Currently, four types of formulation operations are used in the examination, as follows: (a) changing a qualitative value to a quantitative value (for example changing "putting quietly" to "initial velocity zero"), (b) adding a necessary attribute (indication of the necessity of tension T is an example of this formulation operation), (c) rewording a given attribute to a necessary attribute (for example, rewording "work load X" to "change of energy X" in order to use numerical relations of energy), (d) shifting an attribute of one object to the attribute of the other object (shifting "the velocity of the elevator" to "the initial velocity of the ball" in Problem-3 is an example).

When the two problems have the same surface and constraint structures, one of the two might be a partial problem. When the solution structure of one problem can be generated by changing the derived attribute to required or given attributes, the former problem is a partial problem for the latter problem.

When the surface, solution and constraint structures of one problem can be generated by specializing the three structures of the other problem, the former problem is a specialized problem for the latter problem. Currently, the specialization means changing a value of an attribute to a value which makes it possible to omit the attribute in the constraint structure. Changing the value of a frictional coefficient to zero is an example of the specialization.

In the experiment of problem simplification by human tutors, 15 college students with experience in tutoring were subjects. Assuming that their pupils couldn't solve a problem, the subjects were asked to simplify the problem to help the pupils. Three mechanical problems were provided for the subjects. They generated 65 problems in total.

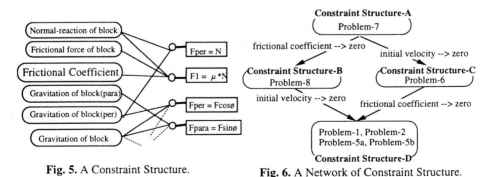

Fig. 5. A Constraint Structure.

Fig. 6. A Network of Constraint Structure.

All types of auxiliary problems were generated by the subjects and only two problems were outside the auxiliary problems. These results suggest that the definition of auxiliary problems contributes to simulate problem simplification performed by human tutors in order to help learners solve the original problems.

In the analysis of practice books, first, the problem pairs of the original problem and a problem which was supposed to help learners solve the original problem were collected. Then the relations of the two problems in the pairs were examined whether or not the relations could be explained by the definition of auxiliary problems. The following three types of problem pairs were collected: (1) a problem and a hint for it, (2) a problem and a reference problem for it and (3) a pair of problem items. We collected 487 pairs in total. Then, 359 pairs were explained by the definition of auxiliary problems (see [9]).

3. A Facility of Problem Simplification

The facility to simplify problems requires some characteristic descriptions based on the definition of the auxiliary problems. By using the descriptions, the facility can generate or retrieve auxiliary problems. Although the quantity of descriptions for each problem increases, the descriptions can be written independently of context of problem practice.

3.1 Description of Problems

The facility requires writing not only (1) surface structure, (2) solution structure, and (3) constraint structure, but also (4) problem sentences for the surface structure, (5) formulated structure, (6) formulation operators which are used to explain the change from surface structure to formulated structure and (7) problem sentences for formulated structure. Currently, modeling of formulation process isn't enough, so people who prepare the problems are required to write surface structure, formulated structure and the formulation operators by themselves for each problem. Because the facility cannot generate natural language from surface and formulated structures, problem sentences for these structures are also required.

The way to write the constraint structure is clear, but the number of numerical relations is often too many to write for each problem. However, one constraint structure includes many problems and there aren't so many constraint structures in the domain of mechanics in high school. So, a network of the constraint structures connected by specialization links is prepared. Fig. 6 shows a part of such a network of the constraint structures. In the situation of Constraint Structure-A, the block has the initial velocity and the frictional coefficient. A specialized constraint structure by changing the initial velocity to zero is Constraint Structure-B. Problem-8 shown in Fig. 2 belongs to Constraint Structure-B. When Constraint Structure-A is specialized by changing the initial velocity to zero, the specialized constraint structure is Constraint Structure-C which includes Problem-6. When Constraint Structure-A is specialized by changing both the frictional coefficient and initial velocity to zero, the specialized constraint structure is Constraint Structure-D. Problem-1, Problem-2, Problem-5a and Problem-5b belong to the Constraint Structure-D. By using this network, the constraint structures don't have to be written for each problem.

3.2. Generation of Equivalent Problems

The facility provides learners with problem sentences for formulated structures as equivalent problems. The simplification operators are used to explain the change from the original problems to the equivalent problems. Therefore, a problem usually has only one equivalent problem. However, a formulated structure sometimes relates to several surface structures. So, when there are two surface structures related to the same formulated structure and one surface structure is more formulated than the other, it is possible to use the problem with the more formulated surface structure as an equivalent problem for the other problem. Currently, the connection of the two problems should be written by people who prepare problems. The formulated structure shown in Fig. 3 includes an object "ball" instead of a more formulated object "particle." Because "particle" isn't familiar to learners, it may be difficult for them. So, currently, familiar objects, like "ball," are used in the formulated structure.

3.3 Generation of Partial Problems

Partial problems have the same surface structure as the original problems. So, the facility provides learners with hints which suggest changing the original problem to a partial problem. There are two types of hints: one is a comment in order to change a derived attribute to a required attribute. A suggestion for Problem-5b, "find first the acceleration of the block in parallel direction to the incline," is an example of this type of hint. In Problem-5b, "the acceleration of the block in parallel direction to the incline" is a derived attribute. This hint changes the derived attribute to the required attribute. The other is a hint in order to change a derived attribute to a given attribute. In Problem-5b, assuming that "the acceleration of the block in parallel direction to the incline" is "a," means to change a derived attribute to a given attribute. So, this hint make it possible to omit to derive "the acceleration of the block in parallel direction to the incline" in the calculation process.

3.4 Generation of Specialized Problem

In order to generate specialized problems, the network of constraint structure is used. The facility provides learners with suggestions which specialize problems. For example, in Fig. 6, Constraint Structure-1 can be specialized to Constraint Structure-2 by defaulting the initial velocity to zero or to Constraint Structure-3 by defaulting the frictional coefficient to zero. Because Problem-7 belongs to Constraint Structure-A, the facility can provide a suggestion which suggests changing the frictional coefficient to zero, or a suggestion which suggests changing the initial velocity to zero. These suggestions mean specialization of problems. So, specialized problems are provided as a suggestion to specialize problems.

4. Helping Problem-Solving by using Problem Simplification

Currently, a learning environment allowing learner-directed problem practice is being developed. In the problem practice, when learners cannot solve problems, the problem simplification described in section 3 is used to help learners solve the problems. This help of using problem simplification is a kind of environment-directed help because the environment requires the learners to solve the simplified problems. Although the environment-directed help doesn't allow the learners to select problems freely, this help is only used when the learners cannot solve problems. The situation provides the learners with motivation to learn in order to solve the problems. So, the environment-directed help can foster the learners' motivation.

When the learners can solve the original problems by solving the simplified problem, the learner-directed problem practice is restarted. When the learners can solve the simplified problems but cannot solve the original problem, the difference between the simplified problems and the original problems is explained. In this case, although the learners cannot solve the original problems by themselves, the simplified problems are useful to make clear what the learners need to solve the original problems. When the learners cannot solve the simplified problem, the simplified problems are further simplified.

In the help of using problem simplification, first, the equivalent problems for the original problems are used. For the learners who cannot solve the equivalent problems, the partial problems for the equivalent problems are used. For the learners who cannot solve the partial problems, the specialized problems for the partial problems are used.

4.1 Helping by Equivalent Problem.

When a learner cannot solve a problem, the equivalent problem for the original problem is provided to the learner. When the learner can solve the equivalent problem, the difficult elements in the problem-solving for the learner should be included in the differences between the original problem and the equivalent problem. When the learner can solve the original problem by solving the equivalent problem, the help is finished and the learner-directed problem practice is restarted. When the learner cannot solve the original problem, the learners have to learn the operations which are used in the formulation process. So, in the help, the formulation operations are explained to the learner.

4.2 Helping by Partial Problems

When the learner cannot solve the equivalent problems, the difficult elements in the problem-solving for the learner aren't included in the difference between the original problem and the equivalent problem. Then, a partial problem is provided to the learner. The partial problem is generated by partitioning the solution structure of the equivalent problem which the learner cannot solve. The partial problem is provided as a subgoal which is generated by changing a derived attribute to a required attribute in the solution structure. When the learner can solve the partial problem, the difficult elements shouldn't be included in the problem-solving process in the partial problem. So, the next partial problem is provided to the learner. In order to generate the partial problems, derived attributes are changed to required attributes following the same order in which the derived attributes are derived in the solution structure. Solving every partial problem is equivalent to solving the original problem. So, when the learner can solve every partial problem, the help is finished.

4.3 Helping by Specialized Problems

When the learner cannot solve a partial problem, the difficult elements should be included in the problem-solving process in the partial problem. The surface structure of the partial problem is the formulation structure. Then, the solution structure includes only one numerical relation. Therefore, the difficult elements should be included in the numerical relation. Simplification of numerical relations can be realized by specialization of the constraint structure. So, a specialized problem is provided to the learners. The specialized problem is generated by specializing the partial problem which the learner cannot solve. Usually, there are several ways of specialization depending on the network of constraint structures. Currently, the way will be decided based on the context of the learner's problem practice. The attribute which isn't included in the problems the learner has solved is specialized. When there are two such attributes or no such attributes, the preference of attributes designed based on the learner's text book will be used.

When the learner can solve the specialized problem, the difficult elements are the specialized attribute. When the learner can solve the partial problem by solving the specialized problem, the learner is provided the original problem again. When the learner can solve the original problem, the help is finished. When the learner cannot solve the original problem, the learner is provided the next partial problem.

When the learner cannot solve the partial problem, the learner has to learn the numerical relation including the attribute. So, the way to solve the partial problem is taught directly. Then, the original problem is provided again. When the learner can solve the original problem, the help is finished. When the learner cannot solve the original problem, the next partial problem is provided.

When the learner cannot solve the specialized problem, the specialized problem is further specialized.

5. Concluding Remarks

A promising way to foster learners' motivation in problem practice is to allow learners to freely select problems. However, in such a learner-directed problem practice, it becomes difficult to design the methods to help the learners who cannot solve the problems. In this paper, a help by using simplified problems was proposed as a resolution.

In the help, a learner who cannot solve the original problem is provided a simplified problem. To solve the simplified problem is useful to make clear what the learner needs to solve the original problem. When the learner cannot solve the simplified problem, the simplified problem is further simplified. Currently, the learning environment allowing learner-directed problem practice by using this help is being developed. Modeling of learner's context in problem practice is also important future work to realize an elaborate use of simplified problems.

References

[1] Koffman, E.B., and Blount, S.E. "Artificial Intelligence and Automatic Programming in CAI", Artificial Intelligence, Vol.6, pp.215-234(1975).
[2] Barr, A., Beard, M., Atkinson, R.C., "The Computer as a Tutorial Laboratory: the Stanford BIP Project", Int. J. Man-Machine Studies, Vol.8, pp. 567-596(1976).
[3] MaCalla, G.I. "The Search for Adaptability, Flexibility, and Individualization: Approaches to Curriculum in Intelligent Tutoring Systems", In Jones, M. and Winne P.H.(Eds.), Adaptive Learning Environment: Foundation and Frontiers, Springer-Verlag, pp.91-122(1990).
[4] Hirashima, T., Kashihara, A., Toyoda, J., "Providing Problem Explanation for ITS", In C. Frasson, G. Gauthier, G. I. McCalla(Eds.), Proc. of ITS'92(Lecture Notes in Computer Science 608), Springer-Verlag, pp.78-83(1992).
[5] Schank, R.C., "Teaching Architectures", Northwestern Univ. Institute for the Learning Science, TR#3(1990).
[6] VanLehn, K., R.M.Jones & M.T.H.Chi: "A Model of the Self -Explanation Effect", Journal of the Learning Science, 2(1), pp.1-59(1992).
[7]Polya, G., "How to Solve It - A New Aspect of Mathematical Method", Princeton, New Jersey: Princeton University Press(1945).
[8] Hirashima, T., T. Niitsu, A. Kashihara and J. Toyoda. "An Indexing Framework for Adaptive Setting of Problems in ITS", Proc. of AI-ED93, pp.90-97(1993).
[9] Hirashima, T., A. Kashihara and J. Toyoda. "A Formulation of Auxiliary Problems and Its Evaluations", Proc. of AI-ED95, pp.186-193(1995).

Acknowledgments

The authors would like to thank the members of L3D group at the University of Colorado for their valuable comments. This research is supported in part by Grant-in-Aid for Scientific Research No. 07458070 from the Ministry of Education, Science and Culture of Japan.

Focusing Problem Solving
in Design-Centered Learning Environments

James C. Lester, Brian A. Stone, Michael A. O'Leary, and Robert B. Stevenson

Multimedia Laboratory
Department of Computer Science
North Carolina State University
Raleigh, NC 27695-8206

Abstract. Design-centered learning environments offer great promise for providing effective, grounded learning experiences. Learners are given a set of design criteria and a library of components which they use to design artifacts that will satisfy the specified criteria. Despite their appeal, design-centered learning environments are plagued with complexities that can overwhelm learners. To address this problem, we have developed a proactive problem-solving focus mechanism that helps learners cope with the complexities inherent in design-centered learning. By exploiting a rich model of the design context, the focus mechanism selects design problems and intervenes with multimedia advice. The mechanism has been implemented in DESIGN-A-PLANT, a design-centered learning environment for botanical anatomy and physiology. Formative evaluations with middle school students are encouraging.

1 Introduction

Constructivism holds as its most central tenet that learning *is* building knowledge structures [11]. To promote constructivist learning episodes, it follows that learning environments should facilitate knowledge construction, and recent years have witnessed a remarkable growth in learning environments that purport to do exactly this. The resurgence of interest in microworlds [13, 7, 2, 8] demonstrates the growing belief that manipulable simulations offer experiences that are qualitatively different from more didactic approaches.

One of the most promising techniques in the constructivist's arsenal is *design*. Whether it is a child assembling a house from building blocks, an engineering student laying out a circuit, or a graduate student in mathematics constructing an axiomatic theory, the learner is actively engaged in a process that requires them to grapple with fundamental issues in their respective domains. In each case, they emerge from their experience with a deep appreciation for the rich conceptual interconnections that define their subject matters.

Unfortunately, it is precisely the characteristics of design-centered environments that offer the greatest potential that also pose the greatest challenge to their development. Because the size of the search space for design problems constantly threatens to overwhelm the learner, techniques must be developed to focus problem-solving activities on the most critical aspects of the concepts under consideration. While providing advice for design tasks is a much investigated topic [4] and efforts have been made to study how to automate the instruction of design per se [6], the primary contributions of other design-centered learning environments lie not in focusing problem-solving but rather in theories of remindings [3] and constraint negotiation [12].

To address this issue, we have developed a proactive problem-solving focus mechanism that helps learners cope with the complexities inherent in design-centered learning environments. The mechanism has been implemented in DESIGN-A-PLANT, a design-centered learning environment for botanical anatomy and physiology. DESIGN-A-PLANT provides middle school children with the opportunity to explore the physiological and environmental considerations that govern plants' survival. Given a set of environmental conditions, children use DESIGN-A-PLANT to graphically assemble a customized plant that can survive in the specified environment. To help focus students' problem solving as they graphically create plants from a library of "plant prostheses," the system monitors their interactions, adaptively selects environmental conditions, and provides both spoken and animated advice.

2 Design-Centered Problem Solving

The design-centered approach to learning can be applied to a broad range of domains. Design-centered learning environments can be developed for domains as diverse as biology (e.g., designing plants), chemistry (e.g., compound synthesis), or the social sciences (e.g., the popular Maxis SIM series). In each domain, design-centered problem solving revolves around a carefully orchestrated series of design episodes. Problems in design episodes are defined by a pair $(\mathcal{E}, \mathcal{L})$:

- $\mathcal{E}$: An *environment* consisting of a high-level set of design specifications defined by environmental factors $E_1 \ldots E_n$; a particular environment may specify only a subset of the E_is.
- $\mathcal{L}$: An *artifact component library* containing the "building blocks" from which artifacts are assembled; $\mathcal{L}$ is partitioned into component clusters $L_1 \ldots L_m$, where each L_i contains components of a particular type, and each component is defined by a feature vector of attribute-value pairs.

The student's task is to create an *artifact A*, which is a compound object composed of objects from $\mathcal{L}$. Critically, A must be able to function successfully in $\mathcal{E}$.

To illustrate, consider design episodes in the domain of botanical anatomy and physiology. Students are given an environment that specifies biologically critical factors in terms of qualitative variables. Environmental specifications for these episodes include the average incidence of sunlight, the amount of nutrients in the soil, and the height of the water table, as illustrated by several environments from DESIGN-A-PLANT (Table 1). Students consider these conditions as they inspect components from a library of plant structures that is segmented

Environment	Feature	Value
Alpine Meadow	water table	high
	temperature	low
	rain	low
	wind	high
Southern Marsh	rain	high
	sunlight	low
	water table	high
	temperature	high

Table 1. Sample Environments from Design-A-Plant

into roots, stems, and leaves. Each component is defined by its structural characteristics such as length and branching factor. Employing these components as their building blocks, students work in a "design studio" to graphically construct a customized plant that will flourish in the environment. Each iteration of the design process consists of inspecting the library, assembling a complete plant, and testing the plant to see how it fares in the given environment. If the plant fails to survive, students modify their plant's components to improve its suitability, and the process continues until they have developed a robust plant that prospers in the environment.

Constraints relating environmental factors to artifact structures govern the composition of artifacts. For example, a design-centered learning environment for botanical anatomy and physiology might include the constraint that a low incidence of sunlight requires large leaves. Hence, in the course of designing artifacts for a variety of environments, students acquire an understanding of the (possibly complex) effects of the environment on artifact functionalities. By continuously designing and redesigning artifacts until they satisfy the given specifications, students gradually bridge the conceptual gap that separates specific environmental factors from specific artifact components.

3 Focusing Design Episodes

Because design decisions require students to consider multiple environmental factors, multiple components, and multiple constraints simultaneously, it is critically important to focus their problem solving. In the absence of a mechanism for helping students attend to the most relevant aspects of their domain, they would easily become lost in the details and the pedagogical advantages of the design process would vanish. To address this problem, we have developed a proactive focus mechanism that exploits a representation of the evolving design context.

3.1   A Tripartite Model of the Design Context

Because students signal which sub-goal they are currently attempting through their design actions and because they indicate the conceptual difficulties they may be experiencing through their partial solutions (i.e., their incomplete arti-facts), the focus mechanism can carefully monitor the design process. To make decisions about how and when to take actions that will focus problem solving, the focus mechanism maintains a tripartite contextual representation of design episodes. It consists of an environmental context, an artifactual context, and an advisory context:

- *Environmental Context:* Critical features of the environment which have been presented to the student:
    - Current Environment: Environmental factors (and their values) in the current design episode.
    - Environmental Intent: Associated with each environment presented to the student is the set of object types from the artifact library which that environment is intended to exercise, e.g., some environments are presented to exercise students' knowledge of leaf morphology.
- *Artifactual Context:* Critical features of the artifact under construction:
    - Partial Solutions: Selections of components for the current artifact under construction, e.g., the student may have completed the roots and leaves.
    - Focused Component: Artifact component to which the student is currently attending, e.g., the stem.
    - Design Evaluation: When the student completes the design, the artifact is evaluated as successful or not successful in the current environment.
- *Advisory Context:* Critical features of the advisory dialogue, where each entry consists of:
    - Topic: Environmental factors, artifact components, constraints, and/or design decisions explained.
    - Frequency Annotations: Indicate the number of times that the student has been advised about the topic(s).
    - Problem-Solving Idle Time: Time expired since the student's last action.
    - Media Annotations: Indicate the media, e.g., audio or animation, that were employed to communicate the advice.

3.2   The Proactive Focus Mechanism

By exploiting the tripartite model of the design context, the focus mechanism can proactively help students focus their problem solving on the most salient aspects of the problem at hand. It can inspect the environmental context to identify the design criteria that the student is attempting to satisfy and to determine which aspects of the design are most critical from a pedagogical perspective; it can inspect the artifactual context to monitor the student's progress and to note possible impasses; and it can inspect the advisory context to determine the nature of the student's request and to track previously presented advice. As the focus mechanism observes the design process, it selects environments, determines when and what type of interventions are appropriate, and presents spoken and/or animated advice.

Environment Selection. In a series of design episodes, the focus mechanism attempts to obtain a comprehensive coverage of artifact components. As the design process unfolds, it chooses environments with different *environmental intents* (see above). It bases its choice of environment on the student's rate of progress, which is indicated by the history of design evaluations. To make these decisions, the focus mechanism navigates its way through an *environment matrix*, each cell of which is a particular environment.[1] Environments in a given column have the same intent, e.g., they all exercise the student's knowledge of stems. Environments in a given row have the same complexity; the complexity of the activated constraints are the same, and they require students to grapple with the same number of components. For example, environments in the second row involve constraints with two components (the other components are "don't cares" with respect to the environment). Beginning in the upper-left cell, the focus mechanism selects an environment. If the student meets with success (as indicated by the quality of the partial solutions), they advance diagonally to an environment in the next column and the next row; if they experience difficulty, they remain in the same row (the same level of complexity) but move to a different column. The session ends when the student successfully completes a design for an environment in the final row, which represents the highest level of complexity.

Intervention. To proactively focus the design process, decisions must be made about when and how to intervene during problem solving. The focus mechanism monitors the state of the artifactual context to determine when the student requires assistance. If the student makes an incorrect design decision (as indicated by his or her partial solutions), or if the problem-solving idle time exceeds a threshold, then the focus mechanism will intervene. When an intervention is triggered, the focus mechanism must determine the topic of the advice it will provide to the student. If the current partial solution indicates that only a single component is inappropriate for the current environment, it will provide advice about that component. If multiple components are inappropriate, the focus mechanism inspects the focused component (the component to which the student is currently attending); if this component is incorrect, advice will be provided about it. Otherwise, the focus mechanism inspects the environmental intent of the current environment and determines if one of the inappropriate components is the subject of the environmental intent. If so, it will provide advice about that component.

Advice Presentation. Once the decision to intervene has been made and the topic of the intervention has been determined, a critical issue in learning environments

---

[1] This process is analogous to the navigation of discourse management networks [14].

is how to provide appropriate advice [9]. These decisions are governed by presentation strategies that first select the appropriate level of *directness* of the advice and then select a communication medium. Note that our emphasis is not on the generation of explanations per se but on selecting the "directness" of presentations and on intelligent media selection [1, 5, 10]. The directness spectrum of advisory presentations represents the degree of explicitness with which presentations inform students about design decisions. The least direct advice discusses the information about constraints, e.g., the functional relation between environmental factors and artifact components; the most direct advice suggests a specific design decision. While direct advice is easily operationalized, the opportunity for learning is reduced, so indirect advice is generally preferred.

The focus mechanism first selects a point on the directness spectrum, and then uses this decision to determine the presentation media. To select a point on the directness spectrum, the focus mechanism weighs four factors: (1) if the topic of the advice is the environmental intent, indirect advice is preferred; (2) as the student advances to higher levels of complexity (as indicated by their position in the environment matrix), indirect advice is preferred; (3) if the student is experiencing difficulty (as indicated by his or her partial solutions), more direct advice is preferred; and (4) if advice about a particular topic has already been presented (as indicated by the advisory context), more direct advice is preferred. The selected level of directness is then used to make media selection decisions. In general, the more indirect the advice is, the more likely it will be presented as animations depicting interactions between environmental factors and artifact components; the more direct the advice is, the more likely it will be presented as speech. Finally, the topic, the selected level of directness, and the selected medium are used to index into the *multimedia advice library*, and the advice is presented to the student.

4　Focusing Problem Solving in Design-A-Plant

DESIGN-A-PLANT is a design-centered learning environment that we and our colleagues have developed for middle school botanical anatomy and physiology.[2] Throughout the design process, students are accompanied by an animated agent in the form of a bug, which serves as the vehicle for both the animated and spoken advice. It presents natural environments to them, and they graphically assemble customized plants that will survive in those environments. Environments are rendered as intriguing landscapes, and specific environmental factors are depicted iconically. The roots, stems, and leaves in the artifact component library are 3D objects. "Rollover" definitions are provided for all environmental factors and components. DESIGN-A-PLANT currently includes:

---

[2] All of the 3D graphics and animations were designed, modeled, and rendered on Macintoshes and SGIs by a twelve-person graphic design team from North Carolina State University's School of Design. DESIGN-A-PLANT runs on a Power Macintosh 9500/132.

- an environment matrix with sixteen environments (four types of environments, each with four complexity levels);
- an artifact component library with eight types of roots, eight types of stems, and eight types of leaves;
- a domain model with thirty-one constraints that relate six environmental factors to the anatomical structures and six physiological functions;
- a multimedia advice library with thirty animations on botanical anatomy and physiology[3] and one hundred and sixty audio clips.

To illustrate its behavior, suppose that a student has just completed designing a plant for the first environment on complexity level one.

> Level 2 is selected because the first environment was completed after only a single error. The first environment focused on leaves. In this environment, roots and leaves are both in focus. The key environmental factors (those that affect objects in the environmental intent) are low temperature and high water table.

Animated Agent: Hooray, a pretty place. It's absolutely lovely. Of course the ground reminds me of a skating rink. Maybe that's because of the low temperature and high water table. Make sure that the stems are thick and well protected and that the roots and leaves can handle the pretty but harsh conditions.

> To focus on roots and leaves, the introduction gives specific advice about the stem only. At this point, the student clicks on the upper portion of the plant construction area to begin working on leaves.

Student: Spends thirty seconds going back and forth with the mouse from the rollover textual descriptions of the environment to the rollover textual descriptions of the leaf choices but cannot make a decision.

> The problem-solving idle time threshold is exceeded. There are three constraints that map cold temperature to leaf features. Because this is the first time that the student has required advice during leaf selection in this environment and leaves are in focus, three animated explanations are played in sequence. They explain the relationship between cold temperature and leaf size, leaf thickness, and leaf skin thickness. These explanations are followed by the first animated lesson on leaf anatomy.

Student: Makes two more unsuccessful attempts at selecting a correct leaf.

> The leaf choice still violates a constraint, but now the student has already seen a detailed animated explanation and has been given a verbal reminder. Therefore, short direct verbal advice is given.

Animated Agent: Why don't you try a small thick leaf with nice thick skin.

---

[3] Approximately twenty are in the 20—30 second range and ten are in the 1–2 minute range.

5 Formative Evaluation

DESIGN-A-PLANT, an ongoing project begun in 1994, has been the subject of a formative evaluation involving middle school students. Informal observational studies with thirteen students were conducted to obtain feedback about the layout and operation of the design studio, the pace, the appeal of the storyline (not discussed here) and the animated agent, and most importantly, the clarity of the advice and the behavior of the focusing mechanism. Each student interacted with the system for forty-five minutes to one hour.

Students seemed to benefit considerably from the design experience in general and the focus mechanism in particular. They enjoyed interacting with the learning environment and appreciated its animations, music,[4] and agent. Detailed design profiles were automatically accumulated for four of the students. Each profile records all of the environments, design decisions, and advice (both topic and media) in the series of design episodes undertaken by a student. Perhaps most encouraging is the fact that the vast majority of mistakes occurred on the components which were in the intent of their respective environments. This indicates that most of students' time was spent in making design decisions about features of the design that were most critical.

6 Conclusion

Because design-centered learning environments enable students to iteratively make, evaluate, and reconsider design decisions, they offer great promise for providing grounded, personalized learning experiences. Design episodes may become so complex, however, that decisions about multiple environmental factors, multiple artifact components, and multiple constraints could easily overwhelm students. By incorporating a proactive problem-solving focus mechanism that exploits environmental, artifactual, and advisory context models, a design-centered learning environment can help students focus on the most critical aspects of complex design episodes. In particular, it can select environments and intervene with multimedia advice to help students more effectively form, test, and refine their hypotheses about complex interrelationships.

Acknowledgements

Thanks to: the animation team which was lead by Patrick FitzGerald of the North Carolina State University School of Design; the students in the Intelligent Multimedia Communication, Multimedia Interface Design, and Knowledge-Based Multimedia Learning Environments seminars; and Chris Tomasson and the students in her seventh grade class at Martin Middle School of Raleigh, North Carolina. Support for this work was provided by the IntelliMedia Initiative of North Carolina State University and donations from Apple and IBM.

---

[4] The soundtrack uses the design context to adapt its tempo, mood, and number of instrumental voices to the student's progress.

References

1. E. André, W. Finkler, W. Graph, T. Rist, A. Schauder, and W. Wahlster. WIP: The automatic synthesis of multi-modal presentations. In M. T. Maybury, editor, *Intelligent Multimedia Interfaces*, chapter 3. AAAI Press, 1993.

2. E. Cauzinille-Marmeche and J. Mathieu. Experimental data for the design of microworld-based system for algebra. In H. Mandl and A. Lesgold, editors, *Learning Issues for Intelligent Tutoring Systems*, pages 278–286. Springer-Verlag, New York, 1988.

3. D. C. Edelson. Learning from stories: Indexing and reminding in a socratic case-based teaching system for elementary school biology. Technical Report 43, The Institute for the Learning Sciences, Northwestern Univeristy, Evanston, Illinois, July 1993.

4. M. Eisenberg and G. Fischer. Programmable design environments: Integrating end-user programming with domain-oriented assistance. In *CHI '94: Human Factors in Computing Systems: Celebrating Interdependence*, pages 431–437, 1994.

5. S. K. Feiner and K. R. McKeown. Coordinating text and graphics in explanation generation. In *Proceedings of the Eighth National Conference on Artificial Intelligence*, pages 442–449, Boston, MA, 1990.

6. M. D. Gross. Design and use of a constraint-based laboratory for learning design. In R. W. Lawler and M. Yazdani, editors, *Artificial Intelligence and Education*, volume 1, pages 167–181. Ablex, Norwood, NJ, 1987.

7. J. D. Hollan, E. L. Hutchins, and L. M. Weitzman. STEAMER: An interactive, inspectable, simulation-based training system. In G. Kearsley, editor, *Artificial Intelligence and Instruction: Applications and Methods*, pages 113–134. Addison-Wesley, Reading, MA, 1987.

8. R. W. Lawler and G. P. Lawler. Computer microwolrds and reading: An analysis for their systematic application. In R. W. Lawler and M. Yazdani, editors, *Artificial Intelligence and Education*, volume 1, pages 95–115. Ablex, Norwood, NJ, 1987.

9. A. Lesgold, S. Lajoie, M. Bunzo, and G. Eggan. SHERLOCK: A coached practice environment for an electronics trouble-shooting job. In J. H. Larkin and R. W. Chabay, editors, *Computer-Assisted Instruction and Intelligent Tutoring Systems: Shared Goals and Complementary Approaches*, pages 201–238. Lawrence Erlbaum, Hillsdale, NJ, 1992.

10. M. T. Maybury. Planning multimedia explanations using communicative acts. In *Proceedings of the Ninth National Conference on Artificial Intelligence*, pages 61–66, Anaheim, CA, 1991.

11. J. Piaget. *The Construction of Reality in the Child*. Basic Books, New York, 1954.

12. M. Smith. CONNIE: An intelligent learning environment for creative tasks based on negotiation of constraints. In *Proceedings of the Artificial Intelligence in Education Conference*, pages 397–404, 1995.

13. P. W. Thompson. Mathematical microworlds and intelligent computer-assisted instruction. In G. Kearsley, editor, *Artificial Intelligence and Instruction: Applications and Methods*, pages 83–109. Addison-Wesley, Reading, MA, 1987.

14. B. Woolf and D. D. McDonald. Building a computer tutor: Design issues. *IEEE Computer*, 17(9):61–73, 1984.

Une utilisation de la modélisation qualitative pour la planification pédagogique

Frédéric Blanc

Laboratoire API, IUT Paul Sabatier, 50 ch. des maraîchers, 31077 Toulouse Cedex, France
et
IUT de Bayonne Dept Informatique, Place Paul Bert, 64100 Bayonne, France

Résumé. Dans cet article, nous présentons une technique de planification pédagogique basée sur une séparation entre les connaissances et les mécanismes d'inférence. La modélisation qualitative est utilisée pour représenter les connaissances. Le modèle, qui n'inclut pas de contrôle pédagogique, n'impose pas un ordonnancement de tâches a priori. Il fournit des critères d'évaluation du travail de l'élève permettant l'adaptation. Le contrôle est externe et répond à des paramètres pédagogiques définis par l'auteur (styles d'enseignement, stratégie pédagogique...). Les règles du système de décision du Système Tuteur Intelligent (STI) sont générales. Elles sont basées sur des techniques de programmation par contraintes, ici de natures pédagogiques (paramètres) et structurelles (état qualitatif du modèle mis à jour par les effets des activités).

1 Introduction

La représentation des connaissances pédagogiques dans les STI fait souvent appel à des techniques de planification issues de l'Intelligence Artificielle [4] [11]... Ces techniques sont en général fondées sur une représentation hiérarchique des tâches pédagogiques. QUIZ [7], SIIP [8] ou IDE [9] sont des exemples de planificateurs pédagogiques. L'enseignant y rassemble un ensemble d'actions pédagogiques et décide un ordonnancement. Des métarègles assurent le dynamisme en sélectionnant et en remettant en cause un plan dans une situation donnée.

Dans cet article, nous présentons une approche de planification pédagogique différente. Après avoir défini les raisons qui nous ont conduit à proposer notre démarche, nous présentons les modèles et les formalismes proposés, basés sur des techniques de raisonnement qualitatif. Enfin, nous décrivons les mécanismes de planification et de prise de décision qui en découlent.

2 Les Fondements de Notre Approche

Point critique de la conception des STI, l'adaptation à l'apprenant bute sur deux types de problèmes :

1. Un problème d'évaluation du travail de l'élève,
2. Un problème de planification : comment modifier la stratégie didactique en fonction de cette évaluation ?

2.1 Démarche Habituelle

Les techniques de planification habituelles considèrent un ordre sur un ensemble d'étapes. L'ordre représente la précédence temporelle et chaque étape une action pédagogique. Pour prendre en compte le caractère dynamique et interactif du STI, des règles de réorientation, intervenant dans des situations pédagogiques étudiées, sont utilisées (changement ou modification de plan).

Cette démarche pose un certain nombre de problèmes, liés à l'ordonnancement :
1. *Par rapport au problème de planification :*
   Un pédagogue a du mal à écrire les règles ou les préconditions d'activation des tâches, spécifiques à des situations particulières. Quelle situation pédagogique étudier ? Quelle tâche choisir ? Il existe un grand nombre d'états ou de situations particulières à prendre en compte.
2. *Par rapport au problème de l'évaluation du travail de l'élève :*
   Les impacts des actions de l'apprenant sont rarement modélisés de manière explicite. Ces effets permettent pourtant d'évaluer la qualité du travail réalisé.

Notre approche vise à résoudre ces problèmes :
- en n'imposant pas un ordonnancement temporel ou une hiérarchie de tâches a priori,
- en spécifiant explicitement les effets des actions de l'élève,
- en basant le développement sur un modèle indépendant d'une stratégie particulière, pour éviter l'étude des conditions d'activation de chaque tâche.

2.2 Principe de Notre Approche

Le principe de base consiste à créer un modèle de représentation des connaissances neutre sur le plan pédagogique, mais intégrant un module d'acquisition de connaissances sur le travail de l'élève explicite. L'objectif est de séparer les connaissances des mécanismes d'inférence, tout en fournissant des moyens d'évaluation. Le modèle est pauvre : il n'inclut pas de contrôle pédagogique. Sa construction est facilitée. Le contrôle est externe et répond à des critères pédagogiques définis par l'auteur, mais gérés par le système (stratégie pédagogique, style d'enseignement).

Le but est d'éviter à l'enseignant l'écriture des règles de production assurant le guidage. Ces règles, générales, embarquées par le système, utilisent les connaissances du modèle et sont paramétrées par les critères pédagogiques spécifiés. Les paramètres permettent d'assurer la planification pédagogique. Le modèle, fondé sur des techniques de raisonnement qualitatif, donne les moyens d'assurer cette planification en fournissant des critères d'évaluation.

3 Quel Modèle pour la Planification ?

Les modèles de planification, qui reposent en général sur un *modèle des tâches* reflétant une organisation hiérarchique très stricte (des tâches de haut niveau sont définies à partir de sous-tâches élémentaires) impliquent de nombreuses révisions de plans lors des activités effectives de l'apprenant. Les critères de changement sont difficiles à cerner car il n'existe pas de modèle des activités intégré par le planificateur.

Un *modèle explicite des activité*s favorise cette adaptation en fournissant des données sur l'interaction élève-système. Une nouvelle forme de planification apparaît, non plus basée sur une organisation hiérarchique, mais intégrant les effets des activités sur les tâches. Ces influences donnent des critères de changement dynamique clairement identifiés. Grâce à ce *modèle des influences* entre tâches et activités, des moyens d'adaptation explicites sont disponibles.

3.1 Objectifs de la Modélisation Qualitative

La modélisation qualitative est la technique utilisée pour représenter les modèles de tâches, d'activités et d'influences. Axée sur la représentation explicite de ces connaissances, on lui assigne dans notre environnement trois fonctions essentielles : une *fonction de prédiction* basée sur la simulation, une *fonction de diagnostic* d'étude des effets immédiats d'une action sur l'état du système et une *fonction de contrôle*, qui permet de déterminer la tâche à réaliser, à partir de l'état actuel et des objectifs à atteindre. Cet article porte essentiellement sur la dernière fonction.

La modélisation qualitative, qui a été conçue au départ pour la description de situations physiques, a donnée naissance à trois grandes théories [2] [3] [6]. Son utilisation dans les STI a principalement résidé dans des environnements d'apprentissage basés sur la simulation du fonctionnement de dispositifs [5] [10]. La connaissance du domaine y est souvent découpée en plusieurs modèles qualitatifs de complexité croissante; l'élève progresse de modèle en modèle au cours de l'apprentissage. Notre objectif est différent, puisqu'il s'agit de modéliser qualitativement, non pas le sujet sur lequel porte l'apprentissage (par exemple le fonctionnement des circuits électriques, comme dans QUEST [12]), mais la planification pédagogique, c'est-à-dire le fonctionnement du didacticiel lui-même.

Comme la majorité des approches de modélisation qualitative, le modèle qualitatif comprend un ensemble de *composants*, un ensemble de *paramètres* agissants sur ces composants et un ensemble de *relations* entre composants et paramètres (Figure 1).

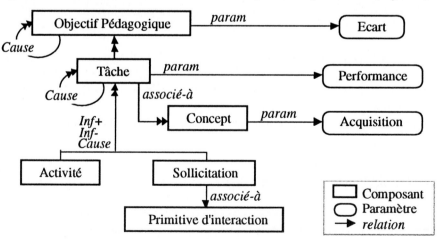

Fig. 1. Modèle qualitatif des données d'un STI

3.2 Description des Composants

Le premier niveau de modélisation, issu de la spécification des besoins, conduit à définir trois types d'entités :

- Les *objectifs pédagogiques*, buts assignés à l'apprenant, sont indispensables pour finaliser le STI et obtenir une planification pédagogique efficace [13]. L'état du système, critère principal de la prise de décision didactique, est mesuré par rapport à ces objectifs.

- Les *tâches* définissent les besoins nécessaires pour atteindre les objectifs. Le but du STI est de prescrire à l'apprenant la tâche qu'il juge la plus adaptée, en se basant sur l'état courant du système.

- Les *concepts* sont les objets liés aux tâches. Leur rôle n'est pas ici de constituer un curriculum explicite à la base de la planification pédagogique, mais d'offrir un critère de décision supplémentaire, grâce à la donnée de leur taux d'acquisition (il n'existe pas de structuration pédagogique du domaine).

Le deuxième niveau de modélisation décrit les moyens mis en œuvre pour répondre aux besoins énoncés (éléments proposés à l'apprenant pour remplir les tâches fixées) :

- Les *primitives d'interaction* sont les formes d'interaction visuelles disponibles, formant une bibliothèque d'objets réutilisables instanciables dans toute nouvelle application créée : *Cours, Définition, Simulation, QCM, Corrélation, Diagnostic, Calcul, Explication, Résultat, Aide, Exemple...*

- Les *sollicitations* permettent de proposer une primitive d'interaction à l'apprenant, en vue de lui faire remplir une tâche particulière. Chaque sollicitation est attachée à une primitive, mais plusieurs sollicitations peuvent être liées à une même tâche : il existe toujours plusieurs moyens de remplir une tâche. Trois types de sollicitations sont définies, en fonction de la primitive d'interaction associée :
  - *Donner lorsque la primitive associée est de l'enseignement (Donner un cours),*
  - *Poser s'il s'agit d'entraînement (Poser une question),*
  - *Proposer si la primitive associée est de l'assistance (Proposer de l'aide).*

- Les *activités* concernent les actions réalisées par l'apprenant sur une sollicitation. Il s'agit de faire un diagnostic du comportement possible de l'élève : type d'erreur commise à un exercice, demande d'aide... Dans le cas d'une activité sur une primitive d'interaction pour l'entraînement, le diagnostic correspond à un modèle d'erreurs.

3.3 Description des Paramètres Qualitatifs

Les paramètres qualitatifs doivent rendre compte de la qualité de la stratégie pédagogique employée. Ce sont des baromètres de la qualité de la session d'enseignement. On les associe donc aux objectifs pédagogiques et aux tâches fixés : l'objectif est-il atteint; la tâche est-elle bien effectuée ? Ils permettent ainsi de déterminer si les primitives d'interaction proposées et les activités réalisées sur ces primitives satisfont les besoins exprimés. La qualité de ces indicateurs est évidemment étroitement liée à la qualité du diagnostic d'activités effectué.

Trois paramètres qualitatifs sont définis :

- *Ecart : distance par rapport à l'atteinte des objectifs pédagogiques,*
- *Performance : efficacité dans la réalisation d'une tâche,*
- *taux d'Acquisition : degré de compréhension des concepts.*

L'*état qualitatif* EQ d'un paramètre p est composé de sa valeur à un instant donné et de sa tendance d'évolution : EQ (p, t) = ([p], δp).

- La *tendance* d'un paramètre qualitatif p, notée δp, est la valeur qualitative de sa dérivée par rapport au temps, c'est-à-dire δp = [dp / dt]. Ses valeurs possibles sont {(-∞,0), 0, (0,+∞)}, c'est-à-dire {*Décroissant, Stable, Croissant*}. La tendance permet d'évaluer l'évolution des paramètres. C'est un critère très important pour déterminer la pertinence de la stratégie pédagogique employée.

- La *valeur* d'un paramètre est composée d'un triplet [p] = (*current, goal, mini/maxi*)
  où :   - *current : valeur courante du paramètre, à partir de laquelle est calculée sa tendance,*
  - *goal : valeur à atteindre,*
  - *mini : valeur minimale des paramètres Performance et Acquisition ,*
  - *maxi : valeur que ne doit pas dépasser Ecart.*

Les valeurs *mini* et *maxi* sont des valeurs limites des paramètres, à partir desquelles s'effectue le contrôle dans le système. La valeur courante d'un paramètre doit toujours rester dans l'intervalle qui lui est associé. Plus cet intervalle est large, moins le contrôle est important.

3.4   Description des Relations d'Influences

Les variations de valeurs de paramètres sont effectuées à partir de connaissances sur les interactions de l'élève. Chaque interaction, c'est-à-dire chaque activité sur une sollicitation proposée, a une influence sur l'évolution des valeurs de paramètres. Or, il existe de nombreux liens entre activités, tâches et objectifs pédagogiques. Le fait d'effectuer une tâche peut ainsi, par exemple, permettre d'atteindre plusieurs objectifs. Une seule activité a donc un effet sur plusieurs tâches et objectifs pédagogiques. Comme on associe un paramètre à chaque tâche et objectif, une seule activité entraîne plusieurs modifications de valeurs de paramètres. Il faut donc mettre en place un mécanisme de propagation d'influences dans le réseau d'activités, tâches et objectifs pédagogiques. Ce mécanisme doit permettre la prise en compte des influences indirectes d'une action de l'apprenant.

D'autre part, il est parfois difficile, voire impossible, de déterminer l'effet d'une action de l'élève sur l'acquisition d'un concept, l'atteinte d'un objectif pédagogique ou la réalisation d'une tâche. Comment savoir par exemple si le fait de proposer la définition d'un concept a réellement une influence positive sur la connaissance de ce concept ? Il faut donc prévoir une relation d'influence neutre (ni positive, ni négative), dans le cas où le pédagogue ne peut déterminer le type de l'influence.

L'implantation récursive des fonctions d'influences permet la propagation et la prise en compte des influences indirectes :

$$\forall x, \ \forall y, \ \forall z \ \ Influence\_positive \ (x, \ y) \Leftarrow Inf+ \ (x, \ y) \ \vee$$
$$(\ Inf+ \ (x, \ z) \wedge Inf+ \ (z, \ y) \ ) \ \vee$$
$$(\ Inf+ \ (x, \ z) \wedge Influence\_positive \ (z, \ y) \ ) \ \vee$$
$$(\ Cause \ (z, \ y) \wedge Influence\_positive \ (x, \ z) \ )$$

x, y et z représentent les composants du modèle qualitatif (objectif pédagogique, tâche ou activité). S'il existe une influence entre x et y, alors la valeur du paramètre lié à y est augmentée ou diminuée, suivant le type d'influence. Des fonctions d'évolution permettent cette mise à jour dynamique des valeurs de paramètres directement lors d'une session. La relation de causalité *Cause* sert uniquement de propagateur d'influence.

4 Quel Paramétrage Pédagogique ?

Le modèle qualitatif est en fait très pauvre, en ce sens qu'il n'encode pas de choix pédagogique. Il est neutre sur le plan pédagogique, c'est-à-dire indépendant d'une stratégie particulière. Cette indépendance entre la représentation des connaissances et l'utilisation, c'est-à-dire le contrôle pédagogique, garantit le caractère général de l'architecture proposée. Le problème du paramétrage pédagogique est alors de définir plusieurs stratégies applicables à un même modèle.

Quatre grands paramètres pédagogiques sont choisis par l'auteur : le *style d'ensei-gnement* (Guidé, Semi-guidé, Supervisé, Libre), le *niveau de l'apprenant* (Novice, Moyen, Confirmé, Expert), le *degré d'inertie* (régulation du STI) et la *stratégie pédagogique* (tutorat, entraînement conseillé, enseignement conseillé, entraînement, enseignement).

Le tableau qui suit fait un résumé des caractéristiques principales de ces paramètres pédagogiques et de leur utilisation par le système de décision (Table 1).

Paramètre Pédagogique	Commentaire	Système de Décision
Style d'enseignement *2 attributs :* - degré de guidage - degré de liberté	Le *degré de guidage* définit le niveau d'orientation de l'élève par le système. Si le degré de guidage est élevé, le STI choisira d'orienter en priorité l'élève vers les objectifs pédagogiques les moins atteints.	+ le degré de guidage est élevé + le choix des objec-tifs pédagogiques est sélectif (par rapport aux Ecarts)
	Le *degré de liberté* définit le niveau de contrôle de l'élève par le STI. Cette variable agit sur l'état qualitatif du système, en particulier sur l'intervalle des valeurs possibles des paramètres qualitatifs. Si le degré de liberté est élevé, l'intervalle est large : de nombreuses activités à influences négatives sont possibles avant de sortir de l'intervalle et provoquer l'intervention du tuteur.	+ le degré de liberté est élevé - l'intervention du système est rapide

Niveau de l'élève	Les valeurs buts (goal) des paramètres qualitatifs sont modulées en fonction du niveau de l'élève.	+ le niveau est élevé + les valeurs buts sont difficiles à atteindre
Degré d'inertie	Le degré d'inertie agit sur la rapidité de changement de style d'enseignement (régulation). Le STI choisit de modifier son guidage en fonction de ce paramètre et des tendances d'évolution des paramètres qualitatifs (qualité du travail).	+ le degré d'inertie est élevé - l'adaptation du système est rapide
Stratégie pédagogique	La stratégie pédagogique permet de définir le type de primitive d'interaction à proposer ainsi que leur ordre d'activation.	Choix d'une primitive en fonction de la stratégie employée

Table 1. Résumé des paramètres pédagogiques et de leurs actions

Ce paramétrage est complexe du fait de la multiplicité des paramètres pédagogiques. C'est pourquoi des techniques de simulation ont été mises au point pour permettre à l'auteur d'étendre la compréhension du STI. Ces techniques permettent au pédagogue de comprendre le fonctionnement souhaitable du système pour le paramétrage testé et d'ajuster en conséquence le modèle qualitatif (les valeurs de son état qualitatif initial notamment). Cette simulation est longue et fastidieuse, mais indispensable car elle garantit un paramétrage satisfaisant. Le lecteur intéressé pourra consulter [1] pour une description du procédé utilisé.

5 Fonctionnement de base d'un STI basé sur le Modèle Qualitatif

5.1 Cycle Didactique de base

Le STI intègre un cycle didactique comprenant six étapes (Figure 2) :

1. Le cycle commence par une activité de l'apprenant sur une sollicitation proposée par le système, par exemple une réponse à une question.

2. L'activité réalisée a un effet sur l'état du STI, mesuré par les paramètres qualitatifs (*Ecart*, *Performance* et *Acquisition*). Cet effet est pris en compte par les fonctions d'influences directes du modèle.

3. Ces influences directes sont propagées dans le réseau de composants et de relations d'influences.

4. Les paramètres associés aux composants touchés par une influence sont mis à jour en fonction de la nature de cette influence. Par exemple, si l'apprenant a répondu faux à une question, la valeur de la performance dans la réalisation de la tâche liée à la question est diminuée.

5. Le STI se trouve alors dans un nouvel état, qui est pris en compte dans le choix d'une nouvelle tâche, puis primitive d'interaction, en fonction de l'état à atteindre. Une sollicitation peut alors être proposée à l'apprenant (décision).

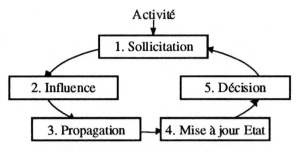

Fig. 2. Cycle didactique de base

5.2 Processus de Prise de Décision

Les règles effectuant le choix de la tâche sont prédéfinies et paramétrées par le modèle qualitatif et les paramètres pédagogiques. Elles définissent le contrôle pédagogique dans le modèle en fonction des paramètres pédagogiques fixés. Si le paramétrage pédagogique de départ est incorrect, le système est capable d'en changer dynamiquement, grâce aux règles de régulation. Ces règles permettent également de changer de style d'enseignement : adaptation sans intervention du pédagogue.

Ces règles sont basées sur des techniques de résolution de contraintes. Elles conduisent à éliminer des tâches successivement, parmi les tâches candidates, en fonction de contraintes pédagogiques (formalisées par les paramètres pédagogiques) et structurelles (état qualitatif du STI).

1. Les *règles de paramétrage* fixent les valeurs initiales des paramètres en fonction du paramétrage pédagogique choisi (niveau de l'apprenant et style d'enseignement).

2. Les *règles d'orientation* sont les règles de guidage de l'apprenant, basées sur des techniques de programmation par contraintes :
   - la première étape consiste à éliminer des primitives d'interaction, en fonction de la stratégie pédagogique choisie. Elimination éventuelle de l'assistance.
   - la deuxième étape vise à éliminer des objectifs (donc des tâches) en choisissant les objectifs les moins atteints.
   - la dernière étape consiste à éliminer des tâches candidates, en fonction du niveau de l'apprenant et du degré de guidage, puis de statistiques sur le travail de l'élève (dispersion, répartition, taux d'utilisation notamment).

3. Les *règles de contrôle* servent à maintenir l'élève dans le domaine de travail que le pédagogue lui a fixé (intervalles de valeurs des paramètres) : choix des tâches qui sortent de leur intervalle de valeurs, puis choix d'une primitive d'interaction en fonction du type d'apprentissage fixé dans la stratégie pédagogique.

4. Les *règles de révision* permettent la mise à jour du profil de l'apprenant, en fonction de la rapidité de changement de niveau fixée et des tendances des valeurs de paramètres qualitatifs.

5. Les *règles de régulation* servent à modifier dynamiquement le style d'enseignement, en modifiant les valeurs des intervalles des paramètres (*mini* et *maxi*). On obtient ainsi un ensemble plus ou moins directif. Ces règles s'appuient sur le degré d'inertie fixé et des calculs de tendances.

Ces différentes règles sont donc fondées sur un procédé de filtrage, dont nous ne donnons ici que les grandes lignes. Dans le cas où cet algorithme produit plusieurs primitives d'interaction possibles, le choix est aléatoire et se porte avant tout sur une primitive non encore proposée. Si aucune primitive n'est produite par le processus, on remonte dans l'algorithme pour éliminer des règles de filtrage et obtenir un choix.

6 Conclusion

Nous avons présenté une technique de planification pédagogique basée sur un modèle qualitatif, qui rend la planification dynamique en intégrant de manière explicite les effets des actions de l'élève : évolution du style d'enseignement en fonction du travail effectué.

Nous avons choisi Prolog2 comme langage pour implanter notre système. Le système actuel intègre des mécanismes de modélisation (constitution des différentes bases) et de simulation (propagation d'influences, mise à jour des états qualitatifs). Le système de décision a également été réalisé, puis testé sur un exemple.

Références

1. Blanc, F.: A systemic approach to courseware engineering. 6ème World Conf. on Computers in Education, WCCE'95. Chapman & Hall (1995) 815-828
2. De Kleer, J.: A qualitative physics based on confluences. Revue Artificial Intelligence 24 (1984) 7-83
3. Forbus, K.: Qualitative Process Theory : twelve years after. Revue Artificial Intelligence 59 (1993) 115-123
4. Huang, X., Mac Calla, G.: Instructional planning using focus of attention. 2ème Conf. Int. on Intelligent Tutoring Systems, ITS'92. Springer Verlag LNCS 608 (1992) 443-450
5. Khuwaja, R., Evans, M., Rovick, A., Michael, J.: Knowledge representation for an Intelligent Tutoring System based on a multilevel causal model. 2ème Conf. Int. on Intelligent Tutoring Systems, ITS'92. Springer Verlag LNCS 608 (1992) 217-224
6. Kuipers, B.: Qualitative simulation. Revue Artificial Intelligence 29 (1986) 289-338
7. Labat, J.M., Futtersack, M., Vivet, M.: Planification pédagogique : de l'expertise humaine à sa modélisation dans un STI. 2ème Conf. Int. on Intelligent Tutoring Systems, ITS'92. Springer Verlag LNCS 608 (1992) 515-522
8. Mac Millian, S., Emme, D., Bekowitz, M.: Instructional planners : lessons learned. Intelligent Tutoring Systems : lessosn learned. LEA (1988) 229-257
9. Pirolli, P.: Computer-aided instructional design systems. Intelligent Tutoring Systems: evolutions in design. LEA (1991) 105-126
10. Sime, J.: Why use multiple qualitative simulations in knowledge-based tutoring systems. 7ème Conference Internationale, PEG'93. (1993) 399-407
11. Van Marcke, K.: Instructional expertise. 2ème Conf. Int. on Intelligent Tutoring Systems, ITS'92. Springer Verlag LNCS 608 (1992) 234-244
12. White, B., Frederiksen, J.: Causal model progressions as a foundation for intelligent learning environments. Revue Artificial Intelligence 42 (1990) 99-157

Towards Design Learning Environments - I: Exploring How Devices Work

Ashok K. Goel[1], Andrés Gómez de Silva Garza[1], Nathalie Grué[1], J. William Murdock[1], Margaret M. Recker[1], and T. Govindaraj[2]

[1] Artificial Intelligence Group
College of Computing
Georgia Institute of Technology
801 Atlantic Drive, Atlanta, Georgia 30332-0280
[2] Center for Human-Machine Systems Research
School of Industrial and Systems Engineering
Georgia Institute of Technology

Abstract. Knowledge-based support for learning about physical devices is a classical problem in research on intelligent tutoring systems (ITS). The large amount of knowledge engineering needed, however, presents a major difficulty in constructing ITS's for learning how devices work. Many knowledge-based design systems, on the other hand, already contain libraries of device designs and models. This provides an opportunity for reusing the legacy device libraries for supporting the learning of how devices work. We report on an experiment on the computational feasibility of this reuse of device libraries. In particular, we describe how the structure-behavior-function (SBF) device models in an autonomous knowledge-based design system called KRITIK enable device explanation and exploration in an interactive design and learning environment called INTERACTIVE KRITIK.

1 Motivations and Goals

Design, construction, evaluation, and use of intelligent tutoring systems (ITS) raises a variety of complex issues. Examples include cognitive issues pertaining to how humans solve problems, comprehend, and learn; user interface issues relating to interaction and communication between humans and computers; and knowledge system issues pertaining to the content, representation, organization, and access of knowledge in the computer. Within the context of knowledge system issues, a common difficulty is the enormous amount of knowledge engineering required to construct an ITS for a particular class of users in a specific class of task domains. One potential solution to this problem is to design reusable ITS's. In this paper, we explore another potential solution, namely, the reuse of knowledge systems already built for one set of goals to address related ITS tasks.

In particular, we are interested in the question of whether device libraries in autonomous knowledge-based design systems can be reused for supporting interactive learning of the way devices work. We have developed a family of autonomous knowledge-based device design systems called KRITIK (Goel and Chandrasekaran 1989, 1992; Goel 1991, 1992). KRITIK addresses the extremely common functions-to-structure design task in the domain of simple physical devices. Its high-level process for this design task is case-based: it designs new devices by adapting the designs of old devices. Its method for adapting old designs is model-based: it uses case-specific device models for deciding on the design modifications needed for the current problem. Thus KRITIK contains (i) a library of design cases and device models, (ii) a case-based process model of design, and (iii) a family of model-based methods for design adaptation. In this paper, we examine how an interactive version of KRITIK can enable the learning of how devices work. An accompanying paper will address the related issue of learning about design processes and methods.

We are developing an interactive design and learning environment called INTERACTIVE KRITIK. The new environment provides a user with access to the device models in KRITIK. It also provides explanations of how the devices work and enables the user to explore the device models.

2 KRITIK

KRITIK[3] contains a library of devices and associated structure-behavior-function (SBF) models. The structure-behavior-function (SBF) model of a device, such as gyroscope, explicitly represents (i) the function(s) of the device, (ii) the structure of the device, and (iii) the internal causal behaviors of the device. The internal causal behaviors specify how the functions of the structural components of the device are composed into the device functions. An SBF device model is organized hierarchically so that the device functions reference the causal behaviors responsible for their accomplishment and the causal behaviors index the functions of the device substructures. As a simple example, let us consider the SBF model of a device that cools nitric acid.

Structure: The structure of a device in the SBF language is expressed in terms of its constituent components and substances and the interactions between them. Figure 1(a) shows a diagrammatic view of the structure of a nitric acid cooler. Within the device, substances can interact both *structurally* and *behaviorally*. For example, water can flow from pump to chamber only if they are structurally *connected*, and due to the function *allow* water of the pipe that connects them.

Function: The function of a device in the SBF language is represented as a schema that specifies the input behavioral state of the device, the behavioral state it produces as output, and a pointer to the internal causal behavior of the design that achieves this transformation. Figure 1(b) illustrates the function of the nitric acid cooler. Both the input state and the output state are represented as *substance schemas.* The input state specifies that the substance HNO_3 at *location* p_1 in the topography of the device (Figure 1(a)) includes the property

---

[3] The current version of KRITIK runs under Common Lisp using CLOS.

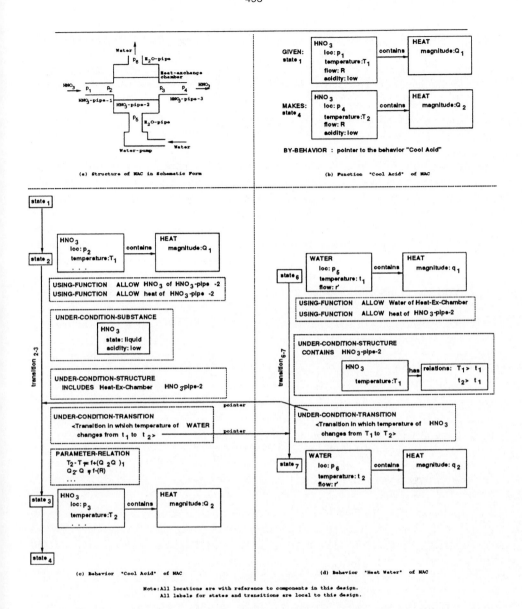

Fig. 1. SBF Model of a Nitric Acid Cooler

temperature and the corresponding parameter T_1. Similarly the output state specifies that this property now has the value T_2. Finally, the slot *by-behavior* points to the causal behavior that achieves the function of cooling acid.

The devices and their SBF models are indexed by the *functions* delivered by the devices. Thus the existing nitric acid cooler is indexed by the function illustrated in Figure 1(b). The functions, in turn, act as indices into the internal causal behaviors of the SBF model through their *by-behavior* slot.

Behavior: The SBF model of a device also specifies the internal causal behaviors that compose the functions of device substructures into the functions of the device as a whole. In the SBF language, the internal causal behaviors of a device are represented as sequences of *transitions* between *behavioral states.* The annotations on the state transitions express the *causal, structural,* and *functional contexts* in which the state transitions occur and the state variables get transformed. The causal context specifies *causal relations* between the variables in preceding and succeeding states. The structural context specifies different *structural relations* among the components, the substances, and the different spatial locations of the device. The functional context indicates which functions of which components in the device are responsible for the transition. Figure 1(c) shows the causal behavior that explains how heat is decreased in the nitric acid. The first two states describe the state of the acid prior to entering the chamber while the last two describe its state after the chamber. The annotation *under-condition-transition* on $transition_{2-3}$ between $state_2$ and $state_3$ indicates that the transition occurs due to the action of the water behavior. Similarly, the annotation *under-condition-structure* specifies that the involved components need to be connected in order for the transition to occur.

3   INTERACTIVE KRITIK

INTERACTIVE KRITIK's architecture consists of two agents: a design reasoning agent in the form of KRITIK and an user interface agent[4]. The architecture is illustrated in Figure 2; in this figure solid lines represent data flow while dotted lines represent control flow.

The interface agent in INTERACTIVE KRITIK has access to all the knowledge of KRITIK. It uses KRITIK's SBF device models to graphically illustrate and explain the functioning of the devices to users. Additionally, as we will describe in an accompanying paper, the interface agent uses task-method-knowledge (TMK) models to describe KRITIK's reasoning.

3.1   Device Explanation in INTERACTIVE KRITIK

INTERACTIVE KRITIK uses SBF device models to explain how a device works to a user. The SBF model provides a functional and causal explanation of how

---

[4] The interface is built using the Garnet tool (Myers and Zanden 1992).

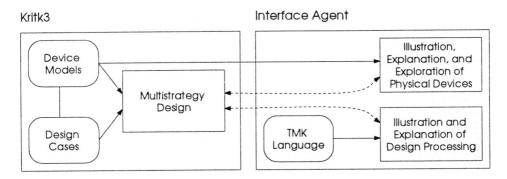

Fig. 2. INTERACTIVE KRITIK's Architecture

the device works in terms of its function, its structure, and its causal behaviors that specify how the functions of the structural elements get composed into the functions of the device. INTERACTIVE KRITIK illustrates the SBF model of a device to the user on several interrelated screens that illustrate the device structure, functions, and behaviors. For example, Figure 3 shows the illustration of part of the behavior of the nitric acid cooler that explains how water is heated; a different screen shows the primary behavior of this device, the cooling of the acid.

3.2 Device Exploration in INTERACTIVE KRITIK

INTERACTIVE KRITIK also enables the user to browse through different aspects of a device design. This exploration of a given device too is enabled by the SBF model. As we explained in Section 2, the SBF language provides a vocabulary for cross-indexing different parts of an SBF model. For example, the *by-behavior* slot in the specification of a function in the SBF model acts as an index to the causal behaviors that accomplish the function (see Figure 1b). Also, the *using-function* slot in the specifications of the state transitions in a causal behavior acts as an index into the functional specifications of the structural components of the device (see Figure 1c). In addition, the *under-condition-transition* slot in the specifications of the state transitions in a causal behavior acts as an index into specific transitions in other causal behaviors of the devices (see Figure 1d). The description of a device component contains a specification of its functions, and points to the causal behaviors in which the component plays a functional role.

This organizational scheme enables the user to browse through the SBF model of the design. The initial view of an SBF model in INTERACTIVE KRI-TIK is a representation of the device's functional specification. From here the user can use push interface buttons to move among the functional, behavioral, and structural representations of the device. Additionally, the user can click on the name of the behavior in the *by-behavior* slot in the functional specification,

498

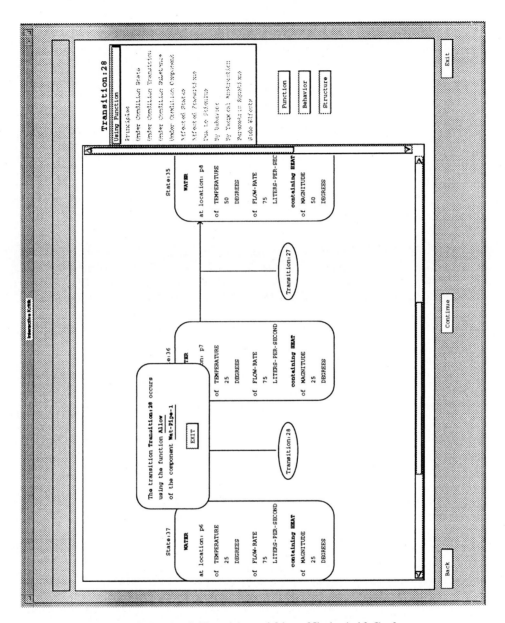

Fig. 3. A Behavioral Transition within a Nitric Acid Cooler

and "jump" directly to that behavior. Figure 3 illustrates a behavior screen. When a user clicks on a particular transition a menu pops up that provides additional information about the transition (as illustrated in Figure 3), and allows direct access to structural and behavioral information relating to that transition. For example, if the transition is dependent on another behavior, the user can jump directly to that behavior by clicking on the name in the *under-condition-transition* slot. The structure screen provides similar capabilities for inspecting the components of a device and the connections between them.

4   Related Work

Explanation of physical devices is a classical issue in intelligent tutoring systems. SOPHIE, designed to teach troubleshooting of electrical circuits, was perhaps the first intelligent tutoring system to encounter this problem (Brown, Burton and de Kleer 1982). Early work on SOPHIE motivated much artificial intelligence and cognitive science research on "qualitative physics" and "naive physics." For example, de Kleer (1984) developed the method of *qualitative simulation* for diagnosing and predicting the behavior of electrical circuits, while Forbus (1984) developed a *qualitative process theory* to describe the behavior of physical processes as opposed to physical devices.

KRITIK's theory of SBF device models evolves from the Functional Representation (FR) scheme (Sembugamoorthy and Chandrasekaran 1986, Chandrasekaran et al. 1993). In FR, the functions are not only represented explicitly, but also used as indices to causal behaviors responsible for their accomplishment. SBF device models build on the FR scheme in three dimensions. First, SBF models are based on a well-defined component-substance ontology in which the structure of a device is viewed as constituted of components, substances and relations between them. This ontology enables explicit representation of behavioral states. Second, SBF models use Bylander's (1991) taxonomy of primitive behaviors to classify the device functions. This taxonomy enables more explicit representation of state transitions. Third, SBF models use Govindaraj's (1987) organization of causal behaviors along the flow of specific substances in the device.

The use of SBF models for device illustration, explanation and exploration is similar to Rasmussen's (1985) earlier work in cognitive engineering. Rasmussen proposed a hierarchical organization for presenting device knowledge to human users. His hierarchically-organized device models specify the structure, the behaviors, and the functions at each level in the hierarchy. TURBINIA-VYASA (Vasandani and Govindaraj 1994), uses a similar organizational scheme in a computer-based instructional system that trains operators to troubleshoot and diagnose faults in marine power plants. But while TURBINIA-VYASA was engineered specifically as an ITS, INTERACTIVE KRITIK reuses KRITIK's knowledge for the ITS task.

ASKHOWITWORKS (Kedar et al. 1993) is a recent prototype of an interactive manual for physical devices. It indexes device information by the kinds of questions and answers that occur in typical dialogs, and enables navigation of the indexed material through question asking. While ASK HOW IT WORKS takes an issue-centered view of device explanations, INTERACTIVE KRITIK takes an artifact-centered view. The latter is a natural result of reusing device libraries in knowledge-based design systems for supporting the learning of device models.

5 Conclusions

Knowledge-based support for learning about physical devices is a classical problem in research on intelligent tutoring systems (ITS). The large amount of knowledge engineering needed, however, presents a major difficulty in constructing ITS's for learning how devices work. Many knowledge-based design systems, on the other hand, already contain libraries of device designs. This provides an opportunity for reusing the design libraries for supporting the learning of how devices work. Our work on INTERACTIVE KRITIK represents an experiment in this reuse of libraries of device designs and associated structure-behavior-function (SBF) models.

There is still a great deal of work to be done on device explanation and exploration within INTERACTIVE KRITIK. Some issues which would need to be addressed before the system could be used in a real world setting include the display of the structure of a device, the building of a better user interface, and provision of additional interaction capabilities. However, our preliminary work on INTERACTIVE KRITIK does indicate the computational feasibility of using SBF models for explaining what a device does and how it does it, and for enabling the user to explore the device model.

Acknowledgments

Much of this research was done during 1993-94 when all the authors were with Georgia Institute of Technology in Atlanta, Georgia, USA. Andrés Gómez is now with the Key Centre of Design Computing, University of Sydney, Sydney, Australia; Nathalie Grué is now with the Institute for Learning Sciences, Northwestern University, Evanston, Illinois, USA; and Margaret Recker is now with Victoria University, Wellington, New Zealand. This work has been funded in part by a grant from the Advanced Research Projects Agency (research contract #F33615-93-1-1338) and partly by internal seed grants from Georgia Tech's Educational Technology Institute, College of Computing, Cognitive Science Program, and Graphics, Visualization and Usability Center.

References

Brown, J.S., Burton, R., and de Kleer, J.: Pedagogical Natural Language and Knowledge Engineering Techniques in SOPHIE I, II, III. Intelligent Tutoring Systems, S. Derek and J. S. Brown, (Ed), Academic Press, New York (1982)

Bylander, T.: A Theory of Consolidation for Reasoning about Devices. Man-Machine Studies **35** (1991) 467-489

Chandrasekaran, B., Goel, A., and Iwasaki, I.: Functional Representation as a Basis for Design Rationale. IEEE Computer **26(1)** (January 1993) 48-56

de Kleer., J.: How Circuits Work. Artificial Intelligence **24** (1984) 205-280

Forbus, F.: Qualitative Process Theory. Artificial Intelligence **24** (1984) 85-168

Goel, A.: A Model-based Approach to Case Adaptation. Proceedings of the Thirteenth Annual Conference of the Cognitive Science Society, Lawrence Erlbaum Associates (1991) 143-148

Goel, A.: Representation of Design Functions in Experience-Based Design. Intelligent Computer Aided Design, D. Brown, M. Waldron and H. Yoshikawa (editors), North-Holland (1992) 283-308

Goel, A., Chandrasekaran, B.: Functional Representation of Designs and Redesign Problem Solving. Proceedings of the Eleventh International Joint Conference on Artificial Intelligence, Morgan Kaufmann Publishers (1989) 1388-1394.

Goel, A., Chandrasekaran, B.: Case-Based Design: A Task Analysis. Artificial Intelligence Approaches to Engineering Design, Volume II: Innovative Design, Tong and D. Sriram (editors), Academic Press (1992) 165-184

Govindaraj, T.: Qualitative Approximation Methodology for Modeling and Simulation of Large Dynamic Systems: Applications to a Marine Power Plant. IEEE Transactions on Systems, Man and Cybernetics, **SMC-17 No. 6** (1987) 937-955.

Grué, N.: Illustration, Explanation and Navigation of Physical Devices and Design Processes. M.S. Thesis, College of Computing, Georgia Institute of Technology (June 1994)

Kedar, E., Baudin, C., Birnbaum, L., Osgood, R., and Bareiss, R.: ASKHOWITWORKS: An Interactive Intelligent Manual for Devices. INTERCHI'93 (1993)

Myers B., Zanden, B.: Environment for rapidly creating interactive design tools. Visual Computer **8** (1992) 94-116

Rasmussen, J.: The Role of Hierarchical Knowledge Representation in Decision Making and System Management. IEEE Trans. Systems, Man and Cybernetics **15** (1985) 234-243

Sembugamoorthy, V., Chandrasekaran., B.: Functional representation of devices and Compilation of Diagnostic Problem Solving Systems. Experience, Memory and Reasoning, J. Kolodner and C. Riesbeck (editors), Elbaum, Hillsdale, New Jersey (1986) 47-73

Vasandani, V., Govindaraj, T.: Knowledge structures for a computer-based training aid for troubleshooting a complex system. The Use of Computer Models for Explication, Analysis and Experiential Learning, D. Towne (editor) NATO ASI Series F, Programme AET, Springer-Verlag (1994)

Un modèle de simulation basée sur une représentation de type "objets - règles" pour l'enseignement des métiers de ventes *

ce travail s'inscrit dans le cadre du pôle de recherche régional, Picardie, NTE

D. Leclet[1] and G. Weidenfeld[1]

1 Université de Picardie Jules Verne, IUP Miage, Faculté des Sciences,
33 rue Saint Leu, 80039 Amiens Cedex 1, France
DominiqueLeclet @ca.u-picardie.fr - GerardWeidenfeld@ca.u-picardie.fr

Résumé. DISTRIACTIF est un projet entrepris en collaboration avec l'Association de Formation et d'Education Continue et subventionné par la Mission Etat Région pour les Technologies de Formation de Picardie pour l'étude et la mise en oeuvre d'un STI des métiers de vente. Destiné à des vendeurs, ce système les aide à structurer leur raisonnement. La caractérisation du problème a permis d'aboutir à un mode d'interaction privilégié, la *simulation*, par rapport aux objectifs d'acquisition des connaissances de nature *abstraite* dans un contexte *pratique*. La pratique courante des experts a mis en évidence des démarches impliquant simultanément des règles "contradictoires" et une complexité ne pouvant être gérée uniquement par Système Expert. Cette constatation nous a conduit à construire un modèle mixte alliant des objets et des règles, où ces dernières sont appliquées dans un ensemble de situations référencées : les simulations de cas.

Mots-clés. Système Tutoriel Intelligent, architecture pour STI, Enseignement des métiers de vente, simulation de cas, objets.

Abstract. The DISTRILEARN's system results from a cooperation with the AFEC with the support of the MERTF. It consists in the study and implementation of an Intelligent Tutoring System to learn the sales's profession. The target audience are sale's mens. The system purpose is to train these people, helping them to structure reasoning. Our analysis lead to the use of simulation in order to acquire *abstract* knowledge in a *practical* job context. Experts' current practice has shown problem solving steps involving simultaneously "contradictory" rules and a complexity that expert systems are not able to solve. We adopt a mixt model combining objects and rules in order to overcome this situation. This rules are applied in a referenced set of situations : cases' simulations.

Keywords. Intelligent Tutoring Systems, ITS' Architecture, Teaching sale's profession, case' simulations, objects.

1   Introduction

Cet article a pour objet de définir un cadre de référence pour des Systèmes Tutoriels Intelligents (16) mettant en jeu des domaines de connaissances dites "mixtes". Nous entendons par là des domaines dans lesquels des connaissances bien formalisées au moyen de règles strictes, quantitatives ou qualitatives coexistent avec des savoir-faires empiriques principalement justifiables par une pratique professionnelle. Une situation concrète a été analysée, le "marchandisage", mais le contexte est bien plus large et les problèmes généraux de formation qu'il soulève s'appliquent à maintes autres professions.

Ces connaissances mixtes sont actuellement dispensées dans le cadre d'enseignements professionnels, encore récemment centrés autour de l'apprentissage de procédures. La nécessité d'intégrer des éléments de prévision, de planification et d'anticipation pose la difficulté "classique" d'associer théorie et pratique dans l'enseignement et nous a naturellement conduit à rechercher des apports dans les nouvelles technologies et plus particulièrement dans la simulation.

La première partie de cet article, caractérise le problème et dégage les objectifs pédagogiques. La deuxième partie justifie la préconisation d'un mode d'interaction privilégié, la *simulation*. En effet, l'approche la plus classique consisterait à établir un système de règles permettant de générer le placement. Bien qu'il existe quelques systèmes experts de ce type, leur utilisation n'est guère possible parce qu'ils prennent difficilement en compte le caractère contextuel de certaines des règles utilisées. L'analyse de cette situation permet de proposer une première représentation des *connaissances mixtes*. Cette représentation n'est pas *constructiviste* comme dans le cas des règles d'un système expert, mais elle est basée sur la description des erreurs, un peu à la manière de *Buggy* (4). La situation est cependant différente dans la mesure où le domaine de référence n'est pas formalisé a priori. Les erreurs qui sont décrites sont générales et ne peuvent être exprimées qu'en référence à des situations spécifiques, qu'il faudra à chaque fois décrire ou préciser : c'est le domaine de *l'étude de cas*. La dernière partie de cet article décrit la structure de données et les algorithmes utilisés pour l'implémentation.

2   Caractérisation du problème

L'objectif de ce projet vise à étudier les connaissances mises en oeuvre dans l'agencement de surfaces de ventes, en vue de former des personnels de qualification initiale faible : niveau 5 dans la nomenclature de la formation professionnelle. D'une façon statistique, ces personnels déjà en place, vendeurs ou magasiniers et les apprenants en formation initiale (CAP ou BEP) sont plus familiers avec des approches concrètes qu'avec des formalisations mathématiques ou logiques. De ce fait, l'agencement des surfaces de vente modernes (hypermarché, supermarché, supérette, etc...) fait de plus en plus appel à des techniques et raisonnements sophistiqués. Ainsi, le "marchandisage" a pour objet principal d'organiser un rayon, de manière à inciter le consommateur à acheter des produits d'impulsion (produit attrayant, séduisant, attirant, etc...) en plus des achats prévus. Deux techniques sont principalement utilisées : l'implantation des rayons dans la surface de vente et l'implantation des produits dans le linéaire. Cet article se focalisera essentiellement sur la première technique (l'implantation des rayons dans la surface), la seconde étant très similaire mais plus simple.

2.1   Les principes d'aménagement de la surface de vente

Le principe général d'aménagement d'une surface de vente est régi par des règles d'optimisation, dont voici quelques exemples :

R1 Attirer les consommateurs avec des produits d'appel, en plaçant les produits de promotion en zone chaude (zone dans laquelle les clients sont forcés de passer).

R2 Ne pas perdre un mètre carré de surface de vente.

R3 Placer dans les zones dites froides, zones vers lesquelles le consommateur n'est, à priori, pas attiré, les produits "prévendus" (produits frais et l'épicerie).

R4 Placer les produits lourds et volumineux en début de circuit de manière à remplir convenablement les chariots.

R5 Ne pas placer des produits incompatibles (par exemple, l'alimentaire et les produits dangereux) à proximité.

R6 Les produits saisonniers sont dans l'allée principale.

R7 Les rayons nécessitant des laboratoires de préparations doivent être à proximité de ceux-ci.

D'autres contraintes pèsent également sur l'agencement : la forme du magasin ; l'emplacement des réserves ; l'emplacement de certains rayons (R6, R7)) ; la nécessité d'assurer une surveillance de certains rayons (disques, cosmétiques, etc…) ; des impératifs de sécurité, assurer l'accès aux dégagements mais aussi gérer les incompatibilités entre rayons (R5) ; etc….

De nombreuses règles complètent ces exemples représentatifs des problèmes du marchandisage. Le paragraphe suivant répertorie les types de connaissances sous jacentes à cette activité.

2.2 Typologie des connaissances mises en œuvre

Le marchandisage est souvent présenté comme une activité entièrement formalisable. Cependant, la description des connaissances permet de mettre en évidence une cohabitation entre des règles strictes et des comportements empiriques.

Les faits. Les faits sont des prérequis pour les opérations d'agencement. Ainsi, les classifications des produits en famille et sous familles définit la notion de rayon qui est à la base de l'agencement. Un autre prérequis est la connaissance des divers types de surface car certaines règles en dépendent.

Les règles strictes. Les règles strictes induisent des placements déterministes. L'application d'une règle stricte à un rayon, permet d'inférer exactement sa place dans la surface. Les règles R6 et R7 en fournissent des exemples.

Les règles contextuelles. L'application d'une règle contextuelle ne détermine pas *univoquement* une solution mais détermine un *ensemble* de positions possibles. Les règles R1 à R5 en fournissent des exemples. Généralement, il y a plusieurs façons acceptables de placer un rayon tout en satisfaisant à chacune de ces règles prise isolément. Par contre, on rencontrera fréquemment des situations mettant en jeu simultanément plusieurs de ces règles et pour lesquelles il n'existe pas de solution formelle. Par exemple, la règle R1 indique de placer les produits d'appel en zone chaude et la règle R3, de placer les produits frais en zone froide. Mais il peut y avoir des produits d'appel parmi les produits frais !

De tels conflits existent aussi dans les systèmes à base de règles de production et sont généralement résolus par des méta-règles ou des schémas plus complexes (priorité, vraisemblances, fréquences, etc...) (6), (8). Ici, les vendeurs et les magasiniers, constamment confrontés, à ce type de problème, les résolvent de façon empirique. Le choix d'une priorité entre les règles est alors déterminé par des références à une situation connue, plutôt qu'à un schéma général formalisé. La définition, par nos experts, de ces situations s'effectue donc selon un schéma plus associatif qu'inductif. Cependant, un mécanisme de prise de décision a pu être dégagé afin de structurer ces situations somme toutes hétérogènes. Il est présenté ci-dessous.

2.3 Les stratégies de résolution de problème

Les règles strictes ou contextuelles appartiennent à diverses catégories représentant des "orientations stratégiques" comme : la sécurité, le confort du client, le "marketing", l'organisation, la rentabilité, etc.... Cette typologie fournit une "entrée" pour résoudre les conflits de placements que nous avons évoqués ci-dessus. Le mécanisme de prise de décision combine alors des étapes ayant à trait à :

1. L'analyse de la situation, pour en extraire les informations qui vont être les "déclencheurs" de certaines règles. Cette analyse suppose la connaissance d'un modèle de la situation permettant de discriminer les divers éléments présents.

2. La prévision et l'anticipation pour évaluer les conséquences des règles correspondantes. Les conflits seront identifiés au cours de cette phase et l'application prioritaire des règles strictes permettra de restreindre les solutions admissibles.

3. L'évaluation des coûts des diverses solutions restantes. Ce coût est relatif à chacune des "catégories" (sécurité, confort, etc...).

4. La hiérarchisation des solutions possibles, par exemple en se référant à une stratégie basée sur des priorités dans la liste des "catégories" précedentes.

2.4 Objectifs de formation et principales difficultés :

Il ressort de la discussion précédente, qu'il existe trois types d'objectifs pédagogiques, correspondants à :

1. L'acquisition des connaissances (les faits, les règles strictes et contextuelles).

2. La maîtrise des procédures de placement. En fait, la mise en œuvre des connaissances précédentes de façon contextuelle et non isolée.

3. La capacité de choisir et de mettre en œuvre une stratégie.

L'appréciation des difficultés d'acquisition se fait évidemment en référence aux compétences des apprenants. Ce public de niveau 5 connaît souvent des difficultés scolaires antérieures et en particulier en "mathématique". Or les problèmes de placement que nous avons analysés, entrent complètement dans la catégorie hypothético-déductive. Il s'agit d'ailleurs, d'un raisonnement très souvent adopté pour des problèmes de diagnostic (1). En effet, la méthode hypothético-déductive permet de bâtir des raisonnements à partir d'hypothèses (données d'un problème, propositions reçues sans se soucier de leur vérité ou de leur fausseté, etc...) émises et dont l'exactitude sera jugée a posteriori, c'est à dire selon une capacité ou une incapacité à produire comme conséquences logiques un ensemble donné de propositions (13).

Il importe donc, pour prévenir une probable difficulté d'acquisition, par des moyens classiques (apparentés à des résolutions de problèmes mathématiques, sous une forme plus ou moins adaptée), de concevoir un dispositif adapté à cette formation n'utilisant pas de prérequis et des méthodes excluantes pour le public visé.

3 Un dispositif de formation centré sur la simulation

Les deux premiers objectifs pédagogiques énoncés dans le 2.4, qui permettent d'une part la compréhension des règles qui régissent le placement et d'autre part celle des diversités (variations) liées aux types de surface, ne posent pas véritablement de problème. L'acquisition de ces connaissances peut être facilitée par des interactions de type *hypermédia*. Ainsi, les règles strictes, la sécurité, les zones chaudes et froides, la complémentarité des produits et les règles d'optimisation de la surface de vente, sont présentées la forme d'un "diaporama" intégrant des commentaires vocaux. Par contre, la mise en œuvre de ces connaissances dans un contexte particulier fait appel à un mécanisme de prise de décision bien plus complexe. Les modèles alors entièrement déductifs, comme Geometry Tutor (2), Guidon (5), Sphinx (7), Socrate (12), ou encore Aplusix (14) ne sont pas ici adaptées. Ainsi, le paragraphe suivant propose un mode d'interaction privilégié pour pallier ces inconvénients.

3.1 Les apports didactiques attendus de l'usage de la simulation :

Face aux difficultés de conceptualisation diagnostiquées, deux hypothèses de base utilisant les nouvelles technologies sont à l'origine du choix effectué.

La première est l'approche constructiviste, illustrée à l'origine, par le langage LOGO (15). Dans ce contexte, l'apprenant construit un monde (micromonde), dont il peut éprouver puis modifier les propriétés.

La seconde est la mise en situation simulée par un dispositif technologique. Cette méthode a été utilisée à l'origine en physique et en biologie, puis dans l'apprentissage du maniement de mécanismes complexes. Elle permet notamment d'expérimenter des situations ayant une modélisation mathématique trop complexe pour qu'elle soit utilisable telle quelle par un opérateur. Les simulations reposent généralement sur un modèle déterministe, exprimé au moyen de fonctions mathématiques ou d'un ensemble de règles. On a cependant montré préalablement que, de par l'existence de règles contextuelles, la présente situation est un peu différente. L'activité considérée ne peut être *entièrement* régie par un modèle de ce type.

Nous avons donc été amené à construire un dispositif intermédiaire, basé à la fois sur les règles dont la description a été esquissée en 2.1 et 2.2, et sur leur mise en application dans un ensemble de situations référencées (proposées par des experts sur la base de leur importance dans le cadre professionnel). Dans chacun de ces contextes, les experts ont isolé un sous ensemble de l'ensemble des règles, qui soit cohérent et dépendant du contexte.

Dans ces conditions, il devient alors possible, pour chacune de ces situations, de proposer aux élèves un environnement de simulations dans lequel il peuvent *explorer* librement tous les placements possibles, comme dans une approche micromonde. De plus, ce dispositif permet de suivre pas à pas l'activité des apprenants, de *diagnostiquer* et *d'expliquer* toutes leurs entorses aux règles. Nous allons maintenant décrire l'interaction correspondante.

3.2 Description de l'interaction (apprenant)

L'interaction avec l'apprenant s'effectue sous la forme d'exercices permettant de simuler une situation réelle afin qu'il puisse aménager un magasin. La forme générale de l'interaction est la suivante :

1. L'exercice débute par une présentation du magasin partiellement installé.

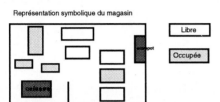

Les informations nécessaires à la compréhension de la situation sont accessibles sous forme iconique au moyen d'une consultation hypermédia.

2. Un problème, de type arithmétique, est alors posé à l'élève. Par exemple :

   "Le magasin est agencé comme ci-dessous, vous devez maintenant le compléter en plaçant les rayons fromage et épicerie. Le rayon fromage comporte 37 produits et le rayon épicerie 52 de cinq types".

3. L'élève pourra dans ce cas, effectuer et ce dans n'importe quel ordre, les actions suivantes : sélectionner un linéaire L, mettre les fromages ou l'épicerie dans L, sélectionner un linéaire dans lequel l'élève avait déjà placé quelque chose et annuler cette opération.

4. Le système vérifie alors que les actions sont conformes aux règles actives (cf paragraphe 4.2) dans l'exercice.

5. Chaque fois qu'une règle est en défaut une explication est générée. Celle-ci est a deux niveaux : la première est intrinsèque et correspond à une reformulation en langage naturel de la règle considérée ; la seconde, contextuelle, est générée situation par situation, par les auteurs (cf page 8).

3.3 Description de l'interaction (auteur)

Un environnement général est préalablement formalisé : la surface et ses contraintes propres, les rayons vides et leurs dispositions, les produits et leurs contraintes, les règles strictes (définies une fois pour toute) et les règles contextuelles (ensemble pouvant être étendu par l'auteur). Le système de création des exercices permet, alors, à l'auteur de :

1. Désigner la portion de surface de vente sur laquelle porte l'exercice.

2. Choisir les rayons à placer.

3. Fixer les contraintes initiales (un module de "cohérence" de placement facilite cette mise en place, cf 4.3).

4. Spécifier les règles strictes ou contextuelles applicables dans l'exercice.

5. Compléter les explications par contextualisation.

3.4 L'évaluation

Le système DISTRIACTIF est utilisé dans le cadre d'une formation, sous la responsabilité d'un formateur. L'évaluation vise à lui fournir, ainsi qu'aux apprenants, une "radiographie" de l'activité. Le domaine est structuré en une dizaine d'objectifs auxquels sont associés des situations, en l'occurrence des exercices. Ceux-ci sont construits de façon à ce que chaque règle soit appliquée et que les différents contextes soient illustrés. Cette représentation permet d'obtenir une évaluation globale, ou par objectifs.

4 L'implantation

4.1 Une représentation mixte " objets règles "

Comme nous l'avons déjà souligné dans le paragraphe 2.2, les connaissances du système n'ont pu être représentées sous la forme de règles de production. En effet, nous avons constaté que certaines règles pouvaient s'exclure mutuellement, générant ainsi des conflits (3). Les magasiniers, confrontés à ces situations contextuelles, exploitent des stratégies différenciées pour résoudre ces conflits.

C'est pour cette raison, que les connaissances du système ont été représentées sous un formalisme associant, d'une part des règles (10), (11) et d'autre part des objets (9). En effet, les règles du système sont de nature mixte : *règles strictes* (quantitatives ou qualitatives) et *règles contextuelles* (savoir-faires empiriques principalement justifiables par référence à des pratiques professionnelles). Ces règles évoluent généralement en fonction de la politique de l'établissement, du responsable de rayon, des aspects promotionnels, etc.... Le formalisme objets a permis, quant à lui, de représenter la surface de vente, les produits, rayons, laboratoires, etc..., sous la forme de hiérarchies taxonomiques permettant ainsi, de constituer des classifications représentatives des connaissances utilisées. Pour intégrer ces deux approches, le langage de programmation utilisé est le C++.

De plus, nous avons observé que, dans leur pratique courante, face à des situations mettant en jeu simultanément plusieurs règles "contradictoires", les experts résolvaient le conflit en se référant à des situations connues. Nous avons donc naturellement recherché, une solution faisant appel à un système de règles appliquées dans un ensemble de situations référencées : les simulations de cas. A cette fin, les experts ont, pour chaque cas, extrait de la base de connaissances, un sous-ensemble de règles significatif, cohérent et dépendant du contexte.

4.2 La structure de données

Une famille de produits possède les caractéristiques suivantes :

```
┌──────────────────────────────────────────┐
│         STRUCTURE = FAM_PROD              │
├──────────────────────────────────────────┤
│ Prevendu : CHAINE                         │
│ Renouvellement : LISTE (chaine)           │
│ Saisonnier : CHAINE                       │
│ Promotion : CHAINE                        │
│ Sécurité : CHAINE                         │
│ Laboratoire : ^ Classe_Laboratoire        │
└──────────────────────────────────────────┘
```

L'attribut *renouvellement* correspond à un des items de la liste (fort, moyen, faible).

L'attribut *laboratoire* associe (s'il existe), la description du laboratoire, lui même, relié à un rayon. Les représentations des laboratoires et des rayons constituent, alors des hiérarchies "taxonomique" issues du formalisme objet.

Une surface est représentée par la structure suivante :

```
┌──────────────────────────────────────────┐
│           CLASSE = Surface                │
├──────────────────────────────────────────┤
│ Type_surface : CHAINE                     │
│ Plan_surface : FICHIER BMP                │
│ Linéaires : ^Classe_Linéaire              │
│ Laboratoires : ¨Classe_Laboratoire        │
│ Fond_magasin : LISTE (^Classe_rayon)      │
│ Zone_chaude : LISTE (^Classe_rayon)       │
│ Zone_froide : LISTE (^Classe_rayon)       │
└──────────────────────────────────────────┘
```

Les emplacements d'une surface sont représentés par des entiers.

L'attribut *linéaire* associe la description du linéaire représenté sous la forme d'une hiérarchie "taxonomique".

L'attribut *fond_magasin* associe une liste de "pointeur", pointant sur la hiérarchie des rayons, etc.

Un exercice quant à lui est représenté par :

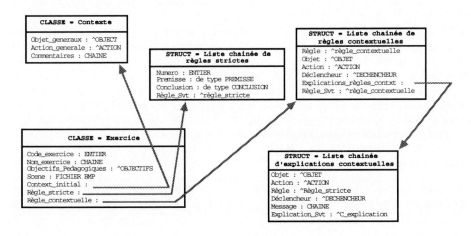

La structure de l'exercice montre qu'il existe deux types d'explications. Les explications "strictes" (affichage de la règle stricte correspondante) et des explications "contextuelles" reconstruites en intégrant des informations spécifiques à la situation contextuelle donnée (fournies par l'auteur lors de la création de l'exercice).

4.3   Un exemple d'algorithme

Cet algorithme s'applique lors de la constitution d'un exercice (cf 3.3 étape 3). En fonction des rayons (produits) restant à placer et des emplacements libres, les tests successifs suivants sont effectués dans l'ordre suivant :

Applications des règles strictes. On applique successivement les règles strictes : *"si le rayon R comporte un laboratoire L et si la position courante de R correspond au laboratoire L alors on peut placer R"* (règle de proximité - R7) ; *"si l'attribut saisonnier de R est vrai dès que l'attribut allée de N est vrai alors placer R en N"* (règle de produits saisonniers - R6) ; etc….

En cas d'échecs. On applique successivement les règles suivantes qui correspondent à une priorité choisie : *"si N-1 est occupé par R' et si R et R' s'excluent alors incrémenter N"* (proximité) ; *"si R est un rayon à renouvellement alors si l'attribut fond est vrai pour N alors placer R"* (renouvellement achat) ; *"si R est un rayon de promotion alors dès que l'attribut chaud est vrai pour N alors placer R en N"* (promotion) ; *"si R est un rayon prévendu alors dès que l'attribut froid est vrai pour N alors placer R en N"* (prévendus) ; *"si R' occupe N-1 et si R et R' sont complémentaires alors on peut placer R en N"* (complémentarité).

Cet algorithme ne détermine pas nécessairement une solution. Il suggérera généralement des placements, dont la solution définitive incombera à l'auteur.

5   Conclusion

Cet article présente un projet de recherche et de développement relatif à la formation au "marchandisage". L'objectif de réalisation d'un produit diffusable nous a conduit à adopter une approche "empirique" centrée sur une prise en compte de besoins concrets de l'organisme de formation. Ceux-ci ont pu être explicités avec le concours d'un expert pleinement disponible durant ce projet. L'approche retenue a été déterminante dans le choix de l'interaction proposée : la simulation. Ce choix est motivé principalement par les caractéristiques du public visé et ses difficultés à effectuer des acquisitions de connaissances sous une forme " abstraite ". Une seconde conséquence concerne le mode de représentation des connaissances. La forme initialement prévue, qui était l'utilisation de règles de production, s'est révélée insuffisante et un modèle mixte "règle-objet" a été conçu. Ces deux aspects, que nous souhaitions mettre en évidence constituent les résultats principaux de la première phase de ce projet. Les aspects liés à la réalisation proprement dite du produit, (deuxième phase du projet), n'ont de ce fait, pas été évoqués ici. Le système, qui comporte par ailleurs des enrichissements multimédia, est actuellement en cours d'achèvement dans sa version Bêta et fera l'objet d'une expérimentation pratique sur le terrain. Un protocole d'évaluation, mobilisant notamment les professionnels, a été construit afin de déterminer avec précision les impacts constatés ainsi que les situations et règles concrètes non prises en compte par le produit. A l'issue de cette phase d'expérimentation, le modèle présenté ici sera affiné.

Références

1. P. Agearter : "Consult-Eao : un tuteur pour l'apprentissage du diagnostic médical destiné aux travailleurs de santé dans les pays en développement" - Extrait du livre de M. Quéré : SE et EAO - Ed Ophrys.

2. J.R. Anderson : "The geometry tutor". In proceedings of ninth international joint conference on AI. IJCAI9, 85

3. A. Bonnet : "L'intelligence artificielle : promesses et réalités" - InterEditions, 88

4. J.S. Brown & R.R Burton : "Diagnostic models for procedural bugs in basic mathematical skills". Cognitive Sciences, Vol.2, 78.

5. W. Clancey : "Guidon". In Barr and Feigenbaum. The hanbook of AI, 82

6. J.P. Delahaye : "Systèmes experts : organisation et programmation des bases de connaissances en calcul propositionnel" - Ed Eyrolles 87.

7. D. Fieschi : "Contribution au système expert Sphinx : application à l'enseignement médical". Thèse 3ècycle, Paris VI, 84

8. M. Fieschi : "IA en médecine - des systèmes experts" - Ed Masson 86.

9. J. Ferber - 1990 - "Conception et programmation par objets" - Ed Hermès 90.

10. M. Joubert : "Conceptualisation, représentation et utilisation des connaissances dans les systèmes experts" - Systèmes experts en médecine - 88.

11. B. Meyer : "Conception et programmation par objets" - InterEditions - Ed 91.

12. J. Moustafadiès : "Socrate : an expert system for training in troubleshouting", Avignon 86.

13. J. Moustafadiès : "Formation au diagnostic technique" - Masson - Ed 90.

14. J.F. Nicaud : "Aplusix : un expert en résolution pédagogique d'exercices d'algèbre". Thèse Paris XI, 87

15. S. Papert : "Jaillissement de l'esprit". Ed Flammarion. 80

16. M. Vivet, J.F. Nicaud : "Les tuteurs Intelligents. Réalisations et tendances de recherches" - T.S.I. - vol. 7, 88

Generic Approaches in Developing

Practical Intelligent Industrial Training Systems

John Liddle, Roy Leitch, Keith Brown
Intelligent Systems Laboratory
Department of Computing and Electrical Engineering
Heriot-Watt University, Edinburgh, Scotland, UK

Abstract. Intelligent training systems have been developed using techniques advanced within the AI in education community. Each new system developed, however, exhibits its own inherent idiosyncrasies and does not address the problems of high development costs. This paper describes two generic approaches adopted within the Mobit project for building Intelligent Training Systems. The first being our approach to acquiring domain specific knowledge which initially requires a decomposition of the training objective into primitive generic tasks. The second being our approach to training based on domain independent learning styles and training strategies.

1   Introduction

Learning how to control a complex industrial process takes years of practice and training [11]. In an attempt to reduce this learning period intelligent training systems have been developed which use techniques [3] advanced within the AI in education community. Each new system developed, however, exhibits its own inherent idiosyncrasies and does not address the problems of high development costs. In order to reduce the development time and cost, we believe that training systems should be developed in a more general and practical manner.

The Mobit project is part of the ESPRC/DTI Intelligent Systems Integration Programme (ISIP) and is involved in developing a generic system and associated methods which will facilitate industrial companies in building their own training systems at a fraction of the present cost. The developed system being capable of delivering training which will aid the trainee in acquiring a deeper understanding of the domain. The project is based on previous work done within the ITSIE project [4] that was funded by the European Community under the ESPRIT Programme.

Described within this paper are the generic approaches adopted within the Mobit programme for acquiring the domain specific knowledge and applied to training based on domain independent "learning styles" and training strategies. In acquiring the domain knowledge we describe a method for decomposing the training objective into primitive tasks. These tasks specify the behaviour of a competent operator and as such can be mapped directly to training goals. We then describe how the domain knowledge is specified on three distinct levels. The knowledge level required to satisfy the training goals being identified from the *level of expertise* at which the trainee will be expected to perfom.

With our approach to domain independent training we describe how the system selects the knowledge level at which the subject matter will be communicated based on the trainee's preferred *learning style.* Further, we describe how the training strategy employed at run-time controls the style of presentation and how much interaction the trainee has with the system.

2 A Generic Approach to Acquiring Domain Knowledge

Two major tasks in developing training systems include identifying and specifying the domain specific training goals and expertise [1]. To date, these tasks have been carried out by the person responsible for developing the system. Starting with a training objective (e.g. "control process x in both normal and abnormal situations"), the initial task is in finding any prerequisite knowledge required to achieve the objective. This knowledge is then decomposed such that the training goals can be specified. The manner in which this decomposition process is carried out is almost certain to vary from individual to individual, and across different industrial domains. If intelligent systems are to be built out with the research lab then these tasks must be performed in a general and consistent manner.

A method for decomposing the training objective to identify tasks which we believe to be generic across all industrial domains is proposed. These generic tasks can be directly mapped to the training goals, as they specify the behaviour expected of a competent operator, and thus that expected of the trainee at the end of training. Having identified the training goals, the domain expertise can then be specified.

2.1 Generic Task Decomposition

The problems of decomposing an instuctional objective are well understood [10]. As the subject domain in industrial training is, almost always, the physical world, we use a task decomposition based on reasoning tasks about the present, past or future behaviour of the industrial system. A generic task classification [5], using five primitive tasks, has been adopted for this purpose; Figure 1 shows the five primitive tasks that a trainee may have to do to achieve a specific instructional objective. These are essentially behavioural sub tasks and are described below:

Interpretation: The process of generating the current state of the world from observation and/or physical measurements. This task is a necessary pre-cursor to the other tasks in the classification.

Identification: This involves determining the *past* values from the current (interpreted) values of the state of the system. It can be used to determine the causes of a given situation and also to identify rates of change of process conditions.

Prediction: This is the dual of identification in that *future* values of the system state are estimated or predicted from the current state.

Decision: This is the process of generating conclusions from the interpreted, identified or predicted state of the system.

Execution: Once decisions have been made the process of turning these into actions has to be performed. This may be a direct translation of decisions or may involve prioritising or ordering of actions. It is the dual of the interpretation task, i.e., converting state into actions rather that observations into state.

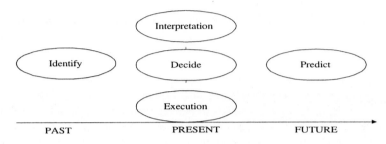

Fig.1 Generic Tasks

Although rather abstract, these primitive tasks have the advantage of being complete, with respect to time, abstraction and specialisation, and are therefore canonical, a useful property in any approach to decomposition.

Some tasks to do with 'understanding' will involve interpretation, identification and then decision. For example, interpret sensors, identify what caused these readings and then decide what to do. Similar groupings of tasks can be found for any instructional objective that is required in a training system. In fact, three major task *cliques* are envisioned:

- Interpret, Identify, Decide, (refers to the trainee's view of the past)
- Interpret, Decide, Execute (refers to the trainee's actions in the present)
- Interpret, Predict, Decide, (refers to the trainee's view of the future)

It should also be clear that each of these tasks can be recursively decomposed into a combination of the same primitive tasks. For example, an identification task, i.e. a task that has the goal of determining the past states, can itself be decomposed into a set of sub-tasks. This leads to a hierarchical decomposition of the training goals until a base level is achieved.

2.2   Specifying the Domain Expertise

Expertise in training is considered to be the ability to exhibit the correct behaviour in a given situation. This requires the definition of three aspects of domain expertise: the desired *behaviour*, the required knowledge, represented as *models*, and the ability or '*expertise*' to use these models to achieve the desired behaviour. This is shown diagramatically in figure 2.

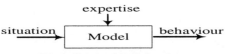

Fig. 2 Generating Behaviour

It is crucial to recognise that *the same behaviour can be generated by using different models, depending on the situation.* For example, in normal situations, models can be used that do not need much reasoning, requiring only that set procedures are executed. Conversely, in uncommon situations decisions may have to be made on very general models that require a significant amount of expertise and time to generate conclusions. This multiple representation of models, and hence expertise, is fundamental to, and the defining characteristic of, the Mobit approach. It is therefore essential to have a clear definition and understanding of the *types of models* and the *levels of expertise* to be used.

Types of Models

A major contribution of AI to engineering problem solving, including training, is the recognition of the multiplicity of approaches to modelling that can be used, depending upon the situation. These techniques range from strictly procedural representations to declarative equations, all of which can be interpreted in numerical, qualitative or symbolic formats. A review of these techniques is beyond the scope of this paper. However, the crucial aspect is that the model should reflect the 'natural' characteristics of the knowledge as closely as possible.

In reasoning about the physical world we can identify three distinct types of knowledge [6] that reflect a trade-off between generality and efficiency. It is believed that human knowledge is a continuous spectrum and is not held as distinct types in different knowledge representations. However, we are creating artificial experts in the domain expertise; what is important is that the properties of the knowledge is captured rather than the way in which it is held. It is argued, therefore, that three distinct artificial representations is better than one such representation. We present these in the order of increasing abstraction.

Procedures: Knowledge of this type is utilised in highly specific situations where the solution involves selecting a 'fixed' sequence of actions. No reasoning about the knowledge is done; the sequence of actions is performed autonomously. It is often used in start-up and shut-down procedures or in safety critical situations.

Associations: This knowledge is used to associate particular situations to possible solutions. It exists as a set of observation - conclusion pairs, with more than one pair being applicable in a given situation It is typical of knowledge gained from direct experience and is often represented as a set of rules.

Principles: These represent the fundamental physical laws underlying the operation of a device or physical system. The knowledge is normally represented in equation form (numeric or qualitative). This type of knowledge is used in classical (numerical) modelling, traditional simulators and qualitative models.

Levels of Expertise

It has been recognised that the same behaviour can be generated by using different knowledge. This is important when consideration is given to what knowledge should be communicated to the trainee. There is little point teaching an operator, whose job is to solder the pins of a CPU chip to its motherboard, the architecture of the chip. An engineer may carry out the same task; the reason for doing so, however, may be based on knowledge regarding the chip's internal structure. The two individuals require different knowledge yet exhibit the same behaviour. What is important is that both the knowledge used and the process to produce the behaviour (expertise) are different in the two cases. Based on work by Rasmussen [9], we identify 3 levels of expertise.

Skill based expertise: The characteristic of this level of expertise is that actions are performed without conscious reasoning i.e. the operator is using 'stored' procedures to complete the task.
Rule based expertise: This level of expertise can be recognised where the operator is associating particular situations to possible solutions and coming to a conclusion i.e. the operator selects appropriate associations for the situation and activates them to produce the desired behaviour.

Model based expertise: This level of expertise is utilised when unfamiliar circumstances arise and no rules or procedures exist which could be used to generate the desired behaviour. The operator must use knowledge pertaining to the fundamental physical laws underlying the device or system to find a solution.

For any training task it is important to identify the level of expertise at which particular classes of operators will be expected to perform, and hence the most effective model in achieving the training objective.

3   Domain Independent Training

During a training session it is vitally important that all interaction with the trainee is done in a fashion which will facilitate the trainee in acquiring the knowledge necessary to exhibit the desired behaviour. We approach this problem by deciding what is communicated to the trainee based on the individual's preferred *learning style*. The style of presentation and how much interaction the trainee has with the system is based upon which *training strategy* is employed during a training session.

The main points here are that the learning styles are based upon levels of knowledge that can represent the domain, not the actual knowledge therein and are therefore domain independent. Similarly, the strategies employed are done so on the basis of the trainee's background and preferences, and are therefore also independent of the domain.

3.1 Learning Styles

Knowledge communicated to the trainee need not be at the same level as the knowledge required for the trainee to perform at the pre designated level of expertise. The type of knowledge used during instruction may be at the same level, at the level above, or at the level below the knowledge required for the expected level of expertise. This leads to three distinct learning styles [7]. Selection of the 'correct' model for the level of expertise expected is shown in figure 3.

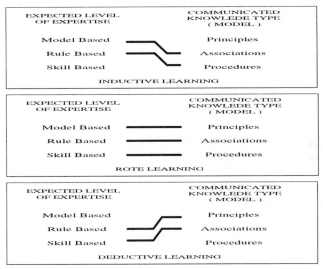

Fig. 3 Learning Styles

If knowledge is taught at the level 'above' that required, then the trainee must *deduce* the relevant knowledge through a process of deduction. For example, a trainee may be expected to operate at the rule base level of expertise and yet may be taught the relevant principles. This requires the trainee to reason deductively in order to generate the appropriate rules to perform the task.

If knowledge is taught at the level 'below' the required level of expertise then the trainee is encouraged to *induce* more general relationships from examples in order to attain the desired level of expertise. For example, a set of rules may be inductively generalised from examples of procedural knowledge.

Finally the level of knowledge required for a given level of expertise may be taught at the same level: procedures for skill based expertise, associations for rule based expertise and principles for model based expertise. This third mode of instruction is based on *rote* learning. In summary we propose three modes of instruction:

- Indirectly, by *deductive learning* The presentation of knowledge at the level above that at which the trainee is expected to perform.
- Indirectly, by *inductive learning*: through a series of examples given at the level below that at which the trainee is expected to perform.

- Directly, by *rote learning* through memorisation and recall of the given knowledge.

The actual learning style adopted at run time is dependent upon the style which has proven to be most effective in past training sessions.

3.2   Domain Independent Instruction

The Mobit system allows different domain independent instructional interactions to be used during training. These interactions range from presenting the trainee with text through to interactive simulations where the trainee has to apply newly acquired expertise to control complex plant. *Training Units* are the mechanisms employed by the system to interact with the trainee while the style and amount of interaction the system has with the trainee is controlled via *domain independent training strategies.*

Training Units

All dialogue with the trainee is controlled through training units (TU) which provide atomic 'chunks' of training interaction. Training Units group services provided by the domain modules of the Mobit system together and deliver the training via the trainee interface. A variety of types of TU have been identified and organised in a class hierarchy. The subset of 'test' is shown in Figure 4.

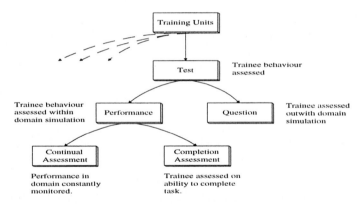

Fig. 4 Subset of Training Unit Class Hierarchy

The main types of training units correspond to basic tutoring interactions as follows:

Present: This is the presentation of the actual subject matter. What is presented depends upon what knowledge (model) is required to satisfy the training goal based upon the trainee's preferred learning style.

Demonstrate: This is used whenever the tutor wishes to demonstrate correct or incorrect behaviour to the trainee. The trainee observes the domain expert's behaviour within a simulation of an industrial process.

Practice: Utilising this allows the trainee a free play environment where they can practise their expertise in a problem solving role within the domain simulation.

Test: Methods must be incorporated which allow the tutor to form beliefs regarding the trainee's knowledge state. In general, assessment involves monitoring the behaviour of the trainee within the domain simulation. If satisfactory performance has been achieved, then the next instructional goal is fetched. If remediation is required, then a new goal is generated.

Domain Independent Training Strategies

In general the training philosophy adopted is one of "learning by doing" i.e. after training of some concept the trainee would be expected to demonstrate the correct behaviour on a simulation of the working environment.   The training delivered conforming to the current strategy employed. Major[8] has shown that there is no definitive agreement on the role of a strategy within tutoring systems. Within the Mobit system the strategies control the style and amount of interaction the trainee has with the system and in a similar fashion to GDT [2] are broadly based on a philosophy of decreasing intervention.. The strategy employed by the system is however dependent upon both the trainee's background and experience and that which has proven most successful in previous training sessions.

Domain independent training strategies are realised by selecting an appropriate training plan to satisfy a particular training goal. Training goals form a dependency hierarchy which is used in guiding the tutor to select the next goal to satisfy. This hierarchy is traversed until the lowest level sub-goal is reached. Training plans are then used in actually delivering the subject matter which is capable of satisfying the current goal. This process is repeated until all sub-goals have been satisfied. The training plan selected delivers instruction by conditionally controlling the order of the training units activated. This allows a spectrum of system to trainee interaction for each item of expertise to be learned irrespective of the training domain.

If the current strategy is proving ineffective then a new one is selected which may simply involve changing the style of interaction i.e. using a different training unit. Numerous strategies can thus be employed in order to satisfy the training goal. This allows for adaptive training and ensures non restrictive delivery of the required knowledge. The training strategies which have proven most successful in aiding the trainee's learning are then recorded for future reference.

4   Conclusion

Within the Mobit project we have developed a generic architecture and generic methods which can be utilised in building practical industrial intelligent training systems. This paper described two approaches adopted with the Mobit programme. The first being a generic approach to acquiring domain specific knowledge. The second being our approach to training based on domain independent learning styles and training strategies.

A Mobit prototype system has been developed for a process control application. In addition, two industrial demonstrator systems are being developed in two contrasting domains. The first domain is that of training operators in nuclear power plant operation, whilst the second is training electronic component assembly workers. A full evaluation of these systems is planned, where it is hoped that the approaches described will be validated.

Acknowledgement
- The work described in this paper has been undertaken in the Mobit project, part of the EPSRC/DTI Intelligent Systems Integration Programme (ISIP), by the following partners: Scottish Nuclear Limited, Digital Equipment (Scotland), Scomagg and Heriot-Watt University. The authors wish to acknowledge the contribution of all the members of the project team whilst taking full responsibility for the views expressed herein.

References

1. Anderson J. "The Expert Module", *Foundations of Intelligent Tutoring Systems*, Polson M & Richardson J. (Eds.). Hillsdale NJ: Lawrence Erlbaum Associates, 1988

2. Elsom-Cook, M.T., "Guided Discovery Tutoring: A Framework for ITS research", Paul Chapman Publishing, 1990

3. Dillenbourg P. "The role of artificial intelligence techniques in training software", paper presented at LEARNTEC 1994, Karlsruhe, November 1994.

4. ITSIE: Final Report, Deliverable D7 of Esprit project 2615 ITSIE 1992

5. Leitch, R.R, Gallanti, M. "Task Classification for Knowledge Based Systems In Industrial Automation", *IEEE Transactions on Systems, Man and Cybernetics*, 22, 1, pp142-152.

6. Leitch, R. R, Ponnapalli P V S, Slater A "The Representation of Domain Knowledge in Intelligent Training Systems", *Proceedings of the 1st. Int. Conf. on Intelligent Systems Engineering*, 269-274 (1992)

7. Leitch R.R. and Sime J-A. "A Specification Methodology for Intelligent Training Systems", *Computers in Education Journal*, Vol. 20, No1, pp 73-80,1993

8. Major N. "Modelling Teaching Strategies" in *Journal of Artificial Intelligence in Education*, Vol. 6 No 2/3 1995 pp117-152

9. Rasmussen J. "Information Processing and Human-Machine Interaction" North-Holland, Amsterdam. 1986

10. Tait K. "The description of Subject Matter and Instructional Methods for Computer-Based Learning", *Instructional Models in Computer-Based Learning Environments*. Dijkstra S, Krammer H, Merrienboer J. (Eds.) Springer-Verlag 1992

11. Woolf B. "Teaching a Complex Industrial Process", *AI and Education: Learning Environments and Intelligent Tutoring Systems*. Lawlwer R, & Yazdani M. (Eds.) Ablex Publishing, Norwood, NJ 1987

12. Wenger E. "Artificial Intelligence and Tutoring Systems", Morgan Kaufmann, 1987

The Transfusion Medicine Tutor: Using Expert Systems Technology to Teach Domain-Specific Problem-Solving Skills[*]

Jodi Heintz Obradovich, Philip J. Smith,
Stephanie Guerlain, Sally Rudmann, Patricia Strohm, Jack Smith,
Larry Sachs, Rebecca Denning

Cognitive Systems Engineering Laboratory
The Ohio State University
210 Baker Systems, 1971 Neil Ave.
Columbus, Ohio
jobradov@magnus.acs.ohio-state.edu (614) 292-1296
psmith@magnus.acs.ohio-state.edu (614) 292-4120

ABSTRACT. This study provides data regarding the effectiveness of the expert system-based Transfusion Medicine Tutor (TMT) when used by medical technology students to learn an important problem-solving task, the identification of alloantibodies in a patient's blood for the purpose of finding compatible blood for transfusion. The results show that the students who were taught by an instructor using TMT to provide the instructional environment went from 0% correct on a pre-test case to 87%-93% correct on post-tests (N=15). This compares with an improvement rate of 20% by a control group (N=15) who used a passive version of the system with the tutoring functions turned off. The results also demonstrate the importance of relying on objective performance data rather than questionnaire data to evaluate systems, as there was no difference in the subjective responses of the students to these two different versions of the system.

1 Introduction

We have conducted a series of empirical studies aimed at understanding how to engineer computer systems to successfully aid students in learning strategies to solve complex problems (Smith, Smith, & Svirbely et al., 1991a; Smith, Miller, Fraser et al., 1991b). The study presented here provides data regarding the learning effectiveness of the expert-system-based Transfusion Medicine Tutor (TMT) when used by medical technology students learning an important problem-solving task, the identification of alloantibodies in a patient's blood for the purpose of finding compatible blood for transfusion. Below, the problem-solving context is described and important design features are explicitly identified. Then, the results of a rigorous empirical evaluation are discussed.

2 The Transfusion Medicine Tutor

2.1 Context
Antibody identification is a laboratory workup task where medical technologists must run a series of tests and analyze a large amount of data to detect antibodies in a patient's blood (to avoid potentially fatal reactions when transfusing blood). This task has the classical characteristics of an abductive reasoning task, i.e., reasoning to the best

---

[*] This research is supported by a grant from the National Heart, Lung, and Blood Institute.

explanation of the data.   Some of the important general characteristics include the following:

- Multiple primitive solutions can be true at the same time (i.e., the patient could have several such antibodies).
- One or more antibodies can mask, or cover up, the presence of another antibody.
- The data is noisy (i.e., the quality of the data is questionable).
- The data is costly, so it is important to carefully select which tests should be run.
- There is sometimes time stress when completing the task.
- The solution space is very large. (There are more than 400 different alloantibodies that have been identified.)
- Practitioners get very little feedback on the accuracy of their answers. This lack of feedback may lead the blood banker to assume she or he is performing adequately when in reality she or he may not be.

2.2 Background Studies

Several empirical studies were conducted to understand the strategies used by both expert immunohematologists and students in the task of antibody identification. The results of these studies identified common errors and misconceptions of students while performing antibody identification tasks (Smith, Miller, et al., 1991a; Smith, Miller, et al., 1991b).   These results also gave insight into the types of knowledge and problem-solving strategies used to support expert performance.   One-on-one human tutoring in the task of antibody identification was also studied.

2.3 Design Concepts and Principles

The design of the system evaluated in this study was based on several underlying design concepts and principles.

Principle 1   If the goal is to offer students an opportunity to actively apply relevant knowledge and develop important problem-solving skills, provide a problem-solving environment that allows them to integrate this declarative knowledge into the procedural knowledge that they need to develop.

The application of this principle, which is supported by previous research on learning procedural knowledge and on the design of problem-based learning environments, was realized by developing an on-line equivalent of the actual laboratory task.   In this problem-solving environment where the computer plays a central role in tutoring, students solve actual patient cases, requesting test results and interpreting these results in order to arrive at an answer. (cf. Albanese and Mitchell, 1993; Anderson, 1983; Gordon, 1994; Lajoie and Lesgold, 1989).

Principle 2   Use expert systems technology to efficiently provide students with immediate, context-sensitive feedback or critiques as they perform the problem-solving tasks.

TMT has embedded in its architecture an expert system that monitors the student's performance (Burton, 1982; Fox, 1993) for evidence of errors of commission (erroneous inference), errors of omission (lacking an expected inference), errors due to incomplete protocols (insufficient converging evidence), and errors due to lack of consistency with the available data.

Principle 3   Design a user interface that allows the expert system to unobtrusively collect data on the student's reasoning during the problem-solving tasks, thus allowing the computer to give immediate, context-sensitive feedback.

The very tools that allow the students to do antibody identification tasks are the same tools that let the computer monitor what the student is doing. The TMT interface design has the on-line equivalents of tasks that are already part of the normal activities of the antibody identification task, allowing the student to proceed with the task without adding extra steps or workload.

Principle 4   Design the system to support rather than replace the teacher.

The TMT interface design potentially improves the instructor's ability to diagnose students' problems and misconceptions by making more explicit to the teacher the student's thought processes (Bailey, 1993; Dempsey and Sales, 1993). The teacher is able to look at the screen and understand where in the task the student is encountering difficulty. The teacher is also able to pull up a summary of the student's work on each case, allowing for a more complete diagnosis of the student's process and progress.

Principle 5   If appropriate, decompose a complex task into subtasks, and teach the subtasks first.

Originally, TMT consisted only of complete patient cases for the student to solve. Initial formative evaluations produced disappointing results. Many of the students seemed overwhelmed by the amount of material that TMT was attempting to teach (even though the students had already covered this material in their normal coursework). Due to these results, five initial lessons were designed that are intended to teach the students a number of the critical subtasks before asking them to solve a complete case (Gagne, 1985).

Principle 6   Use a mixture of proactive and reactive teaching methods to teach and reinforce the student's knowledge.

Based on initial formative evaluations, we also concluded that a computer system that is only reactive to a students errors may not be the most efficient or effective method of teaching (at least with the extensive number of difficulties these students were encountering). To remedy this situation, we designed a checklist that made explicit the high-level goals embedded in TMT's expert model and that summarized some of the key knowledge necessary to achieve these goals. The checklist serves several purposes:
- As an external memory aid it acts as a reminder of certain types of knowledge necessary for antibody identification.
- As a representation of the kinds of knowledge the expert system is expecting the user to apply in solving a case.

3   An Empirical Evaluation

The study reported in this paper explored the question: What is the impact on learning of an environment in which a human teacher uses the computer as a tool to provide a problem-based learning environment and to assist with teaching by providing context-sensitive feedback?

3.1 Procedure

Participants.
Thirty students in the Medical Technology Program at a major U. S. university were tested on TMT. These students were college juniors and had completed the didactic portion of their immunohematology coursework and an associated student lab, but had not yet begun their clinical rotation. Participation in the study was voluntary, but the students were paid for their participation. The study was conducted at another university where the staff had not been involved in the development of the system.

Experimental Design.
Participants were randomly assigned to one of two groups: Half were assigned to be in the Control Group and half to the Treatment Group. All of the participants were tested on the same cases in the same order with the exception of the pre-test case and first post-test case, which were randomized with respect to their order of use for each student. These first two matched cases were garden-path cases where a single antibody looked like a plausible answer when, in fact, two other antibodies were actually generating the patterns of reactions. All participants went through the same lessons in the same order, with the same practice cases and quizzes for each lesson.

The first case (Training Case 1) was used to give both groups the same initial training on the use of the system's interface. This training was identical for both groups (the intelligence was turned off for the Treatment Group).

The second case was used as a "pre-test," allowing the experimenter to get a benchmark on the student's current performance in solving an antibody identification case and to identify the problem-solving strategies they used prior to tutoring. This pre-test case was performed by both groups with the system's critiquing functions turned off, and was matched with the first post-test case.

Following the pretest case, the students completed five lessons; each of the first four lessons consisted of subtasks involved in solving a complete case. The fifth lesson consisted of solving complete patient cases, and included the use of all the subtasks covered in the first four lessons, along with more global strategies for gathering converging evidence to test a hypothesis.

Experimental Treatment.
Control Group. Following the pre-test, the students in the Control Group were shown an example of the summary they would see at the end of each case. This summary pointed out any differences between their answer and the correct answer. It also described how an expert would have solved the subtasks or cases. Thus, the Control Group had access to a passive tutor that only provided tutorial messages at the end of a subtask or case. After being shown this example summary, the Control Group began the lessons without any further instructions.

In other words, this group received no immediate feedback from TMT during the course of solving the subtasks or cases in each lesson. Only by comparing their final answers with the system's, and by utilizing and processing the information in the summary at the end of a case, could they learn what errors they had made and then use that information to avoid making the same errors in solving future cases.

Treatment Group. Following the pre-test, the students in the Treatment Group were introduced to the intelligent tutoring provided by the system. During the first case in Lesson 1, they were instructed to purposely make an error. By doing this, they were able to experience the kind of intelligent feedback the computer would provide following an error. They were told to read the error message and to note that included in the message was the reason their answer was incorrect. Like the Control Group, these students were also shown the information contained in the summary available of the end of each case.

Checklist. In addition to the immediate, context-sensitive tutoring provided by the computer, these students were given a paper checklist that made explicit the high-level goal structure that guided the expert system's error detection and tutoring. This checklist consisted of the step-by-step procedure the students should follow to successfully solve the full cases contained in the tutorial. It was explained that different steps in the checklist corresponded to different lessons and that Lesson 5 included using all the steps that were appropriate for solving each antibody identification case.

Instructor Assistance. The students in the Treatment Group had access to an instructor for any questions or difficulties that they encountered while working on the lessons.

Treatment Differences. As described above, the Control Group represented a very passive system, but one that nevertheless provided students with access to a full description of expert performance on each case. The Treatment Group differed in three ways from the Control Group (context-sensitive, immediate tutoring by the computer, access to the checklist, and access to a teacher). Thus, the Treatment Group represented an attempt to provide a "best-case" environment for teaching students, using the tutoring system to provide a learning environment and to provide active tutoring in order to assist the instructor's activities.

Post-test Cases. Following Lesson 5 (Complete Cases), two "post-test" cases were given to all students. The first was the case that matched the pre-test case. The second case (in which one antibody masked a second that was also present) was the same for all subjects. For the two post-test cases, the intelligence was turned off and no end-of-case summaries were provided. The students in the Treatment Group were, however, allowed to use the checklist for each post-test case.

Questionnaire.
Following use of the system, a questionnaire was administered to each student to gather demographic data, to assess the students' subjective reactions to TMT and its various functions, and to elicit suggestions for improvement in its design and use.

3.2 Data Collection

The computer system logged all of the student's actions, including final answers. In addition, each student was videotaped during the entire session. (Both groups were videotaped even though the instructor was present only for the Treatment Group.)

3.3   Results

The results showed that there was no significant difference in the misdiagnosis rates on the pre-test case for the Control and Treatment Groups (p=0.50; see Table 1). However, using McNemar's chi square test, the students in the Treatment Group showed a significant (p<0.001) improvement in performance (a reduction from 100% to 20% misdiagnosis error rate) from the pre-test case to the matched post-test case. Students in the control group showed a 20% reduction in errors that was not statistically significant from the Pre-Test to Post-Test Case 1.

The between-subject analysis using Fisher's Exact Test showed significant difference in performance on the post-test cases between the two groups (see Table 1). On Post-Test Case 1, subjects in the Treatment Group had a misdiagnosis rate of 13% while subjects in the Control Group had a misdiagnosis rate of 73% (p=0.0046). On Post-Test Case 2, students in the Treatment Group had a 7% misdiagnosis rate, while students in the Control Group had a 73% misdiagnosis rate (p=0.0002). Each of these differences is significant .

Table 1. Misdiagnosis rates for students in the Treatment Group (n=15) vs. the Control Group (n=15).

	Pre-Test	Post-Test Case 1	Post-Test Case 2
Treatment	100% wrong	20% wrong	7% wrong
Control	93% wrong	73% wrong	73% wrong

Thus, something about the Treatment Group (the use of intelligent tutoring, the checklist and/or instructor assistance) produced a sizable and statistically significant improvement in performance.

Classes of Errors.
In order to better understand the impact of the Treatment condition on learning, we used the computer logs to identify error frequencies for five classes of errors (see Table 2). On the pre-test, there were no significant differences between the Control and Treatment Groups (p≥0.17). On the matched first post-test case, Errors 2, 3a, 3b, and 4b each showed significant differences (p<0.05) between the Treatment and Control Groups, with the Treatment Group making fewer errors (see Table 2).

Thus, tutoring appeared to be effective for errors that the computer could detect during the process of solving a case, as well as for errors that were detected after the student marked a final answer for a case.

Remediation.
A second question studied concerned the triggering of the tutoring episodes that occurred (see Table 3).

Table 2. Classes of errors made by the Treatment and Control Group participants on the Pre-Test and Post-Test Case 1.

| | Subjects committing error at least once on: | | | |
| | Pre-Test Case | | Post-Test Case 1 | |
Error	Treatment	Control	Treatment	Control
1. Ruling out correct answer due to ruling out incorrectly.	7	5	2	4
2. Failure to rule out when appropriate.	13	13	5	11
3. Failure to collect converging evidence.				
a. Failure to do antigen typing.	9	8	1	8
b. Failure to satisfy the 3+/3- rule.	7	6	1	6
4. Failure to check for consistency of data with answer.				
a. Failure to ensure there are no unexplained negative reactions.	1	3	1	2
b. Failure to ensure there are no unexplained positive reactions.	14	11	2	8

Table 3. Remediation following computer-detected error (number of interactions and % of total for each student in the Treatment Group)

Student	Computer detected error; no student/ teacher interaction	Instructor taught following computer-detected error	Student initiated tutoring following a computer-detected error	Total number computer-detected errors
T-A	39 (87%)	5 (11%)	1 (2%)	45
T-B	57 (93%)	3 (5%)	1 (2%)	61
T-C	16 (89%)	1 (5.5%)	1 (5.5%)	18
T-D	63 (89%)	4 (5.5%)	4 (5.5%)	71
T-E	10 (100%)	0 (0%)	0 (0%)	10
T-F	117 (96.7%)	3 (2.5%)	1 (.8%)	121
T-G	39 (100%)	0 (0%)	0 (0%)	39
T-H	14 (78%)	2 (11%)	2 (11%)	18
T-I	21 (95.5%)	1 (4.5%)	0 (0%)	22
T-J	9 (82%)	0 (0%)	2 (18%)	11
T-K	*	*	*	*
T-L	31 (94%)	0 (0%)	2 (6%)	33
T-M	33 (94%)	1 (3%)	1 (3%)	35
T-N	16 (89%)	1 (5.5%)	1 (5.5%)	18
T-O	*	*	*	*
Totals	465 (92.6%)	21 (4.2%)	16 (3.2%)	502

Note that:

1. A large proportion of the remediation episodes were handled by the computer alone when the computer detected an error.
2. Detection of an error by the computer also triggered a significant number of teaching episodes by the instructor. Such episodes were initiated by either the teacher or the student.
3. The teacher and students initiated a significant number of teaching episodes without relying on the computer to detect an error.

Video Analysis.

Each student was videotaped while working with TMT. The analysis of the tapes produced some interesting observations regarding the interactions between the instructor and the students in the Treatment Group. For example, of the 66 teaching interactions between students and the instructor, the video indicates that on 8 (12%) of these interactions, the teacher misdiagnosed the student's problem. Also, the instructor utilized several different strategies in the course of the teaching episodes, and students learned to recognize where they needed help and asked for assistance before they made an error.

TMT Questionnaire.

Finally, the questionnaire results (shown below) provided valuable, supportive data about student perceptions regarding the system's usefulness and usability.

Table 5. Questionnaire Results

Statements about Computer Tutorial	Version	S D	D	N	A	S A
1. The program was easy to use.	Control	-	-	-	4	11
	Treatment	-	-	1	5	9
2. I learned a great deal from the program.	Control	-	-	2	4	9
	Treatment	-	-	1	8	6
3. The program would be useful as a study tool.	Control	-	-	-	2	13
	Treatment	-	-	-	5	10
4. The lessons contributed to my understanding of the topic.	Control	-	-	-	4	11
	Treatment	-	-	1	5	9
5. I would recommend this program to other students.	Control	-	-	-	3	12
	Treatment	-	-	-	3	12
Statements about Checklist*						
8. The checklist was easy to use.	Treatment	-	1	-	8	6
9. The checklist was well organized.	Treatment	-	-	-	7	8
10. The checklist was useful.	Treatment	-	1	-	8	6

*The students in the Control Group did not use the Checklist.

Key: Strongly Agree = SA; Agree = A; Neutral = N; Disagree = D; Strongly Disagree = SD

Of the students in both groups, 100% agreed or strongly agreed with Statements 3 and 5. Also 97% of the students agreed or strongly agreed with Statements 1, 4, and 6. It is important to note how insensitive such questionnaire results are to actual performance differences between the Control and Treatment Groups. Responses to open-ended questions were similarly positive, as summarized below.

"What did you like best about the tutorial?"
Treatment Group: "It made antibody screens much easier to do, by hand it's easy to lose your place." "Immediate feedback on wrong answers." "It was a good new, easy way of learning." "It was very informative and easy to use." "It was fun, it was a refresher; it reinforced my understanding of blood banking. It also boosted my confidence." "The explanations that told you why your answer was wrong." "Everything" "It made antibody screening easier to do. I actually had fun while working -- it was like a game."

Control Group: "It's very easy to learn about antibody id." "It explains what you did wrong when you make a mistake. Very easy to use." "Colors made the panel solving much simpler." "The ease of checking off on the panels, the ability to go back and forth between tests; no papers to shuffle around." "Challenges knowledge of antibody id."

"What did you like the least about the tutorial?"
Treatment Group: "Would be more convenient if the results from enzyme panels, etc. could be listed next to normal panel, would make it easier to compare and see patterns." "Nothing." "Nothing -- it was very beneficial." "None." "N/A" "The loud buzzing noises." "The beep! ha ha" "The noise it made when you do something wrong. It should give you a chance to correct your mistakes."

Control Group: "Nothing. but in one of the enzyme panels I didn't know that you can't rule out MNSs and Duffy." "Nothing." "I didn't retain enough information from class to put a better effort forward. I remembered the basics, but forgot why certain tests are done and how to evaluate these tests." "Since this program is a tutorial the whole purpose of it is to help teach students about blood. However, even though it is pretty much user friendly, it did not help or give reasoning as you were using the program. What I may suggest is to have a help screen pop up every time you rule out a wrong Ab. This should help in understanding why we made an error."

4 Conclusion
The results of this study provide strong evidence that an effective learning environment was developed. Furthermore, although the relative contributions of the computer vs. teacher vs. checklist cannot be determined from this study, analyses of the videotapes suggest that the computer played a frequent role in detecting errors and in helping to teach. Thus, this study provides a model for use of an expert system in teaching that has been rigorously evaluated. Future studies are planned to try to tease out the relative contributions of the different components of this attempt at a "best-case" environment (computer vs. the teacher vs. the checklist), and to analyze the data to determine what teaching strategies should be employed to make effective use of such a tool.

5 References

Albanese, M. and Mitchell, S. (1993) Problem-based learning: A review of literature on its outcomes and implementation issues. *Academic Medicine*, 68, 52-81.
Anderson, J.R. (1983) The Architecture of Cognition. Cambridge, MA: Harvard University Press.
Bailey, G.D. (Ed.) (1993) Computer-based integrated learning systems. Englewood Cliffs, NJ: Educational Technology Publications.

Burton, R.R. (1982) Diagnosing bugs in a simple procedural skill. In D. Sleeman and J.S. Brown (eds.), Intelligent Tutoring Systems, London: Academic Press, 157-184.

Dempsey, J.V. and Sales, G.C. (Eds.) (1993) Interactive Instruction and Feedback. Englewood Cliffs, NJ: Educational Technology Publications.

Fox, B. (1993) The Human Tutorial Dialogue Project: Issues in the Design of Instructional Systems. Hillsdale, NJ: Lawrence Earlbaum.

Gagne, R.M. (1985) The Conditions of Learning and Theory of Instruction (4th Edition). New York: Holt, Rinehart and Winston.

Gordon, S.E. (1994) Systematic Training Program Design: Maximizing Effectiveness and Minimizing Liability. Englewood Cliffs, NJ: Prentice Hall.

Lajoie, S.P. and Lesgold, A. (1989) Apprenticeship training in the workplace: Computer-coached practice environment as a new form of apprenticeship. *Machine-Mediated Learning*, 3, 7-28.

Smith, P.J., Galdes, D., Fraser, J., Miller, R., Smith, J.W., Svirbely, J.R., Blazina, J., Kennedy, M., Rudmann, S., & Thomas, D.L. (1991a.) Coping with the complexities of multiple-solution problems: A case study. *International Journal of Man-Machine Studies*, 35, 429-453.

Smith, P.J., Miller, T.E., Fraser, J., Smith, J.W., Svirbely, J.R., Rudmann, S., Strohm, P.L., & Kennedy, M. (1991b) An empirical evaluation of the performance of antibody identification tasks. *Transfusion*, 31, 313-317.

Evaluation of a Knowledge-Based Tutorial Program in Rheumatology – A Part of a Mandatory Course in Internal Medicine

Stefan Schewe[1], Thomas Quak[1], Bettina Reinhardt[2], Frank Puppe[2]

1) Medizinische Poliklinik der Universität München, Pettenkoferstr. 8A, D-80336 Munich, e-mail: schewe@pk-i.med.uni-muenchen.de

2) Lehrstuhl Informatik VI der Universität Würzburg, Allesgrundweg 12, D-97218 Gerbrunn, e-mail: reinhard/puppe@informatik.uni-wuerzburg.de

Abstract

A serious limitation of medical tutoring software in Germany is the lacking integration in the university education routine. In this study, we propose a scenario for such an integration and discuss the results of an evaluation. The scenario is to complement lectures with patient presentations by the use of a training system showing the same cases in a formalized form, so that the students can consolidate their newly acquired knowledge. Then, the students may test themselves by solving a symptomatically similar case with a potentially different diagnosis while being criticized by the training system. Technical prerequisites for this scenario are a knowledge based training system for solving the newly entered cases that were discussed in the lectures and a case-comparison component for finding symptomatically similar cases from a large case base. Both are provided by the diagnostic shell box D3.

1. Introduction

While medical training programs are broadly available they are currently not very well integrated in the education curricula of universities. For example, real patient presentations in lectures are quite popular but most case based training programs are unable to adapt themselves to these particular patient data. In the following, we present a scenario in which the same patient data is both presented in real life and in a computer training system. This scenario has been evaluated in two successive rheumatology courses at the University of Munich with very encouraging results.

Section 2 and 3 describe the technical and the organisational part of the evaluation environment. Section 4 and 5 present and discuss the results.

2. The tutoring shell

Tutoring systems for medical education have become quite popular (see e.g. [Eysenbach 94]). While many of them are based on the hypertext / hypermedia technique consisting of links between predefined windows, the idea of intelligent tutor systems (e.g. [Wenger 87]) is to generate the presentation of the tought subject of the underlying domain as well as didactic knowledge. Case oriented tutoring systems, for example, can be designed in both ways: The patient case can be presented with a hypermedia system in which the sequence and the contents of the windows are prepared for one particular case. Another approach is the construction of a knowledge base capable of solving cases and using real cases for tutorial purposes. While the costs of building hypermedia based training systems are directly proportional to the number of cases included, knowledge based training systems require a large initial effort to build and test the knowledge base. However, afterwards only minimal financial means for the addition of any number of new cases are needed. The first system exploring this approach was GUIDON [Clancey 87], a tutoring system based on the expert system MYCIN. Insights gained from this work are that a general problem solving method like the backward chaining of rules in MYCIN severely restricts the explainability of the program for tutorial purposes and that an unstructured rule format makes it difficult for the students to differentiate the key clause in the rule precondition from the context and activation clauses. Commercially available knowledge based training systems are the tutor versions of ILIAD [Lincoln et al. 92] and QMR [Miller & Masarie 89]. They avoid the problems of GUIDON/MYCIN by a much simpler knowledge representation.

The general architecture of knowledge based tutorial systems is quite obvious: In addition to the basic components of expert systems - including a knowledge base and a problem solver, a knowledge acquisition as well as an explanation and interviewer component - specific tutorial features are case presentation and components for criticism (see e.g. [Fontaine et al. 94]).

A special feature of our shell D3 is the integration of different problem solving methods, in particular by resorting to heuristic and case-based knowledge [Puppe et al. 94]. Developing a new training system with the D3 requires the construction of a knowledge base and the addition of cases with the interviewer component. An attractive feature is that the author of the lectures may build or modify the knowledge base with a convenient graphical knowledge acquisition facility [Gappa et al. 93]. The knowledge base contains sufficient knowledge about the hierarchical or heterarchical structure of the findings to ensure an automatic generation of (textual) case presentations in several modes ranging from detailed presentations of findings to a concentration on the key diagnostic elements for a better control.

At the beginning of a new case the training system presents initial data about the patient. The user then selects tests to investigate his or her hypotheses. On demand the system provides comments on the users' actions and can also criticise his or her justifications. Criticism of hypotheses is generated by a comparison of hypotheses inferred by the system resorting to the same data the user has interpreted so far. Criticising the users´ justifications is rather difficult because the system bases its conclusions on intermediate (pathophysiological) concepts derived from the raw data. The user is unaware of these intermediate concepts which have to be compiled out to assess how many individual raw findings support the hypotheses. The criticism of the test choices is easily generated since the explicit representation of that knowledge is defined in the knowledge base. For each diagnosis a sequence of useful tests is specified. When the user selects a test the system compares it with its own choices (also considering second rate choices) based on the suspected diagnoses in the present stage of the tutorial session. The user can also justify a test selection referring to his or her suspected hypotheses, the correctness and efficiency of which can be assessed by the system. More details concerning the tutoring component of D3 can be found in [Reinhardt & Schewe 95] and [Puppe & Reinhardt 95].

3. The evaluation scenario

The learning environment

The area of rheumatology is partly covered by a mandatory curriculum for the students of Internal Medicine. The rheumatology class is divided into various groups including two or three persons and is held on a regular basis both on Tuesdays and Wednesdays with a duration of 90 minutes each day.

First, the students are given 30 minutes to find out the medical history of a new patient and to implement the most important medical examinations. After that, the professor thoroughly discusses the case with the student while the patient is still present: further questions relevant for the symptoms of the disease are asked and the essential results of the medical examination demonstrated. Moreover, student and professor consider the future diagnostic measures, delineate the options concerning the differential diagnosis and, presupposing the diagnosis, confer on a therapy.

Each individual group of students is assigned to the rheumatology section for two subsequent weeks. On Tuesdays the students are confronted with a rheumatological case and its discussion in the manner mentioned above whereas on Wednesdays they have to deal with a tutorial computer presentation of the Tuesday case for beginners (Beg.Comp). In addition to that, however, one of 1017 rheumatological cases contained in a data base with a similar medical history but a potentially different diagnosis is presented. The similar case has to be solved by the students. The following week, the same procedure is gone through with a new patient.

Beginning with the winter term in 1994/95 a change in the Wednesday version has been made. Instead of using the tutorial computer program each Wednesday, both the presentation of the Tuesday patient and the corresponding data base case were presented to the students in the form of a structurally identical text version providing exactly the same information as the computer program.

In the summer term of 1995 a newly developed advanced version of the computer program (Adv.Comp) has been tested in the second week of the class whereas in the first the former version for beginners has been applied.

The tutorial program

The program combines both the tutorial environment of the shell box D3 [Gappa et al 93] and the knowledge base of the expert system "RHEUMA" which has been evaluated on numerous patients [Schewe et al 93].

The computer version for beginners (Beg.Comp) provides the information en bloc in a very coherent manner. The questions and the patient's answers with respect to the medical history are followed by the clinical examination, the laboratory results and finally all technical and miscellaneous proceedings. Analogous to the physician's measures, the students are supposed to decide on a diagnosis at the end of each section. Thereby they can make recourse to the hierarchical order of the diseases and merely specify a global diagnosis such as inflammatory rheumatological disease, spondylarthropathy etc. or choose particular diagnoses defined within this diagnostic hierarchy (figure 1) with a global degree of probability (suspected or confirmed). The computer system now criticises the student's choice by comparing it to the solution of the knowledge-based system assuming an equal level of information. The student always has the opportunity to call explanations of terms and concepts as well as justifications of the knowledge-based rules. Also, the student can explain his or her own diagnosis to the computer.

Just like in the beginner version the advanced version (Adv.Comp) of the tutorial computer program supplies the preliminary information on the medical history systematically. Like the physician in his future practise the student can freely choose a wide range of possible laboratory, radiological and other examinations that are considered to be indispensable for the actual case. After that the student again specifies a diagnosis which is also assessed by the computer system. This process of selecting relevant results can be repeated several times until a diagnosis of a specific disease is possible.

The text version encompasses the information provided in the computer version for beginners and consists of a printout of both the known and the unknown similar case. The students also have to try to find a diagnosis after each individual bloc.

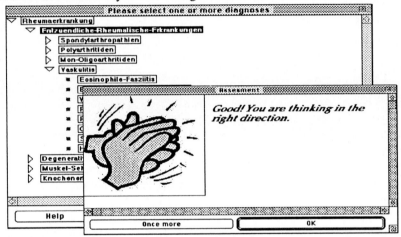

Figure 1: The student chooses one more diagnosis and gets a friendly feedback, because he selected at least one diagnosis in the right category. The use of the dynamic hierarchy is necessary to choose from over 70 diagnoses.

The patients

The patients who volunteer to answer the questions and undergo the students´ examinations are usually ambulatory. Most of them are new to the policlinic and have been referred by general practitioners and hospitals of the area.

The professors, the students

18 professors participate in the Internal Medicine curriculum, partly they are assistant physicians and partly specialists for Internal Medicine or senior physicians. One senior physician is responsible for the field of rheumatology.

All the students are in the eighth or nineth clinical term of medical school. The Internal Medicine curriculum is a mandatory prerequisite held at five Internal University clinics. The students can not choose a course of their choice.

The parameters for evaluation

The students´ opinions are obtained by a questionnaire on each individual day of class. The students assess the quality of the course in Internal Medicine by grading it according to a scale from 1 (does not apply) to 10 (applies) considering their motivation, the organisation of the course, the efficiency, the professor´s achievement as well as their general impression. The questionnaire is anonymous for the students, the professor can freely decide on whether he wants to appear on it namely and be notified of the results towards the end of the term.

In the class on rheumatology the students complete a multiple choice test concerning the disease of the patient presented each week before and after the two days in the course, as well as a 50 item questionnaire after working with the whole computer system or text version in class. The achievement exam concluding the term is also based on multiple choice. Containing questions on Internal Medicine one additional internal and one rheumatological case are described together with brief information on the medical history. The clinical, laboratory and technical examinations necessary to diagnose the disease have to be stated by the students.

Statistics

The statistical analysis used the Student's t-test to compare normal distributed, independent means, the 95% confidence intervals were determined using the same method. The differences of dependent values were tested with Students' t-test or Wilcoxon signed rank test for paired samples depending on the distribution of the data. All statistical tests were two tailed, and a P value of 0.05 or less was taken to indicate statistical significance.

4. Results

In the winter term of 1994/95 there were 22 and in the summer term of 1995 19 students attending the rheuma class. In the curriculum on Internal Medicine (it was only evaluated in the summer term of 1995) 28 students participated, for them 562 student hours were held by 11 professors. 405 hours were evaluated by the students (a response rate of 72.1%), in 22.5% of which suggestions for improvement were made by the students and in 37.5% of which the professors signed.

The opinion of the students in general was very positive (mean value ± 95% confidence interval):

»Today´s class was motivating to me!« (motivation):   8.064 ± 0.165 points,
»It seems like I have learnt a lot!« (efficiency):   8.074 ± 0.170 points,
»The prof. made a considerable effort for my education!« (prof) 8.402 ± 0.163 points,
»The course was well organised!« (organisation):   8.259 ± 0.189 points,

No significant differences in the assessment between the professor of rheumatology and other professors as opposed to considerable differences between individual professors in several categories could be observed. Professors who did not choose to stay anonymous received remarkably better grades than professors who did.

Considering the questionnaires of 41 students (22 students in the winter term of 1994/95 and 19 in the summer term of 1995), the following results with respect to the students´ motivation (excerpt of the results of the 50 item questionnaire, mean value ± standard deviation, minimum, maximum) could be evaluated.

Question: »Do you think the employment of tutorial computer systems in your studies makes sense«:   7.95 ± 1.72; min 2, max 10

Question: »Are you having fun with the computer program ?«:
    7.03 ± 2.06; min 2, max 10

Question: »Do you think that you can effectively study with the program?«:
    6.93 ± 2.30; min 2, max 10

The program was assessed by the students as follows:
Statement: »The program is able to:«
»replace a professor «   1.82 ± 1.61; min 1, max 8,
»support a professor «   6.87 ± 2.24; min 1, max 10,

»improve my diagnostic skills«	6.82 ± 2.15; min 1, max 10,
»support me with specific diagnostic problems«	6.93 ± 2.70; min 1, max 10,
»support independent study«	7.61 ± 2.40; min 2, max 10,
»give practical aids«	4.62 ± 2.71; min 1, max 9.

The students clearly favor an independent study:

Question: »Where would you most frequently use a computerprogram (asume that it is accessible)?«

»computer at the university, independently«	5.63 ± 2.73; min 1, max 10
»computer at home, independently«	7.50 ± 2.67; min 1, max 10
»computer with other students«	3.74 ± 2.70; min 1, max 10
»replacement for practical courses«	1.44 ± 1.18; min 1, max 7
»supplement for practical courses«	7.05 ± 2.78; min 1, max 10

Concerning the satisfaction of the students, both strengths and weaknesses of the program become obvious:

Question: »How satisfied are you with the program concerning:«

| »the plausibility of the text« | 7.43 ± 1.61; min 4, max 10 |
| »the graphic lay-out« | 5.67 ± 2.31; min 2, max 10 |

The following results were obtained concerning the students´ assessment of how their knowledge improved (see figure 2): The students considered their knowledge of rheumatology to be at a level of 3.86 ± 1.83 points on a scale of 1 (no knowledge of rheumatology at all) to 10 (good knowledge of rheumatology) when the winter term started. At the beginning of the summer term the values did not show a significant difference (3.11 ± 1.15). After the two day class, however, the students´ self-assessment ranked at 6.09 ± 1.04 in the winter term and at 5.16 ± 1.26 in the summer term which again doesn´t manifest a significant difference between the two terms but proves a highly significant improvement in how the students estimated their knowledge for both terms. After the tenth day the students considered their rheumatological knowledge to have decreased to the pretest level (3.05 ± 1.36 in summer, 4.41 ± 1.30 in winter, ns). The regular course together with the text version of the system showed an increase in the students´ assessment of their knowledge from 4.41 ± 1.30 to 6.14 ± 1.25 points whereas in the summer term a significantly greater increase from 3.05 ± 1.36 to 6.09 ± 1.04 could be achieved by the regular course and the advanced version (Adv.Comp) together. All the teaching efforts - according to the students - displayed a temporary highly significant increase in the students´ estimated knowledge. After one week, however, it reached the basic pretest values again (fig. 2).

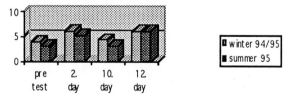

Figure 2: Students´ assessment of their own rheumatological knowledge on an analogous scale of 1 (no knowledge of rheumatology) to 10 (good knowledge of rheumatology), representation of mean values.

Parallel to these results significant increases of the student's knowledge objectively measured in MC tests could be observed. Again the student's knowledge decreased within one week to the pretest level.

The clinical case presented to the students within the written knowledge test after the two day class implied a short delineation of a patient´s medical history similar to the one actually discussed in class. The students had to specify in a free way which additional questions on the medical history they would ask as a physician and which clinical and technical examinations as well as laboratory tests they would require. The answers given by the students were summed up and criticized. Again considerable increases of correct answers could be observed after each 2 day course. In this test, however, the decreases of correct answers after one week were only slight and differed significantly form the pretest values. The summer results showed slower increases of knowledge compared to the winter results. The reason could be a lack of motivation the students´ might have experienced due to the external circumstances. Most summer students did not list the possible examinations completely, so that all specifications - with the exception of the ones concerning the technical examinations - increased significantly during the winter term whereas in the summer term only the enumerated questions on the patient´s medical history improved.

The free exam at the end of the term showed no differences in the number of correct answers between a comparatively easy general internal case (angina pectoris in the winter, pneumonia in the summer term) and a more difficult rheumatological case (sarcoidosis in the winter, spondylitis ancylosans in the summer term). Better results could be obtained in questions concerning clinical problems (medical history, clinical examination) compared to worse results concerning technical exams. Thus, the goal of the course was definitely achieved.

5. Discussion

Similar to the evaluation results of other tutor systems ([Preiss et al 92]), students in an advanced stage of their medical formation hold an overall very positive view on the »RHEUMA« tutor system. They are motivated to work with it and clearly render advantages and areas in which its application makes sense. Thereby it becomes obvious that the use of a computer system for independent study is most frequently welcomed by the students whereas they generally reject all efforts to integrate this tutoring device in universities and clinics without making it part of the regular program. A tutor system can neither substitute a professor nor specific classes, it rather serves as a motivating factor for students to use their books [Lilienfeld et al 94]. This assumption is substantiated by the fact that in the final exam a difficult rheumatological case discussed only with few students during the class is solved with the same results as an easy clinical case of Internal Medicine belonging to the daily routine of the physician. The tutoring system as a replacement for textbooks, however, has not been tested in our study. The equal assessment of the Rheumatology professor by the students was supposed to show that the positive evaluation was not only an expression of the professor´s achievement but a demonstration of how they regarded the complete scenario.

An interpretation of the results of the objective knowledge tests poses a greater challenge. The students´ self-assessment as well as the objective multiple choice test on the students´ rheumatological education clearly show that there exists a temporary increase in their knowledge which is relatively independent of the computer system used during the course (Adv.Comp or Beg.Comp) with slightly better mean results for the advanced version. Similar results were also obtained by [Preiss et al 92]. Even though the students´ knowledge again considerably decreases within a week it is reactivated by the repetition of the whole course with a new emphasis in the field of rheumatology. In the self-assessment of their knowledge by the students the advanced version of the computer system ranked highest even though the difference to the text version was insignificant. The increase in the students´ knowledge throughout a period of 12 days happens wave-like but nevertheless in a continuous manner. The final exam reveals the situation of a student: Being able to achieve the same results in the specialized subject of rheumatology (which at least in Germany is often considered not so important) as in a standard field of Internal Medicine frequently practiced and generally known to the students such as cardiology (angina pectoris) or infectious diseases (tuberculosis) must be very satisfying.

Of course the students also detected weaknesses of the program which shouldn´t be concealed. Points of criticism were the still missing multimedia-illustration as well as the explanations of the system and especially a lack of relevance for their future daily practical work. Either the students underestimate the meaning of rheumatology for their future work as a physician or they have the opinion that skills needed for the recognition and treatment of rheumatological diseases can´t be acquired by the computer system in a satisfactory manner. The second point is contradicted by the experience of the professor in the rheuma course. The fact that the tutoring system »RHEUMA« is a mere device for diagnostic support and doesn´t deal with individual therapies or therapeutic strategies might also play a role.

In contrast to a great variety of medical tutoring programs ([D´Alessandro et al 93], [Lilienfeld et al 94], [Preiss et al 92]), »RHEUMA« has obvious advantages, a fact that has to be mentioned. The system exclusively presents everyday clinical cases adapted for students and also physicians willing to improve their rheumatological knowledge. Right now the data base consists of 1017 cases of patients with joint complaints diagnosed by the computer system »RHEUMA«, a treasure chest of examples which can be individually chosen to illustrate specific rheumatological diseases. The system does not use artificial patients for educational purposes but real cases of everyday practise, a learning environment which plays an important role concerning the future use of the system (see also [Eliot & Woolf 95]). The use of the tutoring device is integrated within a mandatory curriculum so that it can not be regarded as a method substituting lectures or practical classes. The results also proved that the comparison of a real case with a case of the data base is especially welcomed by the students.

Beside the results of this study, the following aspects have to be taken into account in order to achieve a further development of the system: Considerable additions have to be made to the user interface by implementing new areas of explanations, multimedia use in graphics and sound as well as references to standard literature and textbooks. Another logical development in future versions of the program is the integration of a simulation system, that has the ability to criticize the diagnostic process and the therapy of a patient. This addition can be made in a manner similar to the cardiac tutor [Eliot & Woolf 95].

The program today provides a means of support to normal lectures. The factors of cost and efficiency in diagnostic measures will have to be considered more often in the future while not only the costs have to be calculated but also an optimal and rational diagnostic path will have to be followed (»coaching«, [Burton & Brown 82]). With a combination of textbook and personal computer the horizon of students as well as physicians in the field of rheumatology can be considerably widened, both groups of learners, however, have to be determined to acquire patterns for the solution of exemplary clinical cases at an individual learning pace as well as on an own initiative.

References

Burton A and Brown J: An Investigation of Computer Coaching for Informal Learning Activities. In Sleeman D., Brown J. (Eds) Intelligent Tutoring Systems, Academic Press, London, 1982.

Clancey W: Knowledge-Based Tutoring: The GUIDON-Program, MIT Press, 1987.

Cutts JH et al: a graphics assisted learning environment for computer-based interactive videodisc education. Int J Biomed Comput (England) 31, 141-5, 1992.

D'Alessandro MP et al: The instructional effectiveness of a radiology multimedia textbook (HyperLung) versus a standard lecture. Invest Radiol (U S) 28, 643-8, 1993.

Eliot C and Woolf BP: An Adaptive Student Centered Curriculum for an Intelligent Training System. User Modelling and User-Adapted Interaction 5, 67-86, 1995.

Eysenbach G: Computer-Manual, Urban&Schwarzenberg, 1994.

Fontaine D et al: An Intelligent Computer-Assisted Instruction System for Clinical Case Teaching, Meth. Inform. Med. 33, 433-445, 1994.

Gappa U, Puppe F, and Schewe S: Graphical Knowledge Acquisition for Medical Diagnostic Expert Systems, Artificial Intelligence in Medicine 5, 185-211, 1993.

Lilienfield LS, Broering NC: Computers as teachers: learning from animations. Am J Physiol (United States), 266, 47-54, 1994.

Lincoln MJ et al: Ilias's role in the generalization of learning across a medical domain. Proc Annu Symp Comput Appl Med Care (United States), 174-8, 1992.

Miller R and Masarie F: Use of the Quick Medical Reference (QMR) program as a tool for medical education, Meth. Inform. Med. 28, 340-5, 1989.

Nashel DJ, Martin JJ: Images in Rheumatology: a multimedia program for medical education. Proc Annu Symp Comput Appl Med Care (United States), 798-9, 1992.

Preiss B et al: Graphic summaries of expert knowledge for the medical curriculum: an experiment in second-year nephrology. Methods Inf Med (Germ.) 31, 303-9, 1992.

Puppe F, Poeck K, Gappa U, Bamberger S, & Goos K: Reusable Components for a configurable Diagnostics Shell, (Germ.), KI 2/1994, 13–18, 1994.

Puppe F and Reinhardt B: Generating Case-Oriented Training from Diagnostic Expert Systems, to appear in Machine Mediated Learing, 1995.

Reinhardt B and Schewe S: A shell for intelligent tutoring systems, Proceedings of AI-ED-95

Schewe S, Schreiber MA: Stepwise Development of a Clinical Expert System in Rheumatology. Clin. Investig 71, 139 - 144, 1993.

Wenger E: Artificial Intelligence and Tutoring Systems, Morgan Kaufman, 1987.

Widmer G, Horn W, Nagele B: Automatic knowledge base refinement: learning from examples and deep knowledge in rheumatology. Artif Intell Med (Netherlands) 5, 225-43, 1993.

Iterative Development and Validation of a Simulation-Based Medical Tutor

Christopher Eliot and Beverly Park Woolf

Department of Computer Science
University of Massachusetts
Amherst, MA. 01003-4610
Phone: (413) 545-4248 Fax: (413) 545-1249
{eliot, bev @cs.umass.edu}

Abstract. An iterative development cycle approach is described for building an intelligent tutor. This approach is particularly valuable since most tutoring systems require direct interaction with end-users. One of the advantages of this approach is that feedback from experts about the early prototype training system can be used to refine the questions asked during validation studies. The validation process changes at each cycle of the development process in order to define the scope of the project, correctly implement the domain models and verify the effectiveness of the resulting system. This paper describes development of a real-time medical training system and the iterative development approach that was used for its implementation and evaluation.

1 Introduction

Building a real-time medical simulation system for training requires consideration of the cognitive validity of the system, i.e.; the correctness of the tutor depends not solely on the analytical accuracy of the individual components of the model, but rather upon how the tutor is perceived by its users [7]. We determined the most salient aspects of a medical simulation by refining a prototype following evaluation with expert users. The iterative development approach was particularly valuable since direct interaction with end-users is a fundamental goal for all intelligent tutoring systems. Discussion of domain knowledge was conducted in the context of a working prototype, thus serving to properly focus expert and user reactions on specifications for the tutor. The iterative approach of the implementation improved communication between experts and developers since the evolving tutor served as a visible artifact clarifying the developer's understanding of the domain. The methodology also has some drawbacks, which are discussed below.

The user model for the Cardiac Tutor has been described elsewhere in [2, 3] and the implementation details are described in [4, 5]. This paper briefly outlines these components and then focuses on the development and validation processes. Section 2 provides an overview of the Cardiac Tutor, Section 3 details the iterative development process, and Section 4 describes the evaluation of this system.

2 Overview of the Cardiac Tutor

Training simulations provide students with opportunities to realistically practice important tasks. For a simulation to be realistic it has to run in real-time which constrains the design of the tutor's reasoning, including adaptiveness of the simulation, student modeling and the multimedia environment.

We have built and evaluated a system for training medical personnel in the skills of Advanced Cardiac Life Support (ACLS), the care of patients during heart attacks. Proper training for ACLS requires approximately two years of closely supervised clinical experience in an emergency room, ambulance, or similar medical facility.

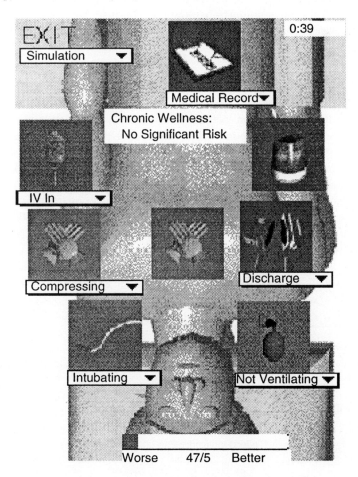

Fig. 1. The Simulated Patient

The high level simulation corresponds closely with the protocols written by the American Heart Association [1] both in terms of level of detail and structure. The treatment protocols are complex flowcharts based upon empirical data that must be memorized by clinicians and used as the basis for patient care.

Figures 1 shows a screen image from a simulation of a patient undergoing treatment. The intravenous line has been installed and the patient is being intubated. The icons on the chest and mouth indicate that compressions are in progress and ventilation is not. At the end of the simulation history a performance review is shown, listing the incorrect actions taken by the student.

Each state transition in the simulation is associated with a different probability as shown in Figure 2. The left side of Figure 2 represents the normal traversal of the system from one arrhythmia (VFIB) to alternative possible arrythmias (VTACH, ASYS and BRADY). The Tutor alters the probabilities of traversal to increase the probability that a specific learning opportunity will be available to the student. Biasing the simulation to reach states with good learning opportunities is a novel way to implement goal directed behavior.

2.1   The Plan Recognition Mechanism

The Cardiac Tutor was based on integrated simulation, tutoring and plan recognition. The relation between these components was cyclic: the plan recognition module monitored the student interacting with the simulation (see User Actions in Figure 3) and produced information that was interpreted by the tutoring module to define goal states. The adaptive simulation responded to the current set of goals so the student spent more time working in problem solving situations considered to have high learning value for the individual student. As the student learned, the system continued to update its model thereby keeping the curriculum focused on the student's most important learning needs.

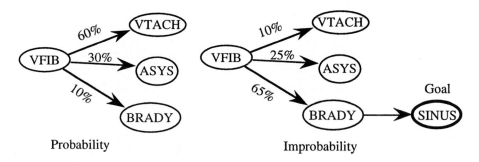

Fig. 2. Underlying Representation of Arrhythmias

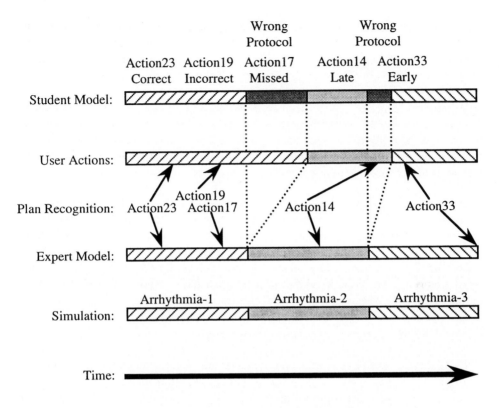

Fig. 3. Functionality of the Simulation and Planning Mechanisms.

Figure 3 shows a time-varying trace of the integrated system reflecting the actions of the student, the system and their effects on each other. The bottom line, *Simulation*, represents clinic reality, in this case, the independent succession of rhythms of the heart during a cardiac arrest. Sometimes the heart spontaneously changes state and goes into one of several abnormal rhythms or arrhythmias. The student is expected to respond to the state changes correctly, *Expert Model*. However, the student's response, *User Actions*, is frequently inconsistent with the behavior of the expert model. During such inconsistencies, a *Plan Recognition* phase predicts what an expert would do and compares this with the student's actions.

The student model was built passively by comparing student actions with expert protocols (similar to plans or scripts) representing expert behavior. Medical interventions by the student were mediated by the computer and compared to protocols representing expert behavior.

2.2   Contributions of the Cardiac Tutor

The system employed planning technology as a knowledge-based critic to determine goal states. Goals are for the student to learn about each component of ACLS, and were satisfied when the simulation moved into a state that provided the student an opportunity to practice a prioritized skill. When a goal, or high priority state, was found to be accessible by searching the simulation model, the tutor considered altering the base probabilities of a choice point, Figure 2. Simulation continued using the new probabilities making goal states more likely but retaining enough non-determinism so that students continued learning to react to unexpected changes.

The protocol recognition algorithm of the Cardiac Tutor demonstrated new techniques for plan recognition in multi-agent, real-time environments using knowledge-based methods for implementing common sense interpretation of plans during unexpected situations [5]. The tutor was capable of classifying many specific student errors and generated feedback specifically informing the student about how individual actions fail to conform with the established protocols. The system ensured that every recommendation was possible in the current situation and conformed to some interpretation of the student's actions applied to the protocols. Extended feedback was provided during retrospective analysis following each simulation.

The ACLS team leader must give unambiguous and timely commands in such a way as to maintain control of a high pressure chaotic situation making confidence and effective communication a major aspect of good ACLS performance. This should be improved by practice, such as is provided by the Cardiac Tutor.

2.3   Hypotheses

Based upon our theory of simulation-based tutoring we claim the Cardiac Tutor has a number of beneficial and empirically falsifiable features. We have yet to obtain data providing definitive support for each of these claims, as explained in Section 4 below. Our purpose in listing these claims is to represent our system as a, potentially falsifiable, scientific theory, rather than as a development effort. We do not compare the simulation to an actual resuscitation effort on a real patient, because the potential of patient risk would make empirical validation difficult.

• Students perceive the cardiac simulation as it was intended, i.e., clinical interventions applied to simulated patients undergoing cardiac arrest.
• Group Practice using the Cardiac Tutor is a particularly effective methodology for creating a positive learning environment.
• An hour of tutoring with the Cardiac Tutor is equivalent in training value to an hour with a human instructor during traditional training.

3   Iterative Development of a Simulation-Based Tutor

Builders of intelligent tutors can not specify ahead of time which tutoring mechanism will work effectively, because tutors are intended to have a specific psychological effect on people, i.e. learning, and because psychological theory has not developed general techniques for predicting student learning, except see Anderson [8]. Thus we selected a more flexible approach using an iterative, user-centered design methodology. The experience of domain experts and common sense knowledge about effective learning techniques was synthesized to develop the tutoring system.

For the simulation-based Cardiac Tutor, the internal accuracy of the mathematical model was less important than the cognitive validity of the model, i.e., it was important that the user perceive the model as realistic. This requirement is different from the needs of a traditional simulation constructed for scientific or engineering analysis in which accurate output and parameter modifications are the top priority. The iterative development process that we selected reflected this difference.

A central aspect of our design methodology was the early demonstration of a prototype system to potential medical users. Successful demonstration of the system in the target environment, not just in the laboratory, is a significant accomplishment of this research.

First, a working prototype was assembled using pre-existing components, scanned images and a minimal quantity of newly developed code. Further discussion with domain experts about the knowledge followed demonstration of this mock-up system. After additional prototype versions were developed, the system was tested with intended users who continued to supply needed corrections about findings, diagnosis and results. Feedback collected from domain experts at each cycle of these iterations was used to drive further development of the system.

The overall structure of the development process is shown in Figure 4. For each scenario implemented in the system, the expert must first describe the domain behavior to the knowledge engineer, who implements an initial model based on the description. The expert compares the behavior of the simulation algorithm to the expected domain behavior of the scenario and provides feedback to the knowledge engineer about how the model must be revised. The knowledge engineer then iteratively refines this model in cooperation with the domain expert until the simulated scenario corresponds with the actual domain behavior.

A medical simulation used for training must model the underlying abnormality along with its clinical appearance. Three important elements must be properly coordinated in order to simulate a specific medical scenario: 1) the findings that would be apparent in that scenario are listed by the expert and a simulation generating those findings implemented by the knowledge engineer; 2) the expert defines the diagnosis and treatment that is appropriate for this scenario; and 3) this process is reversed once the

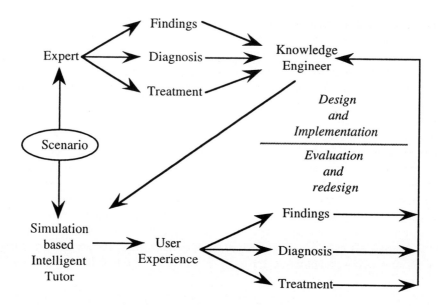

Fig. 4. User-Centered Development of a Tutor

scenario has been encoded as an implemented model. The simulation is unlikely to properly match the intended scenario during the initial implementations and the model must be refined until it does. The knowledge engineer and expert must cooperate to determine if the expert observer perceives the simulation as it was intended. Differences between the intended scenario and the appearance of the simulation are used as feedback to guide incremental refinement of the clinical model.

3.1   Benefits of this Process

End-user perception of a series of prototype tutors provided the primary organizational tools for our iterative development process. The implementation itself served as a conceptual tool for design review during development process. Consequently, errors in the system and awkward aspects of the user interface were salient but coherence of the overall architecture was difficult to perceive.

This methodology has many benefits. For most intelligent tutors, the requirements and specifications can not be clearly identified before the tutor is built. Thus the user-centered methodology serves to:

- Incorporate both the expert's and the user's perceptions.
- Detect simulation steps that don't appear physically.
- Simplify visualization of the presentation based on user needs.
- Guide extension of the system by well-defined user needs.
- Minimize development of extraneous components.

- Detect concepts poorly understood by knowledge engineers.
- Involve domain experts and users.

In the early phases of development it is important for domain experts and knowledge engineers to develop effective means of communication and to learn something of the opposite specialty. Even the most simplistic prototypes enhanced communication by providing an effective common reference. Aspects of the system that could not be interpreted by the domain experts were quickly identified. The simulation not only represented the intended domain, but was developed so it was perceived by users as intended. An iterative development cycle keeps domain experts involved, increasing their sense of purpose and commitment to the project, and gives knowledge engineers feedback concerning the needs and achievements of the system. Obtaining incremental feedback enabled better allocation of resources to the issues of most concern to users.

3.2   Liabilities of this Methodology

The final scope of the project can not be defined at the outset. This introduces challenges that are not found in more narrowly structured development processes. Although problems with the existing system are easily detected, missing components are not easily identified. Development based more on a theoretical analysis of the domain might have provided a more secure basis for defining the scope of the system, but also might have been less sensitive to the psychological needs of the users. Post-development validation is, of course, required for all projects. However, iterative development makes it hard to maintain a verifiable connection between requirements and implementation, so verification must fully address this need.

- Although errors are salient, omissions are not, so an active search for missing knowledge is needed.
- Post-development validation is required, since the design is not based upon a unified theory.

4   Evaluation of the Tutor

Evaluation was used to:

- guide development of the system;
- demonstrate the tutor's effectiveness;
- develop guidelines for use of the tutor; and
- extract general principles and tools about the development methodology and architecture of a tutor.

Initial studies were intended to define the scope of and knowledge in the Tutor. The earliest studies determined what modules and features were needed and involved "brainstorming" among students and domain experts to determine the required high level functionality of the tutoring system.

As development progressed we sought to detect and correct problems or mistakes in modules that had already been implemented. Studies involving two classes of fourth year medical school students to demonstrate the effectiveness of the final tutor were conducted. The original goal, to compare human and computer instruction, was not completed, but we performed a formative evaluation of the system's effectiveness, with encouraging, although inconclusive results.

Two studies were performed in conjunction with regularly scheduled ACLS training courses. The ACLS classes are modular so we were able to replace the appropriate traditional course module with our system. We studied fourth year medical students so that no one currently involved in direct patient care was trained using our unproven system but this reduced the number of subjects available and limited the time and flexibility of our study. Hence the size of our sample was limited and funding constraints restricted our ability to expand the sample size. Consequently, results of this study are informal observations without quantitative data.

Students found the simulation motivating and medically realistic. There were no comments suggesting that the students considered the simulation to be unrealistic or medically impossible. Students observed and commented negatively upon instances of medical inconsistency within a single arrhythmia state but did not object to the tutor's improbable temporal ordering of topics. This suggests that students are better able to judge the consistency of a single state and less able to judge the consistency of a sequence of events.

The students became deeply engaged in trying to "save" the simulated patient and displayed an emotional commitment to the effort. The knowledge-based feedback provided a strong motivation for students to critically review their own knowledge. When several students worked with the system in a group they invariably began an active discussion of the simulated medical situation. The conversation among the students clearly contributed to reflective thought. This situated discussion appeared to help students explore and understand fundamental concepts in the domain and suggests that the system may be most effective when installed to promote group, rather than individual use.

In contrast, the groups being taught by a human instructor were much more passive and appeared reluctant to express their opinions or reasoning.

5   Discussion and Conclusions

An iterative development process was used to build an intelligent simulation-based training system. Feedback from domain experts was used to drive further development of the system. The iterative development approach made system integration an ongoing process rather than a separate development phase. For systems with extensive user-interaction, such as tutoring systems, this development process is well suited, because it is hard to know how a user will actually perceive the system and so the requirements of the system are not known in advance. Students found the simulation medically plausible and motivating.

Tutors need additional capacity to analyze a student's mistakes and to generate corrective feedback. The practice provided by simulation-based intelligent tutors will become more valuable as tutors are better able to explain *how* and *why* the student should have performed certain things and why *not* use the actions selected. Considerable improvements in this area are possible, requiring further research into knowledge representation and explanation [6].

Further effort to develop validation methodologies is important for continued tutor development. Standardized and comparable validation techniques are needed. Currently, each researcher defines a validation procedure specifically for their tutor, making comparison of results across tutors impossible and duplicating the effort required for the design of validation studies.

References

1. American Heart Association, R. O. Cummins, editor: Textbook of Advanced Cardiac Life Support. Dallas, Texas (1994)
2. Eliot, C. R., and Woolf, B. P.: Reasoning about the User within a Simulation-based Real-time Training System. Proc. of the Fourth International Conference on User Modeling (1994) 121-126
3. Eliot, C. R., and Woolf, B. P.: An Adaptive Student Centered Curriculum for an Intelligent Training System. J. of User Modeling and User Interaction (1995) 67-86
4. Eliot, C. R.: An Intelligent Tutoring System Based Upon Adaptive Simulation. Ph.D. thesis, University of Massachusetts, Amherst (1996)
5. Eliot, C. R., and Woolf, B. P.: Multi-agent Protocol Recognition during Simulation. AAAI-96 (to appear)
6. Forbus, K. and Falkenhainer, B.: Self-Explanatory Simulations: Scaling up to large models. AAAI-92 (1992) 685-690
7. Hollan, J., Hutchins, E., and Weitzman, L.: STEAMER: an interactive inspectible simulation-based training system. A. I. Magazine, Summer (1984)
8. Koedinger, K. R., Anderson, J. R., Hadley, W. H., and Mark, M.: Intelligent Tutoring Goes to the Big City. Proceedings AI and Education (1995) 421-428

WULPUS
An Intelligent Problem Solving Environment Delivering Knowledge Based Help and Explanations in Business Management Simulation

Claus Möbus, Olaf Schröder, Heinz-Jürgen Thole[1]

OFFIS Institute, Escherweg 2, D-26121 Oldenburg, Germany
E-Mail: {moebus, schroeder, thole}@informatik.uni-oldenburg.de

Abstract. Business mangement simulation plays an increasing role in schooling and post-qualification. In complex simulation games the interrelationships between decisions and results are intransparent. This is one reason for inefficient knowledge acquisition. Another reason is the *forward chaining* architecture of "classical" simulation games.

In this paper we describe a prototype of a business simulation game based on *hypotheses testing* and *goal oriented backward chaining*. Its design is based on a theoretical framework, the IPSE approach (Intelligent Problem Solving Environment). In order to offer help on the students´ demand, we integrated a hypotheses testing environment, named "simulation in the simulation". The students may state goals and hypotheses about their reachability and about the consistency of decisions with corporate objectives. The system gives feedback and explains the relations in the business marketing simulation by presenting qualitative information, price-demand curves, and by using an "enterprise landscape" which contains the decision and result variables of the system, their dependencies, and the qualities of their influences.

1 Introduction

In managerial schooling and post-qualification management, computer based simulations and management business games are used increasingly to meet education requirements. It is hoped that these systems improve the students´ abilities of problem solving, business analysis, and teamwork. In order not to diverge from reality too much (Cadotte, 1990; Eser, 1992), in "classical" simulation games there is a high degree of interrelatedness of their components. This may lead to intransparency. Moreover, in the "classical" simulation game approach, the students make decisions and then inspect the resulting consequences. Thus business simulation games are forward chaining. If no explanations are offered that help to comprehend the relationships between decisions and results, the students get into difficulties. Thus the students have to know a lot *before* playing the game. The situation is further complicated e.g. by the performance of the competitors, and by the fact that effects may occur with time delay.

---

[1] We thank Klaus Adam and Hagen von Stuckrad for assisting in the implementation.

WULPUS (Wissensbasierte Unterstützung für LUDUS, ein Planspiel für Unternehmensstrategien: Knowledge based support for LUDUS, a marketing simulation game for business strategies) is an Intelligent Problem Solving Environment (IPSE, Möbus, 1995) designed to make the relationships between the various functional areas of a business enterprise transparent. WULPUS does not require a lot of preknowledge from the student. Rather, the intention is that the student acquires this knowledge while working with WULPUS.

In order to support design decisions for the development of knowledge based help systems, a theoretical framework of problem solving and learning is needed. Our IPSE approach is based on a *cognitive science* oriented theory of knowledge acquisition, the ISP-DL Theory (Impasse - Success - Problem Solving - Driven Learning Theory; Möbus, Schröder & Thole, 1994). The theory attempts to integrate *impasse-driven learning* (Laird, Rosenbloom, & Newell, 1986; Newell, 1990; van Lehn, 1988; 1991), *success driven learning* (e. g., Anderson, 1983; 1989), and *phases of problem solving* (Gollwitzer, 1990; Heckhausen, 1989). According to the theory, the student will look for and appreciate help if he is caught in an impasse. Without an impasse there is no need for help. So WULPUS does not interrupt the student but offers help on request. Furthermore the information should be designed to help the student to overcome the impasse and not to trap into a secondary impasse. Thus the information should refer to his preknowledge as much as possible. One way to realize this principle is to let the student test hypotheses about his solutions, and get help, proposals, and explanations from the IPSE. Therefore in WULPUS the hypotheses testing approach (Möbus, 1995; Möbus, Schröder & Thole, 1994; Möbus, Thole & Schröder, 1993) is transferred to the simulation game domain.

A second reason for pursuing the hypotheses testing approach is that stating and testing hypotheses is a key qualification having a beneficial influence on the student´s knowledge acquisition process (Shute & Glaser, 1990).

The domain of WULPUS consists of part of the "classical" business simulation game LUDUS distributed by the German company rado-plan. The main features distinguishing WULPUS from LUDUS and other "classical" business games are:

• *Hypotheses testing before the "real simulation step"*: The hypotheses testing environment allows to state different kind of hypotheses, e.g. the student may state different decision oriented hypotheses one after the other in order to compare their consequences by entering various values for the decision variables. In contrast to LUDUS and other "classical" simulation games, WULPUS supports the decision-making by answering the student´s question: "What happens if ... ?"

• *Forward vs. backward planning*: The student may state goal oriented hypotheses by stating his corporate objectives. The system tries to complete each hypothesis about the reachability of the student´s goals by computing proposals for decisions consistent with these goals. Furthermore the student may state hypotheses about the consistency of his decisions and the desired results, that is, his corporate objectives, by entering both. In contrast to LUDUS, WULPUS supports the decision-making by answering the student´s questions: "How is ... reachable?" and "Is ... reachable if ... ?"

• *Proposing corrections of inconsistent decisions and corporate objectives*. WULPUS gives feedback about the achievability of the student's goals. Furthermore the system offers correction proposals for the decisions if goals cannot be reached.

• *Explanation component*: WULPUS provides knowledge based explanations by answering the student´s questions:
- • How did the results occur given my decisions?
- • Why are the decision proposals suitable to achieve my goals?
- • Why are some goals not reachable?

The remainder of this paper is organized as follows: The next section gives an overview of WULPUS. In the third section, the hypotheses testing facilities of WULPUS are described in some detail. The paper ends with some conulsions.

2 Description of WULPUS

The knowledge based business management simulation game WULPUS has been developed to demonstrate an approach to make the interrelations of a complex simulation game transparent. We wanted WULPUS to offer multiple support for the student´s decision-making. Therefore the concept of a *"simulation in the simulation"* has been developed and realized. Before the next "real simulation step" is performed the student has the opportunity to test alternatives. The student may reverse his former decisions and objectives. After restoring the simulation and entering new values the student may start the WULPUS computation again. So the student is able to compare the relationships between the different values of decisions and corporate objectives. To recognize effects with time delay the student may carry out several trial simulation steps one after the other, focusing on the development of the variables he is interested in, e.g. his sales opportunities.

In order to simulate a realistic market, it is necessary that the student be able to vary the *competitive companies'* goals and decisions as well. Therefore, while using the "simulation in the simulation" for decision-making, the student may enter assumptions about the performance of his competitors.

Furthermore WULPUS supports the knowledge acquisition of the students by offering *explanations*. Since WULPUS contains an integrated expert knowledge base it is able to explain the interrelationships between the variables of the business management simulation. In addition, if the corparate objectives are not reachable, the student may invoke the explanation component of WULPUS. The explanations are taylored in steps which are presented to the student one by one on demand. The feedback steps are: Firstly the answer (yes / no), secondly a qualitative description of the dependencies, and thirdly quantitative information, e.g. price-demand curves. Thus in WULPUS essential knowledge like price-demand curves is not a prerequisite. Rather, this knowledge is *offered* by WULPUS on demand in impasse situations.

There is some evidence that novices get into difficulties while learning business management from complex simulation games. Novices have serious problems in decision-making. They are not able to explain the consequences of their decisions to themselves without further help owing to the lack of preknowledge. On the other hand they have clear-cut ideas concerning their corporate objectives. This is the reason for the opportunity to work in a *goal oriented manner* with WULPUS. During the decision-making in the "simulation in the simulation" the student may enter his goals without specifying the decision variables. Now the system computes the values for the unspecified decision variables in backward direction such that the desired results are reachable. So the conventional roles of the dependent and independent variables of a "classical" business management simulation have been exchanged.

Figure 1 shows the flow of working with WULPUS. According to our theoretical position, the task "accomplishing a simulation step in a business management game" may consist of four phases: Deliberating, planning, executing and evaluating (Heckhausen, 1989; Gollwitzer, 1990). In conventional simulation games just the executing phase is supported: Carrying out the "real simulation step": Entering the decisions and retrieving the results (part between the two broken lines of Figure 1). WULPUS also supports the planning and evaluating processes by offering hypotheses testing and explanations. Control is left to the student. Hypotheses testing and demanding explanations are invoked by the student, that is if the student appreciates them and finds them helpful (rounded boxes).

The student may play up to four hypotheses testing simulation steps to recognize time delayed effects of the mix of marketing tools on the sales opportunities (backward pointing arrow on the upper right of Figure 1). He may save each hypothesis in order to compare its results with future hypotheses (backward pointing arrow on the upper left). He may also ask for explanations for any tested hypotheses.

After finishing the decision-making concerning the mix of marketing tools the student has to accomplish his internal company policy. The budgeting is constrained by the data attained in the market situation, e.g. the values for sales opportunities, and prices. WULPUS offers explanations to support the student's analysis of the results. For the purpose of comparison of alternatives each step of hypotheses testing for internal planning may be repeated with new values too (backward pointing arrow on the left of the middle part of Figure 1). Furthermore the student may reiterate the hypotheses testing about competition in the market situation, e.g. if it becomes obvious that the values for the sales opportunies and the mix of marketing tools are not suitable for a promising internal budgeting. After finishing the complete decision-making process, the real simulation step takes place: Entering decisions and retrieving the results. The student may ask for help by demanding explanations for the unexpected results.

3 Hypotheses Testing in WULPUS

Hypotheses testing within a business simulation will be demonstrated by a sample run with WULPUS. Imagine a student's problem is the decision-making for the next "real simulation step". He may make use of the "simulation in the simulation" by stating hypotheses in order to find out whether his corporate objectives are achievable.

3.1 Hypotheses Testing in the Market Situation

Figure 2 shows the hypotheses testing environment for the market situation. First the student has to select a product and a market (at the top). WULPUS offers several opportunities to state hypotheses. The student can state the following decisions and goals concerning his own business enterprise (left half from top to bottom):

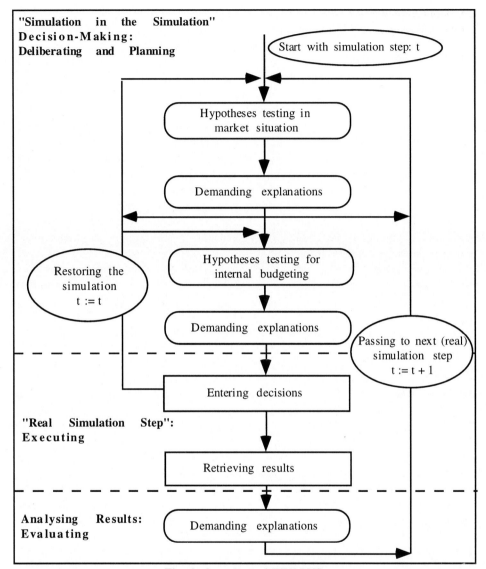

Fig. 1. Overview of WULPUS

The enterprise
- does not change the former (given) decisions for the mix of marketing tools
- decides to use new values for price, advertising, distribution, and research
- pursues the strategy of holding, raising, or decreasing sales opportunities
- sets a value as a goal for the sales opportunities

The assumptions about the performance of the competitor have to be one of the following (right half from top to bottom of Figure 2): The competitor:
- does not change his former marketing decisions
- decides to use new values for price, advertising, distribution, and research
- pursues an equivalent or a contrary strategy for the sales opportunities

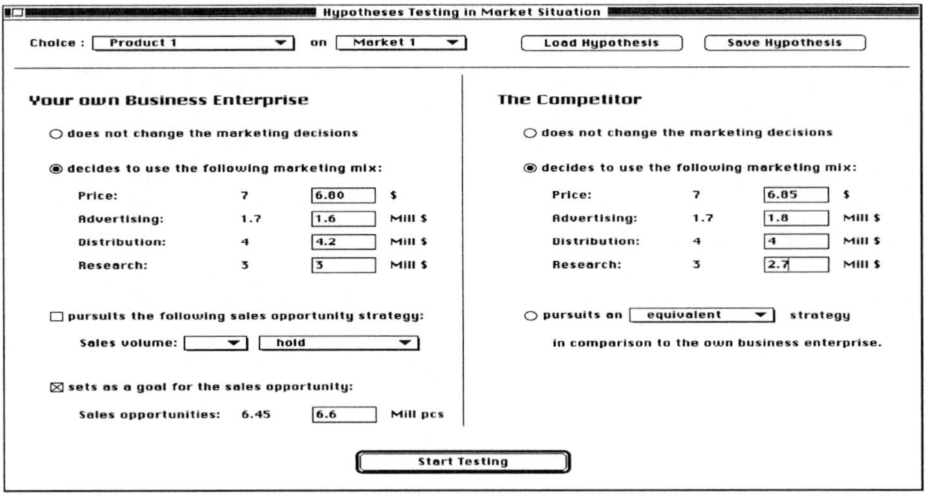

Fig. 2. Consistency hypothesis in the market situation

In the situation depicted in Figure 2, the student may state a *consistency hypothesis* for product 1 on market 1. He has entered the goal for his sales opportunities (6.6 million pieces) and a complete set of values for the decision variables "price" = 6.80 dollars, "advertising" = 1.6 million dollars, "distribution" = 4.2 million dollars, and "research" = 3 million dollars. The values of the last period are also shown: "price" = 7.00 dollars, and so on. Furthermore in this example the learner makes assumptions about the marketing decisions of his competitor. WULPUS analyzes the hypothesis and then gives feedback on the first level: In this case, the value reached falls below the goal set for the sales opportunities. On the second level of feedback WULPUS provides qualitative proposals about how to change the decision variables in order to reach the goal, e.g. to decrease the price or to decrease advertising. The student may test several consistency hypotheses, but this may be a tedious trial and error process.

Therefore the student may state a *goal oriented hypothesis* by leaving at least one decision variable unspecified. WULPUS computes the missing value(s) to reach the objective for the sales opportunity. Figure 3 shows the student´s hypothesis. The price is left unspecified. WULPUS succeeds in computing a price to reach the goal.

On the third level of feedback, the price-demand curve is presented (Figure 4). Looking at the curve the student sees that a considerably higher price can be achieved by a small reduction in the sales opportunities. So he may decide to test another goal oriented hypothesis. He changes neither the values for advertising, distribution, and research, nor his assumptions about his competitor. But he sets a new, slightly lower goal for sales opportunities: 6.35 million pieces. Now even a price of \$ 7.50 is possible. Hypotheses testing can be performed for each product on each market.

3.2 Hypotheses Testing for Internal Budgeting
When the student is satisfied with his marketing decisions, he may start with the internal budgeting. Planning internal budgeting is constrained by the results obtained for the market situation. For internal budgeting, there are the following decision areas

besides marketing: personnel policy, production / stocks of goods, machinery, and finances. Furthermore, there are two reports: sales statistics, and profit and loss account. A student may but need not deal with all variables of the decision areas. As an example we will show the finances dialog (Figure 5). The only decision variable is the value for the line of credit. In our example the student does not decide on this but states $ 290 million as the goal for the "sum of paying out". Now he invokes the hypothesis test. This means that the student states the hypothesis that his marketing decisions can be made without exceeding 290 million dollars for "sum of paying out". As Figure 6 shows, the values left unspecified in figure 5 have been computed by the system. Values consistent with the hypothesis are marked with a friendly smiley button. WULPUS has marked the value for the "sum of paying out" with a sad button. This indicates an inconsistency discovered: This "sum of paying out"-goal is not reachable, given the decisions made. In order to ask for a correction proposal and explanations the student clicks on the sad button. The correct value displayed by WULPUS is $ 296.261 million.

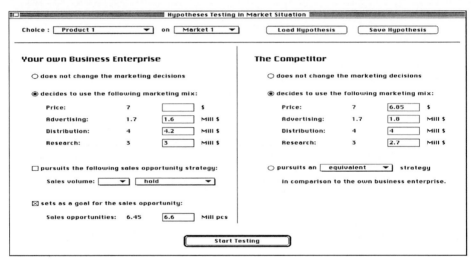

Fig. 3. Goal oriented hypothesis in the market situation

On further request the student may retrieve an overview of the influences on the "sum of paying out". WULPUS opens a landscape of the business enterprise (Figure 7). First the landscape contains only the variable "sum of paying out" and its direct causes (bold ellipses). On demand the landscape is spreading out step by step. The direction of each influence is represented by an arrow. Its quality is symbolized by the sign (+ / -). For example: When the "investments" increase, then the "sum of paying out" will increase too. The student may "walk" through the WULPUS landscape to discover the dependencies between the variables. Reasons for the higher "sum of paying out" may be located in the nodes "paying out without respite" and "investments" because these can be contolled by internal budgeting. The student may explore these possibilities, getting hints for the reasons for his undesirably high sum.

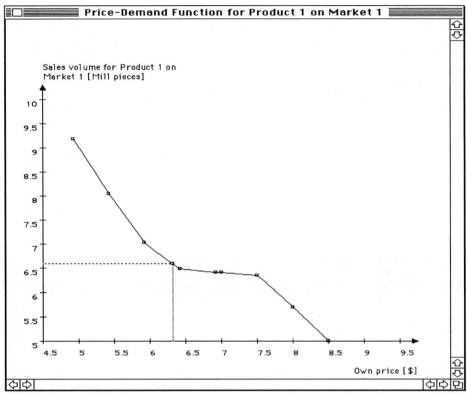

Fig. 4. The price-demand curve corresponding to the goal-oriented hypothesis of Fig. 3

Finances			
Statements of financial positions	**Old values**	**Diff. in %**	**New values**
Sales revenues	228.55		
Short term credit	82.7797		
Line of credit	*82.7797*		
Overdraft facility	0		
Other inpayment	0		
Σ Inpayment	311.329		
Paying out without respite	206.524		
Investments	0		
Redemption for short term credit	97.2156	-14.849303	82.7797
Redemption for overdraft facility	0	0	0
Interest and related expenses	3.40254		
Tax	4.18731		
Σ Paying out	311.329		290
Balance	0		

All values in Mill $.

[Ok]

Fig. 5. Hypothesis for internal budgeting

Finances			
Statements of financial positions	**Old values**	**Diff. in %**	**New values**
Sales revenues	228.55	1.15160156	231.181 ☺
Short term credit	82.7797	-21.381805	65.0799 ☺
Line of credit	*82.7797*	*-21.381805*	65.07996 ☺
Overdraft facility	0	0	0 ☺
Other inpayment	0	0	0 ☺
Σ Inpayment	311.329	-4.8398279	296.261 ☺
Paying out without respite	206.524	0.26565863	207.072 ☺
Investments	0	0	0 ☺
Redemption for short term credit	97.2156	-14.849303	82.7797 ☺
Redemption for overdraft facility	0	0	0 ☺
Interest and related expenses	3.40254	-33.056059	2.27779 ☺
Tax	4.18731	19.1696143	4.99001 ☺
Σ Paying out	311.329	-6.8511841	290 ☹
Balance	0		0 ☺

All values in Mill $.

(Ok)

Fig. 6. Feedback to the hypothesis for internal budgeting

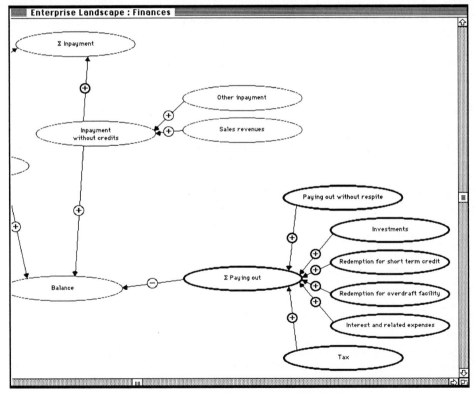

Fig. 7. Part of the Landscape of WULPUS

4 Conclusions

We redesigned a "classical" forward chaining business game. The new game, WULPUS, is "backward chaining" and "goal oriented", thus supporting our hypotheses testing approach. According to our ISP-DL knowledge acquisition theory, hypotheses testing takes place at impasse time when there are knowledge deficiencies on the learner's side.

There is strong empirical evidence that system support in those impasse situations is more efficient than in other problem solving situations. We put forward the empirically testable hypothesis that learners working with the IPSE WULPUS gain more procedural knowledge in less time.

5 References

ANDERSON, J. R., The Architecture of Cognition, Cambridge: Harvard Univ. Press, 1983

ANDERSON, J. R., A Theory of the Origins of Human Knowledge, Artificial Intelligence, 1989, 40, 313-351

CADOTTE, E. R., The Market Place, A Strategic Marketing Simulation, Richard D. Irwin, Inc., 1990

ESER, T. W., Planspiel kommunale Wirtschaftsförderung, in H. SPEHL (Hrgs.), Trierer Schriftenreihe zum Schwerpunkt Tourismus, Regional- und Siedlungsentwicklung Nr. 3, Universität Trier, 1992

GOLLWITZER, P. M., Action Phases and Mind-Sets, in E.T. HIGGINS & R.M. SORRENTINO (eds), Handbook of Motivation and Cognition: Foundations of Social Behavior, 1990, Vol. 2, 53-92

HECKHAUSEN, H., Motivation und Handeln, Berlin: Springer, 1989

LAIRD, J. E. , ROSENBLOOM, P. S. & NEWELL, A., Universal Subgoaling and Chunking. The Automatic Generation and Learning of Goal Hierarchies, Boston: Kluwer, 1986

MÖBUS, C., Towards an Epistemology of Intelligent Problem Solving Environments: The Hypothesis Testing Approach, in: J. GREER (ed), Proceedings of AI-ED 95, World Conference on Artificial Intelligence and Education, 1995, 138-145

MÖBUS, C., SCHRÖDER, O. & THOLE, H.-J., Diagnosing and Evaluating the Acquisition Process of Programming Schemata, in: J. E. GREER & G. McCALLA (eds), Student Modelling: The Key to Individualized Knowledge-Based Instruction (Proc. of the NATO Advanced Research Workshop on Student Modelling, in St. Adele, Quebec, Canada, Berlin: Springer (NATO ASI Series F: Computer and Systems Science, Vol. 125), 1994, 211-264

MÖBUS, C., THOLE, H.-J. & SCHRÖDER, O., Interactive Support of Planning in a Functional, Visual Programming Language, in P. BRNA, S. OHLSSON, H. PAIN (eds), Proceedings AI-ED 93, World Conference on Artificial Intelligence and Education, Edinburgh, 1993, 362 - 369

NEWELL, A., Unified Theories of Cognition, Cambridge: Harvard Press, 1990

SHUTE, V. J. & GLASER, R., A Large-Scale Evaluation of an Intelligent Discovery World: Smithtown, Interactive Learning Environments, 1, 1990, 51-77

Van LEHN, K., Toward a Theory of Impasse-Driven Learning, In: H. MANDL & A. LESGOLD (eds), Learning Issues for Intelligent Tutoring Systems, New York: Springer, 1988, 19-41

Van LEHN, K., Rule Acquisition Events in the Discovery of Problem Solving Strategies, Cognitive Science, 1991, 15, 1- 47

Using Case-Based Reasoning for Exercise Design in Simulation-Based Training

Dong Mei Zhang[1] and Leila Alem[1]

CRC-IDS, 723 Swanston St. Carlton 3053 Australia

[1] CSIRO Division of Information Technology,
Locked Bag 17, North Ryde, NSW 2113, Australia
zhang@syd.dit.csiro.au

Abstract. In many simulation-based training systems, particularly in systems for training operational skills, one of the main issues is the creation of repeated and gradually more complicated training exercises/tasks for the development of the student's skills. In this paper we propose the use of case-based reasoning techniques for representing and designing a follow-up exercise. Such an approach tailors the problems presented in training exercises to facilitate the mastery of specific goals to individual students. An exercise case represents both knowledge concerning the subject area and knowledge of problem situations to be solved within a training exercise. Training goals are defined based on subject topics and problem complexity. A process model for designing training exercises is presented in the context of ATC training.

1 Introduction

Operational skills are nearly always taught or trained by exercises and examples. The training of operational skills requires the use of an intelligent simulation-based training system. Such a system provides an opportunity to practice operational procedures in a dynamic and on-the-job environment [5]. The student is continuously exposed to various training exercises/contexts. In such systems, one of the main issues is the creation of repeated and gradually more complicated training exercises/tasks for developing the student's skills. The ability to produce coherent and appropriate training exercises/tasks can dramatically improve the individualised learning potential of an ITS for training operational skills. For instance, a computer tutor which fails to select problems that are at the "edge" of the individual student's current state of knowledge could not help the student acquire new knowledge effectively. Students may flounder on tasks that are too complex or breeze mindlessly through ones that are too easy.

Like an exploratory learning environment, the situations the student sees and the knowledge the student acquires depend on how the student executes the simulated exercise. As a result, a student may miss key concepts and fail to learn critical operational procedures. In the Air Traffic Control (ATC) domain, human instructors tend to remedy this issue by intervening during the execution of the exercise in order to make sure that the student is faced with the required learning situations. It is therefore critical to design simulation exercises with explicit training goals and contain the exercise. In this paper, we mainly focus on the first issue.

By exercise design, we mean the process used to tailor training exercises/tasks to the student's changing knowledge state. Our exercise design is in line with the curriculum-based problem/task sequencing in ITS, however we do not consider the instructional strategies and methods in the exercise design in current stage. In general, problems presented in the exercise should be chosen to fit the patterns of skills and weaknesses that characterise the specific learner at the time the exercise is designed. Moreover, the exercise/task generated must adhere to major criteria for curriculum planning [6] [8], for example, manageability and individualisation. Given the student's present knowledge state, the training tasks or exercises need to be designed in such a way that they are (a) manageable with skills already possessed by the individual student; (b) easily related to skills already possessed by the individual student.

As part of a project to develop a simulation-based intelligent training system for ATC training, ATEEG [1], we have been investigating the design of the training exercises. Such exercises will provide conflict problem situations where the student resolves conflict by applying separation standards. Our approach uses existing exercises for the design of an exercise that meets the student's training needs. Case-Based Reasoning (CBR) techniques are used to represent and design exercises.

CBR techniques have a significant impact for computer-based tutoring/training designs. Many promising research results have been achieved in this field, for instance, Archie-2 [6], for helping student designers with their architecture projects; a case-based program for teaching law students to argue with cases [2] and CABAT [13] as a tool that supports case-based learning in a simulation environment.

This paper first describes the exercise design process and the three knowledge components it is using. An approach using case-based reasoning techniques to design exercise is developed. The representation of exercise case, training goals and indexing, student evaluation and process model for designing exercise are then respectively described.

2 Exercise Design as Problem Solving

The design of follow-up training exercises in our research is viewed as a problem solving task. It is concerned with two problems: formulating the representation of relevant knowledge to the exercise and training domain, and producing suitable exercises to fit the student's needs by using this representation. Petrushin [12] defines two categories of knowledge used to support exercise design. One is domain specific knowledge concerning the concepts contained in a subject area. The other is knowledge of the problem situation intended to develop habits and skills. In our view, the exercise design process is a problem solving task that searches for an exercise to fit the student's training needs based on present and past evaluation.

An exercise/task design process requires three knowledge components:

(1) Description of subject concepts/topics which reflect training goals ;
(2) Explicit representation of specific training exercises/tasks which present problem situations intended to develop training goals;
(3) Evaluation of the student's mastery of domain knowledge with regard to specific training goals.

From a general ITS view, component (1) deals with the formalisation of curriculum of the training domain. Component (2) provides description of training contexts. Component (3) is referred to the student model. More research in ITS has shown attempts to build frameworks for problem/task sequencing (eg., [3] [16] [11] [10] [4] [15] [5] [8]). Our review here considers features of some systems related to issues in this paper.

The curriculum of the subject forms the basis of any intelligent problem/task sequencing. In many systems, eg., BIP [3] [16]. SCENT-3 [11], ITBA [10], etc., the curriculum is represented as a network of domain concepts connected with relationships. BIP uses a Curriculum Information Network (CIN) which represents programming skills and the salient pedagogical relations among them. In ITBA, a skill network represents relations among various algebra skills based on a component-skill approach. GT-VITA [5] and ITEM/IP [3] develop a curriculum which contains domain concepts related to declarative knowledge, procedural knowledge and operational skill. Such a curriculum supports multiple problem sequencing respectively for training declarative and procedural knowledge, operational skills.

The student's knowledge level is required for problem/task sequencing. An overlay model has been used in most systems to provide the student's knowledge as a subset of expert knowledge, eg., in SCENT-3, ITEM/IP, Sherlock II [8], GT-VITA. A student profile is used in BIP to maintain an assessment of the student's mastery of each skill. ITBA uses past and present student performance to determine a current skill set. In GT-VITA, the measurement of the student's performance is also used to describe the student's knowledge level.

Various strategies for problem/task sequencing/design can be classified into single-concept and multiple-concept according to [4]. For single-concept task sequencing, having selected the current domain concept/element, the system selects the best task/problem or chooses at random a limited set of simple tasks related to the current domain concept. Approaches for multiple-concept task/problem sequencing vary. ITEM/IP makes the choice of the best task based on the measurements of task complexity. BIP selects from a library of a number of preconstructed exercises and presents the task with the greatest number of unlearned skills. ITBA presents the task with the fewest non-target skills.

In our development of an intelligent simulation-based training system for ATC, the student evaluation process is in line with Chu et al.'s approach [5] in the sense that we are using performance measure for the assessment of the operational skills of the trainee, however, we do not deal with training of declarative and procedural skills in the current system. Training goals are defined using ATC subject topics and complexity of problem situations which comprise the curriculum. In our case-based exercise design, a case represents a variety of information relevant to an ATC exercise, including problem situations, complexity of problems, underlying conflict resolution topics. In the generation of follow-up exercises/tasks, we use the existing exercise cases/subcases as starting points and adapt them.

3   Representation of Exercise Cases

Case representation is the process of determining the contents of cases and their organisation. In our approach, a case is a rich representation of both of knowledge concerning the subject area and knowledge of problem situations to be solved within a training exercise. A simulation exercise is composed of a number of subcases, each of which represents a problem situation, that is, the context of particular potential conflict among aircraft. Each subcase represents relevant information to a problem situation, which gives an abstract description of a conflict problem.

A case contains three types of information:

(1)   description of physical information related to problem situations.
(2)   underlying subject concepts/topics that are reflected in problem situations.
(3)   complexity of problems situations.

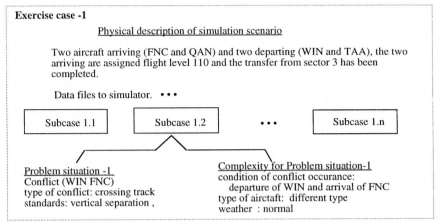

Fig. 1. The representation of an exercise case.

Fig. 1 shows the representation of an exercise case, case-1 which consists of subcases case1.1, case1.2, etc. The physical description represents parameters of an air traffic scenario, eg., airspace and its boundaries, flight plans. Such information forms the context in which the student performs conflict resolution tasks. The underlying subject topics represents ATC training concepts. Currently, our exercises focus on conflict resolution. A training topic is represented by type of conflicts and separation standards applicable for the conflict.

Another type information in our case representation is the complexity description of each problem situation. The representation of a case provides the complexity of each problem situation which composes in the exercise. Problem difficulty can vary widely depending on the overall complexity of the conflict situation. One type of conflict can be reflected by a number of problem situations that differ in complexity. The complexity of problem situations defines the context of ATC scenario. In our case, the complexity of a conflict problem situation is represented by dimensions of the following major features: conditions for conflict occurrence, type of aircraft involved and weather condition.

4 Training Goals and Case Index

In ATC domain, a training goal related to declarative knowledge can be defined based on the particular conflict; a training goal related to procedural knowledge can be the application of separation standard. In our current exercise design, the operational skill training goals relate to conflict resolution. To represent the training goals/aspects, it is necessary to analyse underlying topics/concepts contained in the training domain. In our approach, underlying topics related to conflict resolution includes type of conflict and standards for each type of conflict. For example, the topics can be "same direction conflict among cruising aircraft by time standard", "faster following between departing aircraft by distance standard". These topics are loosely coupled on the conceptual level. Training topics in our approach are represented as a flat list rather than a network. On the other hand, the use of standards depends largely on how complicate the conflict situation is. Therefore, our training goals are defined by

- topics with regarding to conflict resolution and
- complexity of problem situations.

Exercises are designed with explicit training goals. In designing an exercise, relevant exercise cases need to be accessed according to new training goals for the follow up exercise. The retrieval of exercise cases/subcases requires an index representation in order to establish the connection between individual cases/subcases and description of training goals. We adopts an indexing scheme used in a case-based design system, CADSYN [11] [18]. In this indexing representation approach, each design subsystem indicates relevant design subcases which contain specific description of the subsystem. Basically, our cases are indexed at the subcase level, that is, at the problem situation level. A topic-problem list serves as an index representation in retrieving cases. In the topic-problem list, each training topics indicates a list of subcases from multiple cases which contain relevant problem situations to this topic. As illustrated in Fig. 2, the topic "crossing track by vertical separation standard" indicates three relevant subcases, case1.2, case2.2 and case2.4 because these three subcases contain problem situations associated to this topic.

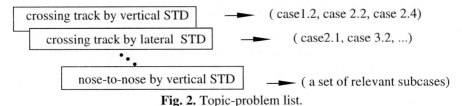

Fig. 2. Topic-problem list.

Such an indexing structure allows the process model to access problem situations and combine them when necessary. The complexity of each problem situation also serves the purpose of indexing. When a set of problem situations is found based on the topic-problem list, the complexity of each problem situation help to identify further the relevance of problem situations to the student's training needs.

5 Evaluation of a Student's Performance

The new training goals for the follow up exercise is identified based on the student's present and past performance evaluation. The student's evaluation is used to generate a student model. The evaluation process is illustrated in Fig. 3.

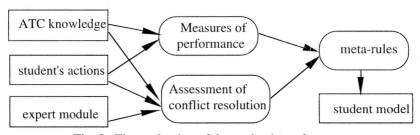

Fig. 3. The evaluation of the student's performance.

The evaluation process uses objective measures of the student's performance, as well as assessment of hight level student's resolution strategy and reasons about this two to derive the student's mastery of training topics presented in the exercise. The evaluation process is further described in [17].

- ATC knowledge represents problem solving knowledge such as separation standards, strategies for resolving conflicts and knowledge for evaluation.
- Objective measures of the student's performance provides a set of performance parameters such as percentage of breakdowns of separation, percentage of conflicts resolved by using optimal standards.
- The assessment of the student's conflict resolution strategy is done using expert module and student's resolution strategy.
- Meta-rules represent heuristics used to assess the student's level of mastery of knowledge.
- Student model provides a statement of the student's knowledge with regard to the training aspects or goal. It is updated after each training session.

6 Process Model for Exercise Design

Our exercise design process consists of four process modules: evaluation, identification of training goals, case retrieval and exercise generation. Fig. 4 shows the process model in our case-based exercise design approach.

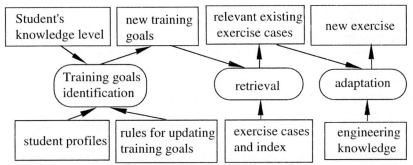

Fig. 4. The process model of exercise design using case-based reasoning.

The process model can be described as follows: first, the evaluation process assesses the student's state of knowledge in terms of training goals achieved and not achieved. The current training goals are then updated by taking into account the student's mastery of relevant training topics reflected in present and previous exercises. A set of heuristic rules is applied to update the current training goals by defining the conflict resolution topics and appropriate complexity of problem situations used to reflect the training topics. Third, relevant exercises and problem situations are retrieved according to the updated training goals. At last, the retrieved exercise and relevant problem situations are combined to produce a new exercise based on ATC exercise engineering knowledge. The rest of this section further describes the updating of training goals, retrieving exercise case and generating a tailored exercise.

6.1 Updating Training Goals

The purpose of this step is to determine new training goals in terms of relevant conflict resolution topics and their complexity level for the follow up exercise.

Promotion and demotion training goals to specific students are determined by considering the student's mastery of relevant training topics reflected in present and previous exercises. A set of heuristic rules is defined to help reasoning about topics and their complexity level. For instance, if the student has correctly resolved a particular type of conflict at certain complexity level in the current and previous sessions, the decision is made to promote the student to the next complexity level of problem. Otherwise, decision related to updating of training goals includes: "demoting the complexity level", "present new problem within same level of complexity".

Some systems described in section 2 use different techniques for identifying relevant training goals for the next task/exercise. BIP uses a simple technique to combine inferential and interactive diagnosis. In the student model, associated with each skill is a pair of numeric values: the system's estimate of the student's mastery and the student's own estimate. In ITBA, training goals are represented by skills and updated in light of changes to the student model. Updating skills relies on the skill network that records logical and conceptual relations between algebraic skills. The main feature of GT-VITA's identification of new training skills is taking into account the relations across declarative knowledge, procedural knowledge and operational skills. If the student failed to master an operational skill, the training goals to be exercised include training of the relevant procedural or declarative knowledge.

6.2 Retrieval of Exercise Cases

Given the description of new training goals, identifying all perfectly or partially matching exercise cases/subcases and selecting the most relevant exercise case are the goal of the retrieval process. The updated training goals indicate (1) the training topics in terms of conflict type and standard and (2) complexities of problem situations associated to those training topics. The retrieval of cases and subcases is based on the topic-problem list and complexity description of problem situations from cases. Based on the training goals, the list of subcases indicated by the matched training topic in the topic-problem list is relevant. The outcome of the retrieval process provides the most relevant exercise case and a set of relevant subcases for each training goal.

The retrieval is conducted in the following way:

(1) For each training topic T and its complexity level C in the training goals
a list of subcases $\{P_1, ... P_i, ...\}$ is found according to the topic-problem list;
For each subcase P_i,
If its complexity level matches C,
then subcase P_i is relevant and kept in the retrieved list.
(2) Compute relevance of exercise cases by counting the number of relevant subcases.
(3) Select the exercise case with the largest number of relevant subcases as the most relevant exercise case.

The most relevant exercise case is then adapted to produce a new exercise to meet the identified training goals. In the adaptation, relevant subcases are combined with the exercis ecase if required.

6.3 Combination of Exercises and Problem Situations

The generation of a new exercise in our approach can be described as adapting the relevant exercise case along with combination of relevant subcases from multiple cases. Such a step aims to produce an exercise which provides the context for the student to perform conflict resolution tasks related to the identified training goals. The overall process for exercise generation includes:

(1) Removing from the selected exercise case the subcases reflecting unnecessary training topics
(2) For each topic identified in the new training goals
    if it is not reflected in the selected exercise
        (2.1) selecting one subcase from the list of relevant subcases;
        (2.2) combining the subcase with the selected exercise case

Step (1) is to ensure that the new exercise does not reflect training topics which are not related to the training goals. Step (2.2) is to integrate relevant problem situations into a new exercise. It must deal with the combination of abstract description of problem situations as well as the combination of physical context of ATC scenarios. In this step, engineering knowledge regarding ATC scenarios is applied to guide the combination of physical contexts. Such knowledge represents how to merge the contexts of various problem situations in the levels of airspace, aircraft performance, flight data, routes etc. The creation of ATC scenarios to meet certain requirements is not a trivial task. Roberts's [14] scenario designer provides a process for constructing physical description of ATC scenarios, which will be applied for combining ATC scenarios in our approach.

7 Conclusions

Exercise design is a key feature in developing intelligent training environment for operational skill training. The design of training exercises is viewed here as a problem solving process that searches for those appropriate training tasks and problem situations to fit the patterns of skills and weaknesses that characterise the individual student. We have identified three knowledge components that an exercise design process requires. An approach for exercise design using CBR techniques has been developed.

The overall process model in this paper is presented. Such a process is not intended as a complete model of training and parts relevant to instruction are excluded. For example, we do not discuss interaction and intervention tactics that are used to guide student through local difficulties. Our system is currently under implementation.

Our further considerations include a three level representation of training goals and more coverage of training tasks in training goals. First, the current training goals is concerned only with operational skill with regard to conflict resolution. This can be extended based on three levels of knowledge: declarative, procedural and operational knowledge. Accordingly, the training exercises can be designed for three types of training goals. Second, currently, the training goals focus on conflict resolution. The extension of coverage of training goals will be another further work, for example, the training goals include traffic handling, coordination between controlled areas.

8 References

1. Alem, L. & Keeling, R. Intelligent simulation environment, an application to air traffic control training, In *Proceedings of SimTecT'96*.
2. Ashley, K. D. and Aleven, V. (1991) A computational approach to case-based concepts of relevance in a tutorial context. *Proceedings of the DARPA Workshop on Case-Based Reasoning*. Morgan Kaufmann: Palo Alto. May 8-10. (Washinton, D.C.)
3. Barr, A., Beard, M. and Atkinson, R. C. (1976) The computer as a tutorial laboratory: the standford BIP project. *Man-Machine Studies,* Vol. **8**: 567-596.

4.   Brusilovsky, P.L. (1992). A framework for intelligent knowledge sequencing and task sequencing. In C.Frasson, G. Gauthier, & G. I. McCalla (Eds.), *Proceedings of 2nd International Conference, ITS'92*, pp. 499-506. Berlin: Springer-Verlag.
5.   Chu, R. W., Mitchell, C. M. and Jones, P. M. (1995) Using the operator function model and OFMspert as the basis for an intelligent tutoring system, *IEEE Transactions on Systems, Man and Cybernetics* Vol. **25**(7): 054-1075.
6.   Domeshek, E. and Kolodner, J. L. (1993) Findings the points of large cases. *Artificial Intelligence for Engineering Design, Analysis and Manufacturing,* Vol **7**(2): 87-96.
7.   Halff, H. M. (1998) Curriculum and instruction in automated tutors. *Foundations of Intelligent Tutoring Systems*, ed., Polson, M. C. & Richardson, J. J. Lawrence Erlbaum: New Jersey.
8.   Katz, S., Lesgold, A., Eggan, G., Gordin, M., and Greenberg, L. (1992). Self-adjusting curriculum planning in Sherlock II. In I. Tomek (Eds.), *Proceedings of 4th International Conferences, ICCAL'92.* pp 345-355. Berlin: Springer-Verlag.
9.   Maher, M. L., Balachandran, M. B. and Zhang, D. M. (1995) *Case-Based Reasoning in Design*, Lawrence Erlbaum: New Jersey.
10. McArthur, D., Stasz, C. and Holla, J. (1988) Skill-oriented task sequencing in an intelligent tutor for basic algebra. *Instructional Science* **17**: 281-307.
11   McCalla, G.I. (1990). SCENT-3: An architecture for intelligent advising in problem-solving domains. In C. Frasson & G. Gauthier (Eds.), *Intelligent Tutoring Systems: At the crossroads of artificial intelligence and education,* Norwood: Ablex.
12. Petrushin, V.A. (1995) Intelligent tutoring systems: architecture and methods of implementation. *Computer and Systems Sciences* , Vol **33**(1) pp 117-139.
13. Reimann, P. and Beller, S. (1993). Computer-based support for analogical problem solving and learning. *Simulation-Based Experiential Learning*, ed., D. Towne, T. de Jong & H. Spada (Hrsg). Berlin: Springer, pp 91-104.
14. Roberts, W. A., Felarca, N. R., Harrington, J. E. and Shiotsuki, C. (1994) An automated tool for designing and producing air traffic control scenarios. http://www.caasd.org/html_files/MP94W06/MP94W06.html.
15. Vassileva, J. (1995). Dynamic Courseware Generation: at the cross point of CAL, ITS and authoring. In D. Jonassen & G. McCalla (Eds.) *Proceedings of International Conference, ICCE'95*, pp. 290297. AACE.
16. Wescourt, K., Beard, M. and Gould, L. (1977) Knowledge-based adaptive curriculum sequencing for CAI. *Proceedings of The National ACM Conf.* (Seattle, Washington), pp 234-240.
17. Yacef, K. and Alem, L. (1996) Student and expert modelling for simulation-based training : a cost effective framework. In *Proceedings of International Conference, ITS'96.*
18. Zhang, D. M. (1994) *A Hybrid Design Process Model Using Case-Based Reasoning,* PhD Thesis, Department of Architectural and Design Science, University of Sydney.

Acknowledgments

We would like to thank Airservices Australia and Royal Australian Air Force for giving us access to the ATC instructors. We are grateful to Grahame Smith, Director of CRC-IDS and all the ATEEG team members, Richard Keeling (from Adacle Pty Ltd), David Kemp (from University of Melbourne), Gil Tihnar and Jamie Curmi (from Australian Artificial Intelligence Institute), Kalina Yacef (from Thomson Radar Australian Corp.) for the discussions on the project. We would also like to thank reviewers for their valuable comments and pointers to the literature.

Adaptive Assessment Using Granularity Hierarchies and Bayesian Nets

Jason A. Collins[1], Jim E. Greer[1], and Sherman X. Huang[2]

[1] ARIES Laboratory, University of Saskatchewan
[2] Alberta Research Council, Calgary AB Canada

Abstract. Adaptive testing is impractical in real world situations where many different learner traits need to be measured in a single test. Recent student modelling approaches have attempted to solve this problem using different course representations along with sound knowledge propagation schemes. This paper shows that these different representations can be merged together and realized in a granularity hierarchy. Bayesian inference can be used to propagate knowledge throughout the hierarchy. This provides information for selecting appropriate test items and maintains a measure of the student's knowledge level.

1 Introduction

Much of the previous work in computer adaptive testing has been concerned with testing a single, atomic learner trait [9, 8]. This approach needs to be extended to be considered useful in the intelligent tutoring systems field. Recent research in student modelling has attempted to allow testing of multiple learner traits in one model [2, 7, 6, 3, 1]. Each of these papers introduces a novel approach towards testing multiple learner traits. The strengths of these separate notions need to be unified in a single adaptive testing environment.

Granularity hierarchies [4] provide the required structure for such a union. Prerequisite relationships can provide test item ordering criteria. Aggregation relationships can be used to break multiple trait components into more fundamental components. Aggregation relationships can also capture multiple model representation and equivalence groups using the AND–OR clustering scheme implicit in granularity. In addition, further controls over the granularity hierarchy can make the testing procedure much more efficient and perhaps more effective than other ad hoc representation schemes.

Martin et al. have suggested that any assessment procedure must be founded in a statistically sound, defensible technique [3]. Their approach uses Bayesian belief networks to update their student model. It is not a difficult extension to superimpose a Bayesian belief network atop a granularity hierarchy. The Bayes net can be used to propagate knowledge from evidence (the observers or test items) through the aggregation and prerequisite links to coarser grain sizes until the coarsest grain size (i.e., the root of the granularity hierarchy) is reached. Bayes nets can accurately update the current belief about a learner's knowledge at all grain sizes contained within the hierarchy.

2 Course Hierarchies

Most types of educational course curricula consist of learning objectives with specific achievement levels, a prerequisite map of the content domain, a set of test items, and varying modes of presentation depending on the needs of the learner. From an adaptive testing point of view, the varying modes of presentation may take the form of asking different learners different types of questions depending upon their internal mental models [6]. Granularity hierarchies provide the structure necessary to capture all of these curriculum requirements.

Granularity refers to the level-of-detail or perspective from which a concept or entity is viewed [4]. A granularity hierarchy captures different levels of detail in a type of semantic network. This semantic network identifies both aggregation and prerequisite relationships in two orthogonal dimensions.

The aggregation dimension allows higher–level concepts to be broken down into subcomponents. Imagine the concept of *elementary arithmetic*. This concept can be broken down, for example, into four subcomponents: *addition, multiplication, subtraction,* and *division.* Figure 1 illustrates such a break down.

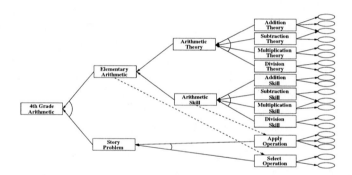

Fig. 1. The *4th Grade arithmetic* domain showing conditional dependencies

Clusters allow us to represent two or more different views of the same concept. For example, one cluster could consist of the practical skills associated with addition, subtraction, multiplication, and division, while another cluster could consist of the theoretical understanding of the four operations. Clusters are depicted by arcs in the hierarchy of Figure 1. Knowledge of at least one of these two clusters might be enough to constitute knowledge of the higher concept *elementary arithmetic.* That is, concepts within one cluster are related through an AND relationship; concepts in different clusters are related through an OR relationship.

Prerequisite links offer a second, orthogonal dimension in which to capture knowledge. For example, the knowledge of *arithmetic skill* can be considered prerequisite knowledge for *apply operation.* This prerequisite relation is indicated by the dashed lines in Figure 1. Clusters can also be used in the prerequisite dimension to capture AND-OR relationships.

Observers are the final component in granularity hierarchies. Any path in the hierarchy through the aggregation dimension is terminated by an observer. In adaptive testing, observers represent test items. The parents of an observer are the primitive learning objectives that are directly measured by that test item.

Primitive learning objectives can be considered the finest–grained level of course decomposition, and consequently are amenable to direct testing. It is at this primitive concept level that most of the work in pure adaptive testing has been done (i.e., at the level of a single, assessable learner trait). Much of that work has been focused on extensive empirical validation [9, 8]. Frequently, however, some higher level unit (e.g., a concept or a course module) consisting of many learning objectives needs to be assessed. Student mastery of these learning objectives must combine together in well–defined ways to form an overall assessment. The aggregation dimension of a granularity hierarchy handles this task nicely. Assessment performed at the finest grain size can now be propagated in some manner to the coarser grain sizes.

A typical weakness of current adaptive testing systems is that there is no guarantee that each learning objective will be adequately tested. That is, there is no guarantee as to the *content balance* of the adaptive test. The aggregation dimension of granularity hierarchies helps to ensure that adaptive tests are content balanced. Once this hierarchy has been built, the adaptive testing routine need only ensure that each node of interest is tested to some instructor–defined extent. This is ensured through Bayesian propagation and clustering both in the aggregation and prerequisite dimensions.

Prerequisite relations help to guide test ordering. For example, it may be desirable to begin to assess students on items having a moderate number of prerequisites. Simple items may bore the learner, difficult items may frustrate the learner. Prerequisites also help reduce test length by adding another dimension across which knowledge propagation may occur. For example, if a learner demonstrates mastery of some concept, one can infer that they have a working knowledge of its prerequisite items. Conversely, if a learner has not mastered some concept, one can draw some fairly strong conclusions about knowledge of follow–up concepts.

Any adaptive testing system needs test items. The test items are modelled within a granularity hierarchy as observers: the leaves of the hierarchy. They can be attached in the aggregation dimension to any concept or learning objective at any of the various levels of granularity. Figure 1 shows a typical set of test items (represented by ellipses). These items are used to directly assess the attached learning objective. These test items do not have to be simplistic, traditional test questions. They can be examples, exercises, or long answer questions provided that there is diagnostic power within the observer to assess the "correctness" of the learner's response; that is, there must be a diagnostic mechanism powerful enough to deem a learner response correct or incorrect.

Clustering can be used to represent AND–OR relationships in the aggregation dimension of the course hierarchy. These clusters may also be used to represent fundamental differences in the mode of presentation to and testing of a learner.

For example, elementary arithmetic consists of theoretical learning objectives OR practical learning objectives (see Figure 1). A learner who can display mastery in at least one of these two clusters is considered to have mastered the overall topic. This method can be used to describe and represent Sime's multiple models [6] and Villano's equivalency groups [7].

3 Adaptive Testing

Granularity hierarchies can merge many different course representations into one consistent scheme. Assessment can be performed at any level of granularity within this hierarchy. However, since testing one node within the hierarchy may have an effect on possibly many nodes, knowledge must be propagated throughout this hierarchy. A Bayesian network, superimposed on top of the granularity hierarchy, becomes a vehicle for this knowledge propagation.

Bayesian networks implicitly represent arbitrary conditional probability distributions without explicitly specifying the full joint distribution. This is accomplished by identifying which variables are truly dependent in a directed graph. Once this is done, conditional probabilities need to be specified only for variables that are directly dependent; all other conditional probabilities can be calculated using Bayesian inference.

There are two important aspects in adaptive testing of multiple learning objectives: accurately updating belief about mastery of each learning objective and selecting the most appropriate test item to pose next. Bayes nets offer a mechanism powerful enough to perform both of these tasks. Using a repetitive process of test item selection followed by knowledge propagation based on a student's answer, an adaptive testing system is produced.

3.1 Knowledge Propagation

There are many different algorithms for propagating belief through a Bayes net. The approach in this paper uses Shachter, D'Ambrosio and DelFavero's SPI algorithm [5]. While issues of Bayesian belief propagation efficiency are not the primary concern in this paper, the complexity of specifying a Bayes net is. In order for it to be truly useful, a course instructor must be able to construct a Bayes net for a course with a minimal amount of effort. It is hoped that the required conditional probabilities can be obtained through empirical measurement or instructor experience and honed over time — additional research is needed on this topic.

There are often a large number of test items for a particular learning objective. If one chooses to make the mastery of the learning objective dependent on the answers to the associated n test items, and assumes the binary result of answering a question (either correct or incorrect), the course instructor must supply 2^n probabilities in order to specify the Bayes net. Clearly, this is impractical for any real world situation. Turning the arrows around (i.e. the answer to the test items is dependent on the mastery level of the learning objective), the course instructor needs to supply only two conditional probabilities for each test item $(2n)$. This latter approach has been found to be empirically plausible [9]. Of course, when test items are attached to multiple learning objectives, the full joint probability (2^k) needs to be specified (where k is the number of learning objectives to which the test item is attached). However, a test item will infrequently be attached to more than two or three learning objectives.

It is desirable further up the course hierarchy to model AND–OR clusters as "noisy-OR" and "noisy-AND" constructs. This improves the computational tractability of the Bayesian inference. To do this, the dependence arrows must point toward the root of the granularity hierarchy. Similarly, the arrows representing prerequisite links must be positioned to make use of AND-OR clustering. Utilizing these noisy gates, the instructor need not supply a full joint distribution for each learning objective, he / she merely has to supply two probabilities for each attached learning objective plus an overall "leakage" value indicating the amount of interaction between the objects in the cluster.

With this construction, the only variables that are not conditioned are the primitive, atomic learning objectives. Without empirical data, the prior probabilities of these nodes may be set to some default level, say 0.5. That is, a given learner may have a 50/50 a priori chance of being a master or nonmaster of any particular atomic learning objective. Arrows in Figure 1 illustrate the conditional dependencies described above.

3.2 Item Selection

In selecting an appropriate test item to pose, a number of factors must be considered. First an item must be informative. The ideal question should perfectly distinguish mastery from non-mastery. Second, content balancing must be ensured. All finer–grained learning objectives of the concept being assessed should be tested. Finally, the notion of item difficulty should be considered.

Decreasing test length is one of the main goals of adaptive testing [9]. In order to quickly terminate a test, an adaptive testing scheme must choose items that most quickly differentiate between mastery and nonmastery. Using Bayes nets, one can calculate both the probability of mastery of a learning objective A given that a student gets a particular test item Q correct $(P(A_M|Q))$, and the probability of nonmastery of A given that the student answers Q incorrectly $(P(A_N|\overline{Q}))$. Each time a question is to be posed, these two values may be calculated for each test item in the hierarchy; the difference between these two values forms a utility score for each test item.

$$utility_Q \leftarrow \left| P\left(A_M|Q\right) - P\left(A_N|\overline{Q}\right) \right|$$

Test items with higher utility have higher discrimination, that is, they give more information towards distinguishing a master from a nonmaster. These items should be favoured in the test item selection.

A well designed hierarchy will make extensive use of clustering and prerequisite links. Choosing appropriate probabilities for the various items, the instructor can ensure a content balanced test. That is, the Bayesian propagation will force the selection of test items such that a content balanced test is formed. Similarly, choosing appropriate probabilities for prerequisite links causes the adaptive test to quickly focus to the learner's skill level. An incorrect response to a prerequisite item should quickly decrease the network's belief in a follow-up item.

3.3 Test Completion

Testing is complete when the knowledge rating of the coarsest–grained concept being assessed (the goal) increases above a certain instructor–specified level (called the mastery level) or below another instructor–specified level (called the nonmastery level). Finer–grained objectives of the concept being assessed may be in one of three states at test completion: mastered, nonmastered, or uncertain. For a more complete assessment, a change in heuristic will force the adaptive testing algorithm to test to completion *all* children of a particular goal node. That is, the algorithm will ask as many questions as is necessary to determine the mastery/nonmastery of each and every child node of a particular goal node. Using this scheme, a formative assessment is created and the instructor can then browse through all of the different grain sizes represented within the granularity hierarchy to see the learner's achievement at any grain size.

4 Preliminary Results

Simulations were performed on three different hierarchies in order to quantitatively show the efficacy of this approach. Hierarchy A (Figure 2(A)) is a form of the granularity hierarchy described in this paper. There are ten primitive learning objectives; each has five questions attached to it. The Bayesian conditional dependencies are indicated by the direction of the arrows. Note that all clusters depicted with arcs are AND clusters. Hierarchy B (Figure 2(B)) is a "flattened" version of A with all intermediate concepts removed. The only ones that remain are the primitive learning objectives and the overall root concept. The overall root concept is conditionally dependent on all of the primitives; each primitive is conditionally dependent on its attached test items. The conditional probabilities for this hierarchy were generated from A, therefore, the two hierarchies are, as close as possible, equivalent. Finally, Hierarchy C (Figure 2(C)) is similar to B except that the arrow directions have been reversed in an effort to reduce the number of conditional dependencies that need to specified. As with B, the conditional probabilities for Hierarchy C were generated from A; and thus the two hierarchies are as similar as possible.

In total, twelve simulations were run. Each simulation repeatedly posed test items to a simulated learner who answered them correctly with a given probabilty (i.e., 1.0, 0.8, 0.2, 0.0). After each learner response to a test item, each hierarchy was updated with the new information and a new test item was posed. This looping continued until the learner was classified a master or a nonmaster at the top level root concept.

Table 1 indicates the results of the twelve simulations. **Conditional Probabilities Required** indicates how many conditional probabilities had to be manually pre–set to specify the corresponding Bayes network. **Probability of**

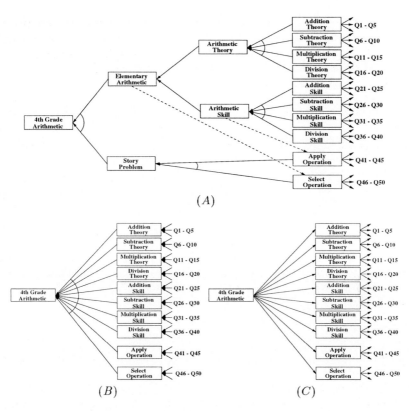

Fig. 2. Course hierarchies used in simulation runs

Correct Answer indicates the probability that the simulated learner would respond correctly to any given test item. **Test Length** indicates the number of test items that were posed before the test completed. Finally, **Coverage** is a ratio indicating the number of learning objectives from which at least one test item was posed divided by the number of learning objectives that must be covered in order to be considered complete. Note that the denominator of this ratio is determined using only the knowledge contained directly in the hierarchy. For example, the number of nodes in Hierarchy B that must be covered is 10, while the number of nodes that must be covered in Hierarchy A is significantly less due to the knowledge provided by prerequisite links and AND–OR clusters.

The results suggest that Hierarchy A seems to win both in terms of test length and content coverage. Hierarchy B is almost as competent in the content coverage aspect, but is more expensive to generate because many more conditional probabilities need be given for the Bayes net specification. In addition, test lengths for Hierarchy B were longer. Hierarchy C is actually somewhat simpler to specify than A, and its test lengths were approximately the same; unfortunately there were no guarantees about content coverage. In fact, the algorithm for Hierarchy C seemed to pick test items almost randomly.

Hierarchy Tested	Conditional Probabilities Required	Probability of Correct Answer	Test Length	Coverage
A	155	1.0	20	1.00
		0.8	21	1.00
		0.2	44	1.00
		0.0	14	0.83
		Average	**24.8**	**0.96**
B	1345	1.0	30	0.90
		0.8	36	0.90
		0.2	39	0.90
		0.0	31	0.90
		Average	**34.0**	**0.90**
C	122	1.0	41	1.00
		0.8	50	1.00
		0.2	12	0.70
		0.0	4	0.40
		Average	**26.8**	**0.78**

Table 1. Adaptive testing preliminary results

5 Discussion

Granularity offers many advantages in the area of student modelling and adaptive testing. Granularity hierarchies provide a structured and well–defined knowledge representation scheme for courses. Bayesian networks can be easily superimposed atop the granularity hierarchy to perform belief propagation. Clusters allow various efficiency gains in the Bayesian inference and conditional probability specification. The granularity hierarchy / Bayesian network symbiosis proves better than a flat concept testing scheme on simulated adaptive testing scenarios in terms of knowledge engineering of conditional probabilities, test length, and content coverage.

The granularity hierarchies discussed here have been very limited in their scope; that is, they have been used for the purpose of adaptive testing only. Much of the power of granularity hierarchies has not been taken advantage of in this simplification. For example, instead of having a test item explicitly selected (active testing), the observers could merely wait passively in the background of an intelligent tutoring system for student behaviour to occur. Once a particular behaviour is observed, the knowledge propagation algorithm can be used to update the belief net. This passive observation is really a form of student modelling. With no significant changes to our representation or algorithms, this system can be used for adaptive testing, student modelling, or some combination of both. For example, a student may be adaptively pretested on entry into a course or module to determine the most appropriate presentation methods. During content presentation and practice, the hierarchy can passively observe the student, perhaps adapting the presentation methods again if problems arise and adjusting belief in the student's mastery level. Once the student has reached certain instructor defined criteria, an adpative posttest can be performed (if desired).

Two further items need to be performed as part of this research. First, the validity of the adaptive assessment must be studied. Through the use of either real data or data based on synthesized students, the precision of the adaptive test must be measured. Second, studies need to be performed using real student data and real course hierarchies. It is not yet completely known how this model will scale up to a real–world situation. Large increases in the test item bank and complex concept interactions may make the exact evaluation of a Bayes network intractable and force the use of an approximation method.

We have shown in this paper that many approaches to course curriculum representation can be merged into the single model presented by granularity hierarchies. Superimposing a Bayesian belief network atop this hierarchy provides the sound belief propagation method. Finally, adaptive testing and student modelling have been merged into a single continuum.

Acknowledgements: We would like to thank the Natural Science and Engineering Research Council of Canada and the Alberta Research Council for funding this work.

References

1. C. Conati and K. VanLehn. POLA: a student modeling framework for Probabilistic On-Line Assessment of problem solving performance. In *Proceedings of the Fifth International Conference on User Modeling*, pages 75–82, 1996. Kailua–Kona, Hawaii.
2. C. E. Dowling and R. Kaluscha. Prerequisite relationships for the adaptive assessment of knowledge. In *Proceedings of the Conference on Artificial Intelligence in Education*, pages 43–58, 1995. Washington, D.C.
3. J. Martin and K. VanLehn. A Bayesian approach to cognitive assessment. In P. Nichols, S. Chipman, and R. L. Brennan, editors, *Cognitively Diagnostic Assessment*, pages 141–165. LEA, Hillsdale, NJ., 1995.
4. G. I. McCalla and J. E. Greer. Granularity–based reasoning and belief revision in student models. In J. E. Greer and G. I. McCalla, editors, *Student Modelling: The Key to Individualized Knowledge–Based Instruction*, pages 39–62. Springer–Verlag, Berlin, 1994.
5. R. Shachter, B. D'Ambrosio, and B. DelFavero. Symbolic probabilistic inference in belief networks. In *Proceedings Eighth National Conference on AI*, pages 126–131. AAAI, August 1990.
6. J.-A. Sime. Modelling a learner's multiple models with Bayesian belief networks. In *Proceedings of the Conference on Artificial Intelligence in Education*, pages 426–432, 1993. Edinburgh, Scotland.
7. M. Villano. Probabilistic student models: Bayesian belief networks and knowledge space theory. In *Proceedings of the Second International Conference on Intelligent Tutoring Systems*, pages 491–498, 1992. Montréal, Canada.
8. D. Weiss and G. Kingsbury. Application of computerized adaptive testing to educational problems. *Journal of Educational Measurement*, 12:361–375, 1984.
9. R. E. Welch and T. W. Frick. Computerized adaptive testing in instructional settings. *Educational Technology Research and Development*, 41(3):47–62, 1993.

Adaptive Assessment and Training Using the Neighbourhood of Knowledge States

Cornelia E. Dowling, Cord Hockemeyer, Andreas H. Ludwig

Technische Universität Carolo Wilhelmina zu Braunschweig
Institut für Psychologie
Abteilung für Mathematische und Sozialpsychologie
38092 Braunschweig, Germany
E–Mail: { C.Dowling | C.Hockemeyer | A.Ludwig } @ tu–bs.de

Abstract. In this paper, we suggest methods for the adaptive assessment and training of students. The main idea is to apply the theoretical concept of the neighbourhood of a knowledge state to adaptive training. We also describe improvements of existing assessment algorithms. These ideas are implemented in a multi–platform tutoring system shell. This shell has been applied to two different fields of knowledge.

1 Introduction

Doignon and Falmagne (1985) suggested a mathematical framework for the adaptive assessment of knowledge. Subsequently, deterministic and probabilistic algorithms were developed which are suitable for posing questions to a student dependent on his/her individual knowledge (Falmagne and Doignon, 1988a,b). Such an adaptive assessment algorithm requires a large pool of *items* from a specified field of knowledge. These items are, for example, classes of equivalent examination questions as they are used in schools.

For each individual student, a small number of questions are sequentially selected from this large item pool, and presented to the student. With each new question, the student's answers to the previous questions are taken into account. In this manner, selecting new questions is increasingly adapted to the student's individual knowledge. As a result of assessing the student, we obtain the student's *knowledge state*. A knowledge state has been defined as the subset of items from the large item pool that can be mastered by the student (Doignon and Falmagne, 1985). Such an adaptive procedure makes use of *prerequisite relationships* between the items. Prerequisite relationships are, for example, obtained by querying experts with the help of a computerized procedure (Dowling and Kaluscha, 1995). The following example illustrates a set of items and their prerequisite relationships.

Example 1. We show five items from a project, in which we developed a system with 77 items from the field of fractions (Baumunk, 1995).

a   Subtraction of fractions without a common denominator.
b   Addition of mixed numbers.

c   Addition of fractions without a common denominator.

d   Addition of fractions with a common denominator.

e   Finding the least common multiple.

For these items, one expert determined the prerequisite relationships represented by the following statements:

1. *If a student masters item a, then he/she masters at least one of its prerequisites b, or c.*
2. *If a student masters item b, then he/she also masters its prerequisite d.*
3. *If a student masters item c, then he/she also masters all of its prerequisites d and e.*

If these prerequisite relationships are valid, then only those subsets of the item set $\{a, b, c, d, e\}$ can be considered to be knowledge states which do not "contradict" the statements 1, 2, and 3 above. For example, the set $\{a, b\}$ is not a knowledge state because it contains item b, but not its prerequisite item d, and hence contradicts statement 2. A subset contradicting statement 1 is, for example, the set $\{a, d, e\}$ which is not a knowledge state, either. Examples of knowledge states are the sets $\{d\}$, $\{b, d\}$, and $\{b, d, e\}$.

For a given set of prerequisite relationships, the set of all knowledge states constitutes a *knowledge space*. A knowledge space $\mathcal{K}$ is a family of subsets of a finite item set Q which contains the empty set $\emptyset$ and the item set Q itself, and which is closed under union, i.e. the set union of each subset of the family $\mathcal{K}$ is an element of $\mathcal{K}$.

Example 2. The set of all knowledge states which are possible if the prerequisite relationships in Example 1 hold, are illustrated by the Hasse–diagram of Fig. 1, which shows that the set is closed under union. The line surrounding some of the states marks the neighbourhood of the knowledge state $\{b, d\}$. The concept of the neighbourhood of a knowledge state will be introduced below.

In one of their probabilistic assessment procedures, Falmagne and Doignon (1988b) use the concept of the *neighbourhood* of a knowledge state which comprises all other states with a distance of at most one. The distance $d(K, K')$ between two knowledge states K and K' is equal to the size of their symmetric set difference, $d(K, K') = |K \Delta K'| = |(K \setminus K') \cup (K' \setminus K)|$. They use this concept to define the *fringe* of a knowledge state which is defined to be the set of items by which the knowledge state differs from its neighbours.

The main suggestion of this paper is to apply the concept of the fringe of a knowledge state not only to assessment but also to training. Suppose that, for each item, we have several equivalent problems which are designed to test whether this item is mastered or not. Equivalent problems for testing item a in Example 1 are, for instance, $\frac{3}{10} - \frac{1}{4}$, and $\frac{2}{15} - \frac{1}{10}$. A method that we recommend for selecting problems for training is to take items from the fringe of the student's knowledge state, and to offer problems belonging to these items as exercises. In that manner we are able to adapt the exercises to his/her individual knowledge.

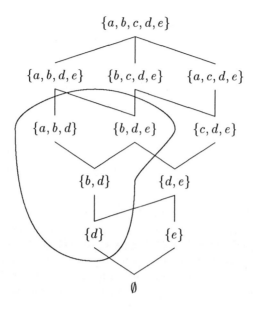

$\{a, b, c, d, e\}$

$\{a, b, d, e\}$ $\{b, c, d, e\}$ $\{a, c, d, e\}$

$\{a, b, d\}$ $\{b, d, e\}$ $\{c, d, e\}$

$\{b, d\}$ $\{d, e\}$

$\{d\}$ $\{e\}$

$\emptyset$

Fig. 1. Neighbourhood of knowledge states

Example 3. Consider the knowledge space $\mathcal{K}$ from Example 2. The neighbourhood of the knowledge state $K = \{b, d\}$ is the set $N(K) = \{\{d\}, \{b, d\}, \{a, b, d\}, \{b, d, e\}\}$. As Fig. 1 shows this is the set of all states which can be reached from the knowledge state $K = \{b, d\}$ in 0 or 1 steps following the edges of the Hasse–diagram. The fringe of the knowledge state K is the set $F(K) = \{a, b, e\}$.

For a student with the knowledge state $\{b, d\}$, it makes sense to practice item b, since it is the item which has been learned most recently. The items a and e are those new items which are recommended to be learned next, since all of their prerequisites are known.

In Sect. 2, we suggest an efficient procedure for the assessment of students' knowledge states and for computing their fringes. In Sect. 3, we describe a robust multi–platform tool which we use for adaptive assessment and training in the neighbourhood of knowledge states, and as a system for authoring new problems. The system is a shell which enables the usage of different assessment and training algorithms with different structures of prerequisite relationships and sets of items.

2 Efficient Procedures for the Adaptive Assessment and Training

Applications of knowledge space theory to different fields of knowledge have shown that the resulting knowledge spaces can grow very large, and nevertheless be efficient for assessment (Baumunk, 1995). For these large knowledge spaces, the algorithms by Falmagne and Doignon (1988a,b) for assessing a knowledge state and for computing its fringe need a large amount of computer memory, and computing time. In this section, we introduce more efficient algorithms for the adaptive assessment, and for determining the fringe of a knowledge state. The structural information about the knowledge domain represented by knowledge spaces can also be represented by other, equivalent structures used by the new algorithms.

A knowledge state K is called *minimal* for an item $q \in K$ if there exists no other knowledge state K' which contains item q, and is a subset of K. A knowledge state can be minimal for several items and, vice versa, an item can have several minimal states. These minimal states cannot be built as a union of other knowledge states. The set of all knowledge states which are minimal for at least one item is called the *basis* of a knowledge space. The basis is the smallest family of knowledge states from which the complete knowledge space can be reconstructed by closure under union (Doignon and Falmagne, 1985).

Example 4. Figure 1 shows a knowledge space $\mathcal{K}$ on the item set $Q = \{a, b, c, d, e\}$. The basis $\mathcal{B}$ of this knowledge space is the set of the knowledge states $\{d\}$, $\{e\}$, $\{b, d\}$, $\{a, b, d\}$, $\{c, d, e\}$, and $\{a, c, d, e\}$. These states are minimal for the items d, e, b, a, c, and a, respectively.

The main idea behind the basis–based assessment algorithm is to interpret the basis as a set of rules, as follows (Hockemeyer, 1993). For any set of items, we say that a student *masters* the set of items if and only if he/she masters all the items within the set. Since each knowledge state can be constructed as a union of elements of the basis, the following two statements are valid:

(i) *A student masters an item q if and only if he/she masters at least one of its minimal states.*

(ii) *A student masters an element of the basis if and only if he/she masters all the items contained in this element.*

Our assessment procedure constructs a constraint network in the following manner. The variables of this network are the mastery of the items, as well as the mastery of the elements of the basis. The relations between these variables are statements of the form (i) and (ii) above. The variables can have one out of three values: *"is mastered"*, *"is not mastered"*, and *"mastery is unknown"*. The assessment procedure can now be considered as solving a constraint satisfaction problem.

Simulation studies have shown that, as a rule, the space–based assessment procedure developed by Falmagne and Doignon (1988a,b) tests a slightly smaller number of items to complete an assessment than the basis–based procedure. On the other hand, the basis–based procedure needs much less computing time and memory than the space–based procedure (Hockemeyer, 1993).

Example 5. Consider the knowledge space used throughout this paper. The left side of Fig. 2 shows the constraint network with the items and basis elements as described above. Suppose that item b is presented to the student first, and that the student answers the question correctly. Then we can conclude that he/she also masters the basis element $\{b, d\}$, and hence, also the item d and its minimal element $\{d\}$. These items and basis elements are marked with an oval in Fig. 2(i). The items b and d are not considered any longer, since we know that the student masters them. Suppose that item a is asked next and that the student gives a false answer. We can now conclude that he/she does not master the basis elements $\{a, b, d\}$ and $\{a, c, d, e\}$, either. Assume that we choose item e next and that the student does not master this item. Now, we can infer that he/she does not master the basis elements $\{e\}$ and $\{c, d, e\}$ and hence, that he/she does not master item c either. The right side of Fig. 2 shows the resulting assessment state. We know for all items and basis elements whether the student masters them or not and, therefore, have finished the assessment. The student's knowledge state can be determined as the set of all items or the union of all basis elements which are marked as mastered by the student. This state is the set $\{b, d\}$.

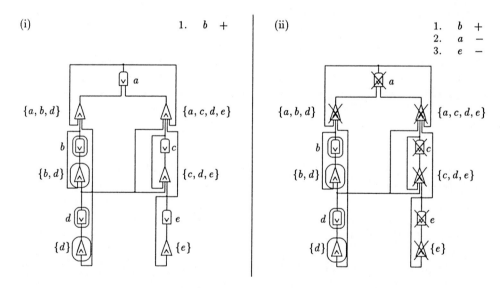

Knowledge state assessed: $\{b, d\}$.

Fig. 2. Knowledge assessment using the basis of a knowledge space

For selecting the training problems from the fringe of a knowledge state, we also need a basis–based procedure to compute it. There are two ways for different cases to test whether or not an item q belongs to the fringe of a knowledge state.

(i) An item q which is not a member of the knowledge state K is an element of the fringe $F(K)$ if there is a minimal element B for the item q such that $B \setminus \{q\} \subseteq K$. (ii) An item q which is a member of the knowledge state K is an element of the fringe $F(K)$ if the set difference of the knowledge state K and the union of specific basis elements is equal to the set $\{q\}$. These basis elements are those which are subset of K but do not contain the item q (Hockemeyer, 1996).

Example 6. Consider the knowledge space and the basis from the Examples 2 and 4. To compute the neighbourhood of the knowledge state $K = \{b, d\}$, we make a case distinction between the items b and d which are elements of the state K, and the items a, c, and e which are not. For item a, we have two minimal elements, $\{a, b, d\}$ and $\{a, c, d, e\}$. Since the set difference $\{a, b, d\} \setminus \{a\}$ is a subset of K, item a is a member of the fringe $F(K)$. The item c has one minimal element, $\{c, d, e\}$. The set $\{d, e\} = \{c, d, e\} \setminus \{c\}$ is not a subset of K. Therefore, c is not a member of $F(K)$. For item e, we get $\{e\} \setminus \{e\} = \emptyset$. The empty set $\emptyset$ is a subset of K and, hence, e is an element of the fringe $F(K)$.

The items b and d are members of the knowledge state K. Therefore, we have to use the other procedure for these items. For item b, there exists one element $\{d\}$ of the basis which is subset of $\{b, d\}$ and does not contain item b. We determine the ordinary set difference $\{b, d\} \setminus \{d\} = \{b\}$. Therefore, the item b is an element of the fringe $F(K)$. For item d, there exists no element of the basis which is a subset of $\{b, d\}$ and does not contain item d. So, we have to compute the set difference of the knowledge state K and the empty set $\emptyset$. This is the state K which is unequal to the set $\{d\}$. Therefore, item d is not a member of the fringe $F(K)$. As a result, we obtain the set $\{a, b, e\}$ to be the fringe $F(K)$.

3 A Tool for Assessment and Training

To put the algorithms introduced above into practice, Ludwig (1995) and Winkelmann (1995) developed a shell for the adaptive testing and training, ADASTRA[1]. ADASTRA provides a graphical user interface, and a programming language for computer–based problems. The motivation for building this adaptive assessment and training tool was to be independent of professional software distributors, and to be able to run it on different platforms.

The problems can be presented either in *assessment mode* or in *training mode*. In both modes, ADASTRA presents the problems on the screen, and evaluates the student's input. The training mode offers *feedback* which informs the student on the type of his/her errors. In this mode, the student is also able to request *help texts*. The language for programming testing and training problems contains elements for the layout of the problems, as well as for the evaluation of the students' answers. These elements are either general or specific for the knowledge

---

[1] ADASTRA is implemented in C++ with the wxWindows 1.5 library and runs under MS–Windows 3.11 and Linux. The wxWindows library was developed by Julian Smart et al., University of Edinburgh, Artificial Intelligence Applications Institute, 80 South Bridge, Edinburgh, UK.

domain. An example of a domain specific function is *'fraction(...)'* which can be used for displaying its arguments above and under the line. ADASTRA includes components for presenting the problems, and a development environment for the author of the problems. The former is called *problem presenter*, the latter *authoring environment*. The architecture of the system ADASTRA is shown in Fig. 3.

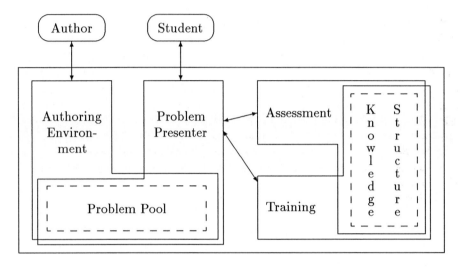

Fig. 3. Architecture of the system ADASTRA

- The authoring environment is a frame, providing file handling, editing, and testing of the problem programs. Additionally, the author can specify which problem programs belong to an item. In the following, the set of all problem programs is called the *problem pool.*
- The problem presenter is the assessment and training environment for the student. It communicates with the assessment or training object, and subsequently presents the problems to the student. This communication is described in more detail below.
- The *assessment object* encapsulates the implementation of an assessment algorithm as, for example, described in Sect. 2. The implemented assessment algorithm accesses the knowledge structure as shown in Fig. 3, and communicates with the problem presenter via the assessment object.
- Figure 3 shows, that the *training object* encapsulates the implementation of the training algorithm described in the Sects. 1 and 2. The implemented training algorithm also accesses the knowledge structure, and communicates with the problem presenter via the training object.

ADASTRA stores the relation on problem programs and items. The problem presenter uses this information. This design has the advantage that the interface between assessment and training object and the problem presenter is simple. In the direction from assessment or training object to problem presenter only an item number is passed and in the reverse direction only a truth value is transmitted. The problem presenter does not access the knowledge structure, and the assessment and training objects do not access the problem pool. The assessment object and its implementation of the assessment algorithm can be exchanged for another one as can the training object with its implementation of the training algorithm and the knowledge structure.

The problem programs are written in the programming language ProLa, an abbreviation for "Problem Language". In each ProLa program, three tasks are specified: (i) Presenting a problem and optionally offering some help text, (ii) reading the student's input, and (iii) checking a student's input for correctness. In step (iii) ProLa programs can display feedback to the student. Figure 4 illustrates how the student sees a problem on the screen. This problem belongs to the item (a) *Subtraction of fractions without a common denominator* from Example 1. It also shows the help frame which is displayed whenever the student clicks on the help button in training mode.

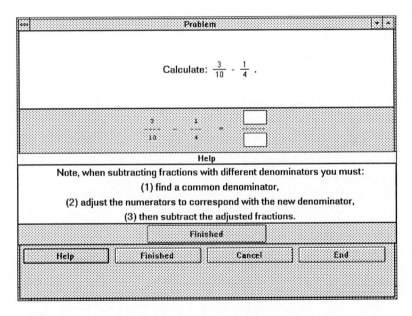

Fig. 4. Display of a problem after clicking on the help button

Presently ADASTRA runs with 77 items from the field of *fractions*. In a second project, a prototype of an assessment and training system in the domain of tax law is being developed.

4 Discussion

We have described an efficient system for the adaptive assessment and training based on the theory of knowledge spaces. It is designed such that the knowledge domains, the knowledge structure representing the prerequisite relationships, and the assessment module can be exchanged easily. Since the teachers are heavily involved in selecting the items, the resulting problem pool is close to the actual curriculum. There are several aspects in which this approach to assessment and training differs from tutoring systems based on cognitive theories as, for example, described by Anderson et al. (1995). The concept of the item as it is used in knowledge space theory integrates both, procedural as well as declarative knowledge. The level of granularity of the items is so fine that items which build on each other differ only very little. Therefore, suitable help can be offered to the student even without cognitive modeling.

References

Anderson, J. R., Corbett, A. T., Koedinger, K. R., and Pelletier, R. (1995). Cognitive tutors: Lessons learned. *The Journal of the Learning Sciences*, 4:167–207.

Baumunk, K. (1995). Die empirische Erhebung einer Struktur von Schulwissen im Fach Mathematik. Diplomarbeit, Technische Universität Carolo-Wilhelmina, Braunschweig, Germany.

Doignon, J.-P. and Falmagne, J.-C. (1985). Spaces for the assessment of knowledge. *International Journal of Man-Machine Studies*, 23:175–196.

Dowling, C. E. and Kaluscha, R. (1995). Prerequisite relationships for the adaptive assessment of knowledge. In Greer, J., editor, *Artificial Intelligence in Education, 1995*, pages 43–50, Charlottesville, VA. Association for the Advancement of Computing in Education (AACE).

Falmagne, J.-C. and Doignon, J.-P. (1988a). A class of stochastic procedures for the assessment of knowledge. *British Journal of Mathematical and Statistical Psychology*, 41:1–23.

Falmagne, J.-C. and Doignon, J.-P. (1988b). A Markovian procedure for assessing the state of a system. *Journal of Mathematical Psychology*, 32:232–258.

Hockemeyer, C. (1993). Wissensdiagnose auf Wissensräumen. Diplomarbeit, Technische Universität Carolo-Wilhelmina, Braunschweig, Germany.

Hockemeyer, C. (1996). Determining the fringe of knowledge states. Submitted.

Ludwig, A. H. (1995). Eine themenorientierte Programmiersprache für die Präsentation und Auswertung computergestützter Test– und übungsaufgaben. Diplomarbeit, Technische Universität Carolo-Wilhelmina, Braunschweig, Germany.

Winkelmann, J. (1995). Ein objektorientiertes Maschinenmodell für die Präsentation und Auswertung computergestützter Test– und übungsaufgaben. Diplomarbeit, Technische Universität Carolo-Wilhelmina, Braunschweig, Germany.

SINT – a Symbolic Integration Tutor

Antonija Mitrović

Computer Science Department,
University of Canterbury, Private Bag 4800,
Christchurch, New Zealand

Abstract. We present an intelligent tutoring system in the area of symbolic integration. The system is capable of solving problems step-by-step along with the student. SINT monitors the student while solving problems, informs the student of errors and provides individualized help and advice when appropriate. The main focus of the research was on student modeling. The technique developed, referred to as INSTRUCT, builds on two well-known paradigms, reconstructive modeling and model tracing, at the same time avoiding their major pitfalls. The approach is not only incremental but truly interactive, since it involves the student in explicit dialogues about his/her goals. The student model is used to guide the generation of instructional actions, like generation of explanations and new problems.

1 Introduction

The effectiveness of Intelligent Tutoring Systems (ITS) depends critically on their ability to offer individualized instruction. These systems employ student models, which enable the selection of instructional content and tutorial strategy, as well as the confirmation of diagnoses. We proposed INSTRUCT, a novel knowledge-driven technique for student modeling. In order to test its effectiveness, we developed an ITS in the area of symbolic integration. The choice of the domain for our system was guided by the availability of domain-specific knowledge, tutors, and students taking relevant university courses. However, the same approach can be utilized in any procedural domain.

In the next section we introduce the architecture of SINT, and present the most important characteristics of its components in the following ones. Finally, conclusions and directions for further research are given in the last section.

2 Architecture of SINT

The basic components of the SINT system are the domain expert, pedagogical module, student modeler and the interface. The expert module is capable of solving problems posed to the student, generating new problems according to the his/her achievements and learning status, and generating explanations in order to remedy student's misconceptions. The student modeler determines the learning status of the student, as detected by the system through the dialogue.

The pedagogical module determines the way of communication, that is the timing, style and content of tutor's interventions. The interface serves as a mediator between the student and the system. It provides information about the system and facilitate learning by reducing working memory load, vizualizing the problem space, aiding conceptualization of domain knowledge and problem solving strategies. These components are illustrated in figure 1 and further described in the following sections.

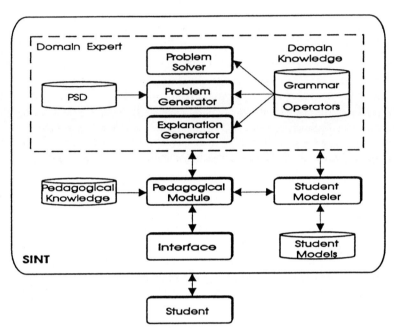

Fig. 1. The architecture of SINT

3   Knowledge Bases

SINT uses three knowledge bases, the domain knowledge base located in the domain expert, pedagogical knowledge used by the pedagogical module and the base of student models generated and maintained by the student modeler.

Domain knowledge consists of grammar rules which define regular expressions in the domain and basic problem-solving knowledge. Grammar rules are not only used when checking syntactic correctness of the input, but also when defining the partial ordering which determines the structure of the problem space.

The basic knowledge in the domain of symbolic integration, like in other procedural domains, can be decomposed into a set of primitive operators and a set of conditions of their applicability. One of the operators from this domain is:

OP69: (coefficient out) $\int r\, f(x)\, dx\ =\ r\, \int f(x)\, dx$

where r stands for any real constant and $f(x)$ for any real function of x. These included symbolic integration and differentiation rules, as well as trigonometric and algebraic transformations.

In general, pedagogical knowledge consists of general tutoring knowledge governing timing and style of instructions, and domain–specific knowledge which describes the structure of the domain and is used when choosing problems to be presented. The domain-dependent part of pedagogical knowledge is presented in SINT in the form of a PSD – Pedagogical Structure of the Domain. In essence, it is a directed graph, with nodes corresponding to concepts in the domain and with arcs determining prerequisite relations between them. In the domain of symbolic integration, nodes describe classes of integrals and ways of solving them. As can be seen in figure 1, this knowledge is a part of the domain expert. The intention behind such a fragmentation of pedagogical knowledge is to make the system as domain-independent as possible. If an ITS is required for a different domain, the domain expert's knowledge bases are the only components of the system that need to be changed.

Student models are represented in SINT as sets of production rules of the form:

$$Applicability\, Condition\ \Rightarrow\ Operator,$$

where *Applicability Condition* is the description of all problem states to which the operator in the "then–part" of the rule has been applied. A reliability indicator is associated with every production rule, which is increased with each successful prediction of the rule's application and decreased contrariwise. Also, there is a threshold parameter, which defines the minimal reliability of a rule needed for it to remain in the model. The mechanism provided by the reliability indicator, threshold, increment, and decrement provide for a rudimentary, yet effective way of dealing with uncertainty in student modeling.

4 Student Modeler

In an ideal case the model of a student should illustrate his/her knowledge, learning strategies preferred, areas of interest beside that of instruction, presentation style, level of concentration and so on. At present, there are no agreed–on techniques of student modeling, but rather several prototypes have been developed for particular domains, generality of which is yet to be determined by applying them elsewhere. Now we turn to the basic characteristics of INSTRUCT.

4.1 Foundations of INSTRUCT

If the instructional process is to be tailored to the student, the student model becomes the critical component. The task of building a student model is extremely difficult and laborious. Several researchers have pointed to the inherent intractability of the task [6] [8]. However, it was recognised by the same researchers that a student model can be useful even if it is not completely cognitively valid and accurate. This claim is supported by findings that human teachers also use very loose models of their learners, and yet are highly effective in what they do.

Another important dimension of the student modeling is the sensitivity of the model to the problem–solving strategy applied by the student. Some approaches assume that a student systematically uses a single procedure for the task at hand. However, Ohlsson [7] shows that each student applies just one of a family of procedures applicable to the problem at hand, and that the procedure selection strategy is ad hoc. This phenomenon is known as the *radical strategy variability*, and means that it cannot be assumed that the student will apply the same procedure when solving distinct problems of the same type.

These were the starting points for our approach, referred to as INSTRUCT (INteractive STudent modeling using techniques of pRocedure indUCtion from Traces). The approach uses a novel knowledge-driven technique for student modeling suited to modeling procedural tasks. Student modeling in such domains consists of inferring the applicability conditions and the definitions of operators known by the student. The underlying assumption of our approach is that student errors come from incorrect application of correct operators (that is, strategic errors) or from application of incorrect operators. It is the later that makes our approach avoid the major shortcoming of reconstructive student modeling [6], [9], where it is believed that the operators are primitive and students never err when applying them.

The other disadvantage of reconstructive modeling, its off-line nature, is avoided in INSTRUCT as well. Advantages of on-line student modeling are of enormous importance. First, it enables the tutor to react to student errors with no delay. There is psychological evidence that immediate feedback of errors is the most effective pedagogical action [2], because it is far easier for a student to localize and analyze the mental state that led to the error and to identify the bugs in his/her knowledge straightaway than after the delayed reaction of the tutor. Also, the possibility of student frustration due to a lack of knowledge and floundering is much less than in the off–line case.

In our approach, we use student traces to enable the model to be built on–line. Traces contain (some or all) steps performed by the student and the sequencing information. Having a trace does not tell everything, though. The trace may not be a valid path through the procedure because some of the steps in the trace may not match exactly the corresponding ones in the procedure. For example, the steps in the procedure could be more general than those performed by the student. This points to the need for a generalization component in procedure induction.

By introducing traces, we also have something in common with model tracing, an approach used in numerous tutors based on ACT theory [1]. ACT tutors model students by forcing them to stay on the problem solving path deemed best by the tutor. Every student's step is compared to the step performed by the domain expert: therefore, the modeling task is computationally cheap, since the problem of student modeling is reduced to inferring from single problem solving steps to single rules. However, this approach suffers from three major shortcomings. Student's steps have to be trivial; in other words, each step is the result of application of a single operator in the domain. In INSTRUCT, we allow the student to combine several primitive operators in a larger chuck (macrooperator) and to perform them at once. Second, although model tracing can be very successful with inexperienced students, knowledgeable students may be frustrated buy not being able to freely explore the problem space. INSTRUCT does not impose any problem-solving methodology on its students. Finally, ACT tutors are based on enumerative bug modeling: they model individual student steps by comparing them to predefined domain knowledge base, which consists of both correct knowledge and a collection of typical bugs and misconceptions observed in real situations. Although this modeling technique is very efficient, its effectiveness is limited by the completeness and precision of the collection of misconceptions. This is a very important limitation, since the process of acquiring such a collection is time–consuming and laborious. It has also been shown that the bug libraries acquired on some population of students are not directly transferable to other populations [7]: such an observation may question the basic assumption and effectiveness of enumerative bug modeling. INSTRUCT does not require such a library of bugs.

4.2 Learning algorithm

INSTRUCT uses an interactive technique for generating a student model. Domain knowledge and the student model are used to focus the search on the portion of the problem space that the student is likely to traverse while solving the problem at hand.

The generalization process is illustrated in figure 2. After the student has been observed using the operator OP69 for the first time, the currently accepted description is $\int 8x^3 dx$. Let us assume that the next application of the same operator is identified at the problem state $\int 4x^9 dx$. One of the hypotheses that could be generated using this second example is $\int kx^i dx$, where k and i stand for integers. The learning algorithm uses the turning–constants–into–variables rule, the dropping condition rule and the climbing generalization tree rule [3], only first being illustrated in figure 2.

Figure 3 summarizes the modeling algorithm that INSTRUCT uses to generalize an action trace into a student model. INSTRUCT uses both *implicit* and *explicit* information about the student. Implicit information consists of the steps the student performed while solving the problem (the student's trace), the explanations or help he asked for and similar observable facts, like typing errors, response time, misuse of system's facilities etc. Explicit information is gained from a student's answers to direct questions posed by the system about his knowledge, preferences, goals or the operations he is trying to perform. There are opinions that explicit dialogues may be undesirable, since they may place a burden on the user. However, human instructors have been observed using explicit questions in order to eliminate ambiguities in the student model and to

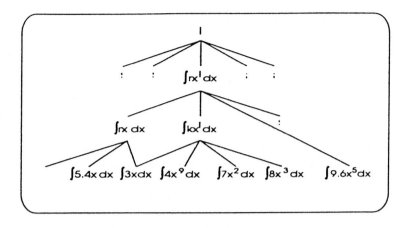

Fig. 2. A segment of the problem space

justify expensive operations of generalization inherent in the modeling process [5]. Such dialogues are also in unison with Self's recommendations for reducing the complexity of the student modeling task, by having the student provide necessary information instead of the system having to infer it.

Each step the student performed is compared to the steps suggested by the expert and those predicted by the student model. If there is a match, it is considered enough evidence for making a hypothesis concerning the operator the student applied. The current problem state (situation) is treated as a positive example for the applicability condition of the hypothesized operator, and a similarity–based learning (SBL) algorithm is called, which generalizes the situation part of the corresponding rule. Otherwise, the modeler checks whether the student is trying to apply *the basic operator* for the problem. This is the operator that defines the strategy for solving the problem at hand, and is determined by the expert module dynamically. If the student acknowledges this assumption, the similarity–based learner takes the lead. In the opposite case, the modeler queries the student about his goal, and relies on SBL to infer the knowledge state of the student. Detailed discussion of the algorithm is beyond the scope of this paper and the interested reader is referred to [4].

5 Domain Expert

The expert module consists of a problem solver, a problem generator and an explanation generator, where all three components share the same knowledge base. The problem solver is a production system which uses the definitions of operators in order to determine a solution for the problem. It provides services for the student modeler – it determines the "best" action, the list of legitimate next actions or the complete solution of the problem. The control strategy employed by the problem solver was forward chaining. The problem solver implemented

1. Initialize the student model and the current problem.
2. Let SA be the student's action.
3. Predict the student's next action from the student model.
4. If there is a prediction PA and PA matches SA,
   > then hypothesize that the student is applying the operator that yielded PA,
   > update the model and go to 12.
5. If there is a prediction PA, but it does not match SA,
   > then update the model.
6. If SA matches the "best" action suggested by the expert,
   > then hypothesize the student uses the same operator H the expert did,
   > update the model and go to 12.
7. If SA matches any action from the list of legitimate actions,
   > then let H be the corresponding operator,
   > update the model and go to 12.
8. If SA matches an action from the solution path,
   > then let M be the corresponding macrooperator,
   > update the model and go to 12.
9. Let B be the "basic" operator suggested by the expert.
10. If the student acknowledges the application of B,
    > then update the model and go to 12.
11. Ask the student about the operator H he applied
    > and update the model.
12. If the problem is solved, stop.
13. Go to 2.

Fig. 3. Summary of the learning algorithm

in the first prototype of SINT was capable of solving only a limited number of integrals, due to the small knowledge base. The limitations placed on the knowledge base size were made arbitrarily and do not reflect a limitation of the modeling approach. Indeed, currently we are implementing the second prototype of SINT whose domain knowledge will be much larger.

The Problem Generator (PG) uses the student model and domain–dependent pedagogical knowledge to determine the next problem to be posed to the student. When determining a problem for a new student who has declared his/her knowledge to be sparse, the problem generator starts with those problems corresponding to sources in the PSD. For other students, the problem is determined on the basis of the model of their knowledge, by finding a node in PSD with all prerequisites satisfied.

The explanation generator (EG) is activated when a deviation is found in the student's knowledge. In such a case, EG compares the applicability condition induced by the SBL learner to the ideal one from the domain expert's knowledge base, and creates an explanation based on the differences found. The current version of EG uses canned text to form explanations, but natural language generation is planned for future work.

6 Pedagogical Module

The pedagogical module is based on the computer coach paradigm, one of the most frequently used pedagogical strategies in ITSs. The system remains silent while the student is doing well and intervenes only in situations when the student is stuck or asks for help. Students are offered different levels of help, depending on their learning status (described by the student model), like browsing existing operators, viewing applicable operators or the preferred operator, viewing the history, asking for a new problem or for a complete solution of the problem.

The pedagogical module is a production system which uses the student model as a working memory. It is invoked after every change in the student model and determines whether to intervene in the tutoring process. Its knowledge base is domain–independent, since all pedagogical domain–dependent knowledge is transferred to the expert module in the form of PSD, as discussed in section 3.

7 Conclusions

In this paper we presented the current state in the development of SINT, an ITS for the domain of symbolic integration. The main focus of our research is student modeling, which is reflected in the paper as well. Our approach is suitable for inducing models of procedural skills from observed student performance. The underlying assumption is that student errors come from applying correct operators to wrong situations (strategic errors) or from bugs in the definitions of operators. INSTRUCT does not assume that the student applies operators in a consistent manner. It will take any problem state as an example for the generalization process, so there is no bias toward the applied strategy.

The framework presented in this paper overcomes the basic limitations of reconstructive modeling, the need for primitive operators and off–line modeling, by being able to identify incorrect operators and induce macrooperators, and by its interactive nature. INSTRUCT is applicable to more complex domains than reconstructive modeling, because it exploits domain knowledge and knowledge about the student to constrain the search in the modeling process. It also engages the student to obtain necessary information which would be very resource-consuming for the system to infer. Such activities are in accordance with recommendations for making student modeling more tractable. INSTRUCT is superior to model tracing techniques, in that it does not rely on bug libraries and enables the student to solve the problems using more complex steps.

The first prototype of SINT system has been tried on a number of students, who showed great interest in it. This informal study provided hints for the user interface and style of interaction. The students felt that they progressed more rapidly when working with the system. However, a fuller user study is in order with a larger population of students and a more sophisticated expert module.

Theoretical evaluation of INSTRUCT was based on the computational complexity of the modeling process [4]. INSTRUCT was evaluated against the modeling procedure performed by ACM. It was found that the processing time of

INSTRUCT is r times smaller, where r was the size of the domain knowledge base in the number of operators. This demonstrates the effect of using domain knowledge in the modeling process.

A preliminary psychological evaluation has been carried out. We asked human teachers to assess the actions taken by INSTRUCT for given student's trace. At the time of the experiment the number of problems that the problem solver could handle was limited, due to the small knowledge base. We have found that human experts mostly agreed with INSTRUCT's actions.

There are numerous ways for advancing the research reported here. Currently, the knowledge base is being enlarged in order for more problems to be handled by the expert module and to allow further evaluation. The pedagogical knowledge base is being refined as well. We also plan to implement ITS systems in other domains in order to manifest the applicability of the approach; the research has started on implementing an ITS for fire training. Additional future directions include broadening the types of input for modeling, implementing more sophisticated model maintenance techniques and developing ways of learning individualized pedagogical rules.

References

1. Anderson, J.R., Boyle, C.F., Corbett, A.T. and Lewis, M.W.: Cognitive Modeling and Intelligent Tutoring. AI **42** (1990) 7-49
2. Lewis, M.W., Milson, R., Anderson, J.R.: The Teacher's Apprentice: Designing Authoring System for High School Mathematics. In: G.P. Kearsley (ed.): Artificial Intelligence and Instruction – Applications and Methods. Reading: Addison-Wesley (1987) 269-301
3. Michalski, R.: A Theory and Methodology of Inductive Learning. AI **20** (1983) 111–161
4. Mitrović, A., Djordjević, S: Interactive Reconstructive Student Modeling: a Machine Learning Approach. Int. J. Human-Computer Interaction **7**(4) (1995) 385-401.
5. Moore, J.D., Paris, C.L.: Exploiting User Feedback to Compensate for the Unreliability of User Models. User Modeling and User–Adapted Interaction **2**(4) (1992) 287-330.
6. Ohlsson, S., Langley, P.: Psychological Evaluation of Path Hypotheses in Cognitive Diagnosis'. In: H. Mandl and A. Lesgold (eds.): Learning Issues for Intelligent Tutoring Systems, New York: Springer-Verlag (1988) 42-62.
7. Ohlsson, S: Constraint–based Student Modeling. In: J.E. Greer and G.I. McCalla (eds.): Student Modeling: the Key to Individualized Knowledge–based Instruction. Berlin: Springer–Verlag NATO ASI Series (1994) 167-189.
8. Self, J.: Formal Approaches to Student Modeling. In: J.E. Greer and G.I. McCalla (eds.): Student Modeling: the Key to Individualized Knowledge–based Instruction. Berlin: Springer–Verlag NATO ASI Series (1994) 295-352.
9. Sleeman, D.H., Langley, P., Mitchell, T.M.: Learning from Solution Paths: an Approach to the Credit Assignment Problem. AI Magazine **3**(1) (1982) 48-52.

A Belief Net Backbone for Student Modelling

Jim Reye

Queensland University of Technology
Brisbane, Q 4001, Australia
j.reye@qut.edu.au

Abstract. In this paper, I present a belief-net-based approach to student modelling which assists an ITS make determinations as to the extent of the student's knowledge. This approach also has advantages for structuring and ensuring the consistency of the student model. As well, the paper shows the desirability of using dynamic belief networks for modelling the dynamic evolution of the student's state of knowledge.

1   Introduction

In discussing the approaches of human instructors, Collins and Stevens (1982) state:

> Rather we assume only a partial ordering on the elements in the teacher's theory of the domain. ... The teacher's assumption is that students learn the elements in approximately this same order. Therefore, it is possible to gauge what the student will know or not know based on a few correct and incorrect responses.

In this paper, I present a belief-net-based approach to student modelling which assists an ITS make similar determinations as to the extent of the student's knowledge. This approach also has advantages for structuring and ensuring the consistency of the student model.

2   Belief Net Backbone

2.1   Probabilistic student modelling

For the purposes of this paper, I (minimally) assume that the domain may be viewed as an abstract collection of *topics* (or "curriculum elements"), each of which represents some piece of conceptual or skill knowledge which the student should acquire. For each such topic, there is a corresponding *student-knows* probability measure in the student model, e.g. p (student-knows (A)) = 0.7. In general, such measures of belief are dynamically updated as tutoring proceeds, e.g. see Corbett and Anderson (1992); Shute (1995). This initial student-modelling approach allows each probability in the student model to be updated independently of all the others. In the following section, I show why this is generally undesirable and why we need to model the impact of a change of belief on related beliefs.

2.2 The importance of the prerequisite relationship for structuring beliefs

When building a domain model (based on an expert's knowledge), there is really no need to specify prerequisite relationships between parts of that knowledge, as such relationships are only important for educational purposes and not for problem-solving within the domain. However, when student models are considered, the prerequisite relationship becomes very important. In the earlier quote from Collins and Stevens, the "partial ordering" is effectively a prerequisite relationship.

This prerequisite relationship is important both for modelling student beliefs at any one point in time and for deciding how best to alter those beliefs over a period of time. At any point in time, if knowledge of topic A is a *prerequisite* for knowledge of topic B, then it is inconsistent to assert that both p (student-knows (A)) = 0 and p (student-knows (B)) = 1. Expressed in terms of predicate logic, we want to enforce the constraint: ¬student-knows (A) ⇒ ¬student-knows (B), or student-knows (B) ⇒ student-knows (A) (equivalently). In probability theory, this constraint is represented as a *conditional probability*: p (student-knows (A) | student-knows (B)) = 1. This can also be expressed in a variety of logically-equivalent forms, e.g.: p (student-knows (B) | ¬student-knows (A)) = 0, which can be paraphrased as: "You can't know B if you don't know A."

2.3 Student modelling via belief networks

Probability theory provides the necessary methods for automated inferencing based on conditional probabilities. *Belief networks* (Pearl, 1988) provide a graphical way of designing probabilistic models based on the concept of conditional probability. As well, the resulting structure is used for subsequent automated reasoning about such models, in the most efficient manner for that structure. Being based on probability theory, belief networks also allow the representation of constraints which are not enirely certain. For example: p (student-knows (A) | student-knows (B)) = 0.9 can be interpreted as "Most students who know B, also know A." Being able to represent and reason with such knowledge is a valuable advantage over approaches based on traditional logic alone. Although the earlier description was only in terms of a pair of related topics, conditional probabilities allow the specification of relationships which are more complex than those given above. For example, we can specify that *both* P and Q are prerequisites for R.

As well as numeric values for the conditional probabilities, we also must specify the prior probabilities of all propositions which are not determined by the conditional probabilities. These prior probabilities specify the system's initial set of beliefs about a (typical) student, prior to the first interaction with that student. As the student uses the system, it directly updates its beliefs about the student's knowledge of topics where these are observable. These changes in belief are then propagated through the belief net, changing the system's belief in the likelihood that the student knows other (as yet) unobserved topics.

2.4   A backbone of conditional probability links

The use of conditional probabilities easily extends to much longer chains and networks of prerequisite dependencies. For example, if we know that A is a prerequisite for B, which is a prerequisite for C, and so on up until Z (say), then if we discover that the student knows Z, then we don't have to ask about the earlier prerequisites. Likewise, if we find out that the student knows F, but not G, then we don't have to ask about A..E or H..Z.

In the general theory of belief networks, there are no restrictions on the structure of the network (apart from the prohibition of directed cycles). However, in any system that uses a belief network, an actual structure must be specified. In this paper, I propose that the appropriate belief network structure for an ITS is based on two categories of nodes:

(a)   a *belief net backbone*, which links all the "student-knows" nodes together in a partial ordering, according to their prerequisite relationships;

(b)   a *topic cluster* for each node in the backbone, which consists of a single "student-knows" node together with a standard set of additional belief nodes. Most such nodes are *local* to the topic cluster, e.g. "student-interested-in (*topic*)". That is, there is a separate instance for each topic. However, some nodes are *global* in that there is only one instance in the whole student model, e.g. student-overall-aptitude ().

Thus these two categories overlap in that each of the "student-knows" *nodes* occurs once in the backbone and once in its topic cluster. However, the links (or "arcs") between these nodes (i.e. the conditional probabilities) do not overlap.

This proposal has two advantages. Firstly, it gives the designer a standard methodology for creating the structure of an ITS belief network, regardless of the particular domain. Secondly, there are computational advantages in that updates to the beliefs in any one topic subnet only affects the other topic subnets via the backbone, rather than there being any direct connection. In particular, this means that the impact of belief updates in a given topic subnet on its "student-knows" node can be calculated locally by considering just the nodes in that topic subnet, rather than having to propagate such updates through the entire network in order to determine their nett results. The efficiency gained by such local computation is very important during instructional planning, when the impacts of large numbers of possible plans must be determined rapidly. (Once a plan has been chosen and is executed, its effects update one or more topic subnets, and these effects must be propagated through the backbone. Although computationally more expensive, such updates occur much less frequently than those needed during planning.)

3   Dynamic belief networks

In ordinary belief networks, it is assumed that the properties of the external world, modelled by the network, are unchanging. That is, even though the system may gather information from the external world which causes it to modify its measures of belief about items in that world, those items remain either true or false.

Such an approach is clearly inadequate for student modelling in a tutoring system, where we must be able to represent the dynamic evolution of a student's knowledge over a period of time. Dynamic belief networks (Dean and Kanazawa (1989)) allow for reasoning about change over time. This is achieved by having a sequence of nodes which represent the state of the external item over a period of time, rather than having just a single temporally-invariant node. For real-world continuous processes, the sequence of nodes may represent the external state as it changes over a sequence of time-slices. For tutoring, it is often more useful to represent changes in the student model over a sequence of interactions, rather than time-slices, as the following example illustrates.

To avoid any possible misunderstanding, I point out that dynamic belief networks model a (moving) snapshot of the student's knowledge. They do not model the evolution itself, in the sense of providing a history of the development of such knowledge. Such a history may well be required, e.g. (i) for deciding to revisit domain areas which were previously of major difficulty to the student; and (ii) to dynamically adapt the system to the student's learning style. Clearly, the complete history of any dynamic model can be captured (and reviewed) by keeping a tuple-based log of redo/undo changes, analogous to the logging done by many database systems. (Such a log may already be present in any system which is able to resume a tutorial session following a system failure.) The subsequent usage of such historical data for instructional planning is outside the scope of this paper.

3.1 A basic dynamic belief network: probabilistic modelling in the ACT Programming Languages Tutor

The ACT Programming Languages Tutor (Corbett and Anderson (1992)) uses a simple two-state psychological learning model with no forgetting, which is updated each time that the student has an opportunity to show their knowledge of a production rule in the ideal student model. There are four parameters associated with each rule:

$p(L_0)$ the probability that a rule is in the *learned* state prior to the first opportunity to apply the rule (i.e. from reading text);

$p(T)$ the probability that a rule will make the transition from the *unlearned* state to the *learned* state following an opportunity to apply the rule;

$p(C|U)$ the probability that a student will guess correctly if the applicable rule is in the *unlearned* state;

$p(E|L)$ the probability that a student will slip and make an error when the applicable rule is in the *learned* state.

In general, the values of these parameters may be set empirically and may vary from rule to rule, but Corbett and Anderson describe a study in which these parameters were held constant across 21 rules, with $p(L_0) = 0.5$, $p(T) = 0.4$, $p(C|U) = 0.2$ and $p(E|L) = 0.2$. Note that there are no conditional probabilities linking different rules i.e. no prerequisite constraints. In an appendix to their paper, the authors briefly state equations for calculating $p(L_n|C_n)$ and $p(L_n|E_n)$, which then can be used to determine the probability that a production rule is in the learned state following a correct (C_n) or erroneous (E_n) student response, at the nth opportunity.

In this section, I illustrate the applicability of dynamic belief networks by showing how Corbett and Anderson's equations can be rederived from the dynamic belief net shown in Figure 1. Structurally, this is the simplest possible dynamic belief network for student modelling (where simplicity may be a virtue rather than a vice). (In their paper, Corbett and Anderson did not describe how they derived these equations. Even though they did not refer to dynamic belief networks, their learning model is most likely mathematically isomorphic to Figure 1, leading to an analogous derivation of the formulae below. My goal here is not just to rederive their results, but to show that their formulae may be viewed as a special case of the general approach of using dynamic belief networks.) To fully specify the dynamic belief net in Figure 1, we need:

(a)   the prior probability that a rule is in the learned state, prior to the first opportunity, i.e. $p(L_0)$, as given by the authors;

(b)   the conditional probabilities linking L_{n-1} and C_n in Figure 1, i.e.:

-     the probability of a correct response when the rule is in the learned state just prior to the nth opportunity, i.e. $p(C_n|L_{n-1}) = p(C|L) = 1 - p(E|L)$, where the latter two parameters are used by the authors; and

-     the probability of a correct response when the rule is in the unlearned state just prior to the nth opportunity, i.e. $p(C_n|\neg L_{n-1}) = p(C|U) = 1 - p(E|U)$, where the latter two parameters are used by the authors.

(c)   the conditional probabilities linking L_{n-1} and L_n in Figure 1, i.e.:

-     the probability of remaining in the learned state when the rule is already in the learned state just prior to the nth opportunity, i.e. $p(L_n|L_{n-1}) = 1$, where this value is specified by the authors' assumption of no forgetting; and

-     the probability of a transition to the learned state when the rule is in the unlearned state just prior to the nth opportunity, i.e. $p(L_n|\neg L_{n-1}) = p(T)$, where the latter parameter is used by the authors.

Given a value for $p(L_{n-1})$, it is easy to calculate $p(C_n)$ via:

$$p(C_n) = p(C_n|L_{n-1}) \ p(L_{n-1}) + p(C_n|\neg L_{n-1}) \ p(\neg L_{n-1}) \tag{1}$$

This value can then be used to revise the belief in $p(L_{n-1})$ when C_n is true (i.e. the response is correct):

$$p(L_{n-1}|C_n) = p(C_n|L_{n-1}) \ p(L_{n-1}) \ / \ p(C_n) \quad \text{(Bayes' theorem)} \tag{2}$$

Finally, the revised belief in $p(L_{n-1})$ can be used to calculate the new belief $p(L_n)$, when C_n is true:

$$p(L_n|C_n) = p(L_n|L_{n-1}) \ p \ (L_{n-1}|C_n) + p(L_n|\neg L_{n-1}) \ p \ (\neg L_{n-1}|C_n) \tag{3}$$

Under Corbett and Anderson's assumption that $p(L_n|L_{n-1}) = 1$, equation (3) becomes:

$$p(L_n|C_n) = p \ (L_{n-1}|C_n) + p(L_n|\neg L_{n-1}) \ p \ (\neg L_{n-1}|C_n)$$

or equivalently (rewriting in terms of their original parameters):

$$p(L_n|C_n) = p \ (L_{n-1}|C_n) + p(T) \ (1 - p \ (L_{n-1}|C_n))$$

which is the same as their equation [1]. Likewise, equation (1) above can be substituted into equation (2) and then also be rewritten in terms of their original

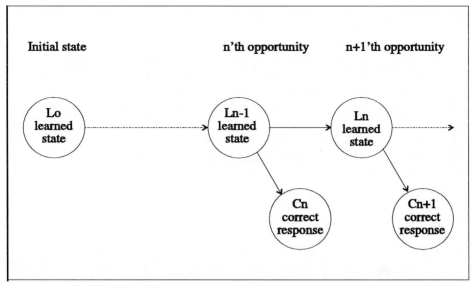

Figure 1   A basic dynamic belief network for student modelling

parameters:
$$p(L_{n-1}|C_n) = p(C|L)\ p(L_{n-1})\ /\ (\ p(C|L)\ p(L_{n-1})\ +\ p(C|U)\ p(U_{n-1})\ )$$
which is their equation [3]. For space reasons, I omit the analogous derivation of equations for $p(L_n|\neg C_n)$ and $p(L_{n-1}|\neg C_n)$, equivalent to Corbett and Anderson's equations [2] and [4].

3.2   A more elaborate dynamic belief network

Figure 2 shows a somewhat more elaborate dynamic belief network for a topic cluster, corresponding to the topic cluster attributes introduced earlier in this paper. This figure is intended to further illustrate the general approach, rather than attempting to be a comprehensive network. As before, each arrow represents a conditional probability which is usually a cause-effect relationship.

4   Diagnosis: determining the state of student knowledge

The earlier quote from Collins and Stevens described how human teachers are able to gauge the extent of a student's knowledge based on a relatively small number of probing questions. This teaching strategy may be modelled as a problem-solving procedure within the framework of a classic AI diagnostic task. In particular, de Kleer and Williams's (1987) research on their General Diagnostic Engine (GDE) system is helpful, even though it cannot be used directly as it is based on some assumptions which do not apply to student modelling. That research is based on the idea of minimising the number of measurements (analogously, minimising the number of questions asked of the student) by making a series of measurements,

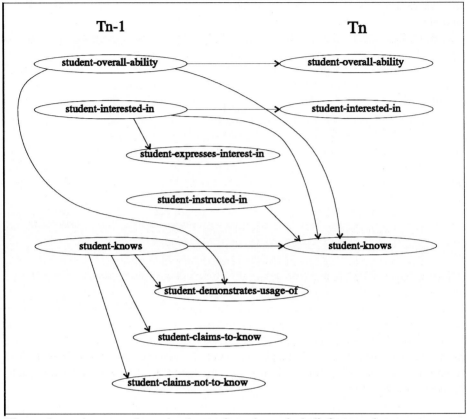

Figure 2   An example topic cluster, in a dynamic belief network

each of which maximises the expected amount of information gained by that measurement. Technically, minimising the expected entropy (H) of the belief network after making that measurement: $H = -\sum p_i \log p_i$. So, the expected entropy (H_e) after asking a student whether they know topic t_n is given by the weighted sum of the two possible responses:

$$H_e(t_n) = p\ (t_n)\ H\ (t_n)\ +\ p\ (\neg t_n)\ H\ (\neg t_n)$$

One of the difficulties faced by the GDE procedure is that the number of possible combinations of faults grows exponentially with the number of components. Fortunately, for student diagnosis, the number of possible combinations is far less. This is because, whenever an ITS considers a possible diagnosis involving a particular faulty node, then all subsequent (partially ordered) nodes must also be faulty (at any one point in time). By comparison, in an electronic circuit, subsequent nodes need not be faulty and so there are more cases to consider.

For example, consider a simple chain of four items: $A \rightarrow B \rightarrow C \rightarrow D$. If this is taken as representing an electronic circuit of buffers, then there are 16 (= 2^4) possible combinations of possibly faulty components. Alternatively, if this chain is a belief net backbone representing the prerequisite relationships linking four topics, then there are only five combinations which model possible states of the student's knowledge, as given by the following sets: {}, {A}, {A, B}, {A, B, C}, {A, B, C, D}. Such linear growth is clearly better than exponential growth, especially when creating domains containing hundreds of topics.

I now give a small example to illustrate the approach. In this example, I omit the "student-knows" predicate for conciseness and clarity, e.g. "p (A)" should be taken as "p (student-knows (A))". *Example:* $A \rightarrow B \rightarrow C \rightarrow D$, with

p (A)	= 0.75	$\therefore$	$p_{prior}(A)$	= 0.75
p (B $\mid$ A)	= 0.75	$\therefore$	$p_{prior}(B)$	= 0.56
p (C $\mid$ B)	= 0.75	$\therefore$	$p_{prior}(C)$	= 0.42
p (D $\mid$ C)	= 0.75	$\therefore$	$p_{prior}(D)$	= 0.32

There are four topics, so there are four possible questions which could be asked. The expected entropy for each of these possibilities are calculated as:

$$H_e(A) = p (A) H(A) + p(\neg A) H(\neg A) \qquad = 0.98$$
$$H_e(B) = p (B) H(B) + p(\neg B) H(\neg B) \qquad = 0.67$$
$$H_e(C) = p (C) H(C) + p(\neg C) H(\neg C) \qquad = 0.69$$
$$H_e(D) = p (D) H(D) + p(\neg D) H(\neg D) \qquad = 0.95$$

These values confirm what one would expect intuitively in this case, i.e. that more information is gained by asking about B or C, rather than A or D. More precisely, topic B has the lowest expected entropy (i.e. highest expected gain of information) and so should be asked first. The student's reply can then be used to update the probabilities in the student model. These revised probabilities can then be used in subsequent calculations of expected entropy, in order to determine which topic should be queried next. The resulting dialogue models the behaviour of the human teachers described above.

5   Related research

Most existing ITSs use fairly coarse-grained measures for representing the student's knowledge. For example, some systems associate one of three values with each domain topic: student knows, student does not know, and not sure if student knows or does not know. Such a coarse-grained measure limits the modelling power of the system and so limits its decision-making capabilities.

For example, consider a situation in which an ITS has to choose between two equally important topics to teach next (both with prerequisites satisfied). Assume that the probability that the student already knows the topic is 0.4 in one case and 0.7 in the other (based on observations of the student). Most systems would be forced to represent both these as "not sure if student knows or does not know", and thus could pick either topic to teach next. This is an inferior approach, as it is clearly better to be able to distinguish the two. For example, if the student has been doing well so far, then we may wish to cover the topic which the student appears more likely not to know. On the other hand, if the student has been doing poorly, then we may wish to work on the topic which the student is more likely to know, in order to improve their self-confidence.

It is only recently that ITS researchers have started investigating the use of probability theory for student modelling. Villano (1992) provides a good but very brief discussion of some of the basic issues in using a belief network for student modelling, such as the need to obtain the structure, prior probabilities and conditional probabilities for the belief network — issues which are also covered in this paper. Pirolli and Wilson (1992) discuss the important diagnostic issue: how to estimate probabilistic student modelling parameters from complex events. The last section of their paper also addresses the basic idea of using belief networks for student modelling. While limited in scope, this section illustrates these ideas, by presenting screen snapshots from Hugin (a belief network shell) showing three different states of a small (seven node) belief network. Shute's (1995) work on updating probabilistic measures of a student's skills is important for the future development of more sophisticated student models based on belief networks, even though she just considers the updating of individual measures in the student model.

Acknowledgments

I thank the anonymous referees for their constructive comments.

References

1. Collins, A., and Stevens, A.L. (1982) Goals and strategies for inquiry teachers. In Glaser, R. (ed.) *Advances in Instructional Psychology (vol. II)*, 65-119.
2. Corbett, A.T., and Anderson, J.R. (1992) Student modeling and mastery learning in a computer-based programming tutor. In Frasson, C., Gauthier, C. and McCalla, G.I. (eds.) *Intelligent Tutoring Systems (ITS'92)*, 413-420.
3. de Kleer, J., and Williams, B.C. (1987) Diagnosing multiple faults. *Artificial Intelligence* 32, 97-130.
4. Dean, T., and Kanazawa, K. (1989) A model for reasoning about persistence and causation. *Computational Intelligence* 5, 142-150.
5. Pearl, J. (1988) *Probabilistic reasoning in intelligent systems: networks of plausible inference*. Morgan Kaufmann.
6. Pirolli, P., and Wilson, M. (1992) Measuring learning strategies and understanding: a research framework. In Frasson, C., Gauthier, C. and McCalla, G.I. (eds.) *Intelligent Tutoring Systems (ITS'92)*, 539-558.
7. Shute, V. (1995). SMART evaluation: cognitive diagnosis, mastery learning & remediation. In Greer, J. (ed.) *Artificial Intelligence in Education, 1995*, 123-130.
8. Villano, M. (1992) Probabilistic student models: bayesian belief networks and knowledge space theory. In Frasson, C., Gauthier, C. and McCalla, G.I. (eds.) *Intelligent Tutoring Systems (ITS'92)*, 491-498.

Adaptation of Problem Presentation and Feedback in an Intelligent Mathematics Tutor

Mia Stern, Joseph Beck, and Beverly Park Woolf

Center for Knowledge Communication
Department of Computer Science
University of Massachusetts
Amherst, MA 01003-4610
{stern, beck, bev}@cs.umass.edu
Phone: (413) 545-0582; Fax: (413) 545-1249

Abstract. We have developed an intelligent tutor for teaching remedial mathematics to community college students. This domain is fairly narrow in scope and is an important component of the college curriculum. The target audience often retains fragments of knowledge from previous courses which can aid them in learning; alternately, misconceptions can present conceptual stumbling blocks if students have misremembered what they learned previously. Thus, a system built with a strong student model can greatly benefit the teaching process. The tutor described in this paper tracks student skills along with a general acquisition factor, and uses this information for topic selection, problem generation, problem presentation, and dynamic feedback.

1 Introduction

Designing an intelligent tutoring system (ITS) to teach remedial mathematics presents several difficulties. As the number of steps to solve a problem increase, as well as the possible operations at each step, determining which path a student took to arrive at his response is problematic [13]. Additionally, within several mathematics domains such as fractions or algebra, many different incorrect solution paths exist that can lead to the same result. Thus, inferring the precise cause of a student's difficulties is impossible without some method of tracing his intervening steps [10].

In spite of these difficulties, an effective mathematics ITS needs a mechanism for evaluating a student's abilities. Our system uses a strong student model that tracks proficiencies on every topic, as well as general factors such as acquisition. This model is then used for topic selection, problem generation, problem presentation, and several varieties of scaffolding and feedback mechanisms.

2 Target Audience

At the college level, an increasing number of incoming students do not meet basic levels of mathematical proficiency [4]. The purpose of this tutor is to help these students work through a remedial mathematics course that is typical for many first year community college students.

This tutor differs from most other attempts at teaching this domain in that the target audience is adults (on average 30 years old). This has strong implications for ITS design. Conversations with expert teachers indicate that, at a gross level, students can be partitioned into two groups: group 1 students learned the material before and have forgotten some of the procedural skills, and group 2 students never successfully learned this material. This is certainly an over generalization, as students will retain fragments of what they learned previously, but it illustrates the wide variation in incoming student knowledge.

Our goal for group 1 students is to help them remember topics they may have forgotten. For this group, the instructional emphasis is on demonstrating procedural problem solving skills. Thus the tutor must be flexible in its teaching, so that these students are not presented with unnecessary material. Group 2 students present more difficulty: traditional instruction enables few students from this group to pass the course. This second group of students will be presented with "concrete-operational" symbols, not just the procedures that produce a correct answer [11]. Furthermore, many of these students are math anxious, and are therefore discouraged by difficult looking problems [16]. Thus, constructing problems at the right level of difficulty presents many challenges for the tutor.

3 Tutoring Environment

This remedial mathematics tutor differs from most other intelligent mathematics environments, and tutors in general, in that it is structured as a "game". The student travels to different rooms where he is presented with various mathematics problems. Rather than simple drill and practice, the student will sometimes interact with the tutor through puzzle-type games (Figure 1), which are meant to make the learning environment more stimulating [17]. However, the student will also be asked traditional mathematics problems, but even these interactions will be based on graphics, sounds, and animations.

Because the student's learning is the most important goal of the system, we do not let his choice of the game scenario entirely determine the mathematics. Rather, regardless of the game room chosen by the student, the system uses the student model to select an appropriate topic and decide at what level the problem will be posed. The problem presentations are governed by this selection.

4 Domain Topics in the Tutor

The specific topics covered by the tutor include addition, subtraction, multiplication, and division of whole numbers, fractions, mixed numbers, and decimals. Each topic is composed of various subskills, which are themselves topics. Figure 2 illustrates the subskill hierarchy for "add mixed numbers". Furthermore, each topic has pretopics indicating which skills a student must understand before a

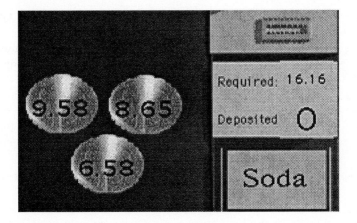

Fig. 1. Sample Puzzle Game. Vending machine where student must deposit exact change to receive a soda

problem of this type will be generated. Some of the pretopics for a skill are also subskills of that skill.

Additional items in the topic network include conceptual "skills"; these are used to track the student's understanding of higher level knowledge. For example, the student must understand the concept of a fraction, and to test this, he will be asked to select from a group of pizzas the one corresponding to $\frac{1}{4}$.

Topics are internally represented with their component parts, and problems are often broken down by the tutor into these parts. Thus the student's actions can be observed at a fine grain size, which enables the tutor to detect subskills that the student did not perform correctly and provide feedback based on a more accurate student model.

Some "buggy" knowledge is also stored [3]. However, the tutor does not know all the permutations of valid rules. Instead, since there are many possible misconceptions and it would not be feasible to include them all, only the most likely student mistakes are encoded. Unless there is a specific remediation mechanism that demonstrates the fallacy of a student's misconception, there is little point in adding the misconception to the tutor's domain knowledge [15].

5 Student Model

In order to construct a tutor with an adaptive curriculum, a model of student performance must be constructed. Based on the community's history of student models which collect more information than the pedagogical module can handle [13], we sought a clear use for the student knowledge gathered. To construct the student model, the system tracks student actions in the problem solving process.

The students using this tutor are more heterogeneous in their recall of prior material than the more traditional learning situation in which students have little background knowledge about the domain. Thus we need to have an adaptive

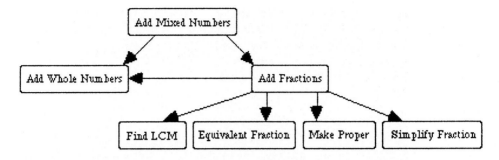

Fig. 2. Subset of topic network, displaying subskill hierarchy of "add mixed numbers"

curriculum that allows students to receive more instruction and perform more problem solving in areas in which they are relatively weak, and to receive a summary for topics they have remembered from previous instruction. Additionally, students may have "bad" knowledge in the form of misconceptions about the domain as a result of earlier educational experiences. Thus, a method of detecting and remediating common misconceptions is needed.

For several reasons, building a student model in this domain is not as problematic as in other domains:

1) The domain of mathematics has been studied extensively, and domain experts are plentiful.
2) A restricted number of correct mathematical transformations are available at each step in the problem solving process; this reduces the "combinatorial explosion" described previously.
3) Conversations with domain experts and literature from previous researchers [10] indicate that the most common student misconceptions are from a relatively small set. Thus extensive "bug libraries" are not needed.

5.1 Representation of the Student Model

The tutor tracks the student's "proficiency" on all topics, both procedural and conceptual. This proficiency rating is numerical, and a history of the student's performance is stored. When the student solves a problem, his performance is appended to the tutor's model.

In addition to maintaining a history of the student's performance, the tutor calculates his acquisition factor, i.e. how quickly he learns new information. Data is gathered by examining the first few trials of every topic to see how quickly the student learns new topics. Future versions of the tutor will include a retention factor, which measures how well the student recalls the material over time. Data is gathered by examining how well the student performs at skills that have not been presented for a certain length of time.

Prior research indicates that examining general factors such as acquisition and retention can be beneficial for student modeling. Work with the LISP tutor [1] and with Stat Lady [14] indicates that general factors extracted from student learning data are predictive of overall learning and allow for a more accurate response to the idiosyncrasies of the student.

5.2   Gathering Modeling Data

Most problems in this domain require several steps to solve, and radically different student knowledge can produce equivalent responses. Therefore, a model tracing system was not implemented. Instead, a set of heuristics is applied to the student's answer to determine with which part of the problem he had difficulties.

The first step in this process is to list all the skills that are needed to solve the problem. Each of these has a heuristic function associated with it that takes as input the student's answer and the current problem. This function indicates whether or not it is likely the student made a mistake applying the skill with which it is associated. For example, the "create equivalent fraction" skill's heuristic function examines the student's answer, and if the denominator is valid (i.e. the correct denominator, or a multiple of it), but the answer is incorrect, it concludes that the student failed to properly find an equivalent fraction.

As a result of this process, a list of skills the student may not understand is collected, and further analysis is performed to determine how the tutor will respond. Currently the tutor examines the list of candidate skills and selects the one with the lowest proficiency for use by the pedagogical module. Obviously, the tutor cannot be certain of the exact reason for the student's error, but for this domain, the method described is reasonably accurate.

Because the system "knows" the skills the student performed correctly or incorrectly, the student model is adjusted based on the level of hint at which the student got the answer correct. Each hint has a "level" associated with it that indicates how much information it provides to the student. The less specific hints a student requires to get the correct answer, the more his proficiency in that skill is incremented. If no hints are required, the student's proficiencies on all subskills of the problem are increased at the maximum rate. This mechanism is similar to the one described by Shute [14].

6   Uses of Student Model

The student model is utilized to adapt the tutor's responses in terms of topic selection, problem generation, feedback, and scaffolding.

6.1   Topic Selection

The tutor selects a new topic by excluding those that are too difficult as well as those already mastered; it then selects from those remaining. A random component to this process ensures that a student will occasionally receive a review problem in an area he knows or will be nudged ahead to a topic not yet mastered.

The random factor has several benefits. Since topic selection is not deterministic, practice tends to be distributed over time; this avoids the problems associated with mass practice [2]. Also, since we cannot be certain of our model's accuracy, a random element will allow the tutor to determine the student's true ability faster by providing more data points for better prediction.

The rate at which new topics are introduced is affected by the student's acquisition factor: the higher this rating is, the faster new topics are introduced. Additionally, when the student answers a problem correctly, his proficiencies on the appropriate topics are increased at a rate which is influenced by his acquisition factor.

6.2 Problem Generation

Once a topic has been selected, a specific problem must be generated. This is accomplished by examining the student's levels of proficiency on the selected topic and its subskills. The higher the student's level of proficiency on the selecte topic, the more subskills he will have to apply to solve the problem; this acts as a means of controlling problem difficulty. For example, a difficult addition of fractions problem is $\frac{2}{3} + \frac{3}{4}$, which requires students to find a valid denominator, convert both fractions to equivalent forms using that denominator, add the numerators, and then convert the result to a mixed number. On the other hand, a simple problem such as $\frac{1}{3} + \frac{1}{3}$ requires few subskills.

As in topic selection, subskill selection has a random component that creates problems with different levels of difficulty. The purpose of this is that since there is a fair probability the tutor's model is not perfectly accurate, it is worthwhile to sometimes present problems that are slightly easier or harder than the model thinks the student can handle. This allows the system to examine other possible states of the student model, which makes future predictions more accurate.

The final stage of problem generation is resolving conflicts between subskills. For example, if one of the subskills chosen requires that the denominators of the two fractions be the same, and another requires that the denominators not be multiples of each other, a contradiction results. A constraint satisfaction algorithm is used to resolve this; subskills at which the student needs more practice (i.e. have a lower proficiency value) have a higher priority of being used. This biases problems to contain features on which the student needs more work.

6.3 Feedback to Students

Giving students the right amount of help in their problem solving efforts is difficult. There are obvious problems with not providing enough support to students, including frustration and floundering [1]. However, there is also evidence that a certain cognitive load must be placed on students for learning to occur and too much help can interfere with learning [5].

The ITS we have developed uses the student's proficiencies to select an appropriate hint. The more proficient he is at a particular skill, the more subtle the hint is. For example, a skilled student may simply be prompted to reexamine his answer. At the other extreme, a student with low proficiency in a skill would be presented with a more obvious hint. In this case, the tutor could call attention to an incorrect denominator or break the problem up into smaller steps. This is superior to requiring students to wade through several levels of hints before being presented with material that is appropriate to their level of knowledge [6].

Furthermore, if the student is having difficulties after a hint is presented, progressively more specific hints will be given until he answers the problem correctly. As the student demonstrates his ability to solve problems, this support is gradually withdrawn; this is similar to Vygotsky's concept of scaffolding [7].

6.4   Scaffolding

In order to aid students in attaining procedural skills, the tutor provides a variety of scaffolding techniques:

Visualization: Before a topic is presented in its abstract mathematical form, students are shown a non-numeric, concrete representation of the problem, i.e. a graphic representing the physical basis of the problem. For example, when demonstrating the concept of one-fourth, the tutor will show a pizza cut into quarters. The goal is to allow students to build a conceptual model of the topic that will allow them to reason about it [8] [12]. Once they acquire this knowledge, the tutor's goal is to relate it to the symbolic mathematics that are normally used to solve problems involving this concept. If the student has difficulties making this transition, the tutor is able to map the abstract symbols back into pictorial form to aid the student. This component has been added to the tutor to address concerns that students only learn rote manipulation of abstract mathematical symbols without any conceptual understanding [9]. The tutor's goal is to provide a mapping from real world objects to the mathematical symbols for the student when he is first learning the skill, but to gradually withdraw this help to motivate him to learn the symbols involved.

Animations: The animations used by the tutor are designed to explicitly show the foundations of the mathematics by breaking up problems into their natural components, and showing the connectivity between those components. For example, in animating the procedure for adding mixed numbers, the tutor breaks the problem into the subparts of adding the whole numbers and then adding the fractions. The system then illustrates how these two individual subparts can be combined to form the final answer.

Virtual Manipulatives: Virtual manipualtives are "glass-box" devices which enable a student to perform a mathematical operation beyond his current (abstract mathematical) capability, in a manner that enables the student to see the underlying process. These manipulatives show students procedural steps and, with the use of pictures, can teach students conceptual knowledge about the domain. For example, one manipulative shows equivalent fractions (Figure 3) by displaying a pictorial representation of $\frac{3}{5}$ of a pizza and $\frac{6}{10}$ of a pizza, to demonstrate that they are really the same quantity.

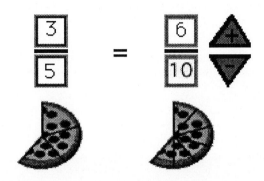

Fig. 3. Equivalent Fractions Virtual Manipulative

7   Discussion and Future Work

The domain of remedial mathematics is amenable to considerable student modeling efforts. First, the wide variation in students' initial knowledge (and partial knowledge) places a strong emphasis on directing instruction to topics in which students need the most help. Second, fractional mathematics is less complex compared to domains many ITSs try to tackle. Thus, the difficulties in building an accurate representation of students' knowledge are reduced. The tutor we have developed uses a strong student model for topic selection, problem generation, and hint selection. This allows students to concentrate their efforts on topics they have not mastered, ensures that problems are at a level of difficulty just beyond what they have mastered, and provides "appropriate" hints. We are investigating how to better incorporate acquisition and retention factors into these mechanisms and how to expand the tutor's repertoire of teaching strategies as a result of this new information.

Future plans also include using scaffolding techniques in problem presentation in a manner similar to the LEAP system [7]. For example, when students are first introduced to an addition of fractions problem for which the operands have different denominators, the tutor could provide the student with the least common multiple of the fractions.

This system has been shown to numerous mathematics teachers, and all are excited at the possibilities provided by it. It has been deployed and is currently being used by community college and high school students as part of a formative evaluation.

Acknowledgments:

This research was supported by a subcontract from Apple Computer, Inc. as part of an ARPA Technology Reinvestment Project under NSF Cooperative Agreement No. CDA-9408607. We acknowledge the work of Dan Neiman and Chris Eliot for help in the implementation, and the advice of Ted Slovin on psychological and pedagogical topics.

References

1. J. Anderson. *Rules of the Mind.* Lawrence Erlbaum Associates, NJ, 1993.
2. H.P. Bahrick and E. Phelps. Retention of spanish vocabulary over 8 years. In *Journal of Experimental Psychology: Learning, Memory, and Cognition*, volume 13, pages 344–349, 1987.
3. R. Burton. Diagnosing bugs in a simple procedural skill. In Sleeman and Brown, editors, *Intelligent Tutoring Systems*, pages 157–182. Academic Press, 1982.
4. C. Finn, Jr. A nation still at risk. In *Commentary*, volume 87(5), pages 17–23, 1989.
5. A. Kashihara, A. Sugano, K. Matsumura, T. Hirashima, and J. Toyoda. A cognitive load application approach to tutoring. In *Proceedings of the Fourth International Conference on User Modeling*, pages 163–168, 1994.
6. S.P. Lajoie. Computer environments as cognitive tools for enhancing learning. In S.P. Lajoie and S.J. Derry, editors, *Computers as Cognitive Tools*, pages 261–288, NJ, 1993. Lawrence Erlbaum Associates.
7. F. Linton. *The Learn, Explore, and Practice (LEAP) Intelligent Tutoring System.* PhD thesis, University of Massachusetts, 1995.
8. N. Mack. Learning fractions with understanding: Building on informal knowledge. In *Journal for Research in Mathematics Education*, volume 21, pages 16–32, 1990.
9. J. Murray. In K.M. Hart, editor, *Children's Understanding of Mathematics*, pages 11–16, London, England, 1986.
10. H. Nwana and P. Coxhead. Towards an intelligent tutoring system for fractions. In *Proceedings of Intelligent Tutoring Systems*, pages 403–408, 1988.
11. National Council of Teachers of Mathematics. *Professional Standards for Teaching Mathematics.* NCTM, Reson, VA, 1991.
12. S. Peterson, M. Ridenour, and S. Somers. Declarative, conceptual, and procedural knowledge in the understanding of fractions and acquisition of ruler measuerment skills. In *Journal of Experimental Education*, volume 58(3), pages 185–193, 1990.
13. J.A. Self. Bypassing the intractable problem of student modelling. In C. Frasson and G. Gauthier, editors, *Intelligent Tutoring Systems: at the Crossroads of Artificial Intelligence and Education*, pages 107–123, Norwood, NJ, 1990.
14. V. Shute. Smart evaluation: Cognitive diagnosis, mastery learning and remediation. In *Proceedings of Artificial Intelligence in Education*, pages 123–130, 1995.
15. D. Sleeman. Some challenges for intelligent tutoring systems. In *Proceedings of the 10th International Joint Conference in Artificial Intelligence*, pages 1166–1168, 1987.
16. S. Tobias. *Overcoming Math Anxiety.* Houghton Mifflin, Boston, MA, 1978.
17. B. Woolf and W. Hall. Multimedia pedagaogues: Interactive multimedia systems for teaching and learning. In *IEEE Computer*, pages 74–80, May 1995.

Student and Expert Modelling for Simulation-Based Training: A Cost Effective Framework

Kalina Yacef[1,2] and Leila Alem[2]

CRC-IDS, 723 Swanston st, Carlton, VIC, Australia

[1] Thomson Radar Australia Corp. & Lab. d'Intelligence Artificielle de Paris 5
[2] CSIRO DIT, Locked bag 17, North Ryde 2113 NSW, Australia
Email: kalina@syd.dit.csiro.au

Abstract. The complexity of student models and expert models is often an obstacle in Intelligent Tutoring Systems research, particularly in the field of simulation-based training where the learner's actions are less contained and can therefore lead to unpredictable paths. In this paper we propose a framework for student modelling and expert modelling in the context of the design of a simulation-based learning system for training of operational skills which is incremental and cost effective as it allows the evaluation of student performance as well as the evaluation of his knowledge in certain aspects of the air traffic control activity. This framework is currently used in the design of an intelligent simulation-based training system for air traffic controllers.

1. Introduction

Simulators are widely used and appreciated in the training process of complex dynamic operations, because of their instructional power [Duchastel 91]. They are particularly helpful for the training of operational skills where students can apply the declarative and procedural knowledge acquired previously without dire consequences on the real world. These constitute the three main types of target knowledge types [Chu et al. 95, Anderson 88] in the various stages of training of any kind of operators. *Declarative knowledge* is a set of facts about the domain being taught, its components, characteristics, rules, standards, etc.. *Procedural knowledge* is about standard practices and activities that skilled operators use. *Operational skill* is about the ability to use the two previous types in a timely, accurate manner, and the ability to cope with dynamic problem solving situations which involve multiple activities and goals [Woods 88]. Bisseret's study [79] on "experience" shows that experienced air traffic controllers had developed a "prudence", or "systematic uncertainty" which was not present in the beginners' behaviour: they in fact change their decision threshold to ensure more safety. These results show that the training of operators is not only about learning facts, rules, etc.. but also about developing a careful instinct and applying knowledge with good sense: this is what we call operational skill.

Operational skills can only be acquired when the student is facing the real world in a "on-the-job" training environment or an artificial but accurate representation of the real world (ie. simulation). In critical and complex domains such as Air Traffic Control, the on-the-job training stage cannot occur before an extensive stage on a simulator [Lucat 88].

Whilst a lot of work has been done in designing systems with the aim of teaching declarative and procedural knowledge (Sherlock II [Katz et al. 92], Cardiac Tutor [Eliot &Woolf 94], Steamer [Hollan et al. 84], Sophie [Brown et al. 75], Scholar [Carbonell 70], SeeChess [Reiman 93],...), less attention has been given to the domain of operational skill. GT-VITA [Chu et al. 95] addresses the overall training of operators of a NASA satellite ground control (real-time environment), from the declarative phase to the operational phase, and adapts its instructional strategies to each step of the training. The context of our research is the training of operational skills in the domain of Air Traffic Control. The type of simulations we are interested in here is an interactive high-fidelity representation of some world, where the learner manipulates the elements of the situations (the control is actually shared between the student and the system), and these situations reflect an accurate representation of the real world (we exclude uses of simulations as a demonstrating tool or any other use where the student does not interact with the model).

As de Jong [91] stated, learning with simulation is only efficient if good support is also provided. Very often this support is represented by a human instructor sitting with the student and assisting him in his tasks: this is the case for air traffic control training. Our research is done in the context of designing an Intelligent Tutoring system for Air Traffic Controllers (ATEEG project, [Alem & Keeling 96]), which aims to provide both the student and the instructor with an intelligent tool that will:

(1) allow the learner to practice his operational skills by providing assistance in the execution of his exercise,

(2) reduce the instructor's workload by allowing him to walk away from the student, and by presenting useful information at the end of the exercise to help the instructor to assess the student and assist him in designing the next exercise appropriate for that particular student [Zhang & Alem 96].

Our interest, in this paper, is focused on the student and expert modelling for ATEEG. The issues central to this work are:

(1) what type of student model should be built in the context of simulation based learning environment for training highly complex skills such as in air traffic control ?

(2) what are the consequences of this choice for the expert model ?

This paper proposes a student modelling approach that is pragmatic, incremental and cost effective. We present our work in the context of the ATEEG project. Section 2 presents the implications for student and expert modelling in such a context, section 3 presents our approach and then comes the conclusion.

2. Implications for student and expert modelling in the simulation-based ITS

A lot of research has been done in the 70-80's on cognitive student modelling, but its popularity decreased when the intrinsic difficulty of the modelling became apparent. As Burger & DeSoi [92] among others stated, student diagnosis is the most difficult tutoring task. It requires long term basic research before a solution can be found. These observations have lead to designing ITS with little student modelling: such systems are not stand-alone systems, the human instructor is still required for adapting the instruction to changes in student knowledge. Gugerty & Hicks [94] refer to such systems as non diagnostic ITS. However, as John Self [95] says, "the tide is turning again", since a good intelligent tutoring system must have a student model to allow individualised instruction. Self [89] and Cialdea [91] have shown the usefulness of formalising the learner modelling process.

Student diagnosis is a particularly difficult task when training complex problem solving skills such as troubleshooting, identifying aircraft from radar display: eg INCOFT [Newman et al 89], or identifying vessel class from sonar signature: eg TOITS [Alem 94]. When building simulation-based tutors, researchers face a non-trivial problem, since the highly dynamic nature of simulators introduce an additional level of complexity to the modelling of the task: the learner's actions being less contained, they can lead to unpredictable paths and each step of a simulation exercise, or session, depends on previous actions of the student. The exploration domain is very large, which makes the task of modelling the student and the expert very fastidious. Furthermore in air traffic control, the complexity of the domain and the lack of formalisation of instructional and operational expertise have dramatic consequences on the design cost of the student and expert models.

Such difficulties reflect the need for a cost effective, feasible framework for student modelling and expert modelling in the context of the design of a simulation-based learning system. Our approach is aligned with Gugerty and Hicks's in the sense that we are aiming at supporting the human instructor rather than replacing him. In fact researchers working in the field of ATC automation tend to think that the earliest we can expect an automatic controlling system is in 20-30 years, and even then the human component must keep the decision side of such system [Leroux 92]. The work done in this field at Eurocontrol Experimental Centre, for example, is aiming beyond 2015 [Eurocontrol].

The next section presents our proposed approach for student and expert modelling, which uses a "translucent" expert model and a hybrid student model.

3. Proposed approach for student and expert modelling

Expert models represent the knowledge or performance of an expert in the domain of instruction. They vary from "Black-box" or fully opaque models to "Glass-box", or fully transparent models [Anderson 88]. "*Black-box*" models produce correct solutions using methods unlike humans, such as algorithmic processors. Although they can judge the correctness of students' actions, they cannot generate instructionally useful explanations of their behaviour. "*Glass-box*" models simulate the human thought processes used in the task being instructed, providing an accurate diagnosis of students' knowledge and misconceptions. But these models are very expensive to build and the feasibility of their achievement is not proved in many domains.

Our expert model is called a "*translucent box*" expert model and combines features of glass box and black box models: it models the general frame of the activity in which the student is being instructed, with some parts being transparent and some others being opaque. We can then judge of the correctness of the student's actions as well as provide some diagnosis of his knowledge.

Student models provide the understanding of the student and a means to support individualised instruction [Polson & Richardson 88, Self 89]. Ohlsson [86] proposed four types of student models leading to different types of cognitive diagnosis: A "*performance model*" represents how successfully the student solves problems in the area of knowledge by using the student's answers and some measurement functions. An "*overlay model*" represents a student by the set of subject matter units he or she has mastered by relating the student's (good or bad) performance on a task to the acquisition (or non acquisition) of knowledge items. This model could guide the choice of best next topic to teach. An "*error description model*" represents student errors based on a defined library of errors. This model could enable the definition of remedial instruction. A "*simulation model*" generates the student's behaviour by constructing the student's problem solving path step by step. This model can explain the student's problem solving approach as well as the solution itself.

In a complex simulation environment, human instructors observing students have problems following their behaviour, although they have access to more information than our computerised system (such as body language). In such a system, a simulation student model is costly to build and its feasibility has not been demonstrated. Our student model is of a hybrid type as it uses performance and overlay structures. The performance structures provide measures which not to rely on subjective rating.(objective measures are essential in the domain of air traffic control [Hopkin 80]), and the overlay structures allow to understand which topics the student has seen and handled correctly: these are particularly useful for the design of the best follow-up exercise [Zhang & Alem 96].

3.1 Expert model

Our expert model is a translucent type and uses a generic model of the activity and its associated expert knowledge. ATC activity consists of a set of underlying operative tasks, each of which is performed according to certain principles based on relevant ATC knowledge. Modelling the expert requires understanding these underlying tasks and their associations as well as formalising the ATC knowledge. We adopt a generic model of the activity to describe the ATC tasks and the problem solving activity as proposed in Alem's methodology [95]. Associated with each task is the relevant knowledge to guide its performance.

3.1.1 The generic model of the activity

The purpose of modelling the activity is to effectively develop a simulation of the problem solving activity in which the knowledge is decomposed into pieces corresponding to meaningful human operations. Each of these operations is modelled as a generic task. The activity model describes the knowledge that the system must have in order to help the student to carry out his or her task during the exploration learning process. It is a representation of "how to do it" knowledge in order to get the intended task accomplished. Alem [94] proposed a task model for modelling the activity and demonstrated its use for the design of the student model and the instructor model for TOITS, an intelligent tutor for sonar operators. In her model, a task contains knowledge about its function, structure and behaviour. We propose to use a similar approach and extend the model to account for the new requirements related to the ATC activity. Similar types of task models have been developed using the MAD methodology [Sebillotte & Alonso 94].

Task analysis as well as a number of interviews and observations with ATC instructors have been conducted in order to elaborate a model of the ATC activity. This model is composed mainly of three major tasks : INSPECT, CONTROL and SEPARATE.

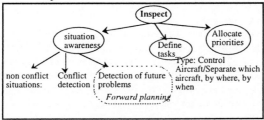

Fig.1. Inspection task

The *inspection* task (fig. 1) plays a key role in the activity, since this is where the air picture appreciation (or mental representation of the airspace) is developed and where the action plan is elaborated and revised. The air traffic controller scans his/her board regularly, and decides on all the tasks he/she has to do. This inspection is done on a regular basis, the frequency depending on the traffic load, and is also triggered by certain types of event: the arrival of a new aircraft in the controller's zone, a pilot call, or a call from another controller. This task is currently black-boxed: the conflict detection for example is done using an automatic conflict detection system.

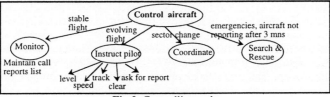

Fig.2. Controlling task

The *controlling* task (fig. 2) is a routine task involving monitoring of aircraft and coordination with adjacent sectors. It includes the monitoring of cruising flights, which have to "report" to the controller at certain points in space or time. It becomes the controller's responsibility to investigate missing call reports (Search & Rescue task). The controller must provide instructions and monitoring to the pilot of an evolving aircraft to achieve his requested level/speed/heading change. Controlled airspace is divided into sectors, each of them being under the responsibility of a controller. Coordination work must be done between the controllers involved in the trajectory of an aircraft before it can depart, and also before it changes sector.

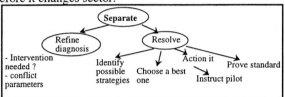

Fig.3.. Separation task

The *separation* task (fig. 3) consists of separating aircraft in conflict by applying a specific separation standard and proving it. When he has detected a conflict, the controller must firstly evaluate the parameters of the conflict, such as aircraft involved, estimated time of conflict, and then resolve the conflict : after identifying a possible set of strategies, he will apply one and instruct the pilot accordingly. This task is glass-boxed.

The purpose of such a model is to effectively develop a simulation of the ATC problem solving activity. In this model, some of these tasks are of a black-box type and some others are of a glass-box type, with a knowledge-based system associated to them.

3.1.2 Expert knowledge

As described above, the generic model of the ATC activity develops a simulation of problem solving activity for each ATC task. Performing or executing these tasks requires certain domain knowledge which is called expert knowledge in our case. Expert knowledge provides guidelines for handling specific situations in each task, including procedural knowledge and declarative knowledge. For example in the task SEPARATE, expert knowledge covers :
- definition of conflict situations
- planning of problem solving strategies

An example of definition knowledge is:

IF the two aircraft are on reciprocal tracks.
   AND the shortest distance between their trajectories is below separation standards
THEN it is a nose-to-nose conflict.

Fig. 4. Definition of nose to nose conflict

An example of strategy knowledge to be applied when a requested change of level introduces a nose to nose conflict can be shown as follows:

IF the conflict is not true (= if longitudinal separation is maintained)
   THEN stA1- Apply longitudinal separation and then vertical separation
ELSE
          stA2- Let the aircraft climb/descent to the limit of vertical separation, maintain vertical separation until aircraft have passed each other and let the aircraft change level (after estimate passing/definite passing time standard)

Fig. 5. Part of strategy knowledge for nose to nose conflicts

Some expert knowledge is applied to identify a particular situation and some is used to handle the identified situation. For example, declarative knowledge such as definition of conflict situation in Figure 4 helps INSPECT task identify a "nose-to-nose" conflict, procedural knowledge such as problem solving strategy in Figure 5 is applied for SEPARATE task to resolve the conflict by generating the best conflict resolution strategies.

The next section presents the task of building the student model which is referred to as student evaluation process.

3.2 Student modelling/evaluation

The student model is a data structure built and maintained by the process of evaluation of the student [Polson & Richardson 88], [Wenger 87]. Our approach to student modelling here is inspired from the way human instructors construct their view of the student. Evaluating operational skills implies a certain level of abstraction: there may be several (or infinite) ways of achieving a set of tasks in a good and timely manner, but the important element is the result itself. If the tasks were all accomplished, safely, timely and efficiently then it is good: the assessment of the student is done on his/her performance. The final result of the student's problem-solving can actually be used to make inferences about the knowledge and/or skills behind it [Gugerty & Hicks 94]. We propose to provide the instructor with performance measures of the student, i.e. elements of "how well" the exercise went. Such a model is then enriched with information regarding the quality of the strategies followed by the student and topics that the student has already seen/not seen. This is provided by the additional overlay model structures.

Our student evaluation process is described below:

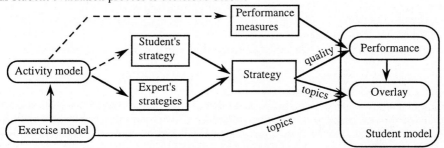

Fig. 7. Evaluation process

The *model of the exercise* defines the instructional context in which the trainee's activity is taking place, and is described in terms of training goals. Zhang & Alem in [96] describe the exercise design process using Case-Based Reasoning techniques. It determines the topics of the overlay model that will be visited and instancies the general *model of the activity* , which gives information about the context in which the student's activity is taking place, initiates the generation of expert's problem solving strategies when a glass-box component is available, and provides the context in which performance measures are done.

The *performance measures* are done on the overall ATC task activity as well as on specific tasks. Meta-rules may be used to derive some information about the student's knowledge, or the measures may be provided bare at the evaluation report. These measures form the performance structures of the student model which is further detailed in 3.2.1.

The *student's strategy* and *expert's strategies* (there are often more than one) when considered at high level are defined by :
a) the order of resolution of conflicts (if more than one at the same time)
b) for each conflict:
    - the aircraft chosen to be moved
    - the separation standard applied (vertical, lateral, or longitudinal)

The *topics* addressed in the particular strategy followed by the student and in the model of the exercise are used to update the relevant fields of the overlay model (number of times the particular topics were seen by the student). The *quality of strategy* is assessed with the strategies suggested by the expert and some adequate performance and cost measures related to safety, expedition and economy. These performance measures are then translated into levels (1 to 5, poor to excellent), and finally stored in the student overlay model for the particular topic visited.

3.2.1 Performance measures

The performance student model is composed of a set of objective performance measures, which could be used as a basis for the provision of tailored explanation/feedback as well as for recommendations for the next training session.

There are a number of performance measures, some relate to specific ATC tasks. For the "conflict detection" task for example:
- number and % conflict detected
- average, min, max, variance time to detect a conflict
- average, min, max, variance time before breakdown to detect a conflict
- number and % of separation breakdown

An example of measure for the "inspect" task is:
- accuracy of strip positioning

Measures relating to the overall ATC activity are:
- Economy : Percentage of deviation from initial flight plans
- Workload: Number of conflicts introduced by the student (not planned in the exercise)
- Timeliness of certain actions
- Safety level. Although the controller keeps all the aircraft separated, he/she might keep the aircraft very close to each other (eg, by resolving the conflicts at the last minute). This measure should actually increase as the controller gains experience, since he/she becomes more prudent [Bisseret 79].

An important advantage of these measures is that they provide a testbed that human experts and instructors can manipulate and, by observing them interpreting the results achieved upon completion of each exercise, help considerably for the cognitive engineering of the evaluation process.

3.2.2 Overlay structures

As mentioned earlier, the overlay model for the conflict resolution task is constructed using the information from the problem solving strategy used by the student in this particular task.

The glass box component for the task SEPARATE, for example, allows an insight on the knowledge used by the student by detecting and recording the exposure and the degree of mastering by the student of the visited topics.

Due to the fact that we are measuring operational skills, ie the ability of applying declarative and procedural knowledge previously acquired, the topics of the overlay structures have to be related to the particular context in which they occurred. The structure of the overlay model is an array in which dimensions are the topics and the situations. In conflict resolution, the topics of the overlay model are declarative or procedural knowledge such as for example Vertical/ Lateral/ Longitudinal separation standards, DME distance standards, time standards, resolution strategies, and the conflict situations are defined by:
- type of sector: enroute, approach
- conditions of conflict occurrence:
    level change
    new entering aircraft (from another sector)

new active aircraft (aircraft status changes from pending to active)
route change
- weather condition (wind, storm, turbulence)
- type of aircraft involved in the conflict: heavy/medium/light
- flight phases of aircraft: departing/climbing/cruising/pre-descending/descending
- navigational aids
- general current workload

4. Conclusion

We have presented our approach to student and expert modelling in the context of the design of an intelligent simulation-based learning system for Air Traffic Control. This approach is based on two types of models: a performance/overlay student model, with measurable performance parameters of the student activity and specific knowledge about the topics visited by the student, and a translucent box expert model which partially models the activity in which the student is being instructed. This approach allows an assessment of the student's performance as well as the provision of tailored help in certain aspects of the activity. The advantages of this approach are twofold: first, its flexibility, with regards to the cost of development, and second, its possibility to be upgraded progressively to a fully transparent model (by replacing the black box components with glass box ones) which would improve the evaluation process.

Currently in ATEEG we have implemented a performance model of the student for some specific parts of the activity (conflict detection, conflict resolution) and we are currently designing the overlay structures for the student model. Then progressively we will extend these to the other parts of the activity: Coordination, controlling tasks.

There are many directions in which research can focus next to improve our approach. We could enrich further the student model with an error model. We have already done some knowledge engineering work to detect the most common student problems and we believe that it would be useful to add this dimension to our evaluation of the student.

Acknowledgments

We acknowledge the CRC-IDS for their coordination and funding on the ATEEG project. We are very grateful to Air Services Australia and Royal Australian Air Force for the time and effort their personnel are spending with us on the project. We also thank all the ATEEG team members: Richard Keeling, Dong Mei Zhang, Ian Mathieson, Bernard Lucat, David Kemp, Gil Tidhar and Jamie Curmi.

5. References

L. Alem (1995), ITS design methodology based on a model of the activity, *Proceedings of Computer in Education*, Singapore.

L. Alem & R. Keeling (1996), Intelligent simulation environments: an application to air traffic control, *Proceedings of SimTect'96*, Melbourne, Australia.

L. Alem & M. Lee, 1994, "An intelligent tutoring system for sonar application in Australia", *Proceedings of The second World Congress on Expert Systems*, Portugal.

J.R. Anderson (1988), The Expert Module, in *Foundations of Intelligent Tutoring Systems*, M. Polson & J. Richardson, Lawrence Erlbaum Associate Publishers, Hilldale, New Jersey.

A. Bisseret (1979), Utilisation de la theorie de la detection du signal pour l'etude de decisions operatives: effet de l'experience des operateurs, Rapport INRIA Rocquencourt CO 7911R60, France.

J.S. Brown, R.R. Burton & A.G. Bell (1975), SOPHIE: a step towards a reactive learning environment. *International Journal Man-Machine Studies*, 1975, vol 7, pp 675-696.

M.L Burger & J.F DeSoi (1992), The cognitive apprenticeship analogue : A strategy for using ITS technology for the delivery of instruction and as a research tool for the study of teaching and learning, *International Journal of Man-machine Studies*, 36, 775-795.

J.R. Carbonell (1970), Mixed-Initiative Man-Computer Instructional Dialogues, Doctoral dissertation, Massachusetts Institutes of Technology, Cambridge, Massachusetts.

R.W Chu, C.M, Mitchell & P.M Jones (1995), Using the Operator Function Model and OFMspert as the basis for an intelligent tutoring system: towards a tutor/aid paradigm for operators of supervisory control systems, *IEEE transactions on systems, man and cybernetics*, July 1995 vol 27, No 7.

M. Cialdea (1991), Meta-reasoning and student modelling, *New directions for Intelligent Tutoring systems*, E. Costa eds, Berlin: Springer-Verlag, pp 183-197.

M. Cox (1992), The cognitive aspects of the air traffic control task: a literature review, IAM report 718, RAF Institute of Aviation Medicine, Farnborough, UK.

P. Eliot & B.P. Woolf (1994), Reasoning about the user within a simulation-based real-time training system, *Proceedings of User Modeling* .

T. de Jong (1991), Learning and Instruction with computer simulations, *Education & Computing* 6, pp 217-229.

P. Duchastel (1991). Instructional strategies for simulation-based training, *Journal of Educational Technology Systems*, 19, 265-276.

Eurocontrol Experimental Centre, B.P. 15, 91222 Bretigny sur Orge cedex, France.

L. Gugerty & K. Hicks (1993), Non-diagnostic intelligent tutoring systems, Proceedings of the 15th interservice/industry training systems and education conference, Orlando, Florida, pp 450-459.

J.D. Hollan, E.L. Hutchins & L.Weitzman (1984), STEAMER: an interactive inspectable simulation-based training system, *The AI Magazine*, Summer 1984, pp 15-27.

V.D. Hopkin (1980), The measurement of the air traffic controller, *Human factors*, 22(5), 547-560.

S. Katz, A. Lesgold, G. Eggan & M. Gordin (1992), Modelling the student in SHERLOCK II, *Proceedings of AI and Education* , vol 3, N. 4.

M. Leroux (1992), How to define a philosophy of automation in ATC, April 1992, CENA document AG-SO-008-T20D R 01.0, France.

B. Lucat (1998), A new approach to ACT simulation, *ICAO Bulletin*, May 1988, pp 30-32.

D. Newman, M. Grignetti, M. Gross & L.D. Massey (1989), Intelligent conduct of fire trainer: Intelligent technology applied to simulator-based training. *Machine-Mediated Learning*, 3,29-39.

S. Ohlsson (1986), Some principles of intelligent tutoring, *Instructional science* 14 293-326, Amsterdam, Elsevier Science Publishers B.V.

A. Paiva & J. Self (1995), TAGUS- A user and learner modeling workbench, *User modeling and User-adapted interaction*, 4:197-226, Kluwer Academic Publishers.

M.C Polson & J. Richardson (1988), Foundations of Intelligent Tutoring systems, Hillsdale, New Jersey, Lawrence Erlbaum Associates Publishers.

P. Reiman (1993), Supporting exploratory learning by providing reminders automatically, *Proceedings of AI-ED 93 workshop: Simulations for Learning: Design, Development and Use*.

S. Sebillotte & B. Alonso (1994), Description MAD de la tache de "controle aerien" executee par deux controleurs, Document Interne INRIA Rocquencourt, Le Chesnay, France.

J.A. Self (1989), The case of formalising student models (and intelligent tutoring generally). *Proceedings of AI and Education*, Amsterdam.

J. Self (1995), The ebb and flow of student modeling, Invited talk at Computer and Education Dec. 1995, Singapore.

E. Wenger (1987), Artificial Intelligence and Tutoring systems, Morgan Kaufmann publishers, Los Altos, CA.

D.D. Woods (1988), Coping with complexity: the psychlogy of human behavior in complex systems, *Tasks, errors and mental models*, Goodstein, Andersen and Olsen eds. London: Taylor & Francis, pp 128-148.

D. Zhang & L. Alem (1996), Case-based exercise design for ATC training, *Proceedings of ITS'96 conference*, Montreal, Canada.

A Programming Learning System for Beginners
--- A Completion Strategy Approach

Kuo-En Chang[1], Bea-Chu Chiao[1], and Rong-Shue Hsiao[2]

[1]Department of Information and Computer Education
National Taiwan Normal University
Taipei, Taiwan, R.O.C.

[2]Department of Electronic Engineering
National Taipei Institute of Technology
Taipei, Taiwan, R.O.C.

Abstract. The purpose of this research is to develop a programming learning system using the completion strategy for beginners. The completion strategy was proved to have feasible result for beginners. Based on the previous works, most of programming tutors require students to write programs and then to evaluate and explain the program correctness. This "program generation" approach is not suitable to beginners. Therefore, the purpose of this research adopts the completion strategy to have beginners learn programming. The completion strategy is to utilize the well-designed programs to let students engage in completing, modifying, and extending their program. This research first investigates the programming learning theories; then initiates the system structure of the programming learning system. Template technique is used to implement the proposed system.

1. INTRODUCTION

Programming teaching systems have been studied for many years with the purpose of helping students to establish programming concept. The programming tutors are Lisp Tutor (Corbett & Anderson, 1992), PROUST (Johnson & Soloway, 1987), Bridge (Bonar & Cummingham, 1988), ELM-PE (Weber & Mollenberg, 1994), and CAPRA (Maite Urretavizcaya & Felisa Verdejo, 1992), etc,. The purpose of these systems is to instruct students how to develop program and assist them to learn programming skills. In general, the common characteristic of these systems is to ask students to design a computer program independently. In other words, these systems often display a problem on the screen, with an editor, to allow students to design a program freely, or utilize a function list to have students choose plans to organize a program. Later, syntax and semantics errors are picked by the computer to engage in teaching. These systems will tell students where and why the mistakes are made and initiate corrections. The approach of asking students to independently design and write a complete program is named as the Program Generation Strategy.

However, to ask a beginner to initiate a program out of the blue will cause frustration to students and further lower their learning motive. In addition, the program solutions for a problem often are not limited to one, so for a problem the system takes much time to trace the program solution that may be different for each student. To avoid the above stated problems, this research adopts a very different approach -- the Completion Strategy (van Merrienboer, 1990, 1992) as the basis of programming tutor for beginners. The so called Completion Strategy is to use the well-designed program (a program designed by expert) to allow students to make completion, modification and extension.

The benefits of adopting this strategy are: firstly, the practice patterns can be multi-phased to stimulate learning motivation; secondly, the correct answer can be limited to a small area to simplify the complex diagnosis process of tracing program. Therefore, the purpose of this research is founded on the completion strategy to develop a programming tutoring system and further allow students to systematically establish the concept of programming.

In the next section, let's explore the learning theories of programming, which also include completion strategy and the fundamental structure of programming; later, introduce our tutoring structure and template technique to implement it; as well as conclusions.

2. LEARNING THEORIES OF PROGRAMMING

Deimel and Moffat (1982) suggested that there are four steps in an introduction course of programming. The first step is to have students execute program to observe its execution and evaluate its benefits and limitations; the second step is to have students study fine structured programs; the third step is to engage in modification and extension; and the fourth step is to independently design and write a new program.

Anderson, Farrell and Sauers (1984) also pointed out that students often use good examples as blue prints to solve new problems, which means to rewrite the original model program to adapt for the quests of new problems. Adelson (1981) indicated that students should establish problem solving knowledge through program functions, pay attention to the similarity of well-known program functions, distinguish program sections, and apply them into the newly designed program. It is known that, for beginners, using examples to conduct the first three steps of programming training is a fine strategy.

Due to the nature of beginners being not familiar with the programming approaches, van Merrienboer and Krammer (1987) initiated the completion strategy. The completion strategy is to use the existing well-designed programs (programs written by experts) as bases to be completed, modified and extended. Under the learning environment based on the completion strategy, the learning contents or programming skills exist in the fine model (or well-design) programs. These model programs may be complete or incomplete, and it is the students' duty to modify or extend the original one. van Merrienboer (1990, 1992) has proved the completion strategy would produce feasible result for beginners.

In terms of completion strategy, the content is a combination of model programs and matching operation patterns, such as cloze (filling in blanks), modification, and extension. We call these patterns as the learning operators to give birth to variety of questions for beginners to learn. The three operators are:

(1). Clozing operator: Leave out several parts of the complete program, and have students to fill in the correct answers. The blanks represent the important concepts the system want students to learn. For the instances of the first and second questions shown on Figure 1, the first question is to train students to know how to find the accumulation, and the second question is to train students to know how to obtain the average.

(2) Modifying operator: Rewrite the program to make it better, more simple, or use another program to reveal the same function. The third exercise in Figure 1 is a typical example. The purpose of this modifying operator is to allow students to understand the meaning of algorithm and the role that each statement plays in the program.

(3) Extending operator: Add new criterias or new commands to the original questions, and have students rewrite the old program by adding or subtracting some steps. For instance, the fourth exercise in Figure 1 adds new commands to the original question, and students have to rewrite the model program for satisfying the new requirements. The purpose of extending operator is to stimulate students' ability to, and further earn the ability to establish problem solving strategies.

Question Input a series of number, calculate their average. As 99999 being input, the calculation is completed.	Exercise 1 Complete the missing portion of line 80 on the model program.

| Examples
10 count = 0
20 sum = 0
30 print "Enter value:";
40 input no
50 while no <> 99999 do
60 temp = count
70 count = temp + 1
80 ....
90 print "Enter next value:";
100 input no
110 wend
120 if ....
    then avg = sum/count: print "the average is:";
    avg else print "No data entered" | Exercise 2
Complete the missing portion of line 120 on the model program.

Exercise 3
Rewrite the model program, simplify line 60-70 to one line.

Exercise 4
Rewrite the model program, only positive numbers are permitted to be input, and calculate the average. |

Figure 1. The programming tutor exercise (completion strategy application)

Another benefit for using completion strategy is to force students to study model program carefully. The students may also put it as the analogical foundation through analyzing and imitation, the programming knowledge will be established. However, when most of students first engage in programming, they do not study exercises in the textbooks in details. In average, fragment knowledge are accumulated through skimming. Only problems encountered while doing assignments, student may return to textbooks and carefully study the context. The completion strategy can force students to carefully study the models for doing program exercises.

To sum the above, we know the completion strategy is the more appropriate learning method for beginners; hence, we use completion strategy to develop programming learning system.

3. SYSTEM STRUCTURE

The purpose of this research is to develop a completion strategy programming learning system to allow students to practice clozing, modifying, and extending various degrees of difficulty, complexing program, and practice how to use the existing program. The proposed system is operated as follows. The system first offers student a problem description and a model program, and the student may engage in clozing, modifying, and extending the program. Then, the system will make evaluations on the student's augmentations. According to the evaluations, the system will make a feedback to the student and record the student's learning status. Next, the system will choose the next problem based on the student's learning status. This procedure shall continuously repeat until the student has learned the programming skill.

There are five units in the system as shown in Figure 2. The problem database is a collection of problems, and these problems may be selected for students to practice programming. The problem generator can select appropriate problems from database. Using the template library, the problems will be transformed into appropriate exercises according to the student's learning status in the student model. These exercises will be displayed on the user interface for the student to practice. The evaluator will check the correctness of student's answers, make an evaluation on the patterns of his/her mistakes, and initiate proper explanations. Furthermore, it informs the student of his/her mistakes and methods of correction. The student model will be recorded through the conclusions from evaluator, and sum up all the student's learning data to decide the learning concepts that the student has to learn. Therefore, while problem generator makes the next problem, the system is able to initiate appropriate exercises that cater to the student's demands.

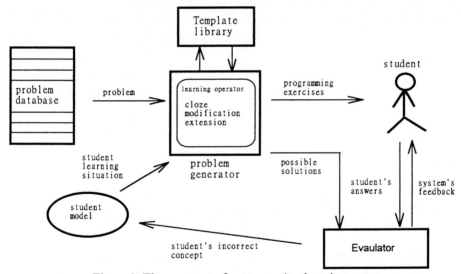

Figure 2. The structure of programming learning system.

3.1 Problem Database
The problem database collects various problems which the contents emphasize on certain portions of the programming concepts, for instance, loop or conditional branch. In terms of this system, when an exercise is presented to student, an incompleted model program is displayed along with problem description. To comply with the problem generator to design exercises and to ensure the produced problems meaningful, the system has designed a set of simple language to describe the core problem. Each problem in problem database is represented as Figure 3.

In which, the "text" portion is the problem description. The "solution" portion describes the model program. The model program is defined by the templates. In each "(template.....)", the name of the template directly follows the alphabets of "template", then is a series of parameters. For an instance of (template sum-initialize sum 0), the template is named as sum_initialize, sum and 0 are parameters. Each template is defined as a representation of a basic programming concept. The basic programming concepts that the system want the students to learn in the problem are described in the "key" portion. The "key" portion represents the important concepts (or a collection of templates) in this problem that may offer problem generator to select. The definition of template will be discussed in the next subsection. The "sequence" portion illustrates the ordering sequence of templates in program. The "modification" and "extension" respectively indicate the exercises evolving from modification and extension operating of learning operators. Figure 3 shows that the question No. 3 (such as no. 3) may evolve one "modification" exercise (modification 1) and two "extension" exercises (extension 2).

```
(Problem (no. 3)
(text "(input a series of numbers, calculate their average. As 99999 being input, the calculation is
completed))
(solution "(template sum_initialize sum 0)"
        "(template counter_initialize count 0)"
        "(template sentinel_control-input no count sum no<>99999)"
        "(template average sum count average)"
        "(template output average=average)" )
(sequence sum_initialize counter_initialize sentinel-control- input average output)
(modification 1) (extension 2)
(key sum_initialize sum_value counter_initialize counter_value sentinel-control-input average
output input input-invalid getmax- initialize getmax_action))
```

Figure 3. The main portions of problem description

```
(modification        (belong-to 3) (no 1)
(text "modification model, may input the computer grades of a given class, when the grades equal
to 999, means the close of input, please print out the students count and the average value")
(solution "(template sentinel-control-input no count sum <>999)"
        "(template output students count)"
        "(insert output 0 output)" ))
```

Figure 4. The description of modification operator problem.

In addition, every problem also defines the "modifying and "extending" operators such as Figures 4 and 5 are for the problems defined in Figure 3. In the example of Figure 4 or 5, besides indicating the problem that the exercise belongs to (belong-to portion) and exercise description (text portion), it also defines the solution of exercise (solution portion). The solution will be referred by evaluator for comparing with the student's answer. While modifying or extending the model program, some templates in model program may be replaced, inserted, or deleted for getting exercise solution. The template operators (replace, insert, and delete) will be given in the solution portion. . The function of "replace" operator is to replace old template with new template. For example, the first problem (noted no. 1) in Figure 5, is to check the correctness of positive input, the original "input" template is replaced by the "input_invalid" template. The function of "insert" operator is to add a new template (or means a new step is added to program). As shown in the second problem (noted no. 2) of Figure 5, the "(insert sum_value counter_value getmax_action)" represents to add "getmax_action" template between "sum_value" and "counter_value" templates. The "delete" operator means subtracting unnecessary templates.

```
(extension          (belong-to 3) (no 1)
(text "extend model program to positive value input  only and print out the average value")
(solution "(template input-invalid no no<0)"
          "(replace input input-invalid)"))
(extension          (belong-to 3) (no 2)
(text "(extend model program to be able to input the computer grades of students of a certain class,
when grades equals to 99999, means the end of input, please print out the highest score of the class
and the  average value."))
(solution "(template getmax_initialize max-99999)"
          "(insert 0 sum_initialize getmax_ initialize)"
          "(template sentinel0control0input no count sum no <> 999)"
          "(template getmax_action max no)"
          "(insert sum_value counter_value getmax_action)"
          "(template output highest= max)"
          "(insert output 0 output)"  ))
```

Figure 5. The description of extension operator problem.

3.2 Template Library

A fine problem description should be able to allow evaluator to "understand" program, easily knows the modifications made by students, and further evaluates their solutions. If model programs are only described by the source statements, then the only method it can judge the correctness of students' modifications is to engage in program code comparison. The work of comparison is impractical and difficult because all possible "correct" program codes have to be pre-stored. For instance: there are many alternates to express the statement of "sum=a+b+c", it is impossible to store each one of them. Therefore, the other representations except "pre-store" method have to be used for overcoming the difficulty in the work of code comparison. For example, LISP tutor (Corbett & Anderson, 1992) used rule-based representation as the definition of problem. The system uses template technique.

Template library collects all templates of problem solutions. In general, all problem solutions have their implications of programming skills and concepts, especially to the program fragment in small problems. In other words, each template that defines the program fragment to solve a problem represents an important concept which the student has to learn. Thus, when students learn a certain template, means to learn the concepts that contain within this template. For the example of Figure 6, the template represents the concept of "the divisor may not be zero", hence, to learn this template may allow students to understand the content of "the divisor may not be zero". The meanings of template structurem are explained as below.

In Figure 6, the sign of "name" indicates the name of template; the "code" portion is to solve problems with BASIC Language. Refer to Figure 3, in the template of (template average sum count average), it will respectively replace the ?sum, ?cnt, ?avg by sum, count, average in the "average" template.

3.3 Problem Generator

Based on the completion strategy of van Merrienboer, we offer some learning operators which include cloze, modification and extension. Utilizing the recorded data of student model, in comply with these operators, the problem generator may produce appropriate exercises which cater to student's weakness to reinforce or correct their concept learning.

The existence of these operators brings another benefit, that is the diverse exercise patterns. This may well stimulate student's motivation to learn accordingly.

```
(template name    :average
        parameter:?sum ?cnt ?avg
        code    : if?cnt>0 then ?avg=?sum/?cnt :
                        (template output ?avg)
                  else print "no data"
```

Figure 6 The definition of a template

Suppose a student is having a problem with addition or ignores the concept of "divisor may not be zero". At this time, the problem generator will look for the template of "sum_value" in the problem library for the student to reinforce his addition concept; or to look for the problem in "average" template to correct his concept of division.

After the exercises affirmed, the problem generator will transfer the problem "solution" defined in problem database into BASIC model programs through the use of templates in template library. As shown in the problem of Figure 3, because the "sum_value" template and "average" template are the ones that students would like to learn, so, the problem generator will automatically reserve these two templates for students to fill in, these become the cloze exercises.

As the students are familiar with certain templates, the problem generator will elevate the complexity of the problems, and design more difficult exercises, which means the modification or extension programs. "Modification" and "extension" are added onto every problem in the problem database (refer to Figure 3 - Figure 5). When engaging in modification or extension, the problem generator may reveal the exercise description and model program for students to rewrite.

Considering the learning situation of the "beginner", when facing "modification" and "extension" exercises, the proposed system adopts the "guide-based" learning approach that makes the extending or modifying portions of model program in cloze form to have students only fill them out but not rewrites the whole program. To beginners, the cloze pattern will guide them to learn the content. At the same time, this cloze form may avoid large changes to model program and simplify the work of evaluator.

The problem generator will produce appropriate exercises based on the student's learning records in the student model. The method is described as follows. The problem generator first marks the templates in the solution portion of the problem definition in problem database. To mark templates means that these marked templates have to be learnt by students. Student's learning records state a series of misunderstood concepts or wrong doing templates. The generator marks the corresponding templates according to the student learning record. After this, the generator will translate the codes in templates into the BASIC program according to the above stated cloze, modification and extension principle. During the translating process, if marked templates have been found, the clozing portions will be determined.

3.4 Evaluator
The system offers model programs for students to practice and fill. Regardless of the modification of model program, the evaluator has to be able to explain and justify the correctness of the answer. To evaluate the student's answers, the evaluator has to know the correct solution (or a list of templates) which will be derived from the problem

generator. The evaluator then compares the derived templates with student's answer. In the event of mismatch, the error can be determined. The nature of the error is decided through the buggy rules in evaluator. The evaluator will further offer appropriate explanation. At the same time, the evaluator will change the student's learning records in the student model.

The student model records the template name of student's error or student's misunderstood concept. When a misunderstood template XXX is found, a (Student (attribute XXX)) will be recorded. If the evaluator has detected the correct answer achieved by the student and the template is in the record, the template will be deleted from the record.

The buggy rules are founded on the template, analyzing each template's structure and the cause of the formation, then to derive each error. When a wrong answer is found, the evaluator will affirm the type of the error and check the template name. Based the template name, the evaluator may match with the corresponding buggy rules to get related explanations

Student's answer	Correct answer in system
40 no <> 99999	40 no <>99999
50 sum +1	50 sum + no
90 count <> 0	90 count<>0

Figure 7. The error example of a student

Taking Figure 7 for an example, while matching the student's and system's correct answer, it is obvious that the error occurs on line 50. When the evaluator finds the error relating to "sum_value" template, it will search for buggy rules of the "sum_value" template and find the related rules, then determines the error pattern, and initiate corresponding explanation to the student. Students can further understand their key problems from the explanation.

In the rules, the first step is to check the correctness of syntax. if it is correct, the evaluator will confirm the correctness of the arithmetic operator "+", then check if there is a variable following the operator "+". If the student fills in a constant like "1" or "2", the evaluator will explain to the student the error of this type. If the student fills in an incorrect variable name, it will also explain the error.

4. CONCLUSIONS

The traditional programming tutoring systems require students to write a complete program, which can be fairly depressive to the students and may cause low willingness to learn. This research adopts the completion strategy to guide students to learn programming. The completion strategy focuses on the utilization of well-designed cloze, modification and extension learning program for beginners.

Through the researches (van Merrienboer, 1990, 1992), the completion strategy has the following benefits:
1. It would produce feasible result for beginners.
2. It forces students carefilly study the models for doing program exercises.
3. The practice patterns used in the strategy can be multiphased to stimulate learning motivation.

Consequently, founded on this theory, this completion strategy system is developed to allow students systematically establish the programming concept.

In the paper, we tried to implement the completion strategy and proposed a learning system of programming for beginners. The system consists of problem database, template library, student model, problem generator, and evaluator. Template technique is used to implement the system. We developed this programming learning system on MS-Windows. The language taught in the system is BASIC Language. In this system, the difficulty and the complexity of the problem design is limited for the beginners. The present problem library has 8 subjects, and there are at least 4 exercises in every subject. This system puts emphases on the learning of programming skills, instead of language teaching, thus users must have the basic language knowledge.

Acknowledgment

This work was supported in part by the National Science Council R.O.C. under contract NSC-85-2511-S-003-043.

References

1. Adelson, B. (1981). Problem solving and the development of abstract categories in programming languages. *Memory and Cognition*, 9(4), 422-433.
2. Anderson, J. R., Farrell, R., and Sauers, R. (1984). Learning to program in Lisp. *Cognitive Science*, 8(2), 87-129.
3. Bonar, J. G., and Cummingham, R. (1988). BRIDGE: tutoring the programming process. In J. Psatka, L. D. Massey, and S. A. Nutter (Eds.), *Intelligent Tutoring Systems: Lessons Learned, LEA*. New Jessey, Hillsdale.
4. Corbett, A. T. and Anderson, J. R. (1992). LISP intelligent tutoring system: research in skill acquisition. In J. H. Larkin and R. W. Chabay (Eds.), *Computer-assisted instruction and intelligent tutoring system: shared goals and complementary approaches*. New Jessey, Hillsdale.
5. Deimel, L. E. and Moffat, D. V. (1982). A more analytical approach to teaching the introductory programming course. In J. Smith and M. Schuster (Eds.), *Proceedings of the NECC*, Columbia.
6. Johnson, W. L., and Soloway, E. (1987). PROUST: An automatic debugger for Pascal programs. In G. P. Kearsley (Eds.), *Artificial Intelligence & Instruction: Applications and Methods. California*, Menlo Park.
7. Maite Urretavizcaya, and Felisa Verdejo, M. (1992). A cooperative system for the interactive debugging of novice programming errors. In S. Dijkstra, H. P. M. Krammer,
    and J. J. G. Van Merrienboer (Eds.), *Instructional Models in Computer-Based Learning Environments*, New York, Springer-Verlag.
8. van Merrienboer, J. J. G. and Krammer, H. P. (1987). Instructional strategies and tactics for the design. *Computers and Education*, 10, 375-378.
9. van Merrienboer, J. J. G. (1990). Strategies for programming instruction in high school: program completion VS. program generation. *Journal of Educational Computing Research*, 6(3), 265-285.
10. van Merrienboer, J. J. G. and De Croock, M. B. M. (1992). Strategies for computer-based programming instruction: program completion VS. program generation. *Journal of Educational Computing Research*, 8(3), 365-394.
11. Weber, G. and Mollenberg, A. (1994). ELM-PE: A knowledge-based programming environment for learning LISP. In *Proceedings of ED-MEDIA 94*, (pp. 557-562), Vancouver, BC, Canada.

Generating and Revising Hierarchical Multi-turn Text Plans in an ITS

Reva Freedman

Department of EECS
Northwestern University
freedman@delta.eecs.nwu.edu

Martha W. Evens

Department of CSAM
Illinois Institute of Technology
mwe@schur.math.nwu.edu

Abstract. CIRCSIM-Tutor v. 3 is a natural-language based ITS for cardiac physiology. In this paper, we describe TIPS, a new text planning engine for CIRCSIM-Tutor based on current research in text generation. Since conversations cannot be completely planned in advance, TIPS plans and executes iteratively. It maintains a goal hierarchy for the tutor while carrying on a conversation with the student. It can handle multi-turn plans on the part of the tutor, and it can back up and replan when the student gives an unexpected answer. In this paper we sketch the design of TIPS using an analysis of human-to-human tutoring transcripts to shape the requirements.

1   Introduction

The negative feedback loop which maintains a steady blood pressure in the human body is one of the more difficult topics for first-year medical students to master. CIRCSIM-Tutor v. 3 is the latest in a series of CAI systems intended to help students master the concepts involved. This paper describes TIPS, a new text planner for CIRCSIM-Tutor v. 3. TIPS stands for "Text generation Interactively, a Planning System". We chose this acronym because of the pun it gives rise to: after all, one of the main goals of CIRCSIM-Tutor is to generate verbal hints to help the student, i.e. tips.

TIPS views responding to the student in an ITS as a text planning problem. It searches a library of plan operators to determine possible responses. The text controlled by plan operators ranges in size from the whole conversation down to primitive speech acts. Constraints on the plan operators can be used to take other knowledge sources into account, such as the domain knowledge base, the dialogue history, and the student model.

We start by analyzing previously collected human-to-human tutoring sessions from a text planning perspective. We characterize the aspects of the tutor's productions which are the most significant to model in a computer-based tutoring system. Then we sketch the design of the new planner and demonstrate that it satisfies the design goals. Finally, we describe the relationship between TIPS and other text planning systems which handle dialogues.

This research was conducted at the Illinois Institute of Technology as part of the CIRCSIM-Tutor project. It was supported by the Cognitive Science Program, Office of Naval Research under Grant No. N00014-94-1-0338, to Illinois Institute of Technology. The content does not reflect the position or policy of the government and no official endorsement should be inferred.

2   A Look at Some Naturalistic Data

2.1   Background

Over the last four years, the CIRCSIM-Tutor project has collected over 75 hours of transcripts of human-to-human tutoring sessions in order to model the pedagogical and linguistic strategies needed for CIRCSIM-Tutor. The sessions were conducted as keyboard-to-keyboard sessions instead of verbally in order to collect text samples which were as close as possible to potential CIRCSIM-Tutor input and output. Our domain experts, who are highly experienced professors of physiology, served as tutors. The students were volunteer medical students.

In their beginning physiology course, the students are given a simplified qualitative model of the heart. Then they are given problems to solve. In each problem, something happens to change the processing of the heart. The student is then asked to predict the direction of change of seven core variables at three points in time: the DR or *direct response* phase immediately after the disruption, the RR or *reflex response* phase, which shows the effect of the negative feedback loop controlled by the nervous system, and the SS or *steady state* phase after a new steady state has emerged.

In the experimental tutoring sessions, the students solve the same type of problem. After each phase, the tutor conducts a dialogue with the student. The tutor discusses each incorrect variable with the student until both are satisfied that the student understands.

2.2   Major Features of the Transcripts with Respect to Planning

Previous studies of the CIRCSIM-Tutor transcripts have concentrated on the syntactic structure of our human tutors' productions [Seu et al. 1991] and their pedagogical goals [Hume et al. 1996, Evens et al. 1993]. We reanalyzed the corpus of texts using a text planning model in order to determine which aspects of the human tutors' productions were the most significant in terms of text planning. The following points summarize our major conclusions.

1) The tutor maintains a hierarchy of goals, visible via the hierarchical structure of the resulting conversation, while at the same time carrying on a conversation with an agent whose responses can't be predicted in advance.

2) The tutor can teach the same thing in more than one way. If the student doesn't understand one method, the tutor has several alternatives:

   a) Explain the concept, then continue.
   b) Use a nested method to go into more detail.
   c) Drop that attempt and try a different method.

3) The tutor sometimes attempts to correct the student's understanding using a multi-turn process. If the student doesn't respond as expected, the tutor can shift smoothly to a different explanation.

4) The tutor can say the same thing in more than one fashion.

2.3   Conversation as a Hierarchical Structure

The high-level organization of the collected dialogues can be succinctly described as follows:

- Within each stage, the text is divided into segments, one for each incorrect core variable.

- The student must explicitly state the correct value of each variable before the tutor proceeds to the next one.

- The variables are discussed in a partially ordered sequence which corresponds to the solution trace of the problem.

Within the basic outline, tutors can follow an idiosyncratic pattern, depending on the student's initial skill at solving the problems, the student's ability to respond to the tutor's help, the tutor's personal style, and a certain amount of free variation. Thus the tutoring session cannot be implemented as a simple algorithmic process. Instead, we have identified twenty or so "correction mechanisms" in the transcripts. These discourse mechanisms form the basis of the TIPS planner. As the planner runs, it produces a hierarchically organized discourse with correction attempts nested inside variables for each physiological stage.

2.4   Making Multiple Attempts To Teach The Same Concept

The correction of each variable is divided into attempts. Once the student gets the right answer for the value of the variable, the tutor goes on to the next variable:

> Correct a variable:
>   Introduce variable (explicitly or implicitly)
>   Make first attempt at correction
>   Make another attempt at correction
>
>   ...

The following excerpt from the transcripts shows an incorrect prediction by the student followed by two attempts at correction. Each attempt ends with the tutor asking for the value of the variable to see if the student understands yet. After the second attempt, the student gives the correct answer.

(1)   S: CC increases.
       T: Yes, that's the effect of increased sympathetic stimulation on the myocardium. However, what happens to CC in the DR period?
       S: CC increases.

T: Reminder, the DR occurs before there are any reflex (neural) changes. What happens to CC in the DR?

S: CC remains constant.

2.5 Use of Multi-Turn Processes

Some of the tutors' most frequently used tutorial mechanisms are recurrent two- and three-turn sequences. In the following excerpt, the tutor points out a contradiction to the student. The variables MAP, CO and TPR are connected by the equation $MAP = CO * TPR$.

(2)　　T:　… What are the determinants of MAP?

　　　　S:　CO and TPR.

　　　　T:　Correct. And you have predicted CO increases and TPR increases. So how can you say MAP decreases?

If the student had not "played along" with the tutor by correctly answering the first question, the tutor would have been unable to continue as planned. In fact, that's exactly what happens in the next example:

(3)　　T:　Now look at your predictions: MAP decreases, TPR increases, CO doesn't change. Is that possible?

　　　　S:　Yes.

　　　　T:　Let's try again. $MAP = CO * TPR$. CO doesn't change. TPR increases…

In this example, the tutor recovers by trying the same plan again but wording it differently. The cue phrase "let's try again" is used to mark a repetition. The tutor could also have chosen any of the alternatives in Section 2.2 for the second attempt. We call these multi-turn plans *interactive explanations* or *directed lines of reasoning*.

2.6 Conversation as a Process Controlled by Two Agents

In the preceding sections, we have described the correction of the core variables as a hierarchical process. Within each attempt, an individual goal, for example the tutor's desire to get the student to state a particular fact, might engender subprocesses which could themselves spawn multiple attempts. At the same time the tutor must maintain a dialogue. In the typical dialogue pattern, predicted by the Conversation Analysis school [Sinclair & Coulthard 1975, Stenström 1994] and observed in our transcripts, every turn has the following basic structure:

Turn:
　　Response to student's previous statement (optional)
　　New material
　　Question for the student (or an imperative)

The response can take many forms. Here is a sampling:

- A response with no physiology content
  - A simple *yes* or *no*
  - A more extensive acknowledgment, such as "Yes, you're right"
- A restatement of the student's last statement
  - Using the student's words: "Yes, <statement>"
  - Using more precise or otherwise preferred language
- A denial of the student's last statement or some aspect of it
  - "No, <contradictory statement>"

In the transcripts the closing question is sometimes left implicit. For example, if the tutor gives the student a hint, the student will usually spontaneously make another attempt to solve the problem. CIRCSIM-Tutor always terminates its turns with a question because people expect computers to be explicit about their requests for data.

The response at the beginning of the tutor's turn usually closes out a tutoring goal, and the new material which follows is generated by a different goal. Even though the parts of a turn are derived from unrelated goals, they must still fit together to form cohesive text. Furthermore, a single sentence may contain material from multiple tutorial goals. For these reasons, we treat turn planning as a parallel process which fashions turns from material provided by the tutorial planner. We accumulate tutorial goals for a turn and pass them to the turn planner as a unit.

2.7 Multiple Ways of Saying the Same Thing

In addition to using a variety of argumentative forms to tutor each concept, the tutor can also express the communicative acts which comprise the forms in more than one way. The sentences below show several locutions which the human tutors use to start the dialogue. Although each of these sentences has a slightly different semantic range, they serve the same purpose within CIRCSIM-Tutor. In addition to the pedagogical value of variety, multiple realizations may be necessary in order to have one which fits into the turn being planned.

(4)	T:	... Now let's review some of your predictions...
(5)	T:	... Let's take a look at some of your predictions...
(6)	T:	... let's talk about your predictions...
(7)	T:	... There are some errors here. Let's start with this issue...

3 Design of the TIPS Planner

3.1 Requirements for the Planner

From the discussion above, we can deduce the following criteria which we want our planner to satisfy. The first four goals deal with the tutor's ability to make and carry out plans while maintaining a dialogue with the student. The final two goals are concerned with the expressive power of the tutor.

1) The tutor must be able to handle interspersed planning and execution, since we can't and don't want to plan the whole conversation in advance.

A game-playing program is a good analogy. A chess program may employ multi-turn strategies, but it cannot predict its opponent's response to intermediate steps of those strategies. Additionally, since we may want to revise the plan later on, we do not want to waste time working out details of later plan steps which may not be needed.

2) The tutor must be able to maintain the tutor's goal hierarchy while carrying on a natural-sounding conversation with the student.

3) The tutor must be able to back up and replan when the student gives a wrong or unexpected answer.

4) The tutor must be able to handle multi-turn plans.

The final two goals ensure that the tutor can generate text for concepts in a variety of ways both at the pedagogical and linguistic levels. Variety at the pedagogical level is important if the tutor is to be able to help the greatest number of students. At the linguistic level, variety is important to ensure that students continue to read the tutor's output and do not resort to solving the problems by rote.

5) The tutor must be able to teach the same concept in multiple ways.

6) The tutor must have the ability to say the same thing in more than one fashion.

3.2   Syntax of the Plan Operators

The TIPS planner is an enhanced "classical" (i.e. STRIPS-style) planner. The plan operators have four fields:

- Name
- Effects
- Constraints
- Decomposition

The intended interpretation of the plan operator is as follows:

1) The *name* field identifies the communicative act which the rule is intended to implement.

2) The *effects* field identifies any state changes which can be assumed to be true as a result of the operator.

3) The *constraints* field refers to *a priori* preconditions which must be true before the operator will be considered.

4) The *decomposition* field describes how to implement the communicative act represented by the *name*, or equivalently how to obtain the state described by the *effects*, in terms of lower-level operators or primitive speech acts. If it contains more than one entry, the entries must be satisfied sequentially. We also have a notation which means "as many times as possible" so that indefinite repetition, such as iterating over each incorrect variable, can be expressed in a simple fashion.

A plan operator may be selected for use if its name (including the arguments) or its effects can be matched against the current entry in the decomposition of the plan operator currently being expanded. The *effects* field permits the specification of the result of an action instead of specifying how the action is to be carried out.

The planning literature contains three kinds of preconditions for plan operators: those which must be true *a priori* (the planner will not try to make them true), those which the planner will try to satisfy if they are not already true, and those which the planner must instantiate even if they are already true. The TIPS planner can handle all three types of preconditions.

We use the *constraints* field of the plan operator to implement the first type of precondition, which is useful for reducing the search space. The second and third types of preconditions both occur in the decomposition field of the plan operator. Since we allow plan operators to match either on the operator name or on the effects, we adopt the convention that entries which contain the name of an operator must be implemented, while entries stated in terms of a desired effect are skipped if the effect is already true. The intention is that if the operator calls for a specific communicative act on the part of the tutor, the tutor must perform that act. If the operator simply requests that a state be true, no action need be taken if the state is already true.

4 Relationship to Previous Work

4.1 Explanation Systems

Other large-scale interactive generation systems have been implemented by Cawsey [1992], Maybury [1992], and Moore [1995]. Of these, Cawsey's EDGE system is the closest in spirit to the work described here, as it teaches concepts from a causal model and embeds the content in a naturally structured conversation. However, EDGE always considers an explanation as a unit. In contrast, CIRCSIM-Tutor needs the ability to drop an incomplete tutoring plan if the student cannot answer intermediate questions.

Maybury's TEXPLAN system illustrates the ability to have multiple ways to explain a concept, including several types of definitions and descriptions. One aspect of TEXPLAN which resembles our system is that plan operators may match on either the *header* field, which identifies the speaker's communicative act, or the *effects* field, which contains the intended effect on the hearer. Moore's PEA system focuses on the intended effect on the student of the tutor's statements. The goal of Moore's work is to be able to ask more intelligent follow-up questions by understanding the meaning of the student's response in context. CIRCSIM-Tutor obtains similar knowledge about the student's understanding by asking further questions.

As each of these systems is primarily an explanation system which accepts follow-up questions rather than a tutoring system, none of them needs to generate the variety of tutoring mechanisms which CIRCSIM-Tutor requires. While explanation is one of the methods which CIRCSIM-Tutor uses to enhance the student's understanding, it is not a major focus of our work. In general, we only give an explanation after the failure of a method such as hinting, which requires more active participation on the part of the student. Furthermore, in each of these systems, the dialogue terminates when the student is satisfied. In contrast, CIRCSIM-Tutor does not terminate the dialogue until the student has answered every question correctly.

4.2 Planning Systems

Wilkins' SIPE system [1988] is an advanced classical planning system used for activities such as robot planning. Wilkins' work is relevant to ours because it is one of the few planning systems using the classical model which can cope with unexpected events happening during plan execution. For example, the robot might arrive at a room and find the door locked. Wilkins presents a taxonomy of actions which the plan execution module can attempt in order to correct the plan, such as grafting new steps onto a plan in progress.

Text planning differs from robot planning is that the tutor cannot "unsay" anything. If the robot drops a screw, it can pick up another screw and try again with few or no untoward consequences. If the student does not understand an idea and the tutor decides to try again, the second attempt must be different in some way, and the first attempt remains in the conversation.

5 Conclusions

This paper describes a new planner called TIPS which will be used to generate natural language dialogue for v. 3 of CIRCSIM-Tutor, and could be used by any similar dialogue-based ITS. TIPS views the generation of a response as primarily a text planning problem. We have shown that TIPS can generate discourse structures similar to those used by expert human tutors. We expect that CIRCSIM-Tutor v. 3 will generate text which is more natural, more varied and more cohesive than previous ITSs, and thus contribute to greater student understanding of cardiac physiology.

6 Acknowledgments

This work could not have been completed without our co-investigators and domain experts, Professors Allen A. Rovick and Joel A. Michael of Rush Medical College. Reva Freedman would also like to thank Professor Gilbert K. Krulee of Northwestern University for his support.

7 References

Cawsey, Alison. *Explanation and Interaction: The Computer Generation of Explanatory Dialogues.* Cambridge, MA: MIT Press, 1992.

Evens, Martha W., John Spitkovsky, Patrick Boyle, Joel A. Michael and Allen A. Rovick. "Synthesizing Tutorial Dialogues," *Proceedings of the 15th Annual Conference of the Cognitive Science Society,* Boulder, 1993. Hillsdale, NJ: Lawrence Erlbaum, 1993.

Hume, Gregory D., Joel A. Michael, Allen A. Rovick and Martha W. Evens. "Hinting as a Tactic in One-on-One Tutoring," *Journal of the Learning Sciences,* 5(1): 32–47, 1996.

Maybury, Mark T. "Communicative Acts for Explanation Generation," *International Journal of Man-Machine Studies* 37(2): 135–172, 1992.

Moore, Johanna D. *Participating in Explanatory Dialogues: Interpreting and Responding to Questions in Context.* Cambridge, MA: MIT Press, 1995.

Seu, Jai, Ru-Charn Chang, Jun Li, Martha W. Evens, Joel A. Michael and Allen A. Rovick. "Language Differences in Face-to-Face and Keyboard-to-Keyboard Tutoring Sessions," *Proceedings of the 13th Annual Conference of the Cognitive Science Society,* Chicago, 1991. Hillsdale, NJ: Lawrence Erlbaum, 1991.

Sinclair, John M. and Richard M. Coulthard. *Towards an Analysis of Discourse: The English Used by Teachers and Pupils.* London: Oxford University Press, 1975.

Stenström, Anna-Brita. *An Introduction to Spoken Interaction.* London: Longman, 1994.

Wilkins, David E. *Practical Planning: Extending the Classical AI Planning Paradigm.* San Mateo, CA: Morgan Kaufmann, 1988.

Towards the Design of More Effective Advisors for Learning-by-Doing Systems

Sandra Katz, Alan Lesgold, Gary Eggan, Linda Greenberg

Learning Research and Development Center
University Of Pittsburgh
Pittsburgh, PA   15260

Abstract. This paper focuses on the advising capabilities of intelligent learning-by-doing systems. We demonstrate the importance of finding out how students use the coaching resources that ITS's make available to them. In particular, which coaching affordances do students use, and which do they ignore? To what extent do system designers' expectations about usage match actual use? We present our observations and analysis of students' use of the advising capabilities of a learning-by-doing system for electronic fault diagnosis called **Sherlock II** (e.g., [3] and [4]). We found that students sometimes depend upon coaching resources to solve the problem for them, and thereby miss opportunities to learn from these resources. Two main principles about the design of effective advising resources stem from this work: (1) design for learning conversations in which students play an active role, and (2) facilitate the integration of different types of knowledge (e.g., conceptual and procedural knowledge).

1   Introduction

The fundamental belief underlying learning-by-doing systems is that learning is produced by *extended engagement* of learners in *complex cognitive activities*, often involving peers, experts, teachers, and intelligent learning systems as partners. In keeping with this belief, learning-by-doing systems offer the means for (1) generating ideas, (2) reflecting on recent cognitive activity, (3) accessing useful information, (4) motivating learner participation, (5) scaffolding students' performances, and (6) developing a long-term agenda for learning. Through these means, learning-by-doing systems respond to a fundamental problem with several other types of learning systems, especially exploratory environments. Exploratory environments provide opportunities that might stimulate learning among peers and with teachers, but such systems characteristically lack an advisor to explain and scaffold learning. Consequently, students often travel down the "garden path", and may quit before they have a chance to learn from their mistakes.

This paper focuses on the advising capabilities of learning-by-doing systems. We demonstrate the importance of finding out how students use the coaching resources that systems make available to them. In particular, which coaching affordances do students use, and which do they ignore? To what extent do system designers' expectations about usage match actual use? Our observations and analysis of students' use of the advising capabilities of a learning-by-doing system for electronic fault diagnosis called **Sherlock II** (e.g., [3] and [4]) enabled us to identify principles of effective advisor design, and ways of carrying out these principles, that we would not otherwise have been able to derive.

2 Sherlock, the Sherlock II Advisor

The domain of **Sherlock II** is avionics for F15 fighter aircraft. More specifically, it was designed to train technicians who work in the "back shop", where aircraft modules suspected of malfunction are sent by flightline technicians for inspection and repair. Shop technicians attach a suspect aircraft module—referred to as a *Unit Under Test* (UUT)—onto a manually controlled testing station. The hard part of the job occurs when the test station malfunctions. Then the avionics technician's job is to troubleshoot the *test station*. Whereas a UUT contains only a handful of circuit cards, the test station contains about 70 cubic feet of circuitry! Sherlock's[1] job is to train technicians in the skills needed for this complex diagnostic task.

Sherlock II is a computer simulation of the actual job environment. Sherlock presents trainees with a series of exercises of increasing difficulty. There are two main phases of a **Sherlock II** problem: problem solving, followed by a review session called Reflective Follow-up [1]. During problem solving, the student runs a set of checkout procedures on a simulation of a test station with a particular UUT attached. Using interactive video, the student can set switches and adjust dials on test station drawers, take measurements, and replace suspect components. These and other activities are realized through a menu-driven interface.

Perhaps most importantly, the student can ask Sherlock for advice at any time. The main principle underlying Sherlock's advising resources is *learner responsibility*—i.e., students should have control over the type of coaching they receive, and the level of detail in that coaching. Sherlock does not intervene unless the student commits a safety violation (e.g., carrying out an ohms measurement when power is on).[2]

Three main types of advice are available: **How to test**, **How it works**, and **Technical data**. **Technical data** provides help with using the documents that avionics technicians work with—e.g., tracing through schematic diagrams of the test station circuitry, following the check-out procedures for a particular UUT, etc. The coaching messages are hand-coded and "static" across problems.

The heart of coaching lies in the **How it works** and **How to test** hints. **How it works** hints describe the functions of components and circuits, and explain how they carry out these functions. The emphasis here is on *conceptual knowledge*. Graphic diagrams of components and circuits are presented along with text. The **How to test**

---

[1]We use boldface to refer to the tutoring system, **Sherlock II**, and regular typeface to refer to the coach, Sherlock.

[2]This policy of learner control carries over to Reflective Follow-up, where students select review activities [1].

hints recommend troubleshooting goals to try next, and—if the student needs additional help—suggest how to achieve these goals. **How to test** hints thus emphasize *procedural knowledge*; in particular, determining what to do in a particular situation and planning an overall strategy. The **How to test** hints are dynamic; they take into account previous actions and their effects. These interpretations are reflected in color-coded circuit diagrams—e.g., red indicates components and signals known to be bad. (See Figure 1.) Like the coaching messages, these displays are updated dynamically to reflect changes in the troubleshooting status of the circuitry. These displays thereby reify an expert's mental model of the active circuitry and its status. We call the diagrams "hypergraphic" because they update themselves, and because students can select components in order to get an explanation about their status.

Students can get increasingly detailed advice in two ways. First, the student can re-select a hint. Second, he or she can request a more detailed hint from the coaching menus. Menu options are arranged from least to most directive advice. For example, a student who was just told which troubleshooting goals remain to be achieved in testing a component (*parts left to test*) may not know *how* to carry out these goals. If the student selects *how to do preferred next test*, Sherlock will suggest a specific measurement to make, including which pins to place the probes on.

3 Student Interactions with Sherlock the "Coach"

To what extent did students' interactions with Sherlock adhere to this principle of learner responsibility? Which coaching options did students use most, and which did they tend to ignore?

To address these and related questions, we examined the data from two phases of formative evaluation. The first phase was field trials of **Sherlock II** at several U.S. Air Force bases. We analyzed the automatically produced "solution trace" files of a random set of students tutored on the system. The second phase of formative evaluation was an observational study of collaborative learning in **Sherlock II** [2]. Eight dyads, consisting of students from local avionics technical schools, collaborated on **Sherlock II** problems. An experienced avionics technician served as "mentor". The mentor provided advice when one student, who assumed the role of "coach", could not help his or her peer; when students did not know which **Sherlock II** advice option to select; or when the advice they received was inadequate. Two dyads were not mentored; they relied on each other and Sherlock for advice.

The first set of data strongly showed that students favored some coaching options over others. Our colleagues at Armstrong Laboratory, Brooks Air Force Base, did gross counts of students' advice selections. They examined 324 trace files from 21 technicians tutored on **Sherlock II**. The results show that students used the **How to test** options much more than they used the **How it works** and **How to trace** options (93% of advice menu selections, versus 6% and 1%, respectively). In other words, students requested procedural advice more than they requested conceptual advice. Furthermore, students accessed particular **How to test** options more often than other options. In general, students often used the **How to test** options that invoke the color-

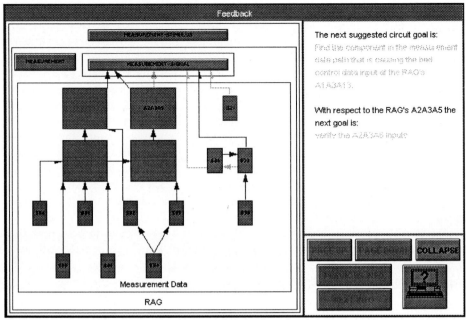

Fig. 1. Color-coded hypergraphic displays of the active circuitry

coded circuit diagrams. Within this class of options, students used the **How to test**/*how to do preferred next test* option the most (32% of all advice selections). This is the most directive coaching option; it tells students which pins to test next.

This preliminary analysis raised several questions, such as: Did students request advice more heavily during some phases of learning than others—e.g., a lot during early sessions, followed by a decline as students gained competence? Did some students use coaching more than others? To answer these questions, we ran an analysis of variance (ANOVA) and paired difference t-tests on the coaching usage data of twelve subjects. These analyses were done on four of the advice *categories* (**How to test this circuit, How to test a particular component, How this component works,** and **How this circuit works**[3]), rather than on particular options within these categories. ANOVA (Session Number x Coaching Option) was significant ($p < .05$) for the **How to test a component** and **How this circuit works** options. This result suggested that selection of these options changed across sessions, but it did not say in which direction the change occurred.

The t-test results reveal the distribution of advice selections across sessions. Table I shows the mean number of selections of each advice category, for three sequential groups of problem-solving sessions (abbreviated as MAPG; e.g., MAPG1 = "the **M**ean number of **A**ccesses for **P**roblem **G**roup 1"). As shown in Table I, there was a significant decrease in the total number of advice selections, from the second

---

[3]The wording of these advice menu options has been modified slightly for clarity.

group of sessions to the third. Access of **How to test the circuit** hints increased across session groups, with a significant increase in problem group 3 relative to group 1. Access of **How to test a component** hints followed a similar "upward" pattern, with a significant increase from problem group 1 to 2, although use decreased from problem group 2 to group 3—perhaps as students made more use of the **How to test the circuit** options. A reversed trend is shown for the **How it works** options. Overall, we see that use of **How it works** either decreased or stopped entirely, across the three sets of sessions.

Why did students use the **How to test** options substantially, especially those that invoked the circuit diagrams (Figure 1), and practically ignore the **How it works** and **How to trace** options? There are several possible explanations. First, students may have found the **How to test** options helpful when they reached an impasse. Perhaps the **How it works** and **How to trace** hints did not satisfy students' desire to find out quickly what to do next, so they tended to ignore these options. The **How to test** option, *how to complete next test*, may have been accessed the most because it lets students take the easy way out; Sherlock tells them what pins to place their probes on. A strategy for testing a component can be *inferred* from information about how the component works and how a signal gets routed through it—as provided by the **How it works** and **How to trace** options, respectively. Understandably, most students took the more direct route to strategy advice offered by the **How to test** hints. Similarly, a possible explanation for students' abundant use of the **How to test** options that invoke the hypergraphic diagrams is that these diagrams provide efficient, visual cues about what to do next. Data supporting this explanation is presented below.

We wanted to make it easy for students to get the information they need, but not to "game" the tutor into solving the problem for them. The latter violates the principle of learner responsibility central to the tutor. One of the goals of **Sherlock II** was to train students in diagnostic skills that *transfer* across avionics jobs. Learning expert troubleshooting procedures and strategies is important for transfer, but it is not enough. Procedural knowledge enables students to "go through the motions", but not necessarily *understand* what they are doing. Conceptual knowledge—e.g., in avionics, knowledge about how circuits and their components work and how signals get routed through them—may be even more important to be able to handle novel situations. We were therefore interested in discovering more about *how* students used **Sherlock**'s coaching resources; in particular, the much-used circuit diagrams. To what extent did students use these diagrams to find out what to do next? To what extent did they request explanations for the procedural cues in these diagrams?

To address these questions, we turned to the second set of data—in particular, the protocols of dyads collaborating on **Sherlock II** problems. We focused on the two dyads who did not have access to a human mentor. (Not surprisingly, mentored dyads used Sherlock as a "coach" less frequently than they used the human mentor.) Our analysis of the protocols showed that students often used the diagrams to find out what to test next, or what to replace. However, they seldom selected components to receive an explanation about their designated status ("good", "bad", or "unknown"). The following excerpt illustrates this pattern of usage. PS stands for the student solving the problem (problem solver), and SC stands for the student coach. Students

Analysis	T-Test Results, Showing Mean Access to Coaching Options in 3 Groups of Problems				
	Total Coaching Requests	How To Test Circuit	How To Test Component	How It Works Circuit	How It Works Component
Problem group (1,3) **X Hint Type**	MAPG1: 5.6 MAPG3: 6.1 (-.5)	MAPG1: 1.3 MAPG3: 1.7 (-.4)*	MAPG1: 3.7 MAPG3: 4.2 (-.5)	MAPG1: .1 MAPG3: 0 (.1)	MAPG1: .4 MAPG3: .2 (.2)
Problem group (1,2) **X Hint Type**	MAPG1: 5.6 MAPG2: 7.0 (-1.4)	MAPG1: 1.3 MAPG2: 1.6 (-.3)	MAPG1: 3.7 MAPG2: 5.2 (-1.5)*	MAPG1: .1 MAPG2: 0 (.1)	MAPG1: .4 MAPG2: .3 (.1)
Problem group (2,3) **X Hint Type**	MAPG2: 7.0 MAPG3: 6.1 (.9)*	MAPG2: 1.6 MAPG3: 1.7 (-.1)	MAPG2: 5.2 MAPG3: 4.2 (1)	MAPG2: 0 MAPG3: 0 (0)	MAPG2:.3 MAPG3:.2 (.1)

* = significant (p < .05)
Number of problems in groups: group 1 = 59
          group 2 = 59
          group 3 = 67
Mean difference is shown in parentheses

Table I

sat at separate workstations, and communicated via a teletyping facility. Our comments are in brackets:

Protocol Excerpt 1
(101) PS: "I just saw the schematics [referring to the circuit diagrams] for A2A3A10. Where does the voltage go into it and stuff. Why are there volts going IN but none comming [sic] OUT?"
(102) SC: "the test you just performed showed that there is a 28 V output. I'm studying the schmatic [sic] now" ...
(103) PS: "I realize that that is not good. What does it mean, bad A2A3A10?"
(104) SC: "The data going into a2a3a10 is good. The data going out is bad. What to do?"

The problem solver requested an explanation about the color coding of the A2A3A10; i.e., about the "green" signals going in, but red signals coming out (101). The student coach was apparently unable to account for the unexpected 28 V output (102), which the problem solver knew indicated a problem (103). He relied on the color coding to suggest the next move: replace the A2A3A10 card (104). The students were able to carry out a successful action (swapping the A2A3A10), but because they did not ask Sherlock for an explanation, they did not understand how Sherlock "knew" the card had bad output.

Contrast this use of advising resources with that shown in the next protocol excerpt. The "pipe" referred to is the system's icon for Sherlock:

Protocol Excerpt 2

(201) SC: "I'm on track, but lets [sic] hit the pipe and check the colors"

[PS selects **How to test circuit** coaching, *parts ruled out.*]

(202) Sherlock:

"Goals completed so far: By verifying that the output at pin 6 and pin 36 of the UUT is good you have shown that: The UUT is good. The test equipment is bad. The measurement functional area is bad....

(203) SC: "whadda ya see?"

(204) PS: "I see that the A1A3A9 must be receiving a bad signal from somewhere. Either, the A2A3A7 or the A2A3A10"

(205) SC: "sort of, it is getting one good signal and two untested ones and giving a bad one."

(206) PS: "So, the question is wil [sic] we be testing pins 33,31, 32, etc... with respect to ground?"

(207) SC: "sounds good, as long as you know what each should read. wake me up when you're done with the grunt work....." [PS tests these pins with respect to ground....]

(208) SC: "hey what should these [readings] be at?"

(209) PS: "Zero!!!!"

(210) SC: "nope"

(211) PS: "What do you mean?"

(212) SC: "ok, do you know how a relay works?"

(213) PS: "Only one point should give a voltage and the rest should read zero."

(214) SC: "nope, lets see what Sherlock has to say about how this circuit operates"

[PS selects HOW IT WORKS—COMPONENT COACHING.]

(215) SC: [restating Sherlock's explanation] "every relay gets 28 volts on the high side. a relay is selected by giving it zero on the low side, causing it to turn on. so, the relay selected should have 28 on one side and zero on the other, while all the rest have 28 on both sides. "

(216) PS: "O.K the light bulb is getting a little brighter."

Note how the student coach prompts the problem solver to *interpret* readings (207, 208); checks the solver's understanding of how a relay card works (212); directs the solver to **How it works** advice on relays when he notices poor understanding (214), and summarizes Sherlock's advice (215). This student is *modelling* active learning for his peer. Unfortunately, students often let Sherlock tell them what to do next, but not *why* to do it, as illustrated in the first protocol excerpt. The two phases of formative evaluation were necessary to reveal these differences. Our observations prompted us to reflect on how to encourage and support active learning.

4 Implications for ITS Design: Towards More Effective Learning Conversations

The 'doing' in *learning-by-doing systems* includes discourse—between students, teachers, and the tutoring system. Below we discuss two principles to guide the design of more effective learning conversations which stem from our analyses of students' interactions with Sherlock.

1. *Get students engaged in the <u>process</u> of overcoming an impasse, beyond giving them control over the type and amount of information they receive.* Despite the fact that **Sherlock's** coaching is non-interventive and students can select the kind of information they receive, coaching is nonetheless passive in this tutoring system, as it is in most tutors. Sherlock sends a message; the student reads it. Students are not guided in finding the information they need. Students catch on that they can "game" the tutor and solve problems by selecting the most directive coaching options, or by following "cues" such as the color coding in the circuit diagrams, as illustrated in **Protocol Excerpt 1**. However, studies of human tutoring suggest that it is highly *interactive.* Human tutors prompt students with questions to guide them over an impasse, a process that Merrill and his colleagues call *collaborative error repair* [5]. This approach is illustrated in **Protocol Excerpt 2**.

We have been working on a redesign of coaching that will prompt students with questions that experts ask themselves—and that human tutors ask students—when students are stuck. For example, Sherlock would list the measurements the student made and prompt the student to interpret the results of these measurements. Graphics tools would allow students to color code the circuit diagrams *themselves*, rather than have Sherlock do this for them. Feedback on the student's responses would be provided. This learning conversation would thereby guide students through an expert's approach to overcoming an impasse—e.g., deciding what to do based on what he or she knows about the circuitry and how its components work.

Of course, the hardest challenge in designing for learning conversations is to balance prompting and informing. More research is needed on how human tutors do this, and encourage learner self-reliance in general. Providing feedback and selecting questions according to the student's ability level should help to make "collaborative error repair" effective as well as tolerable. As students reach higher levels of competency, the system could also assign "costs" to requests for coaching—e.g., adjust the performance rating, by taking reliance on coaching into account. More directive advice would cost more than reminder hints.

2. *Facilitate the integration of procedural and conceptual knowledge. Hypertext can help.* There are advantages to parcelling advice across several categories of options—e.g., according to different types of information, and different levels of detail—as we did. For one thing, this approach reduces the amount of text displayed. It also makes it easier for system developers to construct advice that progresses from very general or "reminder" hints to more specific, detailed hints.

However, some of the problems we discussed might stem from this approach to coaching. For instance, what if the student does not know what information he or she needs? The student may need to access several hints before receiving useful advice. Also, distributing information over several options makes it difficult for students to keep track of the information available from each option. In **Sherlock II**, for example, the student may continually use **How to test** coaching and be unaware of what **How it works** coaching has to offer. Lastly, parcelling out information divides the relevant information into useful "episodes" while making the "whole story" less explicit. Even if a student asks for all of the hints available on any particular component or circuit, the burden of synthesizing that information rests on the student, who may not be ready to rise to the task.

If we want students to integrate different types of knowledge—e.g., procedural and conceptual knowledge—we need to make it convenient for them to do so. Hypertext is one way to achieve this. Hypertext is incorporated in the ITS for flightline avionics that we are developing, called **EagleKeeper**. The student is able to expand general statements, as desired, as well as select particular terms and phrases in order to receive further information about these items. The student need not "flip" between advice menu options to do this. Hypertext also has the nice effect of allowing students to see elaborated explanations in *context*, while limiting the amount of text displayed.

But hypertext and hypergraphics are not the full answer to the problem of helping students integrate different types of knowledge. Further research is needed on how and when (i.e., in what contexts) skilled human tutors do this. We also need to learn more about how experts draw upon conceptual knowledge while carrying out highly procedural tasks, especially when their procedural "rules" fail them and need to be refined. Our current research on the interactions between collaborating peers, between students and mentors, and between skilled avionics technicians [2] aims to address these sorts of issues.

Acknowledgement

The research reported in this article was supported by the US Air Force and by a grant from The Spencer Foundation. The data presented, the statements made, and the views expressed are solely the responsibility of the authors.

References

1. Katz, S., & Lesgold, A. (1994). Implementing post-problem reflection within Coached Practice Environments. In P. Brusilovsky, S. Dikareva, J. Greer, and V. Petrushin (Eds.), *Proceedings of the East-West International Conference on Computer Technologies in Education* (pp. 125-30), Crimea, Ukraine.
2. Katz, S. (1995). Identifying the support needed in computer-*supported* collaborative learning systems. In Schnase, J.L., and Cunnius, E.L, *Proceedings of CSCL '95: The First International Conference on Computer Support for Collaborative Learning* (pp. 200-203), Bloomington, Indiana. New Jersey: Lawrence Erlbaum Associates.
3. Katz, S., Lesgold, A., Hughes, E., Peters, D., Eggan, G., Gordin, M., Greenberg., L. (in press). Sherlock II: An intelligent tutoring system built upon the *LRDC Tutor Framework*. In C.P. Bloom and R.B. Loftin (Eds.), *Facilitating the Development and Use of Interactive Learning Environments*. New Jersey: Lawrence Erlbaum Associates.
4. Lesgold, A., Eggan, G., Katz, S., & Rao, G. (1992). Possibilities for assessment using computer-based apprenticeship environments. W. Regian & V. Shute (Eds.), *Cognitive approaches to automated instruction* (pp. 49-80). Hillsdale, NJ: Lawrence Erlbaum Associates.
5. Merrill, D.C., Reiser, B.J., Ranney, M., & (1992). Effective tutoring techniques: A comparison of human tutors and intelligent tutoring systems. *Journal of the Learning Sciences, 2(3)*, 277-305.

Collaborative Dialogue with a Learning Companion as a Source of Information on Student Reasoning

Eva L. Ragnemalm

Dept. of Computer and Information Science, Linköping University, Sweden.
E–mail: elu@ida.liu.se

Abstract: This report focuses on a problem within the area of Intelligent Tutoring Systems; that of analysing student's reasoning (student diagnosis). A novel approach to collecting information for this analysis, complementary to traditional student modelling techniques, is presented. This technique is based on using a Learning Companion, a computer based agent, as a collaboration partner to the student. In the dialogue between the student and the Learning Companion, information on their problem-solving process is revealed. This information would then be extracted and used for student modelling purposes. Analysis of the proposed solution is commenced in a small experiment and an explorative implementation described here.

Keywords: Learning Companion Systems, Student Modelling, Student Diagnosis, Collaborative Dialogue, Troubleshooting.

1 Introduction

One of the important components in an Intelligent Tutoring System, ITS, is a *Student Model*. This is a collection of data about the current student which is used at runtime by the other components in the system in a number of different tasks. Such tasks include for instance planning the sequence of instruction, remediating misconceptions, generating feedback and explaining the reason for an error made by the student (see e.g. [23], [18], [12]). The complexity of the student modelling problem has caused researchers to question the necessity of student modelling (see e.g. [16] and for counter–arguments [15]). This question will not be discussed further in this paper, in the following it is assumed that student modelling is worthwhile.

In this paper *student modelling* is defined as the process of dynamically gathering information about the student and storing that in a student model. Student modelling is a part of *Student Diagnosis*, which is the process of analysing the student's actions and converting that to a foundation for educational decisions [20].

Most ITS adhere to some variation of the pedagogic principle of learning-by-doing. That is, most ITS are designed to allow the student to exercise the skill to be learned (e.g. LISP tutor [6], Sherlock [13], Sophie, [1], Scent [11]). It is in this context that student modelling takes place. The student modelling process is usually a covert activity, even though overt and negotiated student modelling have been proposed (e.g. [10], [16]). In covert student modelling student diagnosis is based on the input available as the student solves the exercises presented by the ITS. The benefit of covert modelling is that the student is not distracted from the problem solving by (to him) irrelevant questions.

The problem of student diagnosis can be subdivided into three phases [20]. These phases are the *data acquisition* phase, the *transformation* phase and the *evaluation* phase. Data acquisition refers to the collection and refinement of the input, including the abstraction of actual input (such as mouse movements or whatever peripherals are used) to concepts in the domain (such as an action or an answer). Transformation refers to the conversion done either by reconstructing the knowledge causing the student action or by applying knowledge of how to solve the exercise and comparing the result to the student's action. The evaluation refers to the judgement of whether what the student is believed to know is correct or not in relation to the goal of the teaching situation. The student model is constructed either before or after the evaluation phase, thus student modelling covers either the first two or all three phases.

One problem in the data acquisition for covert student modelling is that of gathering sufficient data. If a procedure is taught, procedure oriented evaluation should be used, not goal oriented, but if the procedure is mental it will be inaccessible to the ITS.

Techniques for extrapolating the student's unobservable behaviour from what can be observed include plan recognition and path finding techniques (see e.g. [23]). These techniques have the drawback that they are dependent on the complexity of the exercise the student is doing. When there are many paths or plans that explain observed activities, they quickly become intractable.

There are also techniques that attack the problem of data acquisition by having the student provide additional information to the system, information which is normally not expressed during problem solving. FITS [18] and EPIC [22] require that the student specify what subproblem he wishes to work on. Other systems provide a tool interface through which information is collected while the student uses the tool in the problem solving. An example of this is the program editor in the LISP tutor [6].

This paper proposes another approach to this problem: the use of collaborative dialogue with a Learning Companion, LC. Collaborative dialogue reveals the reasoning of the collaborating partners. The dialogue can thus provide additional information for the data acquisition process. First an example domain is presented. The alternate method is then presented and analysed. A preliminary experiment and explorative implementation are presented. These initial studies indicate that the method will probably suffice but is computationally complex.

2 Example: student modelling of Diagnosis

An example of a situation where the data available is scarce is learning to diagnose faults in a pulp mill by practising with a simulator–based ITS. Diagnosis is here defined as the identification and remediation of faults in a process. The strategy of diagnosis is a cognitive procedure with 10 steps[1] to be executed in specific order [21]. The steps are presented in Table 1 and the observed sequence illustrated in Figure 1.

---

1. The original list [21] contained 8 steps, (1-7, 10), but the author found evidence for another, the ordering of repairs, 8. The application of repair is also shown as an explicit step, 9.

Table 1: The steps to take for a correct diagnosis.

1	**Identification of symptoms.** All symptoms should be identified in order to "see the whole situation".
2	**Judgement.** How serious is the problem (the consequences of it, and do we need to take immediate action to avoid danger or other serious complications).
3	**Determination of possible faults.** All possible faults should be considered.
4	**Ordering of faults** according to likelihood, potential damage and other criteria.
5	**Testing.** Finding evidence for/against a certain fault. (Repeat for all faults. If we rule out all the previously identified faults, return to step 1 or step 3 to think of more.)
6	**Determination of repairs** or remedies. When a fault has been identified, it can often be repaired in a number of different ways, and all must be considered.
7	**Determination of the consequences** of the application of repairs. The side effects of the different repairs must be examined for desirability.
8	**Ordering of repairs** according to desirability of side effects.
9	**Application of repair.**
10	**Evaluation.** Has the situation improved? See if the repair action has the intended effects. If not, either try the next repair or conclude it wasn't that fault, and try another.

As shown in Figure 1, the difference in the top–level strategy between novices and experts is significant. Conversely, the (mental) execution of the top–level strategy (which steps and the order they are taken) is thus significant indication of the student's level of expertise.

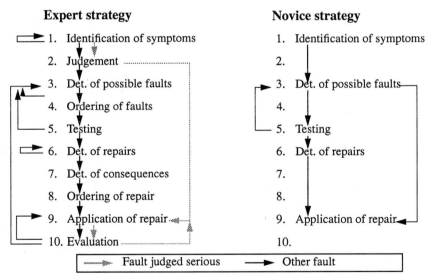

Fig. 1. Models of the diagnostic strategy, employed by experts and novices respectively.

Consider an ITS with the goal of teaching the novices to use the same strategy as the experts. The differences in the models imply that modelling the student's strategy of diagnosis is necessary to judge his competence. The student's strategy of diagnosis is thus an important part of the student model in this ITS. This strategy, however, is mental. The only step which is normally overt is the application of a repair, which shows as input to the simulator. This makes covert data acquisition difficult.

The data acquisition techniques mentioned previously are not suited to this problem. Path finding and plan recognition are unsuitable since there are *many* possible reasons for applying one specific repair. The problem is of exponential complexity.

It would be possible to have the student specify to the ITS which subproblem (i.e. strategy step) he is working on. The drawback with this is that in order to be non–obtrusive, a menu would be the logical choice for interaction. This would provide the student with reminders of the steps that are often forgotten, which would not be present in the real working situation. Similarly, a tool on top of the simulator changes the task into something different from the real working situation. These solutions thus seem to be less than ideal.

3 Collaborative dialogue as a source of information

A technique that is sometimes used by teachers is that of listening to two students talking about a problem. A similar technique is used by researchers in decision making when studying the cognitive procedures of taking a decision. The task is converted into one requiring collaboration between two subjects and the dialogue protocol used as a source of data on the decision making [25]. Such collaborative dialogue could be tapped by a system capable of parsing it, and used in the student diagnosis.

This approach, however, requires the presence of two students. One option is to use a computer–based agent as the collaboration partner. Chan and Baskin [4] propose the concept of Learning Companion Systems, LCS, which are ITSs equipped with an additional agent, the Learning Companion, LC. The LC is a pedagogic tool in the form of a "fellow student" that can either collaborate, teach or compete with the student. LCs have been constructed for competition and reciprocal tutoring [3], [5], concurrent collaboration [8], [7], and learning–by–teaching [17].

The purpose of the LC as proposed here is the possibility of using the dialogue arising from the collaboration as a source of data for the student modelling process. In this case we are only interested in the collaborative LC, since the interesting dialogue does not occur in the competitive or teaching–related settings.

The situation envisioned is a LCS, where the task of the simulator–based ITS component is to present exercises to the student, based on its student model, and evaluate the results. The task of the LC is to collaborate with the student on solving the exercises. The LC's reasoning should be restricted so that the LC does not rush off and solve the problem on its own, since the student should be working on the problem as well. The ITS then takes the arising dialogue and uses it as input to the student modelling procedure. This input will reflect the student's reasoning in greater detail than the input provided to the simulator alone.

Given the greater detail of student input, existing student modelling techniques would then be used in the ITS. For instance, issue tracing [2] can be used, although the definition of recognisers will rely on the quality of the speech recognition system in the case where spoken language is used.

4 Design of a Learning Companion

Creating a LC is a challenging problem. In general the LC is a kind of computer–based intelligent agent and as such appears to be AI complete. The observation that collaborative dialogue reveals reasoning was based on spoken natural language dialogue, thus the LC may need to communicate using spoken natural language. In order to collaborate, it needs to be capable of solving the problem the student is presented with. To be perceived as a believable fellow student, it might also have to learn along with the student. These are complex problems.

It is possible, however, that the specific LC required to cause the student to reveal his reasoning need not be so complex. It must not be so simple as to cause the student to be irritated with it, but it might not require complete capacity on all the above aspects. Its main purpose is to encourage the student to speak his mind, and Weizenbaum's Eliza [24] and Mauldin's Julia [9] show the extent to which a simple design can be acceptable.

A preliminary study of the feasibility of using a LC to elicit collaborative dialogue which could be used to inform the student modelling process was performed. It focused on three questions:

1. Does the collaborative dialogue really reflect such a high level strategy as that of diagnosis? The original models captured by Schaafstal [21] were based on think–aloud protocols and deep interviews. Is it possible to get enough information from uncontrolled dialogue? Is the information that is needed to identify the student's strategy really present in dialogue generated by collaborative problem solving?
2. How computationally complex is the problem of extracting the pertinent information from the spoken dialogue? Specifically, are keywords usable (making the speech–recognition technique *keyword–spotting* [14] usable)?
3. How complex would the construction of this simplified "intelligent" agent be? How would it be designed?

A small experiment was carried out in order to study the first question, and the data was also used in a preliminary study of the second. The third question was studied in an explorative implementation of a prototype LC. The experiment and the implementation are briefly described below. A more detailed description can be found in [19].

5 Dialogue experiment

In order to examine the information content of collaborative dialogue, an experiment on diagnosis of an evaporator in a collaborative setting was performed. A simulator was used to illustrate the fault situation, and the subjects were to identify the fault and compensate for it. Five subjects with no previous skill in process control or diagnosis were used. They were instructed in the expert strategy and told to collaborate on the exercises.

The subjects were divided into three pairs[2] of subjects, for each pair two exercises were video-taped and transcribed, divided into utterances based on speaker and con-

---

2. One subject participated twice, in order to see if a learning effect was achieved during the experiment. None was detected.

tent. Table 2 shows a sample of dialogue at the beginning of an exercise. The statements were analysed and classified by two different raters as to what diagnostic step was reflected, if any. All the ten steps could be found in the dialogue. The dialogue

Table 2: Collaborative dialogue, diagnosing an evaporator

No	Speaker	Statement	Strategy step
4	Anne	But now ... the pressure is dropping.	Symptom (1)
5	Anne	There is a possibility that that one *<points to steam input>* is ...	Faults (3)
6	Beth	Let's see	-
7	Anne	but ... the level is increasing marginally	Symptom (1)
8	Beth	... decreasing ...	Symptom (1)
9	Beth	L2 is in...creasing ...	Symptom (1)
10	Beth	T2 is decreasing	Symptom (1)
11	Anne	Mm.	-
12	Anne	Mhm?	-
13	Anne	So what shall we do?	Faults (3)
14	Beth	Serious error? Noo, is it?	Judgement (2)
15	Anne	No, pressure is okay,	Symptom (1)
16	Anne	the separator is ... rising.	Symptom (1)
17	Anne	We must fix this, but it's not so serious ...	Judgement (2)
Later:			
50	Anne	Come to think of it, it's probably the pressure we should increase,	Repair (6)
51	Anne	this *<points to steam input>* has probably decreased, because this *<points to separator>* doesn't evaporate as much as it should,	Model reasoning

contained a high percentage of statements classified as coming from one of the ten steps (68% classified, another 26% difficult to classify, as evidenced by different classification by the raters, but still classifiable).

The fact that all the ten steps could be identified indicates that sufficient information to recognise the different steps was present in the dialogue. Provided that sufficient techniques for extracting that information can be developed, it should be possible to use the dialogue for student modelling. The high percentage of classifiable statements indicates that much of the dialogue is task oriented, eliminating the need to allow for small talk.

With respect to the second question, an attempt at finding keywords for identifying strategy steps failed. For instance, sets of keywords that cover more than 50% of the utterances pertaining to Identification of Symptoms start yielding false hits. This implies that the problem of information extraction requires further study.

6 Explorative implementation: Else

As a first step of assessing the possibility of simplifying the design of the LC, an explorative implementation of key aspects of an LC was made. The program was called Else. The dialogue from the experiment above was studied in order to identify recurrent characteristics and the behaviour of the subjects was used as a source of inspiration on the behaviour of Else. The existing LCs were thought to be too different from the aims of the current one to be copied. Only the core functionality (problem solving and simple dialogue management) were included in Else, no parsing or language generation was implemented. Else was designed to be capable of solving a diagnostic problem in the simulator and to interact with the student in the process. A more complete report on this implementation is found in [19].

The first of the identified properties was the fact that the majority of the utterances consisted of straightforward statements of facts (claims, cf. statements 4–10 in Table 2) and a minor part was a claim backed by one or more observations (as in statements 15–17 in Table 2). These two types of claims are formed in terms of *results* of subproblems in the strategy. Discussions related to the subproblems themselves (as in statements 50-51 in Table 2) account for no more than 4% of all statements, and were thus thought less important at this point. This led to a decision to leave out models of the subproblems and the evaporator functionality from the design, making Else incapable of discussing anything but the top level strategy. This decision is also supported by the finding by Schaafstal [21], that the novices were already skilled in the subproblems, thus not necessarily requiring training of them.

Another property observed was that parts of the dialogue were not dialogue but intertwined monologues, as in statements 2–10 in Table 2. In these parts it was not possible to identify any underlying plan or intention except for the diagnostic strategy itself and subsequently no other overall plan was identified either. Else has a model of diagnosis but no explicit plan for the dialogue or the collaboration and contains no model of the collaboration partner (the student). It is strictly reactive.

The fact that much of the interaction consisted of providing an alternate result or the next result led to the view that collaboration could be seen as using the companion's expressed results in the private problem solving, and expressing subsequent results. This was realised through an architecture based on the separation of problem solving and dialogue management. Although they interact, neither component controls the other. The fact that these components together cause Else to appear collaborative, since Else uses the student's utterances in its own reasoning, can be seen as an emergent property. Else was also given the ability to choose whether to attend the student's statements or not, based on a collaboration mood.

The subjects were also found to repeat themselves and to express themselves in non–grammatical and incomplete sentences. The first behaviour was allowed for in the implementation by having Else "forget" facts, while the second will have to be implemented in the parsing part of a complete LC. The interaction with Else is purely symbolic, so no parsing is done. Else allows for interruptions and also hesitating students by giving the option to "speak" or be silent regardless of whether the student is currently speaking.

Else is capable of participating in a dialogue similar to that in statements 4–17 in Table 2, but can not produce or respond to statements like those in 50–51. Else is an explorative implementation, and further analysis of its properties is required. Specifically, the sufficiency of collaboration as an emergent property requires further study.

The basic criteria is that Else must be capable of eliciting dialogue from the student, such that the student's strategy is revealed. The data acquisition in student modelling also remains to be designed for extracting the novel data provided in the dialogue.

7 Summary

This paper introduced the problem of how to trace a student's reasoning for student modelling purposes, specifically when modelling the student's strategy of diagnosis in a simulator–based environment.

The proposed solution to the problem of data acquisition is based on the use of collaborative problem–solving dialogue. A small experiment supported the belief that the dialogue between two students collaborating on diagnosing a fault presented on a simulator does reflect their reasoning, and thus reveals the diagnostic strategy they apply. The data thus elicited would then be used by the student modelling process to build and maintain a student model. The experiment also indicated that the problem of parsing the spoken language and constructing recognisers for the student modelling process is a complex problem still to be solved.

The explorative implementation of a prototype LC, Else, indicated the possibility of modelling collaboration as an emergent phenomenon, where dialogue and problem solving are modelled as equal processes, neither controlling the other. Further research will continue the exploration of the design of a LC.

References

[1] Brown, J. S., Burton, R., and de Kleer, J. Pedagogical, natural language and knowledge engineering techniques in SOPHIE I, II, and III. In Sleeman, D. and Brown, J. S., editors, *Intelligent Tutoring Systems*, chapter 11, pages 227–282. Academic Press, 1982.

[2] Burton, R. R. and Brown, J. S. An investigation of computer coaching for informal learning activities. In Sleeman, D. and Brown, J. S., editors, *Intelligent Tutoring Systems*, chapter 4, pages 79–98. Academic Press, 1982.

[3] Chan, T.-W. Integration kid: A Learning Companion system. In *Proceedings of IJCAI'91*, pages 1094–1099, Sydney, Australia, 1991.

[4] Chan, T.-W. and Baskin, A. B. Learning companion systems. In Frasson, C. and Gauthier, G., editors, *Intelligent Tutoring Systems: At the Crossroads of Artificial Intelligence and Education*, pages 6–33. Ablex, New Jersey, 1990.

[5] Chan, T.-W. and Chou, C.-Y. Simulating a learning companion in reciprocal tutoring systems. In *Proceedings of Computer Supported Collaborative Learning (CSCL'95), on-line version*, 1995. http://www-cscl95.indiana.edu/cscl95/chan.html (accessed Nov 7, 1995).

[6] Corbett, A. T. and Anderson, J. R. LISP Intelligent Tutoring System: research in skill acquisition. In Larkin, J. H. and Chabay, R. W., editors, *Computer Assisted Instruction and Intelligent Tutoring Systems: Shared Goals and Complementary Approaches*, chapter 3, pages 73–109. Lawrence Erlbaum Associates, 1992.

[7] Dillenbourg, P. and Self, J. A. PEOPLE POWER: A human-computer collaborative learning system. In Frasson, C., Gauthier, G., and McCalla, G. I., editors, *Proceedings of ITS'92*, pages 651–660. Springer Verlag, 1992.

[8] Dillenbourg, P. J. *Human-Computer Collaborative Learning*. PhD thesis, University of Lancaster, Department of Computing, 1991.

[9] Foner, L. N. What's an agent anyway? a sociolgical case study. Technical Report 93-01, Agents Group, MIT Media Lab, MIT Media Laboratory, 20 Ames St. Camebridge, MA 02139., 1993. Available via Foner's home page http://lcs.www.media.mit.edu/people/foner/ (as of 19th of March 1996).

[10] Goodyear, P. and Tait, K. Learning with computer-based simulations: Tutoring and student modelling requirements for an intelligent learning advisor. In *Learning and instruction: European research in an international context*, pages 463–481, 1991. Proceedings of the 3rd conference of the European Assoc. for Research on Learning and Instruction, 1989.

[11] Greer, J., Mark, M., and McCalla, G. Incorporating granularity-based recognition into SCENT. In Bierman, D., Breuker, J., and Sandberg, J., editors, *Proc. of the 4th International Conference on AI and Education*, pages 107–115, Amsterdam, 1989.

[12] Holt, P., Dubs, S., Jones, M., and Greer, J. The state of student modelling. In Greer, J. E. and McCalla, G. I., editors, *Student Modelling: The Key to Individualized Knowledge-Based Instruction*, NATO ASI Series F, pages 3–35. Springer-Verlag, 1994.

[13] Lesgold, A., Lajoie, S., Bunzo, M., and Eggan, G. Sherlock: A coached practice environment for an electronics troubleshooting job. In Larkin, J. H. and Chabay, R. W., editors, *Computer-Assisted Instruction and Intelligent Tutoring Systems: Shared Goals and Complementary Approaches*, chapter 7, pages 201–238. Lawrence Erlbaum Associates, 1992.

[14] Markowitz, J. Keyword spotting in speech. *AI Expert*, pages 21–25, October 1994.

[15] McCalla, G. The central importance of student modelling to intelligent tutoring. In Costa, E., editor, *New Directions for Intelligent Tutoring Systems*, pages 107–131. Springer-Verlag, 1992.

[16] Newman, D. Is a student model necessary? Apprenticeship as a model for ITS. In Bierman, D., Breuker, J., and Sandberg, J., editors, *Proc. of the 4th International Conference on AI and Education*, pages 177–184, Amsterdam, 1989.

[17] Nichols, D. Issues in designing learning by teaching systems. AAI/AI-ED 107, Computing Department, Lancaster University, Lancaster, LA1 4YR, UK, July 1994. Accessed via Internet, Sept. 1995. http://www.comp.lancs.ac.uk/computing/research/aai-aied/.

[18] Nwana, H. S. User modeling and user adapted interaction in an intelligent tutoring system. *User Modeling and User-Adapted Interaction*, (1):1–32, 1991.

[19] Ragnemalm, E. L. Towards student modelling through collaborative dialogue with a learning companion. Licentiate thesis Thesis No 482, Linköping University, 1995.

[20] Ragnemalm, E. L. Student diagnosis in practice; Bridging a gap. *User Modelling and User Adapted Interaction*, 5(2):93–116, 1996.

[21] Schaafstal, A. M. *Diagnostic Skill in Process Operation: A Comparison Between Experts and Novices*. PhD thesis, University of Groningen, Institute for Perception TNO, P.O. Box 23, 3769 Soesterberg, The Netherlands, September 1991.

[22] Twidale, M. Intermediate representations for student error diagnosis and support. In Bierman, D., Breuker, J., and Sandberg, J., editors, *Proc. of the 4th International conference on AI and Education*, pages 298–306, Amsterdam, May 1989.

[23] VanLehn, K. Student modeling. In Polson, M. C. and Richardson, J. J., editors, *Foundations of Intelligent Tutoring Systems*, chapter 3, pages 55–78. Lawrence Erlbaum Associates, 1988.

[24] Weizenbaum, J. ELIZA – a computer program for the study of natural language communication between man and machine. *Communications of the ACM*, 9(1):36–45, 1966.

[25] Woods, D. D. Process–tracing methods for the study of cognition outside of the experimental laboratory. In Klein, G. A., Orasann, J., Calderwood, R., and Zambok, C., editors, *Decision-Making in Action: Models and methods*, chapter 13, pages 228–251. Ablex publishing, 1993.

Arguing with the Devil: Teaching in Controversial Domains

Symeon Retalis[1], Helen Pain[2] and Mandy Haggith[2]

[1] Department of Electrical Engineering, National Technical University of Athens,
Athens, Greece
email: retal@softlab.ntua.gr

[2] Department of Artificial Intelligence, University of Edinburgh,
80 South Bridge, Edinburgh, EH1 1HN, UK
email: helen@aisb.ed.ac.uk, hag@aisb.ed.ac.uk

Abstract. There are certain problems inherent in teaching in controversial domains. In this paper, we present a prototype of an intelligent tutoring system called OLIA which addresses some of these problems. We focus here on OLIA's **Devil's advocate** strategy which is a method for teaching through a debate between the user and the system.

This paper takes advantage of existing work using a meta-level argumentation framework for knowledge representation in controversial domains. In this framework statements are linked by primitive relations such as disagreement, equivalence and justification, and higher order meta-level ones such as counter-arguments and corroborations. We investigate the use of this framework as the basis for the OLIA system.

1 Introduction

Teaching in controversial domains can be problematic. There is not one viewpoint to be taught as the correct one; teaching has to encourage students to explore different and often conflicting opinions, consider their justifications and weigh up the various arguments for and against a position. Tutoring systems, however, tend to focus on teaching a particular expert view. Cases of inconsistency or various beliefs are handled but usually considered to be evidence of misconceptions on the part of the student. However, in the real world absolute consensus or consistency is rare.

In this paper we present a prototype of an intelligent tutoring system called OLIA, which teaches in controversial domains. The OLIA tutoring system is based on a meta-level argumentation framework (Haggith 1995). It is the application of this framework to teaching in controversial domains that is addressed in this paper. This framework, unlike traditional knowledge based systems, supports controversy and is used for handling and exploring inconsistency. The OLIA tutor supports multiple teaching strategies (see Retalis, 1995), playing primarily the role of a Coach and also the role of a **Devil's Advocate**.

In the Devil's Advocate approach the user debates with the system on a controversial topic and both parties try to defend their opinions using supporting arguments. This teaching method is an innovative one and aims to provide the student with a global knowledge of the domain in order to avoid him jumping to a conclusion without being made aware of the various opinions in the domain.

2 Teaching in Controversial Domains

Conflicting opinions are not a problem but an opportunity to teach; an opportunity for interesting reasoning. For example people were interviewed in order to get their opinions about the greenhouse effect (Haggith 1993). Their viewpoints are conflicting.

Edinburgh will be submerged in a foot of water, claims an informant, as *It is near the sea* and *The sea level will rise* because:

1. The polar ice-caps are mostly ice.
2. The polar ice will melt.
3. When the ice becomes water then the level of the sea will rise.

On the other hand, other informants state: Mm... *Edinburgh won't be submerged in a foot of water* since *There wont be anywhere near the amount of sea level change people make out, ... The ice melting doesn't matter.* Why? Because:

1. The ice will melt.
2. The majority of ice-melt will be at the Arctic.
3. Arctic ice sits on the sea and displaces the water.
4. When the ice melts, all that volume is replaced by water.
5. Nine-tenths of the ice sits below the surface of the water, and its density is lower.

Although some of the above opinions of the scientists are equivalent (*The ice will melt* and *The polar ice will melt*) they are used to justify conflicting viewpoints which disagree. In a case where different opinions exist in the domain we need a tool for exploring the disagreements or the equivalences or for navigating around the domain by following the justifications of the propositions.

Different opinions on a topic often appear in different knowledge bases. Traditional knowledge based systems tend to present the knowledge of only one expert since they have difficulty in coping with the inconsistencies: their goal is usually to get rid of them. There is little work on the benefit that might be gained from exploring rather than removing such inconsistencies. However, Haggith (1995) proposes a meta-level argumentation framework for the exploration of multiple knowledge bases in which conflicting opinions are expressed. It is used as a basis for building the OLIA intelligent tutoring system for teaching in controversial domains. We focus here only on the Devil's Advocate strategy.

Systems such as DOMINIE (Spensley & Elsom-Cook 1988), or Meno-tutor (Woolf 1987) are not committed by design to a single tutoring approach but, as OLIA, support multiple teaching strategies. The difference between these systems and OLIA is that they deal with the viewpoints of only one expert and do not deal with controversies. Systems designed to support learning where several opinions are handled are rare, though there are examples such as Nicol's Intelligent Student System (Nicols 1993) and Belvedere (Suthers & Weiner 1995), and those where disagreement is permitted in relation to the student model (Bull et al, 1995). A number of others, which focus primarily on argumentation in relation to dialogue strategies, are discussed in (Treasure-Jones 1995). The success of systems such as Belvedere suggests that research in this area is of interest and benefit.

This paper introduces the Devil's Advocate strategy. In the previous example we had two scientists presenting their arguments. In OLIA one informant is the user and the other is the system who plays the role of the Devil's Advocate. A Devil's Advocate is a person who champions the weaker case for the sake of argument (Columbia 1950). The two parties debate by each presenting their arguments, and supportor justification for their respective arguments. The debate goes on until either the user has learned enough or the system gives up arguing (because of lack of arguments) saying "I rest my case!"

The **Devil's Advocate** term is commonly used in journalism, literature and law. In the Roman Catholic Church the *advocatus diaboli* was an official appointed to argue against a candidate (*advocatus Dei*) for a beatification or canonisation (Columbia 1950). In this paper we introduce the Devil's Advocate as a teaching approach in order to facilitate teaching in controversial domains into the ITS literature.

3   A knowledge representation framework for conflicting points of view

In Haggith (1995) a framework is described which enables multiple conflicting bodies of knowledge to be represented. This is achieved by restricting the knowledge representation to a high level of abstraction, in which the contents of statements are not formalised in any particular object level language, such as predicate logic; instead, what is formalised are the relationships between statements. The framework is thus meta-level - it enables reasoning *about* the statements in the knowledge base, and their relationships, rather than reasoning *with* them to draw particular conclusions. A basic assumption is that where controversies exist, it is useful to reason about the nature of the controversy, ie to argue. No attempt is made to resolve the conflict.

In this paper we explore how this framework makes possible the teaching of topics involving controversy. We assume that students are not trying to decide which of two conflicting points of view is 'correct', but rather learning about the nature of the controversy thus enabling them to weigh up the various sides of the argument. Understanding arguments, and how they relate, is necessary before a student is able to decide which argument is actually persuasive.

This meta-level framework treats statements or propositions as atoms, which do not contain internal structure which can be reasoned with. The primitive notions in the framework are four binary relations between propositions or sets of propositions.

1. *equivalent* - two propositions mean the same thing, or are in agreement; e.g. equivalent('The ice will melt.', 'The polar ice-caps will melt.').
2. *disagree* - two propositions state points of view which are in conflict; e.g. disagree('The level of the sea will rise', 'I don't think there'll be anywhere near the amount of sea-level change people make out.').
3. *justification* - a proposition is justified or supported by a set of other propositions; e.g. justification('I don't think there'll be anywhere near the amount of sea-level change people make out.', ['The ice melting does not affect sea-level', 'The ice will melt.']).
4. *elaboration* - a proposition is expanded upon by a set of other propositions; e.g. elaboration('The ice melting does not affect sea-level', ['The majority of ice-melt will be at the Arctic.', 'Arctic ice sits on the sea and displaces the water.', 'When the ice melts, all that volume is replaced by water.']).

The most important structures in the framework are arguments. An argument is a recursive structure with a conclusion and a collection of propositions which lend support to that conclusion. For example, if P is a conclusion supported by propositions Q, R and S, this would be written :

P <= [Q, R, S].

Each support can in turn be supported, so if R is itself supported, we get the argument in which R's argument is nested within the argument for P :

P <= [Q, R <= [U,V], S].

The argument connective <= represents that what is on its left hand side is supported by what comes on its right hand side, and the framework allows for various interpretations of the idea of support. For example, if we allow support to include equivalences, justifications and elaborations, we can construct a 'hybrid argument' for the statement above that the informant does not think that there will be much sea-level rise. This would be as follows :

'I don't think there'll be anywhere near the amount of sea-level change people make out.' <= ['The ice melting does not affect sea-level' <= ['The majority of ice-melt will be at the Arctic.', 'Arctic ice sits on the sea and displaces the water.', 'When the ice melts, all that volume is replaced by water.'] 'The ice will melt.']

Substituting single letters for the propositions we can see this structure more clearly :

P <= [Q <= [R, S,T], U]

P is supported by both Q and U. Q in turn is supported by all three of R, S, and T. Using this nesting structure, arbitrarily complex arguments can be constructed. The loss of detailed representational expressiveness of the contents of the propositions is compensated for by being able to represent very rich structures of connections between propositions.

The framework also provides definitions of more complex structures, 'higher order objects' which express relationships between arguments. These structures commonly occur in debates and in the literature on argumentation, and some of them exploit the existence of disagreements within the knowledge base. They include definitions of rebuttal (when an argument has a conclusion which disagrees with the conclusion of another argument), corroboration (two arguments whose conclusions are equivalent or support each other), enlargement (two arguments one of which argues for an elaboration of the conclusion of the other) and counterargument (when an argument's conclusion disagrees with any statement in another argument). Details of these structures and the rest of the framework can be found in Haggith 1995.

4 Devil's advocate strategy

We introduce the Devil's Advocate strategy as a method for tutoring through debate. The system will play the role of the Devil's Advocate and it will try to oppose any proposition that the user presents as support to his viewpoint. The user has selects one of the propositions from the *top level disagreements* in order to defend it. The Devil's Advocate will oppose this opinion and will support the opposite one. The possible options that are offered to the user are: *Support*, *Users higher order objects* and *Devils higher order objects*.

With the **Support** choice the user presents the *supports* for the propositions that he defends. However, the Devil's Advocate presents its supporting propositions in order to defend its part. Each interaction is a new level of debate. The new propositions that appear belong to this *New Level*. All the levels of debate are shown to the user (i.e. propositions that both parties – user and Devil's Advocate – have presented) in order that he be informed of how the discussion is "going". If the user cannot present any other support propositions to defend his opinion because all the propositions of the last level are self evident or assumptions then he is asked to stop interacting or to use only the options for higher order arguments. On the other hand if the Devil's Advocate cannot oppose anything he "rests his case" but the user can continue supporting his opinion since this is a way to learn more about the domain.

Two choices *Users higher order objects* and *Devils higher order objects* present information about the way the propositions that one party defends relate via higher order meta-level relations (rebuttals, undercuttings, counterarguments, etc.) to the ones of the "opponent" party. The following example is an instance of a debate between the user and OLIA as the Devil's Advocate. OLIA allocates one window to the user when they are debating with the system and another similar window presents the opinions of the Devil.

>   **User**: Edinburgh won't be submerged in a foot of water
>   **DEVIL**: Edinburgh will be submerged in a foot of water

User chooses to support his opinion

User: Edinburgh won't be submerged in a foot of water because:
- It is built on hills
- There won't be anywhere near the amount of sea level change people make out

DEVIL: No, no, no! Edinburgh will be submerged in a foot of water because:
- It is near the sea
- The sea level will rise

The user is now called to try again to defend his opinions or try to learn how his opinions and those of his opponent are related to each other via higher order relations
User selects support

User: Edinburgh is built on hills is self evident.
There won't be anywhere near the amount of sea level change people make out because:
- The ice will melt
- The ice melting does not affect sea level

DEVIL: Edinburgh is near the sea is self evident. The sea level will rise because:
- The polar ice-caps will melt.
- The polar ice-caps are mostly ice.
- When the ice becomes water then the level of the sea will rise.

The debate ends when the Devil's Advocate *rests his case* because of lack of arguments.

The Devil's Advocate allows the user to learn about the domain while debating with the system on a subject. However, there are situations in a discussion about a theme where different parties use the same arguments in a different way in order to defend their opinion. The Devil's Advocate strategy that is implemented in the OLIA tutoring system gives the user the option to learn more about the agreements between the "opponents" while they debate. It checks the possibility of equivalent points of view that the different parties have used and it shows some pieces of information such as which proposition an argument supports, with what other arguments it supports that proposition and so on. For example, the equivalent opinions *The ice will melt* and *The polar ice-caps will melt* are being used with different viewpoints to support conflicting opinions.

5   Evaluation and Discussion

Three initial studies were undertaken in order to carry out preliminary evaluation of the OLIA tutoring system. The focus here is primarily on the feasibility of the approach, and does not assess the effect on students' learning. In the long term, we would hope to use such an approach for improving both student's understanding of the arguments in specific domains, and their general understanding of arguments per se.

The first study: involved six postgraduate students, taking an MSc Knowledge Based Systems course. They used a small knowledge base concerning the greenhouse effect and arguments for and against the opinion that Edinburgh will be submerged in a foot of water. This involved a short briefing on the domain representation and the philosophy of the OLIA tutoring system, and a period of unguided exploration of the domain, exploring OLIA's Coaching strategy (see Retalis, 1995, for details) in addition to the Devil's Advocate strategy. Their interaction with the system was observed. This was followed by an informal interview, including questions on the friendliness, usability and limitations of the system.

In general, the results of the evaluation were encouraging. All six users agreed that OLIA was potentially useful for learning about controversial domains. The way in which they interacted with the system varied. They chose different routes (options) for learning the domain. All of them selected the Devil's Advocate strategy as the most interesting strategy. OLIA appeared to be of use to users who already have some idea of the domain or who expect more sophisticated information about the domain. In general, they found that OLIA was user friendly and almost all information was clearly presented.

The users commented that the Devil's Advocate strategy was interesting and potentially useful for tutoring about domains where conflicting opinions exist. They agreed that this strategy was necessary to prevent them from jumping to a conclusion without having general knowledge about the subject that they were exploring. The users also indicated that the Devil's Advocate was useful for teaching how the different opinions are related to each other when it was used with the option of *showing the agreements*.

The second study: involved 10 undergraduate students taking a first year course in Artificial Intelligence. In this study, an alternative domain was implemented: two sets of propositions represented alternative positions in relation to the mind-body problem, the Materialist position (Minsky) and the Dualist position (Descartes). Students were asked to interact with OLIA using both the Devil's Advocate and Coaching strategies, in order to try to answer questions about the mind-body debate. This study took place during a routine practical session, and provided a follow up to material that had been discussed in a previous tutorial.

Students were asked to comment, in writing, after the session. Example questions were, "Did you learn anything about the mind-body problem in this session? Did you learn anything about argumentation structure?" They were also asked to compare working with this material in tutorials to working with it in the OLIA system, and to suggest improvements to the system. We do not go into a detailed analysis of their responses here, but focus on general formative comments on the system that may influence design modifications and a provide a preliminary assessment of its potential use.

The general findings were that all students who expressed a preference preferred using the Devil's Advocate to the coaching strategy. The majority felt that they improved their understanding of the mind-body problem in the course of using OLIA. 5 students felt that using OLIA also improved their knowledge of argument structure. Some students said they preferred using OLIA to learning in a tutorial, because it was 'more systematic', and the arguments 'were presented better', Most students who expressed a preference preferred working in tutorials because the arguments could be 'deeper', they could ask their tutor for clarification, and they could express their own 'personal arguments and opinions'. A number of improvements were suggested, both to the interface and to the way in which the system might be used. Most felt that OLIA's Devils' Advocate strategy provided a useful means of exploring arguments, particularly when presented in relation to other means of presenting these arguments, such as reading texts.

The third study: used the same knowledge base (the mind-body problem), but here OLIA was used as an evaluation exercise for a group of seven postgraduate and honours level students taking a specialist course in Artificial Intelligence and Education. The structure and questions were similar to those of the second study, though there was no comparison with coverage of the material by other means (such as tutorials).

The results indicated that several students learned something about the mind-body problem in the session, though others felt not (though several commented that they were already familiar with the arguments). Most were able to answer a fairly complex question, after working with the Devil's Advocate, that they were not able to answer before using it: "Did you find any proposition that supports two other propositions which disagree with each other?" Some commented that they learned something about argument structure, though felt that the distinctions between some of the relations were not made clear by the system. Most preferred the Devil's Advocate strategy to the basic Coaching strategy. All made useful suggestions for improving the interface.

6 Limitations and Conclusions

Evaluation of the use of the Devil's Advocate strategy in the OLIA system is only in preliminary stages. There are a number of limitations to the approach, some of which will be considered briefly here. The Devil currently always uses the same type of argument move as the user. More flexiblility should be provided to enable a wider variety of interaction. The performance of this strategy has not been tested when more than two opinions appear as *top level disagreements*. If there were more than two conflicting opinions on a topic then the user could choose one and the Devil's Advocate could defend each one of the others. The current algorithm for this strategy should support this option. Nonetheless, we need to investigate ways which the user might debate with two **Devil's advocates** who in their turn might debate with each other. The graphical interface (built in Prolog) as it is at the moment does not enable the implementation of more than one Devil's Advocate. Additionally, there are no facilities at present for the student to add their own propositions: this would be a vital extension for more widespread use.

We have demonstrated the use of the argumentation framework for teaching in controversial domains. We believe that the meta-level argumentation framework could facilitate the use of other strategies such as the Socratic one. This would be further evidence of how powerful this framework is for tutoring. Both the meta-level framework and the OLIA intelligent system are designed to be domain independent (Haggith 1995): it is straightforward to use OLIA with other knowledge bases representing knowledge about other controversial domains, as we have demonstrated through our second and third studies. Further analysis of the data collected is currently being carried out, and improvements to the design of the tutor being considered. Evaluation of the effectiveness of this approach in respect of improving students' learning is also needed. Further study of student's use and understanding of the argument structures and relations is also required.

References

S. Bull, H. Pain and P. Brna. (1995). Mr. Collins: A A Collaboratively Constructed, Inspectable Student Model for Intelligent Computer Assisted Language Learning. *Instructional Science*, 23:65–87.

The Columbia Encyclopedia. Columbia University Press, 1950.

M. Haggith. Towards a formal analysis of disagreement. Discussion Paper 128, 1993.

M. Haggith. A meta-level framework for exploring conflicting knowledge bases. In J.Hallam, editor, *Hybrid Solution, Hybrid problem*. IOS Press, 1995.

M. Minsky. *The Society of mind.* Simon and Schuster, New York, 1988.

D. Nicols. *Intelligent Student Systems: An Application of Viewpoints to Intelligent Learning Environments.* Unpublished PhD thesis, University of Lancaster, 1993.

S. Retalis. Investigating the use of a meta-level argumentation framework as a basis for tutoring in controversial domains. Unpublished M.Sc. thesis, Edinburgh University, 1995.

F. Spensley and M.T. Elsom-Cook. Dominie: Teaching and assessment strategies. Technical Report 37, Milton Keynes, UK: Centre for Information Technology in Education, The Open University, 1988.

D. Suthers and A. Weiner. Belvedere: Engaging students in critical discussion of science and public policy issues. In *Proc. 7th World Conference on Artificial Intelligence in Education (AI–ED 95)*. Washington, D.C, 1995.

T. Treasure-Jones. Support and exploration of disagreement within intelligent tutoring systems. First Year PhD Report. Computing Department Lancaster University, 1995.

B. Woolf. Theoretical frontiers in building a machine tutor. In Kearsley G., editor, *Artificial Intelligence and Instruction. Applications and Methods*, pages 229–265. Addison-Wesley, 1987.

Acknowledgements

We would like to thank Amy Isard for her comments on this paper.

Learning by Learning Roles:
A Virtual Role-Playing Environment for Tutoring

Brian M. Slator[1] and Harold "Cliff" Chaput[2]

1. The Institute for the Learning Sciences, Northwestern University,
Evanston, IL 60201, slator@ils.nwu.edu
2. Department of Computer Sciences, The University of Texas at Austin
Austin, TX 78712, chaput@cs.utexas.edu

Abstract. People will invest extraordinary time and effort into learning how to play and win a game. Virtual role-playing environments can be a powerful mechanism of instruction, provided they are constructed such that learning how to play and win the game contributes to a player's understanding of real-world concepts and procedures. This paper describes a pedagogical architecture and an implemented application where students assume a role in a simulated multi-media environment and learn about the real world by competing with other players. The game, which teaches principles of micro-economics, is an implementation of a networked, multi-player, simulation-based, interactive multi-media, educational environment that illustrates the principles of learning by learning roles.

Introduction

Marshall McLuhan [7] maintained that 20th century people do not want goals so much as they want roles. Authentic simulated environments enable learners to assume roles in particular contexts and have meaningful, near-real experiences. When these experiences are structured and arranged, even loosely, such that playing a role in the environment can illustrate the important concepts and procedures of the simulated domain, students are able to "learn by doing" [4]. Experiences are the best teachers.

Meanwhile, the value of play in learning can hardly be over-stressed. Students quickly tire of rigid tutorial systems designed to teach at any cost and at some predetermined pace [8]. However, since simulations can be adaptive and responsive, playing a role in a simulation can be fun. Players will throw themselves terrier-like into an environment if it feels like a game. Insofar as possible, educational software should be engaging, entertaining, attractive, interactive, and flexible: in short, game-like.

Designing educational games is an exercise in balancing trade-offs. Educational content should be foremost, but not by occluding playability and simple fun. Simulated situations should be familiar, or at least easily recognizable, but not at the cost of slavishly replicating all the tedious detail of "real life". Experience in the simulated environment should be authentic, but not utterly predictable. Further, we believe that educational technology should capitalize on the natural human propensity for role-playing. Students will be willing to assume roles if the environment promotes that cognitive mind-set by making it easy to do, and if the environment reinforces role-playing through careful crafting of the explicit tutorial components of the game.

Finally, to support student learning by learning roles, the tutorial components of a simulated environment should only present conceptual and procedural instruction within their strategic contexts. In other words, the goal in a role-playing environment should mirror the goals of a mythical law school professor: "We are not here to teach you the law, we are here to teach you to think like a lawyer."

This paper describes a networked, multi-player, simulation-based, interactive multi-media, educational game constructed on the principles listed above. The pedagogical domain is micro-economics, in particular retailing. The teaching goals revolve around the strategic importance of "targeting" specific customer groups in order to gain competitive advantage in the retail marketplace. The game is called **"Sell!"**; the point of the game is to make money.

The premise of the game is that the player has inherited a sum of money from a long-lost uncle --- but the bequest is on condition they go to the old home town of Springfield and enter the retail economy by taking over the family store. Thus the player is immediately assigned a well-defined role --- shopkeeper.

The architecture of the virtual role-playing simulation was designed to meet the following criteria:
1. The role of the player should be explicit from the outset;
2. The player's success at learning their role in the environment should translate directly into their success at playing the game;
3. Player actions should have a "real" effect on the simulated environment and the environment should react in realistic ways;
4. The simulated environment should be unintrusively pro-active --- the system should be watchful and active, but the player should always be in control of the experience;
5. The simulated environment should be rich, complex, and filled with interesting and yet plausible detail;
6. Complexity in the environment should be limited to those tasks and functions that relate directly to the teaching goals of the system --- other elements should be trivial, or used for diversion and purely entertainment purposes;
7. Interfaces should be easy to use and obviously representative of the environment being simulated --- the simulated environment should be visually iconic and metaphorical rather than photo-realistic, in order to promote the player's "willing suspension of disbelief" (immersion) and further their acceptance of their role in the environment;
8. Finally, of course, players should be able to receive context sensitive help and advice at virtually any point in the game.

The teaching goals of the system are for the player to learn about marketing so they can compete for sales. Everything the student needs to know is available in the form of video advice and online help. Everything the player needs to succeed is available somewhere in the system. As a first approximation towards learner assessment, the student is said to have mastered the material if they succeed in quadrupling their "inheritance".

The Simulated Town of Springfield

The town of Springfield is simulated by building a graphical user-interface onto a MOO ("MUD, Object-Oriented", where MUD stands for "Multi-User Domain"). MUDs are typically text-based electronic meeting places where players build societies and fantasy environments, and interact with each other [3]. Technically, a MUD is a multi-user database and messaging system. The basic components are "rooms" with "exits", "containers" and "players". MUDs support the object management and inter-player messaging that is required for multi-player games, and at the same time provide a programming language for writing the simulation and customizing the MUD. One of the major shortcomings of MUDs, however, is their low-tech communication system: text. The Sell! game supplies a graphical user interface layered on top of the networked multi-user database and messaging system that MUDs provide.

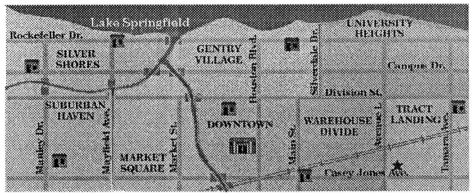

Fig. 1: The map of Springfield

The town of Springfield is built out of an "entryway room" visually represented as a map of Springfield, which is divided into 8 neighborhoods. Every store in town is visible on the map and is implemented as a "room" within a neighborhood. Stores are located on the streets (which are also "rooms", albeit long, thin ones), and players are free to leave their store and visit others, either by moving up and down the streets outside their store, or by "zooming" up to the map and clicking a store icon to visit it (see figure 1).

Roaming the city is both fun and useful. Players are encouraged to keep track of their competition (this is one of the principles of successful marketing, and perfectly consistent with the storekeeper's role), and one straightforward way of doing this is to visit competitors and check their prices. In addition, each neighborhood has its own unique characteristics, that players can only experience by visiting. The players who find themselves in financial trouble can arrange a loan, but must visit the Downtown Bank to do so.

It is important that the environment be sufficiently iconic, because icons impart more (metaphorical) information than photo-realistic images, and because they promote the willing assumption of role and character within the simulated environment [2]. It is also important that the metaphor be consistent and believable. For example, the spatial metaphor is preserved in the city of Springfield, but the map, which is useful by itself as a map, is also a "transporter" device for instantaneous travel.

Playing the Game: Learning to Compete in Springfield

In the current version of the game, the players each "inherit" a store and an initial stake of disposable cash ($25,000 in the current version of the game); the store is located in a randomly assigned neighborhood and is stocked with a small inventory of products (in the current version, either sporting goods or consumer electronics). The initial store configuration is deliberately constructed to be a stagnant one; i.e. their store is in "trouble", and if the player does nothing to improve their competitive position, their products will not sell and they will lose the game.

In the game, players are able to do many of the things real retailers do. Players can buy advertising (on radio or in newspapers), they can order products from a variety of distributors and they can shop around for better prices and volume discounts. They can explore the city, checking the competition and do market research looking for likely customers. They can review their accounts, hire and fire staff, read the newspaper, "listen" to the radio, return slow moving stock to the distributor, and change their prices. And at any point they can stop and ask for help in various forms or seek expert advice. They can even change their own appearance.

Fig. 2: The interior of a store.

The Economic Simulation

It is important that the economic simulation be sufficiently realistic that players can learn to count on their actions having explainable effects on their results. It is crucial to the teaching goals of the system that players be rewarded for effectively learning their roles by success in the game. It is equally important that the simulation be transparent at some level so that players can inspect the inner workings well enough to make strategic generalizations about the environment, and to pass beyond trial-and-error problem-solving.

An economic model was developed to generate consumer behavior for the game [10]. The model takes as input the decisions the players have made, and returns a level of demand for each of the stores. In the game, players compete for market share against other human players trying to learn the same role in the simulated environment.

Different areas of Springfield are home to different types of people with different wants, interests, and media viewing habits. A retailer, in order to succeed in this game, must match business strategy to target population, while also taking into account the activities of competitors. Springfield is composed of eight neighborhoods, each with a spatial orientation relative to the others. Sellers must search for population groups receptive to their business.

Neighborhoods are composed of several homogeneous population groups such as:
° "Up-scale-Urban-Couples/Homeowners/Highly-Educated",
° "Younger/Large-Families/Blue-Collar-Laborers",

° "Center-City/Middle-Age/Low-Income/Fewer Kids/Female-Headed-House",
      and
° "College-Student".

Each Neighborhood also has physical features that may influence the level of demand for certain products. For example, an area called Gentry Village is an upper middle-class area with a large number of young singles and a low number of married couples with children. Gentry Village has bike facilities (i.e. bike paths) which increase the Neighborhood's potential demand for bikes.

To play the game, players must assume their role and make decisions which will determine their success or failure in the market place. The must decide what to sell, how much stock to buy, what prices to set, what service level to set, what level and type of advertising to buy, and, in future versions of the game, where to locate.

The major pedagogical goal of the game is to teach "targeting", which is a retailer's effort at matching their goods and services to particular "target groups" in order to maximize efficiency and profitability. In the economic simulation of Springfield, the underlying effect of a player's targeting is to adjust the simulated consumer's real cost. Real cost is not only price, but also transportation and search costs; also, real cost accounts for the benefits from service and added features or discounts. A store that offers the lowest real costs to a consumer group will win a majority of that groups business (and this is the underlying lesson for the player to learn). The game adopts the economic assumption that consumers are utility maximizers and cost minimizers (i.e. they try to get the most for their dollar) while allowing for considerable variation in what is valued by different consumer groups.

The Market Research Tool (MRT) is a particularly important component of the game since it enables the player to view the economic model in a useful way. In particular, the MRT allows the player to
   1. identify buyers (population groups) interested in particular products;
   2. identify complementary products the same buyers will also want;
   3. identify the advertising media most likely to reach those buyers; and
   4. find those buyers geographically on the map.

The Pro-active Environment: Help and Advice

Information about the real world is offered to the player through the help and advice network (see figure 3), modeled loosely on the Ask System [5]. These interfaces allow the player to ask subject matter experts (SME's) pertinent questions. The information offered by the SME's is in the form of video and text. It consists of theoretical principles that guide business decisions, examples of how these theoretical concepts are applied, and personal experiences or stories. It is, however, up to the player to determine how to use this knowledge in the game. The SME's currently consist of an advertising executive, a marketing professor, a corporate marketing professional, a banker, and a bike store manager.

The SMEs are accessible in two ways, either through advice buttons, which are ubiquitous throughout the program, or through the intervention of the pro-active tutor.

The advice system is context-sensitive which promotes the player's acceptance of their role in the game. For example, if the player is using the advertising interface, pressing the advice button will take them into the advice network at a video clip answering the question,
      ° "As a new retailer, do I need to advertise?".

The video answer, delivered by the advertising executive, covers the fundamental issues of understanding who the customers are in order to choose advertising that appeals to the right groups.

In addition, following the Ask System model, the player is given the opportunity to ask follow-up questions like,

° "What are some reasons that my advertising might be ignored?"
° "What are some ways for a store to benefit from its advertising""
° "What should I consider when advertising my products?"
° "How important is advertising when starting a business?"

The video answer, again delivered by the advertising executive, outlines the dangers of over-extending an advertising campaign to a point where it's not cost-effective.

Again following the Ask System model, every video clip answers a question, and every answer has further follow-up questions. The user is free to browse as they choose. Further, every video clip in the advice network is connected to context-sensitive help, which explains how the real-world advice in the browsing network translates into actions in the game.

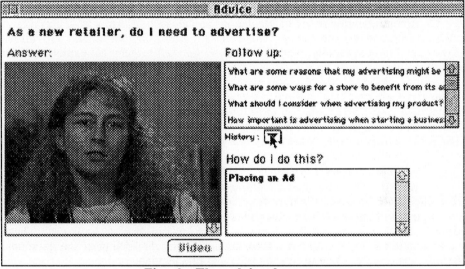

Fig. 3: The advice browser

The Pro-active Environment: Tutoring

Perhaps the most important element of the educational environment is the pro-active tutoring component. This is effected by implementing a set of rules about retailing, and having the simulation monitor player actions, looking for rules to be "broken". For example, a player may decide to try and maximize profits by pricing their products at ten times the wholesale price. This is a naive strategy that says, "I might not sell very many, but each sale will be very profitable". The simulation recognizes this as a losing strategy and knows the player is unlikely to sell anything at all.

When the game detects a strategic mistake it sends a message to the player saying, "You may be setting your prices too high". The player can then decide to ignore the message or pursue it. This unintrusive method of tutoring is implemented to be consistent with the educational game principles of leaving the player in control and letting them make their own mistakes. If the player chooses to pursue the warning, they click on the message and are taken into the tutorial section of the advice network at a video clip answering the question,

° "How do retailers set prices?",

which explains the ideas of profit margin and Manufacturers Suggested Retail Price (MSRP). The special tutorial lessons provide context and explanations, and serve as tutorial bridges to the advice network. Once the player is in the advice network, they may browse through the content matter to the extent they choose.

There is no penalty for ignoring the tutor's warnings, other than the inevitable failure to sell anything, a penalty imposed by the simulation as a consequence of the player's failure to learn their role in the environment. In all cases it is up to the player to decide how the warnings and advice apply to them. The simulation allows the player to win or lose in any way they choose. It is important the environment be an active one, where the player is stimulated by the events occurring in the game. The environment is not just a passive, reactive one, it seeks opportunities to interact and tutor. This model of opportunistic tutoring can be found in the Teaching Executive of Jona [6] and in Burke's SPIEL [1].

A common problem with simulations is that, like the real world, players can foul things up and not know why. Unlike the real world, though, all the information for the simulation is readily available, and can be used to generate explanations or warnings. Rules are based on the design and information in the model, and are fired by user actions. When a rule fires, the player sees a warning; they can ask for more information (bringing them to the Advice Network), or they can ignore it and carry on at their own risk. The idea is that the Proactive Tutor is that guy looking over your shoulder as you play. He should be there when you need him, but when you know what you're doing (or when you think you know), you can ignore him.

The Pro-active Environment: Other "Players"

Another key component of player stimulation in the active environment is the multi-player capability which maintains interest through real interaction and competition with other players. However, it is important the other players, be they human or automaton, appear at the same interface level --- as icons to be manipulated and understood. This is another feature that enhances the feeling of the game and promotes the willing suspension of disbelief and role playing.

In a competitive environment like Sell!, where every player has the same goals and opportunities for cooperation are scarce, there is less value added by interacting with other human players. Although, human nature being what it is, we expect to find some players helping others with hints and advice out of their own generosity, there is little that can be generally anticipated in this regard. We hope, in future games, to devise simulated environments where team-play and cooperation can be rewarded with success in the game.

In the next version of the game, players will be occasionally visited by salesmen offering training course for employees, or Little League coaches soliciting donations for team uniforms. These visitors are Non-Player Characters (NPCs) --- robot players who seek to engage players in sometimes frivolous, sometimes meaningful interactions. These exchanges will promote the feeling of unpredictable reality that can make a simulation seem more "real", while at the same time giving the players opportunities to think on their feet. Some of the NPCs will be offering valuable goods and services, others will be peddling dreck. The player must decide, in their role of shopkeeper, what is worthwhile, and what is not.

Other plans call for robot competitors to populate Springfield even when no humans are playing the game. This will level the field in terms of the advantage we have noticed that goes to players who enter the game first and establish themselves before other players enter the simulated environment. These "agents of retail" will undertake differing retail strategies: conservative vs. risk-taking, expansive vs. cost-conscious, and so forth. They will serve as models for players to copy or avoid, and will form the basis for a case library for competitors that the tutor will retrieve as examples and counter-examples for role-playing.

Preliminary Evaluation

When the Sell! development reached an alpha state, the game was opened for participation within the Institute for the Learning Sciences. Twelve players started playing with little or no pre-game instruction. After about a week, players began improving their game and heavily competing for first place. When interviewed, most reported strategies that were consistent with the pedagogical domain: underpricing the competition or attracting an appropriate customer base with advertising. Few players reported "implementation-related" strategies that took advantage of the software running the simulation. All players improved their play by using Sell!'s Advice Network and Online Help, and without the aid of manuals or additional human instruction. When asked if playing Sell! changed their outlook on the retail business, all players responded affirmatively. While this study was mostly anecdotal, it indicated to us we were on the right track.

Teaching Goals and Learning Roles

The game is an intelligent educational simulation but little is ever explicitly taught in the game. Rather, the game does two things:

1. Assigns a well-defined, understandable role to the player which motivates them to learn more about economics and marketing in order to win the game; and
2. Provides resources that allow the player to learn.

Learning takes place in the game as a consequence of:

1. seeing the results of actions in the simulated world.
2. interacting with the "tutor" (and the real and simulated agents that populate the environment).
3. by browsing advice networks (similar to Ask systems), and seeing stories.

As each turn progresses, players learn their role in the environment and see the results of their actions as well as the impact of other players' actions within the constraints of the simulated world. People like to play, and children have always learned about their society and themselves through role-play, be it playing house, or playing store, or playing doctor.

Learning by doing is the oldest trick in the educator's book, and by leveraging off the natural human proclivity to play and role-play, the game helps players learn about the real world by helping them learn a role in a simulated one. And it helps them learn successful strategies (and win!) by helping them learn their roles exceeding well.

Acknowledgments

The following have all contributed in ways great and small to the development of the Sell! game: Dave April, Mike Bakula, Ray Bareiss, Richard Beckwith, Carol Biolsi, Don Bora, Patrick Brockhagen, Cliff Chaput, Gregg Collins, Ralph DeStephano, Arnease Diggs, Eric Domeshek, Danny Edelson, Andy Fano, Katie Feifer, Ric Feifer, Kerim Fidel, Hamed Hashmy, Jon Hickey, Bob Hooker, Camille Jayne, Debra Jenkins, Neil Josehart, Amy Juhl, Bob Kaeding, Robin Karlov, Alex Kass, Laural Koroncey, Jeff Lind, Marek Lugowski, Rich Lynch, Doug MacFarlane, Scott MacQuarrie, Colette Marine, Doug Miller, Paul Ring, Mark Schaefer, Roger Schank, Don Schultz, Audrey Slator, Brian Slator, Sandor Szego, Pete Tevonian, Kristen Thomas-Clarke, Brendan Towle, Ana Vitek, Paul Wang, Thomas Zeilonka, and Laura Zelinski.

The Institute for the Learning Sciences was established in 1989 with the support of Andersen Consulting, part of The Arthur Andersen Worldwide Organization. The Institute receives additional support from Ameritech, an Institute Partner, and from North West Water.

References

1. Burke, R. D. (1993) *Representation, Storage, and Retrieval of Stories in a Social Simulation*. Ph.D. dissertation, The Institute for the Learning Sciences, Northwestern University. Technical Report #50.

2. Crawford, C. (1990). Lessons from Computer Game Design. *The Art of Human-Computer Interface Design*. Edited by Brenda Laurel. Reading, MA: Addison-Wesley.

3. Curtis, Pavel (1992). Mudding: Social Phenomena in Text-Based Virtual Realities. *Proceedings of the conference on Directions and Implications of Advanced Computing* (sponsored by Computer Professionals for Social Responsibility)

4. Dewey, J. (1900). The School and Society. Chicago, IL: The University of Chicago Press.

5. Ferguson, W., Bareiss, R., Birnbaum, L., Osgood, R. (1992) ASK Systems: An Approach to the Realization of Story-Based Teachers. *The Journal of the Learning Sciences*, 2:95-134.

6. Jona, M. Y. (1995). *Representing and Applying Teaching Strategies in Computer-Based Learning-By-Doing Tutors*. Ph.D. dissertation, The Institute for the Learning Sciences, Northwestern University. Technical Report #.

7. McLuhan, M. (1964). *Understanding Media*. New York: McGraw-Hill Book Co.

8. Schank, R. C. (1991). Case-Based Teaching: Four Experiences in Educational Software Design, *ILS Technical Report #7*, Northwestern University, Evanston, IL.

9. Shute, V. J., & Glaser, R. (1990). A large-scale evaluation of an intelligent discovery world: Smithtown. Interactive Learning Environments, 1(1), 51-77.

10. Slator, B. & Hooker, B. (1995) A Model of Consumer Decision Making for a Mud-based Game. Submitted to the ITS'96 Workshop on Simulation-Based Learning Technology. Montreal, June.

ITS-Engineering: A Domain Independent ITS for Building Engineering Tutors

Chaisak Srisethanil, Nelson C. Baker

School of Civil and Environmental Engineering,
Georgia Institute of Technology, Atlanta, Georgia, USA

Abstract ITS-Engineering provides a developing framework for a tutoring system application in engineering domains. The system is equipped with multiple teaching styles to enable the system to instruct using various teaching styles. These teaching styles are: instructor-oriented; guided-discovery; exploratory; and user-initiated styles. The capability of ITS-Engineering is demonstrated in ITS-CPM (Intelligent Tutoring System for Construction and Project Management); ITS-Shear (Intelligent Tutoring System for Shear Analysis of Reinforced Concrete Beams). The paper proposes a significant improvement in development time and cost reduction when creating an ITS application within ITS-Engineering.

1 Introduction

The research of reusable and domain independent ITSs has recently been discussed as a viable option to bring ITSs out of research labs. Many approaches have been proposed and implemented. The major issue in trying to develop the domain-independent ITS is how the system will cope with various types of domains. A plausible option is to equip the system with the capability to provide multiple teaching styles because there is no single teaching style that can instruct every type of subjects.

ITS-Engineering (Intelligent Tutoring Shell for Engineering) is a domain independent ITS within the range of engineering subjects. It provides a developing shell that supports teaching in a variety of styles adequately adapting to different instructional situations across engineering domains.

This paper focuses on the application of multiple teaching styles to facilitate the implementation of reusable ITS as demonstrated in ITS-CPM (Intelligent Tutoring System for Construction Planning and Management); and ITS-Shear (Intelligent Tutoring System for Shear Analysis of Reinforced Concrete Beams).

1.1 Related works

DOMINIE (DOMain INdependent Instructional Environment) represents an early effort to provide multiple teaching styles in a domain independent system (Spensley et al., 1990). DOMINIE is intended to allow the creation of a tutoring system for training computer interfaces operation. DOMINIE supports several teaching and assessment styles such as: cognitive apprenticeship, successive refinement; guided discovery, abstraction, discovery assessment, Socratic diagnosis, practice and direct assessment. COCA (CO-operative Classroom Assistant) (Major & Reichgelt, 1992) and KAFITS (Knowledge Acquisition Framework for ITS) (Murray & Woolf, 1990) also demonstrate an effort to provide multiple teaching styles in their systems.

However, these systems are not designed with a focus on engineering domains and the need for technical education and training. ITS-Engineering is designed with the recognition of engineering education that is characterized by the needs of visualization, real world experiences, intensive computation, and problem solving. The teaching styles of ITS-Engineering are designed to fulfill these needs.

2. ITS-Engineering

ITS-Engineering is a domain-independent tutoring system intended to support the development of ITS applications within the range of engineering domains (Srisethanil & Baker, 1995). ITS-Engineering includes support for adaptive teaching in multiple styles because in the authors' opinion there is no single best teaching style that is appropriate to all engineering subject domains. Instead the best teaching style is the style (s) that can adapt cognitively and academically to the changing needs of a student. In other words, the teaching style should match the student's cognitive style of learning, the student's aptitude, and the state of the subject knowledge. This capability is even more significant in the shell system such as ITS-Engineering because it has to be able to deliver instructions across various domains. Different types of knowledge, i.e., procedural, declarative, operational, need different instructional approaches to be effective.

ITS-Engineering allows the human instructor to include instructional material in several forms such as text, graphics, audio, and video clips. The availability of multi-instructional media offers several benefits to the user such as real world experience in the form of video clips. Therefore a student can have a better understanding of the subject.

2.1 Adaptive Multiple Teaching Styles

The epitome of ITS-Engineering is the capability to instruct subjects in multiple teaching styles. ITS-Engineering employs four teaching styles each of which supports learning engineering subjects as previously described. These teaching styles are instructor-oriented and guided discovery,, user-initiated, and exploratory. The first two styles represent the instructor-control approach and the last two styles represent the student-control approach.

Instructor-Oriented (I-O)

The instructor-oriented style represents a teaching style that promotes reproduction of knowledge, a process whereby students use previously learned knowledge to produce a desired result. The reproduction of knowledge is achieved via stimulating memory recall and/or task repetition. To adopt the style, the instructor directly presents the information, controls the pace and rhythm of the instruction, provides feedback, and evaluates the performance of students. The possible types of information for this style include declarative knowledge and procedural knowledge.

The instructor-oriented style can achieve several learning outcomes (in Gagné's terminology; Gagné, 1985) pertaining to the reproduction of knowledge such as rule, defined concept and verbal information. The types of learning outcomes are highly correlated to the nature of the subject matter. For instance, if the subject matter is procedural, then the expected learning outcome would be rule. On the other hand, the desired learning outcomes can be defined concept or verbal information if the subject matter is declarative in nature.

Guided Discovery (GD)

In contrast to *"reproduction"* of knowledge in the instructor-oriented style, the guided discovery style emphasizes the *"production"* of new knowledge. The approach invites the learner to think, to infer, and to go beyond the given information and then discover novel information (correct and/or incorrect). The essence of this style is a teacher-student interaction in which the teacher's sequences of information and questions cause corresponding responses that are then discovered by the learner. The cumulative effect of this converging process leads the student to discover a sought concept or principle within the subject.

The most appropriate type of subject matters for guided discovery instruction is declarative knowledge which is unknown and new to the learner such as concept, principle, relationships among entities, order and causal knowledge (Mosston & Ashworth, 1990).

The learning outcomes that can be achieved in this style are problem solving, and defined concept. GD teaching can induce a learner to develop cognitive skills (Mosston and Ashworth, 1990), which is beneficial for problem solving ability. A student can learn the concept of the topic by indirectly presenting the information.

User-Initiated (U-I)

The user-initiated style allows a learner to select the desired topic and its parameters to comprise custom made problems. The U-I style allows a learner to study and practice solving problems in the area that he/she desires to emphasize.

The adequate type of knowledge is procedural knowledge which involves solving/computing mathematical problems. This procedural knowledge is found in most engineering subjects (e.g., CPM computation, calculation of beam shear).

The learning outcomes that could be achieved with the U-I style are rule and problem solving. Rule can be accomplished by repeatedly practicing the relevant exercises. After practicing a student can learn the computation process and the various relationships among problem parameters, i.e., rule. When a student has an opportunity to create his/her own problem comprised of selected parameters, a novel problem may exist for her to practice solving that problem. The more problem situations that a student encounters and solves, the better opportunity that he/she will be able to apply the acquired knowledge to other novel situations, i.e., problem solving.

Exploratory (Ex)

A learner also controls the path and pace of the instruction, in the exploratory style. The learner has the freedom to select which topics to learn without specific sequence. The exploratory style enables a student to look over the content of the subjects without engaging in the elicitation process.

The appropriate type of knowledge for the exploratory style is non-procedural knowledge such as fact and conceptual knowledge. The possible learning outcomes that can be accomplished using the exploratory styles are verbal information, i.e., rote memory, and defined concepts.

There is no eliciting performance process in which a learner is tested. The learner is responsible for learning and sequencing the instructing material. The role of the instructor in this style is during the authoring process where he/she can structure and control the outlook of the teaching materials.

2.2 Switching Strategies

ITS-Engineering's switching strategies are heuristic knowledge synthesized from publications and instructors' input. ITS-Engineering switches its teaching styles based on: learner's preferences; learning outcome; and subject matter. ITS-Engineering implicitly switches teaching style based on learner preferences by allowing a student to select different learning sessions (to be discussed later). Therefore, the first scenario that ITS-Engineering can instruct in multiple styles is by switching between learning sessions. The second scenario for applying the multiple teaching styles occurs within the session (tutoring session). Based the subject matter and learning outcome, ITS-Engineering heuristically switches styles between instructor-oriented and exploratory (e.g., if the subject matter is procedural and the outcome is rule/problem solving); and between instructor-oriented and guided discovery (e.g., if the subject matter is declarative and the learning outcome is defined concept).

2.3 Learning Sessions and Teaching Styles

ITS-Engineering provides three types of learning sessions for applications developed within the framework. They are: browsing session, practicing session, and tutoring session. ITS-Engineering provides mechanisms to create these sessions from the knowledge base defined by human instructors and knowledge engineers. Each session employs different teaching styles reflecting the characteristics of each teaching style and learning session.

Browsing Session.
A student is free to select the topic that he/she wants to learn during the browsing session. The dominant teaching style in this session is exploratory. The browsing session provides two major benefits to a student. First, the browsing session can be used as an introductory session to induce a student to develop a feel and expectation for the forthcoming instruction. Second, a student can use the browsing session as a quick reference as previously discussed.

Practicing Session.
A unique characteristic of the practicing session of ITS-Engineering is the capability to allow students to create their own problems and to practice solving problems. The session commences by displaying the available topics for a student to select. After the desired topic is selected, the system then generates the related available parameters that can comprise a problem (s). A student is required to choose these problem parameters in any combination and submit to the system. Problems are subsequently generated for a student to practice. Correct answers are provided to the student if he/she makes mistakes. These correct answers are dynamically computed based on the knowledge of the subject domain. The practicing session provides unlimited resources for a student to learn and practice solving problems for a particular topic that

he/she is interested in or weak at. Practicing solving mathematical problems represents a major element of engineering curriculum. The dominant teaching style of the practicing session is the user-initiated style.

Tutoring Session.
In the tutoring session, a student has access to all information available in the application developed within ITS-Engineering. Without the freedom to select the topic to learn as seen in the other two sessions, a student's learning path is assessed by the instructor module during the tutoring session. The instruction is generated based on the hierarchical network of the domain. The new student will start right at the beginning of the subject and the old student continues from the last topic.

The tutoring session provides a more complete instruction than the other two sessions described above. The instruction is generated and delivered using the entire set of Gagne's instructional events, i.e., gain attention to retention and transfer. Another major characteristic of the tutoring session is the capability to change and adapt teaching styles when it is appropriate. The major teaching style of the tutoring session is instructor-oriented style. However, if a student has no success with the present topic taught by the instructor-oriented style, the system will heuristically switch to guided-discovery style or user-initiated style as previously discussed in the section describing *Switching Strategies*.

2.4 Current Applications
Within the framework of ITS-Engineering, two domain specific applications have been developed: ITS-CPM (Intelligent Tutoring System for Construction and Project Management) and ITS-Shear (Intelligent Tutoring System for Shear Analysis of Reinforced Concrete Beams). ITS-CPM has been developed along with ITS-Engineering as a prototype system to mainly evaluate the capability of multiple teaching styles to engineering curriculum. ITS-Shear is developed after the skeleton of ITS-Engineering is implemented to assess the shell capability of the system.

ITS-CPM (Intelligent Tutoring System for Construction and Project Management)
There are four objectives in developing ITS-CPM (Srisethanil and Baker, 1995). First, the application is intended to investigate the plausibility of the application of multiple teaching styles to engineering education. The literature indicates the benefit of this paradigm to other domain applications and the author believes that the multiple teaching styles paradigm can be beneficial to engineering domains, as well. Second, ITS-CPM is used as a delivering mechanism to examine the applicability of each (of four) teaching style to certain learning situations, i.e., subject matter, learning outcome and knowledge level. Third, ITS-CPM is implemented to examine the capability of the framework of ITS-Engineering whether it is capable of allowing the development of ITS applications across different engineering domains. Lastly, ITS-CPM is developed to demonstrate a potential source for providing assistance to classroom instruction and/or providing continuing education mechanism for the engineering community (academic and corporate).

The subject domain of the ITS-CPM application includes basic planning and scheduling, CPM, PERT, Line of Balance and resource allocation as can be found in an undergraduate class on Construction. The subsequent sections demonstrate the examples of the learning sessions of ITS-CPM.

Examples of Learning Sessions in ITS-CPM Figure 1 demonstrates the main screen of ITS-CPM and it's learning sessions. The student is free to choose the sessions.

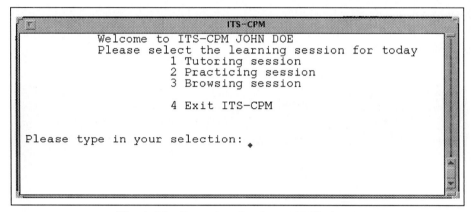

Fig. 1. The Learning Sessions of ITS-CPM

Figure 2 displays the browsing session of ITS-CPM. The screen is generated at run-time depending on the available topics. Therefore, the knowledge base of ITS-CPM (or any application) can be enhanced with more information and/or with more subjects without interfering the interface. Figure 3 demonstrates the main screen of the practicing session of ITS-CPM. Similar to the browsing session, the interface displays the available topics that can teach in the practicing session. After a student selects a topic number to practice, ITS-CPM will generate the another screen of available parameters. A student can choose any combination of these parameters to comprise a problem. The screen shots of detailed practicing session and tutoring session of ITS-CPM are not available due to limited space of the paper. More details of the learning sessions of ITS-CPM can be found in Srisethanil (1996).

ITS-Shear (Intelligent Tutoring System for Shear Analysis of Reinforced Concrete Beams)
ITS-Shear is developed to assess the capability of the ITS-Engineering's framework whether it appropriately allows for the development of other ITS applications of different engineering subjects. The subject of shear analysis of reinforce concrete beam was selected due to several rationales. First, the subject characterizes engineering subjects that contain intensive mathematical computation. Second, information sources (human expert) for the subject is accessible and volunteers to supply information for developing ITS-Shear. Third, there have been several approaches to develop computer based instruction on the subject of shear analysis (ITS-Progress by Braun, 1993; Distributed Problem Generator by Boyd, 1995). Thus, the developing

time/cost, contents and pedagogy of ITS-Shear can be compared to those of these systems.

Developing time The developing time of ITS-Shear is noticeably less than the systems implemented by Braun (1993) and Boyd (1995). Utilizing the framework of ITS-Engineering, the coding time is approximately 40 to 50 man-hour, and the material/domain preparation time is approximately 30 to 40 man-hour (Srisethanil, 1996). Therefore the developing time consumes roughly 70 to 90 man-hours for the instruction that lasts about 60 minutes. Comparing to the industry standard figures (100-300 man-hour to develop an hour instruction) as reported by Murray and Woolf (1992), the developing time of ITS-Shear is less than the best time that an instructional system can be developed from the literature source.

```
┌──────────────────────── ITS-CPM ────────────────────────┐
│ Searching... Found CPM-circle                            │
│ Searching... Found CPM-leadlag                           │
│ Searching... Found BAR_CHART                             │
│ Searching... Found CRASH-COST                            │
│                                                          │
│                                                          │
│     The Available Topics                                 │
│     ====================                                 │
│     1    definition-fundamental                          │
│     2    definition-concept                              │
│     3    scheduling                                      │
│     4    resource-allocation                             │
│     5    PERT-introduction                               │
│     6    PERT-computation                                │
│     7    LOB-introduction                                │
│     8    LOB-MultiProject                                │
│     9    LOB-SoloProject                                 │
│    10    CPM-introduction                                │
│    11    CPM-notation                                    │
│    12    CPM-basic-computation                           │
│    13    CPM-circle-diag                                 │
│    14    CPM-leadlag                                     │
│    15    BAR-CHART                                       │
│                                                          │
│                                                          │
│     Please type in the number of the topics you want to  │
│    learn                                                 │
│     Topic number ( q to Quit):  ◆                        │
│                                                          │
└──────────────────────────────────────────────────────────┘
```

Fig. 2. The Browsing Session of ITS-CPM

Multiple Teaching Styles Capability. ITS-Shear also demonstrates the capability for switching teaching styles provided by ITS-Engineering. The learning sessions of ITS-Shear function properly. In the tutoring session, ITS-Shear adequately switches the teaching style between the instructor-oriented style and the user-initiated style as found in ITS-CPM. However, because the majority of the subject is computationally intensive, the guided-discovery is not appropriate as previously discussed..

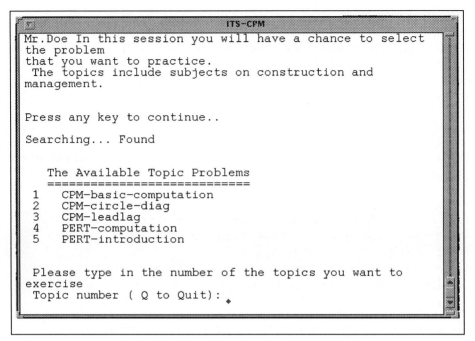

Fig.3. The Practicing Session of ITS-CPM

3. Conclusion and Discussion

ITS-Engineering is a domain-independent tutoring system designed dedicatedly for engineering domains. ITS-Engineering employs a multiple teaching paradigm to enable applications to deliver instruction in various teaching styles. The multiple teaching styles paradigm enables the system to deliver adaptive instruction reflecting the student's preferences, subject matter and type of learning outcome to be achieved. These teaching styles are instructor-oriented, guided-discovery, user-initiated, and exploratory. The application of these teaching styles can be found within the learning sessions and between learning sessions of ITS-Engineering. There are three learning session in ITS-Engineering: tutoring, practicing and browsing session; reflecting the uses of four available teaching styles.

One major issue that arises when trying to implement ITS-Engineering is how to appropriately represent the information to sufficiently support the generation of multiple teaching styles instruction. The readers are encouraged to find more information in the publications by Srisethanil (1996) and Srisethanil & Baker (1995).

ITS-CPM is a intelligent tutoring system for teaching construction planning and scheduling. ITS-Shear is a system for teaching shear analysis of concrete beams. Both systems are developed to demonstrate the shell capability and pedagogy of ITS-Engineering's framework. Users of the system have said that the multiple teaching styles greatly benefit students in learning engineering material, unlike the human ability in a classroom environment-everyone gets the same information in the same style (Srisethanil, 1996).   ITS-Engineering, ITS-CPM and ITS-Shear are all implemented using CLIPS (Giarrantano, 1993).

The focus of this paper is not intended to address the issue of interfaces. However, the role of computer interfaces in learning is evident.   While the interfaces of the system are currently primitive, they are functional and can be enhanced at the later stage of implementation.

4 References

Braun, S. (1993). *Exploration of the functionality requirement associated with devel opment of a problem generation facility to supplement an intelligent tutoring sys tem.* Master Thesis submitted to the School of Civil and Environmental Engineer ing, Georgia Institute of Technology, Atlanta, Georgia, U.S.A.

Boyd, M. (1995). *Global dissemination of the Problem Generator.* Master Thesis submitted to the School of Civil and Environmental Engineering, Georgia Insti tute of Technology, Atlanta, Georgia, U.S.A.

Gagné, R.M. (1985) *The conditions of learning and theory of instruction (4th ed.)* New York: Holt, Rinehart and Winston.

Giarratano, J. and Riley, G., (1993) *CLIPS Reference Manual version 6.0 ,* NASA, Software Technology Branch, Lyndon B. Johnson Space Center.

Major, N., & Reichgelt, H. (1992) COCA: A shell for intelligent tutoring systems. In Frasson, C.,Gauthier, G. & McCalla, G.I. (Eds.) *Proceedings of Intelligent Tu toring Systems 92, Lecture Notes in Computer Science, 608.* 523-530, Berlin:Springer-Verlag.

Mosston, M. & Ashworth, S. (1990). *The Spectrum of Teaching Styles: From Com mand to Discover.* New York:Longman.

Murray, T., & Woolf B. P., (1990) A knowledge acquisition tool for intelligent com puter tutors. *Sigart Bulletin, 2* (2), 1-13.

Spensley, F., Elsom-Cook, M., Byerley, P., Brooks, P., Federici, M., & Scaroni, C. (1990) Using multiple teaching strategies in an ITS. In Frasson, C., Gauthier, G. (Eds.) *Intelligent tutoring systems: at the crossroads of artificial intelligence and education.* 189-205, New Jersey: Ablex.

Srisethanil, C. (1996). *Pedagogical framework for an Engineering Intelligent Tutor ing System.* Ph.D. dissertation submitted to the School of Civil and Environmen tal Engineering, Georgia Institute of Technology, Atlanta, Georgia, U.S.A.

Srisethanil, C., Baker, N. (1995) Application and development of multiple teaching styles to an engineering ITS. In Greer, J. (Eds.) *Proceedings of AI-ED 95-7th World conference on Artificial Intelligence in Education.* Associate for the Ad vancement of Computing in Education (AACE), 315-322.

Woolf, B. P. (1992) Towards a computational model of tutoring. In Jones, M., & Winne, H. P. (Eds.) *Adaptive Learning Environment-Foundations and Frontiers.* NATO ASI Series , Vol.85, 209-231, Berlin: Springer-Verlag.

Acknowledgment: The research is sponsored by under the National Science Foundation's National Young Investigator Award RED-925-8205 and a grant from the GE Foundation.

Author Index

Lecture Notes in Computer Science

For information about Vols. 1–1018

please contact your bookseller or Springer-Verlag